Fourth Canadian Edition

EXPLORING SOCIAL PSYCHOLOGY

DAVID G. MYERS
Hope College

STEVEN M. SMITH
Saint Mary's University

McGraw-Hill
Ryerson

EXPLORING SOCIAL PSYCHOLOGY
Fourth Canadian Edition

ISBN-13: 978-1-25-902470-2
ISBN-10: 1-25-902470-9

2 3 4 5 6 7 8 9   WEB   1 9 8 7 6 5

Printed and bound in Canada.

Care has been taken to trace ownership of copyright material contained in this text; however, the publisher will welcome any information that enables them to rectify any reference or credit for subsequent editions.

Director of Product Management: Rhondda McNabb
Product Manager: Jason Chih
Senior Marketing Manager: Margaret Greenfield
Product Developer: Katherine Goodes
Senior Product Team Associate: Marina Seguin
Supervising Editor: Stephanie Gay
Photo/Permissions Editor: Tracy Leonard
Copy Editor: Valerie Adams
Plant Production Coordinator: Scott Morrison
Manufacturing Production Coordinator: Emily Hickey
Cover and Interior Design: Lightbox Visual Communications Inc.
Cover Image: Rob Broek/ Getty Images
Page Layout: Laserwords
Printer: Webcom

Library and Archives Canada Cataloguing in Publication

Myers, David G., author
Exploring social psychology / David G. Myers, Hope College, Steven M. Smith, Saint Mary's University. — Fourth Canadian edition.
Includes bibliographical references and index.
ISBN 978-1-25-902470-2 (pbk.)

1. Social psychology--Textbooks. I. Smith, Steven M. (Steven Michael), 1971-, author II. Title.
HM1033.M94 2015   302   C2014-905562-5

About the Authors

DAVID G. MYERS is the John Dirk Werkman Professor of Psychology at Michigan's Hope College, where students have voted him "Outstanding Professor." Myers's love for teaching psychology is manifest in his writings for the lay public. His articles have appeared in three dozen magazines and he has authored or co-authored a dozen books, including *The Pursuit of Happiness* (Avon, 1993) and *Intuition: Its Powers and Perils* (Yale University Press, 2002).

Also an award-winning researcher, Myers received the Gordon Allport Prize from Division 9 of the American Psychological Association for his work on group polarization.

His scientific articles have appeared in three dozen journals, including *Science, American Scientist, Psychological Science*, and the *American Psychologist*. He has served his discipline as consulting editor to the *Journal of Experimental Social Psychology* and the *Journal of Personality and Social Psychology*.

In his spare time he has chaired his city's Human Relations Commission, helped found a community action agency that assists impoverished families, and spoken to hundreds of collegiate and religious groups. Drawing on his experience, he has also written articles and a book (*A Quiet World*) about hearing loss, and he is advocating a revolution in American hearing-assistance technology. (Learn more at hearingloop.org.) David and Carol Myers are the parents of two sons and a daughter.

STEVEN M. SMITH is a Professor of Psychology and the Dean of Science at Saint Mary's University in Halifax. He completed his B.A. (Honours) at Bishop's University in Lennoxville, Quebec, and his M.A. and Ph.D. in Social Psychology at Queen's University in Kingston, Ontario. Smith regularly teaches Social Behaviour, Attitudes and Persuasion, and Psychology and Law. His lectures are well received, and he has been nominated for the Saint Mary's University Student Association Faculty of Arts Teaching Award.

He is an active researcher and is dedicated to applying his theoretical work to real-world concerns. His research has been supported by the Social Sciences and Humanities Research Council, the Canadian Institutes of Health Research, the Nova Scotia Health Research Foundation, the Nova Scotia Gaming Foundation, and a number of private organizations. His work has appeared in journals such as the *Journal of Applied Psychology, Law & Human Behavior, Journal of Personality and Social Psychology, Personality and Social Psychology Bulletin, Social Psychology and Personality Science*, and *Psychophysiology*.

He has lent his expertise to a number of community organizations, particularly advising on communication and social marketing issues. His wife, Isabel, is a clinical developmental psychologist, and together they have two fantastic but heavily analyzed children, Sydney and Dylan.

Brief Contents

Table of Contents

Preface

Welcome to the fourth Canadian edition of *Exploring Social Psychology*. Once again, I am very proud to be involved with this textbook. As a student of social psychology myself, I fully comprehend the difficulty people can sometimes have understanding how we influence and are influenced by the world around us. Because I have taught social psychology courses for a number of years, I am well aware of the breadth of choices available to instructors when choosing a text to accompany an introductory social psychology course. I am also aware of the challenges involved in teaching a comprehensive course in a single semester. Most textbooks are simply too long and too expensive. Shorter books often fail to cover the topics instructors want, even in a one-semester course. I believe this text is short enough for a one-term course, yet comprehensive enough to cover the most important topics.

A CANADIAN PERSPECTIVE ON SOCIAL PSYCHOLOGY

When I began teaching social psychology, students often complained that the texts I used were not "Canadian" enough. This common shortcoming is what the Canadian edition of *Exploring Social Psychology* aims to address. This fourth edition has continued this approach. Importantly, the adaptation of the U.S. text was not about dropping in a few Canadian names and changing the spelling of the word *behavior* to *behaviour*. Discussing the topic of social psychology in a Canadian context means exploring the extent to which certain psychological issues may be different in Canada than in the rest of the world. We are very fortunate that many of the world's leading social psychologists are Canadian. One only needs to look at the editorial boards of the major journals to verify this. This book is about delving into social psychology in the Canadian context, addressing issues that are by their nature Canadian-specific (topics such as acculturation, multiculturalism, separatism, and the challenges faced by Aboriginal peoples in Canada), and most important, illustrating why social psychology is relevant to every student.

David Myers wrote *Exploring Social Psychology* from a very personal perspective and I have continued that tradition. The theme running through this book reflects what I feel is at the root of social psychological research: storytelling. When we tell a story, we talk not only about what people did, but also about why they did it. Understanding the *why* of social behaviour is the basis of a great deal of research in the field of social psychology.

FEATURES OF THE CANADIAN EDITION

This book also reflects one of my core principles in the teaching of social psychology, one that is shared by most other teachers—that students learn better when they are engaged with the material. Therefore, one of my primary aims in this book is to engage you, the reader, through the use of critical-thinking exercises, application tasks, and storytelling.

- **Critical-Thinking Approach.** Since I began teaching, I have found that one of the ways to engage students is to have them think critically about questions (e.g., "Do opposites attract?") and ask them to commit to a predicted outcome. I use these "thought experiments" to get students to think about the topic under discussion. I have tried to incorporate this approach into the text by asking the reader, in each module, to think about one of the central issues covered. I do this by including Critical Thinking and Activity boxes throughout the text, which will ask you to answer questions, think about a topic, or seek out some relevant information from your own social world. In many cases I ask you to commit to a response by answering a question or predicting an outcome. In some modules of the book, you are asked to think about a specific experiment or issue that has been described in the module, and to critique it from a methodological or ethical standpoint.

- **Opening Vignettes.** Another goal I have worked toward in my teaching is to make social psychology real for students. I have incorporated this goal into the fourth Canadian edition of the text by opening each module with a story that is relevant to the module content. In some modules, this will be a story about someone or something that has happened. In others, this opening vignette will ask you to put yourself in a particular situation and think about how you might react.

- **Storytelling.** As mentioned earlier, I believe a central element to exploring social psychology is the stories we tell. I believe that using narratives is yet another way to engage people in the subject matter. Therefore, in each module of the book I have tried to incorporate at least one researcher's story about how he or she got involved in a particular topic, or how their research came up with a way to answer an important question in their area. The "Story behind the Research" features have been integrated into the text for this new edition. More detailed stories are also available in the accompanying online material.

- **Applying Social Psychology.** Social psychology is a very applied area of research. However, sometimes the connections between the theory on the page and the application in real life can be difficult to see. Therefore, in every module, I have included an Applying Social Psychology box, either to expand on some of the material to make the applied context easier to understand, or discussed how to apply the themes being explained in the text to your everyday life.

- **Connections.** Social psychology is about the interaction between individuals and the groups they are involved with. You will not be surprised to read that many of the topics that are covered in this book are interconnected. To highlight these links, I have added references to topics in previous or future modules to help the reader understand those links.

NEW IN THE FOURTH CANADIAN EDITION

As with any revision, a number of elements have been updated in the fourth Canadian edition.

The specific changes we have made in the fourth Canadian edition are:

Module 1 contains a number of revisions. I have clarified the opening vignette, as requested by reviewers. I have updated the activities and several other elements. I have added some additional recent research references. I have also made reference to recent well-known events, such as the 2013 Calgary floods and the 2014 Winter Olympic Games, and how they are related to social psychological issues. In addition, a new Applying Social Psychology box has been added, along with Connections to other modules.

Module 2 has an enhanced discussion of methodological issues through the addition of information on observational research methods, as requested by a reviewer. I have also added, as requested, a section on demand characteristics and its link to the need for deception in research. As with Module 1, the Applying Social Psychology box is new, and Connections to other modules have been added.

Module 3 contains many updated references, and I have included updated data. I have added some information on self-presentation while online. Finally, I have revised the section on issues surrounding sexuality and its variations. As with Modules 1 and 2, the Applying Social Psychology box is new, and Connections to other modules have been added.

Module 4 includes several updates, as do previous modules, including the addition of new statistics and the discussion of new and revised research. As with the previous modules, the Applying Social Psychology box is new, and Connections to other modules have been added.

Module 5 contains many new and updated references. As with the other modules, the Applying Social Psychology box is new, and Connections to other modules have been added.

Module 6 contains many updated references and some new research on the fundamental attribution error and the actor–observer bias. I have also updated the examples to make them more current and relevant, highlighting the latest Winter Olympic Games. As with the other modules, the Applying Social Psychology box is new, and Connections to other modules have been added.

For Module 7, along with new and updated references, I have added an Applying Social Psychology box, and Connections to other modules have been added.

Module 8 contains many new studies and updated material. In addition, where new data were available, statistics have been updated. Changing attitudes toward gay marriage are highlighted. As with the other modules, the Applying Social Psychology box is new, and Connections to other modules have been added.

Module 9 has updated research on obedience to authority that touches on recent events and research on these issues. For example, I have included a discussion of "chant" events that happened on several university campuses, and which highlighted sexuality and gender issues at university. As with the other modules, the Applying Social Psychology box is new, and Connections to other modules have been added.

Module 10 is updated, with discussions of new research and new elements in most sections. New examples have also been added. As with the other modules, the Applying Social Psychology box is new, and Connections to other modules have been added.

Module 11 is updated in a number of ways, including the discussion of new research. There is also some updated material on cults, gangs, and terrorist groups, along with new statistics regarding persuasive appeals and smoking rates. I have also added some new examples of hazing in Canada. As with the other modules, the Applying Social Psychology box is new, and Connections to other modules have been added.

Module 12 contains updated coverage of research topics. There is new material on issues such as mobs, hazing, social loafing, and the role of groups on deindividuation, with a focus on the Rehtaeh Parsons case, which involved online bullying and her ultimate suicide. As with the other modules, the Applying Social Psychology box is new, and Connections to other modules have been added.

Module 13 covers groupthink, and I have updated the examples of groupthink used. I have also covered new and developing research on the topic, and discussed groupthink in gangs in Canada. As with the other modules, the Applying Social Psychology box is new, and Connections to other modules have been added.

Module 14 includes a chance to assess the actions of a former prime minister, as well as a discussion of new research and new statistics on violence in Canada. I have added a short section on the work of Konrad Lorenz on the role of instinct in aggression, and made some observations on cyber-bullying. As with the other modules, the Applying Social Psychology box is new, and Connections to other modules have been added.

Module 15 has a discussion of new research on stereotypes and prejudice, and a new, more detailed discussion of issues surrounding stereotypes and prejudice related to gender and homosexuality. I also discuss the topic of bullying in this module. I have also updated some gender-related statistics. As with the other modules, the Applying Social Psychology box is new, and Connections to other modules have been added.

Module 16 includes a discussion of new research, and now has revised sections on domestic abuse, rape, Aboriginal perspectives on stereotypes and prejudice, and how stereotyping can be related to self-protection by certain groups. As with the other modules, the Applying Social Psychology box is new, and Connections to other modules have been added.

Module 17 contains references to recent conflicts and events (such as the Quebec Charter of Values) and the different roles taken by international groups in some conflict zones. I have also updated the research, and discussed how punishment impacts on sharing. As with the other modules, the Applying Social Psychology box is new, and Connections to other modules have been added.

Module 18 contains discussion of recent events and how they relate to issues around helping, including work by major Canadian researchers. I have also expanded the discussion of bullying and the role of bystanders in its reduction. There is also a discussion of the role of religion in helping and pro-social behaviour. As with the other modules, the Applying Social Psychology box is new, and Connections to other modules have been added.

In Module 19 I have updated the content by discussing new research and recent developments. As with the other modules, the Applying Social Psychology box is new, and Connections to other modules have been added.

Module 20 has been revised to reflect several new lines of inquiry that researchers have developed, particularly regarding social media. As with the other modules, the Applying Social Psychology box is new, and Connections to other modules have been added.

Module 21 has also been updated with a specific definition of pornography, as well as new statistics on that topic. Statistics on screen time usage has also been updated, as well as issues surrounding social media. In addition, new research has been discussed, and new statistics and information are included. As with the other modules, the Applying Social Psychology box is new, and Connections to other modules have been added.

In Module 22 I have enhanced the section on the Mr. Big technique, which is used by police to extract confessions from suspects. This is a very expensive and popular technique, but it is problematic from a psychological perspective. In addition, new research has been added and discussed, particularly Canadian research. As with the other modules, the Applying Social Psychology box is new, and Connections to other modules have been added.

Module 23 has many new statistics related to the environment are included, and new and relevant research on the topics covered in the module has been added. Also, I have updated the section on persuasive appeals. As with the other modules, the Applying Social Psychology box is new, and Connections to other modules have been added.

Module 24 has been updated with the addition of new examples, a revised section on mood, and some new elements on the role of fear in persuasion. Reviewers asked for revised content on the stress scale, and some uniquely Canadian health promotion campaigns have been discussed. As with the other modules, the Applying Social Psychology box is new, and Connections to other modules have been added.

Thus, in working through all the modules in this text, students will learn not only about the science of social psychology but also a great deal about themselves and how to apply the principles of social psychology to the real world. Therefore, even more than the previous edition, I believe the fourth Canadian edition of *Exploring Social Psychology* will help achieve the goals set by all good instructors in the field.

PEDAGOGY

- **Module-Opening Vignette:** Each module opens by asking readers to put themselves in a situation that relates to the main topic covered and then prompts them to question their response from a methods-based perspective. This feature encourages readers to think critically about their approach to social psychology.

- **Learning Objectives:** For the fourth Canadian edition, at the beginning of each module I have added Learning Objectives, which correspond to the major headings in the module. This should help students understand how the module is structured and what the key messages are.

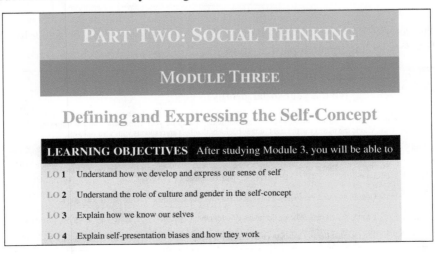

PART TWO: SOCIAL THINKING

MODULE THREE

Defining and Expressing the Self-Concept

LEARNING OBJECTIVES   After studying Module 3, you will be able to

LO 1   Understand how we develop and express our sense of self

LO 2   Understand the role of culture and gender in the self-concept

LO 3   Explain how we know our selves

LO 4   Explain self-presentation biases and how they work

- **Connections:** As noted earlier, every module now has specific links from topics covered in the module you are reading, with topics covered in previous or later modules. Although these links had often been mentioned in the text, reviewers felt this would be a valuable addition, especially with the numerous Connections that have been added. Therefore, I have added this links for this edition.

- **Applying Social Psychology:** New to this edition, the Applying Social Psychology boxes assist students to better connect theory with application in everyday life through either discussion or expanded subject material.

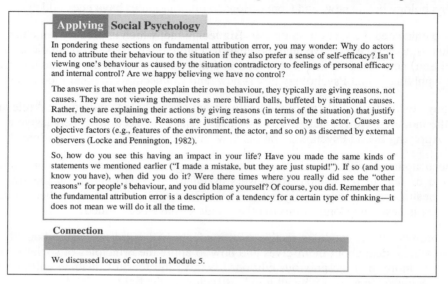

Applying Social Psychology

In pondering these sections on fundamental attribution error, you may wonder: Why do actors tend to attribute their behaviour to the situation if they also prefer a sense of self-efficacy? Isn't viewing one's behaviour as caused by the situation contradictory to feelings of personal efficacy and internal control? Are we happy believing we have no control?

The answer is that when people explain their own behaviour, they typically are giving reasons, not causes. They are not viewing themselves as mere billiard balls, buffeted by situational causes. Rather, they are explaining their actions by giving reasons (in terms of the situation) that justify how they chose to behave. Reasons are justifications as perceived by the actor. Causes are objective factors (e.g., features of the environment, the actor, and so on) as discerned by external observers (Locke and Pennington, 1982).

So, how do you see this having an impact in your life? Have you made the same kinds of statements we mentioned earlier ("I made a mistake, but they are just stupid!"). If so (and you know you have), when did you do it? Were there times where you really did see the "other reasons" for people's behaviour, and you did blame yourself? Of course, you did. Remember that the fundamental attribution error is a description of a tendency for a certain type of thinking—it does not mean we will do it all the time.

Connection

We discussed locus of control in Module 5.

- **Critical Thinking:** These boxes briefly present a specific issue and ask a pointed question, encouraging students to critique the issue from a methodological or ethical standpoint. For the fourth Canadian edition I have doubled the number of Critical Thinking boxes in the text, attempting to have one near the start and one toward the end of each module.

Critical THINKING

Can you think of a role that you play in your life now (e.g., coach, mentor, student, mother, father) that influences how people see you? Maybe it is a social, cultural, or ethic group you belong to. What assumptions do they make about you?

- **Activity Box:** One activity appears in each chapter. Whether a survey, poll, or scenario, they are designed to deepen students' understanding through participation.

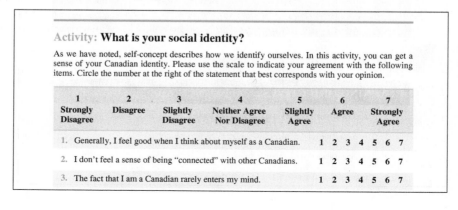

Activity: What is your social identity?

As we have noted, self-concept describes how we identify ourselves. In this activity, you can get a sense of your Canadian identity. Please use the scale to indicate your agreement with the following items. Circle the number at the right of the statement that best corresponds with your opinion.

1 Strongly Disagree	2 Disagree	3 Slightly Disagree	4 Neither Agree Nor Disagree	5 Slightly Agree	6 Agree	7 Strongly Agree

1. Generally, I feel good when I think about myself as a Canadian.   1 2 3 4 5 6 7

2. I don't feel a sense of being "connected" with other Canadians.   1 2 3 4 5 6 7

3. The fact that I am a Canadian rarely enters my mind.   1 2 3 4 5 6 7

- **Key Terms:** Each module ends with a review of the "Key Terms" and their definitions. This list of key terms, combined with the "Summary of Key Points," helps students to review the highlights of each module.

KEY TERMS

Hindsight bias   The tendency to exaggerate, after learning an outcome, one's ability to have foreseen how something turned out. Also known as the I-knew-it-all-along phenomenon.

Hypothesis   A testable proposition that describes a relationship that might exist between events.

Social psychology   The scientific study of how people think about, influence, and relate to one another.

Theory   An integrated set of principles that explains and predicts observed events.

- **Summary of Key Points:** Reviewers noted that it would be helpful to have a summary of the key points from the module to help students review the material. Therefore, in this section I have relisted each of the learning objectives, and reiterated the key points underneath.

SUMMARY OF KEY POINTS

LO1. Understand how our preconceptions bias our thinking.
- Our preconceptions bias how we expose ourselves to, process, judge, and remember information.

LO2. Understand why we ignore base-rate information.
- We make judgments based on representativeness of information, rather than focusing on statistical base rates.

LO3. Explain why we are more persuaded by memorable events.
- We judge the likelihood of events based on how easy it is to recall instances of that event.

LO4. Understand how we misperceive correlation and control.
- When presented with two unlikely events that co-occur, we perceive the strength of that relationship to be greater.
- We believe we have more control over random events than we typically do.

---

connect™

McGraw-Hill Connect™ is a Web-based assignment and assessment platform that gives students the means to better connect with their coursework, with their instructors, and with the important concepts that they will need to know for success now and in the future.

With Connect, instructors can deliver assignments, quizzes, and tests online. Instructors can edit existing questions and author entirely new problems. Track individual student performance—by question, assignment, or in relation to the class overall—with detailed grade reports. Integrate grade reports easily with Learning Management Systems (LMS). And much more.

By choosing Connect, instructors are providing their students with a powerful tool for improving academic performance and truly mastering course material. Connect allows students to practise important skills at their own pace and on their own schedule. Importantly, students' assessment results and instructors' feedback are all saved online—so students can continually review their progress and plot their course to success.

Connect also provides 24/7 online access to an eBook—an online edition of the text—to aid students in successfully completing their work, wherever and whenever they choose.

Key Features

Simple Assignment Management

With Connect, creating assignments is easier than ever, so you can spend more time teaching and less time managing.

- Create and deliver assignments easily, and supply test bank material online.
- Streamline lesson planning, student progress reporting, and assignment grading to make classroom management more efficient than ever.
- Go paperless with the eBook and online submission and grading of student assignments.

Smart Grading

When it comes to studying, time is precious. Connect helps students learn more efficiently by providing feedback and practice material when they need it, where they need it.

- Automatically score assignments, giving students immediate feedback on their work and side-by-side comparisons with correct answers.
- Access and review each response; manually change grades or leave comments for students to review.
- Reinforce classroom concepts with practice tests and instant quizzes.

Instructor Library

The Connect Instructor Library is your course creation hub. It provides all the critical resources you'll need to build your course, just how you want to teach it.

- Assign eBook readings and draw from a rich collection of textbook-specific assignments.
- Access instructor resources, including ready-made PowerPoint presentations and media to use in your lectures.
- View assignments and resources created for past sections.
- Post your own resources for students to use.

eBook

Connect reinvents the textbook learning experience for the modern student. Every Connect subject area is seamlessly integrated with Connect eBooks, which are designed to keep students focused on the concepts key to their success.

- Provide students with a Connect eBook, allowing for anytime, anywhere access to the textbook.
- Merge media, animation and assessments with the text's narrative to engage students and improve learning and retention.
- Pinpoint and connect key concepts in a snap using the powerful eBook search engine.
- Manage notes, highlights, and bookmarks in one place for simple, comprehensive review.

LEARNSMART®

No two students are alike. Why should their learning paths be? LearnSmart uses revolutionary adaptive technology to build a learning experience unique to each student's individual needs. It starts by identifying the topics a student knows and does not know. As the student progresses, LearnSmart adapts and adjusts the content based on his or her individual strengths, weaknesses, and confidence, ensuring that every minute spent studying with LearnSmart is the most efficient and productive study time possible.

SMARTBOOK™

As the first and only adaptive reading experience, SmartBook is changing the way students read and learn. SmartBook creates a personalized reading experience by highlighting the most important concepts a student needs to learn at that moment in time. As a student engages with SmartBook, the reading experience continuously adapts by highlighting content based on what each student knows and doesn't know. This ensures that he or she is focused on the content needed to close specific knowledge gaps, while it simultaneously promotes long-term learning.

INSTRUCTOR SUPPLEMENTS

Connect is a one-stop shop for instructor resources, including:

- **Instructor's Manual** (by Steven Smith, Saint Mary's University): Each chapter in the Instructor's Manual contains key learning points, lecture ideas, class discussion topics, and more.
- **Computerized Test Bank** (by Barbara Bond, Trent University): The Test Bank provides a variety of questions, including multiple choice, true/false, and short answer. The multiple-choice and true/false questions include the answer as well as the reference to the closest heading relating to the question in the main text where the material appears.
- **Microsoft® PowerPoint® Presentations** (by Barbara Bond, Trent University): These visual presentations, crafted for each chapter, include useful outlines, summaries, and visuals.

STUDENT SUPPLEMENTS

Connect for Students

By choosing Connect, instructors are providing their students with a powerful tool for improving academic performance and truly mastering course material. Connect allows students to study and practise important skills at their own pace and on their own schedule with pre- and post-tests, additional quizzing material, social psychology videos, and an eBook for easy reference. Pre- and post-practice tests are tied to learning objectives and allow students to continually review their progress and plot their course to success. Online access to Connect with eBook is included with all Connect printed textbooks—at no extra charge to the student.

SUPERIOR LEARNING SOLUTIONS AND SUPPORT

The McGraw-Hill Ryerson team is ready to help you assess and integrate any of our products, technology, and services into your course for optimal teaching and learning performance. Whether it's helping your students improve their grades, or putting your entire course online, the McGraw-Hill Ryerson team is here to help you do it. Contact your Learning Solutions consultant today to learn how to maximize all of McGraw-Hill Ryerson's resources!

For more information on the latest technology and Learning Solutions offered by McGraw-Hill Ryerson and its partners, please visit us online: **www.mcgrawhill.ca/he/solutions**.

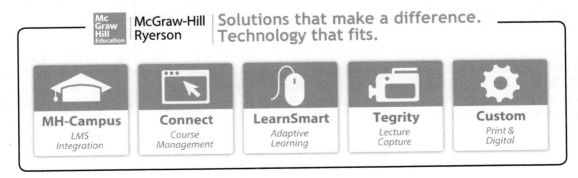

ACKNOWLEDGMENTS

I am very grateful to those people who took the time to review the previous Canadian edition of *Exploring Social Psychology* and who have provided suggestions for this revision. In addition, I am very grateful to the reviewers who took the time to review early versions of modules for the fourth Canadian edition. Many of the reviewers listed below also reviewed *Exploring Social Psychology* in preparation for the first and second Canadian editions, thus I thank them doubly (or even triply). Without the reviewers' help, this book would not have been possible. Thus, I express my heartfelt thanks to:

Anomi G. Bearden, *Red Deer College*

Michael Boisvert, *Fanshawe College*

Gary Bonczak, *Sir Sandford Fleming College*

David Bourgeois, *Saint Mary's University*

Dr. Paul Dupuis, *Algoma University*

Jim Cameron, *Saint Mary's University*

Leora Dahl, *Okanagan College*

Laura Dane, *Douglas College*

Deborah Flynn, *Nipissing University*

Ken Fowler, *Memorial University of Newfoundland*

Dr. Deborah George, *University of Victoria*

William Patrick Hague, *Fanshawe College*

Trista A. D. Hallman, *Georgian College*

Sarah A. Hill, *Royal Military College of Canada*

Gordon Hodson, *Brock University*

Audrene Kerr-Brown, *Humber College*

Connie Korpan, *Grande Prairie Regional College*

Diane Lachapelle, *University of New Brunswick*

Karen McDonald, *Mount Saint Vincent University*

Jennifer M. Ostovich, *McMaster University*

Stephen B. Perrott, *Mount Saint Vincent University*

Loris Peternelli, *Vanier College*

Julie Quinn, *Saint Mary's University*

Ravi Ramkissonsingh, *Niagara College*

Kim Regehr, *Conestoga College*

Greg Tyndall, *College of New Caledonia*

Frank Winstan, *Vanier College*

The fourth Canadian edition has been supported by many people: Katelyn Carter-Rogers who provided important research and editing support; Courtney Merriam, my unshakable administrative assistant in the Dean's office, was vital in protecting my time so that the fourth edition could be completed on schedule; and the dedicated folks at MHR: Jason Chih, Kim Brewster, Katherine Goodes, Stephanie Gay, Valerie Adams, and the many people who worked on this project through its development.

Finally, and most personally important, I could never have accomplished this without the love and constant support of my family: my wife, Isabel; my daughter, Sydney; and my son, Dylan. All three of them tolerated many late nights while I worked on the book. You make it all worthwhile. I would also like to thank my parents, Bob and Louise—I never would have made it this far without their support, encouragement, and faith in me. Dad—I am just sorry you are not around to see it.

STEVEN M. SMITH

PART ONE: SOCIAL PSYCHOLOGY: WHAT IS IT AND HOW DO WE DO IT?

MODULE ONE

Introduction to the Science of Social Psychology

Imagine yourself in this situation: you have just returned home from a trip to Winnipeg, where you were visiting family. You get a call from the RCMP, who want to drop by to "ask you a few questions." Being the honest and innocent person that you are, you agree. Once the police arrive, they begin to question you about your trip and ask if you remember buying coffee at a donut shop before you left town. You reply, "Of course, I always need coffee before a long drive." A crime was committed at a coffee shop, but you are not worried—you have an ironclad alibi—you were visiting sick children at a hospital when the crime occurred. Before leaving, the police ask permission to take your picture. Again, you believe you are innocent of any crime and agree to be photographed.

Much to your surprise, three days later the police are back and you are arrested. You are taken to a Winnipeg police station where you are fingerprinted and put in a cell. Later, you are subjected to a humiliating strip search and questioned for 13 hours. The police show you pictures of the horrific murder that occurred at the donut shop you visited. The teenager who worked there had been strangled and left for dead. The police have an eyewitness who says he saw you running from the scene of the crime. They tell you your fingerprints were found at the scene. The nurse who provided your alibi is now saying she doesn't remember seeing you. The police start to question your mental state.

Critical THINKING

> What would you do? Would you continue to deny your involvement? Would you confess and hope for a lenient sentence? Would you ask to see a lawyer? Would the police come to their senses and realize you are innocent? If someone else were in a similar situation and confessed, would you believe he or she was guilty?

LO 1

DEFINING THE FIELD OF SOCIAL PSYCHOLOGY

Is this scenario difficult to imagine? Does it seem implausible? This situation was Tom Sophonow's reality. He was convicted, based largely on the mistaken eyewitness (there were no fingerprints). He spent four years in prison for the murder of that Winnipeg teenager and fought for 16 years before he was finally able to clear his name. What would you have done in his position? Many people believe that they would never confess to a crime they didn't commit—that's just common sense. However, innocent people confess to crimes all the time. Why? Police are trained in the application of psychological principles to create a particular social situation that encourages suspects to confess. This is very useful when suspects are guilty, but incredibly dangerous when suspects are innocent. Why is it difficult for us to understand why people might confess? We often say, "I would never do that!" But are you right? You might be surprised.

The French philosopher-novelist Jean-Paul Sartre (1946) would have had no problem accepting the idea that we might confess to a crime we did not commit. He believed that we humans are, first of all, beings in a situation. We cannot be distinguished from our situations, for they form us and decide our possibilities. Social psychology is a science that studies the influences of our situations, with special attention to how we view and affect one another. It does so by asking questions such as

- How and what do people *think about* one another?
- How, and how much, do people *influence* one another?
- What shapes the way we *relate to* one another?

A common thread runs through these questions: As Figure 1-1 shows, they all deal with how people view and affect one another. To put it formally, social psychology is *the scientific study of how people think about, influence, and relate to one another*.

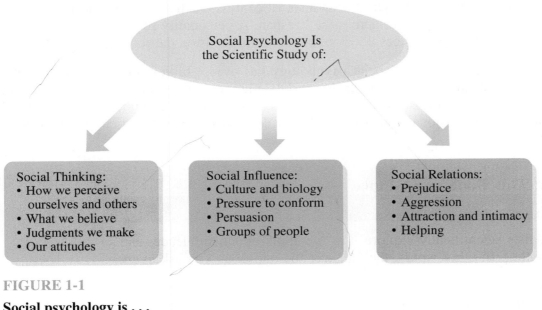

FIGURE 1-1

Social psychology is . . .

LO 2

HOW IS SOCIAL PSYCHOLOGY DIFFERENT FROM OTHER DISCIPLINES?

Social psychology differs from other disciplines in several important ways, but also has many natural links across fields of study. For example, although sociologists also deal with groups and societal influences, the level of analysis is very different. Sociologists focus on the broader societal trends and the impact of factors such as culture and socio-economic status on group-level outcomes. Social psychologists deal with the individual within the group and how outside factors affect the individual. Also, the methods employed differ. Sociologists might typically use survey methods to track changes in attitudes toward a minority group over time, whereas a social psychologist might use experimental procedures to understand how people's attitudes affect their behaviour toward members of that minority group. This is perhaps the most important difference between these two groups. Social psychologists can employ a variety of methods to explore behaviour, whereas sociologists are more limited in what they have to work with. Sociologists generally do not perform controlled experiments, which is the only definitive way to establish cause and effect, where change in one variable *causes* change in another.

However, the fundamental issues addressed within psychology have broader influences. For example, an emerging area within social psychology has been to study how neuroscience can help us understand behaviour, cognition, and emotion. Understanding the neurological bases of behaviour can have important effects on fields outside of psychology, such as biology and medicine. Social psychology also differs in significant ways from other disciplines within psychology. For example, a neuropsychologist will focus on the individual, but will typically explore that individual in isolation, without considering external social influences. A developmental psychologist may study topics with relevance to social psychology (such as lying) or in a social context (such as attachment) but is more focused on the development of behaviour across the lifespan. A personality psychologist focuses on how personality and individual differences develop, but does not focus on the social context.

Also, unlike most scientific disciplines, social psychology has over 7 billion amateur practitioners. People-watching is a universal hobby—in parks, at school, at home, in our communities, and online. As we observe people, we form ideas about how human beings think about, influence, and relate to one another. However, a professional social psychologist does so more systematically, by forming and testing theories.

Connections: This Book at a Glance

Social psychologists scientifically explore how we think about, influence, and relate to one another. In other words, they answer the questions you ask every day. For example, you might ask

- Why do I like the people I do? (See Module 19)
- Does advertising actually work? (See Module 9)
- If I play violent video games, will it make me more violent? (See Module 21)
- When I have a bad day, why do I take it out on the people I love? (See Module 14)
- Are men and women really different? (Covered in several modules)
- How does my cultural background influence my perceptions and behaviour? (Covered in several modules)
- Why did I like Justin Bieber when I was in junior high? (See Module 8)

Those are just some of the questions people ask, and those are the types of questions we will try to answer in this book. Some key points and topics will come up more than once over the course of this text. To help you remember, look for these "Connection" boxes, which will either remind you of where we discussed a topic before, or let you know when we might need the information again in a later module.

LO 3

FORMING AND TESTING THEORIES IN SOCIAL PSYCHOLOGY

We social psychologists have a hard time thinking of anything more fascinating than human existence. If, as Socrates said, "The unexamined life is not worth living," then simply "knowing thyself" seems a worthy enough goal.

As we wrestle with human nature to pin down its secrets, we organize our ideas and findings into theories. A **theory** is *an integrated set of principles that explains and predicts observed events.* Theories are scientific shorthand.

In everyday conversation, "theory" often means "less than fact"—a middle rung on a confidence ladder from guess to theory to fact. For example, it is a fact that global temperatures are increasing. But to many, the idea that our use of fossil fuels is leading to this change in temperature is "just a theory." But to a scientist, facts and theories are apples and oranges. Facts are objective statements about what we observe. Theories are *ideas* that summarize and explain facts. Theories imply testable predictions, called **hypotheses**. Hypotheses serve several purposes. First, they allow us to test a theory by suggesting how we might try to falsify it. Second, predictions give *direction* to research. Any scientific field will mature more rapidly if its researchers have a sense of direction. Theoretical predictions suggest new areas for research; they send investigators looking for things they might never have thought of. Third, the predictive feature of theories can also make them *practical*. As Kurt Lewin, one of modern social psychology's founders, declared, "There is nothing so practical as a good theory."

Consider how this works. Say we notice that after playing violent video games we see our friends behaving more aggressively (roughhousing, driving fast, etc.). We might therefore theorize that playing violent video games *causes* people to be more violent. Alternatively, we might argue that these people are already naturally aggressive, and playing the violent video games is a symptom, rather than the cause, of their behaviour.

But how do we conclude that one theory is better than another? A good theory (1) effectively summarizes a wide range of observations, and (2) makes clear predictions that we can use to (a) confirm or modify the theory, (b) generate new exploration, and (c) suggest practical applications. When we discard theories, usually it's not because they have been proved false. Rather, like old cars, they are replaced by newer, better models.

LO 4

SCIENCE VERSUS COMMON SENSE

Anything seems commonplace, once explained.

DR. WATSON TO SHERLOCK HOLMES

But here's a question for you: Do social psychology's theories provide new insight into the human condition, or do they only describe the obvious? Many of the conclusions presented in this book will probably have already occurred to you, for social psychology is all around you. We constantly observe people thinking about, influencing, and relating to one another. It pays to discern what a certain facial expression predicts, or how to get someone to do something, or whether to regard another person as friend or foe. For centuries, philosophers, novelists, and poets have observed and commented upon social behaviour, often with keen insight. Social psychology is everybody's business.

Therefore, can we say that social psychology is only common sense expressed in different words? Social psychology faces two contradictory criticisms: one is that it is trivial because it documents the obvious; the second is that it is dangerous because its findings could be used to manipulate people. Is the first objection valid? Does social psychology simply formalize what any layperson already knows intuitively? Writer Cullen Murphy (1990) thinks so: "Day after day social scientists go out into the world. Day after day they discover that people's behaviour is pretty much what you'd expect."

One problem with common sense, however, is that we invoke it *after* we know the facts. Events seem far more obvious and predictable in hindsight. Experiments reveal that when people learn the outcome of an experiment, that outcome suddenly seems unsurprising—certainly less surprising than it is to people who are simply told about the experimental procedure and the possible outcomes (Slovic & Fischhoff, 1977). With new knowledge at hand, our efficient memory system purges its outdated presumptions (Hoffrage et al., 2000).

Likewise, in everyday life we often do not expect something to happen until it does. *Then* we suddenly see clearly the forces that brought the event about and feel unsurprised. Consider the Malaysian Airways crash in the spring of 2014, the Swissair plane crash off Peggy's Cove in Nova Scotia in 1998, the devastating floods in Calgary in 2013, the deadly impact of Hurricane Katrina in 2005, the financial crash of 2008, the 2010 BP oil spill in the Gulf of Mexico, and the 9/11 terrorist attacks in 2001—with all of these events, numerous TV and newspaper commentators argued that the individuals involved "should have known" what was coming, and that the devastating consequences should have been avoided. If this hindsight bias (also called the I-knew-it-all-along phenomenon) is pervasive, you may now be feeling that you already knew about it. Indeed, almost any conceivable result of a psychological experiment can seem like common sense—*after* you know the result. As the Danish philosopher-theologian Søren Kierkegaard put it, "Life is lived forwards, but understood backwards."

Often when disasters strike (such as the Calgary flood in in 2013), people say that someone "should have known" the potential risks and should have avoided errors that caused the disaster to occur.

Before reading further, let's do an activity that Steven (one of your authors) regularly gives students in his classes. Look at the questions below, and answer them.

Activity: **Is common sense really that common?**

For each statement, please indicate whether you think it is true or false by circling the letter **T** or **F**.

1. Although women's salaries in 1994 were approximately $14 000 less than men's, women's incomes have gradually increased so that today we are seeing women's salaries at wages comparable to those of their male counterparts.   **T   F**

2. Due to the high cost of living, the number of full-time workers in a single household has increased dramatically over the last ten years.   **T   F**

3. Canada is known for its attitudes of acceptance of others and its respect for human rights and freedoms. It is therefore not unexpected that we would have fewer active terrorist groups here than in any other Western democracy.   **T   F**

4. There is a positive relationship between how much money you make and how many hours you volunteer. The more money you make, the more hours you volunteer.   **T   F**

5. Manitobans are the most likely to say they have more in common with people in Nova Scotia than with Americans just south of them in North Dakota.   **T   F**

6. Nine out of every ten Canadians strongly or somewhat support "having more women in elected office to achieve a well-functioning political system."   **T   F**

7. Most of us have quite accurate insight into the factors that influence our moods.   **T   F**

8. Most people rate themselves as worse than average on socially desirable characteristics.   **T   F**

9. Memory is like a storage chest in the brain into which we deposit material and from which we can withdraw it later if needed. Occasionally, something gets lost from the chest, and then we say we have forgotten.   **T   F**

10. The greater the reward promised for an activity, the more one will come to enjoy the activity.   **T   F**

How did you do? Go to the end of the module to find out.

Once students have responded to the items, Steven asks them to explain why they gave the answers they did. For example, let's look at number 10. Does this make sense to you? Many students say yes.

When asked why, students will say it is because we want to be rewarded for our work, and when we are, we enjoy it. Yet you might also argue that doing something is its own reward—we do not need to be compensated. As it turns out . . . it depends, but typically once we are paid for doing something, we do not enjoy it as much. (To see the answers to all of these items, and look up the reasons for those answers, check the end of the module).

Applying Social Psychology

On June 23, 2012, a section of the roof parking lot at the Algo Centre Mall in Elliot Lake, Ontario, collapsed onto shoppers and employees, killing two people and injuring more than 20 others. The media and residents of Elliot Lake heavily criticized the mall's owners, as well as the structural engineer who inspected the structure prior to its collapse. Couldn't more have been done to prevent the death and destruction in this case? Maybe. However, given what we know about the hindsight bias, is this extent of criticism fair?

We tend to exaggerate our ability to have foreseen how something would turn out, *after* learning the outcome. Demakis (1997) reported hindsight bias in connection with pre- and post-verdict predictions of the outcome of a criminal trial. Students who made post-verdict ratings were more likely to say they expected a not guilty verdict and less likely to have expected a hung jury than those who made pre-verdict predictions. Russo and Schoemaker (1989) suggest that we see more reasons for an event when it *has already happened* than when we simply ask why it *might occur*. They asked managers and MBA students who had been given a brief description of a new employee why he *might* quit six months from now. They generated a mean of 3.5 reasons per person; however, when told that the new employee had already quit, the hindsight group generated 25 percent more reasons on average (4.4 reasons). Moreover, the reasons were more specific and more closely tied to the description of the employee. The investigators further suggested that by merely pretending that an event has occurred leads us to see more reasons for its occurrence and ultimately to assign it a higher probability of becoming reality. For example, they indicated that people who imagined (in 1988) that a woman *would* been elected president of the United States in 2004 came up with more reasons why this might occur than those who are simply asked why a woman *might* be elected in 2004. Moreover, when finally asked to estimate the probability of the hypothetical event becoming reality, the former gave a higher estimate than the latter.

Are you aware of other situations where the media, and others, make these kinds of mistakes?

Hindsight Bias versus Counterfactual Thinking

When Neal Roese was a student at the University of Western Ontario (he is now a professor at the University of Illinois), he began some research with Dr. James Olson on counterfactual thinking. Counterfactual thinking is very closely related to hindsight bias, but it deals with how people think about the way they could have changed the outcome of an event if only they had acted differently. For example, after a particular event in our lives (such as a failure on an exam), we think about what "could have been" or how things could have been different.

In his initial exploration of counterfactuals, Dr. Roese saw that they were typically seen in the literature as distinct processes; however, he wondered how these two seemingly inconsistent patterns of thinking could be reconciled. He approached Dr. Olson with the problem, and together they devised a project to explain this apparent discrepancy (see Roese & Olson, 1996).

They realized that people engage in hindsight bias when they have a sense of certainty around the specific set of conditions under which an event occurs: "given the way things were, the outcome was inevitable." However, people engage in counterfactual thinking (that is, thinking about alternatives) if they believe some of those conditions could have been changed. For example, if you fail an exam after a night of drinking, you might think, "Well of course I failed; I was out drinking all night!" But you might also think, "If only I hadn't gone out drinking, I could have passed the exam." Thus, counterfactual thinking and the hindsight bias are not inconsistent at all. In fact, the link between the two is quite clear.

Importantly, especially in academic contexts, people are not very good at identifying the causes of their failure, and when they try to (and make mistakes) it can actually inhibit later performance (Petrocelli, Seta, & Seta, 2013; Petrocelli, Seta, Seta, & Prince, 2012). You might think you failed your test because you were out drinking, but if it really was because you did not read the material, simply not drinking the night before the next test will not solve your problems.

Critical THINKING

Consider the last time you failed a test (or had a car accident, or experienced some other negative outcome)? Why did it happen? Is there something you could have done to avoid it? Considering what you now know about the hindsight bias, and counterfactual thinking, how accurate do you think your judgments are in terms of how you could have changed the outcome?

The Importance of Understanding Hindsight Bias

Hindsight bias creates a problem for many psychology students. Sometimes results are genuinely surprising. For example, you may be amazed to learn that that Olympic *bronze* medalists take more joy in their achievement than *silver* medalists. If you watched the 2014 Winter Olympics in Sochi, Russia, you might have noticed this. Why? Medvec, Madey, and Gilovich (1995) propose that the most obvious alternative for a silver medalist is the gold medal (so they are disappointed), whereas the most obvious comparison for a bronze medalist is not getting a medal at all (so they are very pleased).

The I-knew-it-all-along phenomenon can not only make social science findings seem like common sense, but can also have wide-ranging consequences. That is conducive to arrogance—an overestimation of our own intellectual powers. Moreover, because outcomes seem as if they should have been foreseeable, we are more likely to blame decision makers for what are, in retrospect, "obvious" bad choices than to praise them for good choices, which also seem obvious. In 2003, after the seemingly successful invasion of Afghanistan, then-U.S. President George W. Bush made clear his intent to invade Iraq and depose Saddam Hussein.

Across the United States, many people were confident that the "coalition of the willing" could rapidly overwhelm Iraqi defences and "liberate" the country. Within Canada, a debate raged as to whether we should become involved. At the time, joining the coalition was seen as "smart" and "neighbourly" for Canada. Failing to get involved would hurt our relationship with the United States and incur costs in terms of trade relations. Many politicians (including Stephen Harper) argued that getting involved was the right thing to do. Now, more than a decade later, after wars in Iraq and Afghanistan have proved long, expensive, and devastating (for both coalition forces and for innocent civilians), many people have argued that they knew all along that getting involved would be a bad idea and many deny they ever supported involvement. It has also affected more recent decision-making—indeed, when faced with decisions about getting involved in the "Arab Spring" uprising in Egypt, Bahrain, Libya, and Syria, world governments became much more hesitant. They were also reluctant to act after Russia annexed the Ukrainian peninsula of Crimea in the spring of 2014.

We sometimes blame ourselves for "stupid mistakes"—perhaps for not having handled a person or a situation better. Looking back on the event, we see how we should have handled it. "I should have known how busy I would be at the end of semester and started that paper earlier." But sometimes we are too hard on ourselves. We forget that what is obvious to us *now* was not nearly as obvious at the time. Physicians who are told both a patient's symptoms and the cause of death (as determined by an autopsy) sometimes wonder how an incorrect diagnosis could have been made. Other physicians, given only the symptoms, don't find the diagnosis nearly as obvious (Dawson et al., 1988). Indeed, this even extends to judgments of defendants in criminal trials—jurors who know that a crime victim died were more likely to say the defendant should have foreseen the outcome (Evelo & Greene, 2013).

CONCLUSIONS

So can we conclude that common sense is usually wrong? Sometimes it is. At one time, common sense and medical experience assured doctors that bleeding was an effective treatment for typhoid fever—until someone in the mid-1800s bothered to experiment and divided patients into two groups: one that was bled, and one that was given mere bed rest. Other times, conventional wisdom is right. However, it is important to realize that folk wisdom often proposes completely inconsistent patterns of behaviour. For example, we often hear that "birds of a feather flock together" as well as that "opposites attract." Similarly, "out of sight, out of mind" and "absence makes the heart grow fonder" are equally inconsistent. They can't both be right all the time. Undoubtedly, these sayings are all correct at times. What folk wisdom does not do is help us understand when and under what conditions these "common sense" effects occur, when these effects go away, and when they might be reversed.

The point is not that common sense is predictably wrong. Rather . . . it depends. We easily deceive ourselves into thinking that we know, and knew more than we do and did. And this is precisely why we need science—to help us sift reality from illusion and genuine predictions from easy hindsight. So, how do we avoid the hindsight bias? By consciously employing "critical thinking" when we encounter a situation. The key role of critical thinking will be one that we revisit time and again in this textbook.

SUMMARY OF KEY POINTS

LO1. Describe the field of social psychology.

- Social psychology is the scientific study of how people think about, influence, and relate to one another.

LO2. Explain how social psychology differs from other disciplines.

- Social psychology, while covering the role of groups and society, differs in terms of level of analysis, and methods used, focusing on the individual in the group, rather than the individual alone, or the group as a whole.

LO3. Understand how we form and test theories in social psychology.

- A theory is an idea that can be used to explain facts—it suggests specific hypotheses that can be tested, and which provide specific predictions. A good theory

  - Effectively summarizes a wide range of observations.
  - Makes clear predictions that we can use to (a) confirm or modify the theory, (b) generate new exploration, and (c) suggest practical applications.

LO4. Understand the difference between science and common sense.

- When presented with an outcome, we have a natural tendency to believe we "knew it all along."
- We engage in the hindsight bias and counterfactual thinking.
- Science does not rely on hindsight, but focuses on empirical testing of hypotheses, and the unbiased observation of outcomes.

Answers to Activity:

1. F (Module 24)
2. F
3. F
4. F
5. T (Module 3)
6. F
7. F (Module 7)
8. F (Module 4)
9. F (Module 7)
10. F (Module 8)

KEY TERMS

Hindsight bias   The tendency to exaggerate, after learning an outcome, one's ability to have foreseen how something turned out. Also known as the I-knew-it-all-along phenomenon.

Hypothesis   A testable proposition that describes a relationship that might exist between events.

Social psychology   The scientific study of how people think about, influence, and relate to one another.

Theory   An integrated set of principles that explains and predicts observed events.

Module Two

Methods in Social Psychology

LEARNING OBJECTIVES   After studying Module 2, you will be able to

LO 1   Understand the difference between correlation and causation

LO 2   Define independent and dependent variables

LO 3   Understand the importance of random assignment

LO 4   Understand the importance of ethics in psychological research

Now that you know what social psychology is, we are ready to discover how social psychologists answer the questions they are asking. Most of what you will learn about social-psychological research methods you will absorb as you read later modules. But let us go backstage now and take a brief look at how social psychology is done. This glimpse behind the scenes will be just enough for you to appreciate the findings discussed later and to think critically about everyday social events.

Critical THINKING

So, let's go back to a question we asked in the last module. Does playing violent video games lead to violent behaviour? How would you address this question? Fortunately, this is the type of question that social psychologists know how to answer.

Social-psychological research varies by location, how we measure variables, and how we analyze the data we obtain. Research ideas come from many different sources: day-to-day events, cultural trends, government initiatives (such as directed research funding), and even popular TV shows. For example, a downturn in the Canadian economy may lead to a number of different research projects about money, happiness, and resiliency. Research can take place in the *laboratory* (a controlled situation) or in the *field* (everyday situations). Studies can use *observational methods* (observing and recording people in social situations), *surveys* (questionnaires specifically designed to get at particular issues that are administered to individuals), or a variety of other techniques to explore the relationships between variables. Furthermore, social psychologists use both quantitative methods (e.g., using statistics to analyze numeric data) and qualitative methods (e.g., looking for themes in narrative responses given by participants).

LO 1

CORRELATIONAL RESEARCH: DETECTING NATURAL ASSOCIATIONS

How we approach social-psychological questions varies by method—correlational research asks if two or more factors are naturally associated, and experimental research manipulates one or more factors to see if they exert a causal impact on another. If you want to be a critical reader of research reported in newspapers and magazines (or even this text), it pays to understand the difference between correlational and experimental research.

There are some features of correlations we need to understand. Sometimes we will have a positive correlation, indicating that as one variable increases, so does the other (such as age and weight gain in childhood—as we get older, we get heavier). Negative correlations indicate that as levels of one variable increase, the levels of the other variable decrease. For example, we might observe that people who eat more are less healthy. Correlations also vary in strength, from a perfect negative correlation (−1.0, meaning that as one factor increases, the second factor decreases in direct proportion to it) to a perfect positive correlation (1.0, meaning that as one factor increases, the other increases proportionally), and every number in between (e.g., −0.60, 0.10, 0.78, etc.). The closer the relationship is to zero, the weaker the correlation. But what is the value of correlational research? Using some real examples, let's first consider the advantages of correlational research (often involving important variables in natural settings) and the disadvantages (ambiguous interpretation of cause and effect).

Today's psychologists often relate personal and social factors to human health. Soft drink companies have long argued that weight-conscious consumers could help control their weight by drinking diet soft drinks. Sharon Fowler and her colleagues (see Fowler et al., 2008) found that consuming soft drinks was correlated with obesity—the more you drink, the more likely you are to be obese. Given soft drinks' high sugar content, perhaps this finding was not surprising. However, what surprised the researchers even more was that consuming *diet* soft drinks was *even more* strongly related to obesity rates.

As shown in Figure 2-1, we can see that the risk of becoming obese was higher in every consumption category for diet soda drinkers over regular soda drinkers. Why? Could it be that drinking diet soda causes weight to increase? Should obese people who drink diet soft drinks switch to regular to lose weight? What are some of the alternative explanations for this effect? Look at the activity later in this module for some potential explanations.

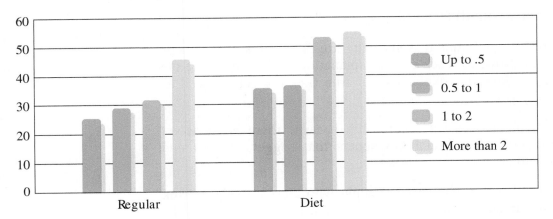

FIGURE 2-1

Percentage risk of becoming overweight by type and amount of pop consumed.
Source: Data from Fowler et al., 2005.

Correlation versus Causation

The diet soda–weight gain question illustrates the most irresistible thinking error made by both amateur and professional social psychologists: When two things go together, it is very tempting to conclude that one is causing the other. Correlational research therefore allows us to *predict*, but it cannot tell us whether changing one variable will *cause* changes in another.

Connection:

We will discuss our tendency to make causal inferences when two things happen at the same time in Module 6, when we discuss attribution theory.

The correlation–causation confusion is behind much muddled thinking in popular psychology. Why do you suppose this is? If we stick with the diet soft drink example, this can make some sense. In

Activity: **Do diet drinks make you fat?**

Ask yourself these questions:

A. Do I drink diet soft drinks?

B. Will this fact influence how I think about these potential explanations?

C. If I am being objective, why do I think drinking diet soft drinks and weight gain are related?

D. Is this a cause-and-effect relationship?

E. Or is there another (third) factor playing a role?

Below are a number of potential reasons that drinking diet soft drinks is related to weight gain. Now, for each of the explanations below, evaluate the extent to which you believe this explanation is true (i.e., correct) as well as why you think the way you do.

1. There is a direct and causal relationship because there is an as-yet unknown property of artificial sweeteners that triggers hunger and causes people to eat more.

2. It is causally related, but reversed: People who are overweight drink diet soft drinks in an attempt to lose weight, but it is too late. Thus the effect is causal, but in the *reverse* direction (being overweight *causes* the drinking of diet soft drinks).

3. There is a third variable involved; thus, there is no causal relationship. People who drink diet soft drinks are less likely to consume good drinks (e.g., milk, juice) and good food (e.g., fruits, vegetables), which can help control weight gain. There is no causal connection.

Now that you have thought this through, ask your friends what they think. Do they agree or disagree with you? Why?

(Adapted from Fowler, 2005, personal communication)

Figure 2-2, we show three ways in which the variables (diet soft drink consumption; weight gain) might be related. Each of the hypothesized relationships in the activity falls into one of the relationships described in Figure 2-2. (Can you figure out which is which?)

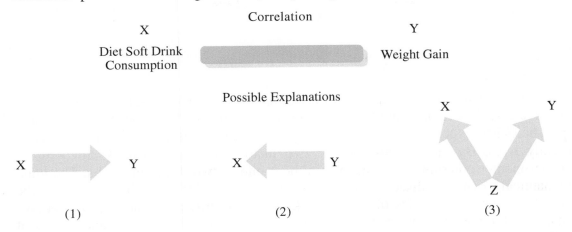

Correlation

X
Diet Soft Drink
Consumption

Y
Weight Gain

Possible Explanations

X ➡ Y   X ⬅ Y   X   Y
                                      Z

(1)   (2)   (3)

FIGURE 2-2

When two variables correlate, any combination of three causal explanations is possible. In (1), for example, drinking diet soft drinks leads to weight gain, whereas in the relationship described by (2), weight gain causes the drinking of diet soft drinks. Finally, in (3), a third variable (Z) causes both the drinking of diet soft drinks and weight gain.

The great strength of correlational research is that it tends to occur in real-world settings where we can examine factors such as race, sex, and social status that we cannot manipulate in the laboratory. Its great disadvantage lies in the ambiguity of the results. If you take nothing else from this module, remember this: Knowing that two variables change together enables us to predict one when we know the other, but *correlation does not specify cause and effect.* If we want to understand a problem and find a solution (such as the cause of obesity, cancer, or why people behave in a certain way), we need to know the real cause of the problem.

This family is drinking Diet Pepsi at breakfast.

LO 2

EXPERIMENTAL RESEARCH: SEARCHING FOR CAUSE AND EFFECT

Control: Manipulating Variables

Because it is nearly impossible to discern cause and effect among naturally correlated events, most social psychologists create laboratory simulations of everyday processes whenever feasible and ethical. Social psychologists experiment by constructing social situations that simulate important features of our daily lives. By varying just one or two factors at a time—called independent variables—the experimenter pinpoints how changes in these one or two things affect us. The wind tunnel helps aeronautical engineers discover principles of aerodynamics; experiments enable the social psychologist to discover principles of social thinking, social influence, and social relations. The ultimate aim of wind tunnel simulations is to understand and predict the flying characteristics of complex aircraft. Social psychologists experiment to understand and predict complex human behaviours. They aim to understand why behaviour varies among people, across situations, and over time.

Social psychologists have used the experimental method in about three-fourths of their research studies (Higbee et al., 1982), and in two out of three studies the setting has been a research laboratory (Adair et al., 1985). To illustrate the laboratory experiment, consider an experiment that typifies a possible cause–effect explanation of correlational findings: the well-known correlation between television viewing and children's behaviour (a question similar to our hypothetical video game violence–aggression hypothesis). Children who watch many violent television programs tend to be more aggressive than those who watch few such programs. This suggests that children might be learning from what they see on the screen. This is a correlational finding. Figure 2-2 reminds us that there are two other cause–effect interpretations that do not implicate television as the cause of the children's aggression.

Social psychologists have therefore brought television viewing into the laboratory, where they control the amount of violence the children see. By exposing children to violent and non-violent programs, researchers can observe how the amount of violence affects behaviour. Chris Boyatzis and his colleagues (1995) showed some elementary schoolchildren, but not others, an episode of the 1990s' most popular—and violent—children's show, *Power Rangers* (a show that ran until 2009, and is now returning). Immediately after viewing the episode, the viewers committed seven times as many aggressive acts per two-minute interval as the non-viewers. The observed aggressive acts we call the dependent variable. Such experiments indicate that television can be one cause of children's aggressive behaviour.

Connection:

Research that examines the link between television, playing violent video games, and aggression will be discussed in greater detail in Module 21.

LO 3

RANDOM ASSIGNMENT: THE GREAT EQUALIZER

So far we have seen that the logic of experimentation is simple: By creating and controlling a miniature reality, we can vary one factor, and then another, to discover how these factors, separately or in combination, affect people. Now let's go a little deeper and see how an experiment is done.

Every social-psychological experiment has two essential ingredients. We have just considered one—*control*. The second key ingredient to proper experimentation is the ability to use random assignment of participants to conditions. It is important to note that simply being able to categorize people into two groups does not make an experiment. Sex and culture are two very popular factors for studies in social psychology. Although we can easily break people into groups based on sex (male versus female), sexual orientation (gay, lesbian, bisexual, transgendered, heterosexual), culture (European Canadian, Australian, Chinese, East Indian), or religious orientation (Catholic, Jewish, Muslim, Hindu, atheist), these are not experimental groups. When someone compares groups like these (and there are important differences), they can describe the differences, but they cannot necessarily imply cause (i.e., that sex or culture caused the difference). The key to experiments is to manipulate one or two independent variables while trying to hold everything else constant.

Recall that we were reluctant, on the basis of a correlation, to assume that viewing violence *causes* aggressiveness. A survey researcher might measure and statistically extract other possibly pertinent factors and see if the correlations survive. For political pollsters and marketers, representative samples, where participants are carefully selected so that responses accurately reflect the responses of the population of interest—are more important. When properly done, representative samples of about 1000 people can accurately predict federal elections with 10 million voters (plus or minus 2.5 percentage points). The Canadian Census, until recently, was such a sampling procedure. However, with new rules making the full-form census optional, Statistics Canada appears to be having difficulty accurately extrapolating from their sample to the population at large—the representativeness of the sample is no longer guaranteed.

Critical THINKING

So, given the changes to how Statistics Canada collects its census data, how might the results be affected? The Government of Canada (and many other groups) use Statistics Canada data to make policy and budgetary decisions. What might happen now that samples may be biased?

But one can never control for all the factors that might distinguish violence viewers from non-viewers. Maybe violence viewers differ in education, culture, intelligence—or in dozens of ways the researcher hasn't considered. Even though we can control for this variation to some extent with proper survey methodology (i.e., using *random selection* of respondents from diverse groups), we can never know cause and effect without the experiment.

Within experiments, and in one fell swoop, random assignment eliminates all such extraneous factors. With random assignment to experimental conditions, each person has an equal chance of viewing the violence or the non-violence. Thus, the people in both groups would, in every conceivable way—family status, intelligence, education, initial aggressiveness—average about the same. Highly intelligent people, for example, are equally likely to appear in both groups. Because random assignment creates equivalent groups, any later aggression difference between the two groups must have something to do with the only way they differ—whether or not they viewed violence (see Figure 2-3).

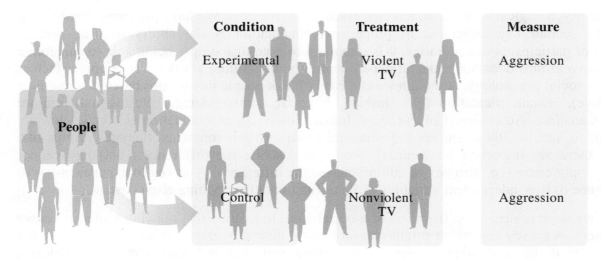

FIGURE 2-3

Random assignment. Experiments randomly assign people to either a condition that receives the experimental treatment or to a control condition that does not. This gives the researcher confidence that any later difference is somehow caused by the treatment.

Unfortunately, true experimental manipulation is not always possible. Some situations (such as cases of child welfare) do not allow for random assignment, or for direct manipulations of independent variables. For example, one cannot randomly assign children to be brought up by "alcoholic" versus "non-alcoholic" parent to see what impact a substance-abusing parent has on a child's welfare (Foster & McCombs-Thorton, 2013). That would be unethical. So some researchers need to try to make causal inferences using observational research methods—where individuals are observed in natural settings, often without awareness, in order to provide the opportunity for objective analysis of behaviour. Observational researchers use sophisticated statistical analysis techniques to make inferences about cause and effect where a true experiment is not possible.

Evaluating Measurement

So far in this module we have discussed how we manipulate variables. But how do we explore the impact of the independent variable? Fundamentally, making our observation of the dependent variable means measuring something. It is no surprise, then, that a tremendous amount of time is spent by social psychologists trying to develop effective ways of measuring all kinds of different phenomena.

Two elements are necessary if we want a good measurement of a particular variable. The first is reliability. A reliable measure is one that will give us the same result over and over again. For example, if you are trying to measure your self-esteem, you should be able to get the same measurement today, tomorrow, and a week from now. However, just because we get the same answer over and over again does not mean we are actually measuring what we think we are.

The measure also needs to have validity. Validity means that you are assessing what you intend to assess. Let's consider a police officer's speed gun. The officer may be reliably measuring cars going at 50 km/h, but if the speed gun is poorly calibrated, this may not be an accurate measure. There is reliability in the measurement (i.e., the same car will be clocked at the same speed every time) but not necessarily validity (is the car actually going 50 km/h?). It is important to note that, by definition, if something is valid, it must be reliable. However, just because something is reliable, does not mean that it is valid.

Applying Social Psychology

Testing theories are vital for psychology to move forward, and for us to get a better understanding of the role of social processes in human behaviour. However, we need to be cautious in generalizing from the laboratory to life. Although the laboratory uncovers basic dynamics of human existence, it is still a simplified, controlled reality. It tells us what effect to expect of variable X, all other things being equal—which, in real life, they never are.

Moreover, as you will see, the participants in many experiments are typically university students. Although this may help you identify with them, students are hardly a random sample of all humanity. Would we get similar results with people of different ages, educational levels, and cultures? This is an open question. Therefore, it is always important to try to conduct *field-based* research as well, where we explore factors in natural settings. We can also use cross-sectional designs, where participants from different groups (e.g., students in Grades 1 through 9) are assessed all at once, and longitudinal designs (where one group of people is followed for several weeks, months, or even years) to help answer questions. However, although these approaches are useful, they do suffer from some of the same problems of control we discussed with correlation research. Essentially, it is almost impossible to arrive at a complete understanding of a phenomenon using one type of research technique. Multiple approaches are always best.

Nevertheless, we can distinguish between the *content* of people's thinking and acting (their attitudes, for example) and the *process* by which they think and act (e.g., how attitudes affect actions and vice versa). The content varies more from culture to culture than does the process. For example, Canadians and Americans tend to have different views on a number of social issues (e.g., attitudes toward gay marriage, Bibby, 2004) and similar views on other topics (e.g., capital punishment, Honeyman & Ogloff, 1996). Yet *how* attitudes and behaviours change is likely to be the same. That is, our behaviours may differ, yet they are still influenced by the same social forces.

We also need to make sure that our measures are not reactive. Reactivity simply refers to the extent to which the measurement influences how people act. For example, if you are trying to measure how prejudiced people are, you might ask a question such as "How comfortable would you be if your sister married outside your religion?" To most readers, it is obvious what this question is getting at.

In addition, most readers do not want to appear to be racist. Therefore, people might answer in a less racist way than would be truly reflective of their attitudes.

Related to this issue, we have to be careful to avoid demand characteristics when doing research. Demand characteristics are elements of the experiment or research that give cues to participants about what the researcher is expecting to find. If a participant knows what the experimenter is expecting, the person may—wanting to be a "good participant"—behave in a way that confirms those expectations, even though that may not be how the participant would behave normally. A real-world analogy of this situation would be how people behave when they are contestants on "reality" TV shows like *Big Brother*, *Survivor*, or *Hell's Kitchen*. The behaviour exhibited by the participants is much more extreme than how they would behave normally, but they know the producers want them to be extreme in order to make "good TV." Indeed, it turns out that many of the "contestants" have professional experience as actors. Therefore, in order to avoid demand characteristics and encourage natural behaviour, sometimes researchers deceive their participants about the purpose of the research. Deception, however, brings with it its own set of ethical issues, which we will discuss shortly.

LO 4

THE ETHICS OF EXPERIMENTATION

Our violent television example illustrates why some experiments are ethically sensitive. Social psychologists would not, over long time periods, expose one group of children to brutal violence. Rather, they briefly alter people's social experience and note the effects. Sometimes the experimental treatment is a harmless, perhaps even enjoyable experience to which people give their knowing consent. Sometimes, however, researchers find themselves operating in a grey area between the harmless and the risky.

In the 1960s Stanley Milgram did a series of experiments where he convinced participants to shock innocent victims up to 450 volts. Despite screams and pleas for release, some participants did not stop shocking their victims (called "learners" in the experiment) until well after they had gone quiet. Although this experiment taught us a great deal about obedience, it did raise several important ethical issues. Indeed, it is not likely that an experiment such as this one could be conducted today due to those ethical issues.

Connection:

The Milgram experiment will be covered in detail in Module 9.

Experiments need not have what Elliot Aronson, Marilynn Brewer, and Merrill Carlsmith (1985) call mundane realism. That is, laboratory behaviour (e.g., delivering electric shocks as part of an experiment on aggression) need not be literally the same as everyday behaviour. But the experiment *should* have experimental realism—it should absorb and involve the participants and result in the real psychological experiences it is intending to create. Experimenters do not want participants consciously play-acting; they want to engage real psychological processes. Forcing people to choose whether to give an intense or mild electric shock to someone else can be a realistic measure of aggression because it functionally simulates real aggression.

A good example of this concept is research done by Rod Lindsay at Queen's University, who specialized in the accuracy of eyewitness identification. Most eyewitness research is done using videotaped crimes, but early on, Lindsay preferred to enact his "crimes" live. Participants were shown into a lab room and seated. The research assistant would then escort a second "participant" into the room and seat him or her nearer the door. After introducing the participants, the research assistant would say she had to leave the room for a while. The second participant was actually a confederate of the experimenter. After engaging the participant in small talk, the confederate would suddenly "steal" something (e.g., a calculator or the research assistant's purse) and run out of the room. Not surprisingly, this often left the participant shaken (as a real crime would). After the participant calmed down, he or she was asked to give a description of the criminal and to try to make an identification from a lineup. Dr. Lindsay's research found that witnesses in these "real" crimes were quite likely to make errors in their lineup identifications.

Achieving experimental realism sometimes requires deceiving people with a plausible cover story. In the Milgram experiments, if the person in the next room actually is not receiving the shocks (they were not actually shocked in the Milgram experiments), the experimenter does not want the participants to know this. That would destroy the experimental realism. Thus, about one-half of social-psychological studies use some form of deception in their search for truth (Hertwig & Ortmann, 2008). Such experiments raise the age-old question of whether the ends justify the means. Do the insights gained justify deceiving and sometimes distressing people? University research ethics boards now review all research that involves human participants. In Canada, the three major federal granting councils have developed a Tri-Council Policy Statement on Ethical Conduct for Research Involving Humans (2010; available at pre.ethics.gc.ca). Only universities that certify compliance with this policy receive research funding from these agencies. The Tri-Council Policy is based on some guiding ethical principles:

- Respect for human dignity
- Concern for vulnerable persons (that is, people who cannot provide free and informed consent—for example, minors—must have appropriate representation, such as parents or guardians)
- Privacy and confidentiality of any information collected from participants
- Justice and inclusiveness

Participants have the right to be completely debriefed at the end of any study and informed of its purpose. Finally, participants have the right to be told if they were deceived, and the reason for that deception.

In terms of appropriate debriefing, the experimenter should be sufficiently informative and considerate that people leave feeling at least as good about themselves as when they came in. Better yet, the participants should be repaid by having learned something about the nature of psychological inquiry. When treated respectfully, few participants mind being deceived (Epley & Huff, 1998; Kimmel, 1998).

Using deception will always be controversial. Deception must be used carefully and with strict guidelines. Antonio Pascual-Leone, Terence Singh, and Alan Scoboria (2010) have developed a checklist for researchers to use in determining if deception is warranted in a given study.

CONCLUSIONS

As the research on children, television, and violence illustrates, social psychology mixes everyday experience with laboratory analysis. Throughout this book we will do the same by drawing our data mostly from the laboratory and our illustrations mostly from life. This interplay appears in our discussion of the link between television and real-life violence. What people saw in everyday life suggested the need for experimental research. Network and government policymakers—those with the power to make changes—are now aware of the results. The consistency of findings on television's effects—in the lab and in the field—is true of research in many other areas, including studies of helping, leadership style, depression, and self-efficacy. The effects one finds in the lab have been mirrored by effects in the field. "The psychology laboratory has generally produced psychological truths rather than trivialities," noted Craig Anderson and his colleagues (1999).

Connection:

Experiments on the causal link between television viewing, video gaming, and violence, will be discussed in Module 21.

SUMMARY OF KEY POINTS

LO1. Understand the difference between correlation and causation.

- Correlation denotes the simple relationship between two variables, whereas causation indicates that changes in one variable actually causes the change in the other variable.
- People must be aware of the "third variable" issue, when a unknown factor is actually creating the relationship between the target variables.

LO2. Define independent and dependent variables.

- The *independent* variable is the experimental factor the researcher manipulates. The *dependent* variable is the variable being measured in terms of change.

LO3. Understand the importance of random assignment.

- Random assignment allows us to control for the impact of variables extraneous to the research.
- With random assignment we can be confident that observed effects are likely to be caused by our manipulations.

LO4. Understand the importance of ethics in psychological research.

- Research must be ethical, with participants receiving respectful treatments. Participants should be informed of the nature of the research, have their personal information treated with confidence, and be treated in a just manner.

KEY TERMS

Correlational research   The study of the naturally occurring associations between two or more factors.

Demand characteristics   Characteristics or cues in a study that suggest to participants what behaviour is expected.

Dependent variable   The variable being measured, so-called because it may depend on manipulations of the independent variable.

Experimental realism   The degree to which an experiment produces the real psychological experiences that it is intended to create.

Experimental research   Studies that seek clues to cause–effect relationships by manipulating one or more factors (independent variables) to determine their impact on other factors (dependent variables).

Independent variable   The experimental factor that a researcher manipulates.

Informed consent   An ethical principle requiring that research participants be told enough to enable them to decide if they wish to participate.

Mundane realism   The degree to which an experiment is superficially similar to everyday situations.

Observational research methods   Research methods in which individuals are observed in natural settings, often without awareness, in order to provide the opportunity for objective analysis of behaviour.

Random assignment   The process of assigning participants to the conditions of an experiment such that all persons have the same chance of being in a given condition. (Note the distinction between random assignment in experiments and random sampling in surveys. Random assignment helps us infer cause and effect. Random sampling helps us generalize to a population.)

Reactivity   The degree to which a measure may itself influence the behaviour we are studying.

Reliability   The extent to which a measure yields the same result when used on more than one occasion to assess some relatively stable characteristic.

Representative samples   Carefully selected samples used by survey researchers so that participant responses accurately reflect the responses of the population of interest.

Validity   The extent to which a measure assesses what it is intended to assess.

PART TWO: SOCIAL THINKING

MODULE THREE

Defining and Expressing the Self-Concept

LEARNING OBJECTIVES   After studying Module 3, you will be able to

LO 1   Understand how we develop and express our sense of self

LO 2   Understand the role of culture and gender in the self-concept

LO 3   Explain how we know our selves

LO 4   Explain self-presentation biases and how they work

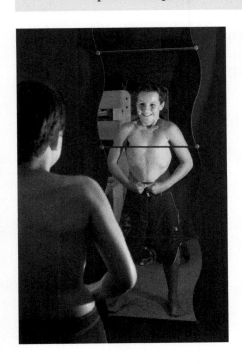

Take a minute and consider this question: If someone came up to you on the street and asked you who you were, what would you say? What factors contribute to your sense of self? Who *are* you? As a unique and complex creature, you undoubtedly have many ways to complete the sentence "I am . . ." Francophone? Anglophone? Muslim? Catholic? Male? Female? Gay? Straight? Black? Asian? Aboriginal? Caucasian? Or some combination of the above? How we answer this question not only affects our perception of the world, but how others perceive us. Perhaps not surprisingly, social psychologists have been interested in this question for some time.

Our self-concept affects how we perceive ourselves and others, as well as how they perceive us. Before you delve into this module, take a minute to complete the questionnaire in the activity, which examines how you see yourself as a Canadian.

Critical THINKING

Who are you? Now, what if you were asked the question during a job interview? Would your answer change? What if you were meeting your partner's parents for the first time? How does context change how we present ourselves? Does it actually change your self-concept? Or make you focus on something else?

Now that you have completed the questionnaire (a scale developed by James Cameron [2004] at Saint Mary's University), think about how you feel about being "Canadian." Is that something that is very central to you? Or is it something that is not even relevant to you? Taken together, your answers help define your self-concept.

Our sense of self organizes our thoughts, feelings, and actions. Whatever we do in our years on this planet, whatever we infer and interpret, whatever we conceive and create, whomever we meet and greet, will be filtered through our self. How, and how accurately, do we know ourselves? What determines our self-concepts?

Activity: **What is your social identity?**

As we have noted, self-concept describes how we identify ourselves. In this activity, you can get a sense of your Canadian identity. Please use the scale to indicate your agreement with the following items. Circle the number at the right of the statement that best corresponds with your opinion.

1 Strongly Disagree	2 Disagree	3 Slightly Disagree	4 Neither Agree Nor Disagree	5 Slightly Agree	6 Agree	7 Strongly Agree

1. Generally, I feel good when I think about myself as a Canadian.	1 2 3 4 5 6 7
2. I don't feel a sense of being "connected" with other Canadians.	1 2 3 4 5 6 7
3. The fact that I am a Canadian rarely enters my mind.	1 2 3 4 5 6 7
4. In general, being a Canadian is an important part of my self-image.	1 2 3 4 5 6 7
5. I often regret that I am a Canadian.	1 2 3 4 5 6 7
6. I feel strong ties to other Canadians.	1 2 3 4 5 6 7
7. I don't feel good about being a Canadian.	1 2 3 4 5 6 7
8. Overall, being a Canadian has very little to do with how I feel about myself.	1 2 3 4 5 6 7
9. I have a lot in common with other Canadians.	1 2 3 4 5 6 7
10. I often think about the fact that I am a Canadian.	1 2 3 4 5 6 7
11. I find it difficult to form a bond with other Canadians.	1 2 3 4 5 6 7
12. In general, I am glad to be a Canadian.	1 2 3 4 5 6 7

SCORING: Items 2, 3, 5, 7, 8, and 11 are all negatively keyed items. Reverse the scoring on those items (7 becomes 1, 6 becomes 2, 5 becomes 3, 4 stays 4, etc.). Now, add up your score. The higher the score, the stronger your Canadian identity.

LO 1

OUR SENSE OF SELF

Schemas are mental templates by which we organize our worlds. Our self-schemas—our perceptions of ourselves as athletic, overweight, smart, or whatever—powerfully affect how we process social information (Markus & Wurf, 1987). These self-defining beliefs influence how we perceive, remember, and evaluate other people and ourselves. If athletics is a central part of your self-concept (i.e., if being an athlete is one of your self-schemas), then you will tend to notice others' bodies and skills. You will quickly recall sports-related experiences, and you will welcome information that is consistent with your self-schema (Kihlstrom & Cantor, 1984). The self-schemas that make up our self-concepts operate like a mental system for cataloguing and retrieving information.

Consider how the self influences memory, a phenomenon known as the self-reference effect: *When information is relevant to our self-concepts, we process it quickly and remember it well* (Higgins & Bargh, 1987; Kuiper & Rogers, 1979; Symons & Johnson, 1997).

The self-reference effect illustrates a basic fact of life: Our sense of self is at the centre of our world. Because we tend to see ourselves on centre stage, we overestimate the extent to which others' behaviour is aimed at us. We often see ourselves as responsible for events in which we played only a small part (Fenigstein, 1984). When judging someone else's performance or behaviour, we often spontaneously compare it with our own (Dunning & Hayes, 1996). And if, while talking to one person, we overhear our name spoken by another in the room, our auditory radar instantly shifts our attention (Wood & Cowan, 1995). However, this effect does not happen the same way for everyone. While Takashi Nakao was a post-doctoral fellow at the University of Ottawa, he found that people who are more altruistic (i.e., who are more likely help others) are less likely to show the self-reference effect (presumably because they tend to think of others more than themselves; Nakao, et al., 2012).

Nonetheless, from our self-focused perspectives we readily presume that others are noticing and evaluating us. Thomas Gilovich and his colleagues (2000) demonstrated this by having individual students don Barry Manilow T-shirts before entering a room with other students. (Barry Manilow is a cheesy ballad singer from the '70s and '80s.) Feeling self-conscious, the T-shirt wearers guessed that nearly half their peers would notice the shirt (only 23 percent did). Keenly aware of our emotions, we often have an illusion that they are transparent to others. The same goes for our social blunders and public mental slips. What we agonize over, others may hardly notice and soon forget (Savitsky et al., 2001).

Jacquie Vorauer at the University of Manitoba and Michael Ross at the University of Waterloo (1999) have demonstrated that the more self-conscious we are, the more we believe this "illusion of transparency." But we do not just worry about people judging us, we actively compare ourselves to them. Jennifer Campbell and her colleagues at the University of British Columbia (e.g., Campbell, Fairley & Fehr, 1986) have demonstrated that we readily compare ourselves to others when judging ourselves as well.

LO 2

SELF, CULTURE, AND GENDER

How did you score on the self-concept activity? That scale was designed to assess your overall feelings about who you are relative to a specific target group. In this case, we discussed your Canadian identity. Each person who lives in Canada has his or her own personal sense of "self." However, what is less clear is the extent to which our perception of self is dependent on who we are versus where we come from.

Canadian Identity

But what is the Canadian identity? Interestingly, there is quite a bit of research that suggests one of the main ideals of being Canadian is that we are "not American" (see Hedley, 1994; Lalonde, 2002; MacGregor, 2003). A 1999 poll published in *Maclean's* reported that Canadians consider the most important elements of the Canadian identity to be our flag, our climate and geography, the achievements of Canadians throughout the world, our healthcare system, our role in international politics, and our multicultural heritage. While 71 percent of Americans thought Canada and the United States were mainly the same, only 49 percent of Canadians agreed.

Truro, Nova Scotia, native Jeff Douglas portrays Joe Canadian in the Molson Canadian beer commercial.

A reflection of the Canadian identity is Molson's award-winning Molson Canadian beer ad campaign featuring "Joe Canadian." This ad, which first appeared during the 2000 Academy Awards, had the following text:

Hey. I'm not a lumberjack, or a fur trader . . . I don't live in an igloo, or eat blubber, or own a dogsled . . . and I don't know Jimmy, Sally, or Suzy from Canada, although I'm certain they're really really nice.

I have a Prime Minister, not a president. I speak English and French, not American. And I pronounce it "about," not "a boot."

I can proudly sew my country's flag on my backpack. I believe in peace keeping, not policing, diversity, not assimilation, and that the beaver is a truly proud and noble animal. A toque is a hat, a chesterfield is a couch, and it is pronounced "zed." Not "zee"—"zed"!!!!

Canada is the second largest landmass! The first nation of hockey! And the best part of North America! My name is Joe!! And I am Canadian!!!

An instant hit, "I am Canadian" is still the signature motto for Molson.

The Self and Culture

Most of us have multiple identities (e.g., male, Muslim, Canadian, and gay; female, Baptist, Black, and straight). However, can these different identities cause conflict? Do you see conflict in the multiple identities that define who you are? Many immigrants, or children of recent immigrants, report high levels of interrole conflict. Often, their life satisfaction and well-being is related to their ability to balance the values of their traditional culture with their new language and cultural reality (e.g., Lee & Chen, 2000). Yet new Canadians can encounter some difficulties that Canadian-born people may not appreciate. Vicki Esses and her colleagues (2006) at the University of Western Ontario, and Peter Grant (2008) at the University of Saskatchewan have demonstrated that immigrants can have a difficult time finding a job because their skills are undervalued by Canadian employers.

Critical THINKING

So, once again, we ask: "Who are you?" In 2006, Quebec was hailed in Parliament as a "nation within a nation," thereby formally recognizing Quebec's unique identity within Canada. But is this the only group that should be formally recognized? What other groups within Canada warrant this type of acknowledgement?

Culture can be defined as the enduring behaviours, attitudes, and traditions shared by a large group of people and transmitted from one generation to the next. For some people, especially those in industrialized Western cultures, individualism prevails as the self-concept. The psychology of Western culture (e.g., Canada, the United States, Western Europe) assumes that your life will be enriched by defining your possible selves (that is, the person you could be) and believing in your power of personal control.

Cultures native to Asia, Africa, and Central and South America place a greater value on collectivism. They nurture what Shinobu Kitayama and Hazel Markus (1995) call the *interdependent self*. Steven Heine and his colleagues at the University of British Columbia have demonstrated that people with interdependent self-construals are more self-critical, have less need for positive self-regard, and are less likely to try to self-enhance—that is, make themselves look better relative to others (e.g., Heine, 2010; Falk et al., 2009). Identity is defined more in relation to others.

However, making general statements about a culture's individualistic or collectivist orientations is an oversimplification. Even within Canada, there are differences. For example, people might argue that Quebecers tend to be more liberal, whereas Albertans are more conservative. Conservatives tend to be economic individualists ("don't tax or regulate me") and moral collectivists ("do legislate against immorality"). Liberals tend to be economic collectivists and moral individualists. Despite these differences, however, researchers still make the individualist/collectivist distinction, notes Ulrich Schimmack at the University of Toronto (Schimmack et al., 2005), at the cultural level.

With an *inter*dependent self, one has a greater sense of belonging. Uprooted and cut off from family, colleagues, and loyal friends, interdependent people would lose the social connections that define who they are. They have not one self but many selves: self-with-parents, self-at-work, self-with-friends (Cross et al., 1992). As Figure 3-1 suggests, the interdependent self is embedded in social memberships. The goal of social life is not so much to enhance one's individual self as to harmonize with and support one's communities. The hyper-individualized latté—"decaf, non-fat, single shot, skinny, extra hot"—that seems just right at a North American espresso shop would seem a bit weird in Seoul, note Kim and Markus (1999; see also Kim & Sherman, 2007). In Korea, people place less value on uniqueness and more on tradition and shared practices (Choi & Choi, 2002). For example, Korean advertising tends to focus on groups of people, rather than individual choice or personal freedom (Markus, 2001; Morling and Lamoreaux, 2008).

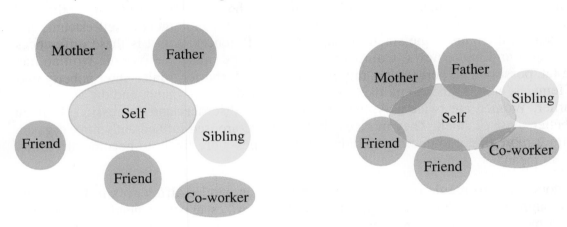

Independent view of self   Interdependent view of self

FIGURE 3-1

Self-construal as independent or interdependent. The independent self acknowledges relationships with others, but the interdependent self is more deeply embedded in others.

From Markus & Kitayama, 1991.

Self-esteem in collectivist cultures correlates closely with "what others think of me and my group." Self-concept is malleable (context-specific) rather than stable (enduring across situations). In one study, Romin Taforodi and his colleagues at the University of Toronto found that 80 percent of Canadian students but only a third of Chinese and Japanese students agreed that across different activities, the beliefs you hold about your inner self vary (Taforodi et al., 2004). For those in individualistic cultures, "outside" appraisals of oneself and one's group matter somewhat less (Crocker, 1994; Kwan et al., 1997). Self-esteem is more personal and less relational. Threaten our *personal* identity and we feel angrier and gloomier than when someone threatens our collective identity (Gaertner et al., 1999).

Self and Gender

Later, we will consider how culture and gender—the characteristics people associate with being male and female—affects the way others regard and treat us. For now, let's consider how gender affects our sense of self.

First, it is worth noting that gender can be considered as distinct from sex, although most people use the terms interchangeably (Kessler & McKenna, 1978). Sex is biological, and determines whether we are male or female. However, gender is more psychological. A good example of this is a transsexual male, who is biologically male but perceives himself as psychologically female. Typically, in this book, when we discuss gender effects, we are really comparing males with females.

Your first question might be: "Are men and women really different?" We frequently read about gender differences in popular magazines like *Cosmopolitan* and *Men's Health*. We see these gender differences and stereotypes portrayed on countless TV shows. But are these differences real? Well, yes, but only to a point.

Females and males are similar in many physical traits, such as the age at which we sit, teethe, and walk, as well as the development of overall vocabulary, creativity, intelligence, self-esteem, and happiness. Nonetheless, there are some small but significant differences, and it is these differences that capture attention and make news. Compared to the average man, the average woman has 70 percent more fat, possesses 40 percent less muscle, and is 12 cm shorter. Males enter puberty two years later than females, are 20 times more likely to have colour-deficient vision, and die an average of five years earlier. Women are twice as vulnerable to anxiety disorders and depression. Women have a slightly better sense of smell. They more easily become re-aroused immediately after orgasm. Men are three times more likely to commit suicide and five times more likely to become alcoholic. But what does it all mean?

One of your authors (Steven) regularly discusses the research on gender differences in his classes. Interestingly, although most students smile and nod as he describes apparent gender differences, there are always a handful of people who object and say: "But that's wrong! This doesn't describe me!" Maybe, but it is important to remember when we talk about gender differences we are talking about average differences—the distribution of traits for males and females definitely overlaps. For example, Figure 3-2 describes a hypothetical distribution of how nurturing men and women are. Although the average rates of nurturing are different, many men and women overlap. There will be men who nurture, and women who do not.

But how does gender affect the self? Well, the differences surface in childhood. Boys tend to strive for independence; they define their identities in separation from the caregiver, usually their mothers. Girls tend to welcome *inter*dependence; they define their identities through their social connections. Boys' play often involves group activity. Girls' play occurs in smaller groups, with less aggression, more sharing, more imitation of relationships, and more intimate discussion (Lever, 1978). Perhaps this is because, even when young, girls are also more talkative than boys and use more affiliative speech, whereas boys use more assertive speech (although these differences are small; Leaper & Smith, 2004).

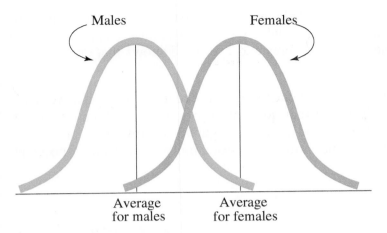

FIGURE 3-2

Hypothetical distribution of nurturing behaviour in males and females.

Adult relationships continue these small but significant gender differences. Women describe themselves in more relational terms, experience more relationship-linked emotions, and are more attuned to others' relationships (Gabriel & Gardner, 1999; Tamres et al., 2002). In conversation, men more often focus on tasks and on connections with large groups; women focus on personal relationships (Tannen, 1990). In groups, men talk more to give information; women talk more to share lives, give help, or show support (Dindia & Allen, 1992; Eagly, 1987). Among first-year American college students, five in ten males and two in three females say it is *very* important to "help others who are in difficulty" (Sax et al., 1999). In an interesting study conducted by Debbie Moskowitz and her colleagues at McGill University in Montreal, women and men, across a 20-day period, monitored their interpersonal behaviour (Moskowitz et al., 1994; Suh et al., 2004). Moskowitz found that, in general, women were more communal and agreeable than men, but especially when they were interacting with other women. Men interacting with men were more likely to show dominance-oriented behaviours.

This difference has an impact on what we do later in life as well: studies of 640 000 people's job preferences reveal some tendency for men more than women to value earnings, promotion, challenge, and power, and for women more than men to value good working hours, personal relationships, and opportunities to help others (Konrad et al., 2000). Indeed, in most North American caregiving professions, such as social work, teaching, and nursing, women outnumber men. Women spend more time caring for both preschoolers and aging parents (Eagly & Crowley, 1986). Compared with men, they buy three times as many gifts and greeting cards, write two to four times as many personal letters, and make 10 to 20 percent more long-distance calls to friends and family (Putnam, 2000). Asked to provide photos that portray who they are, women include more photos of parents and of themselves with others (Clancy & Dollinger, 1993). For women, especially, a sense of mutual support is crucial to marital satisfaction (Acitelli & Antonucci, 1994). Again, however, this depends on culture. In typically Western, independent cultures (e.g., Canada, New Zealand), the difference between male and female self-concept is larger than in collectivist cultures (e.g., China, Ethiopia), where men are more likely to hold collectivist or relational views of the self (see Watkins et al., 1998a, 1998b). Overall, the varying expectations we have for ourselves (and others have for us) define our **gender roles**.

Our gender roles can have an important impact on our behaviour, but does culture construct gender roles and expectations? Or do gender roles merely reflect behaviour that is naturally appropriate for men and women? The variety of gender roles across cultures and over time shows that culture does indeed construct our gender roles.

For example, you might ask: Who generally makes a better political leader—a man or a woman? When the Pew Global Attitudes (2010) survey posed that question to people in 56 countries, most said that men and women were equally good leaders. However, as Figure 3-3 shows, the country-to-country differences were considerable. Even so, there are still substantially more men in political positions of power than women.

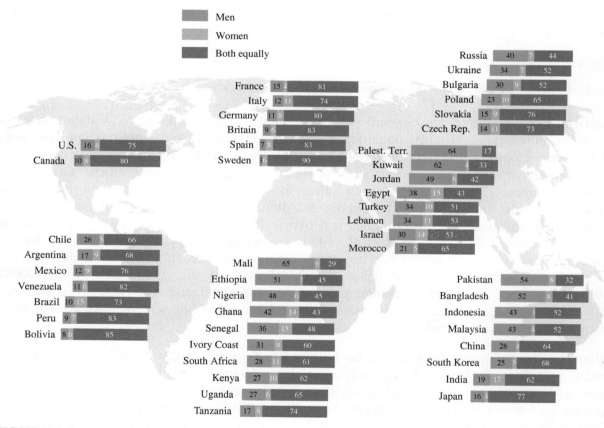

FIGURE 3-3

Opinions about whether men or women make better political leaders vary from culture to culture.

Data from the 2010 Pew Global Attitudes Survey.

In industrialized societies, roles vary enormously. Women fill one in ten managerial positions in Japan and Germany, and nearly one in two in Australia and the United States (ILO, 1997; Wallace, 2000). Although there are differences across countries (e.g., in North America, most doctors and dentists are men; in Russia, most doctors are women, as are most dentists in Denmark), attitudes toward women vary as well. The Pew Global Attitudes survey reported in 2010 that although 97–99 percent of people in Western countries support gender equality, in Egypt, 60 percent support gender equality; in Nigeria only 45 percent do (Pew, 2010). The International Labour Organization reported in 2010 that ". . . the circumstances of female employment—the sectors where women work, the types of work they do, the relationship of women to their jobs, the wages they receive—bring fewer gains . . . to women than are brought to the typical working male" (p. *x*). Interesting research by Catherine Ott-Holland and her colleagues (2013) showed that vocational interests are influenced by cultural norms. Typical vocational tests assess an individual's personality and match them to occupations. These researchers found that link between personality traits and occupational interests was stronger in individualistic than collectivist cultures.

Consistent with these findings, Wendy Wood and Alice Eagly (2010) believe that a variety of factors, including biological influences and childhood socialization, predispose a sexual division of labour. In adult life, the immediate causes of gender differences in social behaviour are the *roles* that reflect this sexual division of labour. Men, because of their strength and speed, tend to be found in roles demanding physical power. Women's capacity for childbearing and nursing inclines them to more nurturant roles. Each gender then tends to exhibit the behaviours expected of those who fill such roles and to have their skills and beliefs shaped accordingly.

Most importantly, however, Wood and Eagly (2000) conclude that "the behaviour of women and men is sufficiently malleable that individuals of both genders are fully capable of effectively carrying out organizational roles at all levels" (see Figure 3-4). Thus, the differences in roles can largely be attributed to cultural and social norms rather than innate abilities.

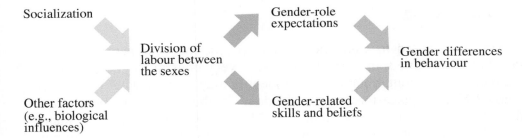

FIGURE 3-4

Social-role theory of gender differences in social behaviour. Various influences, including childhood experiences and factors, bend males and females toward differing roles. The expectations, skills, and beliefs associated with these differing roles affect men's and women's behaviour.

The Self and Sexuality

Sexuality and sexual identity are very important to our self-concept. There is no one "homosexual identity," and indeed, there is much debate about how identity develops among non-heterosexuals. There is an important distinction to make that might influence the development of self-identity in homosexuals however. There is no question that prejudice exists in our world, and prejudice toward gay, lesbian, bisexual, and transgendered individuals certainly exists as well. Thus, even in Canada, being "not heterosexual" is a salient characteristic; it is something that will play a significant role in the development of self-concept (e.g., see Aldrerson, 2003). There is, in fact, a substantial debate in the literature about how homosexual identity forms (see, for example, Horowitz & Newcomb, 2002). But we must recognize that regardless of how the self-concept forms, context is very important.

Connection:

Prejudice and discrimination will be discussed further in Modules 15 and 16.

There are unique experiences that might influence the development of the self-concept for gay, lesbian, bisexual, and transgendered individuals. For example, Neil Pilkington at McGill and his colleagues (e.g., Pilkington & D'Augelli, 1995; see also Saewyc et al., 2006) have demonstrated that most gay, lesbian, and bisexual youth experience victimization (ranging from verbal abuse to armed assault), and that for LGBT youth, no social environment (e.g., family, school, work, and community) is free from risk. Youth who disclosed their sexuality at an early age, or for whom concealing their sexuality was more difficult, were most likely to be victimized.

Interestingly, there are areas where homosexuality might buffer against social norms. Sherry Bergeron and Charlene Senn at the University of Windsor (1998) found that although both heterosexual and lesbian women were aware of socio-cultural norms for female body image, lesbians felt more fit, felt better about their bodies, and internalized the social norms less than heterosexual women.

Applying Social Psychology

Earlier in this module, you were asked to complete a scale to describe your perceptions of yourself as a Canadian. Is being Canadian something that is very central to you (or even applicable)? If you are a recent immigrant, your Canadian identity may be somewhat weaker or absent. How did you score? Now, replace the word "Canadian" in the scale with some other word that can be used to describe you (maybe Catholic, or Muslim, or Aboriginal, gay, man, woman, or any other word that describes a group you belong to). Most of us have multiple identities. Can these different identities cause conflict?

Answer the items and give yourself a new score based on whatever term you selected. Are you more Canadian than the other trait? Do you see conflict in the multiple identities that define who you are? How does this make you feel? Often, life satisfaction and well-being are related to our ability to balance the relative importance of the multiple roles we have.

LO 3

SELF-KNOWLEDGE: HOW DO WE KNOW OURSELVES?

"Know thyself," admonished the Greek philosopher Socrates. We certainly try. We readily form beliefs about ourselves, and we don't hesitate to explain why we feel and act as we do. But how well do we actually know ourselves? Sometimes we *think* we know ourselves, but our information is wrong.

Explaining and Predicting Our Feelings and Behaviour

Why did you choose your current school? Why did you yell at your roommate? Why did you fall in love with that special person? Why did you post that picture? Sometimes we know. Sometimes we don't. Asked why we have felt or acted as we have, we produce plausible answers. Yet, when causes are subtle, our self-explanations are often wrong.

Donald Dutton at the University of British Columbia conducted a clever study to explore how people misattributed fear responses as sexual attraction (Dutton & Aron, 1974). Men were interviewed by a female research assistant after crossing the fear-arousing Capilano Suspension Bridge in Vancouver. These men, compared with men who crossed a more solid bridge, used more sexual imagery in a later projective test and they were more likely to phone the female research assistant for a "follow-up." Clearly, these men were misattributing the fear arousal they felt to attraction for the research assistant.

Sometimes people think they have been affected by something that has had no effect. For example, researchers asked people to record their moods, along with factors that might affect their moods—the day of the week, the weather, the amount they slept, and so forth (Stone et al., 1985; Weiss & Brown, 1976; Wilson et al., 1982). At the end of each study, the participants judged how much each factor had affected their moods. There was little link between their perceptions of how important a factor was and how well that specific factor actually predicted their mood. As Dan Gilbert (2007) notes, we are remarkably bad at predicting what will make us happy.

People also make mistakes when predicting their behaviour. For example, dating couples predict the longevity of their relationships through rose-coloured glasses. Dr. Tara MacDonald (at Queen's University) explored whether parents and friends of students were better judges of the students' romantic relationships than the students themselves (see MacDonald & Ross, 1999). She found that the outsiders were more accurate in their predictions than the people involved in the relationships, likely because someone involved in the relationship is not able to make an objective assessment of the relationship and thus cannot accurately predict its outcome.

When predicting negative behaviours such as crying or lying, self-predictions are more accurate than predictions by one's mother and friends (Shrauger et al., 1996). Close friends are at least as good as you at predicting your daily routine as well (Vazire & Mehl, 2008). However, when planning for the future, you need to be careful predicting how long it will take you to do something. In one study, students predicted how long it would take them to finish a term paper (Buehler et al., 2002). On average, it took three weeks longer than they predicted as "realistic" and one week longer than their "worst case" scenario. Nevertheless, the surest thing we can say about your individual future is that it is sometimes hard for even you to predict. When predicting your behaviour, the best advice is to consider your past behaviour in similar situations (Osberg & Shrauger, 1986, 1990).

Many of life's big decisions involve predicting our future feelings. Sometimes we know how we will feel—if we fail that exam, win that big game, or soothe our tensions with a half-hour jog. But often we don't. People have mispredicted how they would feel some time after a romantic breakup, or when receiving a gift, losing an election, winning a game, or being insulted (Gilbert & Ebert, 2002). Here are some examples:

- When male youths are shown sexually arousing photographs, then exposed to a passionate date scenario in which their date asks them to "stop," they acknowledge the possibility that they might not stop. If they are not first shown sexually arousing pictures, they more often deny the possibility of being sexually aggressive (Loewenstein & Schkade, 1999). When not aroused, one easily mispredicts how one will feel and act when aroused—a phenomenon that leads to many unintended pregnancies.

Connection:

The impact of pornography on thinking and behaviour will be discussed further in Module 21.

- Only one in seven occasional smokers (of less than one cigarette per day) predict they will be smoking in five years. But they underestimate the power of their drug cravings; nearly half will still be smoking (Lynch & Bonnie, 1994).
- Undergraduates who break up with a partner are less upset than they thought they would be (Eastwick et al., 2007). European track athletes were similarly less upset than they thought they would be if they did not meet their goals at a key track meet (van Dijk et al., 2008).

Connection:

We will talk more about romantic relationships in Modules 19 and 20.

- When people being tested for HIV predict how they will feel five weeks after getting the results, they expect to be feeling misery over bad news and elation over good news. Yet, five weeks later, the bad-news recipients are less distraught and the good-news recipients are less elated than they anticipated (Sieff et al., 1999).

Wilson and Gilbert (2005) argue that this bias in perceptions of the impact of events is important, because people's "affective forecasts" influence their decisions. In *focusing* on the negative *event*, we discount the importance of everything else that contributes to happiness and so over-predict our misery. Moreover, people underestimate the speed and power of their psychological immune system, which includes their strategies for rationalizing, discounting, forgiving, and limiting emotional trauma. We are resilient.

LO 4

SELF-PRESENTATION BIASES

Much of how we perceive ourselves depends on how we present ourselves to others. As we will see in the next module, we sometimes interpret our social world in a very self-serving way. Similarly, we spend a significant amount of time being careful to present ourselves in a positive light. There is significant evidence that people present a different self than the one they may be feeling.

Role-Playing

Think of a time when you stepped into some new role—perhaps your first days on a job or at a new school. That first week on campus, for example, you may have been supersensitive to your new social situation and tried valiantly to act appropriately and to root out your high school behaviour. At such times we feel self-conscious. We observe our new speech and actions because they aren't natural to us. Then one day we notice something amazing. Our faked enthusiasm or our pseudo-intellectual talk no longer feels forced. The role has begun to fit as comfortably as our old jeans and T-shirt. The take-home lesson: What is unreal (an artificial role) can evolve into what is real. Take on a new role—as club member, teacher, soldier, or salesperson—and it may shape your attitudes and behaviour.

False Modesty

Interestingly, often people present themselves in a more negative light than a more positive one. For example, you probably have a friend who always says after an exam, "I did terribly! I know I failed!" but consistently ends up with high grades. This is known as *false modesty*. Why might people do this? Such self-disparaging remarks can actually be self-serving: The comment "I look terrible in this outfit" is usually countered with "No, you look great!"

We may present ourselves differently depending on the situation. In a job interview, we want to manage the impression we make on others.

False modesty also appears in people's accounts of their successes in life. In acceptance speeches, people often thank all of those who have helped them achieve their successes. But do people really believe that others are the cause of their success? Interestingly, the audience of the speech makes a difference. Roy Baumiester and Stacy Ilko (1995) asked people to write a description of an important success experience in their life. Participants who signed their names and expected to present their description to an audience were much more likely to acknowledge the help and support of others than participants who wrote anonymously. Indeed, those who wrote anonymously were much more likely to attribute their successes to their own efforts—suggesting that the gratitude expressed by the non-anonymous writers was shallow and superficial.

Self-Handicapping

Sometimes, people can sabotage their own chances for success. Take, for example, the student who goes out drinking the night before a final exam. Surprisingly, Daniel Bailis at the University of Manitoba has demonstrated that this type of self-destructive behaviour often has a self-protective aim (see Bailis, 2001). Why? Because it allows the person to say, "I'm really not a failure—if I hadn't gone out the night before, I would have done well on the exam." Thus, self-handicapping protects both our self-esteem and our public image. If we fail, we have an outside factor to blame; if we succeed, we must really be competent.

For example, Bailis (2001) has shown that university athletes who are prone to self-handicapping prepare less for events and have poorer nutrition. Yet self-handicapping is not all bad. Self-reported self-handicapping dispositions are positively related to both performance at the athletic events, and the athletes' experience of the event—thus there are real benefits. Interestingly, people who have strongly identified with their academic goals are less likely to exhibit self-handicapping in academic settings, presumably because they are motivated to do well, and prepare, rather than creating the excuse for failure.

Impression Management

To varying degrees, we are continually managing the impressions we create. Self-presentation refers to our wanting to present a desired image both to an external audience (other people) and an internal audience (ourselves). We want others to perceive us as good, friendly, and competent people, and for the most part we want to see ourselves in that light as well. In familiar situations (such as with family), this may occur with little effort and we may be less modest. In unfamiliar situations (such as at a party), we are acutely aware of the impression we are creating (Leary et al., 1994; Tice et al., 1995) and will modify our behaviour accordingly.

For some people, conscious self-presentation is a way of life. Others are less concerned about how they are seen by others. To assess this occurrence, Mark Snyder developed the self-monitoring scale (see Snyder & DeBono, 1989). People who score high in self-monitoring act like social chameleons, adapting easily to social situations. People who are low in self-monitoring care less about what others think and are more focused on, and tend to act on, their internal thoughts and beliefs (McCann & Hancock, 1983). For example, when low-self-monitoring British university women answered questions about their gender-related attitudes, they were not affected by how the female interviewer dressed. However, high-self-monitoring women answered in more feminine ways if the interviewer was dressed in a feminine manner (Smith et al., 1997). Self-presentation strategies vary online as well. Singaporeans were more likely than Americans to upload photos of themselves (Rui & Stefanone, 2013)—and people from collectivist cultures tend to disclose less personal information (Chen & Marcus, 2012). Women also tend to compare themselves to others online more so than men do, and women tend to use social networking sites to search for information. Men are more likely to look at profiles to find friends. Women also tend to post portrait photos (upper body and face), whereas men are more likely to post full body shots (Haferkamp et al., 2012).

CONCLUSIONS

Overall, our self-concept is defined by how we perceive ourselves. Yet how we perceive ourselves is also dependent on how others perceive us. Thus, our self-concept will always to some extent be influenced by others. Culture, gender, and sexuality also play very important roles. Perhaps most importantly, self-concept is not a static unchanging thing. Self-concept changes, both over time and adaptively, depending on the context and situation we are in. Where we are, who we are with, and what we are trying to accomplish all interact to affect our self-concept.

SUMMARY OF KEY POINTS

LO1. Understand how we develop and express our sense of self.

- Our self-schemas guide how we process social information, and we tend to remember things best if they are relevant to the self.

LO2. Understand the role of culture and gender in the self-concept.

- Our sense of self is influenced in large part by our culture and upbringing.
- Men and women share many similarities, but small, significant differences, do exist.

LO3. Explain how we know our selves.

- We are not always very good at predicting our future feelings and behaviour.
- Often, family and friends are at least as good, if not better, at making predictions about our behaviour.

LO4. Explain self-presentation biases and how they work.

- We are motivated to present ourselves in the best light, and use several different techniques to present ourselves in the most positive light possible.

KEY TERMS

Collectivism   Giving priority to the goals of one's groups (often one's extended family or work group) and defining one's identity accordingly.

Culture   The enduring behaviours, attitudes, and traditions shared by a large group of people and transmitted from one generation to the next.

Gender roles   Sets of behavioural expectations (norms) for males and females.

Gender   In psychology, the characteristics, whether biological or socially influenced, by which people define male and female.

Individualism   The concept of giving priority to one's own goals over group goals and defining one's identity in terms of personal attributes rather than group identifications.

Role   A set of norms that define how people in a given social position ought to behave.

Self-concept   A person's answers to the question, "Who am I?"

Self-presentation   Wanting to present a desired image both to an external audience (other people) and an internal audience (ourselves).

Self-reference effect   The tendency to process efficiently, and remember well, information related to oneself.

Self-schemas   Beliefs about self that organize and guide the processing of self-relevant information.

MODULE FOUR

Self-Serving Bias

How do you feel about yourself? Do you like yourself? Or are you your worst critic? In general, college and university students have somewhat higher self-esteem than the general public. For many of you, this might seem surprising. College and university often challenge us as we have never been challenged before. We get frequent (and sometimes harsh) feedback from professors. So, how do we deal with negative information about ourselves, how does this information influence our outlook on life, and why is it that our self-esteem can handle these constant threats?

Critical THINKING

Was this crash a result of the driver's ability or external factors? If you had been in this accident, what would you blame it on?

Despite what we have just read, it is widely believed that most of us suffer from low self-esteem. Actually, most of us have a good reputation with ourselves. Before you go on, take a minute and answer the items in the following activity. We will come back to it a little later in the module.

Activity: **How good are you?**

Compared to other students in the same year and of the same gender as yourself, how would you rate yourself on the following characteristics? Use the following scale in making your response.

1 = well below average

2 = below average

3 = slightly below average

4 = average

5 = slightly above average

6 = above average

7 = well above average

_____   1. leadership ability

(Continued)

_____   2. athletic ability

_____   3. ability to get along with others

_____   4. tolerance

_____   5. energy level

_____   6. helpfulness

_____   7. responsibility

_____   8. creativity

_____   9. patience

_____   10. trustworthiness

_____   11. sincerity

_____   12. thoughtfulness

_____   13. cooperativeness

_____   14. reasonableness

_____   15. intelligence

Now that you have answered all of these items, take a look at your responses again. Do you see yourself in a positive light? A negative one? How good are you compared to others? Chances are, you rated yourself above average on most of the characteristics. Most people do.

Interestingly, in studies of self-esteem, even low-scoring people respond in the midrange of possible scores. (A low-self-esteem person responds to statements such as "I have good ideas" with a qualifying adjective, such as "somewhat" or "sometimes.") Moreover, one of social psychology's most provocative, yet firmly established, conclusions concerns the potency of self-serving bias: the tendency to perceive and present oneself favourably. Are you likely to succumb to this bias?

LO 1

EXPLAINING POSITIVE AND NEGATIVE EVENTS

People accept credit when they have succeeded. They attribute their success to their ability and effort, but attribute failure to external factors such as bad luck or the problem's inherent "impossibility" (Campbell & Sedikides, 1999). Similarly, in explaining their victories, athletes commonly credit themselves, but they attribute losses to something else: bad breaks, bad referee calls, or the other team's superior effort or dirty play (Grove et al., 1991; Lalonde, 1992; Mullen & Riordan, 1988). And how much responsibility do you suppose car drivers tend to accept for their accidents? On insurance forms, drivers have described their accidents in words such as these: "An invisible car came out of nowhere, struck my car, and vanished"; "As I reached an intersection, a hedge sprang up, obscuring my vision, and I did not see the other car"; "A pedestrian hit me and went under my car" (*Toronto News*, July 26, 1977).

Such biases in allocating responsibility contribute to marital discord, dissatisfaction among workers, and impasses when bargaining (Kruger & Gilovich, 1999). It is a small wonder that divorced people usually blame their partner for the breakup (Gray & Silver, 1990) or that managers usually blame poor performance on workers' lack of ability or effort (Imai, 1994; Rice, 1985). Workers are more likely to blame something external—inadequate supplies, excessive workload, difficult co-workers, and ambiguous assignments. It is also a small wonder that people evaluate fat raises as fairer when they receive a bigger raise than most of their co-workers (Diekmann et al., 1997).

This bias appears in academics as well, particularly when considering authorship on research papers. Typically, the person who contributed most to the project ought to be the first author. Consistent with this anecdotal evidence, one of your authors, Steven, has found (see Parks et al., 2005) that if three authors provide a percentage estimate of how much they contributed to a published paper, the total percentage value assigned by the first, second, and third authors combined adds up to 158 percent!

Critical THINKING

In 2013, the CBC reported that students at Dalhousie University who were failing their classes blamed Facebook for their poor performance. These students claimed that Facebook was addictive and thus they could not get their work and studying done. What do you think about this? Can using Facebook be an addiction? Who is really to blame here?

Students who do well tend to accept personal credit. They judge the exam to be a valid measure of their competence (Arkin & Maruyama, 1979; Davis & Stephan, 1980; Gilmor & Reid, 1979; Griffin et al., 1983). Those who do poorly are much more likely to criticize the exam. Blaming failure on something external, even another's prejudice, is less depressing than seeing oneself as undeserving (Major et al., 2003). We will acknowledge our distant past failings—those by our "former" selves, note Anne Wilson at Wilfrid Laurier University and Michael Ross at the University of Waterloo

(2001). Describing their old pre-university selves, Waterloo students offered nearly as many negative as positive statements. Yet when describing their present selves, they offered three times more positive statements: "I've learned and grown, and I am a better person." Interestingly, Wilson and her colleagues (e.g., Wilson, Gunn, & Ross, 2009) have found that positive events are perceived to have happened "more recently" than negative events (even when they happen at the same time). Wilson and her colleagues propose that this helps people stay positive about themselves—negative events are "in the past." Interestingly, Peetz, Wilson, and Strahan (2009) have shown that this works for future events—future success on an upcoming midterm seems closer than future failure.

LO 2

CAN WE ALL BE BETTER THAN AVERAGE?

Have you done the activity from earlier in the module yet? If not, please do so before moving on. Self-serving bias also appears when people compare themselves to others. On most *subjective* and *socially desirable* dimensions, most people see themselves as better than average:

- Dr. Lionel Standing at Bishop's University has found that university and college students who were asked to judge the "accuracy" of a personality profile were more likely to rate the positive traits as accurately describing themselves than negative traits (MacDonald & Standing, 2002), and that students who smoke perceive themselves as smoking "less than" their friends (Standing, 2002).

- Ninety percent of business managers rate their performance as superior to that of their average peer (French, 1968). In Australia, 86 percent of people rate their job performance as above average, and 1 percent as below average (Headey & Wearing, 1987).

- When presented with versions of their own face morphed to look both more and less attractive, people were asked to pick the one that was their actual face. People tended to pick a version of their face that was more attractive than their actual face (Epley & Whitechurch, 2008).

- Most drivers—even most drivers who have been hospitalized for accidents—believe themselves to be safer and more skilled than the average driver (Guerin, 1994; McKenna & Myers, 1997; Svenson, 1981).

- Most people perceive themselves as more intelligent than their average peer, better looking, and much less prejudiced (*Public Opinion*, 1984; Wylie, 1979).

How often did you rate yourself as above average on the items in the activity earlier in the module? Research would suggest more frequently than you should have. Subjective behaviour dimensions (such as "helpful") trigger greater self-serving bias than objective behavioural dimensions (such as "punctual"). Students are more likely to rate themselves superior in "moral goodness" than in "intelligence" (Allison et al., 1989; Van Lange, 1991). And community residents overwhelmingly see themselves as *caring* more than most others about the environment, about hunger, and about other social issues, though they don't see themselves as *doing* more, such as contributing time or money to those issues (White & Plous, 1995). Interestingly, a number of factors appear to moderate the occurrence of self-serving biases. Education doesn't eliminate self-serving bias; even social psychologists exhibit it, by believing themselves more ethical than most social psychologists (Van

Lange et al., 1997). Nancy Higgins at St. Thomas University and Gira Bhatt at Kwantlen University College (Higgins & Bhatt, 2001) have demonstrated that Canadian students are less likely to engage in self-serving biases than Indian students (see also Joshi & Carter, 2013). However, Steven Heine has found Canadians are more self-serving than the Japanese (Falk, Heine, Yuki & Takemura, 2009; see also Rose et al., 2008). Furthermore, Hildy Ross and her colleagues (Ross et al., 2004) have demonstrated that as children get older they are more likely to engage in self-serving explanations for their behaviour.

Subjective qualities give us leeway in constructing our own definitions of success (Dunning et al., 1989, 1991). Rating your "athletic ability," you might ponder your basketball play, not the agonizing weeks you spent as a Little League baseball player hiding in right field. Assessing your "leadership ability," you might conjure up an image of a great leader whose style is similar to yours. By defining ambiguous criteria in our own terms, each of us can see ourselves as relatively successful. In one U.S. College Entrance Examination Board survey of 829 000 high school students, *none* rated themselves below average in "ability to get along with others" (a subjective, desirable trait), 60 percent rated themselves in the top 10 percent, and 25 percent saw themselves among the top 1 percent!

Researchers have asked if people really believe these inflated self-assessments, or if they are a product of how the question was asked (Krizan & Suls, 2008). It turns out they do—when researchers had students bet actual money on the accuracy of their estimates, they found that people truly did believe these inflated self-assessments (Williams & Gilovich, 2008).

UNREALISTIC OPTIMISM

Optimism predisposes a positive approach to life. Many of us, however, have what researcher Neil Weinstein (1980, 1982) terms "an unrealistic optimism about future life events." Partly because of their relative pessimism about others' fates (Shepperd, 2003), students perceive themselves as far more likely than their classmates to get a good job, draw a good salary, and own a home, and as far less likely to experience negative events, such as developing a drinking problem, having a heart attack before age 40, or being fired. Similarly, parents have unrealistic expectations for their children's success (Lench et al., 2006).

People, overall, tend to be more optimistic than pessimistic (Fischer & Chambers, 2008). Unrealistic optimism can lead to problems, however. Dillard and her colleagues (2009) found that students who were unrealistically optimistic about their ability to control their drinking at university were more likely to exhibit problems with alcohol years later.

In Scotland, most older teens think they are much less likely than their peers to become infected with HIV (Abrams, 1991; Pryor & Reeder, 1993). This type of thinking is apparent after disasters as well. For example, before Hurricane Juan struck Halifax in September 2003, residents did not believe that the hurricane would do much damage even if it struck (CBC, 2003). Juan did more than $100 million in damage. Interestingly, in the fall of 2007, as the remnants of Hurricane Noel crept north from the devastated southern United States, Nova Scotia residents predicted dire consequences (CBC, 2007). Of course, Noel did little damage. Famously, U.S. President Obama was quoted as saying that deep sea oil rigs almost never cause oil spills—three weeks before the 2010 BP oil spill in the Gulf of Mexico (easily the worst single oil spill ever; CBC, 2011).

People wade through flood water on Lakeshore West during a storm in Toronto on Monday, July 8, 2013.

However, illusory optimism can rebound. For example, after the September 11, 2001, terrorist attacks in the United States, 80 percent of Canadians thought their lives would be deeply and permanently changed, but one year later only 16 percent still believed this (*Toronto Star*/EKOS, 2002).

Linda Perloff (1987) notes how illusory optimism increases our vulnerability. Believing ourselves immune to misfortune, we do not take sensible precautions. In one survey, 137 marriage licence applicants accurately estimated that half of marriages end in divorce, yet most assessed their chance of divorce as zero percent (Baker & Emery, 1993). Sexually active undergraduate women who don't consistently use contraceptives perceive themselves, compared to other women at their university, as much less vulnerable to unwanted pregnancy (Burger & Burns, 1988). When gambling, optimists persist more than pessimists, even as the losses pile up (Gibson & Sanbonmatsu, 2004).

Optimism definitely beats pessimism in promoting self-efficacy, health, and well-being (Armor & Taylor, 1996). Being natural optimists, most people believe they will be happier with various aspects of their lives in the future—a belief that surely helps create happiness in the present (Robinson & Ryff, 1999). Half of 18- to 19-year-old Americans believe that they are "somewhat" or "very likely" to "be rich"—a belief shared by progressively fewer people with age (Moore, 2003). Yet a dash of realism—or what Julie Norem (2000) calls "defensive pessimism"—can save us from the perils of unrealistic optimism. Self-doubt can energize students, most of whom—especially those destined for low grades—exhibit excess optimism about upcoming exams (Proshaska, 1994; Sparrell & Shrauger, 1984). Students who are overconfident tend to underprepare. Their equally able but more anxious peers, fearing that they are going to bomb on the upcoming exam, study furiously and get higher grades (Goodhart, 1986; Norem & Cantor, 1986; Showers & Ruben, 1987).

FALSE CONSENSUS AND UNIQUENESS

We have a curious tendency to further enhance our self-images by overestimating the extent to which others think and act as we do—a phenomenon called the false consensus effect. On matters of *opinion*, we find support for our positions by overestimating the extent to which others agree (Krueger & Clement, 1994; Marks & Miller, 1987; Mullen & Goethals, 1990).

When we behave badly or fail in a task, we reassure ourselves by thinking that such lapses are common. After one person lies to another, the liar begins to perceive the other as dishonest (Sagarin et al., 1998). They guess that others think and act as they do: "I lie, but doesn't everyone?" If we harbour negative ideas about another racial group, we presume that many others also have negative stereotypes (Krueger, 1996). If we like a celebrity, we assume others do as well (Bui, 2012). Elite athletes who use drugs are more likely to assume other elite athletes do as well (Dunn et al., 2012).

False consensus might occur because we generalize from a limited sample, which prominently includes ourselves (Dawes, 1990). Also, we're more likely to associate with people who share our attitudes and behaviours and then to judge the world from the people we know.

Applying Social Psychology

In the previous module we discussed the self-presentation strategies of false modesty, self-handicapping, and impression management. In this module we have discussed attribution processes, how we compare ourselves to others, and our unrealistic optimism. How do you think these topics are related?

Our discussions on these topics can be readily extended using Edward E. Jones's (1990) taxonomy of self-presentational strategies. Jones argued that the motive underlying impression management is the desire to maintain or augment social power. Does this apply to you? The major strategies include ingratiation, intimidation, self-promotion, exemplification, and supplication.

Through *ingratiation*, people try to elicit the affection of others by conforming to others' opinions, by doing favours, or by praising others' achievements. Through *intimidation*, people try to elicit fear in others by projecting both the capacity and inclination to deliver negative outcomes. Typically, this strategy is used in relationships that are non-voluntary rather than in freely formed relationships among peers. Through *self-promotion*, people try to elicit the respect of others by highlighting their prior successes and excusing previous failures. Through *exemplification*, people try to elicit guilt in others by creating the impression of moral superiority. They may do this by deliberately seeking out ways to make their own self-sacrifice and self-denial public. Through *supplication*, people try to elicit the nurturance of others through self-deprecation and entreaties for help. This is the last resort and is typically used by low-power persons who have little else going for them.

Now consider why, and how, you do impression management. What are you trying to accomplish, and do you use any of these techniques? Is it easier to see in others?

On matters of *ability* or when we behave well or successfully, a false uniqueness effect more often occurs (Goethals et al., 1991). We serve self-image by seeing our talents and moral behaviours as relatively unusual. Interestingly, Cathy McFarland at Simon Fraser University has found that people can demonstrate both false consensus and false uniqueness effects in the same context (see McFarland & Miller, 1990). She presented participants with two aversive situations and asked them to indicate which they would least like to be involved with. Participants were then asked to rate the percentage of other students who would choose to avoid that same situation, and predict their and the "typical student's" emotional reactions to the situation. Interestingly, students overestimated the percentage of students who would choose to avoid the situation they chose to avoid (demonstrating false consensus) and they predicted that their emotional reactions would be stronger than the typical student (demonstrating false uniqueness). Another example of this finding might be tattoos. At one time, tattoos were a sign of social rebellion—a diversion from the norms of society—clearly a case of people trying to be unique. However, now tattoos are quite common (some estimates suggest that 40 percent of people under 40 have tattoos). Is having a tattoo now just a sign of conformity to the norm (O'Neill, 2012)? Even when tattoos were rare, they were still common among certain groups (e.g., military, bikers). So when estimating the percentage of young people with tattoos now, people might overestimate (i.e., demonstrating false consensus) but might underestimate the percentage of older people with tattoos (i.e., demonstrating false uniqueness).

To sum up, these tendencies toward self-serving attributions, congratulatory comparisons, illusory optimism, false consensus, and false uniqueness are major sources of self-serving biases (see Figure 4-1).

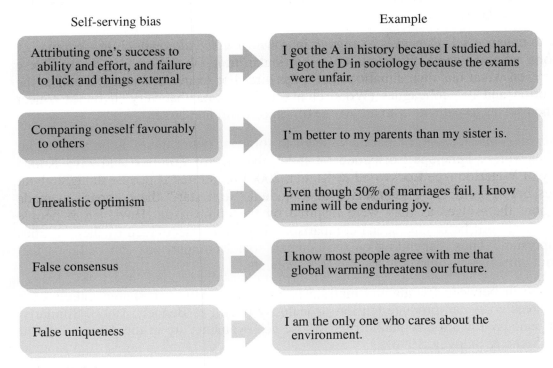

Self-serving bias	Example
Attributing one's success to ability and effort, and failure to luck and things external	I got the A in history because I studied hard. I got the D in sociology because the exams were unfair.
Comparing oneself favourably to others	I'm better to my parents than my sister is.
Unrealistic optimism	Even though 50% of marriages fail, I know mine will be enduring joy.
False consensus	I know most people agree with me that global warming threatens our future.
False uniqueness	I am the only one who cares about the environment.

FIGURE 4-1

How self-serving biases work.

Connection:

False modesty, self-handicapping, and impression management were discussed initially in Module 3.

SELF-ESTEEM MOTIVATION

Why do people perceive themselves in self-enhancing ways? One explanation sees the self-serving bias as a by-product of how we process and remember information about ourselves. Recall the study in which married people gave themselves credit for doing more housework than did their spouses. Might this not be due, as Michael Ross and Fiore Sicoly (1979) believe, to our greater recall for what we've actively done and our lesser recall for what we haven't done or merely observed others doing?

Are the biased perceptions, then, simply a perceptual error, or are self-serving *motives* also involved? It's now clear from research that we have multiple motives. Questing for self-knowledge, we're eager to assess our competence (Dunning, 1995). Questing for self-confirmation, we're eager to *verify* our self-conceptions (Sanitioso et al., 1990; Swann, 1996, 1997). Questing for self-affirmation, we're especially motivated to *enhance* our self-image (Sedikides, 1993). Self-esteem motivation, then, helps power our self-serving bias. As social psychologist Daniel Batson (2006) surmises, "the head is an extension of the heart."

One common way to enhance self-esteem is to engage in *downward social comparison*—comparing yourself to someone who is worse than you on a particular trait (Wood et al., 2000). These comparisons occur even when our own situations are quite dire. For example, Joanne Wood at the University of Waterloo and her colleagues (Wood et al., 1985) found that very ill breast cancer patients compare themselves to patients who are worse off, in order to feel better.

So, does *upward social comparison*—comparing yourself to someone better than you on a particular trait—make you feel worse? Penelope Lockwood (at the University of Toronto) and Ziva Kunda from the University of Waterloo (see Lockwood & Kunda, 2000) found that if people thought about their "usual" selves before comparing themselves to a student "superstar," the comparison made them feel better about themselves as they were inspired by the comparison. However, if people thought about their "best" self before the social comparison, they were discouraged by their abilities relative to the "superstar." Thus, depending on the context, social comparisons can make us feel better or worse about ourselves—something we can all appreciate.

Self-esteem threats occur between friends and married partners, too. Although shared interests are healthy, *identical* career goals can produce tension or jealousy (Clark & Bennett, 1992). Similarly, people feel greater jealousy toward a romantic rival whose achievements are in the domain of their own aspirations (DeSteno & Salovey, 1996).

What underlies the motive to maintain or enhance self-esteem? Mark Leary (1998, 1999) believes that our self-esteem feelings are like a fuel gauge. As we noted earlier, relationships are conducive to our surviving and thriving. Thus, the self-esteem gauge alerts us to threatened social rejection, motivating us to act with greater sensitivity to others' expectations. Studies confirm that social rejection lowers our self-esteem, strengthening our eagerness for approval. Spurned or jilted, we feel unattractive or inadequate. Like a blinking dashboard light, this pain can motivate action—self-improvement and a search for acceptance and inclusion elsewhere.

The Role of Culture

Perhaps not surprisingly, culture plays an important role in self-serving cognitions and self-enhancement. Indeed, self-serving biases are largely a product of Western individualistic cultures (e.g., Heine, 2003, 2010). In many Asian cultures, self-effacement, that is, holding a negative self-view, is more common. In a demonstration of this, University of British Columbia professor Del Paulhus and his colleagues (Yik, Bond, & Paulhus, 1998) asked students to rate the personality characteristics of people they had worked with in a group, as well as their own. Canadian students showed typical self-serving biases by rating themselves more positively than other group members did. Asian students in Hong Kong were asked to make similar ratings, and showed the opposite effect—they rated the other students more positively than themselves. Interestingly, in follow-ups to the research described in previous sections, Penelope Lockwood and her colleagues (Lockwood et al., 2005) found that Asian Canadians were more motivated by negative role models, whereas European Canadians were more motivated by positive role models.

LO 3

THE POSITIVES AND NEGATIVES OF SELF-SERVING BIAS

The Self-Serving Bias as Adaptive

Self-serving bias and its accompanying excuses also help protect people from depression (Snyder & Higgins, 1988). Non-depressed people excuse their failures on laboratory tasks or perceive themselves as being more in control than they are. Depressed people's self-appraisals are more accurate: sadder but wiser.

In "Terror Management Theory," Jeff Greenberg, Sheldon Solomon, and Tom Pyszczynski (1997; see also Vail et al., 2010) propose another reason why positive self-esteem is adaptive—it buffers anxiety, including anxiety related to our certain death. In childhood, we learn that when we meet the standards taught us by our parents we are loved and protected; when we don't, love and protection may be withdrawn. We therefore come to associate viewing ourselves as good with feeling secure. Greenberg and his colleagues argue that positive self-esteem—viewing oneself as good and secure—even protects us from feeling terror over our eventual death. Their research shows that reminding people of their mortality (say, by writing a short essay on dying) motivates them to affirm their self-worth. Moreover, when facing threats, increased self-esteem leads to decreased anxiety.

As this new research on depression and anxiety suggests, there may be some practical wisdom in self-serving perceptions. It may be strategic to believe we are smarter, stronger, and more socially successful than we are. Cheaters may give a more convincing display of honesty if they believe themselves honourable. Belief in our superiority can also motivate us to achieve—creating a self-fulfilling prophecy—and can sustain a sense of hope in difficult times.

The Self-Serving Bias as Maladaptive

Although self-serving pride may help to protect us from depression, it can, at times, be maladaptive. People who blame others for their social difficulties are often unhappier than people who can acknowledge their mistakes (Anderson et al., 1983; Newman & Langer, 1981; Peterson et al., 1981). Moreover, the most self-enhancing people often come across to others as egotistical, condescending, and deceitful (Colvin et al., 1995). In human history, expansive egos have marked genocidal dictators, white supremacists, and drunken spouse-abusers (Baumeister et al., 1996). When someone's inflated self-esteem is challenged by others' criticisms or taunts, the result is sometimes an abusive or murderous rage.

Self-serving biases also inflate people's judgments of their groups. When groups are comparable, most people consider their own group superior (Codol, 1976; Jourden & Heath, 1996; Taylor & Doria, 1981). For example, almost two-thirds of parents, when asked to rate *their child's* school, gave a grade of A or B. But nearly as many—64 percent—give the *nation's* public schools a grade of C or D (Whitman, 1996).

Are You More Narcissistic than Your Parents?

Have things changed over time? Is self-esteem more of a problem now than it was in your parents' day? Narcissus, an ancient Greek hero, was a handsome man. So handsome in fact, that one day, as he walked through the woods, he saw his own reflection in a pool of water and fell instantly in love. He subsequently died (either by accidentally drowning himself in the pool, or of thirst, depending on whose version of the story you believe). Narcissism leads to all kinds of behaviours, including taking more resources for yourself, lack of empathy, and a greater likelihood to cheat on a romantic partner (Campbell et al., 2005; Twenge, 2006; Twenge & Campbell, 2009).

There have been suggestions that today's young people (you) are more self-centred, self-absorbed, and have a greater sense of entitlement than previous generations. Is this true? Research conducted at the University of Western Ontario by Dr. Kali Trzesniewski and her colleagues (Trzesniewski et al., 2008) says no. They examined trends in narcissistic personality across 30 years and almost 27 000 college students, and found no meaningful changes in overall levels of narcissism. Furthermore, in a study of 410 000 high school students, the authors found no increases in self-enhancement (as indexed by the differences between perceived intelligence and academic performance).

But not everyone agrees. Jean Twenge and her colleagues (e.g., Twenge, 2006; Twenge & Campbell, 2009; Twenge et al., 2006) argue that, indeed, overall narcissism has increased among university-aged students (N = 17 000). Twenge argues that the pursuit of self-esteem for its own sake (such as we do in elementary and high school, where children can no longer fail) is problematic as it gives youth an unrealistic set of expectations such that they are doomed to be disappointed when they enter the "real world."

Critical THINKING

What do you think? Are you more narcissistic than your parents? Or is it a self-serving bias of older adults to make themselves feel better about themselves compared with today's youth? What we do know is that whether we as individuals "notice" an effect over time depends on a number of *heuristics* (or mental shortcuts) we regularly use, and can be influenced by potential biases.

Narcissus fell in love with his own reflection—are you more prone to narcissism than your parents were?

Connection:

Heuristics will be further discussed in Module 7.

Self-esteem has its dark side, but it also has a bright side. When good things happen, high- more than low-self-esteem people tend to savour and sustain the good feelings (Wood et al., 2003). Critics question popular psychology's assumption that positive self-esteem is the secret to successful, happy living. Low self-esteem does predict an increased risk of depression, drug abuse, and some forms of delinquency. High self-esteem fosters initiative, resilience, and pleasant feelings (Baumeister et al., 2003). Yet, teen males who engage in sexual activity at an "inappropriately young age" tend to have *higher* than average self-esteem. So do teen gang leaders, extreme ethnocentrists, and terrorists, notes Robyn Dawes (1994, 1998). "Hitler had very high self-esteem," note Baumeister and his colleagues (2003).

Steven Spencer at the University of Waterloo has demonstrated in numerous studies (e.g., Fein & Spencer, 1997; Spencer et al., 1998) that when people's self-esteem is threatened, they tend to stereotype members of minority groups. In Spencer's studies, students are randomly assigned to receive positive or negative feedback about their own performance on a task, and then they are asked to evaluate a member of a stereotyped group (e.g., Blacks, Asians). People who received negative feedback were more likely to demonstrate stereotypic attitudes and behaviours toward these group members.

Brad Bushman and Roy Baumeister (1998) showed that among student writers who received criticism, those with the highest self-esteem were "exceptionally aggressive," delivering three times the punishment (in this case loud noises) on their critics than those with normal self-esteem. High-self-esteem people are more likely to be obnoxious, to interrupt, and to talk *at* people rather than *with* them (in contrast to the shyer, more modest, self-effacing folks with low self-esteem). Yet, people expressing low self-esteem are somewhat more vulnerable to assorted clinical problems, including anxiety, loneliness, and eating disorders. When feeling bad, or threatened, they are more likely to view everything through dark glasses—to notice and remember others' worst behaviours and to think their partners don't love them (Murray et al., 1998, 2002; Ybarra, 1999).

Self-esteem, like attitudes, comes in two forms—explicit (conscious) and implicit (outside of one's awareness). Psychologists measure explicit self-esteem using questionnaires ("I feel I am a person of worth"), but measure implicit self-esteem with subtler methods, ranging from preferences for letters from one's name to computer-measured reaction times classifying positive and negative words related to the self. Those scoring high in explicit self-esteem may or may not score high in implicit self-esteem (women are more consistent across the top types of measures than men; Pelham et al., 2005). However, Christian Jordan at Wilfrid Laurier University, along with his colleagues, found that when people are consistently positive across explicit and implicit measures, they appear more secure, behave less defensively, and display less prejudice (Jordan et al., 2003, 2005).

CONCLUSIONS

Unlike a fragile self-esteem, a secure self-esteem—one rooted more in feeling good about who one is than on grades, looks, money, or others' approval—is conducive to long-term well-being (Kernis, 2003; Schimel et al., 2001). Jennifer Crocker and Lora Park (2004) confirmed this in studies with University of Michigan students. Those whose self-worth was most fragile—that is, most contingent on external sources—experienced more stress, anger, relationship problems, drug and alcohol use, and eating disorders than those whose worth was rooted more in internal sources, such as personal virtues. Ironically, those who pursue self-esteem, perhaps by seeking to become beautiful, rich, or popular, may lose sight of what really makes for good quality of life. Moreover, if feeling good about ourselves is our goal, then we may become less open to criticism, more likely to blame than empathize with others, and more pressured to succeed at activities rather than simply to enjoy them. Over time, such a pursuit of self-esteem can fail to satisfy our deep needs for competence, relationships, and autonomy. To focus less on one's self-image, and more on developing one's talents and relationships, eventually leads to greater well-being.

SUMMARY OF KEY POINTS

LO1. Understand how we explain events.

- We explain events by making attributions as to the cause of behaviour.
- How we make those attributions may differ depending on the nature of the event.

LO2. Define and explain self-serving biases.

- We regularly engage in misattributions, false consensus, false uniqueness, and unrealistic optimism.
- This serves to modify and improve our view of ourselves relative to others.

LO3. Understand the positive and negative elements of self-serving biases.

- Self-serving biases have a number of benefits, such as buffering us from anxiety and depression.
- Self-serving biases can have negative consequences, including denigrating others, or members of groups other than our own.

KEY TERMS

False consensus effect   The tendency to overestimate the commonality of one's opinions and one's undesirable or unsuccessful behaviours.

False uniqueness effect   The tendency to underestimate the commonality of one's abilities and one's desirable or successful behaviours.

Self-serving bias   The tendency to perceive and present oneself favourably.

MODULE FIVE

Self-Efficacy

LO **1**   Understand locus of control

LO **2**   Understand the distinction between locus of control and self-determination

LO **3**   Understand the negative aspects of too much freedom to choose

Terry Fox is a Canadian icon. He was born in Winnipeg, Manitoba, and grew up in Port Coquitlam, British Columbia. At 18, Terry was diagnosed with bone cancer, and his right leg was amputated 15 cm above the knee. During his time in the hospital, Terry was touched by the suffering of his fellow patients and decided to run across Canada to raise money and awareness about cancer. His *Marathon of Hope* began on April 12, 1980, in St. John's, Newfoundland, and lasted over 5000 kilometres, until his illness returned and he was forced to quit in September. He died June 28, 1981, at the age of 22. Although he did not make it across Canada, his efforts inspire over 2 million people annually to run in his memory to raise money for cancer. To date, the Terry Fox Run has raised over $650 million for cancer research (Terry Fox Foundation, 2014).

Critical THINKING

Put yourself in Terry Fox's situation. How would you deal with a diagnosis of cancer (yours or someone else's)? Chances are cancer (or another serious illness) has already touched your life. How did you react to it? How did the person who was ill react (if it wasn't you)? In your view, how does your personality have an impact on your ability to cope with life's challenges?

Studies of self-serving biases expose deep truths about human nature. But single truths seldom tell the whole story because the world is complex. Indeed, there is an important complement to these truths. High self-esteem—a sense of self-worth—is adaptive. Compared to those with low self-esteem, people with high self-esteem are happier, less neurotic, less troubled by ulcers and insomnia, and less prone to drug and alcohol addictions. They respond more resiliently to threats to rejection, and they are less likely to become anorexic; high self-esteem even buffers us against the negative cardiovascular reaction induced by stress (Brockner & Hulton, 1978; Brown, 1991; Ford & Collins, 2010; Nicholls & Viner, 2009).

Connection:

Self-serving biases were discussed in Module 4.

Additional research on *locus of control*, optimism, and *learned helplessness* confirms the benefits of seeing oneself as competent and effective. Albert Bandura (1986), who was born in northern Alberta, and did his undergraduate degree at the University of British Columbia, merges much of this research into a concept called self-efficacy—an optimistic belief in our own possibilities that pays dividends (Bandura et al., 1999; Maddux & Gosselin, 2003, Klassen, 2010). People with strong feelings of self-efficacy are more persistent, less anxious and depressed, and more academically successful (Gecas, 1989; Maddux, 1991; Scheier & Carver, 1992). Robert Klassen at the University of Alberta has found that adolescents with learning disabilities who have self-efficacy regarding their ability to learn got better grades (Klassen, 2010). Improving your self-efficacy can have meaningful effects. It has been demonstrated that increasing smokers' self-efficacy can help them quit smoking (Warneck et al., 2001).

Your self-efficacy is how competent you feel to do something; your self-esteem is your sense of self-worth. For example, a skilled burglar might feel high self-efficacy but low self-esteem (interestingly, a criminal with high self-efficacy may be less likely to stop his or her criminal activity; Brezina & Topalli, 2012). If you believe you can do something, will this belief necessarily make a difference? That depends on a second factor: Do you have *control* over your outcomes? You may, for example, feel like an effective driver (high self-efficacy), yet feel endangered by drunken drivers (low control). You may feel like a competent student or worker, but fearing discrimination based on your age, gender, or appearance, you may think your prospects are dim.

LO 1

LOCUS OF CONTROL

What do you think? Are people more often captains of their destinies or victims of their circumstances? Are they the playwrights, directors, and actors of their own lives or prisoners of invisible situations? Julian Rotter called this dimension locus of control. With Jerry Phares, he developed 29 paired statements to measure a person's locus of control. Do the following activity to discover yours.

Activity: **Locus of control**

Here is the test Rotter and Phares developed. Below you will see a list of statements. For each of these pairs of statements, select the one that best reflects your views.

Rotter's Locus of Control Scale

1. a.   Children get into trouble because their parents punish them too much.

    b.   The trouble with most children nowadays is that their parents are too easy with them.

2. a.   Many of the unhappy things in people's lives are partly due to bad luck.

    b.   People's misfortunes result from the mistakes they make.

3. a.   One of the major reasons why we have wars is because people don't take enough interest in politics.

    b.   There will always be wars, no matter how hard people try to prevent them.

4. a.   In the long run people get the respect they deserve in this world.

    b.   Unfortunately, an individual's worth often passes unrecognized no matter how hard he tries.

5. a.   The idea that teachers are unfair to students is nonsense.

    b.   Most students don't realize the extent to which their grades are influenced by accidental happenings.

6. a.   Without the right breaks, one cannot be an effective leader.

    b.   Capable people who fail to become leaders have not taken advantage of their opportunities.

7. a.   No matter how hard you try, some people just don't like you.

    b.   People who can't get others to like them don't understand how to get along with others.

8. a.   Heredity plays the major role in determining one's personality.

    b.   It is one's experiences in life which determine what they're like.

9. a.   I have often found that what is going to happen will happen.

    b.   Trusting fate has never turned out as well for me as making a decision to take a definite course of action.

10. a.   In the case of the well-prepared student there is rarely, if ever, such a thing as an unfair test.

    b.   Many times, exam questions tend to be so unrelated to course work that studying is really useless.

11. a.   Becoming a success is a matter of hard work, luck has little or nothing to do with it.

    b.   Getting a good job depends mainly on being in the right place at the right time.

12. a.   The average citizen can have an influence in government decisions.

    b.   This world is run by the few people in power, and there is not much the little guy can do about it.

SCORING. Give yourself one point for each of these answers:

2. a, 3. b, 4. b, 5. b, 6. a, 7. a, 9. a, 10. b, 11. b, 12. b

The higher you score, the more external your locus of control. The lower your score, the more internal. Your results may surprise you—what do you think they say about you?

Given your answers, do you believe you control your own destiny (*internal* locus of control)? Or that chance or outside forces determine your fate (*external* locus of control)? Those who see themselves as internally controlled are more likely to do well in school, successfully stop smoking, wear seat belts, practise birth control, deal with marital problems directly, make lots of money, and delay instant gratification in order to achieve long-term goals (Findley & Cooper, 1983; Lefcourt, 1982; Miller et al., 1986). External locus of control is linked to anxiety and depression (Cheung et al.,

Applying Social Psychology

Now that you have read about locus of control, what do you think about your own locus of control? Are you more internal or more external? Based on what you have learned in the text, and about yourself, how do you think locus of control might affect some of the following?

• What relationship would you anticipate between locus of control and gender, age, race, religious affiliation, conformity to peer pressure, academic achievement, and participation in lotteries?

• How would this dimension influence the extent to which people are superstitious, and believe in horoscopes, quack remedies, and magical rituals?

• Who is most likely choose a delayed but valuable reward over an immediate momentary pleasure?

• Do you feel more or less external in some areas of life (e.g., politics) than others (e.g., academic)?

• What childhood experiences or characteristics of your family may have contributed to your own locus of control expectancies?

2013). Daniel Bailis, Alexander Segall, and Judith Chipperfield (2010) at the University of Manitoba have demonstrated that health locus of control predicts people's sense of autonomy, which may prepare them to handle the inevitable experiences of negative health as they age.

LO 2

LEARNED HELPLESSNESS VERSUS SELF-DETERMINATION

The benefits of feelings of control also appear in animal research. Dogs taught that they cannot escape shocks while confined will learn a sense of helplessness. Later, these dogs cower passively in other situations when they *could* escape punishment. Dogs that learn personal control (by escaping their first shocks successfully) adapt easily to a new situation. Researcher Martin Seligman (1975, 1991) notes similarities to this learned helplessness in human situations. Depressed or oppressed people, for example, become passive because they believe their efforts have no effect. Helpless dogs and depressed people both suffer paralysis of the will, passive resignation, even motionless apathy (see Figure 5-1).

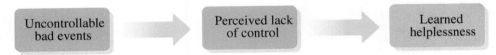

FIGURE 5-1

Learned helplessness. When animals and people experience uncontrollable bad events, they learn to feel helpless and resigned.

This dog, kept in a shelter, may develop learned helplessness.

Here is a clue to how institutions—even benevolent ones—can dehumanize people. Such service may appear good to outsiders, but it is bad for people's health and survival. Losing control over what you do and what others do to you can make unpleasant events profoundly stressful (Pomerleau & Rodin, 1986). Several diseases are associated with feelings of helplessness and diminished choice. So is the rapidity of decline and death in both concentration camps and nursing homes. Hospital patients who are trained to believe they can control stress require fewer pain relievers and sedatives, and exhibit less anxiety (Langer et al., 1975).

Critical THINKING

Before you read on, take a second and think about where you would want your grandmother or grandfather to live out their old age. Imagine what the building would look like, imagine what their room would look like, and imagine how they could be treated by the staff there. You may actually have a grandparent or family member in one of these institutions right now. What could be better in terms of how they are treated? Most of you thinking about this would say, "In the best seniors' home, everything would be done for my grandma: they would bring her all her food, they would clean her room, and they would help her with all of her personal care." Does that sound like a good-quality establishment?

Many researchers (e.g., Ruthig et al., 2007; Chipperfield et al., 2004; Bailis et al, 2006) have shown that perceived control over a situation is very important to health outcomes for older adults. These researchers asked participants to estimate their risk of suffering a hip fracture compared with other people their age. They also measured how much control (self-efficacy) people felt they had over the risk they are exposed to. Next, they measured how people's perception of risk predicted their well-being. Chipperfield and her colleagues found that perceived control was very important: For older adults with high perceived control, being optimistic about risk (i.e., having a low perceived risk) was associated with positive well-being. On the other hand, people who were pessimistic (i.e., having a high perceived risk) were associated with negative outcomes. However, this effect held for people who felt in control. For people with low perceived control, perceived risk did not predict outcomes. Thus again, control (or perceived control) is important. Daniel Bailis and his colleagues conducted a study using Statistics Canada data demonstrating that people who believe themselves to have control over their lives have more positive health outcomes (Bailis et al., 2006). Interestingly, Dr. Bailis has also found evidence that having less perceived control over their lives could be an important reason why people with lower socioeconomic status have poorer physical and mental health overall.

Studies confirm that governing and managing people in ways that promote personal control will indeed promote health and happiness (Deci & Ryan, 1987):

- Prisoners given some control over their environments—by being able to move chairs, control TV sets, and operate the lights—experience less stress, exhibit fewer health problems, and commit less vandalism (Ruback et al., 1986; Wener et al., 1987).

- Workers given leeway in carrying out tasks and making decisions experience improved morale (Miller & Monge, 1986), as do telecommuting workers who have more flexibility to balance work and family life (Valcour, 2007). Control of work tasks acts a buffer for stress in the workplace and reduces counterproductive behaviours (Sprung & Jex, 2012).

- Institutionalized residents allowed choice in such matters as what to eat for breakfast, when to go to a movie, or whether to sleep late or get up early, may live longer and certainly are happier (Timko & Moos, 1989).

- Homeless-shelter residents who perceive little choice in when to eat and sleep, and little control over their privacy, are more likely to have a passive, helpless attitude regarding finding housing and work (Burn, 1992).

- In all countries studied, people who perceive themselves as having free choice experience greater satisfaction with their lives. And countries where people experience more freedom have more satisfied citizens (Inglehart & Welzel, 2005; Inglehart et al., 2008).

- Students with higher self-efficacy regarding drinking self-control strategies were less likely to binge drink, particularly in situations where they feel more in control (e.g., at home, versus at a bar or party; Bonar et al., 2011).

LO 3

THE COSTS OF EXCESS CHOICE

Can there ever be too much of a good thing like freedom and self-determination? Barry Schwartz (2004) contends that individualistic modern cultures indeed have "an excess of freedom," causing decreased life satisfaction and increased clinical depression. Too many choices can lead to paralysis, or what Schwartz calls "the tyranny of freedom." After choosing from among 30 kinds of jams or chocolates, people express less satisfaction with their choices than those choosing among six options (Iyengar & Lepper, 2000). With more choice comes information overload and more opportunities for regret.

We do not like uncertainty. Read the excerpt below, and see how you would feel:

Imagine the following scene and see if you can picture yourself in it. You are sitting on the couch one evening at home. Your loving partner is across the darkened room playing with the stereo. Suddenly overcome with uncharacteristic emotion, you pour out your feelings of love. Once you finish, you sit back, anticipating a response from your love. However, instead of responding to your expression of love, he or she stands up and walks into the kitchen, not saying a word. Naturally, the fact that your partner does not return your heartfelt expression bothers you. That was not like him or her at all. It was not until you see what your partner is doing in the kitchen that you understand why he or she did not respond. Up until that point, the uncertainty, not knowing the reason for the behaviour, was very unsettling to you. Only after you notice what your partner is doing in the kitchen does your considerable discomfort subside.

What is the end of the story? Are you wondering? That's because, just like in the story, we do not like uncertainty. You want to know the ending. With uncertainty comes a lack of control. In order to retain control, we want to know the end of the story.

Christopher Hsee and Reid Hastie (2006) illustrate how choice may enhance regret. Give employees a free trip to either Paris or Hawaii and they will be happy. But give them a choice between the two and they may be less happy. People who choose Paris may regret that it lacks the warmth and the ocean. Those who choose Hawaii may regret the lack of great museums. Something like that may explain why the final-year students from 11 colleges in one recent study, who spent the most time seeking and assessing various job possibilities, ended up with higher starting salaries but lower satisfaction (Iyengar et al., 2006).

In other experiments, people have expressed greater satisfaction with irrevocable choices (such as those made in an "all purchases final" sale) than with reversible choices (as when allowing refunds or exchanges). Ironically, people like and will pay for the freedom to reverse their choices. Yet that freedom "can inhibit the psychological processes that manufacture satisfaction" (Gilbert & Ebert, 2002).

That principle may help explain a curious social phenomenon (Myers, 2000a): National surveys show that people expressed more satisfaction with their marriages several decades ago when marriage was more irrevocable ("all purchases final"). Today, despite greater freedom to escape bad marriages and try new ones, people tend to express somewhat less satisfaction with the marriage that they have.

IMPLICATIONS

Although psychological research on perceived self-control is relatively new, the emphasis on taking charge of one's life and realizing one's potential is not. We find it in Norman Vincent Peale's 1950s best-seller, *The Power of Positive Thinking*, and more recently in the best-selling book *The Secret* by Rhonda Byrne, which offers ". . . that if you think positively you will attract positive things to you." We find this positive thinking premise in the many self-help books and videos that urge people to succeed through developing positive mental attitudes and owning their decisions.

For example, Dr. Phil McGraw ("Dr. Phil") repeatedly advises viewers that "we teach people how to treat us" and "when you choose the behaviour, you choose the consequences." (The latter is a phrase Steven uses repeatedly with his teenage children—which they hate!) The underlying implication of all of these messages is that we have control over our behaviour and its outcomes.

Connection:

Think back to our discussion of narcissism in Module 4.

Yet, Bandura emphasizes that self-efficacy does not grow primarily by self-persuasion ("I think I can, I think I can") or by vacuous compliments ("You're terrific!"; see Twenge & Campbell, 2009). Indeed, Joanne Wood and her colleagues at the University of Waterloo (Wood, Perunovic, & Lee, 2009) have found that repeating positive self-statements can improve self-esteem if you already have high self-esteem. This backfires if you have low self-esteem—repeating positive self-statements actually makes you feel *worse* about yourself, presumably because repeating them makes you more aware that you are not achieving them.

CONCLUSIONS

The chief source of self-efficacy is the experience of success (see Perkins, et al., 2012). If your initial efforts to lose weight, stop smoking, or improve your grades succeed, your self-efficacy increases. For example, after mastering the physical skills needed to repel a sexual assault, women feel less vulnerable, less anxious, and more in control (Ozer & Bandura, 1990). After experiencing academic success, students develop higher appraisals of their academic ability, which in turn often stimulate them to work harder and achieve more (Felson, 1984; Marsh & Young, 1997). To do one's best and achieve is to feel more confident and empowered. This can lead to enhanced self-esteem. Perhaps it is for this reason that Mark Baldwin and his colleagues at McGill University have developed a website called "Self-Esteem Games" (search for it—it's fun). These games have been demonstrated to improve individual self-confidence and esteem through a series of tasks that improve implicit self-perceptions. Positive words and images are paired with words about yourself, which creates a positive perception of your own self-worth (see Baccus, Baldwin, & Packer, 2004; Dandeneau & Baldwin, 2004). This work has been successful enough to attract the interest of health insurance companies, who recognize that improving health starts with improving self-efficacy.

SUMMARY OF KEY POINTS

LO1. Understand locus of control.

- Locus of control is the extent to which people see outcomes as internally or externally controlled.

LO2. Understand the distinction between locus of control and self-determination.

- People who believe they have no control over repeated negative events can suffer from learned helplessness.
- Learned helplessness and locus of control can have impacts on people's well-being.

LO3. Understand the negative aspects of too much freedom to choose.

- At times, too much choice can lead people to be less satisfied with the choices they do make.

Answer to Uncertainty Example:

As it turns out, what you see in the kitchen is your partner dancing to the music coming from the headphones he or she is wearing. The reason your partner didn't respond to your outpouring of affection and love was that he or she did not hear you. Do you feel better now?

KEY TERMS

Learned helplessness   The hopelessness and resignation learned by humans or animals who perceive themselves as having no control over repeated bad events.

Locus of control   The extent to which people perceive outcomes as internally controllable by their own efforts and actions, or as externally controlled by chance or outside forces.

Self-efficacy   A sense that one is competent and effective.

MODULE SIX

Explaining Other People's Behaviour

The 2010 Winter Olympics, held in Vancouver and Whistler, British Columbia, came with high hopes. Canada was hosting the world, had what was billed as the best group of athletes ever, and was hoping to "Own the Podium." All of the athletes were under pressure, but perhaps the team under the most pressure was the men's hockey team. Hockey is "Canada's Game" and thus we *should* be the best in the world. At home, there should be no stopping them. Of course, they did win—on Sidney Crosby's "golden goal" in overtime. And with many repeat players, this put a lot of pressure on the men's hockey team for the 2014 Winter Olympics in Sochi, Russia. Russia, as the home team, was under similar pressure, and although they won the most medals overall, the men's hockey team was eliminated without reaching the final round. The team and the fans were devastated. (The Canadian men's and women's hockey teams both won gold.)

Overall, at the 2010 Olympic Games, Canada won more gold medals than it has ever won before at any Olympic games. The games were seen as a tremendous success, which carried over to their success in Sochi (where they won almost as many medals). However, there were many critiques of the games—the cost, the security, the debacle around access to and views of the flame, and the fact that Canada did not win the most total medals.

Critical THINKING

Consider the Russian men's hockey team at the Olympics. Why do you think they did not reach the medal round? Now, let's think back to the 2006 Olympic Games, when the Canadian men's hockey team did not make the medal round. Why do you think that happened?

LO 1

MAKING ATTRIBUTIONS ABOUT OTHERS

Our judgments of ourselves and others depend on how we explain behaviours. Depending on our judgments, we may decide a behaviour is perfectly reasonable or completely uncalled for. Is a person's death a murder, manslaughter, self-defence, justified, or an accident? We might judge squeegee kids as lazy and lacking initiative, or as victims of society and a bad home environment. Depending on our explanation, we might judge someone's friendly behaviour as genuine warmth, a way to make a sale, or a sexual come-on. In this module, we will explore how we make those attributions and some of their consequences.

Attributing Causality to the Person or the Situation

We endlessly analyze and discuss why things happen as they do, especially when we experience something negative or unexpected (Bohner et al., 1988; Weiner, 1985). If you have been in a traffic accident, was it because the other guy was a bad driver, or as found in some recent research, did you just make a mistake (Lennon et al., 2011).

Spouses in unhappy relationships typically offer distress-maintaining explanations for negative acts ("she was late because she doesn't care about me"). Happy couples more often externalize ("she was late because of heavy traffic"). With positive partner behaviour their explanations similarly work either to maintain distress ("he brought me flowers because he wants sex") or to enhance the relationship ("he brought me flowers to show he loves me") (Gelinas et al., 1995; Hewstone & Fincham, 1996; Weiner, 1995).

Attribution theory analyzes how we explain people's behaviour. Fritz Heider (1958), widely regarded as attribution theory's originator, concluded that people tend to attribute someone's behaviour either to *internal* causes (e.g., the person's disposition) or *external* causes (e.g., something about the person's situation). A teacher may wonder whether a child's underachievement is due to lack of motivation and ability (a **dispositional attribution**) or to physical and social circumstances (a **situational attribution**). Some people are more inclined to attribute behaviour to stable personality; others tend to attribute behaviour to situations (Bastian & Haslam, 2006; Robins et al., 2004).

Inferring Traits

As Edward Jones and Keith Davis (1965) noted, we often infer that other people's actions are indicative of their intentions and dispositions. If I observe Rick making a sarcastic comment to Linda, I infer that Rick is a hostile person. Jones and Davis's "theory of correspondent inferences" specifies the conditions under which such attributions are most likely. For example, normal or expected behaviour tells us less about the person than does unusual behaviour. If Samantha is sarcastic in a job interview, where a person would normally be pleasant, this tells us more about Samantha than if she is sarcastic with her siblings.

The ease with which we infer traits is remarkable. In one set of experiments James Uleman (1989) gave students statements to remember, like "The librarian carries the old woman's groceries across the street." The students would instantly, unintentionally, and unconsciously infer a trait. When later they were helped to recall the sentence, the most valuable clue word was not "books" (to cue librarian) or "bags" (to cue groceries) but "helpful"—the inferred trait that we suspect you, too, spontaneously attributed to the librarian.

Why is this student asleep? Is she lazy? Or overworked?

Common Sense Attributions

As these examples suggest, attributions often are rational. In testimony to the reasonable ways in which we explain behaviour, attribution theorist Harold Kelley (1973) described how we use information about "consistency," "distinctiveness," and "consensus" (Figure 6-1).

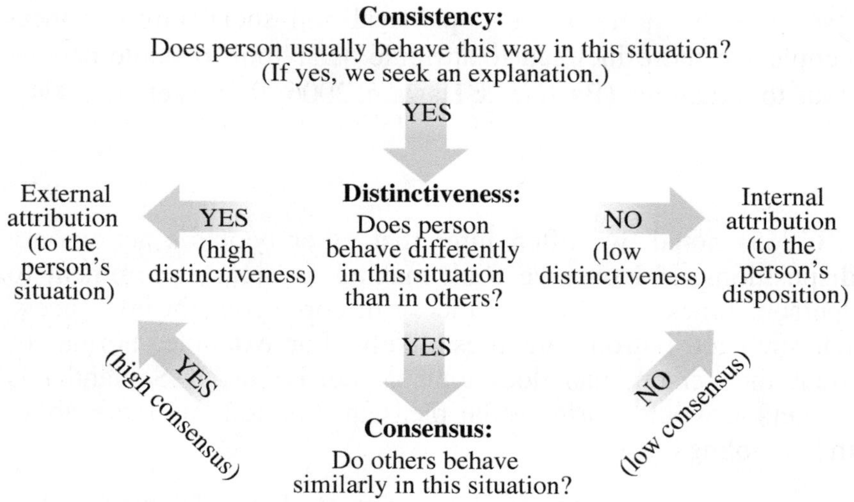

Consistency:
Does person usually behave this way in this situation?
(If yes, we seek an explanation.)

YES

| External attribution (to the person's situation) | ← YES (high distinctiveness) | **Distinctiveness:** Does person behave differently in this situation than in others? | NO (low distinctiveness) → | Internal attribution (to the person's disposition) |

YES

(high consensus)   **Consensus:** Do others behave similarly in this situation?   *(low consensus)*

FIGURE 6-1

Harold Kelley's Theory of Attributions.   Three factors—consistency, distinctiveness, and consensus—influence whether we attribute someone's behaviour to internal or external causes.

- Consistency: How consistent is the person's behaviour in this situation?
- Distinctiveness: How specific is the person's behaviour to this particular situation?
- Consensus: To what extent do others in this situation behave similarly?

When explaining why Marc is having trouble with his Chevy Malibu, most people use information concerning *consistency* (Does Marc usually have problems with his Malibu?), *distinctiveness* (Does Marc have trouble with other cars, or only his Malibu?), and *consensus* (Do other people have similar problems with Malibus?). If we learn that Marc alone consistently has trouble with this car and other cars, we likely will attribute the troubles to Marc, not to defects in this car.

So our common sense psychology often explains behaviour logically. But Kelley also found that people often discount a contributing cause of behaviour if other plausible causes are already known. If we can specify one or two reasons a student might have done poorly on an exam, we may ignore or discount other possibilities (McClure, 1998).

LO **2**

THE FUNDAMENTAL ATTRIBUTION ERROR

Attribution researchers have found that when explaining someone's behaviour, we often underestimate the impact of the situation and overestimate the extent to which it reflects the individual's traits and attitudes. Do you make these same kinds of mistakes? Consider your performance on a recent exam. Why did you do well (or poorly)? You probably gave some of the following reasons: "The exam was unfair." "I didn't sleep well the night before." "I had too much work to do." "There were too many distractions in the class." In other words, these reasons highlight the situational aspects of why you did poorly. Next, you might consider why a friend did poorly on a similar exam. You might give somewhat different reasons: "He would rather party than study." "She doesn't study hard enough." "He isn't that smart" and so on. These reasons highlight your friend's internal attributes, and you probably ignored or minimized the situational reasons for his or her poor performance. We commit the fundamental attribution error when we explain *other people's* behaviour, but we often explain *our own* behaviour in terms of the situation. When referring to ourselves, we typically use verbs that describe our actions and reactions ("I get annoyed when . . ."). Referring to someone else, we more often describe what that person is ("He is nasty") (Fiedler et al., 1991; McGuire & McGuire, 1986; White & Younger, 1988). And these reactions can have serious consequences. Husbands who attribute their wives' criticisms to being "mean and nasty" are more likely to become violent (Schweinle, et al., 2002). This discounting of the situation, what Lee Ross (1977) called the fundamental attribution error, appears in many experiments.

THE FUNDAMENTAL ATTRIBUTION ERROR IN EVERYDAY LIFE

If we know the checkout cashier is taught to say, "Thank you and have a nice day," do we nevertheless automatically conclude that the cashier is a friendly, grateful person? We certainly know how to discount behaviour that we attribute to ulterior motives (Fein et al., 1990). The discounting of social constraints was further revealed in a thought-provoking experiment by Lee Ross and his collaborators (Ross et al., 1977). The experiment recreated Ross's firsthand experience of moving from graduate student to professor. His doctoral oral exam had proved a humbling experience as his apparently brilliant professors quizzed him on topics they specialized in. Six months later, *Dr.* Ross was himself an examiner, now able to ask penetrating questions on *his* favourite topics. Ross's hapless student later confessed to feeling exactly as Ross had a half-year before—dissatisfied with his ignorance and impressed with the apparent brilliance of the examiners.

Connection:

We will revisit the fundamental attribution error in Module 9 when we discuss conformity and obedience.

In an experiment, Ross set up a simulated quiz game. He randomly assigned some Stanford University students to play the role of questioner, some to play the role of contestant, and others to observe. The researchers invited the questioners to make up difficult questions that would demonstrate their wealth of knowledge. Any one of us can imagine such questions using our own domain of competence: "Where is Bainbridge Island?" "How did Mary, Queen of Scots, die?" "Which has the longer coastline, Europe or Africa?" If even these few questions have you feeling a little uninformed, then you will appreciate the results of this experiment.*

---

* Bainbridge Island is across Puget Sound near Seattle. Mary, Queen of Scots, was beheaded while in the custody of her cousin, Queen Elizabeth I. Although the African continent is more than double the area of Europe, Europe's coastline is longer. (It is more convoluted, with lots of harbours and inlets, a geographical fact that contributed to its role in the history of maritime trade.)

Everyone had to know that the questioner would have the advantage. Yet both contestants and observers (but not the questioners) came to the erroneous conclusion that the questioners *really were* more knowledgeable than the contestants (see Figure 6-2). Follow-up research shows that these misimpressions are not a reflection of low social intelligence. If anything, intelligent and socially competent people are *more* likely to make the attribution error (Block & Funder, 1986). We find it difficult to escape the illusion that the scripted behaviour reflects an inner disposition. Perhaps this is why Leonard Nimoy, who played Mr. Spock on the original *Star Trek*, entitled his 1975 autobiography *I Am Not Spock*.

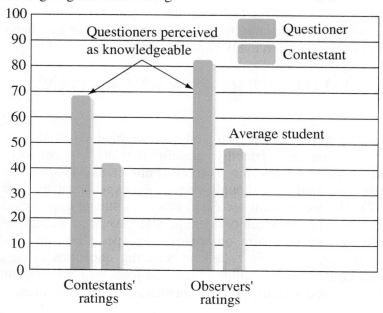

Rating of general knowledge

FIGURE 6-2

Both contestants and observers of a simulated quiz game assumed that a person who had been randomly assigned the role of questioner was far more knowledgeable than the contestant. Actually, the assigned roles of questioner and contestant simply made the questioner seem more knowledgeable. The failure to appreciate this illustrates the fundamental attribution error.

Critical THINKING

Can you think of a role that you play in your life now (e.g., coach, mentor, student, mother, father) that influences how people see you? Maybe it is a social, cultural, or ethic group you belong to. What assumptions do they make about you?

In real life, those with social power usually initiate and control conversations, which often leads underlings to overestimate their knowledge and intelligence. Medical doctors, for example, are often

Connection:

We will discuss perceptions of social groups more in Modules 15 and 16.

presumed to be experts on all sorts of questions unrelated to medicine. Similarly, students often overestimate the brilliance of their teachers. When some of these students later become teachers, they are usually amazed to discover (your authors certainly were . . .) that teachers are not so brilliant after all.

To illustrate the fundamental attribution error, most of us need look no further than our own experiences. Determined to make some new friends, Bev plasters a smile on her face and anxiously plunges into a party. Everyone else seems quite relaxed and happy as they laugh and talk with one another. Bev wonders to herself, "Why is every-one always so at ease in groups like this while I'm feeling shy and tense?" Actually, everyone else is feeling nervous, too, and making the attribution error in assuming that Bev and the others *are* as they *appear*—confident. Attributions have very practical importance as well. Attributions of responsibility are at the heart of many judicial decisions (Fincham & Jaspars, 1980).

Applying Social Psychology

In pondering these sections on fundamental attribution error, you may wonder: Why do actors tend to attribute their behaviour to the situation if they also prefer a sense of self-efficacy? Isn't viewing one's behaviour as caused by the situation contradictory to feelings of personal efficacy and internal control? Are we happy believing we have no control?

The answer is that when people explain their own behaviour, they typically are giving reasons, not causes. They are not viewing themselves as mere billiard balls, buffeted by situational causes. Rather, they are explaining their actions by giving reasons (in terms of the situation) that justify how they chose to behave. Reasons are justifications as perceived by the actor. Causes are objective factors (e.g., features of the environment, the actor, and so on) as discerned by external observers (Locke and Pennington, 1982).

So, how do you see this having an impact in your life? Have you made the same kinds of statements we mentioned earlier ("I made a mistake, but they are just stupid!"). If so (and you know you have), when did you do it? Were there times where you really did see the "other reasons" for people's behaviour, and you did blame yourself? Of course, you did. Remember that the fundamental attribution error is a description of a tendency for a certain type of thinking—it does not mean we will do it all the time.

Connection:

Recall that we discussed locus of control in Module 5.

LO 3

WHY DO WE MAKE THE ATTRIBUTION ERROR?

So far we have seen a bias in the way we explain other people's behaviour: We often ignore powerful situational determinants. Why do we tend to underestimate the situational determinants of others' behaviour but not of our own? See the following activity to see how this works.

Activity: How do we assess people's traits?

This demonstration was adapted from work by Richard Nisbett. For each of the following ten pairs of traits, circle the one trait in each pair that is most characteristic of Jon Stewart of *The Daily Show* (actually, you can use any celebrity you wish if you object to Jon Stewart). If neither of the traits in a trait pair is the most characteristic, indicate that by circling "depends on the situation."

serious	fun-loving	depends on the situation
subjective	analytic	depends on the situation
future oriented	present oriented	depends on the situation
energetic	relaxed	depends on the situation
unassuming	self-asserting	depends on the situation
lenient	firm	depends on the situation
reserved	emotionally expressive	depends on the situation
dignified	casual	depends on the situation
realistic	idealistic	depends on the situation
intense	calm	depends on the situation

Go back and complete the same responses for *you*.

Now, go back and count the number of times you circled "depends on the situation" for Jon Stewart, and how many times you circled it for you. Are you more willing to ascribe traits to Jon Stewart than yourself? Were you more likely to circle "depends on the situation"? If so, why? If so, it is probably because, as the actor, you are better able to see the external factors that influence your behaviour than you are able to see them for a celebrity.

Perspective and Situational Awareness

Differing Perspectives

Attribution theorists point out that our perspective differs when we observe others than when we act (Jones, 1976; Jones & Nisbett, 1971). This is often referred to as the actor–observer bias. When we act, the environment commands our attention. When we watch another person act, that person occupies the centre of our attention and the situation becomes relatively invisible. See if you can predict the result of a clever experiment conducted by Michael Storms (1973). Picture yourself as a subject in Storms's experiment. You are seated facing another student with whom you are to talk for a few minutes. Beside you is a TV camera that shares your view of the other student. Facing you from alongside the other student are an observer and another TV camera. Afterward, both you and the observer judge whether your behaviour was caused more by your personal characteristics or by the situation.

Which of you—subject or observer—will attribute the least importance to the situation? Storms, like many researchers, found the classic actor–observer difference (also known as the actor–observer effect). You—the actor—see your behaviour as due to the situation, while the observer sees your behaviour as reflecting your personality. But what if we reverse points of view by having you and the observer each watch the videotape recorded from the other's perspective? (You now view yourself, while the observer views what you saw.) This reverses the attributions: The observer now attributes your behaviour mostly to the situation you faced, while you now attribute it to your person. *Remembering* an experience from an observer's perspective—by "seeing" oneself from the outside— has the same effect (Frank & Gilovich, 1989). For another example, remember the attributions you made about your own and a friend's performance on exams. Most people focus on the situation to explain their own poor performance and personal attributes to explain another's performance.

Bertram Malle and his colleagues (Malle, 2006, 2007; Malle et al., 2007) have recently argued that a key element on how actor–observer effects occur is the observer's perception of the intentionality of the act. If we perceive someone as having acted intentionally, then we will make certain types of attributions ("He cut me off in traffic because he is a jerk"). Explanations for these types of events focus around the actor's reasons for the behaviour. However, if we see the actor (or ourselves) as having acted unintentionally, we make other types of attributions ("He must not have seen me; he must be distracted"). Explanations for these events focus more around the external causes for these events.

In some experiments, people have viewed a videotape of a suspect confessing during a police interview. If they viewed the confession through a camera focused on the suspect, they perceived the confession as genuine. If they viewed it through a camera focused on the detective, they perceived it as more coerced (Lassiter et al., 2005). The camera perspective influenced people's guilt judgments even when the judge instructed them to disregard it (Lassiter et al., 2005, 2010). In courtrooms, most confession videotapes focus on the confessor. As we might expect, note Daniel Lassiter and Kimberly Dudley (1991), such tapes yield a nearly 100 percent conviction rate when played by prosecutors. Perhaps a more impartial videotape would show both interrogator and suspect (see Kassin, 2005; Kassin et al., 2009).

Connection:

We will discuss more about confession evidence and false confessions in Module 22.

Perspectives Change with Time

As the once-visible person recedes in their memory, observers often give more and more credit to the situation (Burger, 1991). Circumstances can also shift our perspective on ourselves. Perhaps this is why Leonard Nimoy's second autobiography, published 20 years after the first, was titled *I Am Spock*. He realized that, just as he was part of the Spock character, Spock was part of his own identity. Seeing ourselves on television or in a mirror redirects our attention to ourselves, focusing our attention inward, making us *self*-conscious instead of *situation*-conscious. To see this in your own experience, do the activity. How did you respond to the questions? Did you say "depends on the situation" more for yourself than for Jon Stewart? We do this with our past as well. If instead of asking you to describe Jon Stewart, we had asked you to describe yourself five years ago, you would be more likely to circle a trait description than "depends on the situation." Why? When recalling our past, we become more like observers than actors (Pronin & Ross, 2006). For most of us, the "old you" is someone other than the "real you."

Leonard Nimoy, tired of being confused with his most famous character, called his first book I Am Not Spock. *Two decades later, he wrote another book, which he entitled* I Am Spock.

Because we are acutely aware of how our behaviour varies with the situation, we see ourselves as more variable than other people (Baxter & Goldberg, 1987; Kammer, 1982; Sande et al., 1988). The less opportunity we have to observe people's behaviour in context, the more we attribute to their personalities. Thomas Gilovich (1987) explored this by showing people a videotape of someone and then having them describe the person's actions to other people. The secondhand impressions were more extreme, partly because retellings focus attention on the person rather than on the situation (Baron et al., 1997).

Cultural Differences

Cultures also influence the attribution error. A Western worldview predisposes people to assume that people, not situations, cause events. Internal explanations are more socially approved (Jellison & Green, 1981): you get what you deserve and deserve what you get. Thus, we often explain bad behaviour by labelling a person "sick," "lazy," or "sadistic." As children grow up in Western culture, they learn to explain behaviour in terms of the other's personal characteristics (Rholes et al., 1990; Ross, 1981). As a Grade 1 student, one of (your author) David's sons brought home an example. He unscrambled the words "gate the sleeve caught Tom on his" into "The gate caught Tom on his sleeve." His teacher, applying the Western cultural assumptions of the curriculum materials, marked this wrong. The "right" answer located the cause within Tom: "Tom caught his sleeve on the gate."

Connection:

Remember that we discussed cultural differences in self-perception in Module 3.

The fundamental attribution error occurs across all cultures studied (Krull et al., 1999). Yet, people in Eastern Asian cultures are somewhat more sensitive to the importance of situations. Thus, they are less inclined to assume that others' behaviour corresponds to their traits (Choi et al., 1999; Farwell & Weiner, 2000; Masuda & Kitayama, 2004).

Some languages promote external attributions. Instead of "I was late," a Spanish idiom allows one to say, "The clock caused me to be late." In collectivist cultures, people less often perceive others in terms of personal dispositions (Lee et al., 1996; Zebrowitz-McArthur, 1988). They are less likely to spontaneously interpret behaviour as reflecting an inner trait (Newman, 1993). When told of someone's actions, Hindus in India are less likely than Americans to offer dispositional explanations ("She is kind") and more likely to offer situational explanations ("Her friends were with her"; Miller, 1984).

HOW FUNDAMENTAL IS THE FUNDAMENTAL ATTRIBUTION ERROR?

Like most provocative ideas, the presumption that we're all prone to a fundamental attribution error has its critics. Granted, say some, there is an attribution *bias*. But in any given instance, this may or may not produce an "error," just as parents who are biased to believe their child does not use drugs may or may not be correct. In some settings, people may see their own behaviour as *less* constrained than do observers (e.g., Robins et al., 1996). So it's an overstatement to say that at all times and in all settings observers underestimate situational influences. For this reason, many social psychologists follow Edward Jones in referring to the fundamental attribution error—seeing behaviour as corresponding to an inner disposition—as the correspondence bias. Nevertheless, experiments reveal that the bias occurs even when we are aware of the situational forces. It is sobering to think that we can know about a social process that distorts our thinking and still be susceptible to it. Perhaps that's because it takes more mental effort to assess social effects on people's behaviour than it does merely to attribute it to their dispositions (Gilbert et al., 1988, 1992; Webster, 1993). It's as if the busy person thinks, "This isn't a very good basis for making a judgment, but it's easy and all I've got time to look at."

What is clear is that attributional processes colour our explanations in basic and important ways. Researchers in Britain, India, Australia, and the United States have found that people's attributions predict their attitudes toward the poor and unemployed (Furnham, 1982; Pandey et al., 1982; Skitka, 1999; Wagstaff, 1983; Zucker & Weiner, 1993). Those who attribute poverty and unemployment to personal dispositions ("They're just lazy and undeserving") tend to adopt political positions unsympathetic to such people (see Figure 6-3). French investigators Jean-Leon Beauvois and Nicole Dubois (1988) report that "relatively privileged" middle-class people are more likely than less-advantaged people to assume that people's behaviours have internal explanations. In other words, those who have made it tend to assume that you get what you deserve.

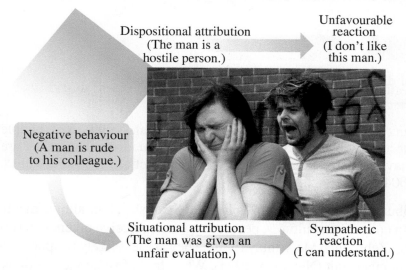

FIGURE 6-3

Attributions and reactions. How we explain someone's negative behaviour determines how we feel about it.

CONCLUSIONS

Can we benefit from being aware of the attribution error? As faculty members, the authors of this textbook are frequently called upon to participate in the hiring of new teachers at our respective institutions. David once assisted with some interviews for a faculty position. One candidate was interviewed by six people at once; each person had the opportunity to ask two or three questions. David came away thinking, "What a stiff, awkward person he is." He met the second candidate privately over coffee, and they immediately discovered they had a close, mutual friend. As they talked, he became increasingly impressed by what a "warm, engaging, stimulating person she is."

Only later did he remember the fundamental attribution error and reassess his analysis. He had attributed the first candidate's stiffness and the second candidate's warmth to their dispositions; in fact, David later realized, such behaviour resulted partly from the difference in their interview situations. Had he viewed these interactions through their eyes instead of his own, he might have come to different conclusions. We should always keep potential situational factors in mind when considering why people behave the way they do.

SUMMARY OF KEY POINTS

LO1. Describe Kelley's attribution theory.

- Three factors—consistency, distinctiveness, and consensus—influence whether we attribute someone's behaviour to internal or external causes.

LO2. Describe the fundamental attribution error.

- It is the tendency for observers to underestimate situational influences and overestimate dispositional influences upon others' behaviour.

LO3. Understand why we make the fundamental attribution error.

- We make this error because although we may know the situational influences on our own behaviour, we are not as aware of the influences on others' behaviour.
- Our perspective changes over time.
- People are more likely to make this error in some cultures than in others.

KEY TERMS

Actor–observer bias   When we are the actor, we tend to attribute behaviour to the environment, whereas when we observe others, we tend to underestimate the impact of the environment.

Attribution theory   The theory of how people explain others' behaviour—for example, by attributing it either to internal dispositions (enduring traits, motives, and attitudes) or to external situations.

Correspondence bias   A tendency for people to view behaviour as coming from inner dispositions.

Dispositional attribution   Attributing behaviour to the person's disposition and traits.

Fundamental attribution error   The tendency for observers to underestimate situational influences and overestimate dispositional influences upon others' behaviour. This is also called the correspondence bias, because we so often see behaviour as corresponding to a disposition.

Situational attribution   Attributing behaviour to the environment.

Heuristics and Errors in Reasoning

LO 1 Understand how our preconceptions bias our thinking

LO 2 Understand why we ignore base-rate information

LO 3 Explain why we are more persuaded by memorable events

LO 4 Understand how we misperceive correlation and control

LO 5 Understand how we overestimate the accuracy of our judgment

LO 6 Understand confirmation biases

Thomas Mulcair

Stephen Harper

Justin Trudeau

What good fortune for those in power that people do not think.

ADOLF HITLER

Perhaps it may seem odd to you to start a module with a quote from one of the worst war criminals of the twentieth century (one might say he was *the* worst, but many since have tried to outdo him); but his point is a good one. Political leaders through the ages have counted on this fact. It was perhaps most famously written down in the sixth century BCE, in Sun Tzu's *The Art of War*, yet past and current political leaders have continued to use propaganda to get us onside so we'll vote for them. They count on us not to pay too close attention to what they say, because if we do, their arguments can fall apart.

Political parties take shots at their opponents all the time. But are such ads really effective? We don't have time to actually think about everything, and advertisers are counting on that. It is a sort of mental sleight of hand. We take mental shortcuts. However, when we cut corners we sometimes make mistakes, and that is the focus of this module.

Applying   Social Psychology

Although most advertisements don't garner a great deal of scrutiny, some do. For example, Super Bowl commercials are watched more (by some people) than the game itself!

We see thousands of advertisements in a given week. Picture one advertisement you see a lot— do you think about it much? Consider it now—take a minute and think about what the message is, and what it is trying to sell. What is your first reaction to the advertisement? Is it trying to sell something that you would normally buy or use? If so, your reaction may be quite positive. If it is something you do not use, your response may be quite negative.

Advertisers know that people have quick, almost automatic, responses to ads, so they use tricks to overcome our natural shortcuts and biases.

Now, look at the advertisement again. What methods are the advertisers using to overcome (or reinforce) your initial reaction?

Connection:

We will discuss advertising in greater detail in Module 10.

Our cognitive powers outstrip the smartest computers in recognizing patterns, handling language, and processing abstract information. Our information processing is also wonderfully efficient. With such precious little time to process so much information, we specialize in mental shortcuts. Scientists marvel at the speed and ease with which we form impressions, judgments, and explanations. In many situations, our snap generalizations—"That's dangerous!"—are adaptive. They promote our survival. But our adaptive efficiency has a trade-off: we are not perfect. Our helpful strategies for simplifying complex information can lead us astray. To enhance our own powers of critical thinking, let's consider six reasons for our mistakes:

1. Our preconceptions bias our thinking.

2. We ignore base-rate information.

3. We are more swayed by memorable events than by facts.

4. We misperceive correlation and control.

5. We tend to be overconfident in our judgments

6. Our beliefs can generate their own confirmation.

LO 1

OUR PRECONCEPTIONS BIAS OUR THINKING

Our preconceptions guide how we perceive and interpret information. We construe the world through theory-tinted glasses. Your attitude toward the prime minister is largely determined by whether you support the Conservatives, the Liberals, the NDP, the Bloc Québécois, or the Green Party. People grant that preconceptions influence social judgments, yet fail to realize how great the effect is.

Pro-Israel supporters march with the Israeli flag.

An experiment by Robert Vallone, Lee Ross, and Mark Lepper (1985) reveals just how powerful preconceptions can be. They showed pro-Israeli and pro-Arab students six network news segments describing the 1982 killing of civilian refugees at two camps in Lebanon. As Figure 7-1 illustrates, each group perceived the networks as hostile to its side. The phenomenon is commonplace: Political candidates and their supporters rarely view the news media as sympathetic to their cause. Sports fans perceive referees as partial to the other side—for example, after the 2002 Olympic women's hockey final in Salt Lake City, where the Canadian team was assessed many more penalties than the U.S. team, commentators in Canada (your author, Steven, included) were outraged by the supposed "bias" shown by the referees. Indeed, people continued to feel slighted for years (CBC, 2010). At the women's hockey final in the 2010 Winter Olympics in Vancouver, commentators were still referring to the "unfair" penalty calling in the 2002 game—eight years later! Consistent with this phenomenon, people in conflict (married couples, labour and management, opposing racial groups) see impartial mediators as biased against them.

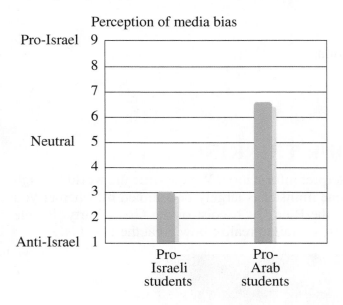

FIGURE 7-1

Pro-Israeli and pro-Arab students who viewed network news descriptions of the "Beirut massacre" both believed the coverage was biased against their point of view.

We start by selectively exposing ourselves to information that is consistent with our existing preconceptions, in order to avoid any "unpleasant surprises" (e.g., Festinger, 1957; Smith et al., 2007). Even if we are presented with contradictory evidence, our perceptions of that evidence can change it to seem more supportive. For example, Ross and Lepper assisted Charles Lord (1979) in asking students to evaluate the results of two supposedly new research studies. Half the students favoured capital punishment and half opposed it. One study confirmed and the other disconfirmed the students' beliefs about the deterrent effect of the death penalty. The results: Both proponents and opponents of capital punishment readily accepted evidence that confirmed their beliefs but were sharply critical of disconfirming evidence. Showing the two sides an *identical* body of mixed evidence had therefore not lessened their disagreement but *increased* it.

Connection:

We will revisit biased information processing in Module 11 when we discuss resistance to persuasion.

Activity: How well do we predict the future?

The following are some examples of things that various political, military, or business leaders have said over the last 100 years or so. Take a look at them and see what you think about their accuracy. These examples have been adapted from Russo and Schoemaker (1989):

"There is no reason anyone would want a computer in their home." (Ken Olson, president of Digital Equipment Company, 1977)

"Heavier-than-air flying machines are impossible." (Lord Kelvin, British mathematician, physicist, and president of the British Royal Society, 1895)

"Reagan doesn't have the presidential look." (United Artists executive, when asked whether Ronald Reagan should be offered the starring role in the movie *The Best Man,* 1964. Reagan went on to be governor of California and later a two-term president of the United States)

"A severe depression like that of 1920–21 is outside the range of possibility." (Harvard Economic Society, *Weekly Letter,* November 16, 1929, just before the stock market crash that led to the Great Depression)

"Impossible!" (Jimmy "The Greek" Snyder when asked whether Muhammad Ali could last six rounds in his upcoming bout with heavyweight champion Sonny Liston, 1964; Ali won.)

"They couldn't hit an elephant at this dist—" (General John B. Sedgwick, Union Army Civil War officer's last words, uttered during the Battle of Spotsylvania, 1864)

Although these quotes were obviously wrong (laughably so, perhaps), consider the context in which they were made. Why might the Harvard Economic Society want to believe that a severe depression could not occur? Consider the comments made today by politicians. Despite the bankruptcy of many companies, banks, and investment firms in the fall of 2008, the U.S. government was not willing to admit the United States was in a recession. During the same period, the Bank of Canada continued to claim that Canada would be isolated from and unaffected by the poor showing of the U.S. economy (CBC, 2008).

Now, look at the other statements above. Can you think of reasons why these comments may have seemed perfectly reasonable in their context? Don't fall victim to the hindsight bias. Look carefully at each comment.

Connection:

Remember that we discussed the hindsight bias in Module 1.

LO 2

WE IGNORE BASE-RATE INFORMATION

Now, consider the following: imagine we tell you about the 100 people that work at JMS Building Supplies. We tell you that 20 of them are in sales, and 80 of them are engineers. Next, we ask you to consider "Rick":

> Rick works at JMS Building Supplies. Rick is a happy-go-lucky guy. He enjoys sports. He drives a nice car. Although he has been divorced, he tries to see his two children as frequently as he can. However, his hectic schedule keeps him busy. His friends would describe him as outgoing, energetic, and the life of the party. *Question:* How likely is it that Rick is one of the salespeople at JMS?

So, what is your answer? You probably guessed that there is a high likelihood Rick is one of the salespeople, even though there is only a 20 percent chance that this is true (if 80 percent of the employees are engineers, there is an 80 percent chance Rick is an engineer).

Baruch Fischhoff and his colleagues (1984) have demonstrated that people are more likely to judge a person like Rick as a salesperson, regardless of the base rates, because he seems more *representative* of salespeople in general. When we judge someone or something by comparing it to our mental representations it is called using a *representativeness heuristic* (Tversky & Kahneman, 1973). These heuristics, or mental shortcuts, are very useful. Typically, they provide us with easy and simple decision criteria for which to guide our decisions and behaviour. However, sometimes they can lead us astray (as it probably did for you).

LO 3

WE ARE MORE SWAYED BY MEMORABLE EVENTS THAN BY FACTS
Critical THINKING

Consider the following questions. Before you read the next paragraph, write down your estimates . . . make a commitment to your responses.

1. Does the letter *k* appear in print more often as the first letter of a word or as the third letter?

2. Do more people live in Cambodia or in Tanzania?

How did you do? Go to the end of the module to find out. Were you right? Why?

You probably answered in terms of how readily instances of *k*'s, Cambodians, and Tanzanians come to mind. If examples are readily *available* in our memory—as words beginning with *k* and as Cambodians may be—then we presume that such are commonplace. Usually it is, so we are often well served by this cognitive rule of thumb, called the availability heuristic. For example, most marketing surveys ask us how often we take trips or use products. The ease with which instances of these types of actions come to mind is usually an excellent estimate of our behaviour.

But sometimes the rule deludes us. Stuart McKelvie, at Bishop's University, has explored how the availability heuristic can affect our judgments. If people hear a list of famous people of one sex (Mother Teresa, Oprah Winfrey, and Madonna) intermixed with an equal size list of unfamous people of the other sex (Donald Scarr, William Wood, Mel Jasper), the famous names will later be more cognitively available. Most people will therefore recall having heard more (in this instance) women's than men's names (McKelvie, 1995, 1997). Our use of the availability heuristic highlights a basic principle of social thinking: People are slow to deduce particular instances from a general truth, but they are remarkably quick to infer general truth from a vivid instance. No wonder that after hearing and reading stories of rapes, robberies, and beatings, nine out of ten Canadians overestimate—usually by a considerable margin—the percentage of crimes that involve violence (Doob & Roberts, 1988). Perhaps not surprisingly, South Africans, after a series of headline-grabbing gangland robberies and slayings, estimated that violent crime had doubled between 1998 and 2004, when in fact it had decreased (Wines, 2005). What do you think? Has crime gone up in the last five years, or down? Most people say up, but it is actually down 17 percent in the 2000s, and violent crime was down 5 percent (Statistics Canada, 2010).

The availability heuristic explains why powerful anecdotes are often more compelling than statistical information and why perceived risk is therefore often badly out of joint with real risks (Allison et al., 1992). Because news footage of airplane crashes is readily available in memory for most of us, and we can often identify specific cases of downed planes (such as the Malaysia Airlines flight that was shot down over Ukraine in July 2014, or the other Malaysia Airlines flight that went missing in the spring of 2014), we often suppose we are more at risk travelling in commercial airplanes than in cars. Actually, figures released on 2010 airline accidents data by the International Civil Aviation Administration demonstrate that it continues to be very safe to fly. There is less than one fatal accident per two *million* commercial departures in North America. That translates to an airline fatality rate of 0.0005 for every 100 million kilometres travelled (ICAO, 2005). In other words, one person dies for every 20 billion kilometres flown. This compares to a rate of 1.00 (or one death) per 100 million kilometres travelled in cars (and a frightening 17.5 for motorcycles; ATSB, 2005). Thus, by distance travelled, you are 200 times more likely to die in a car crash than in a plane crash. Even after terrorists crashed four airplanes into U.S. targets on September 11, 2001, Americans were much safer on planes than in cars. Not surprisingly, however, the 9/11 attacks on the World Trade Center and the Pentagon dramatically influence people's assessments of their risk of being the victim of a terrorist attack, even more than a decade later. Because more people chose to drive out of fear of flying after these attacks, it is estimated that 350 more people died in car crashes in the three months after the September 11 attacks than would have been expected (Gigerenzer, 2004). Perhaps as we would expect, although both Canadians and Americans perceive themselves to be at risk, Americans perceive a greater risk of such an attack than Canadians (see Bailis et al., 2005).

The horrific images of September 11, 2001, are still cognitively available and have influences on our perceptions of the risk of flying.

LO 4

WE MISPERCEIVE CORRELATION AND CONTROL

Another influence on everyday thinking is our search for order in random events, a tendency that can lead us down all sorts of wrong paths.

Illusory Correlation

It's easy to see a correlation where none exists. When we expect to find significant relationships, we easily associate random events, perceiving an illusory correlation. An excellent example of this is the perceived relationship between sugar consumption and hyperactivity in children. Although there is no evidence that sugar causes "bad" behaviour in children, David DiBattista, at Brock University, found that 80 percent of 389 primary school teachers surveyed believed that consuming sugar resulted in behavioural problems in hyperactive children and increased activity levels in children overall (DiBattista & Sheppard, 1993). Further, 55 percent of the teachers had counselled parents to reduce their child's sugar intake in order to control activity level.

Other experiments confirm that people easily misperceive random events as confirming their beliefs (Crocker, 1981; Jennings et al., 1982; Trolier & Hamilton, 1986). If we believe a correlation exists, we are more likely to notice and recall confirming instances. If we believe that overweight women are less happy, we perceive that we have observed such a correlation when we have not (Viken et al, 2005). If we believe that premonitions predict events, we notice and remember the joint occurrence of the premonition and the event's later occurrence. We seldom notice or remember all the times unusual events do not coincide with a premonition. If, after we think about a friend, the friend calls us, we notice and remember this coincidence. We don't notice all the times we think of a friend without any ensuing call or receive a call from a friend about whom we've not been thinking.

Illusion of Control

Our tendency to perceive random events as related feeds an illusion of control—*the idea that chance events are subject to our influence.* This is what keeps gamblers going and what makes the rest of us do all sorts of unlikely things.

Gambling

Ironically, the illusion of control is important in games of chance. Gambling is a major money-maker in North America. In Canada alone, there are currently 87 000 slot machines and video lottery terminals (VLTs), 60 casinos, 250 race tracks, and 25 000 licences for bingo-type games. Provincial government-run gambling revenues in 2008 were $13.7 billion (Statistics Canada, 2010). A group of Saint Mary's University researchers has found that although family income is a significant predictor of gambling (that is, the more we make the more likely we are to gamble), lower-income households are overrepresented among high-spending gamblers, and they tend to spend a greater percentage of their income on gambling products (e.g., games and lotteries; Macdonald & Perrier, 2004). Less-educated people are also overrepresented among the "big spenders." In addition, the games (and the casinos) themselves are designed to increase spending and time playing the games. Robert Ladouceur and his colleagues at Université Laval (Ladouceur & Sévigny, 2005) have demonstrated that putting a device on a VLT that allows the player to stop the machine actually increases the player's illusion of control, resulting in gamblers playing for a longer time (and thus spending more money). Interestingly, when people have lost consistently for a long time, they begin to believe they are "due for a win," not realizing that the probability of winning is not additive for each game played (e.g., you *must* win 20 percent of the time) but resets for every new game (you have a 20 percent chance of winning any particular game). This belief in additive probability increases people's perception of control, as well as how long they will gamble (and lose). Moreover, pathological gamblers are more susceptible to the illusion of control (Orgaz et al., 2013).

Dr. Michael Wohl at Carleton University noticed one day while watching a game of craps, that many of the players performed certain rituals before they threw the dice (e.g., blowing on the dice or shaking them a certain way; clinical psychologists call this "superstitious" behaviour), and he wondered why. In his research (see Wohl & Enzle, 2002, 2003, 2009), he found that, indeed, some people perceive themselves as personally lucky and try to use whatever luck they believe themselves to possess to maximize gambling-related outcomes. Participants were seated in front of a "slot machine" that was rigged to provide certain outcomes. Each player started with five tokens that were worth 20 cents each. Players would be able to remit their tokens for cash at the end of the experiment; thus, they were motivated to maximize their winnings. The researchers manipulated people's success on the slot machine by creating a situation where participants either just missed a big win ($14), or just missed a big loss (bankruptcy). Although people in both conditions won an equal amount of money ($2), the people who avoided bankruptcy felt luckier, and they were more likely to continue to play the game (ultimately losing more money) than people who had missed a big win.

Critical THINKING

Have you ever gone to a casino? Have you ended up spending more money that you expected to? Why or why not. What strategies did you use to control your spending? If you did go a bit out of control, what strategies could you use next time?

Regression Toward the Average

In a classic work published in 1974, Amos Tversky and Daniel Kahneman (the latter of whom was for a time a faculty member at the University of British Columbia and ultimately won a Nobel Prize for his work) noted another way by which an illusion of control can arise: We fail to recognize the statistical phenomenon of regression toward the average. Because an individual's exam scores fluctuate partly by chance, most students who get extremely high scores on an exam will get somewhat lower scores on the next exam. Because their first score is near the top limit of performance, their second score is more likely to fall back ("regress") toward their own average than go higher. This is why groups and teams that are initially successful (e.g., early in the season) will inevitably face failures. Conversely, the lowest-scoring students on the first exam are likely to improve (assuming they return to class). If those who scored lowest go for tutoring after the first exam, the tutors are likely to feel effective when the student improves, even if the tutoring had less of an effect that they might think.

Indeed, when things reach a low point, we will try anything, and whatever we try—going to a psychotherapist, starting a new diet and exercise plan, reading a self-help book—is more likely to be followed by improvement than by further deterioration.

LO 5

WE OVERESTIMATE THE ACCURACY OF OUR JUDGMENTS

So far we have seen that our cognitive systems process a vast amount of information efficiently and automatically. But our efficiency has a trade-off; as we interpret our experiences and construct memories, our automatic intuitions sometimes err. Usually, we are unaware of our flaws. The "intellectual conceit" evident in judgments of past knowledge ("I knew it all along") extends to estimates of current knowledge and predictions of future behaviour. As was found by Michael Ross at the University of Waterloo and Ian Newby-Clark at the University of Guelph, although we know we've messed up in the past, we have more positive expectations for our future performance. This can be in terms of meeting deadlines, managing relationships, following an exercise routine, and so forth (Ross & Newby-Clark, 1998). To explore this overconfidence phenomenon, Daniel Kahneman and Amos Tversky (1979) gave people factual questions and asked them to fill in the blanks, as in the following: "I feel 98 percent certain that the air distance between New Delhi and Beijing is more than _____ miles but less than _____ miles."* Most individuals were overconfident: About 30 percent of the time, the correct answers lay outside the range they felt 98 percent confident about.

_____
* Distance is 3798 km.

To find out whether overconfidence extends to social judgments, David Dunning and his associates (1990) created a little game show. They asked Stanford University students to guess a stranger's answers to a series of questions, such as "Would you prepare for a difficult exam alone or with others?" and "Would you rate your lecture notes as neat or messy?" Knowing the type of question but not the actual questions, the participants first interviewed their target person about background, hobbies, academic interests, aspirations, astrological sign—anything they thought might be helpful. Then, while the targets privately answered 20 of the two-choice questions, the interviewers predicted their target's answers and rated their own confidence in the predictions.

The interviewers guessed right 63 percent of the time, beating chance by 13 percent. But, on average, they felt 75 percent sure of their predictions. When guessing their own roommates' responses, they were 68 percent correct and 78 percent confident. Moreover, the most confident people were most likely to be overconfident. People also are markedly overconfident when judging whether someone is telling the truth or when estimating things such as the sexual history of their dating partner or the activity preferences of their roommates (DePaulo et al., 1997; Swann & Gill, 1997).

Ironically, incompetence feeds overconfidence. It takes competence to recognize what competence is, note Justin Kruger and David Dunning (1999). Students who score at the bottom on tests of grammar, humour, and logic are most prone to overestimate their gifts at such. Those who don't know what good logic or grammar is are often unaware that they lack it. If you make a list of all the words you can form out of the letters in "psychology," you may feel brilliant—but then stupid when a friend starts naming the ones you missed. Deanna Caputo and David Dunning (2005) recreated this phenomenon in experiments, confirming that our ignorance of our ignorance sustains our self-confidence. Follow-up studies indicate that this "ignorance of one's incompetence" occurs mostly on relatively easy-seeming tasks, such as forming words out of "psychology." On really hard tasks, poor performers more often appreciate their lack of skill (Burson et al., 2006).

This ignorance of one's own incompetence helps explain David Dunning's (2005) startling conclusion from employee assessment studies that "what others see in us . . . tends to be more highly correlated with objective outcomes than what we see in ourselves." In one study, participants watched someone walk into a room, sit, read a weather report, and walk out (Borkenau & Liebler, 1993). Based on nothing more than that, their estimate of the person's intelligence correlated with the person's intelligence score (0.30) about as well as did the person's own self-estimate (0.32)!

Are people better at predicting their own behaviour? To find out, Robert Vallone and his colleagues (1990) had students predict in September whether they would drop a course, declare a major, elect to live off campus next year, and so forth. Although the students felt, on average, 84 percent sure of those self-predictions, they were wrong nearly twice as often as they expected to be. Even when feeling 100 percent sure of their predictions, they erred 15 percent of the time.

In estimating their chances for success on a task, such as a major exam, people's confidence runs highest when removed in time from the moment of truth. By exam day, the possibility of failure looms larger and confidence typically drops (Gilovich et al., 1993; Shepperd et al., 2005). Roger Buehler and his colleagues (1994, 2002, 2003) report that most students also confidently underestimate how long it will take them to complete papers and other major assignments. They are not alone:

- *The "planning fallacy."* How much free time do you have today? How much free time do you expect you will have a month from today? Most of us overestimate how much we'll be getting done, and therefore how much free time we will have (Zauberman & Lynch, 2005). Professional planners, too, routinely underestimate the time and expense of projects. In 1969, Montreal Mayor Jean Drapeau proudly announced that a $120 million stadium with a retractable roof would be built for the 1976 Olympics. The roof was completed in 1989 and cost $120 million by itself. The final payment for the project was made in 2006, 30 years after the Olympics. In 1985, officials estimated that Boston's "Big Dig" highway project would cost $2.6 billion and take until 1998. The cost ballooned to $14.6 billion and the project took until 2006.

- *Stockbroker overconfidence.* Investment experts market their services with the confident presumption that they can beat the stock market average, forgetting that for every stockbroker or buyer saying "Sell!" at a given price, there is another saying "Buy!" A stock's price is the balance point between those mutually confident judgments. Thus, incredible as it may seem, economist Burton Malkiel (2004) reports that mutual fund portfolios selected by investment analysts have not outperformed randomly selected stocks.

- *Political overconfidence.* Overconfident decision makers can wreak havoc. It was a confident Adolf Hitler who from 1939 to 1945 waged war against the rest of Europe. It was a confident Saddam Hussein who in 1990 marched his army into Kuwait and in 2003 promised to defeat invading armies. It was a confident George W. Bush in 2003 who proclaimed "Mission Accomplished" and that peaceful democracy would soon prevail in a liberated and thriving Iraq. It was a confident Stephen Harper who said in 2008 that the global recession would not affect Canada.

What produces overconfidence? Why doesn't experience lead us to a more realistic self-appraisal? For one thing, people tend to recall their mistaken judgments as times when they were almost right. Phillip Tetlock (1998, 1999) observed this after inviting various academic and government experts to project—from their viewpoint in the late 1980s—the future governance of the Soviet Union, South Africa, and Canada. Five years later, communism collapsed, South Africa had become a multiracial democracy, and Quebec had not seceded from Canada. Experts who had felt more than 80 percent confident were right in predicting these turns of events less than 40 percent of the time.

Yet, reflecting on their judgments, those who erred believed they were still basically right. "I was 'almost right,'" said many. "The hardliners almost succeeded in their coup attempt against [the Soviet leader] Gorbachev." "The Québécois separatists almost won the secessionist referendum." "But for the coincidence of [South African President] de Klerk and [Nelson] Mandela, there would have been a lot bloodier transition to black majority rule in South Africa." Among political experts—and stock market forecasters, mental health workers, and sports prognosticators—overconfidence is hard to dislodge.

People also tend not to seek information that might disprove what they believe. P. C. Wason (1960) demonstrated this, as you can, by giving participants a sequence of three numbers—2, 4, 6—that conformed to a rule he had in mind. (The rule was simply any three ascending numbers.) To enable the participants to discover the rule, Wason invited each person to generate additional sets of three numbers. Each time, Wason told the person whether or not the set conformed to his rule. As soon as participants were sure they had discovered the rule, they were to stop and announce it.

The result? Seldom right but never in doubt: 23 of the 29 participants convinced themselves of a wrong rule. They typically formed some erroneous belief about the rule (e.g., counting by twos) and then searched for confirming evidence (e.g., by testing 8, 10, 12) rather than attempting to disconfirm their hunches. We are eager to verify our beliefs but less inclined to seek evidence that might disprove them, a phenomenon called the confirmation bias. We see this in many contexts, such as in criminal investigations (Rassin et al., 2010), in the interpretation of forensic evidence (Kassin et al., 2013), the interpretation of scientific evidence by researchers (Hergovich et al., 2010), and in psychiatric diagnoses (Mendel et al., 2011).

Connection:

We will discuss the role of confirmation biases in police investigations in Module 22.

Remedies for Overconfidence

What lessons can we draw from research on overconfidence? Even when people are sure they are right, they may be wrong. Confidence and competence need not coincide. Two techniques have successfully reduced the overconfidence bias. One is prompt feedback (Lichtenstein & Fischhoff, 1980). In everyday life, weather forecasters and those who set the odds in horse racing both receive clear, daily feedback. And experts in both groups do quite well at estimating their probable accuracy (Fischhoff, 1982).

To reduce "planning fallacy" overconfidence, people can be asked to "unpack" a task—to break it down into its subcomponents—and estimate the time required for each. Justin Kruger and Matt Evans (2004) report that doing so leads to more realistic estimates of completion time. When people think about why an idea might be true, it begins to seem true (Koehler, 1991). Thus, another way to reduce overconfidence is to get people to think of one good reason why their judgments might be wrong; that is, force them to consider disconfirming information (Koriat et al., 1980). Managers might foster more realistic judgments by insisting that all proposals and recommendations include reasons why they might not work.

Still, we should be careful not to undermine people's reasonable self-confidence or to destroy their decisiveness. In times when their wisdom is needed, those lacking self-confidence may shrink from speaking up or making tough decisions. Overconfidence can cost us, but realistic self-confidence is adaptive.

LO 6

UNDERSTANDING CONFIRMATION BIASES

There's one additional reason why our intuitive beliefs resist reality: They sometimes lead us to act in ways that produce their apparent confirmation. Our beliefs about other people can therefore become self-fulfilling prophecies.

In his well-known studies of "experimenter bias," Robert Rosenthal (1985, 2006) found that research participants sometimes live up to what is expected of them. In one study, experimenters asked participants to judge the success of people in various photographs. The experimenters read the same instructions to all their participants and showed them the same photos. Nevertheless, experimenters led to expect high ratings obtained higher ratings than did those who expected their participants to see the photographed people as failures. Even more startling—and controversial—are reports that teachers' beliefs about their students similarly serve as self-fulfilling prophecies.

Do Teacher Expectations Affect Student Performance?

Teachers do have higher expectations for some students than for others. Perhaps you have detected this after having a brother or sister precede you in school, after receiving a label such as "gifted" or "learning disabled," or after being tracked with "high-ability" or "average-ability" students. Perhaps conversation in the teachers' lounge sent your reputation ahead of you. Or perhaps your new teacher scrutinized your school file or discovered your family's social status. Do such teacher expectations affect student performance?

By Rosenthal's own count, in only 39 percent of the 448 published experiments do expectations significantly affect performance (Rosenthal, 1991, 2002). Low expectations do not doom a capable child, nor do high expectations magically transform a slow learner into a valedictorian. Human nature is not that pliable. High expectations do seem to influence low achievers, for whom a teacher's positive attitude may be a hope-giving breath of fresh air (Madon et al., 1997). How are expectations transmitted? Rosenthal and other investigators report that teachers look, smile, and nod more at "high-potential students." Teachers also may teach more to their "gifted" students, set higher goals for them, call on them more, and give them more time to answer (Cooper, 1983; Harris & Rosenthal, 1985, 1986; Jussim, 1986).

Reading the experiments on teacher expectations makes us wonder about the effect of *students*' expectations upon their teachers. RateMyProfessor and similar sites allow students to give free and open feedback to their colleagues about a professor's performance in class. You no doubt begin many of your courses having heard or read that "Professor Bourgeois is hilarious" and "Professor MacDougall is a bore." Do these expectations have an impact? Perhaps.

One experiment found that if women were led to believe their male professor was sexist, they had a less positive experience, performed worse, and rated him as less competent (Adams et al., 2006). Another research team led by David Jamieson (1987) experimented with four Ontario high school classes taught by a newly transferred teacher. During individual interviews, they told students in two of the classes that both other students and the research team rated the teacher very highly. Compared to the control classes, the students given positive expectations paid more attention during class. At the end of the teaching unit, they also got better grades and rated the teacher as clearer in her teaching. The attitudes that a class has toward its teacher are as important, it seems, as the teacher's attitude toward the students.

Do We Get What We Expect from Others?

Although the expectations of experimenters and teachers are usually fairly accurate assessments, they do occasionally act as self-fulfilling prophecies. How general is this effect? Studies show that self-fulfilling prophecies also operate in work settings (with managers who have high or low expectations), in courtrooms (as judges instruct juries), and in simulated police contexts (as interrogators with guilty or innocent expectations interrogate and pressure suspects; Kassin, 2005; Rosenthal, 2003, 2006). There are times when negative expectations of someone lead us to be extra nice to that person, which induces them to be nice in return—thus *dis*confirming our expectations. But a more common finding in studies of social interaction is that, yes, we do, to some extent, get what we expect (Olson et al., 1996).

Connection:

We will discuss self-fulfilling prophecies in the context of confessions in Module 22.

Do intimate relationships prosper when partners idealize one another? Are positive illusions of the other's virtues self-fulfilling? Or are they more often self-defeating, by creating expectations that can't be met and that ultimately spell doom? Among University of Waterloo dating couples followed by Sandra Murray and her colleagues (1996, 2000), positive ideals of one's partner were good omens. Idealization helped buffer conflict, bolster satisfaction, and turn self-perceived frogs into princes or princesses. When someone loves and admires us, it helps us become more the person he or she imagines us to be. Among married couples, too, those who worry that their partner doesn't love and accept them interpret slight hurts as rejections, which motivates them to devalue the partner and distance themselves. Those who presume their partner's love and acceptance respond less defensively, and even may be closer to their partner (Murray et al., 2003). Love helps create its presumed reality.

Several experiments conducted by Mark Snyder (1984) at the University of Minnesota show how, once formed, erroneous beliefs about the social world can induce others to confirm those beliefs, a form of self-fulfilling prophecy called **behavioural confirmation**. In a now-classic study, Snyder, Elizabeth Tanke, and Ellen Berscheid (1977) had male students talk on the telephone with women they thought (from having been shown a picture) were either attractive or unattractive. Analysis of just the women's comments during the conversations revealed that the supposedly attractive women spoke more warmly than the supposedly unattractive women. The men's erroneous beliefs had become a self-fulfilling prophecy by leading them to act in a way that influenced the women to fulfill the men's stereotype that beautiful people are desirable people.

These experiments help us understand how social beliefs, such as stereotypes about people with disabilities or about people of a particular race or sex, may be self-confirming. We help construct our own social realities. How others treat us reflects how we and others have treated them.

CONCLUSIONS

We have reviewed some reasons why people sometimes come to believe what may be untrue. We cannot easily dismiss these experiments.

Research in cognitive social psychology thus mirrors the mixed review given humanity in literature, philosophy, and religion. Many research psychologists have spent lifetimes exploring the awesome capacities of the human mind. We are smart enough to have cracked our own genetic code, to have invented talking computers, and to have sent people to the moon. But intelligence does not make us immune from these biases (Stanovich & West, 2008).

Three cheers for human reason. Well, two cheers—because the mind's premium on efficient judgment makes our intuition more vulnerable to misjudgment than we suspect. With remarkable ease, we form and sustain false beliefs. Led by our preconceptions, overconfident, persuaded by vivid anecdotes, perceiving correlations and control even where none may exist, we construct our social beliefs and then influence others to confirm them. "The naked intellect," observed novelist Madeleine L'Engle, "is an extraordinarily inaccurate instrument."

SUMMARY OF KEY POINTS

LO1. Understand how our preconceptions bias our thinking.

- Our preconceptions bias how we expose ourselves to, process, judge, and remember information.

LO2. Understand why we ignore base-rate information.

- We make judgments based on representativeness of information, rather than focusing on statistical base rates.

LO3. Explain why we are more persuaded by memorable events.

- We judge the likelihood of events based on how easy it is to recall instances of that event.

LO4. Understand how we misperceive correlation and control.

- When presented with two unlikely events that co-occur, we perceive the strength of that relationship to be greater.
- We believe we have more control over random events than we typically do.

LO5. Understand how we overestimate the accuracy of our judgment.

- We tend to look for information than confirms our beliefs, rather than disconfirming them.

LO6. Understand confirmation biases.

- Self-fulfilling prophecies (where our behaviour elicits the behaviour we expect from others) can also be manifested in behavioural confirmation, where social expectations elicit specific behaviours from individuals.

Answer to Question 1: The letter k appears in print two to three times more often as the third letter. Yet most people judge that k appears more often at the beginning of a word. Words beginning with k are more readily available to memory, surmise Tversky and Kahneman (1974), and ease of recall—availability—is our heuristic for judging the frequency of events.

Answer to Question 2: Tanzania's 40 million people greatly outnumber Cambodia's 14 million. Most people, having more vivid images of Cambodians, guess wrongly.

KEY TERMS

Availability heuristic   An efficient but fallible rule of thumb that judges the likelihood of things in terms of their availability in memory. If instances of something come readily to mind, we presume it is commonplace.

Behavioural confirmation   A type of self-fulfilling prophecy whereby people's social expectations (based more on social beliefs than personal expectation) lead them to act in ways that cause others to confirm the expectations.

Confirmation bias   We are eager to verify our beliefs but less inclined to seek evidence that might disprove them.

Illusion of control   Perception of uncontrollable events as subject to one's control or as more controllable than they are.

Illusory correlation   Perception of a relationship where none exists, or perception of a stronger relationship than actually exists.

Regression toward the average   The statistical tendency for extreme scores or extreme behaviour to return toward one's average.

Self-fulfilling prophecy   The tendency for one's expectations to evoke behaviour in others that confirms the expectations.

MODULE EIGHT

Attitudes, Behaviour, and Compliance

LEARNING OBJECTIVES After studying Module 8, you will be able to

LO **1**   Understand when attitudes influence behaviour

LO **2**   Understand that behaviours can at times influence attitudes

LO **3**   Describe the principles of compliance

LO **4**   Describe cognitive dissonance theory

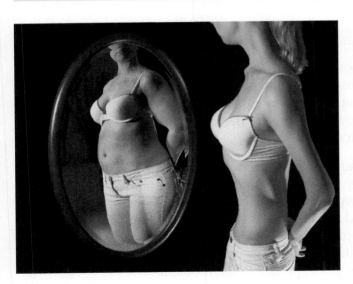

For years, social psychologists have been asking themselves the following question: Which comes first, belief or behaviour? Inner attitude or outer action? Character or conduct? What is the relationship between who we *are* (on the inside) and what we *do* (on the outside)? Underlying our teaching, preaching, politics, and counselling is the assumption that private beliefs determine public behaviour: If we want to alter people's actions, we need to change their hearts and minds. We need to understand *attitudes* if we are going to understand *behaviour*.

Critical THINKING

The picture below shows a victim of the Rwandan genocide living in a refugee camp. Can changing the way people think about one another help prevent violence and human catastrophe in places such as Syria, Rwanda, Bosnia, and Darfur? Is genocide becoming more common in our world? Or are we just hearing about it more?

A young Tutsi refugee gazes upon the Tutsi camp of Nyarushishi, Rwanda.

LO 1

DO ATTITUDES INFLUENCE BEHAVIOUR?

An attitude is a general evaluation of some person, object, or issue along a continuum from positive to negative. However, attitudes encompass a variety of elements, including both cognition (beliefs about the object—our "minds") and affect (our emotions or feelings toward that object—our "hearts"). Our beliefs and feelings can influence our reactions. If we *believe* that someone is threatening, we might *feel* dislike and therefore *act* with hostility.

Believing that attitudes were the key to behaviour prediction, social psychologists during the 1940s and 1950s studied factors that influence attitudes. However, numerous studies showed that attitudes did not always predict behaviour. Most damaging to attitude–behaviour researchers, Allan Wicker (1971) found that the relationship between attitudes and behaviour was weak to non-existent. At the time, attitudes were among the most studied topics in social psychology—but if attitudes did not predict behaviour, what was the point in studying them? In response to these studies and others, researchers studying attitudes devised a three-pronged approach to the problem:

1. *Specificity:* General attitudes are not good predictors of specific behaviours. To predict specific behaviours, one must ask specific questions. For example, James Olson of the University of Western Ontario and Mark Zanna at the University of Waterloo (1981) found that attitudes toward jogging predicted jogging behaviour well. Diane Morrison (1989) found that attitudes toward contraceptive use predicted contraceptive use. Interestingly, general attitudes can

predict classes of behaviour as well: Russell Weigel and Lee Newman (1976) found that general attitudes toward the environment can predict classes of pro-environmental behaviours. Thus, if we measure the relationship properly, attitude will be a good predictor of behaviour.

2. *Behavioural models:* Martin Fishbein and Icek Ajzen (1980) developed the *theory of reasoned action*, and later Ajzen (1990) proposed the *theory of planned behaviour* to explain when attitudes would predict behaviour. As shown in Figures 8-1 and 8-2, both models have attitudes and behaviour in them, but also include a number of factors external to the attitudes themselves (that is, perceived social norms, perceived behavioural control, behavioural intentions). For example, most smokers have negative attitudes toward smoking and want to quit, yet they do not. Many feel they do not have control over their behaviour. When combined, these factors have been found to be excellent predictors of behaviour in a variety of domains.

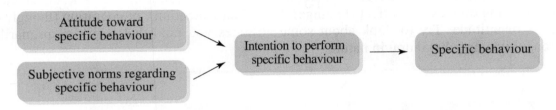

FIGURE 8.1

Theory of reasoned action.

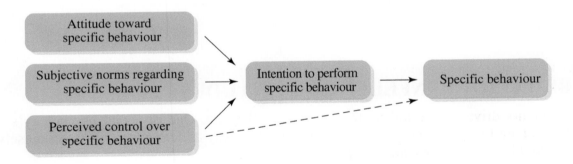

FIGURE 8.2

Theory of planned behaviour.

3. *Attitude strength:* A final approach to understanding the sometimes tricky attitude–behaviour relation was to explore the role of attitude strength. Strong attitudes (those we feel passionately) are persistent over time, resistant to change, and influence perception and judgment of attitude-relevant information. Most importantly, strong attitudes consistently predict behaviour. Weak attitudes are less likely to do so (see Krosnick & Petty, 1995).

Thus, early research that explored the attitude–behaviour relationship often looked at attitudes that were poorly assessed, did not take external factors into account, or examined both strong and weak attitudes. So, do attitudes predict behaviour? The answer is, quite clearly, yes—under certain conditions.

Applying Social Psychology

When you read about attitudes in this text, some thoughts may have come to mind about the types of attitudes people hold. For example, as you know, some attitudes are positive and some are negative. Also, some attitudes may be more "cold" (i.e., based on beliefs and cognitions), whereas others may be more "hot" (i.e., based on emotions). Finally, some attitudes are simply based on your previous behaviours—for example, you might buy Pepsi because you always drink Pepsi.

An attitude may be exhibited in beliefs, feelings, or intended behaviour. It is important to understand the distinctions this can create. If you want to convince your sister to buy a new smartphone, then your approach should be different than if you wanted her to buy a kitten. The underlying basis of the attitude is different. Thus when assessing attitudes, we should tap at least one of the following dimensions: affect (feelings), behaviour (intention), or cognition (thoughts) —the ABC's of attitude. Try to think about some attitudes you hold that might be primarily affective, cognitive, or behavioural in nature.

Connection:

We will revisit attitudes when we discuss resisting persuasion in Module 11.

LO 2

DOES BEHAVIOUR INFLUENCE ATTITUDES?

But can behaviours drive our attitudes? In some cases, they do. One of social psychology's big lessons is that we are likely not only to think ourselves into a way of acting but also to act ourselves into a way of thinking. Sometimes *attitudes follow behaviour*.

Role-Playing

Critical THINKING

Imagine you are part of a research study. You are sitting in the office of a researcher who tells you that you have been randomly assigned to be one of the "guards" in an experiment about prison life. What kind of guard would you be? Would you be "tough but fair"? Would you be strict? Would you be sadistic and cruel? How would you behave? How do you think you *should* behave? What if the researcher had told you that you had been assigned to be a prisoner? Would that make a difference? Would you act any differently?

Philip Zimbardo wanted to know the answers to the questions we posed in the Critical Thinking box, so he constructed a mock prison in the basement of a Stanford University building. How do you think his participants (normal students like you) behaved? Did being assigned to being a prisoner instead of a guard matter? Does the role you are given affect your behaviour? In Zimbardo's study, student volunteers spent time in a simulated prison (Zimbardo, 1971; Haney & Zimbardo, 1998). Zimbardo wanted to know if prison brutality is a product of problem prisoners and malicious guards, or if the institutional roles of guard and prisoner embitter and harden even compassionate people. Do the people make the place violent? Or does the place make the people violent?

So, by a flip of a coin, Zimbardo designated some students as guards and some as prisoners. He gave the guards uniforms, billy clubs, and whistles, and instructed them to enforce the rules. Prisoners were locked in cells and made to wear humiliating outfits. After a jovial first day of "playing" their roles, the guards and prisoners, and even the experimenters, got caught up in the situation. The guards began to disparage the prisoners, and some devised cruel and degrading routines. The prisoners broke down, rebelled, or became apathetic. There developed, reported Zimbardo (1972), a "growing confusion between reality and illusion, between role-playing and self-identity. . . . This prison which we had created . . . was absorbing us as creatures of its own reality."

Zimbardo was forced to call off the planned two-week simulation after only six days. You cannot appreciate the power of this study without seeing the video. Look online and you will see the remarkable impact role-playing can have on people's behaviour. The take-home lesson: What is unreal (an artificial role) can evolve into what is real. Take on a new role—as a teacher, soldier, or salesperson—and it may shape your attitudes. Perhaps this is why we often hear that actors who play a romantically involved couple on screen often end up together off-screen (e.g., Brad Pitt and Angelina Jolie from *Mr. and Mrs. Smith*; Kristen Stewart and Robert Pattinson from the *Twilight* movies; Ryan Gosling and Rachel McAdams from *The Notebook*). Many of these relationships do not last.

You might think that the Zimbardo Prison Study could not happen again, but it has—the *BBC Prison Study* replicated the basic approach taken by Zimbardo, assigning people to be either a guard or a prisoner (see Haslam & Reicher 2007a). The researchers found that many of the same authoritarian leadership approaches developed over time. To be fair though, while some people may become sadistic in these situations, others do not (Mastroianni & Reed, 2006; Zimbardo, 2007). But consider also what has happened in similar situations in the real world—torture and humiliation of military detainees in the Abu Ghraib Prison in Iraq, and torture of prisoners in Guantanamo Bay. These are just two salient examples. Being assigned to a role or a task can make people behave in a manner that is highly inconsistent to their beliefs and values. Also, we have to recognize the importance of leadership, compliance, and obedience in these situations—a powerful leader and/or a strong group can exert tremendous influences on individual behaviour.

Connection:

Obedience will be discussed further in Module 9.

It is important to note, however, as more recent work has shown (Haslam & Reicher 2007b; McFarland & Carnahan, 2009; Carnahan & McFarland, 2007), Zimbardo played an active role in the experiment. As "Prison Warden," he encouraged much of the guards' behaviour—they listened to him and looked to him for leadership. Understanding obedience is very important if we want to explain behaviour. People take cues about how to act from the leaders and the rest of the group.

LO 3

THE PRINCIPLES OF COMPLIANCE

How do people (e.g., our parents, marketers, salespeople) use our attitudes and behaviour against us? How do they get us to do what they want us to do? In other words, how do people persuade us to comply with their requests to buy something, to try something, or to do them a favour? This is the question social psychologist Robert Cialdini has been answering for four decades (see Cialdini, 2006; Cialdini & Goldstein, 2004; Goldstein et al., 2008).

Cialdini is a self-described "patsy." "For as long as I can recall, I've been an easy mark for the pitches of peddlers, fund-raisers, and operators of one sort or another." To better understand why one person says yes to another, he spent three years as a trainee in various sales, fund-raising, and advertising organizations, discovering how they exploit "the weapons of influence." Cialdini uncovered six principles of compliance:

- *Commitment and consistency*: Once we agree to something we do not want to change our minds.
- *Scarcity*: If something is limited in amount or time of availability, we will want it more.
- *Reciprocity*: If someone does something for us, we want to return the favour.
- *Social proof*: We look to others' behaviours when making our decisions.
- *Liking*: We are more likely to accept something coming from someone we like.
- *Authority*: If someone in authority tells us it is good, we will like it.

Marketers and salespeople use these principles to their advantage and have developed them into specific techniques. We will now discuss a few of these techniques.

The Foot-in-the-Door Phenomenon

Experiments suggest that if you want people to do a big favour for you, an effective strategy is this: Get them to do a small favour first. In the best-known demonstration of this foot-in-the-door phenomenon, researchers posing as safe-driving volunteers asked Californians to permit the installation of huge, poorly lettered "Drive Carefully" signs in their front yards. Only 17 percent consented. Others were first approached with a small request: Would they display 3-inch (8 cm) "Be a safe driver" window signs? Nearly all readily agreed. When approached two weeks later to allow the large, ugly signs in their front yards, 76 percent consented (Freedman & Fraser, 1966).

Other researchers have confirmed the foot-in-the-door phenomenon with altruistic behaviours:

- Patricia Pliner and her colleagues (1974) found 46 percent of Torontonians willing to give to a cancer charity when approached directly. Others, asked a day ahead to wear a lapel pin publicizing the drive (which all agreed to do), were nearly twice as likely to donate.
- Paul Markey and his colleagues (2002) requested help in Internet chat rooms. ("I can't get my email to work. Is there any way I can get you to send me an email?") Help increased—from 2 to 16 percent—by including a smaller prior request ("I am new to this whole computer thing. Is there any way you can tell me how to look at someone's profile?")
- Nicolas Gueguen and Celine Jacob (2001) tripled the rate that French Internet users contributed to child landmine victims' organizations (from 1.6 to 4.9 percent) by first inviting them to sign a petition against landmines.

Note that in these experiments, the initial compliance was voluntary. We will see again and again that when people commit themselves to public behaviours *and* perceive these acts to be their own doing, they come to believe more strongly in what they have done.

The Low-Ball Technique

Cialdini and his colleagues (1978) also explored a variation of the foot-in-the-door phenomenon by experimenting with the low-ball technique, a tactic used by some car dealers, who are extremely well versed in the use of these tactics. For example, one of your authors, Steven, likes to shop for cars (although he has only ever purchased one) and has experienced how automobile dealers use these tactics. For example, when he helped his sister-in-law buy a new car, the salesman prepared the bill of sale, which the sister-in-law signed. When he returned, an additional $375 had been added to the cost for "tire fees" and "processing" (a clear example of the low-ball technique). His sister-in-law still purchased the car. Once, when Steven shopped for a vehicle for himself, a saleswoman gave him a car to drive home for the night (an example of employing the commitment and consistency principle—"I am already taking the car home, I must want it"). He did not buy that car, although the same tactic worked a couple of years later.

These compliance principles are well worth learning about. Someone trying to seduce us—financially, politically, or sexually—will usually try to create a momentum of compliance. The practical lesson: Before agreeing to a small request, think about what may follow.

The Door-in-the-Face Technique

Cialdini and his colleagues (e.g., Cialdini et al., 1975; Cialdini & Golstein, 2004) have also identified the door-in-the-face technique—the tendency for people who have first declined a large request to comply with a subsequent but smaller request. The door-in-the-face technique works through the principle of reciprocity.

The basic idea is that an initial large request is presented—one that is so large that people will almost all say no (e.g., "Can you donate $100 for cancer research?"). The requester acquiesces, and then makes a smaller request (e.g., "Well, if you can't donate $100, how about $10?"). We feel bad about saying no at first, so we say yes to the second request to "be nice." Cialdini and his colleagues (1975) have shown that this "request then moderation" procedure is very effective at gaining compliance.

Activity: **Is forewarned forearmed?**

They say that forewarned is forearmed. Now that you know of the six principles of compliance, can you think about how to counter them? Let's take a concrete example. Have you ever received a free sample at a grocery store? Often there is a booth set up for tasting a new product. Conveniently, the product is on display with the samples. People try the sample, and then take the product. It has been demonstrated that people are much more likely to take the product after having a free sample than they are if no sample is provided. This may be an example of the reciprocity principle—we get something (the sample) and we reciprocate by taking the product (although there are likely other elements at play as well, such as the taste of the product, hunger, etc.).

What about other principles? Companies use scarcity with "limited time offers" and "limited quantities." Authority and liking are being used when attractive athletes and performers advertise products. Pull out a magazine. How many of the ads in that magazine use one or more of these principles? Look at the ads on these pages. What principles are they getting at?

Marketing researchers and salespeople have found that these principles work even when we are aware of a profit motive (Cialdini, 1988). A harmless initial commitment—returning a card for more information and a gift, agreeing to listen to an investment possibility—often moves us toward a larger commitment. Remember, just because you have initially agreed to something (and even signed something) does not necessarily mean you have to follow through if the deal changes.

In their initial study, Cialdini had students go out to recruit volunteers to chaperone a group of children from the "County Juvenile Detention Centre" on a trip to the zoo. For half of the participants, this request was preceded by a larger request—to act as a volunteer, unpaid counsellor at the detention centre. When people received the small request only (to chaperone) they agreed 16.7 percent of the time. But when they received the large request first (that no one agreed to), 50 percent of those asked agreed to chaperone the children to the zoo. This technique has also been used to get six- to eight-year-olds to do more school work (Chan & Au, 2011). Clearly, it is a very effective technique.

Immoral Behaviours and Attitudes

The attitudes-follow-behaviour principle works with immoral acts as well, which sometimes result from gradually escalating commitments. To paraphrase La Rochefoucauld's *Maxims* (1665), it is easier to find a person who has never succumbed to a given temptation than to find a person who has succumbed only once.

We not only tend to hurt those we dislike, but also to dislike those we hurt. Harming an innocent victim—by uttering hurtful comments or delivering electric shocks—typically leads aggressors to disparage their victims, thus helping them justify their behaviour (e.g., Berscheid et al., 1968). In studies establishing this, people would justify an action especially when coaxed, not coerced, into it. When we agree to a deed voluntarily, we take more responsibility for it.

This phenomenon also appears in wartime. Concentration camp guards would sometimes display good manners to inmates in their first days on the job. Soldiers ordered to kill may initially react with revulsion to the point of sickness over their act (Waller, 2002). But these reactions do not last. Often soldiers denigrate their enemies with dehumanizing nicknames. Actions and attitudes feed one another, sometimes to the point of moral numbness. The more one harms another and adjusts one's attitudes, the easier harm-doing becomes. Conscience mutates.

Playing a role, such as that of prison guard, elicits certain behaviours from people.

Can a Change in Behaviour Change Attitudes?

If moral action feeds moral attitudes, will positive interracial behaviour reduce racial prejudice? This was part of social scientists' testimony in advance of the U.S. Supreme Court's 1954 decision to desegregate schools. Until that time it was legal and typical for Black and White children to go to separate schools. Following this decision on desegregation, the percentage of White Americans favouring integrated schools more than doubled, the percentage of White Americans who said that Black Americans should be allowed to live in any neighbourhood increased, and there have been decreasing differences in racial attitudes among people of differing religions, classes, and geographic regions (*ISR Newsletter*, 1975; Greeley & Sheatsley, 1971; Taylor et al., 1978).

Considering the objections of some people before same-sex marriage legislation was introduced in Canada, it is worth considering how people's views have changed. One Liberal Member of Parliament was quoted as saying that by 2015 same-sex marriage would not be an issue in Canada. Despite little discussion of same-sex marriage since it was approved by Parliament in 2004, by 2010, 68 percent of Canadians supported same-sex marriage (Environics, 2010). At the time of this writing, 16 U.S. states and the District of Columbia allowed gay marriage, and for the first time ever in 2013, the majority of Americans supported same-sex marriage (Angus Reid, 2013).

LO 4

COGNITIVE DISSONANCE THEORY

Social psychologists agree: Our actions influence our attitudes, sometimes turning foes into friends, captives into collaborators, and doubters into believers. Social psychologists debate: Why?

One idea is that, wanting to make a good impression, people might merely express attitudes that *appear* consistent with their actions. To manage the impression we're creating, we might adjust what we say to please rather than offend. But this isn't the whole story. Experiments suggest that some genuine attitude change follows our behaviour commitments. Cognitive dissonance theory and self-perception theory offer two explanations for this effect.

Cognitive dissonance theory, developed by Leon Festinger (1957), proposes that we feel tension ("dissonance") when two simultaneously accessible thoughts or beliefs ("cognitions") are psychologically inconsistent—as when we decide to say or do something we have mixed feelings about. Festinger argued that to reduce this unpleasant arousal, we often adjust our thinking.

Dissonance theory pertains mostly to discrepancies between behaviour and attitudes. We are aware of both. Thus, if we sense some inconsistency, perhaps some hypocrisy, we feel pressure for change. That helps explain why, in a British survey, half of cigarette smokers disagreed with the near-consensus among non-smokers that smoking is "really as dangerous as people say" (Eiser et al., 1979) and why the perception of risk among those who have quit declines after relapsing (Gibbons et al., 1997).

Before the 2003 U.S. invasion of Iraq, opposition MPs (most notably, then-Leader of the Opposition Stephen Harper) argued that Canada should enter the war. Then-Prime Minister Jean Chrétien declined. At the time, a significant portion of Canadians and Americans supported the war in Iraq, but now, most do not. By 2008, only 58 percent of Americans felt the war in Iraq was justified. With casualties rising, support for the war was declining—only 36 percent of Americans thought the U.S. did the right thing, and 59 percent felt they should have stayed out if it (Pew Research Center, 2008). Similarly, Canadian support for the war in Afghanistan declined as more Canadian troops were killed. In 2002, 67 percent of Canadians supported the increased use of military forces to fight terrorism, but in 2007 only 13 percent strongly supported Canadian troops staying in Afghanistan. Although Canadian troops are no longer in a military role in Afghanistan, they remain in the country. In the fall of 2014, when Canadian and U.S. troops prepared to enter Iraq and Syria to fight ISIS (Islamic State of Iraq and Syria) militants, the public was more supportive, but understandably cautious (CBC, 2014).

So, if we can persuade others to adopt a *new* attitude, behaviour should change accordingly (that's common sense). Or if we can induce people to behave differently, their attitude should change (that's the self-persuasion effect we have been reviewing). How does cognitive dissonance work? Well, imagine yourself as a subject in Festinger and James Carlsmith's classic (1959) study on the topic. For an hour you perform a series of mind-numbing tasks, such as repeatedly turning wooden knobs. At the end of the hour, the experimenter tells you that he is in a bind. The study he is conducting is about expectations and performance. In order for the experiment to work, he tells you, participants have to believe they are going to be doing a fun task. Unfortunately, the confederate he usually has, who would normally brief the next participant, can't make the session. Would you be willing to fill in?

He agrees to pay you, so you go ahead and lie to the next participant and say that it was a very enjoyable and interesting task. Finally, as you are leaving, the secretary asks you to fill out a form, where you are asked how much you really enjoyed the knob-turning task. Festinger and Carlsmith paid participants either $1 or $20 to lie.

Critical THINKING

Before you move on—answer this question: Who do you think had the more positive attitude toward the experiment? Those paid $1 to lie, or those paid $20? Why?

One of your authors, Steven, has performed this thought experiment in a number of classes, and the prediction is always the same—participants paid $20 (a lot of money in 1959) would have the more positive attitudes. Is that what you predicted? Perhaps surprisingly, Festinger and Carlsmith predicted that when participants had insufficient justification for their behaviour, their attitudes toward the task would become more positive. Much to the amazement of many people, consistent with their predictions, when participants were induced to lie for $1 (an insufficient justification), participants' attitudes toward the task became more positive, whereas when participants were provided with sufficient justification ($20), their attitudes remained similar to the attitudes of those in the control condition (who were not asked to lie; see Figure 8-3).

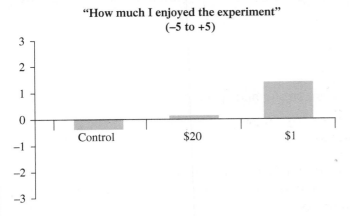

FIGURE 8-3

Dissonance theory predicts that when we have insufficient justification for our behaviour our attitudes will shift accordingly. When given insufficient justification ($1), participants' attitudes toward the tasks became more positive, whereas when people were given sufficient justification ($20) their attitudes remained similar to the control condition.

Data from Festinger & Carlsmith, 1959.

Cognitive dissonance theory assumes that our need to maintain a consistent and positive self-image motivates us to adopt attitudes that justify our actions. Assuming no such motive, self-perception theory says simply that when our attitudes are unclear to us, we observe our behaviours and then infer our attitudes from them.

Dissonance theory best explains what happens when our actions openly contradict our well-defined attitudes. When, say, we hurt someone we like, we feel tension, which we might reduce by viewing the other as a jerk.

Self-perception theory best explains what happens when we are unsure of our attitudes. In proposing self-perception theory, Daryl Bem (1972) assumed that when we're unsure of our attitudes, we infer them by observing ourselves, much as we make inferences about others' attitudes. If we lend our new neighbours, whom we neither like nor dislike, a cup of sugar, our helpful behaviour can lead us to infer that we like them. So it goes with our own behaviour. What we freely say and do can be self-revealing. To paraphrase an old saying—how do I know what I think until I hear what I say or see what I do?

CONCLUSIONS

The debate over how to explain the attitudes-follow-behaviour effect has inspired hundreds of experiments that reveal the conditions under which dissonance and self-perception processes operate. As often happens in science, each theory provides a partial explanation of a complex reality. If human nature were simple, one simple theory could describe it. Alas, but thankfully, we are not simple creatures, and that is why there are great distances to go before psychological researchers can sleep. What research into persuasion and attitudes shows is that attitudes can guide our behaviour, and behaviour can influence our attitudes. Ultimately however, compliance research shows that we can change our behaviour without changing our attitudes at all, and often without understanding why.

SUMMARY OF KEY POINTS

LO1. Understand when attitudes influence behaviour.

- Attitudes can predict behaviours best when they are strong and specific, and models are used to assess them effectively.

LO2. Understand that behaviours can at times influence attitudes.

- Role-playing and habits can result in behaviours than influence attitudes.

LO3. Describe the principles of compliance.

- Commitment and consistency, scarcity, reciprocity, social proof, liking, and authority are all factors that have been demonstrated to influence compliance.

LO4. Describe cognitive dissonance theory.

- Cognitive dissonance is tension that arises when one is simultaneously aware of two inconsistent cognitions.
- Cognitive dissonance theory proposes that we act to reduce such tension.

KEY TERMS

Attitude   A general and enduring evaluation of some person, object, or issue along a continuum from positive to negative.

Cognitive dissonance theory   Cognitive dissonance is tension that arises when one is simultaneously aware of two inconsistent cognitions, as when we realize that we have, with little justification, acted contrary to our attitudes. Cognitive dissonance theory proposes that we act to reduce such tension, as when we adjust our attitudes to correspond with our actions.

Door-in-the-face technique   The tendency—based on the principle of reciprocity—for people who have first declined a large request to comply with a subsequent, smaller request.

Foot-in-the-door phenomenon   The tendency for people who have first agreed to a small request to comply later with a larger request.

Low-ball technique   A tactic for getting people to agree to something. People who agree to an initial request will often still comply when the requester ups the ante. People who receive only the costly request are less likely to comply with it.

Self-perception theory   When unsure of our attitudes, we infer them—much as someone observing us would—by looking at our behaviour and the circumstances under which it occurs.

MODULE NINE

Conformity and Obedience

Imagine you are standing alone on the corner of a busy intersection. You want to cross the street. The Don't Walk signal is clearly flashing. There is a lull in the traffic. Do you cross? (Students living in Nova Scotia may be saying "Absolutely not!" while students living in Montreal may be asking "What's a Don't Walk signal?") Now, let's change the situation a little bit. What if you are not alone on the corner? What if another person crosses in front of you? Would that change your behaviour? What if there were a group of people standing on the corner, all waiting for the Walk signal? Chances are you will conform to what the rest of the group is doing, even if this is very different from what you would normally do. It is not easy to be different. Next time you are at a crosswalk, ask yourself why you are doing what you are doing. What is influencing you?

In this module we will address the topics of conformity and obedience. In Module 8 we covered compliance—agreeing to simple requests—and how different techniques such as the foot-in-the-door and low-balling techniques can increase compliance. In Module 10 we will discuss persuasion—a direct attempt to change people's attitudes and beliefs. Here, however, we deal with conformity and obedience. Conformity is distinct from compliance and persuasion because it involves a change in behaviour that does not involve either an attempt at persuasion or a direct request. For example, when you go to class, you sit down like everyone else. Why? How would you feel if in the middle of class you simply stood up? Would you feel awkward? In order to fit in with society and our peer groups, we frequently conform—we look to others to see what we should do. Obedience is engaging in behaviour because we are given a direct order. It does not involve "convincing" or persuading anyone—you are simply told to do something and you do it.

Researchers who study conformity and obedience construct miniature social worlds: laboratory micro-cultures that simplify and simulate important features of everyday social influence. Consider two noted sets of experiments. Each provides a method for studying conformity and obedience—and some startling findings.

LO 1

ASCH'S STUDIES OF CONFORMITY

Solomon Asch had been fascinated since childhood about the idea of conformity to the group mind. Imagine yourself as one of Asch's volunteer subjects. You are seated sixth in a row of seven people. The experimenter says that you will be taking part in a study of perceptual judgments, then asks you to say which of the three lines shown in Figure 9-1 matches the standard line. You can easily see that it's line 2. So it's no surprise when the five people responding before you all say "Line 2."

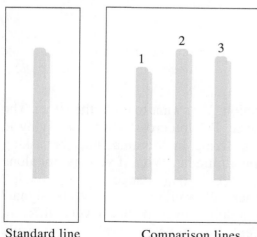

Standard line   Comparison lines

FIGURE 9-1

Sample comparison from Solomon Asch's conformity procedure.
The participants judged which of three comparison lines matched the standard.

The next comparison proves just as easy, and you settle in for what seems a simple test. But the third trial surprises you. Although the correct answer seems just as clear-cut, the first person gives a wrong answer. When the second person gives the same wrong answer, you sit up in your chair and stare at the cards. The third person agrees with the first two. Your jaw drops; you start to perspire. "What is this?" you ask yourself. "Are they blind? Or am I?" The fourth and fifth people agree with the others. Then the experimenter looks at you. Now you are experiencing a dilemma: "What's true? Is it what my peers tell me or what my eyes tell me?"

Dozens of college students experienced this conflict during Asch's experiments. Many conformed—that is, they changed their perceptions, opinions, or behaviour in order to go along with the group norm. Those in a control condition who answered alone were correct more than 99 percent of the time. Asch wondered: If several others (confederates coached by the experimenter) gave identical wrong answers, would people declare what they would otherwise have denied? Although some people never conformed, 75 percent did so at least once. All told, 37 percent of the responses were conforming. Of course, that means 63 percent of the time people did not conform. Thus, most people "tell the truth, even when others do not," note Bert Hodges and Anne Geyer (2006).

But why did most people conform at least some of the time? Researchers studying conformity have shown there are at least two ways in which we are influenced by the group. One type of effect is called normative influence—that is, we change our opinions or actions because we want to fit in with the group (that is, be normal). You can certainly think of situations where you have experienced this type of influence—such as standing at the street corner as we just described. You may feel that in order to fit in, you should cross too.

A good example comes from a series of events that happened at several Canadian universities (Steven's was one of them) in the fall of 2013. Canadian university orientations received a great deal of attention and international scrutiny when a YouTube video of students singing a sexist chant promoting non-consensual underage sex went viral (CBC, 2013). What struck many people was that there were an equal number of men and women singing the chant, and that it had apparently been going on for several years. Why would young women on university campuses, the most likely target of unwanted sexual advances, sing these chants? What most commentators did not address was the issue of normative influence. Undoubtedly, most women singing this chant (and indeed most men) probably recognized the chant was offensive (and promoted illegal activity) but "Everyone was doing it"—right? It is hard to stand up to a group of people you have just met, especially when you are trying to fit in with a new crowd.

Another way groups affect us is through informational influence—that is, we may feel that other people have the information we need in order to make the correct decision. For example, when you are trying to decide what type of smartphone to buy, you might ask your friends and family which is the best. You assume that other people have knowledge that you do not and you may therefore go along with the group.

Connection:

We will discuss normative and informational influence further in Module 13.

So what was happening in the Asch conformity studies? Was normative influence the most likely cause of people changing their responses or was it informational influence? It is likely that most of Asch's participants felt normative pressures. The errors in the lines were significant, and it should have been clear to most people that their responses were incorrect. Indeed, in a videotaped re-creation of the Asch experiments by Anthony Pratkanis at the University of California at Santa Cruz, people who conformed to the group frequently indicated that they just did not want to "stand out" any more (you can find this re-creation online).

In one of Asch's conformity experiments, subject number six experienced uneasiness and conflict after hearing five people before him give a wrong answer.

Asch's results are startling because they involved no obvious pressure to conform—there were no rewards for "team play," no punishments for individuality. If people are this compliant in response to such minimal pressure, how much more compliant will they be if they are directly coerced? Could someone force the average Canadian to perform cruel acts? One would guess not: our humane, democratic, individualistic values would make us resist such pressure. Besides, the easy verbal pronouncements of these experiments are a giant step away from actually harming someone. We would never yield to coercion to hurt another. Or would we? Social psychologist Stanley Milgram wondered the same thing.

Activity: Experiences of conformity

We have all experienced conformity. We have seen it in others and we have done it ourselves. The interesting thing about conformity is that we may not recognize it until we think back. Let's consider a time when we are most likely to conform—high school.

When you were in high school, were there norms that dictated how you were supposed to look?

(Continued)

Take a second and write down what the norm for clothing was in your group.

What about hairstyle? Were there common themes based on popular people in the media?

Now, let's consider the consequences of failing to meet that norm. Do you remember people who weren't groomed that way? How were they regarded and treated? Did they form their own group and their own "cultural" norms?

Have you even, perhaps under others' influence, done something that really wasn't your type of activity?

Did this illustrate *normative* or *informational* influence?

LO 2

MILGRAM'S OBEDIENCE EXPERIMENTS

Milgram's (1965, 1974) experiments testing what happens when the demands of authority clash with the demands of conscience have become social psychology's most famous and controversial experiments—those of obedience—changes in behaviour elicited by the commands of an authority figure. "Perhaps more than any other empirical contributions in the history of social science," notes Lee Ross (1988), "they have become part of our society's shared intellectual legacy—that small body of historical incidents, biblical parables, and classic literature that serious thinkers feel free to draw on when they debate about human nature or contemplate human history." There is no doubting the impact of these studies on the social psychological literature (Benjamin & Simpson, 2009).

Here is the scene staged by Milgram (who was a creative artist who wrote stories and stage plays): Two men come to Yale University's psychology laboratory to participate in a study of learning and memory. A stern experimenter in a grey technician's coat explains that this is a pioneering study of the effect of punishment on learning. The experiment requires one of them to teach a list of word pairs to the other and to punish errors by delivering shocks of increasing intensity. To assign the roles, they draw slips out of a hat. One of the men, a mild-mannered, 47-year-old accountant, who is the experimenter's confederate, pretends that his slip says "learner" and is ushered into an adjacent room. The "teacher" (who is there in response to a newspaper ad) takes a mild sample shock and then looks on as the experimenter straps the learner into a chair and attaches an electrode to his wrist.

Teacher and experimenter then return to the main room (see Figure 9-2), where the teacher takes his place before a "shock generator" with switches ranging from 15 to 450 volts in 15-volt increments. The switches are labelled "Slight Shock," "Very Strong Shock," "Danger: Severe Shock," and so forth. The 435- and 450-volt switches are labelled "XXX." The experimenter tells the teacher to "move one level higher on the shock generator" each time the learner gives a wrong answer. With each flick of a switch, lights flash, relay switches click, and an electric buzz sounds.

If the participant complies with the experimenter's requests, he hears the learner grunt at 75, 90, and 105 volts. At 120 volts, the "learner" shouts that the shocks are painful. And at 150 volts, he cries out, "Experimenter, get me out of here! I won't be in the experiment anymore! I refuse to go on!" By 270 volts, his protests have become screams of agony, and he continues to insist on being let out. At 300 and 315 volts, he screams his refusal to answer. After 330 volts, he falls silent. In answer to the "teacher's" inquiries and pleas to end the experiment, the experimenter states that the non-responses should be treated as wrong answers. To keep the participant going, he uses four verbal prods:

Prod 1: Please continue (or Please go on).
Prod 2: The experiment requires that you continue.
Prod 3: It is absolutely essential that you continue.
Prod 4: You have no other choice; you *must* go on.

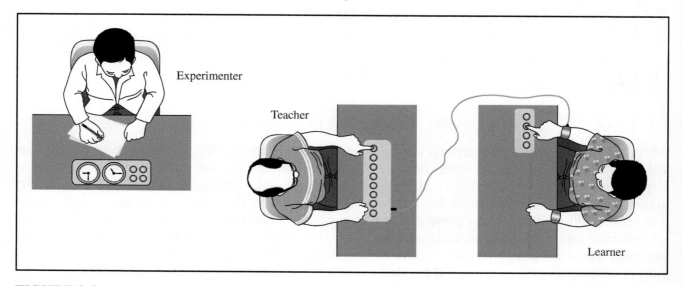

FIGURE 9-2

Milgram's obedience experiment.

How far would you go? Milgram described the experiment to 110 psychiatrists, college students, and middle-class adults. People in all three groups guessed that they would disobey by about 135 volts; none expected to go beyond 300 volts. Recognizing that self-estimates might reflect self-serving bias, Milgram asked them how far they thought *other* people would go. Virtually no one expected anyone to proceed to XXX on the shock panel. (The psychiatrists guessed about one in a thousand.)

But when Milgram conducted the experiment with 40 men—a mix of 20- to 50-year-olds—26 of them (65 percent) went to 450 volts. In fact, all who reached 450 volts complied with a command to continue the procedure until, after two further trials, the experimenter called a halt.

Having expected a low rate of obedience, and with plans to replicate the experiment in Germany and assess the culture difference, Milgram was disturbed (A. Milgram, 2000). So instead of going to Germany, Milgram next made the learner's protests even more compelling. As the learner was strapped into the chair, the teacher heard him mention his "slight heart condition" and heard the experimenter's reassurance that "although the shocks may be painful, they cause no permanent tissue damage." The learner's anguished protests were to little avail; of 40 new men in this experiment, 25 (63 percent) fully complied with the experimenter's demands (see Figure 9-3).

Percentage of subjects still obedient

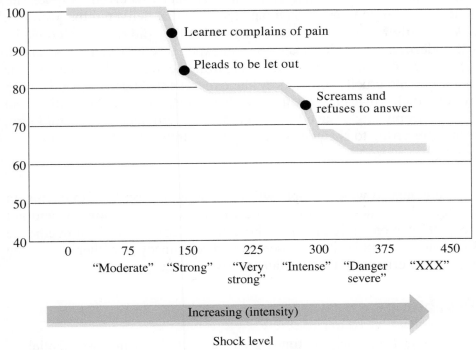

FIGURE 9-3

The Milgram obedience experiment. Percentage of subjects complying despite the learner's cries of protest and failure to respond.

Critical THINKING

So, should Milgram have done his experiments? There are some clear ethical issues here. What are the problems? What are the solutions? Do you think these experiments should have been done at all? Did we learn something?

Milgram's "shock box."

The obedience of his subjects disturbed Milgram. The procedures he used disturbed many social psychologists (Blass, 2004, 2009). The "learner" in these experiments actually received no shock (he disengaged himself from the electric chair and turned on a tape recorder that delivered the protests). Nevertheless, some critics said that Milgram did to his participants what they did to their victims: he stressed them against their will. Indeed, many of the "teachers" did experience agony. They sweated, trembled, stuttered, bit their lips, groaned, or even broke into uncontrollable nervous laughter. A *New York Times* reviewer complained that the cruelty inflicted by the experiments "upon their unwitting subjects is surpassed only by the cruelty that they elicit from them" (Marcus, 1974). Critics also argued that the participants' self-concepts might have been altered. One participant's wife told him, "You can call yourself Eichmann" (referring to Nazi death camp administrator Adolf Eichmann).

What Breeds Obedience?

Milgram did more than reveal the extent to which people will obey an authority; he also examined the conditions that breed obedience. In further experiments, he varied the social conditions and got compliance ranging from zero to 93 percent fully obedient. Four factors that determined obedience were the victim's emotional distance, the authority's closeness and legitimacy, whether or not the authority was institutionalized, and the effects of a disobedient fellow subject.

Applying Social Psychology

The text notes that conformity is at times bad, at times good, and at times inconsequential. Michael J. Saks (1992) raised the question: "When is compliance bad and disobedience good and when the reverse?" What do you think? That question, as Saks noted, seems unavoidable in research and theory on obedience to rules.

Saks observed that an undertone of moral judgment accompanies most research on the topic. The work of Asch and Milgram suggests that conformity to group norms is wrong because it leads to error. But, asked Saks, can we imagine being in the position of one who thinks that Milgram's subjects ought to have obeyed, perhaps because the short-term harm confers longer-term good? (That is both the law's, and most parents' justification for punishment: We do harm when we punish, but do so in the service of a greater social good.)

Certainly, part of the dilemma in these situations is that people are presented with conflicting rules. In any given situation, how are we to know which rule to follow? A political protester who breaks the law may point to a higher principle that demands obedience; however, in a telephone panel study of 1575 Chicago residents, Tom Tyler (1990) found that eight of ten respondents agreed that "people should obey the law even if it goes against what they think is right." Do you agree?

Emotional Distance of the Victim

Milgram's subjects acted with the least compassion when the "learners" could not be seen (and could not see them). When the victim was remote and the "teachers" heard no complaints, nearly all obeyed calmly to the end. When the learner was in the same room, "only" 40 percent obeyed to 450 volts. Full compliance dropped to 30 percent when teachers were required to force the learner's hand into contact with a shock plate.

In everyday life, too, it is easiest to abuse someone who is distant or depersonalized. People will be unresponsive even to great tragedies. Executioners often depersonalize those being executed by placing hoods over their heads. The ethics of war allow one to bomb a helpless village from 10 000 metres but not to shoot an equally helpless villager. In combat with an enemy they can see, many soldiers either do not fire or do not aim. Such disobedience is rare among those given orders to kill with the more distant artillery or aircraft weapons (Padgett, 1989).

Critical THINKING

The face of war is changing every day. What role does (de)personalization have in this process? Increasingly, aerial assaults are carried out by camera-guided missiles fired from remote-controlled drone aircraft. What impact does this have on the operator? They can see the enemy (their targets) through clear HD cameras until the moment the missiles hit. In terms of impact, is this better or worse than shooting someone? Than dropping a bomb from over 10 000 metres?

On the positive side, people act most compassionately toward those who are personalized. That is why appeals for the unborn, the hungry, victims of disasters, or animal rights are nearly always personalized with a compelling photograph or description. Perhaps even more compelling is an ultrasound picture of one's own developing fetus. When queried by John Lydon and Christine Dunkel-Schetter (1994) at McGill University, expectant women expressed more commitment to their pregnancies if they had seen ultrasound pictures of their fetuses that clearly displayed body parts.

Closeness and Legitimacy of the Authority

The physical presence of the experimenter also affected obedience. When Milgram gave the commands by telephone, full obedience dropped to 21 percent (although many lied and said they were obeying). Other studies confirm that when the one making the request is physically close, compliance increases. Given a light touch on the arm, people are more likely to lend a dime, sign a petition, or sample a new pizza (Kleinke, 1977; Smith et al., 1982; Willis & Hamm, 1980).

The authority, however, must be perceived as legitimate. In another twist on the basic experiment, the experimenter received a rigged telephone call that required him to leave the laboratory. He said that since the equipment recorded data automatically, the "teacher" should just go ahead. After the experimenter left, another person, who had been assigned a clerical role (actually a second confederate), assumed command. The clerk "decided" that the shock should be increased one level for each wrong answer and instructed the teacher accordingly. Now 80 percent of the teachers refused to comply fully. The confederate, feigning disgust at this defiance, sat down in front of the shock generator and tried to take over the teacher's role. At this point, most of the defiant participants protested. Some tried to unplug the generator. One large man lifted the zealous confederate from his chair and threw him across the room. This rebellion against an illegitimate authority contrasted sharply with the deferential politeness usually shown the experimenter.

It also contrasts with the behaviour of hospital nurses who, in one study, were called by an unknown physician and ordered to administer an obvious drug overdose (Hofling et al., 1966). The researchers told one group of nurses and nursing students about the experiment and asked how they would react. Nearly all said they would not have followed the order. One said she would have replied, "I'm sorry, sir, but I am not authorized to give any medication without a written order, especially one so large over the usual dose and one that I'm unfamiliar with. If it were possible, I would be glad to do it, but this is against hospital policy and my own ethical standards." Nevertheless, when 22 other nurses were actually given the phoned-in overdose order, all but one obeyed without delay (until being intercepted on their way to the patient). Although not all nurses are so compliant (Krackow & Blass, 1995; Rank & Jacobson, 1977), these nurses were following a familiar script: doctor (a legitimate authority) orders; nurse obeys.

Compliance with legitimate authority was also apparent in the strange case of the "rectal ear ache" (Cohen & Davis, 1981, cited by Cialdini, 1988). A doctor ordered eardrops for a patient suffering infection in the right ear. On the prescription, the doctor abbreviated "place in right ear" as "place in Rear." Reading the order, the compliant nurse put the required drops in the compliant patient's rectum.

Institutional Authority

If the prestige of the authority is this important, then perhaps the institutional prestige of Yale University legitimized the Milgram experiment commands. In post-experimental interviews, many participants said that had it not been for Yale's reputation, they would not have obeyed. To see whether this was true, Milgram moved the experiment to Bridgeport, Connecticut. He set himself up in a modest commercial building as the "Research Associates of Bridgeport." When the usual "heart disturbance" experiment was run with the same personnel, what percentage of the men do you suppose fully obeyed? Though reduced, the rate remained high—48 percent.

The Role of Gender in Conformity and Obedience

Does gender matter? In early work, there was an assumption that women were more susceptible to influence than men (see Crutchfield, 1955), showing that women conformed more than men in many situations. However, when Milgram specifically explored this in the paradigm just given, he found no difference between men and women (Milgram, 1974), and this finding has been replicated recently (Burger, 2009). This may be a factor of the situation—one could argue that women are more likely to obey, but also that they are more likely to be empathic and refuse to hurt someone (Burger, 2009).

Alice Eagly and her colleagues (e.g., Eagly & Carli, 1981; Eagly, 1987) have argued that the early research was incorrect. In a meta-analysis of 145 studies spanning over 21 000 people, they did find that men were slightly less influenceable than women. However, this effect was fairly weak and varied considerably across studies. Interestingly, women were more likely to conform when they were in situations where people could observe the participant's behaviours, such as the group pressure situations in the Asch study. When behaviours were less observable, the difference went away. One of Eagly's findings was particularly notable. They found that studies with male researchers were more likely to find increased conformity effects for women than studies run by women. Why? Eagly argues this is because men tend to choose more male-oriented topics, where women tend to be less knowledgeable, thus leading to increased "informational" conformity. In essence then, the gender difference may be in part a confound effect!

Connection:

Remember that in Module 3 we discussed the difference between men and women in terms of conformity.

There is some research to back up the hypothesis put forward by Alice Eagly. In a study of University of Saskatchewan students, males were found to conform more to female-oriented topics, where women displayed superior skills and/or knowledge. These results are consistent with a study by Sistrunk and McDavid (1971), who found that, in general, men conformed more to topics where women would typically know more (e.g., fashion) whereas women conformed more when the topics were more male-oriented (e.g., mechanics).

The Liberating Effects of Group Influence

These classic experiments give us a negative view of conformity. But conformity can also be constructive. The heroic first responders who rushed into the flaming World Trade Center towers were "incredibly brave," note social psychologists Susan Fiske, Lasana Harris, and Amy Cuddy (2004), but they were also "partly obeying their superiors, partly conforming to extraordinary group loyalty."

Can conformity be constructive? Perhaps you can recall a time you felt justifiably angry at an unfair teacher, or with someone's offensive behaviour, but you hesitated to object. Then one or two others objected, and you followed their example. Milgram captured this liberating effect of conformity by giving the teacher two confederates who were to help conduct the procedure. During the experiment, both confederates defied the experimenter, who then ordered the real subject to continue alone. Did he? No. Ninety percent liberated themselves by conforming to the defiant confederates.

LO 3

CONFORMITY AND OBEDIENCE IN THE REAL WORLD

The common response to Milgram's results is to note their counterparts in recent history: the "I was only following orders" defences of Adolf Eichmann in Nazi Germany and of the perpetrators of "ethnic cleansing" and sectarian violence occurring more recently in Syria, Iraq, Rwanda, Bosnia, and Darfur.

In January 2005, U.S. soldiers were convicted on charges related to the torture and humiliation of numerous prisoners in Abu Ghraib prison in Iraq. U.S. soldiers were accused of similar crimes by human rights group Amnesty International at the U.S. detention centre for "unlawful combatants" in Guantanamo Bay, Cuba.

However, this is not solely an American issue. In 1992, Canadian soldiers of the Airborne Regiment (which has since been disbanded) shot and killed two Somalis, one execution-style. A few days later soldiers captured, tortured, and killed a 16-year-old, taking pictures of themselves with the dead Somali boy as souvenirs.

An inmate of Camp X-Ray is escorted by two guards while other inmates are seen in their cells in Guantanamo Bay Naval Base, Cuba.

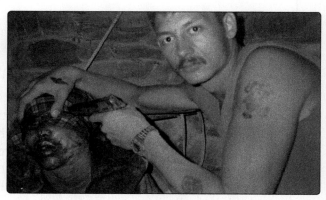

A Canadian soldier posing with 16-year-old Somali Shidane Arone.

What compels people to commit these horrible acts? Soldiers are trained to obey superiors, and often do, even when carrying out clearly unethical and immoral orders. How is this different from the experiments described here?

The "safe" scientific contexts of the obedience experiments differ from the wartime contexts. Moreover, much of the mockery and brutality of war and genocide goes beyond obedience (Miller, 2004). The obedience experiments differ from the other conformity experiments in the strength of the social pressure: Compliance is explicitly commanded. Without the coercion, people did not act cruelly. Yet, both the Asch and Milgram experiments share certain commonalities. They showed how compliance can take precedence over moral sense.

The obedience and conformity studies we have discussed in this module succeeded in pressuring people to go against their own consciences. The studies did more than teach an academic lesson. They sensitized us to moral conflicts in our own lives and they illustrated and affirmed some familiar social psychological principles—the link between behaviour and attitudes, the power of the situation, and the strength of the fundamental attribution error. Importantly too, these studies hold up over time. In a recent re-creation of the Milgram experiments (up to the 150 volt level), Jerry Burger at Santa Clara University found that levels of obedience were comparable to Milgram's original studies (Burger, 2009). Other replications have further found that these experiments were not a product of their time—experiments using immersive video environments found the same pattern of effects as Milgram (Dambrun & Vatine, 2010).

The Power of the Situation

The most important lesson of Module 9 is that immediate situational forces are powerful. For example, new immigrants to Canada frequently find themselves in new social contexts that can affect their conformity behaviour. Consistent with this, Romin Tafarodi and his colleagues at the University of Toronto (Tafarodi et al., 2002) have found that people from ethnic minorities (in this case, Chinese Canadians) trying to assimilate into new cultures may be more likely to conform to the majority group when their physical appearance is made salient—that is, when they are made aware of their appearance. The researchers asked participants to judge artwork while either standing in front of a mirror (that is, making their appearance salient) or without a mirror present. Participants were provided with normative ratings of the paintings supposedly given by the majority group. Participants who were made aware of their appearance judged the artwork in a manner consistent with the norm. Thus culture, and one's position within it, can influence the extent to which one conforms.

Connection:

Attitudes toward and behaviour of different cultural groups will be discussed further in Modules 15 and 16.

So, how comfortable are you with being different from the group? To feel this for yourself, imagine violating some minor norms: standing up in the middle of a class; singing out loud in a restaurant; shaving half your head. In trying to break with social constraints, we suddenly realize how strong they are.

Some of Milgram's own students learned this lesson when he and John Sabini (1983) asked for their help in studying the effects of violating a simple social norm: asking riders on the New York City subway system for their seats. To their surprise, 56 percent gave up their seats, even when no justification was given. The students' own reactions to making the request were as interesting: most found it extremely difficult. Often, the words got stuck in their throats, and they had to withdraw. Once having made their requests and gotten seats, they sometimes justified their norm violation by pretending to be sick. Such is the power of the unspoken rules governing our public behaviour.

The students in a Pennsylvania State University experiment found it similarly difficult to get challenging words out of their mouths. Some students imagined themselves discussing with three others whom to select for survival on a desert island. They were asked to imagine one of the others, a man, injecting three sexist comments, such as, "I think we need more women on the island to keep the men satisfied." How would they react to such sexist remarks? Only 5 percent predicted they would ignore each of the comments or wait to see how others reacted. But when Janet Swim and Lauri Hyers (1999) engaged other students in discussions where such comments were actually made by a male confederate, 55 percent (not 5 percent) said nothing. Does this make you consider the "chant" issue described earlier in a different light? Similarly, although people predict they would be upset by witnessing someone making a racial slur (e.g., by not picking that person as a partner in an experiment), indifference is the more common response (Kawakami et al., 2009). This, once again, demonstrates the power of normative pressures and how hard it is to predict behaviour, even our own behaviour. Normative influence is powerful indeed.

Critical THINKING

Consider the situations just described—people using racial slurs, people chanting inappropriate songs, or people requesting illegal or unethical activities. How do you think you will react the next time you are confronted with one of these situations. Will knowing the underlying psychological process equip you better to resist the pressure? If no, why not; if yes, how?

What about in the "real world"? Will we stand up to a perceived authority? Perhaps not. In a well-publicized string of incidents between 1995 and 2004, presumably well-meaning fast food restaurant managers subjected their employees to humiliating acts and sexual assault all because of a prank phone call. The caller would ask for the manager, identify himself as a police officer and then tell the manager he was investigating a theft (e.g., of a customer's purse). He would then ask the manager to call in a female employee. The manager was then told to search the employee. Typically, these requests started small (empty pockets) but progressed until the employee was strip searched and even sexually assaulted. The man accused of being behind the hoax was charged but ultimately acquitted. Interestingly, in one case, a man who obeyed the caller was sentenced to five years in prison for the sexual assault. To date, many of these cases remain unresolved. In a number of frightening ways, these incidents parallel those of the Milgram experiments. The requests, once adhered to, were difficult to disobey.

A similar string of cases was reported in February of 2011 in Vancouver, where a man posing as a hotel manager called guests and convinced them to activate fire alarms and set off in-room sprinklers. Guests were told that unless they did as they were told, they could be killed in an explosion from a gas leak. Similar calls were made to several fast-food restaurants in the area, where employees were also convinced to set off the fire alarms and sprinkler systems. Damage was estimated in the hundreds of thousands of dollars.

The Fundamental Attribution Error

Why do the results of certain classic experiments so often surprise people? Is it not because we expect people to act in accord with their dispositions? It doesn't surprise us when a surly person is nasty, but we expect those with pleasant dispositions to be kind. Bad people do bad things; good people do good things.

When you read about Milgram's experiments, what impressions did you form of the subjects? Most people attribute negative qualities to them. When told about one or two of the obedient subjects, people judge them to be aggressive, cold, and unappealing—even after learning that their behaviour was typical (Miller et al., 1973). Cruelty, we presume, is inflicted by the cruel at heart.

Connection:

Remember that we discussed the fundamental attribution error in Module 6.

Günter Bierbrauer (1979) tried to eliminate this underestimation of social forces (the fundamental attribution error). He had university students observe a vivid re-enactment of the experiment or play the role of obedient teacher themselves. They still predicted that their friends would, in a repeat of Milgram's experiment, be only minimally compliant. Bierbrauer concluded that although social scientists accumulate evidence that our behaviour is a product of our social histories and current environments, most people continue to believe that people's inner qualities reveal themselves—that only good people do good and that only evil people do evil.

It is tempting to assume that Eichmann and the Auschwitz death camp commanders were uncivilized monsters. But Eichmann himself was outwardly indistinguishable from common people with ordinary jobs (Arendt, 1963; Zillmer et al., 1995). Consider the German police battalion responsible for shooting nearly 40 000 Jews in Poland. Many of the victims were women, children, and elderly people who were shot in the backs of their heads. Like the many, many others who ravaged Europe's Jewish ghettos, operated the deportation trains, and administered the death camps, they were not Nazis, SS members, or racial fanatics (Browning, 1992). They were labourers, salesmen, clerks, and artisans—family men who were too old for military service, but who, when directly ordered to kill, were unable to refuse.

Mohamed Atta, the leader of the 9/11 attacks, reportedly had been a "good boy" and an excellent student from a healthy family. Zacarias Moussaoui, the would-be 20th 9/11 attacker, had been very polite when applying for flight lessons and buying knives. He called women "ma'am." The pilot of the second plane to hit the World Trade Center was said to be an amiable, "laid-back" fellow, much like the "intelligent, friendly, and 'very courteous'" pilot of the plane that dove into the Pentagon. If these men had lived next door to us, they would hardly have fit our image of evil monsters. They were "unexceptional" people (McDermott, 2005).

CONCLUSIONS

"The most fundamental lesson of our study," Milgram noted, is that "ordinary people, simply doing their jobs, and without any particular hostility on their part, can become agents in a terrible destructive process" (Milgram, 1974, p. 6). As Fred Rogers from *Mr. Rogers' Neighborhood* often reminded his preschool television audience, "Good people sometimes do bad things." Perhaps then, we should be more wary of political leaders whose charming dispositions lull us into supposing they would never do evil. Under the sway of evil forces, even nice people sometimes get corrupted, as they construct moral rationalizations for immoral behaviour (Tsang, 2002). Ordinary soldiers may follow orders to shoot defenceless civilians; political leaders may lead their people into ill-fated wars; ordinary employees will distribute harmful products; and ordinary group members will haze new initiates. The key is not to blame the victim or the aggressor necessarily (although people are ultimately responsible for their own behaviour) but to understand that to stop the behaviour, there has to be an understanding of—and willingness to address—the situation underlying the behaviour.

Connection:

Hazing will be discussed further in Module 11.

SUMMARY OF KEY POINTS

LO1. Discuss the Asch conformity studies.

- These were key studies demonstrating how conformity occurs, and the difference between informational and normative influence.

LO2. Describe Milgram's obedience studies.

- These were a key set of experiments to provide evidence for destructive obedience, and explore the limits of that obedience.

LO3. Understand the impact of conformity and obedience in real-world settings.

- Conformity and obedience happen in the real world, and there are many examples of it. Understanding the forces that impact on level of obedience and conformity may help counter "destructive" obedience.

KEY TERMS

Conformity   Changing one's perceptions, opinions, or behaviour in order to be more consistent with real or imagined group norms.

Informational influence   When people change their opinions or actions because they believe that others have the information they need to make the right decisions.

Normative influence   When people change their opinions or actions because they want to fit in with the group (i.e., be normal).

Obedience   Changes in behaviour elicited by the commands of an authority figure.

MODULE TEN

Two Routes to Persuasion

LEARNING OBJECTIVES   After studying Module 10, you will be able to

LO **1**   Describe the central and peripheral routes to persuasion

LO **2**   Understand the role of the source of the message in persuasion

LO **3**   Understand the role of the message content in persuasion

LO **4**   Understand the role of the audience in persuasion

Think of the best advertisement you have ever seen. What made it good? Was it artistic? Was it funny? Was it sad? Was it informative? What was the ad for? Did you buy the product? When asked about their favourite advertisement, most people probably think about a very poignant ad or a very funny one. Interestingly, most people cannot remember what the ad was for, and most never bought the product. Regardless, the advertisement was trying to persuade you to buy whatever product it was selling. Persuasion is everywhere—at the heart of politics, marketing, courtship, parenting, negotiation, conflict resolution, and courtroom decision-making. Social psychologists therefore seek to understand what leads to effective, long-lasting attitude change. What factors affect persuasion? And how, as persuaders, can we most effectively "educate" others?

Imagine that you are a marketing or advertising executive, one of those responsible for the over $600 billion spent annually worldwide on advertising (O'Reilly & Tennant, 2009). Or imagine that you want to promote energy conservation, to encourage breast-feeding, or to campaign for a political candidate. What could you do to make yourself and your message persuasive? If you are wary of being manipulated by such appeals, to what tactics should you be alert?

To answer such questions, social psychologists usually study persuasion by observing the effects of various factors in brief, controlled experiments. The effects are small and are most potent on weak attitudes that don't touch our values (Johnson & Eagly, 1989; Petty & Krosnick, 1995). Yet they enable us to understand how such factors could produce big effects.

LO 1

THE CENTRAL AND PERIPHERAL ROUTES

In choosing tactics, you must first make a decision. Should you focus mostly on building strong *central arguments*? Or should you make your message appealing by associating it with favourable *peripheral cues*, such as sex appeal? Persuasion researchers Richard Petty and John Cacioppo propose that persuasion tends to occur by either a central or a peripheral route. They described this in the Elaboration Likelihood Model of Persuasion (1986; Petty & Wegener, 1999). When people are motivated and are able to think systematically about an issue, elaboration is high and they are likely to take the central route to persuasion—focusing on the arguments. If those arguments are strong and compelling, persuasion is likely. If the message contains only weak arguments, thoughtful people will notice that the arguments aren't very compelling and will counterargue.

If we're not all that motivated or able to think carefully—elaboration is low. If we're distracted, uninvolved, or just plain busy, we might not take the time to think carefully about the message content. Rather than noticing whether the arguments are particularly compelling, we might follow the peripheral route to persuasion—focusing on cues that trigger acceptance without much thinking (e.g., is the source of the message an expert or celebrity?). Billboards, television commercials, and website ads—media that consumers are exposed to for only brief amounts of time—typically use visual images. Our opinions regarding food, clothing, TV shows, and a wide range of products are often based more on feelings than on logic. Instead of providing arguments in favour of Coke or Pepsi, soft drink ads associate the product with images of beauty, youth, and pleasure. On the other hand, car ads, which interested, logical consumers might pore over for some time, seldom feature Hollywood stars or great athletes; instead, they offer customers information on competitive features and prices. Matching the type of message to the route that message recipients are likely to follow can greatly increase the likelihood that any attention will be paid to the persuasive message at all (Petty et al., 2000; Shavitt, 1990).

Even people who like to think form tentative opinions using the peripheral route to persuasion. We all make snap judgments using other rule-of-thumb heuristics: if a speaker is articulate and appealing, has apparently good motives, and has several arguments (or better, if the different arguments come from different sources), we usually take the easy peripheral route and accept the message without much thought (see Figure 10-1).

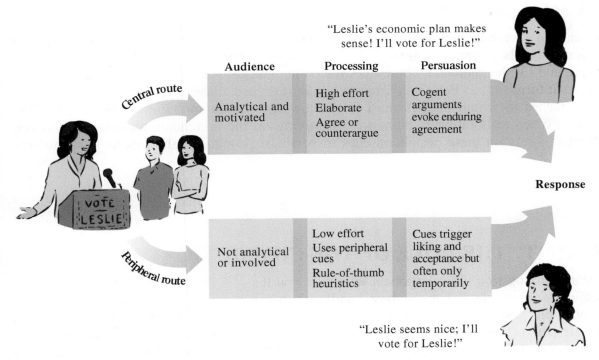

FIGURE 10-1

The central and peripheral routes to persuasion. Some ads take the central route by assuming their audience wants to systematically consider important information and arguments. Other ads can take the peripheral route, by merely associating their product (e.g., a political candidate) with glamour, success, and good moods.

Critical THINKING

Now that you have learned about the central and peripheral routes to persuasion, think of one of your favourite products, something that you have bought recently that you enjoyed (e.g., an iPad, a drink, a song, or a game). What would be the best way to sell that product—the central or peripheral route? Now, find out what kind of advertising the company does for that product—do they do what you think they should? Many advertisers do not use the best approach. What about this ad? What tactics is it using? Do you think it is effective?

THE ELEMENTS OF PERSUASION

In early persuasion research, people explored the factors that influenced the persuasiveness of a communication: (1) the communicator, (2) the message content and how the message is communicated, and (3) the audience. Sometimes the communicator was important. Sometimes he or she was not. As it turns out, as Petty and Cacioppo (1986) argued, elaboration is the key. Who says what by what means to whom matters most in the low-elaboration conditions, when we rely on peripheral cues. When elaboration is high, we are relying on the arguments presented. However, because advertisers rely on these peripheral cues to persuade people, it behooves us to know how they work.

LO **2**

WHO SAYS IT? THE ROLE OF THE COMMUNICATOR

Imagine you are talking to a car salesperson who tells you that the car you are interested in is the most fuel-efficient in its class, has the best handling, and is cheaper than the competition. The salesperson also tells you all her customers have loved the car—no one has complained. Would you believe the salesperson? Would you buy the car? Now, what if you read the same information in *Consumer Reports* magazine, or looked at reviews online? Most people would believe the magazine but not the salesperson. The salesperson clearly has something to gain, whereas the magazine does not.

Social psychologists have found that who is saying something affects how the message gets received. In one experiment, when the Socialist and Liberal leaders in the Dutch parliament argued identical positions using the same words, each was most effective with members of his own party (Wiegman, 1985). It's not just the message that matters, but also who says it. What makes one communicator more persuasive than another?

Any of us would find a statement about the costs of smoking more believable if it came from Health Canada rather than a tobacco company. Credible communicators seem both *expert* (confidently knowledgeable) and *trustworthy*. They speak unhesitatingly and without any selfish motive. Some television ads are obviously constructed to make the communicator appear both expert and trustworthy. Toothpaste companies peddle products using a white-coated speaker who declares confidently that most dentists recommend their product. Given such peripheral cues, people who don't care enough to analyze the evidence might reflexively infer that the product has value.

The effects of source credibility often diminish after a month or so. If a credible person's message is persuasive, its impact can fade as soon as the credible source is forgotten or dissociated from the message. On the other hand, the impact of a non-credible person can *increase* over time, if people remember the message better than the reason for discounting it (e.g., Pratkanis et al., 1988; Kumkale & Albarracín, 2004). This delayed persuasion, after people forget the source or its connection with the message, is called the sleeper effect. You have probably experienced this yourself. Can you think of a time when you were telling a friend about something but could not remember where you initially heard the information? These conversations often start with "they say" as in "They say plastic water bottles are bad for you now," or "Artificial sweeteners make you fat," but you may not remember where you got that information.

Connection:

Hint: You learned about artificial sweeteners in Module 2.

What about how people look or if they are famous? Most people deny that endorsements by star athletes and entertainers affect them. Most people know that stars are seldom knowledgeable about the product they endorse. Besides, we know the intent is to persuade us; we don't just accidentally eavesdrop on Tiger Woods's father telling his son about how to be a better man (a Nike commercial) or why Wayne Gretzky and his father like Fords. Such ads are based on another characteristic of an effective communicator: attractiveness. We may think we are not influenced by attractiveness or likeability, but researchers have found otherwise. Even something as simple as a fleeting conversation is enough to increase our liking for someone and our responsiveness to their influence (Burger et al., 2001). Our liking might open us up to the communicator's arguments (central-route persuasion), or it might trigger positive associations when we see the product later (peripheral-route persuasion).

Attractiveness varies in several ways. *Physical appeal* is one. Arguments, especially emotional ones, are often more influential when they come from beautiful people (e.g., Chaiken, 1979). *Similarity* is another. We tend to like people who are like us, and are influenced by them. As a general rule, people respond better to a message that comes from someone in their "own" group (Van Knippenberg & Wilke, 1992; Wilder, 1990). That's why salespeople act in a friendly manner and try to convince you that they are similar to you—being from the same area, having a sibling who went to your school, or liking the same hobbies as you.

Connection:

We will discuss why *we like* people who *like us* in Module 19.

LO 3

WHAT IS SAID? THE ROLE OF MESSAGE CONTENT

It matters not only who says something, but also *what* that person says. If you were to help organize an appeal to get people to vote for lower tuition or to stop smoking or to give money to disaster relief, you might wonder how to concoct a recipe for central-route persuasion. Common sense could lead to arguments for both sides of these questions:

- Is a purely logical message most persuasive—or one that arouses emotion?
- Is persuasion based on what mood you are in?
- Do fear-based approaches work?
- Do you need to be aware of the process? In other words, do subliminal messages work?

Suppose you were campaigning in support of disaster relief (like many Hollywood stars did after the Haitian earthquake, or in the aftermath of the flooding from Typhoon Haiyan in the Philippines in 2013). Would it be best to itemize your arguments and cite an array of impressive statistics? Or would you be more effective presenting an emotional approach—the compelling story of one injured child or one homeless family, for example? Of course, an argument can be both reasonable and emotional, but, which is more influential?

It depends on the audience. Well-educated or analytical people are more responsive to rational appeals than less-educated or less-analytical people are (Cacioppo et al., 1996). Thoughtful, involved audiences travel the central route; they are most responsive to reasoned arguments. It also depends on the type of attitude people already have—sometimes emotional attitudes are more influenced by emotional appeals, but sometimes more reason-based approaches work (e.g., Fabrigar & Petty, 1999).

Activity: What are the advertisements trying to tell you?

Look at the two advertisements above. Now ask yourself, what elements of these ads are getting at the factors we have just discussed? What about the source of the ad? Who is the source of the burger ad? How are they trying to make it seem "better"? You should also consider the audience. The burger ad would likely be shown to a different audience than the iPad ad—although maybe it would be the same audience—what do you think? Let's turn the tables. If we wanted to appeal to a young male audience, how might we change the iPad ad? If we wanted to appeal to an older audience, how would we change the ad? Can you see how the audience matters?

The Role of Mood

Messages also become more persuasive through associations with good feelings (Hullett, 2005; Wegener et al., 1995). Irving Janis and his colleagues (1965; Dabbs & Janis, 1965) found that Yale students were more convinced by persuasive messages if they were allowed to enjoy peanuts and Pepsi while reading them. Similarly, Mark Galizio and Clyde Hendrick (1972) found that Kent State University students were more persuaded by folk-song lyrics accompanied by pleasant guitar music than they were by unaccompanied lyrics.

Good feelings often enhance persuasion—partly by enhancing positive thinking (when people are motivated to think) and partly by linking good feelings with the message (Petty et al., 1993). In addition, positive moods can either enhance or decrease thinking about a message, depending on people's expectations. If the message is expected to produce positive feelings, people will process it more in a good mood. However, if people expect the message to elicit negative feelings, they will process the message less (Wegener et al., 1995).

People in a good mood view the world through rose-coloured glasses. They also make faster, more impulsive decisions; they rely more on peripheral cues (Bodenhausen, 1993; Braverman, 2005; Moons & Mackie, 2007; Schwarz et al., 1991). Unhappy people ruminate more before reacting, so they are less easily swayed by weak arguments—they also construct more persuasive arguments (Forgas, 2007). Thus, if you can't make a strong case, you might want to put your audience in a good mood and hope they'll feel good about your message without thinking too much about it. This is why many advertisers use humour in their approaches. The idea is this: If I make you laugh, you will associate your good mood with my product and you are more likely to buy it. Indeed, there is research that suggests this technique can work. For example, Jim Lyttle (2001) at the University of Toronto has shown that speakers who use humour (such as cartoons or self-effacing humour) are more persuasive, presumably because people who use humour are seen as more likeable or credible.

Applying Social Psychology

In marketing circles, there is one study that receives a great deal of attention, even today. In 1957, James Vicary claimed to have increased concession-stand sales at a movie theatre by introducing subliminal messages during the movie—messages that were flashed on the screen so quickly people couldn't actually see them. Vicary reported that popcorn sales increased by 50 percent and Coke sales increased by 18 percent after the messages were shown on the screen. Although this study has been accepted, quoted, and marketers have even tried to develop subliminal ads, there is no evidence that subliminal priming actually works. Indeed, Vicary fabricated the whole study in a desperate attempt to save his cash-strapped advertising firm (the ploy worked—even though the study was fake).

Drs. Erin Strahan (now at Wilfrid Laurier University), Steven Spencer, and Mark Zanna at the University of Waterloo decided to find out if subliminal advertising really does work. In their studies, they found that subliminal priming worked when people were already motivated to engage in the behaviour. For example, in a pair of studies (see Strahan et al., 2002, 2005, for details), they found that people who had thirst-related words subliminally flashed in front of them on a screen (e.g., thirst, dry) drank more than participants who did not receive the primes, and were more persuaded by an ad for "SuperQuencher" that claimed to be the best thirst-quenching sports drink on the market. However, these differences were apparent only if the participants came into the study thirsty. Thus, this research suggests that subliminal priming works only if you are already predisposed to the behaviour. So, maybe Vicary's study would have worked after all—on the hungry moviegoers, anyway.

The Effect of Arousing Fear

Messages can also be effective by evoking negative emotions. When trying to convince people to cut down on smoking, to brush their teeth more often, to get a tetanus shot, or to drive carefully, a fear-arousing message can be potent (de Hoog et al., 2007; Muller & Johnson, 1990). The Canadian government requires cigarette makers to include graphic representations of the hazards of smoking on each new pack of cigarettes; it is counting on the fact that showing smokers the horrible things that can happen to people who smoke will create a persuasive anti-smoking message (Newman, 2001). But how much fear should you arouse? Should you evoke just a little fear, lest people become so frightened that they tune out your painful message? Or should you try to scare the daylights out of them?

The effectiveness of fear-arousing communications is being applied in ads discouraging smoking, drinking and driving, and risky sexual behaviours. Does it work? When Claude Levy-Leboyer (1988) found that attitudes toward alcohol and drinking habits among French youth were changed effectively by fear-arousing pictures, the French government incorporated this kind of information into its TV spots. To have one's fear aroused is to become more intensely interested in information about a disease and in ways to prevent it (Das et al., 2003; Ruiter et al., 2001). Fear-arousing communications also increase people's detection behaviours, such as getting mammograms, doing breast or testicular self-exams, and checking for signs of skin cancer.

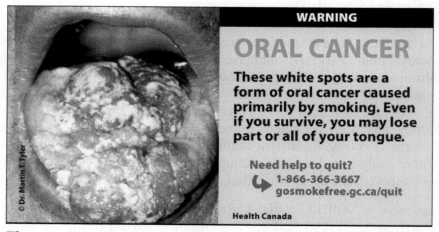

The warning on a cigarette package is designed to warn smokers of the dangers of their habit. But might it backfire?

All indications are that the Health Canada anti-smoking ads depicting diseased lungs and gums may be working (O'Hegarty et al., 2007; Peters et al., 2007; Stark et al., 2008). A study conducted by the Canadian Cancer Society in 2002 found that 58 percent of smokers interviewed said the new ads made them think about the health effects of smoking. Of smokers who attempted to quit in 2001, 38 percent said the new warnings were a factor in their motivations to quit. Importantly, 21 percent of smokers who had been tempted to have a cigarette decided not to because of the new warnings. Finally, Statistics Canada reports that overall cigarette smoking rates declined from 24.3 percent of all Canadians in 1994 to 16 percent in 2012. The biggest declines have been with teenagers and young adults, with only 11 percent of these groups indicating they are current smokers. Overall, anti-smoking campaigns over the decades have clearly had an effect. In 1965, a remarkable 50 percent of Canadians smoked, almost three times more than today.

Connection:

We will discuss fear-based appeals and health again in Module 24.

However, fear-based appeals are not all good—people may engage in denial because, when they aren't told how to avoid the danger, frightening messages can be overwhelming. Fear-arousing messages are more effective if they not only lead people to fear the severity and likelihood of a threatened event but also to perceive a solution (Devos-Comby & Salovey, 2002). Many ads aimed at reducing sexual risks aim both to arouse fear—"AIDS kills"—and to offer a protective strategy: Abstain, or wear a condom, or have sex only in a committed relationship. During the 1980s, fear of AIDS did persuade many men to alter their behaviour. One study of 5000 gay men found that, as the AIDS crisis mushroomed between 1984 and 1986, the number saying they were celibate or monogamous rose from 14 to 39 percent (Fineberg, 1988). However, more recent data suggest that these trends may be reversing. Research by Ted Myers at the University of Toronto (Myers et al., 2004) found that the number of gay men who reported having unprotected homosexual sex in 2002 was double that of a decade earlier.

LO 4

TO WHOM IS IT SAID? THE ROLE OF THE AUDIENCE

It also matters who *receives* a message. Let's consider two characteristics of those who receive a message: their age and their thoughtfulness.

People tend to have different social and political attitudes, depending on their age. Social psychologists give two explanations for the difference. One is a *life-cycle explanation*. Attitudes change (e.g., become more conservative) as people grow older. The other is a *generational explanation*. The attitudes older people adopted when they were young persist largely unchanged, but because these attitudes are different from those being adopted by young people today, a generation gap develops.

The evidence mostly supports the generational explanation. In surveys and re-surveys of groups of younger and older people over several years, the attitudes of older people usually show less change than those of young people (Sears, 1979, 1986). More recent research by Penny Visser and Jon Krosnick (1998; Eaton et al., 2009) suggests that older adults, near the end of the life cycle, may become more susceptible to attitude change, due to a decline in the strength of their attitudes.

Older adults are not inflexible; most people in their 50s and 60s have more liberal sexual and racial attitudes than they had in their 30s and 40s (Glenn, 1980, 1981). Few of us are utterly uninfluenced by changing cultural norms. The teens and early 20s are important formative years (Krosnick & Alwin, 1989), and the attitudes formed then tend to remain stable through middle adulthood (Eaton et al., 2009). Young people might therefore be advised to choose their social influences—the online groups they join, the media they imbibe, the roles they adopt—carefully.

Adolescent and early adult experiences are formative partly because they make deep and lasting impressions. We may therefore expect that today's young adults will remember phenomena such as the explosion of social media, the advent of Web 2.0, Twitter, Instagram, and the election of Barack Obama as turning points in world history.

But what are people thinking? The crucial aspect of central-route persuasion is not the message itself but the responses it evokes in the audience's mind. Our minds are not sponges that soak up whatever pours over them. If the message summons favourable thoughts, it persuades us. If it provokes us to think of contrary arguments, we remain unpersuaded. What circumstances breed counterargument? One is a warning that someone is going to try to persuade you. If you had to tell your family that you wanted to drop out of school, you would likely anticipate their pleading with you to stay. So you might develop a list of arguments to counter every conceivable argument they might make. Jonathan Freedman and David Sears (1965) demonstrated the difficulty of trying to persuade people under such circumstances. They warned one group of California high schoolers that they were going to hear a talk: "Why Teenagers Should Not Be Allowed to Drive." Those forewarned did not budge in their opinions. Others, not forewarned, did. In courtrooms, too, defence lawyers sometimes forewarn juries about prosecution evidence to come. With mock juries, such "stealing thunder" neutralizes its negative impact (Dolnik et al., 2003).

Sneak attacks on attitudes are especially useful with involved people. Given several minutes' forewarning, involved people will prepare defences (Chen et al., 1992). People do not even need to be told about the persuasive attempt—if they recognize it from the structure of the message, they begin to counterargue (Kamalski et al., 2008). When forewarned people regard an issue as trivial, however, they may agree even before receiving the message, to avoid later seeming gullible (Wood & Quinn, 2003).

Critical THINKING

Remember the activity you did earlier? Now let's do the reverse of what you did. Consider how ads affect you.

Describe an advertisement that has been effective in drawing your attention. What method(s) was/were used by the advertisers to get your attention? Which was spoken to more by the advertisement—your emotion or your reason? What effect, if any, did the advertisement have in altering your attitudes or behaviours?

Verbal persuasion is also enhanced by distracting people with something that attracts their attention just enough to inhibit counterarguing (Festinger & Maccoby, 1964; Keating & Brock, 1974; Osterhouse & Brock, 1970). Political ads often use this technique. The words promote the candidate, and the visual images keep us occupied so we don't analyze the words. Distraction is especially effective when the message is simple (Harkins & Petty, 1981; Regan & Cheng, 1973).

The Role of Personality in Elaboration

Analytical people—those with a high *need for cognition*—enjoy thinking carefully and prefer central routes (Cacioppo et al., 1996). People who like to conserve their mental resources—those with a low need for cognition—are quicker to respond to such peripheral cues as the communicator's attractiveness and the pleasantness of the surroundings. In addition, we also need to be motivated and able to understand the message. However, just because we are motivated does not mean we are necessarily able to process it. For example, Carolyn Hafer and her colleagues (Hafer et al., 1996) at Brock University have demonstrated that when the message is particularly complex, people are less able to elaborate it, and any persuasion that occurs will work through peripheral processes. However, if the message is simple, people can elaborate it, and the strength of the argument is what matters.

But the issue matters, too. All of us actively struggle with issues that involve us while making snap judgments about things that matter little (Johnson & Eagly, 1990). As we mentally elaborate upon an important issue, the strength of the arguments and of our own thoughts determines our attitudes.

CONCLUSIONS

The basically simple theory that we have presented—that *what we think in response to a message is crucial*, especially if we are motivated and able to think about it—helps us understand several findings. For example, we more readily believe trustworthy, expert communicators if we're following the peripheral route. When we trust the source, we think favourable thoughts and are less likely to counterargue. But mistrusting an expert source makes us more likely to follow the central route. Because of our careful thought about the message content, we may end up refuting a weak message (Priester & Petty, 1995).

The Elaboration Likelihood Model also has practical implications. Effective communicators care not only about their images and their messages but also about how their audience is likely to react. The best instructors tend to get students to think actively. They ask questions, provide intriguing examples, challenge students with difficult problems, and repeat their arguments. All of these techniques are likely to foster a process that moves information through the central route to persuasion. In classes where the instruction is less engaging, you can provide your own central processing. If you think about the material and elaborate on the arguments, you are likely to do better in the course.

SUMMARY OF KEY POINTS

LO1. Describe the central and peripheral routes to persuasion.

- Central-route persuasion under high elaboration results in critical analysis of arguments presented; peripheral-route persuasion occurs when people rely on heuristics, such as source expertise or attractiveness.

LO2. Understand the role of the source of the message in persuasion.

- The credibility and attractiveness of a source can powerfully influence the persuasiveness of a message.

LO3. Understand the role of the message content in persuasion.

- The structure of a message is important: affective versus cognitive content, mood, fear, and the subliminal versus supraliminal nature of the message all matter.

LO4. Understand the role of the audience in persuasion.

- Age and personality characteristics can influence the persuasive power of a message.

KEY TERMS

Attractiveness   Having qualities that appeal to an audience. An appealing communicator (often someone similar to the audience) is most persuasive on matters of subjective preference.

Central-route persuasion   Persuasion that occurs when interested people focus on the arguments and respond with favourable thoughts.

Credibility   Believability. A credible communicator is perceived as both expert and trustworthy.

Peripheral-route persuasion   Persuasion that occurs when people are influenced by incidental cues, such as a speaker's attractiveness.

Sleeper effect   A delay in the impact of a message; occurs when we remember the message but forget a reason for discounting it.

Subliminal messages   Messages presented in such a manner as to be below a person's threshold of conscious awareness.

MODULE ELEVEN

Resisting Social Influence

We are inundated with up to 15 000 persuasive communications every day (O'Reilly & Tennant, 2009). Most of the time, these communications are mundane (e.g., banner ads on apps or on websites), with little meaning or consequence. Perhaps we buy a chocolate bar, or maybe even a car we had not intended to, but our decisions are typically harmless (except to our bank accounts). However, sometimes we are persuaded to do things that are very harmful, even deadly. People who kill innocent civilians in the name of some cause are good examples. But how does it come to this? No one grows up thinking, "I want to blow up innocent civilians for a cause one day."

At the very least, you should understand by now that social influence is pervasive and often affects us without our knowing. But we do resist. In this module we will discuss some of the ways in which groups use social influence tactics to change individual behaviour, and how we might resist their attempts more effectively.

Critical THINKING

When acts of terrorism such as suicide bombings occur, people often speak about the perpetrators as being outwardly "normal" and having typical childhoods. The Boston Marathon bombing is a good example—the two men who committed the horrendous crime appeared normal, and their conversion to radical beliefs occurred over a long period of time. How does this conversion—from normal law-abiding citizen to terrorist—occur?

Joseph Goebbels, Germany's minister of "popular enlightenment" and propaganda from 1933 to 1945, understood the power of persuasion. Given control of publications, radio programs, motion pictures, and the arts, he undertook to persuade Germans to accept Nazi ideology. How effective were the Nazi propagandists? Did they, as the Allies alleged at one Nuremberg trial, "inject poison into the minds of millions and millions" (Bytwerk, 1976)? Most Germans were not persuaded to feel raging hatred for the Jews. But many were. Others became sympathetic to anti-Semitic measures. And most of the rest became either sufficiently uncertain or sufficiently intimidated to staff the huge genocidal program, or at least to allow it to happen. Without the complicity of millions of people, there would have been no Holocaust (Goldhagen, 1996).

The powers of persuasion were apparent in what a Pew survey (2003, 2008) called the "rift between Americans and Western Europeans" over the Iraq War. Surveys shortly before the war, for example, revealed that Europeans and Canadians opposed military action against Iraq by about two to one, while Americans favoured it by the same margin (Burkholder, 2003; Moore, 2003; Pew, 2003). Once the war began, Americans' support for the war rose to more than three to one (Newport et al., 2003). Except for Israel, people surveyed in all other countries were opposed to the attack. As the 2008 U.S. presidential election approached, support for the war in Iraq waned. the huge rift between Americans and their distant cousins in other countries points to persuasion at work. What persuaded Americans to favour the war? What persuaded most people elsewhere to oppose it? Depending on where you lived, you may have heard and read about either

- "America's liberation of Iraq" or "America's invasion of Iraq"
- "Operation Iraqi Freedom" or "The War in Iraq"
- Headlines such as "Tense Standoff Between Troops and Iraqis Erupts in Bloodshed" (ambiguous passive-voice headline of the *Los Angeles Times*) or "U.S. Troops Fire on Iraqis; 13 Reported Dead" (active-voice headline of the same incident on the CBC)
- Scenes of captured and dead Iraqis, or scenes of captured and dead Americans

Imagine how the story might differ on CTV, Fox News, or Al Jazeera—and those are just the mainstream outlets. Thousands of websites and bloggers reported on the conflict from their own perspectives. When Iran cracked down on people who opposed the re-election of President Mahmoud Ahmadinejad, much of the news was sent from people holding smartphones. This is also true of the uprisings of the 2011 "Arab Spring," which led to the deposition of several leaders in countries such as Egypt, Tunisia, and Libya. Scenes of protest and brutal government crackdowns were recorded on phones and shared via social media sites in Egypt and Syria. Context matters. In Canada, we saw similar discussions about whether or not the Canadian military should remain in a fighting role in Afghanistan and how they should treat Afghani detainees. One Conservative cabinet minister accused a Liberal critic of the war as being "in league with the Taliban." Clearly, propaganda is just as alive and well in the present as it was in the past.

Depending on their perspective, people discuss and believe (and are presented with) somewhat differing information. Persuasion matters. On the positive side of the equation however, persuasive forces have also been harnessed for good—to promote healthier living, safer driving, and better education and child care. For example, the rate of new U.S. university students reporting abstinence from beer has increased—from 25 percent in 1981 to 57 percent in 2005 (Pryor et al., 2005). In the fall of 2011, when the University of Alberta offered 80 spots in an alcohol-free residence, over 200 new students applied. More than at any time in recent decades, health- and safety-conscious educated adults are shunning cigarettes and beer. Nonetheless, because persuasion tactics can be used among a wide variety of groups, we need to be aware of how they work and how to counteract them.

LO 1

HOW GROUPS USE INDOCTRINATION TACTICS

On an early-October evening in 1994, firefighters were called to the scene of a chalet fire in Morin Heights, near Montreal. Inside, they found two dead bodies, badly burned. In an adjoining chalet they found three more dead bodies, clearly murdered, including a three-month-old child. Authorities were shocked. However, they quickly realized that these bodies were linked to the Order of the Solar Temple.

The Solar Temple was started by Luc Jouret and Joseph Di Mambro. Jouret, the more charismatic of the two, became the spiritual leader of the group. They believed that they were the reincarnations of the Knights Templar, the protectors of the Holy Grail. Shortly after the fire in Morin Heights, 43 additional victims were found in Switzerland (and 16 more victims were found in France the following year). The leaders of the Order of the Solar Temple had ordered their members to commit ritualistic suicide (although many members appeared to have been killed before their bodies were burned). Members of the Order believed that burning would purify their souls and prepare them for the spiritual transformation they would achieve when they reached the star Sirius. Members of the **cult** (also sometimes referred to as a *new religious movement*) included prominent businesspeople, journalists, and even a mayor. What would drive these people to kill themselves and others?

Luc Jouret, one of the founders of the Order of the Solar Temple.

The Solar Temple is just one example of cults, which we often only hear about in the news: Marshall Applewhite and 37 "Heaven's Gate" followers committed suicide in 1997, and dozens of David Koresh's Branch Dravidians died during a standoff with U.S. federal law enforcement officials in 1993. But research on cults and their tactics really started after over 900 members of Jim Jones's People's Temple cult collectively committed suicide in Guyana in 1978 by drinking cyanide-laced grape drink.

Shall we attribute cult members' apparently strange behaviours to strange personalities? Or do their experiences illustrate the common dynamics of social influence and persuasion? Do more mainstream groups (e.g., sport teams, the military) use these **indoctrination** techniques as well?

Bear three things in mind. First, this is hindsight analysis. It uses persuasion principles as categories for explaining, after the fact, fascinating and sometimes disturbing social phenomena. Second, explaining *why* people believe something says nothing about the *truth* of their beliefs. That is a logically separate issue. A psychology of religion might tell us *why* a theist believes in God and an atheist disbelieves, but it cannot tell us who is right. Third, we must bear in mind that indoctrination tactics are used by a wide variety of groups, from mainstream religious groups, to bikers and other gangs, to corporations, sports teams, and governments trying to win over the hearts and minds of their citizens. Cults provide useful case studies to explore persuasion because these groups are often intently analyzed. Therefore, we will focus here on some of the tactics they use.

Attitudes Follow Behaviour

As we have discussed previously, people usually internalize commitments made voluntarily, publicly, and repeatedly. Cult leaders seem to know this. New converts soon learn that membership is no trivial matter. They are quickly made active members of the team. Rituals within the cult community, as well as public canvassing and fund-raising, strengthen the initiates' identities as members. The greater the personal commitment, the more we need to justify it.

Connection:

We discussed compliance tactics in Module 8.

One does not suddenly decide, "I'm gonna find a cult." Nor do cult recruiters approach people on the street with, "Hi. I'm a cult member. Care to join us?" Rather, the recruitment strategy exploits the foot-in-the-door principle. Let's consider one man's encounter with a new religious group in Montreal. Craig Silverman (2004) described his first meeting with members of the Raelians, who believe that their leader, Rael, was visited by aliens and is the "brother of Jesus" sent to save us by telling us our true origins and preparing us for the visit from our creators. In the Raelian philosophy, life on Earth was created by extraterrestrials and they will come back once an extraterrestrial embassy is built on Earth.

At the meeting the people were very polite and friendly. They watched a video that asked all of the questions to which we want answers: Why are we here? What is the meaning of life? Where do we come from? The video answered some (but not all) of these questions and the newcomers were encouraged to buy the movement's books and DVDs to learn more and to obtain more answers to their questions. At the end of the session they were invited to sign up for additional lectures. Do you see the foot-in-the-door technique at work? Presumably, once you have bought the book or agreed to a new meeting, you have committed (albeit in a small way) to find out more.

Consistent with their approach at individual meetings, the Raelians operate a visitor's centre in the Eastern Townships of Quebec that is designed to work in a similar way. As it turns out, Steven's brother (interestingly, also a psychologist) was once visiting the Eastern Townships with his wife and saw a sign for a "UFO museum." On a whim, they decided to visit. Upon paying the fee, they gained entry to a building (intriguingly, billed as the largest building made of hay bales in the world) and started to wander through. They found themselves being shadowed by one of the group members, who offered information about the group and asked if they had questions. They were given several opportunities to purchase information, and soon found that the path they were on was deliberately complex with no obvious exits—so that they had to go through all of the exhibits and "sales pitches" before they could leave.

Persuasive Elements

We can also analyze group persuasion by considering the following factor: *Who* (the communicator) said *what* (the message) to *whom* (the audience)?

Connection:

We discussed "who, what, and whom" in Module 10.

Successful groups have a charismatic leader—someone who attracts and directs the members. As in experiments on persuasion, a credible communicator is someone the audience perceives as an expert and trustworthy; for example, Luc Jouret would perform "miracles." He arranged a sophisticated sound and light apparatus when he gave his speeches, and at the appointed time he would perform a miracle (making images of Jesus appear, and so on). These often convinced audiences that he was indeed who he claimed to be, and led to many people joining the group. Trust is another aspect of credibility. Many cult members have been recruited by friends or relatives—people they trust (Stark & Bainbridge, 1980). The vivid, emotional messages and the warmth and acceptance with which the group showers lonely or depressed people can be strikingly appealing: Trust the master, join the family; we have the answer, the "one way." The message echoes through channels as varied as lectures, small-group discussions, and direct social pressure (see Moore, 2009).

Recruits are often young—people under 25 are still at that comparatively open age before attitudes and values stabilize. Some are less-educated people who like the simplicity of the message and find it difficult to counterargue. But most are educated, middle-class people. Potential converts are often at turning points in their lives, facing personal crises, or vacationing, or living away from home. They have needs; the cult offers them an answer (Lofland & Stark, 1965; Singer, 1979). Times of social and economic upheaval are especially conducive to someone who can make apparent simple sense out of the confusion (Moore, 2009).

As you read in the description of the Raelians, members of these groups do not appear scary and intimidating. They are friendly, gentle, and pleasant people. People who join these groups often feel alienated from the larger society and are looking for a group to provide acceptance. Similar processes work with youth and street gangs and religious and political organizations. Humans are social beings and we want to be accepted and liked by people. These groups (gangs, cults, religious groups, political groups) provide the social acceptance and sometimes provide (e.g., as explicitly offered by the Raelians and other religious groups) the answers to life's important questions. These tactics work—the Unification Church (the "Moonies") has successfully recruited about one in ten people who attend its workshops (Ennis & Verrilli, 1989).

Group Effects

Cults also illustrate the next module's theme: the power of a group to shape members' views and behaviour. Groups can shape our behaviour in negative ways—as we assume a role we look to others for guidance (see McFarland & Carnahan, 2009; Carnahan & McFarland, 2007). The cult typically separates members from their previous social support systems and isolates them with other cultists. There may then occur what Rodney Stark and William Bainbridge (1980) call a "social implosion": external ties weaken until the group collapses inward socially, each person engaging only with other group members. Cut off from families and former friends, they lose access to counterarguments. The group now offers identity and defines reality. Because the cult frowns on or punishes disagreements, the apparent consensus helps eliminate any lingering doubts. Moreover, stress and emotional arousal narrow attention, making people "more susceptible to poorly supported arguments, social pressure, and the temptation to derogate nongroup members" (Baron, 2000).

Connection:

We learned about group influence on behaviour in Module 9.

The techniques we have described do not have unlimited power. Toward the end, the leaders of the Solar Temple became increasingly eccentric, and many of the members began to leave. One of the leaders' own sons exposed the frauds of the "religious experiences." Many of the members left and some demanded their "contributions" of money be returned.

It is important to recognize that cult influence techniques are in some ways similar to techniques used by groups more familiar to us. We might also ask why people join gangs. Wendy Craig at Queen's University and her colleagues (e.g., Craig et al., 2002) have demonstrated that the decision can start in childhood. Youth join gangs as young as age 10 or 11, and by 13 their gang membership has become stable. Researchers at the University of Alberta (Grekul & LaBoucane-Benson, 2008) have found that Aboriginal youth join gangs due to their perceptions of discrimination, marginalization, and lack of opportunity, and that joining the gang provides a sense of identity for them. Police in Toronto have blamed a number of structural problems, such as poverty, unemployment, non-integrated neighbourhoods, and a weak legal system, for the upswing in gun violence in that city (Ezonu, 2010). These factors not only encourage participation in gangs, but provide a basis for increasing gang cohesion and influence on its members.

Fraternity and sorority members have reported that the initial "love bombing" of potential cult recruits is not unlike their own "rush" period. Members lavish prospective pledges with attention and make them feel special. During the pledge period, new members are somewhat isolated, cut off from old friends who did not pledge. They spend time studying the history and rules of their new group. They suffer and commit time on its behalf. They are expected to comply with all its demands. Not surprisingly, the result is usually a committed new member. These same techniques are used in sports teams and in the military during "hazing," such as the well-publicized 2012 events that resulted in the women's hockey team at Dalhousie University being suspended for a full year, and the 2013 hazing of Grade 9 and 10 students by senior students at the Lanigan Central High School near Saskatoon. The latter incident resulted in 39 charges being laid against 11 students. Any group that wants cohesion among its members will likely use some form of these tactics.

Much the same is true of some therapeutic communities for recovering drug and alcohol abusers and for people who claim to have recalled repressed memories of sexual abuse. Some self-help groups form a cohesive "social cocoon," have intense beliefs, and exert a profound influence on members' behaviour (Galanter, 1989, 1990). Keep in mind that many groups use these indoctrination techniques. For example, terrorist organizations isolate individuals, and promise benefits in the afterlife as a potential reward (Aslan, 2010). Some movements can be broad-ranging and generally seem socially acceptable (Scientology, and the rise of the Tea Party movement in the United States are examples), but these groups can use similar tactics—even if they are not considered cults. However, aside from terrorist groups, cults are perhaps the most documented and analyzed of these types of groups in terms of their social psychological approaches to persuasion and indoctrination.

Connection:

We will discuss terrorist groups in more detail in Module 13.

Applying Social Psychology

You have learned about the tactics cult leaders can use to convert members and overcome resistance. There is no actual "manual" for cult leaders, but if there were one, it might read like this (see Pratkanis and Aronson, 1992):

1. **Create your own social reality.** Remove all sources of information other than that provided by the cult. Mail should be censored, and relatives should be prevented from visiting members. It's best if cult headquarters are isolated from the rest of the world.

2. **Establish an ingroup of followers and an outgroup of the unredeemed.** Constantly remind members: "If you want to be chosen, then you must act like a chosen one. If you are not chosen, then you are wicked and unredeemed."

3. **Generate commitment through dissonance reduction.** Ensure obedience by establishing a spiral of escalating commitment (foot-in-the-door technique).

4. **Establish the cult leader's credibility and attractiveness.** Many cults have leader myths passed from member to member concerning the life and times of the cult leader.

5. **Send members out to preach to and convert the unredeemed.** This technique not only brings in new members but also ensures that members are constantly engaged in self-sell or self-generated persuasion.

6. **Distract members from thinking "undesirable" thoughts.** For example, never allow new recruits to be alone to think for themselves. Chanting and singing prevents thinking about anything else. Teach that any disagreeable thought is evil and from the devil.

7. **Fixate members' vision on a phantom.** Dangle the notion of the promised land and a vision of a better world before the faithful. By keeping members focused on a future phantom, you provide a powerful incentive to keep working. Phantoms also maintain hope by providing a sense of purpose and mission.

What does this tell us? That you should beware if you see these tactics being used in the groups you belong to. At the very least, it suggests poor decision-making is going on. You should be more critical of groups using these tactics.

Connection:

We discussed cognitive dissonance in Module 8.

Connection:

We discussed the role of source attractiveness in Module 10.

We use the examples of fraternities, political movements, self-help groups, and sports teams not to disparage them but to illustrate two concluding observations. First, if we attribute new religious movements to the leader's mystical force or to the followers' peculiar weaknesses, we may delude ourselves into thinking we are immune to social control techniques. In truth, our own groups—and countless salespeople, political leaders, and other persuaders—successfully use many of these tactics on us. Between education and indoctrination, enlightenment and propaganda, conversion and coercion, therapy and mind control, there is but a blurry line.

LO 2

HOW WE RESIST SOCIAL PRESSURE

Social psychology offers other reminders of the power of the person. We act in response to the forces that push upon us, but we are not just billiard balls. Some of our reactions are more automatic than others, but some are active attempts to resist persuasive communications. All of these processes help us resist.

Attitude Strength and Information Processing

Strong attitudes are more likely to lead to behaviour, whereas weak attitudes are not. Similarly, strong attitudes are consequential in that they bias how we perceive incoming information, whereas weak attitudes do so to a lesser degree (Krosnick & Petty, 1995).

Connection:

We discussed attitude and attitude strength in Module 8.

The process through which your attitudes are formed is also very relevant to the strength of attitudes. Mark Zanna at the University of Waterloo and his colleagues (Fazio & Zanna, 1978) have shown that direct experience with an attitude object creates stronger attitudes toward that object. For example, we might feel more strongly about a car we have actually driven than about a car we have simply seen (remember the example of the car salesperson in Module 8). There has also been research exploring people's subjective beliefs about the strength of their attitudes. Indeed, subjective beliefs are probably the most common approach to assessing attitude strength. Think back to any opinion survey you have ever done. You were probably asked how "certain" you were or how "important" the topic was to you. Certainty refers to the level of subjective confidence or validity a person attaches to his or her attitude. Certainty is high when people have a clear notion of what their attitudes are and believe their attitudes are accurate (Petrocelli, Tormala, & Rucker, 2007). Studies conducted by multiple researchers have found that higher certainty is associated with attitude stability over time (Bassili, 1996), resistance to persuasion (Bassili, 1996; Tormala & Petty, 2002), and impact on social judgments (Marks & Miller, 1985). Thus, the more certain you are, the harder it will be for someone to change your mind.

Information Processing Biases

Connection:

We addressed the issue of information processing biases in Module 7.

Perhaps not surprisingly, given the extensive work on attitude strength and its relation to information processing, strong attitudes have been demonstrated to result in biases in how we process information. Leon Festinger (1957), who developed cognitive dissonance theory, provided one of the earliest discussions and conducted the first systematic research into the impact of attitudes on information processing. Festinger argued that, because individuals are motivated to maintain cognitive consistency, people should be motivated to incorporate information that is consistent with their attitudes and to avoid information that is inconsistent. There is some evidence that we are better at incorporating new information if it is consistent with our existing knowledge. For example, Teena Willoughby at Brock University (Willoughby et al., 2009) has demonstrated that when doing Internet searches for assigned essays, we are much better at getting information if we already know something about the topic. Having that basic knowledge helps both subjectively (how we feel about it) and objectively (how well we write the essay).

Typically, these biases have been broken down by the stages at which they have an influence on information processing: selective exposure and attention to information, selective processing and judgment, and selective memory. Although more sophisticated approaches to the concept of information processing have been developed, and the "stage" model is not as supported as it once was, it is still a useful way to think about information processing biases (Eagly & Chaiken, 1993; Smith et al., 2007).

Selective Exposure and Selective Attention

Early work on exposure found that people were biased in how they exposed themselves to information. **Selective exposure** is the extent to which people's attitudes affect the information they expose themselves to. **Selective attention** is the extent to which people's attitudes affect how much of this information they pay attention to, once they've been exposed to it. For example, Ehrlich and colleagues (1957) found that car owners who had recently made a car purchase read more ads about the cars they purchased than they did ads for cars they had considered but decided not to buy. More recently, Steven Smith (one of this textbook's authors) and his colleagues (2007) found that motivation and the ability to process information is important. In order to be complete information processors, a person must both be able (e.g., have the appropriate cognitive resources, not be distracted) and be motivated (e.g., want to or be predisposed to) to first process all of the available information, and then be unbiased when processing that information. However, as you can imagine, there are many times when motivation to be unbiased may be low, and times when being biased in an attitude-congruent way would be common. Thus, under many conditions, people are indeed biased in how they expose themselves to information. However, there are occasions (e.g., when we are uniquely responsible for decisions or our decisions have important consequences) where we will strive to be unbiased (see Jonas et al., 2005; Smith et al., 2007, 2008).

Selective Perception and Selective Judgment

Perception can be defined as the encoding of information, so selective perception is the extent to which people's attitudes affect their encoding of information. Judgment, on the other hand, can be defined as drawing conclusions about the meaning or relevance of information (Eagly & Chaiken, 1993); selective judgment is the extent to which people's attitudes affect the conclusions they draw about the meaning or relevance of information. Research has provided fairly clear support that people usually evaluate messages negatively when the messages are counter to their pre-existing attitudes. In a classic study, Lord, Ross, and Lepper (1979) demonstrated biased perception and judgment regarding the death penalty. The researchers first assessed people existing attitudes toward the death penalty. Next, participants were presented with the results of two purportedly real studies. One study supported the effectiveness of capital punishment as a deterrent, whereas the other did not. As predicted, participants rated the study that agreed with their own point of view as more convincing and more scientifically rigorous than the study they disagreed with. In general, these selectivity effects have been found to be particularly likely to occur when attitudes are strong. For example, Houston and Fazio (1989) found that people whose attitudes toward capital punishment were more accessible engaged in biased processing to a greater degree than people whose attitudes were not as accessible.

Selective Memory

Of the various attitude-based information processing biases, perhaps the most controversial has been the relationship between attitudes and recall. Within this literature, the dominant perspective has been that attitudes should produce *congeniality* biases in recall. This perspective postulates that people use selective memory when they process social information: they remember information that is congruent with their attitudes better than information that is incongruent with their attitudes (e.g., see Eagly et al., 1999). Meghan Norris at Purdue University and her colleagues (Smith et al., 2008; Norris, 2007; Norris et al., 2014) have shown that, similar to selective exposure effects, people's motivation and ability to be biased are important factors in biased memory.

Overall, however, we can consider that attitude strength and biases in information processing work as somewhat "passive" factors in protecting our attitudes from inconsistent information. Most people are not aware of the natural biases they may be exhibiting (Wegener & Petty, 1996). Yet, the effects are quite consistent. If we cannot ignore the inconsistent information, we can judge it as irrelevant or inconsequential, or we can simply forget it. This does not necessarily require any conscious decision making. However, there are certainly more "active" approaches we can take to defend our attitudes. We will now discuss some of these.

Reactance

Knowing that someone is trying to coerce us may even prompt us to react in the *opposite* direction. For example, think back to some of your early romantic relationships. Did you ever have a relationship with someone your parents did not like? Most of us have had this experience. You bring home the new love of your life, only to discover that your mother or father (or both) absolutely despises him or her. If your parents were social psychologists, they probably said nothing. However, if they were like most parents, they probably told you how they felt about your new sweetheart. How did you react to this information? If you are like many of the students in the authors' classes, you probably liked your new love interest *even more* after you discovered your parents' true feelings about him or her. This is called reactance.

The theory of psychological reactance—that people do indeed act to protect their sense of freedom— is supported by experiments showing that attempts to restrict a person's freedom often produce an anti-conformity "boomerang effect" (Nail et al., 2000). After contemporary female university students in Western cultures think about how traditional culture expects women to behave, they become less likely to exhibit traditional feminine modesty (Cialdini et al., 1998).

Critical THINKING

What role does reactance have in drug use? Marijuana use in the Netherlands, where marijuana use is legalized, is the same or lower than in countries where it is not legal. Indeed, Canada rates highest in the world in youth who smoke marijuana (Statistics Canada, 2012; Huffington Post, 2013). The Netherlands also compares well in terms of the use of illegal drugs (such as cocaine and ecstasy) and drug-related deaths compared to other countries (Keizer, 2001). What do you think this says about the role of reactance in drug use?

Reactance may also contribute to underage drinking. A survey of 18- to 24-year-olds by the Canadian Centre on Substance Abuse (1997) revealed that 69 percent of those over the legal drinking age had been drunk in the last year, as had 77 percent of those under the legal age. In the United States, a survey of students on 56 campuses revealed a 25 percent rate of abstinence among students of legal drinking age (21) but only a 19 percent abstinence rate among students under 21. The researchers, Ruth Engs and David Hanson (1989), also found that 15 percent of the legal-age students and 24 percent of the underage students were heavy drinkers. They suspect this pattern reflects a reactance against the restriction. It probably also reflects peer influence. With alcohol use, as with drugs, peers influence attitudes, provide the substance, and offer a context for its use. This helps explain why post-secondary students, living in a peer culture that often supports alcohol use, drink more alcohol than their non-student peers (Atwell, 1986).

Reactance may also play a role in more antisocial behaviours. Baumeister and colleagues (2002) have suggested that reactance processes may have an impact on sexual assault. They argue that when a woman refuses to comply with a man's desire for sex, he may react with frustration over this restriction, resulting in increased desire for the forbidden activity (in this case, sex). Mix this reactance with narcissism—a self-serving sense of entitlement and low empathy for others—and the result can be forced sex.

Reactance can occur in some rather unexpected situations as well. It may surprise you that in the 2001 census, 20 000 Canadians indicated their religion as "Jedi." The Jedi, as you may know, are the guardians of peace and justice who manipulate the Force to maintain order in the blockbuster *Star Wars* movies. Is this actually a religion 20 000 Canadians follow? Not likely. The move to choose Jedi as a religion was begun by Denis Dion, a man living outside Vancouver, as a protest (that is, reactance) against what he believed to be an intrusive Statistics Canada question. On the census, which Canadians were until recently required to complete, one of the questions concerns religion.

Dion felt this question was none of the government's business and began an email campaign to encourage others to defy the government by giving a bogus response: Jedi. Obviously, many others had a similar reaction, and indicated Jedi as their religion. Interestingly, this reaction has been seen in other countries as well—apparently there were 400 000 Jedi followers in the United Kingdom in 2001 (compared with 260 000 self-identified Jews), and 70 000 Australians listed themselves as Jedi in 2002.

More recently, people have begun to identify themselves as vampires. As you no doubt know, vampires are the fictional undead characters who elegantly drink the blood of unsuspecting victims. The vampire groups, says Adam Possami at the University of West Sydney in Australia, are a form of "hyper real" religion—groups that use elements of existing religions, unique philosophy, and pop culture elements (such as the *True Blood* and *Twilight* novels) to create their own reality (Metcalfe, 2010). These groups are typically harmless and short-lived, but at times can develop into dangerous obsessions. In 2003 a 12-year-old Toronto boy was reportedly stabbed to death by his brother and two friends, who all claimed to be members of a vampire group (CTV, 2005).

Asserting Uniqueness

People feel uncomfortable when they appear too different from others. But—at least in Western cultures—they also feel uncomfortable when they appear exactly like everyone else. In one experiment, Snyder (1980) led students to believe that their "10 most important attitudes" were either distinct from or nearly identical to the attitudes of 10 000 other students. When they then participated in a conformity experiment, those deprived of their feeling of uniqueness were most likely to assert their individuality by non-conformity. For those of us from Western cultures, our distinctiveness is central to our identity (Vignoles et al., 2000).

Both social influence and the desire for uniqueness appear in popular baby names. People seeking less commonplace names often hit upon the same ones at the same time. The top five names for girls in 2013 were Emma, Sophia, Olivia, Emily, and Hailey. For boys, they were Liam, Ethan, Jackson, Jacob, and Noah (BabyCentre, 2014). Although many of these names may seem "unique," they will become very common in schools. For example, Steven named his children Sydney and Dylan, thinking they would be unique. Now there are three Dylans and another Sydney Smith in his kids' school of 160 kids. Although the popularity of some names has faded over time (e.g., Abigail), they do tend to resurface in future generations (Orenstein, 2003).

Seeing oneself as unique also appears in people's "spontaneous self-concepts." William McGuire and his Yale University colleagues (McGuire & Padawer-Singer, 1978; McGuire et al., 1979) report that when children are invited to "tell us about yourself," they are most likely to mention their distinctive attributes. Foreign-born children are more likely than others to mention their birthplace. Redheads are more likely than black- and brown-haired children to volunteer their hair colour. Light and heavy children are the most likely to refer to their body weight. Minority children are the most likely to mention their race. Likewise, we become more keenly aware of our gender when we are with people of the other sex (Cota & Dion, 1986).

As another example, imagine you are sitting in your social psychology class and the person next to you asks you where you live. What would you say? You would probably give the name of the part of the city or the residence you live in. That is what identifies you. However, let's imagine you are visiting Stonehenge in England and someone asks you the same question. What is the most identifying information for you then? Probably that you live in Canada.

These zebras, like many other animals, protect themselves by avoiding uniqueness. Humans, on the other hand, like to express theirs.

It seems that, while we do not like being greatly deviant, we are, ironically, all alike in wanting to feel distinctive and in noticing how we are distinctive But as research on the self-serving bias makes clear, it is not just any kind of distinctiveness we seek, but distinctiveness in the right direction. Our quest is not merely to be different from the average, but *better* than average.

Connection:

Remember our discussion of self-serving bias in Module 4.

Activity: **The need for uniqueness**

So, do you need to express your uniqueness? Complete the following scale, score it, and see how you do. Did you score high? Low? Would you have scored differently if you were of the opposite gender or from another culture? How do our experiences guide our behaviour?

Directions: The following statements concern your perceptions about yourself in a variety of situations. Your task is to indicate the strength of your agreement with each statement, using a scale in which 1 denotes strong disagreement, 5 denotes strong agreement, and 2, 3, and 4 represent intermediate judgments. In the blank preceding each statement, place a number from 1 to 5.

(Continued)

1	2	3	4	5
Strongest Disagreement				**Strongest Agreement**

There are no "right" or "wrong" answers, so select the number that most closely reflects you on each statement. Take your time and consider each statement carefully.

_____ 1. When I am in a group of strangers, I am not reluctant to express my opinion openly.

_____ 2. I find that criticism affects my self-esteem.

_____ 3. I sometimes hesitate to use my own ideas for fear they may be impractical.

_____ 4. I think society should let reason lead it to new customs and throw aside old habits or mere traditions.

_____ 5. People frequently succeed in changing my mind.

_____ 6. I sometimes find it amusing to upset the dignity of teachers, judges, and "cultured" people.

_____ 7. I like wearing a uniform because it makes me proud to be a member of the organization it represents.

_____ 8. People have sometimes called me "stuck-up."

_____ 9. Others' disagreements make me uncomfortable.

_____ 10. I do not always need to live by the rules and standards of society.

_____ 11. I am unable to express my feelings if they result in undesirable consequences.

_____ 12. Being a success in one's career means making a contribution that no one else has made.

_____ 13. It bothers me if people think I am being too unconventional.

_____ 14. I always try to follow rules.

_____ 15. If I disagree with a superior on his or her views, I usually do not keep it to myself.

_____ 16. I speak up in meetings in order to oppose those whom I feel are wrong.

(Continued)

This represents a shortened version of Snyder and Fromkin's (1977, 1980) Need for Unique-ness Scale. To calculate the total Need for Uniqueness Scale score, reverse each of the individual scores on items 2, 3, 5, 7, 9, 11, 13, and 14 (i.e., 1 to 5, 2 to 4, 3 to 3, 4 to 2, and 5 to 1). On these 16 reversed items, have students mark through their original score and put the reversed score in the blank. Finally, add the scores for all 16 items. The higher the score, the higher your need for uniqueness. This scale was developed to measure not how different one actually may be, but rather the magnitude of a person's desire or need to be unique.

What is your score? A score of 50 would be about average, 35 would be very low need for uniqueness, and 65 would be very high. Where do you fall on this scale? Does this seem about right? So, how do you express your uniqueness? Do you have more insight now?

LO 3

ATTITUDE INOCULATION

There is another way to resist. Before encountering others' judgments, make a public commitment to your position. Having stood up for your convictions, you will become less susceptible (or should we say less "open"?) to what others have to say.

How might we stimulate people to commit themselves? From his experiments, Charles Kiesler (1971) offers one possible way: mildly attack their position. Kiesler found that when committed people were attacked strongly enough to cause them to react, but not so strongly as to overwhelm them, they became even more committed. Kiesler explains: "When you attack committed people and your attack is of inadequate strength, you drive them to even more extreme behaviours in defense of their previous commitment. Their commitment escalates, in a sense, because the number of acts consistent with their belief increases" (p. 88). Perhaps you can recall a time when this happened in an argument, as those involved escalated their rhetoric, committing themselves to increasingly extreme positions.

There is a second reason why a mild attack might build resistance. When someone attacks one of our cherished attitudes, we typically feel some irritation and contemplate counterarguments. Counterarguing helps people resist persuasion (Jacks & Cameron, 2003). Refute someone's persuasion, and know that you have done so, and you will feel more certain than ever (Tormala & Petty, 2002; Tormola et al., 2006). Like inoculations against disease, even weak arguments will prompt counterarguments, which are then available for a stronger attack. William McGuire (1964) documented this in a series of experiments. McGuire wondered: Could we inoculate people against persuasion much as we inoculate them against a virus? Is there such a thing as attitude inoculation?

To test this, McGuire started with cultural truisms, such as "It's a good idea to brush your teeth after every meal if at all possible." He then showed that people were vulnerable to a massive, credible assault upon these truisms (e.g., prestigious authorities were said to have discovered that too much toothbrushing can damage one's gums). If, however, before having their belief attacked, they were "immunized" by first receiving a small challenge to their belief, and if they read or wrote an essay in refutation of this mild attack, then they were better able to resist the powerful attack.

Robert Cialdini and his colleagues (2003) agree that appropriate counterarguments are a great way to resist persuasion but wondered how to bring them to mind in response to a political opponent's ads, especially when the opponent (like most political incumbents) has a huge spending advantage. The answer, they suggest, is a "poison parasite" defence—one that combines a poison (strong counterarguments) with a parasite (retrieval cues that bring those arguments to mind when seeing the opponent's ads). In their studies, participants who viewed a familiar political ad were least persuaded by it when they had earlier seen counterarguments overlaid on a replica of the ad. Seeing the ad again thus also brought to mind the puncturing counterarguments. Anti-smoking ads have effectively done this, for example, by re-creating a "Marlboro Man" commercial set in the rugged outdoors but now showing a coughing, decrepit cowboy.

A "poison parasite" ad.

Inoculating Children Against Peer Pressure to Smoke

In a clear demonstration of how laboratory research findings can lead to practical applications, a research team led by Alfred McAlister (1980) had high school students "inoculate" Grade 7 students against peer pressures to smoke. The Grade 7 students were taught to respond to tobacco advertisements. They also acted in role-plays in which, after being called "chicken" for not taking a cigarette, they answered with statements like "I'd be a real chicken if I smoked just to impress you." After several such sessions during Grades 7 and 8, the inoculated students were half as likely to begin smoking as uninoculated students at another junior high school that had an identical parental smoking rate (see Figure 11-1).

Connection:

Remember that we initially discussed reactions to tobacco ads in Module 10.

Other research teams have confirmed that such inoculation procedures, sometimes supplemented by other life-skill training, reduce teen smoking (Botvin et al., 1995; Hirschman & Leventhal, 1989; Ellickson & Bell, 1990). Anti-smoking and drug education programs apply other persuasion principles, too. They use attractive peers to communicate information. They trigger the students' own cognitive processing ("Here's something you might want to think about"). They get the students to make a public commitment (by making a rational decision about smoking and then announcing it, along with their reasoning, to their classmates). Some of these smoking-prevention programs require only two to six hours of class, using prepared printed materials or videotapes. Today, any school district or teacher wishing to use the social-psychological approach to smoking prevention can do so easily, inexpensively, and with the hope of significant reductions in future smoking rates and associated health costs.

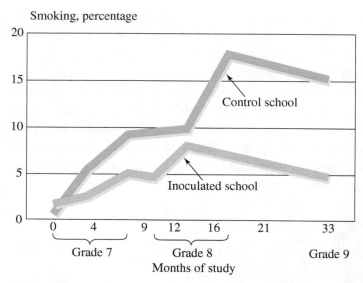

Smoking, percentage

FIGURE 11-1

The percentage of cigarette smokers at an "inoculated" junior high school was much less than the percentage at a matched control school using a more typical smoking education program.

Data from McAlister et al., 1980; Telch et al., 1981.

Inoculating Children Against the Influence of Advertising

Researchers have also studied how to immunize young children against the effects of television commercials. Sweden, Italy, Greece, Belgium, Denmark, and Ireland all restrict advertising that targets children, and other European countries have been discussing doing the same (McGuire, 2002). In the United States, notes Robert Levine in *The Power of Persuasion: How We're Bought and Sold*, the average child sees more than 10 000 commercials a year (2003).

Smokers often develop an "initial brand choice" in their teens, said a 1981 report from researchers at Philip Morris, a major contributor to the $11.2 billion spent annually on tobacco advertising and promotion (FTC, 2003). "Today's teenager is tomorrow's potential regular customer, and the overwhelming majority of smokers first begin to smoke while still in their teens" (Lichtblau, 2003). That explains why some cigarette and smokeless tobacco companies aggressively market to college and university students by advertising, by sponsoring parties, and by offering free cigarettes in an attempt to get at the "entry level" smoker (Farrell, 2005). Because of these approaches, the law in Canada since 2003 has been that tobacco companies in Canada are not allowed to sponsor sporting and cultural events. This legislation has recently withstood a challenge at the Supreme Court.

Hoping to restrain advertising's influence, researchers have studied how to immunize children against the effects of television advertising. This research was prompted partly by studies showing that children, especially those under eight years old, (1) have trouble distinguishing commercials from programs and fail to grasp their persuasive intent, (2) trust television advertising rather indiscriminately, and (3) desire and badger their parents for advertised products (Adler et al., 1980; Feshbach, 1980; Palmer & Dorr, 1980). Children, it seems, are an advertiser's dream: gullible, vulnerable, an easy sell. This is why the American Psychological Association has released guidelines about television and youth—to help reduce these potentially negative effects.

Connection:

The role of media in social influence will be discussed further in Module 21.

Critical thinking and diverse opinions may be key. Inner-city Grade 7 students who are able to think critically about ads are also better able to resist peer pressure in Grade 8 and are less likely to drink in Grade 9 (Epstein & Botvin 2008). Further, people who live amid diverse views become more discerning—changing their views in response to strong arguments, but being less likely to accept weak arguments (Levitan & Visser, 2008).

CONCLUSIONS

We encounter persuasive tactics every single day—from simple advertising, to requests for financial and personal contributions from a variety of groups. The best way to build resistance to persuasion probably isn't stronger indoctrination into your existing beliefs. If you are worried that you or one of your friends might be influenced by such a group, you should become aware of the different groups out there and become a critical thinker about what the purposes of the groups are. In order to resist persuasion, you need to prepare yourself to counter persuasive appeals. Groups apply this principle by forewarning members of how families and friends will attack their beliefs. When the expected challenge comes, the member is armed with counterarguments.

The fact the power of persuasion can be used for negative purposes does not mean persuasion is intrinsically bad. Persuasive power enables us to enlighten or deceive. Knowing that these powers can be harnessed for the negative should alert us, as scientists and as citizens, to guard against them. But the powers themselves are neither inherently bad nor inherently good; how we use them determines whether their effect is destructive or constructive. Condemning persuasion because of deceit is like condemning the rain for being wet.

SUMMARY OF KEY POINTS

LO1. Understand the indoctrination tactics groups use.

- Groups use many tactics to influence new members: having members engage in specific behaviours to change their attitudes, using persuasive messages from charismatic communicators, and having the group reinforce the new attitudes through conformity, compliance, and obedience principles.

LO2. Explain how we resist social pressure.

- We resist social pressure through selective information processing, reactance, and motivations to assert our own uniqueness.

LO3. Define attitude inoculation.

- By exposing people to weakened versions of arguments (such as cigarette ads), they can acquire the resources and knowledge to counterargue those persuasive appeals in the future.

KEY TERMS

Attitude inoculation   Exposing people to weak attacks on their attitudes so that when stronger attacks come, they will have refutations available.

Certainty   Refers to the level of subjective confidence or validity a person attaches to his or her attitude.

Cult   A group typically characterized by (1) distinctive rituals and beliefs related to its devotion to a god or a person, (2) isolation from the surrounding "evil" culture, and (3) a charismatic leader. (A sect, by contrast, is a spinoff from a major religion.)

Indoctrination   A process, used by a number of social groups, to teach members a partisan and uncritical acceptance of the group's perspective on issues.

Reactance   A motive to protect or restore one's sense of freedom. Reactance arises when someone threatens our freedom of action.

Selective attention   The extent to which people's attitudes bias the attitude-relevant information they attend to, once exposed.

Selective exposure   The extent to which people's attitudes bias the attitude-relevant information they expose themselves to.

Selective judgment   The extent to which people's attitudes bias how they draw conclusions about the meaning or relevance of information.

Selective memory   The extent to which people's attitudes bias recall and recognition of attitude-relevant information.

Selective perception   The extent to which people's attitudes bias their encoding of information.

How the Presence of Others Affects Our Behaviour

LEARNING OBJECTIVES   After studying Module 12, you will be able to

LO **1**   Understand why we are aroused by the presence of others

LO **2**   Explain social loafing and how to counteract it

LO **3**   Understand the cause and consequences of deindividuation

Imagine yourself in front of a crowd. Perhaps you are preparing to give a speech to a class of 150 students. How would you feel? Is your heart beating fast? Are your palms sweating? Do you feel ill? You might well be suffering from some performance anxiety—you might be afraid of performing badly. Do you think you would feel differently if you were speaking in front of only three friends instead of 150 strangers? Would your performance anxiety go away? When do you think you would perform your best? Do you perform best on your own, or when there are other people around you?

LO 1

THE PRESENCE OF OTHERS

Our world contains not only over 7 billion individuals but also 200 nation-states, 4 million local communities, 20 million economic organizations, and hundreds of millions of other formal and informal groups—couples on dates, families, churches, housemates. How do these groups influence individuals?

Let's begin with social psychology's most elementary question: Are we affected by the mere presence of another person? "Mere presence" means people are not competing, do not reward or punish, and, in fact, do nothing except be present as a passive audience or as co-actors. Would the mere presence of others affect a person's jogging, eating, typing, or exam performance?

Runners often report that they do better on race day than when they run alone. More than a century ago, Norman Triplett (1898), a psychologist interested in bicycle racing, noticed that cyclists' times were faster when racing together than when racing alone against the clock. Before he peddled his hunch (that others' presence boosts performance), Triplett conducted one of social psychology's first laboratory experiments. Children told to wind string on a fishing reel as rapidly as possible wound faster when they worked with co-actors than when they worked alone.

Critical THINKING

In the late nineteenth century, Norman Triplett discovered competitors' times were faster when they competed together rather than alone. Have you ever experienced this for yourself? If so, when? Did you realize what was causing the difference at the time?

Ensuing experiments found that others' presence also improves the speed with which people do simple multiplication problems and cross out designated letters. It also improves the accuracy with which people perform simple motor tasks, such as keeping a metal stick in contact with a dime-sized disk on a moving turntable (called a "pursuit-rotor apparatus"; F. W. Allport, 1920; Dashiell, 1930; Travis, 1925). This social facilitation effect, as it came to be called, also occurs with animals. In the presence of others of their species, ants excavate more sand and chickens eat more grain (Bayer, 1929; Chen, 1937). In the presence of other sexually active rat pairs, mating rats exhibit heightened sexual activity (Larsson, 1956).

However, other studies revealed that on some tasks, the presence of others *hinders* performance. In the presence of others, cockroaches, parakeets, and green finches learn mazes more slowly (Allee &

Masure, 1936; Gates & Allee, 1933; Klopfer, 1958). This disruptive effect also occurs with people. Others' presence diminishes efficiency at learning nonsense syllables, completing a maze, and performing complex multiplication problems (Dashiell, 1930; Pessin, 1933; Pessin & Husband, 1933).

Saying that the presence of others sometimes facilitates performance and sometimes hinders it is about as satisfying as the typical Newfoundland weather forecast—predicting that it might be sunny but then again it might rain. By 1940, research activity in this area had ground to a halt, and it lay dormant for 25 years.

Social psychologist Robert Zajonc wondered if these seemingly contradictory findings could be reconciled. As often happens at creative moments in science, Zajonc (1965) used one field of research to illuminate another. In this case, the illumination came from a well-established principle in experimental psychology: Arousal enhances whatever response tendency is dominant (see Figure 12-1). Increased arousal enhances performance on easy tasks for which the most likely—"dominant"—response is the correct one. People solve easy anagrams, such as *akec*, fastest when they are anxious. On complex tasks, for which the correct answer is not dominant, increased arousal promotes *incorrect* responding. On harder anagrams, people do worse when anxious.

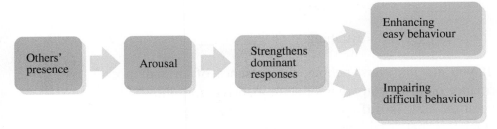

FIGURE 12-1

The effects of social arousal. Robert Zajonc reconciled apparently conflicting findings by proposing that arousal from others' presence strengthens dominant responses (the correct responses only on easy or well-learned tasks).

Could this principle solve the mystery of social facilitation? It seemed reasonable to assume what evidence now confirms—that others' presence will arouse or energize people (Mullen et al., 1997). If social arousal facilitates dominant responses, it should *boost performance on easy tasks and hurt performance on difficult tasks*. Now the confusing results made sense. Winding fishing reels, doing simple multiplication problems, and eating were all easy tasks for which the responses were well learned or naturally dominant. Sure enough, having others around boosted performance. Learning new material, doing a maze, and solving complex math problems were more difficult tasks for which the correct responses were initially less probable. In these cases, the presence of others increased the number of incorrect responses on these tasks. Suddenly, what had looked like contradictory results no longer seemed contradictory. Does this hold for you too? Complete the questions in the Activity box and come to your own conclusions.

After almost 300 studies, conducted with the help of more than 25 000 volunteer participants, the solution has survived (Bond & Titus, 1983; Guerin, 1993, 1999). Several experiments in which Zajonc and his associates manufactured an arbitrary dominant response confirmed that an audience enhanced this response. In one, Zajonc and Stephen Sales (1966) asked people to pronounce various

---

Activity: **The impact of others on everyday behaviour**

How does the presence of others affect you?

On a scale of 1 to 10, where 1 is poor and 10 is excellent, how good are you at:

Playing a musical instrument	_____	Driving a car	_____
Riding a skateboard	_____	Snowboarding	_____
Public speaking	_____	Running	_____

Now, imagine you have an audience (e.g., speaking in front of a group of strangers, driving with your mother, running in a race). On the same rating scale, where 1 is poor and 10 is excellent, how good are you at:

Playing a musical instrument	_____	Driving a car	_____
Riding a skateboard	_____	Snowboarding	_____
Public speaking	_____	Running	_____

Did your ratings change? If you are like most people, the presence of an audience should *improve* your performance on tasks you are good at (e.g., driving, running) but *hinder* your performance when the task is difficult (e.g., public speaking, playing a musical instrument). How does this match with your own experience?

---

nonsense words between one and 16 times. Then they told the people that the same words would appear on a screen, one at a time. Each time, they were to guess which had appeared. When the people were actually shown only random black lines for a hundredth of a second, they "saw" mostly the words they had pronounced most frequently. These words had become the dominant responses. People who took the same test in the presence of two others were even more likely to guess the dominant words (Figure 12-2).

In various ways, later experiments confirmed that social arousal facilitates dominant responses, whether right or wrong. Peter Hunt and Joseph Hillery (1973) found that in others' presence, students took less time to learn a simple maze and more time to learn a complex one (just as the cockroaches do!). James Michaels and his colleagues (1982) found that good pool players in a student union (who had made 71 percent of their shots while being unobtrusively observed) did even better (80 percent) when four observers came up to watch them play. Poor shooters (who had previously averaged 36 percent) did even worse (25 percent) when closely observed.

Athletes perform well-practised skills, which helps explain why they often perform best when energized by the responses of a supportive crowd. Studies of more than 80 000 college and professional athletic events in Canada, the United States, and England reveal that home teams win about 6 in 10 games (somewhat fewer for baseball and football, somewhat more for basketball and soccer). In the last several Olympic games, including the Vancouver 2010 games, home teams did much better than they typically do. The Russians did particularly well during the Sochi 2014 Winter

Average number of responses

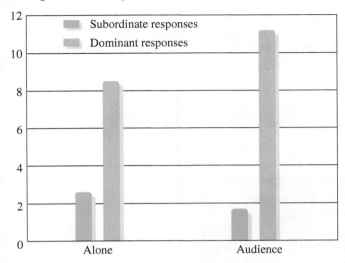

FIGURE 12-2

Social facilitation of dominant responses. People responded with dominant words (practised 16 times) more frequently, and subordinate words (practised only once) less frequently when observers were present.

Olympics, winning the most medals. The Chinese dominance at the Beijing Olympics was a frequent topic of discussion, and as we mentioned Module 6, Canada won more gold medals than any Canadian team has ever won at a winter Olympics when the games were held in Canada.

Connection:

Recall that we discussed athletes' performance in Module 6.

Critical THINKING

Before you read on, consider the following: The idea behind "home-field advantage" is that being in the presence of supporters facilitates the dominant response and enhances simple athletic performance. If this is true, why would it be the case that home advantage typically works for more complex behaviours as well? Curling, for example, is a very complicated sport, yet Canada did very well at the Vancouver Winter Olympics, with the men's and women's teams winning gold and silver medals, respectively (of course, they did even better in Sochi, winning two gold medals). Are there other reasons teams and athletes might do well at home?

Some research by Stephen Bray and his colleagues at the University of Lethbridge (see Bray et al., 2003) suggests that home-field advantage is not always an advantage. In this research, the authors found that home field was more of an advantage for good teams than for poor-performing teams.

More specifically, they found that British professional soccer teams were more likely to tie their home games if they were poor-performing teams. Higher-quality teams were less likely to tie home games. The home advantage may, however, also stem from the players' familiarity with their home environment, less travel fatigue, feelings of dominance derived from territorial control, or increased team identity when cheered by fans (Zillmann & Paulus, 1993).

Connection:

We discussed attributions for the Olympic hockey team performances in Module 6.

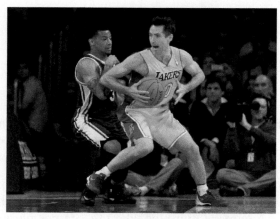

Los Angeles Lakers' Steve Nash, right, in possession of the ball. Would the presence of a crowd hinder or help his performance?

CROWDING: THE PRESENCE OF MANY OTHERS

So people do respond to others' presence. But does the presence of observers really arouse people? In times of stress, a comrade can be comforting. But with others present, people perspire more, breathe faster, tense their muscles more, and have higher blood pressure and a faster heart rate (Geen & Gange, 1983; Moore & Baron, 1983). Even a supportive audience may elicit poorer performance on challenging tasks (Butler & Baumeister, 1998). Having Mom and Dad at your first piano recital likely won't boost your performance.

The effect of other people increases with their number (Jackson & Latané, 1981; Knowles, 1983). Sometimes the arousal and self-conscious attention created by a large audience interferes even with well-learned, automatic behaviours, such as speaking. Given *extreme* pressure, we're vulnerable to failure. Stutterers tend to stutter more in front of larger audiences than when speaking to just one or two people (Mullen, 1986b). College basketball players become slightly *less* accurate in their free-throw shooting when very highly aroused by a packed rather than a near-empty stadium (Sokoll & Mynatt, 1984). In fact, Larry Leith at the University of Toronto (Geisler & Leith, 1997) has demonstrated that, in a sports context, just thinking about failure can cause you to fail. Leith had 80 students try to complete 25 basketball free throws. He randomly assigned participants to a condition where they were asked to think about missing the free throw, or not. He found that simply thinking about failing actually caused participants to miss more free throws.

Applying Social Psychology

When reading about the effects of crowding, some of you may have thought, "But I don't like crowds!" Crowding is very related to the idea of territoriality. Territoriality, in which a specific space is marked out and defended against intrusion from others, is common in many animals. It serves important functions, such as providing a place for food, shelter, and caring for the young.

How is territoriality present in humans? Altman (1975) identified three common types of territory:

1. Primary territories are places over which the occupant has exclusive control (e.g., homes, apartments, and private offices).

2. Secondary territories are areas shared with others but over which regular users have considerable control (e.g., a classroom, church, or neighbourhood bar).

3. Public territories are uncontrolled areas that are used by whoever is the first to arrive (e.g., telephone booths, theatres, and parks).

In each type of territory, people may mark out space as their own and defend it against intrusion. "No trespassing" signs, fences, or hedges are common markers used by homeowners. Leaving articles of personal clothing or books and magazines on tables or chairs protects one's place in secondary or public territories.

Why do people want a territory? There are probably several reasons. It may give people a sense of security and make their lives seem more predictable and important. Some researchers have suggested that territoriality may protect people from those whom they fear or dislike. It may also foster the person's sense of self-identity and uniqueness. People are more assertive and dominant when they are in their own territories. Consider the following:

1. How do the concepts of personal space and territoriality differ? How is human territoriality different from that of non-human species?

2. What are the advantages to being the home team in sports? (Hint: We just learned them.)

3. How do people respond to invasions of their territory?

Being *in* a crowd also intensifies positive or negative reactions. When they sit close together, friendly people are liked even more, and *un*friendly people are *dis*liked even more (Schiffenbauer & Schiavo, 1976; Storms & Thomas, 1977).

Connection:

We will discuss the role of proximity in attraction in Module 19.

In experiments with Columbia University students and with Ontario Science Centre visitors, Jonathan Freedman and his colleagues (1979, 1980) had an accomplice listen to a humorous tape or watch a movie with other subjects. When they all sat close together, the accomplice could more readily induce the subjects to laugh and clap. As theatre directors and sports fans know, and as researchers have confirmed, a "good house" is a full house (Aiello et al., 1983; Worchel & Brown, 1984).

Perhaps you've noticed that a class of 35 students feels warmer and more lively in a room that seats just 35 than when spread around a room that seats 100. This occurs partly because when others are close by, we are more likely to notice and join in their laughter or clapping. But crowding also enhances arousal, as Gary Evans (1979) found. He tested 10-person groups of University of Massachusetts students, either in a room 20 by 30 feet (about 6 by 9 metres) or in one 8 by 12 feet (about 2.4 by 3.7 metres). Compared to those in the large room, those densely packed had higher pulse rates and blood pressure (indicating arousal). Though their performance on simple tasks did not suffer, on difficult tasks they made more errors. In a study of university students in India, Dinesh Nagar and Janak Pandey (1987) similarly found that crowding hampered performance only on complex tasks, such as solving difficult anagrams. So, crowding enhances arousal, which facilitates dominant responses.

WHY ARE WE AROUSED IN THE PRESENCE OF OTHERS?

To this point we have seen that what you do well, you will be energized to do best in front of others (unless you become hyperaroused and self-conscious). What you find difficult may seem impossible in the same circumstances. What is it about other people that causes arousal? There is evidence to support three possible factors (Aiello & Douhitt, 2001; Feinberg & Aiello, 2006): evaluation apprehension, distraction, and mere presence.

Evaluation Apprehension

Nickolas Cottrell surmised that observers make us apprehensive because we wonder how they are evaluating us. To test whether or not evaluation apprehension exists, Cottrell and his associates (1968) repeated Zajonc and Sales's nonsense-syllable study at Kent State University and added a third condition. In this "mere presence" condition, they blindfolded observers, supposedly in preparation for a perception experiment. In contrast to the effect of the watching audience, the mere presence of these blind-folded people did *not* boost well-practised responses.

Other experiments confirmed Cottrell's conclusion: The enhancement of dominant responses is strongest when people think they are being evaluated. In one experiment, joggers on a University of California at Santa Barbara jogging path sped up as they came upon a woman seated on the grass—*if* she was facing them rather than sitting with her back turned (Worringham & Messick, 1983).

Evaluation apprehension also helps explain the following:

- Why people perform best when their co-actor is slightly superior (Seta, 1982).
- Why arousal lessens when a high-status group is diluted by adding people whose opinions don't matter to us (Seta & Seta, 1992).
- Why the people who worry most about others' evaluations are the ones most affected by their presence (Gastorf et al., 1980; Geen & Gange, 1983).

- Why social-facilitation effects are greatest when the others are unfamiliar and hard to keep an eye on (Guerin & Innes, 1982).

The self-consciousness we feel when being evaluated can also interfere with behaviours that we perform best automatically (Mullen & Baumeister, 1987). If self-conscious basketball players analyze their body movements while shooting critical free throws, they are more likely to miss.

Distraction

Glenn Sanders, Robert Baron, and Danny Moore (1978; Baron, 1986) carried evaluation apprehension a step further. They theorized that when people wonder how co-actors are doing or how an audience is reacting, they get distracted. This *conflict* between paying attention to others and paying attention to the task overloads the cognitive system, causing arousal. Evidence that people are indeed "driven to distraction" comes from experiments that produce social facilitation, not just by the presence of another person, but even by a non-human distraction, such as bursts of light (Sanders, 1981a, 1981b).

Mere Presence

Zajonc, however, believes that the mere presence of others produces some arousal even without evaluation apprehension or arousing distraction. For example, people's colour preferences are stronger when they make judgments with others present (Goldman, 1967). On such a task, there is no "good" or "right" answer for others to evaluate, and thus no reason to be concerned with their reactions. Still, others' presence is energizing.

Recall that facilitation effects also occur with non-human animals. This hints at an innate social arousal mechanism common to much of the zoological world. (Animals probably are not consciously worrying about how other animals are evaluating them.) At the human level, most joggers are energized when jogging with someone else, even one who neither competes nor evaluates.

This is a good time to remind ourselves of the purpose of a theory. A good theory is scientific shorthand: it simplifies and summarizes a variety of observations. Social-facilitation theory does this well. It is a simple summary of many research findings. A good theory also offers clear predictions that (1) help confirm or modify the theory, (2) guide new exploration, and (3) suggest practical applications. Social-facilitation theory has definitely generated the first two types of prediction: (1) The basics of the theory (that the presence of others is arousing and that this social arousal enhances dominant responses) have been confirmed, and (2) the theory has brought new life to a long-dormant field of research.

Connection:

Remember we discussed the definition of a good theory in Module 1.

Does it also suggest some practical applications? Many new office buildings have replaced private offices with large, open areas divided by low partitions. Might the resulting awareness of others' presence help boost the performance of well-learned tasks, but disrupt creative thinking on complex tasks? Can you think of other possible applications?

LO 2

SOCIAL LOAFING

Think about the last time you worked on a group project. (Many of you may be doing one right now!) Have you ever been in a group where one person was not pulling his or her weight? Have you ever been that person, slacking off a bit because you know you can get away with it? We all do it, under certain conditions. This can be particularly frustrating when a person who has done little or no work will get the same credit as those who did more work. What can you do in these situations to make that person work harder? Does the culture you come from make a difference? If not, why not?

Social facilitation usually occurs when people work toward individual goals and when their efforts can be individually evaluated. These situations parallel some everyday work situations. A team tug-of-war provides one such example. Organizational fundraising—pooling the proceeds from selling cookies, plants, or candy to pay for the class trip—provides another. So does a class project in which all get the same grade. On such "additive tasks," will team spirit boost productivity? One way to address such questions is with laboratory simulations.

Many Hands Make Light Work

Nearly a century ago, French engineer Max Ringelmann (reported by Kravitz & Martin, 1986) found that the collective effort of such teams was but half the sum of the individual efforts. This suggests, contrary to the common "in unity there is strength" notion, that group members may actually be *less* motivated when performing additive tasks. Maybe, though, poor performance stemmed from poor coordination—people pulling a rope in slightly different directions at slightly different times. A group of researchers led by Alan Ingham (1974) cleverly eliminated this problem by making individuals think others were pulling with them, when in fact they were pulling alone. Blindfolded participants were assigned the first position in the apparatus shown in the photo below and told, "Pull as

The rope-pulling apparatus. People in the first position pulled less hard when they thought people behind them were also pulling.

hard as you can." They pulled 18 percent harder when they knew they were pulling alone than when they believed that behind them two to five people were also pulling. While completing his Ph.D. at Carleton University, Frederick Lichacz replicated the original Ringlemann study and added a couple of other twists (see Lichacz & Partington, 1996). He found that giving feedback to the participants on their performance was effective at increasing their individual efforts. In addition, he found that if people had experience with the task, they exerted a greater effort than if the task were a novel one for them.

Researchers Bibb Latané, Kipling Williams, and Stephen Harkins (1979; Harkins et al., 1980) kept their ears open for other ways to investigate this phenomenon, which they labelled social loafing. They observed that the noise produced by six people shouting or clapping "as loud as you can" was less than three times that produced by one person alone. Like the tug-of-war task, however, noise-making is vulnerable to group inefficiency. So Latané and his associates followed Ingham's example by leading their Ohio State University participants to believe others were shouting or clapping with them, when in fact they were doing so alone.

Their method was to blindfold six people, seat them in a semicircle, and have them put on headphones, over which they were blasted with the sound of people shouting or clapping. People could not hear their own shouting or clapping, much less that of others. On various trials they were instructed to shout or clap either alone or along with the group. People who were told about this experiment guessed the subjects would shout louder when with others, because they would be less inhibited (Harkins, 1981). The actual result? Social loafing: When the participants believed five others were also either shouting or clapping, they produced one-third less noise than when they thought themselves alone. Social loafing occurred even when the subjects were high school cheerleaders who believed themselves to be cheering together or alone (Hardy & Latané, 1986).

John Sweeney (1973), a political scientist interested in the policy implications of social loafing, observed the phenomenon in an experiment at the University of Texas. Students pumped exercise bicycles more energetically (as measured by electrical output) when they knew they were being individually monitored than when they thought their output was being pooled with that of other riders. In the group condition, people were tempted to free ride; free riders benefited from the group but gave little in return. Recent work has found that if we know that we are going to perform a group task, we even prepare less than if we were performing the task alone (Ohlert & Kleinart, 2013).

In this and 160 other studies (Karau & Williams, 1993), we see a twist on one of the psychological forces that makes for social facilitation: evaluation apprehension. In the social loafing experiments, individuals believe they are evaluated only when they act alone. The group situation (rope pulling, shouting, and so forth) *decreases* evaluation apprehension. When people are not accountable and cannot evaluate their own efforts, responsibility is diffused across all group members (Harkins & Jackson, 1985; Kerr & Bruun, 1981). By contrast, the social-facilitation experiments *increased* exposure to evaluation. When made the centre of attention, people self-consciously monitor their behaviour (Mullen & Baumeister, 1987). So the principle is the same: when being observed *increases* evaluation concerns, social facilitation occurs; when being lost in a crowd *decreases* evaluation concerns, social loafing occurs (see Figure 12-3). We even see social loafing in online groups (Shiue et al., 2010; see also Zoghbi-Manrique-de-Lara, 2009) and when members of online groups loaf, group cohesion suffers.

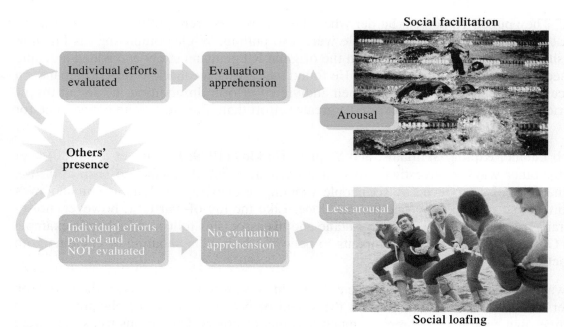

FIGURE 12-3

Social facilitation or social loafing? When individuals cannot be evaluated or held accountable, loafing becomes more likely. An individual swimmer is evaluated on her ability to win the race. In a tug-of-war, no single person on the team is held accountable, so any one member might relax or loaf.

To motivate group members, one strategy is to make individual performance identifiable. Some football coaches do this by filming and evaluating each player individually. Ohio State researchers had group members wear individual microphones while engaged in group shouting (Williams et al., 1981). Whether in a group or not, people exert more effort when their outputs are individually identifiable: university swim team members swim faster in intrasquad relay races when someone monitors and announces their individual times (Williams et al., 1989). Even without pay consequences, actual assembly line workers in one small experiment produced 16 percent more product when their individual output was identified (Faulkner & Williams, 1996).

Social Loafing in Everyday Life

How widespread is social loafing? Surely collective effort does not always lead to slacking off.

The evidence assures us that it does not. People in groups loaf less when the task is *challenging, appealing*, or *involving* (Karau & Williams, 1993). On challenging tasks, people may perceive their efforts as indispensable (Harkins & Petty, 1982; Kerr, 1983; Kerr & Bruun, 1983). When people see others in their group as unreliable or as unable to contribute much, they work harder (Plaks & Higgins, 2000; Williams & Karau, 1991). Adding incentives or challenging a group to strive for certain standards also promotes collective effort (Harkins & Szymanski, 1989; Shepperd & Wright, 1989). Finally, recent research has suggested (e.g., Pearsall et al., 2009) that hybrid reward systems, where the group benefits from cooperation and individuals are also identified for specific activities, further reduces social loafing.

Groups also loaf less when their members are *friends* or identified with their group, rather than strangers (Davis & Greenlees, 1992; Karau & Williams, 1997; Worchel et al., 1998). Even just expecting to interact with someone again serves to increase effort on team projects (Groenenboom et al., 2001). Latané notes that Israel's communal kibbutz farms have actually out-produced Israel's non-collective farms (Leon, 1969). Cohesiveness intensifies effort. So will there be social loafing in group-centred cultures? To find out, Latané and his colleagues (Gabrenya et al., 1985) headed for Asia, where they repeated their sound production experiments in Japan, Thailand, Taiwan, India, and Malaysia. Their findings? Social loafing was evident in all these countries, too.

Seventeen later studies in Asia reveal that people in collectivist cultures do, however, exhibit less social loafing than do people in individualist cultures (Karau & Williams, 1993; Kugihara, 1999; Hong et al., 2008). As we noted earlier, loyalty to family and work groups runs strong in collectivist cultures. Likewise, women tend to be less individualistic than men—and to exhibit less social loafing.

So while social loafing is a common occurrence when group members work collectively and without individual accountability, many hands need not always make light work. So, how do you get other students to do their share of the work when you are working on a joint task? Take a look at the principles outlined in this module and write down a few ideas.

LO 3

THE CAUSES AND CONSEQUENCES OF DEINDIVIDUATION

The suicide attempt and subsequent death of Cole Harbour, Nova Scotia, high school student Rehtaeh Parsons led national and international news for several days in the spring of 2013. In November 2011, Rehtaeh was drinking at a party and while intoxicated was gang-raped by four other teenagers. The assault was photographed and photos of the event were widely distributed on Facebook. Rehtaeh was bullied and teased, and was repeatedly sent messages asking for sex. Though the rape was reported to police, no charges were laid until after her death 17 months later. Ultimately, two of the teenagers who posted photos of the rape were charged with creating and distributing child pornography. But people asked themselves, "How could these kids have done this?" Would they have committed the same crime if they had been on their own, or did being in the group influence their behaviour? Was distributing the photos easier because it could be done essentially anonymously, online?

A woman holds a photo of Rehtaeh Parsons during a community vigil in her memory.

Social facilitation experiments show that groups can arouse people. Social loafing experiments show that groups can diffuse responsibility. When arousal and diffused responsibility combine, and normal inhibitions diminish, the results may be startling. People may commit acts that range from a mild lessening of restraint (swearing at a referee, screaming during a rock concert) to impulsive self-gratification, to destructive behaviour (rioting, gang-rape, beatings). Of course, **deindividuation** does not always have to be negative. We cheer loudly in support of our teams at sporting events, and protesting crowds can lead to positive social change.

However, these unrestrained behaviours have something in common: they are somehow provoked by the power of a group. Groups can generate a sense of excitement, of being caught up in something bigger than one's self. In certain kinds of group situations, people are more likely to abandon normal restraints, to lose their sense of individual identity, to become responsive to group or crowd norms—in a word, to become what Leon Festinger, Albert Pepitone, and Theodore Newcomb (1952) labelled *deindividuated*. What circumstances elicit this psychological state?

A protester clashes with police during an anti-police brutality demonstration in Montreal.

As world leaders meet in Toronto, Ontario, for the G20/G8 summit, protesters and anarchists meet police and burn police cars.

GROUP SIZE

After the Montreal Canadiens won the Stanley Cup in 1993, Montrealers celebrated in a rather unexpected way—they rioted. Similar riots have broken out in cities after local sports teams have won championships (e.g., Chicago, Detroit; CNN, 2001). More recently, after winning in the *first round* of the 2010 playoffs, Montreal Canadiens fans rioted again (CBC, 2010). During the 2006 NHL playoffs, fans of the Edmonton Oilers rioted after the Oilers took the lead in their division series (CBC, 2006)! Riots such as these, as well as those that occurred in Paris in October 2005 (CBC, 2005), in Toronto during the 2010 G20 conference, and after the Vancouver Canucks lost the Stanley Cup final in 2011, can cause millions of dollars in damage and sometimes cost people their lives. Why does this happen? Perfectly normal and respectable people can find themselves involved in and participating in rioting. Indeed, one of Steven's friends—now a tenured professor at a Canadian university—actually participated in the Toronto riot that occurred after the Blue Jays won the World Series.

A group has the power not only to arouse its members but also to render them unidentifiable: they perceive the action as the *group's*. Rioters, made faceless by the mob, are freed to loot. In an analysis of 21 instances in which crowds were present as someone threatened to jump from a building or bridge, Leon Mann (1981) found that when the crowd was small and exposed by daylight, people did not usually try to bait the person. But when a large crowd or the cover of night gave people anonymity, the crowd usually baited and jeered. Brian Mullen (1986a) reports a similar effect of lynch mobs: the bigger the mob, the more its members lose self-awareness and become willing to commit atrocities, such as burning, lacerating, or dismembering a victim.

PHYSICAL ANONYMITY

We can experiment with anonymity to see if it actually lessens inhibitions. In one creative experiment, Philip Zimbardo (1970, 2002) dressed women in identical white coats and hoods, rather like Ku Klux Klan members (see the photo below). This was also the reasoning behind dressing up the guards and prisoners in identical uniforms during his prison experiment. He got the idea for the experiment from his undergraduate students, who wondered how the "good boys" depicted in William Golding's *Lord of the Flies* could so suddenly become monstrous after painting their faces. Women in the experiment (who were wearing the coats and hoods) pressed the shock button twice as long as women who were visible and wearing large name tags when asked to deliver electric shocks to a woman.

Anonymous women delivered more shock to helpless victims
than identifiable women did.

These experiments make us wonder about the effect of wearing uniforms. Preparing for battle, warriors in some tribal cultures (like rabid fans of some sports teams) depersonalize themselves with body and face paints or special masks. After the battle, some cultures kill, torture, or mutilate any remaining enemies; other cultures take prisoners alive. Robert Watson (1973) scrutinized anthropological files and discovered that the cultures with depersonalized warriors were also the cultures that brutalized their enemies. But does this have a consequential impact on behaviour? In Northern Ireland, 206 of 500 violent attacks studied by Andrew Silke (2003) were conducted by attackers who wore masks, hoods, or other facial disguises. Compared with undisguised attackers, these anonymous attackers inflicted more serious injuries, attacked more people, and committed more vandalism. And of course, there is the Stanford Prison Experiment and the recent replications. (If you have not yet watched the original video, now would be a good time).

Does becoming physically anonymous *always* unleash our worst impulses? Fortunately, no. In an experiment at the University of Georgia, women put on nurses' uniforms before deciding how much shock someone should receive. When those wearing the nurses' uniforms were made anonymous, they became *less* aggressive in administering shocks than when their names and personal identities were stressed.

Connection:

Remember we discussed the impact of the role we take on in behaviour in Module 8, and the role of self-concept on behaviour in Module 3.

From their analysis of 60 deindividuation studies, Tom Postmes and Russell Spears (1998; see also Jetten et al., 2004; Van Zomeren et al., 2008) conclude that being anonymous makes one less self-conscious, more group-conscious, and more responsive to cues present in the situation, whether negative (Klan uniforms) or positive (nurses' uniforms). Thus, deindividuation can actually lead to more positive behaviour, depending on the group norms. Given altruistic cues, deindividuated people even give more money (Spivey & Prentice-Dunn, 1990).

This helps explain why wearing black uniforms—which are traditionally associated with evil and death—have an effect opposite to that of wearing nurses' uniforms. Mark Frank and Thomas Gilovich (1988) report that, led by the Los Angeles Raiders and the Philadelphia Flyers, black-uniformed teams consistently ranked near the top of the National Football and Hockey Leagues in penalties assessed between 1970 and 1986. Follow-up laboratory research suggests that just putting on black jerseys can trigger wearers to behave more aggressively.

Being part of a team can have other effects as well. Sports teams frequently use tactics designed to increase group cohesion among its members. One tactic sports teams use at times is the "hazing" of new players. New players are picked on, degraded, and even physically and sexually assaulted. Presumably, if it is difficult to become a member of the team, you will like it more once you become a member. The more effort we put into something, the more we appreciate it. (Think back to cognitive dissonance theory—if it was this hard to get in it must be great!)

However, sometimes hazing rituals go too far. There are a number of well-publicized hazing incidents inside and outside sports. For example, in the fall of 2005, the McGill Redmen football team had its season cancelled after a number of rookies were gagged, forced into degrading positions, and sexually assaulted with a broomstick. As we noted in the previous module, the Dalhousie women's hockey team was suspended for the whole season for their undisclosed hazing behaviour. In 2013, 11 high school students in Saskatchewan were charged after a hazing incident involving Grade 9 and 10 students at a high school. In 2008 three soccer players from the Yukon were suspended for binding their under-14 teammates with athletic tape and plastic wrap and beating them with wet towels. In 2010 two Mississauga Transportation supervisors were suspended for hazing other employees, including video-taping them while they were bound and had water balloons thrown at them. Although these behaviours are widely condemned, they are still disturbingly frequent.

Connection:

In Module 11 we discussed how sports teams can use indoctrination tactics like hazing.

AROUSING AND DISTRACTING ACTIVITIES

Aggressive outbursts by large groups often are preceded by minor actions that arouse and divert people's attention. Group shouting, chanting, clapping, or dancing serve both to hype people up and to reduce self-consciousness.

An excellent example of this is the well-publicized behaviour of a group of fans at a Detroit Pistons game in November 2004. It started innocently enough when Ron Artest of the Indiana Pacers fouled a Pistons player. A fight broke out between the two players and the crowd quickly got involved, throwing beer cups, trash, and other debris at the Pacers players. Remarkably, Ron Artest and two other teammates waded into the crowd and began fighting with the fans. This behaviour likely occurred because the fans believed that they could not be individually identified in the large crowd. Interestingly, many of the fans who caused the trouble were identified shortly after the fight, as television cameras had continued to roll. Many of the fans were subsequently featured in news stories and identified by the public.

A similar approach was used to identify Guns N' Roses fans who rioted in Vancouver after the band cancelled a show at the last minute. The website the police set up received 12 000 hits per day in the first week, producing more than 80 useful tips. The Montreal police announced they would do the same thing after the Canadiens' playoff games. After the Vancouver Canucks lost in the Stanley Cup final in 2011, the riots that followed cost the city millions. Interestingly, the police turned to Facebook and other social media for tips, and received tens of thousands.

When we see others act as we are acting, we think they feel as we do, which reinforces our own feelings (Orive, 1984). Moreover, impulsive group action absorbs our attention. When we yell at the referee, we are not thinking about our values; we are reacting to the immediate situation. Later, when we stop to think about what we have done or said, we sometimes feel chagrined.

DIMINISHED SELF-AWARENESS

Group experiences that diminish self-consciousness tend to disconnect behaviour from attitudes. Dawn Mewhinney at the University of Guelph found that people's expectations of a situation may influence this phenomenon. For example, Mewhinney and her colleagues (1995) found that Canadian students going on spring break in Daytona Beach, Florida, felt anonymous and believed that casual sex was both common and accessible. Perhaps not surprisingly, then, combining the perceptions of anonymity and perceived social norms, these students were more likely to engage in unplanned sexual activity. Consistent with this, experiments by Steven Prentice-Dunn and Ronald Rogers (1989) reveal that un–self-conscious, deindividuated people are less restrained, less self-regulated, more likely to act without thinking about their own values, and more responsive to the situation.

These findings complement and reinforce the experiments on *self-awareness*. We should take a moment to understand the distinction between private self-awareness (being aware of our own internal states) versus public self-awareness (being aware of how others are seeing us at a particular moment).

Self-awareness is the opposite of deindividuation. Those made privately self-aware by acting in front of a mirror exhibit *increased* self-control, and their actions more clearly reflect their attitudes. In front of a mirror, people taste-testing cream cheese varieties eat less of the high-fat variety (Sentyrz

& Bushman, 1998). People made privately self-aware are also less likely to cheat (Beaman et al., 1979; Diener & Wallbom, 1976). So are those who generally have a strong sense of themselves as distinct and independent (Nadler et al., 1982).

Public self-awareness comes from a perception of being watched in person or remotely (or not) by others. With the police using Facebook and other social media for tips, perhaps this will ultimately increase self-awareness. Anonymity leads to reduced public self-awareness. Public self-awareness leads to evaluation apprehension and a sense of needing to adhere to social standards. People who are self-conscious, or who are temporarily made so, exhibit greater consistency between their words outside a situation and their deeds in it. Circumstances that decrease self-awareness, as alcohol consumption does, therefore increase deindividuation (Hull et al., 1983). And deindividuation decreases in circumstances that increase public self-awareness: mirrors and cameras, small towns, bright lights, large name tags, undistracted quiet, and individual clothes and houses (Ickes et al., 1978). When a teenager leaves for a party, a parent's parting advice could well be "Have fun, and remember who you are." In other words, enjoy being with the group, but be self-aware, maintain your personal identity, don't become deindividuated.

CONCLUSIONS

Thus, we have seen that the mere presence of others can affect our behaviour in a number of ways. The extent to which this effect will be positive or negative depends substantially on how we interpret the situation and how confident we feel in our own abilities. The take-home message of this module is simple—we are not isolated in our social worlds; thus, we need to be aware of the influences others have on us if we are to ensure that we make the right choices.

SUMMARY OF KEY POINTS

LO1. Understand why we are aroused by the presence of others.

- The presence of others creates arousal, which can distract us, making it more difficult to perform complex task, but also make it easier to perform simple tasks.

LO2. Explain social loafing and how to counteract it.

- Social loafing can be reduced by assigning tasks and making individual contributions identifiable.

LO3. Understand the cause and consequences of deindividuation.

- Loss of self-awareness and evaluation apprehension can lead people to behave in ways closer to the group norms; this can cause more positive or more negative behaviour, depending on the norm activated.

KEY TERMS

Co-actors   Co-participants working individually on a non-competitive activity.

Deindividuation   Loss of self-awareness and evaluation apprehension; occurs in group situations that foster responsiveness to group norms, good or bad.

Evaluation apprehension   Concern for how others are evaluating us.

Free riders   People who benefit from the group but give little in return.

Private self-awareness   Being aware of our own internal states.

Public self-awareness   Being aware of how others are seeing us at a particular moment.

Social facilitation   (1) Original meaning—the tendency of people to perform simple or well-learned tasks better when others are present. (2) Current meaning—the strengthening of dominant (prevalent or likely) responses in the presence of others.

Social loafing   The tendency for people to exert less effort when they pool their efforts toward a common goal than when they are individually accountable.

MODULE THIRTEEN

How Groups Intensify Decisions

Indo-Canadians celebrate the Canadian men's hockey gold medal win at the 2010 Winter Olympics in Vancouver, B.C.

Have you ever sat on a committee that had to make a decision? Have you ever been part of a student group or a group of friends trying to plan an event? Have you ever seen this turn into an absolute disaster? Typically, when groups get together to make decisions, this is a good thing. Group members can share the effort, as well as provide multiple cognitive resources and different ways of thinking about the problem and solutions. However, group decision-making must be done carefully. Because of the social influences working within them, groups can make poor decisions—decisions that sometimes have devastating consequences.

There is no question that the impact of any group can be both positive and negative. Research helps clarify our understanding of the likelihood of positive versus negative outcomes, and studies of people in small groups have produced a principle that helps explain both bad and good outcomes: *Group discussion often strengthens members' initial inclinations.* The research on this process, called group polarization, illustrates the steps people go through during scientific inquiry—how an interesting discovery often leads researchers to hasty and erroneous conclusions, which ultimately get replaced with more accurate conclusions. This is a scientific mystery that one this textbook's authors, David, can discuss firsthand, having been one of the detectives.

Critical THINKING

In 2013, a scandal erupted in the Canadian Senate. Senator Mike Duffy was forced to pay back housing reimbursements that had been allegedly fraudulent. Later, it was revealed that the prime minister's chief of staff personally reimbursed Duffy $90 000 after he paid the money back. Debate raged about "who knew what when" and whether or not Prime Minister Stephen Harper was involved. Clearly, some very poor decisions were made. What information, if any, do you think would have changed these decisions? Why do you think the decisions seemed so right at the time, but so wrong later?

Mike Duffy, Canadian Senator for Prince Edward Island.

LO 1

THE "RISKY SHIFT" PHENOMENON

Research literature, which now includes more than 300 studies, began with a surprising finding by James Stoner (1961), then an MIT graduate student. For his master's thesis, Stoner tested the commonly held belief that groups are more cautious than individuals. He posed decision dilemmas in which participants were asked to advise imagined characters in stories how much risk to take. How do you think the group decisions compared to the average decision before the discussions? Would the groups be likely to take greater risks, be more cautious, or stay the same?

To everyone's amazement, the group decisions were usually riskier. Dubbed the "risky shift phenomenon," this finding set off a wave of group risk-taking studies. These revealed that risky shift does not just occur when a group decides by consensus; after a brief discussion, individuals, too, will alter their decisions. Researchers successfully repeated Stoner's finding with people of varying ages and occupations in a dozen nations.

Here was a delightful puzzle: The small risky shift effect was reliable, unexpected, and without any immediately obvious explanation. So, what are the group influences that produce such an effect? And how widespread is it? Do discussions in juries, business committees, and military organizations also promote risk taking? Does this explain why teenage reckless driving, as measured by death rates, nearly doubles when a 16- or 17-year-old driver has two passengers rather than none (Chen et al., 2000)? This is one of the reasons that most provinces issue *graduated* drivers' permits to new drivers. These drivers must observe strict limitations (e.g., a 0.00 blood alcohol level, no driving alone after midnight, and no infractions) for a period of years before they can obtain an unrestricted licence.

After several years of study, as the methodology and approach evolved, we learned that the risky shift is not universal. Sometimes people become *more cautious* after discussion with group members. Researchers realized that this group phenomenon was not a consistent shift to risky behaviour, but rather a tendency for group discussion to *enhance* group members' initial leanings. This idea led investigators to propose what Serge Moscovici and Marisa Zavalloni (1969) called a *group polarization*: discussion typically strengthens the average inclination of group members.

LO 2

GROUP POLARIZATION EXPERIMENTS

This new view of the changes induced by group discussion prompted experimenters to have people discuss statements that most of them favoured or most of them opposed. Would talking in groups enhance their initial inclinations, as it did with the decision dilemmas? That's what the group polarization hypothesis predicts (see Figure 13-1).

Dozens of studies confirm group polarization. Moscovici and Zavalloni (1969) observed that discussion enhanced French students' initially positive attitude toward their president and negative attitude toward Americans. Mititoshi Isozaki (1984) found that Japanese university students gave more pronounced judgments of "guilty" after discussing a traffic case. And Glen Whyte (1993) reported that groups exacerbate the "too much invested to quit" phenomenon that has cost many businesses huge sums of money. Canadian business students imagined themselves having to decide whether to invest more money in the hope of preventing losses in various failing projects (e.g., whether or not to make a high-risk loan to protect an earlier investment). They exhibited the typical effect: 72 percent of individuals chose to reinvest money they would seldom have invested if they were considering a project on its own merits as a new investment. When making the same decision in groups, 94 percent opted for reinvestment.

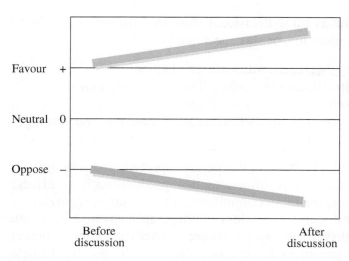

FIGURE 13-1

The group polarization hypothesis predicts that discussion will strengthen an attitude shared by group members. If people initially tend to favour something (say, risk on a life dilemma), they tend to favour it even more after discussion. If they tend to oppose something, they tend to oppose it even more after discussion.

Does discussion with like-minded people strengthen shared views? Does it magnify the attitude gap that separates two opposing sides? One of this textbook's authors, David, and a colleague, George Bishop, wondered. So, they set up groups of relatively prejudiced and unprejudiced high school students and asked them to respond—before and after discussion—to issues involving racial attitudes, such as property rights versus open housing (Myers & Bishop, 1970). They found that the discussions among like-minded students did indeed increase the initial gap between the two groups.

Naturally Occurring Group Polarization

Connection:

The role of similarity in attraction will be discussed in greater detail in Module 19.

In everyday life, people associate mostly with others whose attitudes are similar to their own. Does everyday group interaction with like-minded friends intensify shared attitudes? Do nerds become nerdier and jocks jockier? It happens. The self-segregation of boys into all-male groups and of girls into all-female groups accentuates over time their initially modest gender differences, notes Eleanor Maccoby (2002). Boys with boys become gradually more competitive and action oriented in their play and fictional fare, while girls with girls become more relationally oriented.

Group polarization also occurs in U.S. Courts of Appeals. In the United States, judges at the federal level are appointed by the president. It may not surprise you to learn that judges appointed by a

Republican are more likely to vote more conservatively than Democrat-appointed judges (Schkade & Sunstein, 2003). But such tendencies are accentuated among like-minded judges. Schkade and Sunstein found that a Republican appointee who makes decisions with other Republican appointees makes more conservative decisions than when he or she is making a decision with at least one Democratic appointee.

Polarization also occurs in communities. For example, David Brooks (2005) observed, "Conservative places attract conservatives and become more so." During community conflicts, like-minded people associate increasingly with one another, amplifying their shared tendencies. Gang delinquency emerges from a process of mutual reinforcement within neighbourhood gangs, whose members share attributes and hostilities (Ezeonu, 2010). If, on your block, "a second out-of-control 15-year-old moves in," found David Lykken (1997), "the mischief they get into as a team is likely to be more than merely double what the first would do on his own. . . . A gang is more dangerous than the sum of its individual parts." Indeed, "unsupervised peer groups" are "the strongest predictor" of a neighbourhood's crime victimization rate, report Veysey and Messner (1999). Moreover, experimental interventions that group delinquent adolescents with other delinquents actually increase the rate of problem behaviour—no surprise to any group polarization researcher (Dishion et al., 1999). This is true of politics as well. The percentage of "landslide counties" in U.S. presidential elections (counties where more than 60 percent of voters voted for one candidate) nearly doubled between 1976 and 2000 (Bishop, 2004).

Connection:

Remember we discussed gang membership in Module 11.

Email and electronic chat rooms provide a great medium for group interaction. By 2013, almost 100 percent of Canada's 25.5 million Internet users logged on daily (techvibes.com, 2014). Eighty-five percent of Grade 7 students surveyed in Montreal use the Internet for up to ten hours weekly (Barnett et al., 2008). Fifteen percent of those use the Internet more than ten hours per week. Facebook hit 1.2 billion users in 2013, with 19 million Canadians logging on at least once per month, and almost 10 million using it daily. On average, Canadians are on the Internet over 41 hours per month (Canadian Press, 2013). The Internet's countless virtual groups enable peacemakers and neo-Nazis, geeks and Goths, vegans and vampires, conspiracy theorists and cancer survivors to isolate themselves with one another and find support for their shared concerns, interests, and suspicions (Gerstenfeld, 2003; McKenna & Bargh, 1998, 2000; Sunstein, 2001). Even terrorist groups such as Al Qaeda are using the Internet to recruit new members (CBS, 2009). Indeed, terrorist websites—which grew from about a dozen in 1997 to 4700 in 2005—have increased more than four times faster than the total number of websites (Ariza, 2006).

From their analysis of terrorist organizations around the world, Clark McCauley and Mary Segal (1987; McCauley, 2002) note that terrorism does not erupt suddenly. Rather, it arises among people whose shared grievances bring them together. As they interact in isolation from moderating influences, they become progressively more extreme. The social amplifier brings the signal in stronger. The result is violent acts that these individuals, apart from the group, would never have committed.

Connection:

We discussed the development of terrorist groups in Module 11.

For example, the 9/11 terrorists were bred by a long process that engaged the polarizing effect of like-minded individuals. The process of becoming a terrorist (much like becoming a cult member) isolates individuals from other belief systems, dehumanizes potential targets, and tolerates no dissent (Smelser & Mitchell, 2002). Over time, groups come to categorize the world as "us" and "them" (Moghaddam, 2005; Qirko, 2004). According to one analysis of terrorists who were members of Salafi Jihad—an Islamic fundamentalist movement, of which Al Qaeda is a part—70 percent joined while living as expatriates. After moving to foreign countries in search of jobs or education, they became mindful of their Muslim identity and often gravitated to mosques and moved in with other expatriate Muslims, who sometimes recruited them into cell groups that provided "mutual emotional and social support" and "development of a common identity" (Sageman, 2004). This pattern may also describe what happened with the "Toronto 18," the group of young Muslim men charged with being involved in a terrorist training camp north of Toronto (*Maclean's*, 2008).

Massacres have been found to be a group phenomenon, enabled when the killers egg each other on (Zajonc, 2000). There are very few examples of individuals driven to suicide attacks by personal whim (Merari, 2002). Unfortunately, it is difficult to influence someone from outside the terrorist group to which they belong (Post, 2005). Jerrold Post, after interviewing many accused terrorists, concluded that the most effective way to fight terrorism is to prevent people from joining terrorist groups in the first place. Perhaps this is why in the Middle East one can find commercials debunking the myth that martyrdom will lead to reverence by the community. Parents of suicide bombers are shown crying and tearing the pictures of their deceased children out of family photos.

EXPLAINING GROUP POLARIZATION

Among several proposed theories of group polarization, two have survived scientific scrutiny. One deals with the arguments presented during a discussion, the other with how members of a group view themselves vis-à-vis the other members. The first idea is an example of informational influence (influence that results from accepting evidence about reality). The second is an example of normative influence (influence based on a person's desire to be accepted or admired by others).

Informational Influence

Sometimes we agree with others because we think they have information we need to make the right decision—thus, group members are said to be having an *informational influence* on us. According to the best-supported explanation, group discussion elicits a pooling of ideas, most of which favour the dominant viewpoint. Ideas that were common knowledge to group members will often be brought up in discussion or, even if unmentioned, will jointly influence their discussion (Gigone & Hastie, 1993; Larson et al., 1994; Stasser, 1991).

Other ideas may include persuasive arguments that some group members had not previously considered. When discussing the Canadian military engaging in Libya in the spring of 2011, for example, some people said, "We should go for it, because we have little to lose. If things don't work out quickly, we can always pull out." Such statements often entangle information about the person's *arguments* with cues concerning the person's *position* on the issue. Interestingly, the success of the mission, with no United Nations casualties, might increase the likelihood that we might get involved in a similar conflict in the future. But when people hear relevant arguments without learning the specific stands other people assume, they still shift their positions (Burnstein & Vinokur, 1977; Hinsz et al., 1997). *Arguments*, in and of themselves, matter.

Connection:

We discussed normative and informational influence in Module 9.

Normative Influence

Sometimes, people exert a *normative influence* on us—that is, we change our opinions or actions because we want to fit in with the group (be normal). Thus, a second explanation of polarization involves comparison with others. As Leon Festinger (1954) argued in his influential theory of social comparison, it is human nature to want to evaluate our opinions and abilities, something we can do by comparing our views with those of others. We are the most persuaded by people in our "reference groups"—groups we identify with (Abrams et al., 1990; Hogg et al., 1990). Moreover, wanting people to like us, we may express stronger opinions after discovering that others share our views.

Social comparison theory prompted experiments that exposed people to others' positions but not to their arguments. This is roughly the experience we have when learning the results of an opinion poll or an exit poll on election day. When people learn others' positions—without discussion—will they adjust their responses to maintain a socially favourable position? Merely learning others' choices also contributes to the bandwagon effect that creates blockbuster songs, books, and movies. Sociologist Matthew Salganik and his colleagues (2006) experimented with this phenomenon by engaging 14 341 Internet participants in listening to, and if they wished, downloading previously unknown songs. The researchers randomly assigned some participants to a condition that disclosed previous participants' download choices. Among those given that information, popular songs became more popular and unpopular songs became less popular.

Group polarization research illustrates the complexity of social-psychological inquiry. Much as we like our explanations of a phenomenon to be simple, one explanation seldom accounts for all of the data. Because people are complex, more than one factor frequently affects the outcome.

LO 3

THE CAUSES AND CONSEQUENCES OF GROUPTHINK

Do the social-psychological phenomena we have been considering occur in sophisticated groups like corporate boards, governments, or organizations such as NASA? Social psychologist Irving Janis (1971, 1982) wondered whether such phenomena might help explain good and bad group decisions made by some twentieth-century American presidents and their advisers. To find out, he analyzed the decision-making procedures that led to several major fiascos, such as the lack of preparation for the World War II attack on Pearl Harbor, the ill-fated invasion of Cuba by U.S. sponsored forces in the 1960s, and U.S. involvement in the Vietnam War.

More recently, NASA has suffered through the loss of two space shuttles—the *Challenger*, which exploded shortly after takeoff in 1986, and the *Columbia*, which broke up over Texas on February 1, 2003, when heat shields failed after being damaged during takeoff.

Janis believed blunders such as these were bred by the tendency of decision-making groups to suppress dissent in the interests of group harmony, a phenomenon he called groupthink. In work groups, camaraderie boosts productivity (Mullen & Copper, 1994). Moreover, team spirit is good for morale. But when making decisions, close-knit groups may pay a price. Janis believed that the soil from which groupthink sprouts includes an amiable, *cohesive* group, relative *isolation* of the group from dissenting viewpoints, and a *directive leader* who signals what decision he or she favours.

Symptoms of Groupthink

From historical records and the memoirs of participants and observers, Janis identified eight symptoms of groupthink. These symptoms are a collective form of dissonance reduction that surface as group members try to maintain their positive group feeling when facing a threat (Turner et al., 1992; Turner & Pratkanis, 1994).

The first two groupthink symptoms lead group members to *overestimate their group's might and right*:

- **An illusion of invulnerability:** Groups develop excessive optimism that blinds them to warnings of danger.
- **Unquestioned belief in the group's morality:** Group members assume the inherent morality of their group and ignore ethical and moral issues.

Group members also become *closed-minded*:

- **Rationalization:** Groups discount challenges by collectively justifying their decisions.
- **Stereotyped view of opponent:** Participants in these groups consider their enemies too evil to negotiate with, or too weak and unintelligent to defend themselves against the planned initiative.

Finally, the group suffers from *pressures toward uniformity:*

- **Conformity pressure:** Group members rebuff those who raise doubts about the group's assumption and plans, at times not by argument but by personal sarcasm.
- **Self-censorship:** Since disagreements are often uncomfortable and the groups seem in consensus, members withhold or discount their misgivings.
- **Illusion of unanimity:** Self-censorship and pressure not to puncture the consensus create an illusion of unanimity. What is more, the apparent consensus confirms the group's decision.
- **Mindguards:** Some members protect the group from information that would call into question the effectiveness or morality of its decisions.

"All those in favour say 'Aye'."

"Aye."   "Aye."   "Aye."

"Aye."   "Aye."

Applying Social Psychology

Now that you have learned about informational and normative influence on decision-making, do you think you can counter it? How do we make good decisions? From their extensive research on decision-making in government, business, and private welfare organizations, Janis and Mann (1977) extracted seven principles of effective decision makers:

1. Survey a wide range of objectives to be reached, always taking into account the multiplicity of values involved.

2. Consider a wide range of possible courses of action.

3. Intensively search for new information relevant to evaluating the alternatives.

4. Correctly consider and assimilate new information and expert judgments, even when they do not support the initially preferred course of action.

5. Reconsider both the positive and negative consequences of alternatives originally regarded as unacceptable, before making a final decision.

6. Carefully weigh the negative as well as the positive consequences that could result from the preferred alternative.

7. Prepare detailed provisions for implementing and monitoring the chosen course of action, with particular attention to contingency plans that might be required if known risks were to materialize.

Groupthink in Action

Groupthink symptoms can produce a failure to seek and discuss contrary information and alternative possibilities (Figure 13-2). When a leader promotes an idea and when a group insulates itself from dissenting views, groupthink may produce defective decisions (McCauley, 1989).

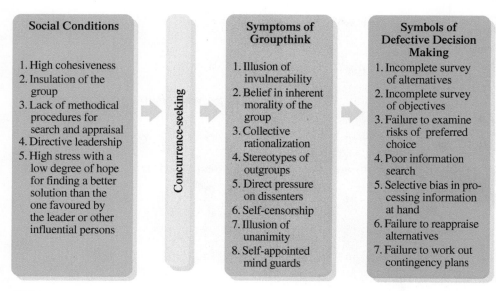

Social Conditions		Symptoms of Groupthink	Symbols of Defective Decision Making
1. High cohesiveness 2. Insulation of the group 3. Lack of methodical procedures for search and appraisal 4. Directive leadership 5. High stress with a low degree of hope for finding a better solution than the one favoured by the leader or other influential persons	Concurrence-seeking	1. Illusion of invulnerability 2. Belief in inherent morality of the group 3. Collective rationalization 4. Stereotypes of outgroups 5. Direct pressure on dissenters 6. Self-censorship 7. Illusion of unanimity 8. Self-appointed mind guards	1. Incomplete survey of alternatives 2. Incomplete survey of objectives 3. Failure to examine risks of preferred choice 4. Poor information search 5. Selective bias in processing information at hand 6. Failure to reappraise alternatives 7. Failure to work out contingency plans

FIGURE 13-2

Theoretical analysis of groupthink.

Groupthink was tragically evident in the decision process by which NASA decided to launch the space shuttle *Challenger* in January 1986 (Esser & Lindoerfer, 1989). Engineers at Morton Thiokol, which made the shuttle's rocket boosters, and at Rockwell International, which manufactured the orbiter, opposed the launch because of dangers posed to equipment by the subfreezing temperatures. The Thiokol engineers feared the cold would make the rubber seals between the rocket's four segments too brittle to contain the super-hot gases. Several months before the doomed mission, the company's top expert had warned in a memo that it was a "jump ball" whether the seal would hold and that if it failed, "the result would be a catastrophe of the highest order" (Magnuson, 1986).

In a telephone discussion the night before the launch, the engineers argued their case with their uncertain managers and with NASA officials, who were eager to proceed with the already delayed launch. One Thiokol official later testified, "We got ourselves into the thought process that we were trying to find some way to prove to them [the booster] wouldn't work. We couldn't prove absolutely that it wouldn't work." The result was an *illusion of invulnerability*.

Conformity pressures also operated. One NASA official complained, "My God, Thiokol, when do you want me to launch, next April?" The top Thiokol executive declared, "We have to make a management decision," and then asked his engineering vice president to "take off his engineering hat and put on his management hat."

To create an *illusion of unanimity*, this executive then proceeded to poll only the management officials and ignore the engineers. The go-ahead decision made, one of the engineers belatedly pleaded with a NASA official to reconsider: "If anything happened to this launch," he said prophetically, "I sure wouldn't want to be the person that had to stand in front of a board of inquiry to explain why I launched."

Thanks, finally, to *mindguarding*, the top NASA executive who made the final decision never learned about the engineers' concerns, nor about the reservations of the Rockwell officials. Protected from disagreeable information, he confidently gave the go-ahead to launch the *Challenger* on its tragic flight.

In 2003, tragedy struck again after NASA removed five members of an expert panel who warned them of safety troubles for its aging shuttle fleet (Broad & Hulse, 2003). NASA said it was only bringing in fresh blood, but some of the panelists said the agency was trying to suppress their criticism, and that NASA was discounting their concerns. This, alas, gained credence when the *Columbia* disintegrated during its return to earth on February 1. Amazingly, when a report on the *Columbia* disaster was released in the summer of 2003, little seemed to have changed at NASA. Seventeen years after the *Challenger* explosion, another shuttle was destroyed, and the report on that disaster was eerily similar to the previous one.

Critical THINKING

British psychologists Ben Newell and David Lagnado (2003) believe groupthink symptoms may also have contributed to the invasion of Iraq by the United States and its allies. These authors and others contend that both Saddam Hussein and George W. Bush surrounded themselves with like-minded advisers, intimidated opposing voices into silence, and received filtered information that mostly supported their assumptions. It is clear that during discussions of the decision to invade, any dissent to the plan to attack Iraq was quashed (e.g., Woodward, 2006). At one point, then-secretary of state Colin Powell was asked, "Are you with us or against us?" As a consequence, Powell stayed quiet about his concerns over the invasion, thus promoting a false sense of unanimity. What would you have done in this situation? How would you have countered these pressures?

Prior to the start of the Iraq War, then-secretary of state Colin Powell had reservations, but agreed with the decision to invade anyway.

More recently, the leaders of most Western countries were stunned by the sudden and deep economic recession in 2008–2009. During the 2008 federal election campaign, Stephen Harper assured Canadians that the economic downturn was not real—Canada had a strong, healthy economy. His advisors assured him things were fine. Indeed, the dip in the market was a great time to invest! Almost no one in the financial community predicted the sudden downturn (although those who did were ridiculed into silence), and once it started, no one believed it would get too bad. Groupthink almost certainly played a part in this situation. Interestingly, in the 2011 election campaign, the Conservatives warned that a change in government would mean a return to the recession.

These high-level examples of groupthink beg the question—can we ever avoid groupthink from happening? The answer is simple—yes. Indeed, U.S. President Barack Obama has purposely surrounded himself with his former opponents (such as Hillary Clinton, and members of the opposing party) in order to avoid groupthink in his cabinet (CTV, 2008). So, how can you avoid groupthink? Go to the following activity and find out.

Activity: **Preventing groupthink**

Earlier, we noted seven strategies to help make high-quality decisions. Now, let's consider a number of strategies you might employ to reduce or even eliminate groupthink in your life. Frequently, as a student, you will need to do group work. Typically, the group will first have to decide how to approach a problem. If you make a mistake early on, it might doom you in the presentation. (Have you experienced this before?) You might also experience groupthink at your work, during a staff meeting or in another group-work context. Again, understanding the following principles will help you avoid the pitfalls of group polarization and groupthink:

1. Be impartial—do not endorse any position (at least initially).

2. Encourage critical evaluation; assign a "devil's advocate." (It is best if this person can remain anonymous to avoid the risk of possible reprisals.)

3. Occasionally subdivide the group; then reunite to air differences.

4. Welcome critiques from outside experts and associates.

5. Before implementing a decision, call a "second-chance" meeting to air any lingering doubts.

These approaches have been well-developed and tested through the years. So, how might you apply these principles to your next group assignment?

LO 4

MINORITY INFLUENCE

We now know that groups can influence those individuals within the group as well as the decisions that both people and groups make. However, before we move on to other topics, let's consider the reverse effect. How can individuals influence their groups? We have discussed how to avoid groupthink, but are there things an individual can do to sway a group's decision?

At the beginning of most social movements, a small minority will sometimes sway, and then even become, the majority. "All history," wrote Ralph Waldo Emerson, "is a record of the power of minorities, and of minorities of one." Think of Copernicus and Galileo. The American civil rights movement was ignited by the refusal of one African-American woman, Rosa Parks, to relinquish her seat on a Montgomery, Alabama, bus. In Manitoba, one man's stand changed the course of constitutional reform in Canada.

In 1990, the Meech Lake Accord was billed as the solution to Canada's constitutional crisis— Quebec had never signed the Constitution. However, many people were disenchanted with the process by which the Meech Lake Accord had been developed. With time running short, in order for debate to begin, the Manitoba Legislature needed to unanimously waive the formality of a waiting period. Elijah Harper, a Manitoba Member of the Legislative Assembly and an Aboriginal leader, was frustrated that the Meech Lake Accord had not taken Aboriginal peoples' views or concerns about constitutional reform into account. Therefore, he alone—against tremendous pressure from federal and provincial parties—voted against the waiver. Shortly after this vote, Newfoundland Premier Clyde Wells announced he would not be putting the Accord forward for discussion in the Newfoundland Legislature. These two actions effectively killed the Meech Lake Accord.

Elijah Harper, then a Manitoba MLA, stood alone in the legislature in opposition to the Meech Lake Accord.

Small groups of people can also have an important impact on the larger group. As another example, at the turn of the last century, women did not have the right to vote in Canada. Many argued that women should not vote, as it would distract them from their "wifely duties." And getting involved in politics would only upset them. Undoubtedly, this would lead to the downfall of society as Canadians knew it. In 1914, Nellie McClung presided over a mock parliament of women who presented arguments about the disasters that would befall society if men got the vote. ("Politics unsettle men, and unsettled men mean unsettled bills, broken furniture, broken vows, and divorce. Men's place is on the farm.") This event was key to turning the public tide in favour of granting women the vote in Canada.

But let's turn to the broader question. What makes a minority persuasive? Experiments initiated by Serge Moscovici have identified several determinants of minority influence: consistency, self-confidence, and defection from the majority.

Consistency

More influential than a minority that wavers is a minority that sticks to its position. Moscovici and his associates (1969, 1985) have found that if a minority consistently judges blue slides as green, members of the majority will occasionally agree. But if the minority wavers, saying "blue" to one-third of the blue slides and "green" to the rest, virtually no one in the majority will ever agree with "green."

Still debated is the nature of this influence (Clark & Maass, 1990; Levine & Russo, 1987). Moscovici believes that a minority's following the majority usually reflects just public compliance, but a majority's following a minority usually reflects genuine acceptance—really recalling the blue slide as greenish. In public, people may wish not to align themselves with a deviant, minority view (Wood et al., 1994, 1996). A majority can give us a rule of thumb for deciding truth ("All those smart cookies can't be wrong"); a minority influences us by making us think more deeply (Burnstein & Kitayama, 1989; Mackie, 1987). Minority influence is therefore more likely to take the thought-filled central route to persuasion.

Experiments show—and experience confirms—that non-conformity, especially persistent non-conformity, is often painful (Levine, 1989). If you set out to be Ralph Waldo Emerson's minority of one, prepare yourself for ridicule—especially when you argue an issue that's personally relevant to the majority and when the group wants to settle an issue by reaching consensus (Kameda & Sugimori, 1993; Kruglanski & Webster, 1991; Trost et al., 1992). People may even attribute your dissent to psychological peculiarities (Papastamou & Mugny, 1990). When Charlan Nemeth (1979) planted a minority of two within a simulated jury and had them oppose the majority's opinions, the duo was inevitably disliked. Nevertheless, the majority acknowledged that the persistence of the two did more than anything else to make them rethink their positions.

A persistent minority is influential, even if not popular, partly because it soon becomes the focus of debate (Schachter, 1951). Being the centre of conversation allows one to contribute a disproportionate number of arguments. And Nemeth reports that in minority influence experiments, as in the group polarization studies, the position supported by the most arguments usually wins. Talkative group members are usually influential (Mullen et al., 1989).

Self-Confidence

Consistency and persistence convey self-confidence. Furthermore, Nemeth and Joel Wachtler (1974) reported that any behaviour by a minority that conveys self-confidence—for example, taking the head seat at the table—tends to raise self-doubts among the majority. By being firm and forceful, the minority's apparent self-assurance may prompt the majority to reconsider its position. This is especially so on matters of opinion rather than fact. In her research at Italy's University of Padova, Anne Maass and her colleagues (1996) report that minorities are less persuasive regarding fact ("from which country does Italy import most of its raw oil?") than regarding attitude ("from which country should Italy import most of its raw oil?").

Defections from the Majority

A persistent minority punctures any illusion of unanimity. When a minority consistently doubts the majority wisdom, majority members become freer to express their own doubts and may even switch to the minority position. In research with university students, John Levine (1989) found that a minority person who had defected from the majority was more persuasive than a consistent minority voice. In her jury-simulation experiments, Nemeth found that once defections begin, others often follow, initiating a snowball effect.

Are these factors that strengthen minority influence unique to minorities? Sharon Wolf and Bibb Latané (1985; Wolf, 1987) and Russell Clark (1995) believe not. They argue that the same social forces work for both majorities and minorities. Informational and normative influence fuels both group polarization and minority influence. And if consistency, self-confidence, and defections from the other side strengthen the minority, such variables also strengthen a majority. The social impact of any position depends on the strength, immediacy, and number of those who support it. Minorities have less influence than majorities simply because they are smaller.

Anne Maass and Russell Clark (1984, 1986) agree with Moscovici, however, that minorities are more likely to convert people to *accepting* their views. And from their analyses of how groups evolve over time, John Levine and Richard Moreland (1985) conclude that new recruits to a group exert a different type of minority influence than long-time members do. Newcomers exert influence through the attention they receive and the group awareness they trigger in the old-timers. Established members feel freer to dissent and to exert leadership.

CONCLUSIONS

Thus, from this module, you should have learned about the power of the group to influence decisions. Groupthink is a serious problem in some decisions, and as we have seen from multiple shuttle disasters, terrorist acts, military engagements, and various other examples, group polarization can lead to extremely bad decision-making with life-and-death consequences. On the other hand, we have also learned that groups have more cognitive resources than individuals. If group contexts are handled well (see the activity) then the decisions made by groups can be superior to those made by individuals. Furthermore, we have learned that a persistent, consistent, and confident minority has a good chance of convincing the majority of their opinions. If you find yourself in a group making a bad decision, don't be afraid to speak up. Remember—someone else is likely to agree with you.

SUMMARY OF KEY POINTS

LO1. Understand the risky shift phenomenon.

- In general, groups make more risky decisions than individuals would in the same situation.

LO2. Explain group polarization.

- Informational and normative influence both act to reduce people's willingness and likelihood to intervene in group decision-making.

LO3. Understand the causes and consequences of groupthink.

- Highly cohesive groups with strong leadership, pressure to make decisions, and poor decision-making methods can result in poor decisions.

LO4. Understand minority influence.

- A consistent and confident minority can influence a group, particularly when members of the majority begin to defect to the minority view.

KEY TERMS

Group polarization   Group-produced enhancement of members' pre-existing tendencies; a strengthening of the members' average tendency, not a split within the group.

Groupthink   "The mode of thinking that persons engage in when concurrence-seeking becomes so dominant in a cohesive in-group that it tends to override realistic appraisal of alternative courses of action." Irving Janis (1971).

Social comparison   Evaluating one's opinions and abilities by comparing oneself to others.

MODULE FOURTEEN

Understanding Aggression

LEARNING OBJECTIVES   After studying Module 14, you will be able to

LO **1**   Define aggression

LO **2**   Explain the different biological influences on aggression

LO **3**   Understand the psychological influences on aggression

LO **4**   Describe effective methods to reduce aggression

In February 1996, Jean Chrétien, then the prime minister of Canada, was wading through a crowd celebrating Flag Day in Hull, Quebec. Suddenly, he was confronted by an anti-poverty protester yelling insults into his face. Canadians were shocked by what happened next—the prime minister grabbed the protestor by the throat and angrily threw him aside. Although the protestor did not resist, RCMP officers who came to the prime minister's aid tackled the protestor, and in the process knocked out two of his teeth (CBC, 1996). The incident raised a number of questions. The RCMP officers were criticized for perhaps being overly violent with the protestor, as well as for letting him get too close to the prime minister. Chrétien was criticized for overreacting by some, but was lauded by others for taking matters into his own hands. Over ten years later, Chrétien still joked about this incident (e.g., pretending to choke comedian Rick Mercer during a November 2007 interview on *The Rick Mercer Report*—you can watch the video online; look for "Mercer: At Harvey's with Chrétien" from the November 20, 2007, episode).

While some theorize that aggression is a fundamental part of human nature, others believe that society teaches humans to be violent. What are some variables that might affect our tolerance of aggression? Is it an act of aggression if someone gives you the finger after you cut them off in traffic?

Critical THINKING

Was what Jean Chrétien did "aggression"? If so, was it justified? If you think it was justified, why? Clearly, we agree that aggression and violence are sometimes acceptable. When do we cross the line? In order to protect players, the NFL has recently enacted a policy to suspend players who enact "brutal" hits on opponents. The NHL has also changed rules to punish players who take "headshots." How do you feel about this?

In his 2003 book *Shake Hands with the Devil*, Canadian Lieutenant-General Roméo Dallaire describes in horrific detail the slaughter of 800 000 Tutsis by rival Hutus in the 1994 genocide in Rwanda. It took a short 100 days to accomplish the killings. Unfortunately, even this level of violence is not unique. In Sudan's Darfur region, the Janjaweed militias have carried out terror campaigns that have killed up to 400 000 and displaced 2.5 million people from their homes (UNHCR, 2008). Similar ethnic violence occurred in Egypt and Libya, during the 2011 "Arab Spring," and more recently by Islamic extremists in Iraq and Syria in the summer of 2014.

LO 1

DEFINING AGGRESSION

During the last 100 years, 250 wars have killed 110 million people (see Figure 14-1). These tolls have come not only from the two World Wars, but also from countless genocides such as the Ottoman Empire genocide of Armenians, the Pakistani genocide of 3 million Bangladeshis, and the murder of 1.5 million Cambodians in a reign of terror that began in 1975 (Sternberg, 2003). Hitler's genocide of millions of Jews, Stalin's genocide of millions of Russians, Mao's genocide of millions of Chinese, and the early genocide of Aboriginal Peoples in North America all attest to the human potential for cruelty.

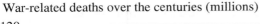

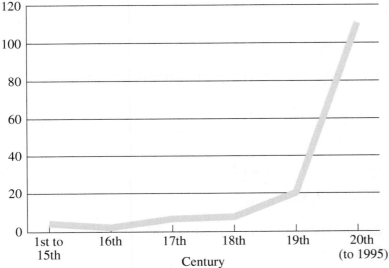

War-related deaths over the centuries (millions)

FIGURE 14-1

The bloodiest century. Twentieth-century humanity was the most educated, and homicidal, in history (data from Renner, 1999). Adding in genocides and human-made famines, there were approximately 182 million "deaths by mass unpleasantness" (White, 2011).

Source: Based on Dollard et al., 1939; and Miller, 1941.

It should be clear to you by now that aggression is actually a very broad term. To a social psychologist, however, aggression is any physical or verbal behaviour intended to hurt someone. This excludes auto accidents, dental treatments, and sidewalk collisions, but includes slaps, direct insults, and gossip.

In psychology, we typically categorize aggression into two forms: hostile aggression (also known as *angry aggression*), where the goal is to injure another; and instrumental aggression, where the goal is also to injure, but only as a means to an end. For example, when you get mad at someone for cutting you off in traffic, you are experiencing hostile aggression. Most murders are acts of hostile aggression, occurring as the result of arguments between friends or family members (Ash, 1999).

However, most wars and terrorist acts are instrumental aggression. "What nearly all suicide terrorist campaigns have in common is a specific secular and strategic goal," concludes Robert Page (2003), after studying all suicide bombings from 1980 to 2001. After the 9/11 attacks, Osama bin Laden noted that for a cost of $500 000 al Qaeda inflicted $500 billion in damage to the U.S. economy; the goal is to "compel liberal democracies to withdraw military forces from territory that terrorists consider to be their homeland" (Zakaria, 2008). Terrorism is rarely committed by someone with a psychological pathology, note Arie Kruglanski and Shira Fishman (2006). It is, rather, a strategic tool used in conflict (Aslan, 2010).

Activity: Defining aggression

How do you define aggression? Below are a number of examples of behaviours that some might see as aggressive. Read each one and indicate whether or not the acts described are aggression.

Yes	No		
____	____	1.	A criminal is executed under China's capital punishment law.
____	____	2.	A father spanks his six-year-old daughter.
____	____	3.	A woman shoots mace at her would-be rapist.
____	____	4.	A batter's line drive hits the pitcher in the knee.
____	____	5.	A frustrated wife yells at her "messy slob of a husband."
____	____	6.	A soldier in Afghanistan shoots at a car whose driver refuses to stop at a checkpoint.
____	____	7.	A professor lowers a student's grade on a late paper.
____	____	8.	A man passes along rumours about his business rival's ethical transgressions.
____	____	9.	A boy tells his little sister that her art project is "dumb and ugly."
____	____	10.	Two teenage girls create a website to spread rumours about another girl at school.

LO 2

BIOLOGICAL INFLUENCES ON AGGRESSION

Philosophers have long debated whether our human nature is fundamentally that of a benign, contented, "noble savage" or that of a potentially explosive brute. In the last century, the "brutish" view—that aggressive drive is inborn and thus inevitable—was argued by Sigmund Freud in Austria and Konrad Lorenz in Germany. Indeed, these views formed the basis for the development of evolutionary psychology. Both Freud and Lorenz agreed that aggressive energy is instinctual (unlearned and universal). Lorenz, an animal behaviour expert, saw aggression as adaptive rather than self-destructive—more aggressive animals might be more successful getting food, or competing for mates, or protecting their offspring. Martin Daly and Margo Wilson at McMaster University (e.g., Daly & Wilson, 1996) have argued that this also explains why parents are more likely to abuse or murder stepchildren than their own biological children. They have less evolutionary "investment" in stepchildren, as they will not pass on their genes. Although Lorenz (1976) also argued that we have innate mechanisms for inhibiting aggression (such as making ourselves defenceless), he feared the implications of arming our "fighting instinct" without arming our inhibitions.

Connection:

We will discuss evolutionary psychology more in Module 19.

The support for aggression as an instinct collapsed as the list of supposed human instincts grew to include nearly every conceivable human behaviour, and scientists became aware how much behaviour varies from person to person and culture to culture. Yet, biology clearly does influence behaviour just as nurture works upon nature. Our experiences interact with the nervous system engineered by our genes.

Neural Influences

Because aggression is a complex behaviour, no one spot in the brain controls it. But researchers have found neural systems in both animals and humans that facilitate aggression. When scientists activate these areas in the brain, hostility increases; when they deactivate them, hostility decreases. Docile animals can thus be provoked into rage, and raging animals into submission.

In one experiment, researchers placed an electrode in an aggression-inhibiting area of a domineering monkey's brain (Moyer, 1976, 1983). One small monkey, given a button that activated the electrode, learned to push it every time the tyrant monkey became intimidating. Brain activation works with humans, too. After receiving painless electrical stimulation in her amygdala (a part of the brain associated with aggression), one woman became enraged and smashed her guitar against the wall, barely missing her psychiatrist's head.

So, are violent people's brains in some way abnormal? To find out, Adrian Raine and his colleagues (1998, 2000, 2005, 2008) used brain scans to measure brain activity in murderers whose violence could not be attributed to childhood abuse or neglect and to measure the amount of grey matter in men with antisocial conduct disorder. They found that the prefrontal cortex, which acts like an emergency brake on deeper brain areas involved in aggressive behaviour, was 14 percent less active than normal in the non-abused murderers and 15 percent smaller in the antisocial men. Did the brain abnormality by itself precipitate violence? Possibly not, but for some violent people it likely is a factor (Davidson et al., 2000).

Genetic Influences

Heredity influences the neural system's sensitivity to aggressive cues. It has long been known that animals of many species can be bred for aggressiveness. Sometimes this is done for practical purposes; sometimes, breeding is done for research. Finnish psychologist Kirsti Lagerspetz (1979) took normal albino mice and bred the most aggressive ones together and the least aggressive ones together. After repeating the procedure for 26 generations, she had one set of fierce mice and one set of placid mice. Beginning in 1959, Russian researchers bred foxes to either be aggressive or friendly toward humans. These traits accentuated over a few generations (Ratliff, 2011). Interestingly, over time, wild foxes bred to be friendly also developed traits we normally associate with domesticated dogs—floppy ears, tail wagging, coat colour variations, and short curly tails.

Aggressiveness naturally varies among primates and humans (Asher, 1987; Olweus, 1979). Our temperaments—how intense and reactive we are—are partly brought with us into the world, influenced by our sympathetic nervous system's reactivity (Kagan, 1989). Identical twins, when asked separately, are more likely than fraternal twins to agree on whether they have "a violent temper" or have gotten into fights (Rowe et al., 1999; Rushton et al., 1986). Yet a person's temperament, observed in infancy, usually endures (Larsen & Diener, 1987; Wilson & Matheny, 1986). A child who is non-aggressive at age eight will very likely still be non-aggressive at age 48 (Huesmann et al., 2003).

Blood Chemistry

Blood chemistry also influences neural sensitivity to aggressive stimulation. For example, U.S. researchers found that drinking four or more servings of sugared soda is linked to aggression in children (Suglia, 2013). Both laboratory experiments and police data indicate that when people are provoked, alcohol unleashes aggression (Bushman, 1993; Bushman & Cooper, 1990; Taylor & Chermack, 1993; Testa, 2002). Violent people are more likely (1) to drink, and (2) to become aggressive when intoxicated (White et al., 1993). Consider the following:

- Geoff MacDonald at the University of Toronto and his colleagues (2000) found that when intoxicated, people administer more painful electric shocks and are angrier.
- Peter Hoaken at the University of Western Ontario has found that both men and women are more susceptible to provocation when intoxicated (Hoaken & Pihl, 2000).
- Statistics Canada reported that in 2004 half of homicide victims and three-quarters of accused persons had consumed alcohol or drugs at the time of the crime.

Alcohol enhances aggressiveness by reducing people's self-awareness, by reducing their ability to consider consequences, and because people mentally associate alcohol with aggression (Bartholow & Hienz, 2006; Ito et al., 1996; Steele & Southwick, 1985). Alcohol deindividuates and disinhibits.

Aggressiveness also correlates with the male sex hormone, testosterone. Although hormonal influences appear much stronger in other animals than in humans, drugs that diminish testosterone levels in violent human males will subdue their aggressive tendencies. After men reach age 25, their testosterone levels and rates of violent crime decrease together.

Testosterone levels tend to be higher among prisoners convicted of unprovoked violent crimes than of non-violent crimes (Dabbs et al., 1997, 2001). And among the normal range of teenage boys and adult men, those with high testosterone levels are more prone to delinquency, hard drug use, and aggressive responses to provocation (Archer, 1991; Dabbs & Morris, 1990; Olweus et al., 1988). Testosterone, says James Dabbs (2000), "is a small molecule with large effects." Injecting a man with testosterone won't automatically make him aggressive, yet men with low testosterone are somewhat less likely to react aggressively when provoked (Geen, 1998). Interestingly, Klinesmith and colleagues (2006) have found that after handling a gun, men's testosterone levels rise. The more they rise, the more men are willing to "punish" another person by making them consume more hot sauce.

Gender and Aggression

Imagine two people. One is "adventurous, autocratic, coarse, dominant, forceful, independent, and strong." The other is "affectionate, dependent, dreamy, emotional, submissive, and weak." If the first person sounds more to you like a man and the second like a woman, you are not alone, report John Williams and Deborah Best (1990a). The world around, from Asia to Africa and Europe to Australia, people *rate* men as more dominant, driven, and aggressive.

These perceptions and expectations correlate with reality. In essentially every society, men *are* socially dominant. In no known societies do women dominate men (Pratto, 1996). Consider the following:

- Women in 2010 were only 19 percent of the world's legislators (22 percent in Canada) and 15 percent of government or house leaders (IPU, 2011). In 2005, only 5 percent of presidents and prime ministers were women (IPU, 2005). However, these women were at least as effective legislators (if not more so) as their male counterparts (*The Economist,* 2014).

- In November of 2010, in Canada, only 13 percent of corporate officers were women, and only 17 percent were directors in Canada's top 500 companies (*Globe and Mail,* 2010), and only 21 of the top 1000 have female CEOs. Women are 1 percent of the chief executives of the world's 500 largest corporations (Eagly et al., 2003). Yet women make up almost 50 percent of the workforce.

- Men are more likely to favour conservative political candidates and programs that preserve group inequality (Eagly et al., 2003; Sidanius & Pratto, 1999).

- Men have been half of all jurors but 90 percent of elected jury leaders and most of the leaders of ad hoc laboratory groups (Davis & Gilbert, 1989; Kerr et al., 1982).

But, do these differences in social dominance bleed into differences in aggression? Throughout the world, hunting, fighting, and warring are primarily male activities. In surveys, men admit to more aggression than women. In laboratory experiments, men indeed exhibit more physical aggression, for example, by administering what they believe are hurtful electric shocks (Knight et al., 1996). In Canada, the male-to-female arrest rate is 7 to 1 for murder and 6 to 1 for assault (Statistics Canada, 2000). Across the world, murder rates vary. Yet, in all regions, men are roughly 20 times more likely to murder men than women are to murder women (Daly & Wilson, 1989; Wilson, Daly & Pound, 2002).

However, the gender difference fluctuates with the context. When there is provocation, the gender gap shrinks (Bettencourt & Miller, 1996). And, within less assaultive forms of aggression—say, slapping a family member, throwing something, or verbally attacking someone—women are no less aggressive than men (Björkqvist, 1994; White & Kowalski, 1994). Indeed, says John Archer (2000), from a statistical digest of 82 studies, women are slightly more likely to commit an aggressive act than men. But men are more likely to inflict an injury; 62 percent of those injured by a partner are women.

Critical THINKING

So why are there gender differences in aggressive behaviour? One explanation that has been suggested is that in many social situations men and women differ in status. Is there a way to influence how this occurs? Would this explain the reduced differences in aggression for some situations?

LO 3

PSYCHOLOGICAL INFLUENCES ON AGGRESSION

There are important neural, genetic, and biochemical influences on aggression. Biological influences predispose some people more than others to react aggressively to conflict and provocation. But there is more to the story.

Frustration and Aggression

One of the first psychological theories of aggression was the frustration-aggression theory. "Frustration always leads to some form of aggression," said John Dollard and his colleagues (1939, p. 1). Frustration is anything (such as the malfunctioning vending machine) that blocks our attaining of a goal. Frustration grows when our motivation to achieve a goal is very strong, when we expected gratification, and when the blocking is complete. When Rupert Brown and his colleagues (2001) surveyed British ferry passengers heading to France, they found much higher aggressive attitudes on a day when French fishing boats blockaded the port, preventing their travel. Blocked from obtaining their goal, the passengers became more likely (in responding to various vignettes) to agree with, for example, an insult toward a French person who had spilled coffee.

As Figure 14-2 suggests, the aggressive energy need not explode directly against its source. We learn to inhibit direct retaliation, especially when others might disapprove or punish; instead, we *displace* our hostilities to safer targets. Displacement occurs in the old anecdote about a man who, humiliated by his boss, berates his wife, who yells at their son, who kicks the dog, which bites the mail carrier. In experiments and in real life, however, displaced aggression is most likely when the target shares some similarity to the instigator and does some minor irritating act that unleashes the displaced aggression (Marcus-Newhall et al., 2000; Miller et al., 2003; Pedersen et al., 2000). When a person harbours anger, even a trivial offence may elicit an explosive overreaction.

Dr. Kathryn Graham, at the Centre for Addiction and Mental Health and an adjunct professor at the University of Western Ontario, has been exploring the role of alcohol in aggressive behaviour for more than 30 years. As a graduate student as part of a course on aggression, she completed a project on alcohol and aggression where it became apparent that most of the research focused on a simplistic causal relationship between alcohol and aggression—namely, that alcohol consumption leads to aggressive behaviour. This relationship was not consistent with the wide range of behaviours that she had observed while working in the bars, specifically that the barroom environment had a large impact on the alcohol–aggression relationship. She was able to demonstrate this effect as part of an observational study of more than 200 bars and clubs in Vancouver conducted for her master's thesis (Graham et al., 1980). A later study examining aggression among adolescents found that drinking in public locations (bars, cars) was especially associated with increased risk of aggression for young men (Graham et al., 2005; Graham et al., 2010).

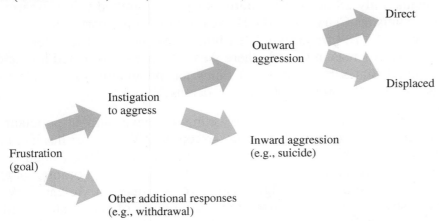

FIGURE 14-2

The classic frustration-aggression theory. Frustration creates a motive to aggress. Fear of punishment or disapproval for aggressing against the source of frustration may cause aggressors to focus the aggressive drive on some other target, or even turn it on themselves.

Source: Based on Dollard et al., 1939; and Miller, 1941.

Laboratory tests of the frustration-aggression theory have generally produced mixed results, however: Sometimes frustration increased aggressiveness; sometimes not. In one laboratory experiment (Vasquez et al., 2005), researchers provoked some students (but not others) by having an experimenter insult their performance on an anagram-solving task. Shortly afterwards, the students had to decide how long another supposed student should be required to immerse his or her hand in a painful cold water bath while completing a task. When the supposed student committed a trivial offence (i.e., by giving a mild insult), the previously provoked participants responded punitively. This may help to explain how an earlier provocation may be displaced on others.

Leonard Berkowitz (1978, 1989) realized that the original theory overstated the frustration–aggression connection, so he revised it. Berkowitz theorized that frustration produces *anger*, an emotional readiness or cue to aggress. But, as we will see, cues associated with aggression amplify aggression (Carlson et al., 1990).

Terrorists understand the anger-eliciting effect of their actions. Social psychologists (McCauley, 2004; Wagner, 2006) have noted that terrorists sometimes aim to commit an act that will induce a strong and angry enemy to overreact, producing effects that ultimately serve the terrorists' interests. Reza Aslan (2010) argues that the "crusade" against terrorism begun by the West after the attacks of September 11, 2001, has led to more, not less, religious extremism and violence.

Berkowitz (1968, 1981, 1995) and others have found that even the sight of a weapon is such a cue, especially when perceived as an instrument of violence rather than recreation (Batholow et al., 2004). In one experiment, children who had just played with toy guns became more willing to knock down another child's blocks. Guns prime hostile thoughts and punitive judgments (Anderson et al., 1998; Dienstbier et al., 1998).

Perhaps it is no surprise, then, that in 2003 two-thirds of U.S. murders were committed with firearms. As a comparison, in 2004 in Canada, only 28 percent of murders were committed using firearms— less than half the U.S. proportion (Statistics Canada, 2007). However, this is only part of the story. In 2002 in the United States, there were 12 129 firearms-related homicides (plus 17 108 suicides and more than 1000 accidental shootings), whereas in Canada there were 152 firearms-related homicides that same year. Although the United States has almost 10 times the population of Canada (305 million versus 33 million), it has 80 times the number of firearms deaths. Why?

Consider that Vancouver, British Columbia, and Seattle, Washington, have similar populations, climates, economies, and rates of criminal activity and assault—except that Vancouver has had one-fifth as many handgun murders as Seattle and a 40 percent lower overall murder rate (Sloan et al., 1988). Can this have to do with the law? After a series of handgun-related deaths in Toronto, tougher gun-crime laws have been put in place. Would a handgun ban have an effect on violence? When Washington, D.C., adopted a law restricting handgun possession, the numbers of gun-related murders and suicides each abruptly dropped about 25 percent (Loftin et al., 1991). (Interestingly, this ban on handguns was successfully challenged in the U.S. Supreme Court as being unconstitutional.) In 1974, Jamaica implemented a sweeping anti-crime program that included strict gun control and censorship of gun scenes from television and movies (Diener & Crandall, 1979). In the following year, robberies dropped 25 percent and non-fatal shootings decreased by 37 percent.

Guns not only serve as aggression cues, they also put psychological distance between aggressor and victim. As Milgram's obedience studies taught us, remoteness from the victim facilitates cruelty. A knife can kill someone, but a knife attack is more difficult than pulling a trigger from a distance.

Relative Deprivation

We often become more frustrated when we compare ourselves to others. An A– on a recent exam can be very uplifting, until we hear that the class average was an A. Similarly, an employee's feeling of well-being will depend (in part) on how his or her salary compares to similar others (Yuchtman, 1976). These perceptions are called relative deprivation (Olson & Hafer, 1996). Relative deprivation has been used to explain why nations with large economic inequalities tend to have lower happiness and higher crime rates than countries with smaller inequalities (Hagerty, 2000).

The Learning of Aggression

Theories of aggression based on instinct and frustration assume that hostile urges erupt from inner emotions, which naturally "push" aggression from within. Social psychologists contend that learning also "pulls" aggression out of us.

The Rewards of Aggression

By experience and by observing others, we learn that aggression often pays. A child whose aggressive acts successfully intimidate other children will likely become increasingly aggressive (Patterson et al., 1967). Collective violence can also have its rewards. For example, in January and

February of 2006, Muslims in a number of European and Middle Eastern countries held sometimes-violent protests over offensive depictions of the Muslim prophet Mohammed in Danish and other newspapers. Although all newspapers in the Western world insisted that they had the right to publish those caricatures, almost none did. Many cited fear of reprisals as a reason for not re-publishing the caricatures. The point is not that people consciously plan riots for their instrumental value, but that aggression sometimes has payoffs. If nothing more, it gets attention.

The same is true of terrorist acts, which enable powerless people to garner widespread attention. "Kill one, frighten ten thousand," asserts an ancient Chinese proverb. "The primary targets of suicide bombing attacks are not those who are injured but those who are made to witness it through media coverage," note Paul Marsden and Sharon Attia (2005). In this age of global communications, killing only a few can frighten tens of millions, as happened after the September 11, 2001, attacks in the United States, when many Western democracies—including Canada, the United Kingdom, and the United States—spent billions of dollars on security and passed legislation limiting the civil rights of their citizens.

These reactions can have serious consequences to individuals. No one knows this better than Maher Arar, a Canadian citizen who was deported to Syria after being stopped by U.S. customs agents in New York. Arar spent almost a year in Syria, during which time he was tortured before finally being released. In 2007, the Canadian government paid Arar $10 million in compensation for their part in his rendition and torture (CBC, 2007). This could not have happened if the anti-terrorism laws did not exist. Deprived of what Margaret Thatcher called "the oxygen of publicity," terrorism might be reduced (although it would be naïve to think it would be eliminated altogether), concluded Jeffrey Rubin (1986).

Observational Learning

Albert Bandura (1997) proposed a social learning theory of aggression. He believes that we learn aggression not only by experiencing its payoffs but also by observing others. As with most social behaviours, we acquire aggression by watching others act and noting the consequences.

Bandura (1979) believes that everyday life exposes us to aggressive models in the family, the subculture, and the mass media. Perhaps not surprisingly, Canadian teenage hockey players whose fathers applaud physically aggressive play show the most aggressive attitudes and style of play (Ennis & Zanna, 1991). Children of physically punitive parents tend to use aggression when relating to others. Their parents often disciplined them by screaming, slapping, and beating—modelling aggression as a method of dealing with problems (Patterson et al., 1982). These parents often had parents who were physically punitive (Bandura & Walters, 1959; Straus & Gelles, 1980). Although most abused children do not become criminals or abusive parents, 30 percent do later abuse their own children (Kaufman & Zigler, 1987; Widom, 1989). Children who are spanked at age three are more aggressive at age five. Recent work (e.g., Homel, 2013) found that people who were bullies in their youth (and who presumably learned that bullying has benefits) were more likely to be aggressive later in life. In Somalia, pirates have made hijacking ships lucrative—gaining more than $150 million in ransom in 2008 alone (BBC, 2008).

Connection:

We will discuss the role of aggression in health and behaviour again in Module 24.

The social environment outside the home also provides models. The violent subculture of teenage gangs, for instance, provides its junior members with aggressive models. Among Chicago adolescents who are otherwise equally at risk for violence, those who have observed gun violence are at double the risk for violent behaviour (Bingenheimer et al., 2005). Gordon Russell at the University of Lethbridge found that watching boxing increased aggression in men, especially if they tended to perceive themselves as "macho" (1992).

Violence in sports is pretty common, but violence in hockey is ubiquitous. In almost no other sport (with the obvious exception of boxing, ultimate fighting, and other combat sports) is aggression so tolerated and even encouraged. What other sport has players specifically designated as "enforcers" to protect "star" players and intimidate the opposition?

Steve Downie of the Philadelphia Flyers was regularly suspended for fights and attacks on other players (CBC, 2008). He was suspended for 20 games for a pre-season hit, and then suspended again for another sucker punch to a Toronto Maple Leafs' player—all in his rookie season! So does this make us redefine aggression? Is it aggression when you check an opposing player into the boards during a hockey game? Most would say no. How about if you sucker-punch another player from behind (like then-Vancouver Canucks player Todd Bertuzzi did to the Colorado Avalanche's Steve Moore, breaking his neck)? Death is not unknown either—in 2009, Ontario AAA player Don Sanderson died after hitting his head on the ice during a fight with an opposing player.

But why is regular violence in hockey tolerated whereas it is not in other sports? We see this bleeding down into the minor leagues. In March 2008, Jonathan Roy of the Quebec Ramparts was suspended for seven games and fined $500 for his part in a fight during a game against the Chicoutimi Sagueneens. His coach and father, Patrick Roy (now coach of the Colorado Avalanche, as well as the controversial former star goalie of the Montreal Canadiens), was also suspended and fined for purportedly encouraging the fight (CTV, 2008).

In November of 2007, two teams of eight-year-olds got into a bench-clearing brawl in Guelph, Ontario (CBC, 2007). What was shocking about that fight was not only the age of the participants (in a league where fighting is clearly not allowed) but the fact that several parents and even the coaches appeared to be encouraging the fight to continue. Ultimately, no coaches were charged with crimes, although both were suspended.

So, people learn aggressive responses both by experience and by observing aggressive models. But when will aggressive responses actually occur? Bandura (1979) contended that aggressive acts are motivated by a variety of aversive experiences—frustration, pain, insults, and so forth. Such experiences arouse us emotionally. But whether we act aggressively depends upon the consequences we anticipate. Aggression is most likely when we are aroused *and* it seems safe and rewarding to aggress.

People learn from past experiences. In many ways, "killing begets killing" (Martens et al., 2007). Andy Martens at the University of Canterbury and his colleagues explored how killing insects in an initial task leads to killing more insects later on. What they found was fascinating. People who killed an insect during a "practice" extermination killed significantly more bugs during a "self-paced" extermination task later on than participants who had not killed an insect during the "practice." Obviously, insects and humans are different, but the principle is the same. In other words—once you have killed something, it is easier to kill again, a hypothesis that is consistent with the progress of homicidal individuals and genocidal groups. Interestingly, this was moderated by how similar one feels to the "victim." As we might expect, for people who did not "practise" killing initially, more similarity led to reduced killing in a subsequent task. However, and perhaps surprisingly, for participants who had killed initially, feeling more similar to the victim (in this case the insects) actually *increased* killing in the subsequent task. Thus, once killing starts, being similar to the killer will not protect the victim.

Environmental Influences

Social learning theory offers a perspective from which we can examine specific influences on aggression. Under what conditions do we aggress? What environmental influences pull our triggers?

Painful Incidents

Researcher Nathan Azrin (1967) wanted to know if switching off foot shocks would reinforce two rats' positive interactions with each other. Azrin planned to turn on the shock and then, once the rats approached each other, cut off the pain. To his great surprise, the experiment proved impossible. As soon as the rats felt pain, they attacked each other before the experimenter could switch off the shock. The greater the shock (and pain), the more violent the attack.

Is this true of rats alone? The researchers found that with a wide variety of species, the cruelty the animals imposed upon each other matched zap for zap the cruelty imposed upon them. As Azrin (1967) explained, the pain–attack response occurred with many types of animals. The animals would attack animals of their own species and also those of a different species, or stuffed dolls, or even tennis balls.

The researchers also varied the source of pain. They found that not just shocks induced attack; intense heat and "psychological pain"—for example, suddenly not rewarding hungry pigeons that have been trained to expect a grain reward after pecking at a disk—brought the same reaction as shocks. "Psychological pain" is, of course, what we call frustration.

Pain heightens aggressiveness in humans, also. Many of us can recall such a reaction after stubbing a toe or suffering a headache. Leonard Berkowitz and his associates demonstrated this by having University of Wisconsin students hold one hand in lukewarm water or painfully cold water. Those whose hands were submerged in the cold water reported feeling more irritable and more annoyed, and they were more willing to blast another person with unpleasant noise. In view of such results, Berkowitz (1998) believes that aversive stimulation rather than frustration is the basic trigger of hostile aggression. Frustration is certainly one important type of unpleasantness. But any aversive event, whether a dashed expectation, a personal insult, or physical pain, can incite an emotional outburst. Even the torment of a depressed state increases the likelihood of hostile aggressive behaviour.

Heat and Attacks

An uncomfortable environment also heightens aggressive tendencies. Offensive odours, cigarette smoke, and air pollution have all been linked with aggressive behaviour (Rotton & Frey, 1985). But the most-studied environmental irritant is heat. William Griffitt (1970; Griffitt & Veitch, 1971) found that compared to students who answered questionnaires in a room with a normal temperature, those who did so in an uncomfortably hot room (more than 32°C) reported feeling more tired and aggressive and expressed more hostility toward a stranger. Follow-up experiments revealed that heat also triggers retaliative actions (Bell, 1980; Rule et al., 1987).

Does uncomfortable heat increase aggression in the real world as well as in the laboratory? Consider the following:

- Brendan Rule and her colleagues (Rule et al., 1987) at the University of Alberta found that adults were more likely to finish stories with an aggressive ending if the temperature were hot (33°C) versus cool (21°C).
- Ehor Boyanowsky (1999) from Simon Fraser University found that people in hot conditions felt both aggressive and threatened relative to people in very cool conditions. Interestingly, the coldest condition led participants to feel the most romantic arousal.
- During the 1986 to 1988 Major League Baseball seasons, the number of batters hit by a pitch was two-thirds greater for games played when the temperature was over 30°C than for games played below 30°C (Reifman et al., 1991). Pitchers weren't wilder on hot days—they had no more walks and wild pitches. They just hit more batters.
- Across the northern hemisphere, not only do hotter days have more violent crimes, but so do hotter seasons of the year, hotter summers, hotter years, hotter cities, and hotter regions (Anderson & Anderson, 1998; Anderson et al., 2000). If a 4-degree global warming occurs, Anderson and his colleagues project that the United States alone would annually see at least 50 000 more serious assaults.

Being attacked or insulted by another is especially conducive to aggression. Numerous experiments (Dengerink & Myers, 1977; Ohbuchi & Kambara, 1985; and Taylor & Pisano, 1971) confirm that intentional attacks breed retaliatory attacks. In most of these experiments, one person competes with another in a reaction-time contest. After each test trial, the winner chooses how much shock to give the loser. Actually, each subject is playing a programmed opponent, who steadily escalates the amount of shock. Do the real subjects respond charitably? Hardly. Extracting "an eye for an eye" is the more likely response.

Crowding

Crowding—the subjective feeling of not having enough space—is stressful. Crammed in the back of a bus, trapped in slow-moving freeway traffic, or living three to a small room in residence diminishes one's sense of control (Baron et al., 1976; McNeel, 1980). Might such experiences also heighten aggression?

The stress experienced by animals allowed to overpopulate a confined environment does heighten aggressiveness (Calhoun, 1962; Christian et al., 1960). But it is a rather large leap from rats in an enclosure or deer on an island to humans in a city. Nevertheless, it's true that dense urban areas do experience higher rates of crime and emotional distress (Fleming et al., 1987; Kirmeyer, 1978). Even when they don't suffer higher crime rates, residents of crowded cities may *feel* more fearful. Toronto's crime rate has been four times higher than Hong Kong's. Yet, compared to Toronto, people from safer Hong Kong—which is four times more densely populated—have reported feeling more fearful on their city's streets (Gifford & Peacock, 1979).

Applying Social Psychology

One common form of aggression is road rage. We have all experienced it. But how do we deal with it? Compare your driving habits with those of adults in a *USA Today*–CNN–Gallup Poll. Of those surveyed about their driving habits during the previous five years, 41 percent admitted to honking at someone whose driving upset them; 39 percent shouted, cursed, or made gestures to other drivers whose driving upset them; 28 percent slowed down when someone behind them honked or flashed their lights; and 16 percent had a verbal exchange with another driver. Males and those ages 18 to 29 admit to more aggressive acts. Self-serving bias was clearly evident in the poll because three-quarters of respondents reported that others were driving more aggressively today than five years earlier, but only 13 percent admitted that they were doing so (Puente & Castaneda, 1997).

Statistics on aggressive driving are difficult to compile because there is no consensus on a definition and most cases go unreported. Nonetheless, the U.S. National Highway Traffic Safety Administration estimates that road rage causes two-thirds of highway deaths (O'Driscoll, 1997). Why does road rage occur? Among the answers psychologists have suggested (Sleek, 1996) are that the swelling congestion on highways is creating more frustration and stress. E. Scott Geller, a psychologist at Virginia Polytechnic Institute and State University, argued that urbanization, dual-income families, and workplace downsizing have left more people in crowded communities with more to do and less time to do it. People feel rushed, and their stress is particularly noticeable when they drive. Other psychologists have suggested that cars promote deindividuation. The loss of self-awareness and evaluation apprehension reduces restraints on aggression. How do you think this links with some of the discussion we have had on crowding and aggression?

Arousal

So we can see that various aversive situations can result in anger and aggressiveness. However, can any type of arousal elicit aggression? Can sexual arousal, for example, or the arousal we experience after exercise also lead to aggression and violence? In a famous experiment (Schacter & Singer, 1962) researchers found that external cues are important to how we interpret our arousal. These researchers injected participants with adrenalin, which resulted in increased heart rates, rapid breathing, and flushing. Half the participants were forewarned about the effect of the injection, and half were told to expect no side effects. Next, the participants were asked to wait with either a euphoric person or a hostile person. Participants who had been forewarned about the drug's effect (i.e., could attribute their arousal to the drug) were not affected by the state of the person they were waiting with. However, those who were not warned attributed their physical reaction to the person they were with. People with a hostile partner became angry; people with the euphoric partner became amused.

Dolf Zillman and his colleagues (1998, 1989) have found that people can easily attribute arousal from exercise and sexual arousal to provocations. Furthermore, different types of arousal (e.g., sexual or from exercise) can amplify one another. For example, erotic stimuli are more arousing to people who have recently been frightened.

Does the Internet Facilitate Bullying?

Bullying has increasingly been in the news over the last few years. Bullying appears to have been at the heart of the death of Rehtaeh Parsons in Nova Scotia. In addition, there have been numerous cases of bullying victims committing suicide, or lashing out at their tormentors. Overall, a recent U.S. study found that cyber-bullying can lead to depression, reduced social skills, and reduced scholastic performance (NIH, 2010). A recent Canadian study (Cassidy et al., 2009) found that adolescents perceive cyber-bullying to be all too frequent.

Connection:

We discussed the Rehtaeh Parsons case in Module 12.

With the increased time children and young adults spend on the Internet, an obvious question arises: Does the Internet facilitate bullying? Recall our discussion of deindividuation in Module 12. What is more anonymous than the Internet? Web pages are largely untraceable. A bully can attack with little threat of reprisal. Without the presence of specific physical threats, the police and authorities can do nothing to stop it.

Connection:

We first discussed deindividuation in Module 12.

Some might consider that cyber-bullying is less harmful, as it does not involve direct physical violence (although threats online can lead to physical violence in real life). However, adolescents view online bullying as potentially more problematic, as the bullies can remain anonymous (Mishna, Saini & Solomon, 2009). Remember what we learned about deindividuation—people behave more aggressively when they believe they cannot be identified.

LO 4

REDUCING AGGRESSION

We have examined instinct, frustration-aggression, and social learning theories of aggression, and we have scrutinized influences on aggression. How, then, can we reduce aggression? Do theory and research suggest ways to control aggression?

Does Catharsis Reduce Aggression?

"Youngsters should be taught to vent their anger" advised Ann Landers (1969).

The near consensus among social psychologists is that, contrary to what Freud, Lorenz, and their followers supposed, catharsis does *not* result from violence (Geen & Quanty, 1977). For example, Robert Arms and his associates report that Canadian and American spectators of football, wrestling, and hockey games exhibit *more* hostility after viewing the event than before (Arms et al., 1979; Goldstein & Arms, 1971; Russell, 1983). Melissa Ferguson at Cornell, and Ran Hasson (2007) at the Hebrew University, found that Americans who watch news regularly are automatically primed to be aggressive and to make more aggressive and negative judgments toward others, compared with people who do not watch television news. Thus, simply watching the news (which over the last several years in the United States has focused a great deal on coverage of the "War on Terror") can make people more, not less, aggressive.

In laboratory tests of catharsis, Brad Bushman (2002) invited angered participants to hit a punching bag while either ruminating about the person who angered them or thinking about becoming physically fit. A third group did not hit the punching bag. Then, when given a chance to administer loud blasts of noise to the person who angered them, people in the punching bag plus rumination condition felt angrier and were most aggressive. Doing nothing at all more effectively reduced aggression than "blowing off steam."

In some real-life experiments too, aggressing has led to heightened aggression. Ebbe Ebbesen and his colleagues (1975) interviewed 100 engineers and technicians shortly after they were angered by layoff notices. Some were asked questions that gave them an opportunity to express hostility against their employer or supervisors—for example, "What instances can you think of where the company has not been fair with you?" Afterward, they answered a questionnaire assessing attitudes toward the company and the supervisors. Did the previous opportunity to "vent" or "drain off" their hostility reduce it? To the contrary, their hostility increased. Expressing hostility bred more hostility.

Should we therefore bottle up anger and aggressive urges? Silent sulking is hardly more effective, because it allows us to continue reciting our grievances as we conduct conversations in our head. Fortunately, there are non-aggressive ways to express our feelings and to inform others how their behaviour affects us. Across cultures, those who reframe accusatory "you" messages as "I" messages—"I'm angry" or "When you leave dirty dishes I get irritated"—communicate their feelings in a way that better enables the other person to make a positive response (Kubany et al., 1995). We can be assertive without being aggressive.

A Social Learning Approach

If aggressive behaviour is learned, then there is hope for its control. Let us briefly review factors that influence aggression and speculate on how to counteract them.

Anticipated rewards and costs influence instrumental aggression. This suggests that we should reward cooperative, non-aggressive behaviour. In experiments, children become less aggressive when caregivers ignore their aggressive behaviour and reinforce their non-aggressive behaviour (Hamblin et al., 1969).

Because most aggression is impulsive—the result of an argument, an insult, or an attack, we must *prevent* aggression before it happens. We must teach non-aggressive conflict resolution strategies.

To foster a gentler world, we could model and reward sensitivity and cooperation from an early age. Training programs encourage parents to reinforce desirable behaviours and to frame statements positively. ("When you finish cleaning your room you can go play," rather than, "If you don't clean your room, you're grounded.") One "aggression-replacement program" has reduced re-arrest rates of juvenile offenders and gang members by teaching the youths and their parents communication skills, training them to control anger, and raising their level of moral reasoning (Goldstein & Glick, 1994).

If observing aggressive models lowers inhibitions and elicits imitation, then we might also reduce brutal, dehumanizing portrayals in films and on television—steps comparable to those already taken to reduce racist and sexist portrayals. We can also inoculate children against the effects of media violence. In one study, Stanford University used 18 classroom lessons to persuade children to simply reduce their TV watching and video game playing (Robinson et al., 2001). They did—reducing their TV viewing by a third—and their aggressive behaviour at school dropped 25 percent compared to that of children in a control school. Maybe there is hope yet.

CONCLUSIONS

Suggestions such as the ones we have outlined can help us minimize aggression. But given the complexity of aggression's causes and the difficulty of controlling them, who can feel the optimism expressed by Andrew Carnegie's forecast that, in the twentieth century, "To kill a man will be considered as disgusting as we in this day consider it disgusting to eat one." Since Carnegie uttered those words in 1900, over 200 million human beings have been killed. It is a sad irony that although today we understand human aggression better than ever before, humanity's inhumanity is hardly diminished.

SUMMARY OF KEY POINTS

LO1. Define aggression.

- Aggression is broad ranging but can be defined as physical or verbal behaviour intended to hurt someone.

LO2. Explain the different biological influences of aggression.

- There are multiple approaches to explaining aggression, but most theorists now know that there are multiple biological factors that influence the expression of aggression: neural, genetic, and blood chemistry; as well as gender and social dominance.

LO3. Understand the psychological influences on aggression.

- Early theories focused on the role of frustration on aggression, but more recent work focuses on social elements, such as learning through rewards and observation, as well the role of the environment and the Internet.

LO4. Describe effective methods to reduce aggression.

- Although catharsis is not an effective way to reduce aggression, many social learning methods have been successfully employed.

KEY TERMS

Aggression   Physical or verbal behaviour intended to hurt someone.

Catharsis   A belief, derived from instinct theories of aggression, that acting out violently will reduce the need or desire to be violent.

Crowding   A subjective feeling that there is not enough space per person.

Displacement   The redirection of aggression to a target other than the source of the frustration. Generally, the new target is a safer or more socially acceptable target.

Frustration   The blocking of goal-directed behaviour.

Hostile aggression   Aggression with the aim of injuring someone driven by anger.

Instrumental aggression   Aggression that provides a means to an end.

Relative deprivation   The perception that you are less well-off than others with whom you compare yourself.

Social learning theory   The theory that we learn social behaviour by observing and imitating, and by being rewarded and punished.

MODULE FIFTEEN

Defining Stereotypes, Prejudice, and Discrimination

What does this photo mean to you? These Ku Klux Klan (KKK) members support a white supremacist mandate. The Klan was founded by Confederate (Southern) loyalists after the American Civil War. The Klan is active primarily in the American south, but although they receive significant media attention when they are active, they actually represent a viewpoint that is no longer supported by the vast majority of people. Should the KKK be allowed freedom of speech? Do they have the right to spew their hatred the same way tolerant people preach acceptance? Interestingly, in the United States, this is clearly the case. In Canada, it is not so clear.

James Keegstra was a high school teacher and mayor in Eckville, Alberta, when it came to light that he was teaching his social studies classes that the Holocaust had not occurred. He described Jews as "treacherous, subversive, and sadistic." He was stripped of his teaching licence and charged under the Criminal Code of Canada for "wilfully promoting hatred against an identifiable group." He was convicted, but challenged that conviction all the way up to the Supreme Court of Canada. Ultimately, the Supreme Court found that there were limits to free speech. More recently, David Ahenakew, an Aboriginal leader and Order of Canada winner, was charged under the hate crimes law for telling a reporter that he admired how Hitler had "fried" the Jews. In a later trial he was ultimately acquitted, although his comments were called "revolting, disgusting, and untrue" by the judge.

Critical THINKING

In Canada, we have anti–hate speech laws that preclude the type of hatred-based public demonstrations we might see in the United States and other countries. But which is better? Restricting speech so that the hateful language does not come out? Or allowing it to surface so it can be undermined and counterargued? What do you think? What would you do if you made the laws?

Prejudice comes in many forms—against Asians, Blacks, Aboriginals, Jews, women, men, homosexuals, transsexuals, bisexuals; against Arab "terrorists" or Jewish Zionists or Christian fundamentalists; against people who are short, fat, old, young, or unattractive; against the poor, the disabled, or the marginalized. Think of a group and there are probably people who are prejudiced against them. Some people are even prejudiced against members of groups they belong to (so-called "autophobias"; e.g., Finlay, 2005; Herek et al., 2009; Wester et al., 2007). Consider a few actual examples of discrimination and/or prejudice that we might have observed in our everyday lives:

- Aboriginal peoples have been fighting for their land claim and treaty rights for decades, making little progress. Most recently, the Supreme Court of Canada found against an Aboriginal group because they had waited too long before challenging the 100-year-old violation of their treaty rights. Meanwhile, people living on reserves suffer from the highest levels of illness, suicide, alcohol and drug dependence, and unemployment in Canada (CBC, 2013). Aboriginal women are four times more likely to be murdered than the rest of the Canadian population (CBC, 2014). In 2012, the Health Council of Canada reported that Aboriginals also face racist stereotypes when seeking treatment in the Canadian health care system.

- In response to the debate over "reasonable accommodation" in Quebec, the town of Herouxville adopted a "code of conduct" for immigrants in the town. The code reminded immigrants that women should be allowed to show their faces in public, that they should be allowed to drive cars and write cheques, and they should not be stoned or burned alive in public. Although many were shocked, the town council received thousands of supportive emails, and seven towns in the region also supported the code of conduct (CBC, 2007). More recently, in 2013 the Parti-Québécois government in Quebec moved to ban the wearing of religious symbols (including yarmulkes and head scarves, but not small crucifixes) in the public sector (which includes all school and government employees). The legislation died when the government was voted out of office in 2014.

- Research by Stewart Page at the University of Windsor has shown that being homosexual can hurt your chances of finding a place to live (Page, 1998, 1999). He found that if the caller mentioned being HIV-positive, landlords were *five times* more likely to say the accommodation was unavailable. Further, two-thirds of gay high school students report being bullied (Hunt and Jenson, 2007), and 20 percent of lesbian and gay adults report being harassed, insulted, or assaulted (Dick, 2008).

RCMP officers Jason Lee and David Conners made national headlines when they announced their engagement. In general, the reaction to their announcement was positive.

RCMP officer Baltej Singh Dhillon also made headlines when he challenged the RCMP uniform policy on religious grounds. Reaction to him was less positive.

- Harkening back to the tactics of the KKK, Justin and Nathan Rehberg were convicted in 2010 of a hate crime for burning a cross on the front lawn of a mixed-race couple near Windsor, Nova Scotia. Shayne Howe (a Black man) and Michelle Lyon (a White woman, who was actually related to the Rehberg brothers) were at home when the cross was lit on fire. The two men were convicted of inciting hate—the first time in Canada that burning a cross has been deemed a hate crime.

- When RCMP Constables Jason Lee and David Connors announced their plans to marry in 2006, the story made national news headlines (CTV, 2006). Both constables said that their co-workers, friends, managers, and residents of the small Nova Scotia town they worked in supported the marriage. This stands in sharp contrast to the case of Baltej Singh Dhillon, a Sikh cadet who wanted to keep his beard and turban, in direct challenge to RCMP regulations in 1990 (CBC, 1990). He received hate mail and threats. Ultimately, the solicitor general of Canada, who is responsible for the RCMP, ruled in favour of Dhillon, who is still an officer and still wears his turban.

Gay rights activist Cathy Marino-Thomas, centre, of Brooklyn, chants slogans during a demonstration in front of the Russian consulate in New York prior to the Sochi Winter Olympics.

- In the year leading up to the 2014 Sochi Winter Olympics in Russia, the Russian government passed a law that made "gay propaganda" illegal in order to "protect the children" from the influence of gays. Many human rights organizations complained, boycotts were proposed, and some countries changed the make-up of their Olympic delegations in protest. For example, U.S. President Barack Obama declined to attend, and sent openly gay tennis star Billie-Jean King as the U.S. representative.

- Shortly after September 11, 2001, hostilities flared against people perceived to be of Arab descent. In suburban New York City, a man tried to run down a Pakistani woman while shouting that he was "doing this for my country" (Brown, 2001). In Denton, Texas, a mosque was firebombed (Thomson, 2001). At Boston University, a Middle Eastern student was stabbed, and at the University of Colorado, students spray-painted the library with "Arabs Go Home." These were not isolated events. The American Arab Anti-Discrimination Committee catalogued more than 250 acts of violence against Arab-American students on college campuses in the week following the attacks (CNN.com, 2001). Negative views of Middle Eastern immigrants have persisted. In one U.S. survey six months after the attacks, Pakistanis and Palestinians were rated as negatively as drug dealers (Fiske, 2002). More recently (Cohen, 2006), 46 percent of Americans have expressed a negative view of Islam, with 58 percent believing that Muslims are disproportionately likely to be violent extremists.

- When seeking love and employment, overweight people—especially overweight White women—face slim prospects. In both correlational studies and in experiments (in which people are made to appear overweight or not), overweight people marry less often, gain entry to less-desirable jobs, make less money, and are perceived as less attractive, intelligent, happy, self-disciplined, and successful (Gortmaker et al., 1993; Hebl & Heatherton, 1998; Pingitore et al., 1994). Weight discrimination is, in fact, notably greater than race or gender discrimination and occurs at every employment stage—hiring, placement, promotion, compensation, discipline, and discharge (Roehling, 2000; Roehling et al., 2008, 2009). A recent Ipsos-Reid poll of 1500 Canadians revealed that 54 percent of Canadians believe that people who are seriously overweight should pay more for employee health benefits. Clearly, people who are overweight are seen as responsible for their situation.

LO 1

DEFINING PREJUDICE

Prejudice, stereotyping, discrimination, racism, sexism—the terms often overlap. Let's clarify them. Each of the situations just described involved a negative evaluation of some group. And that is the essence of prejudice: a negative attitude toward a group. Prejudice biases us against a person based on the person's perceived group. Prejudice is typically considered the affective or emotional component of outgroup bias.

Prejudice is an attitude. The negative evaluations that mark prejudice can stem from emotional associations, from the need to justify behaviour, or from negative *beliefs*, which are called stereotypes. To stereotype is to generalize. To simplify the world, we generalize: The British are reserved; the French are arrogant; professors are absent-minded.

Occasionally, there may be a "kernel of truth" in beliefs about particular groups. However, the problem with stereotypes arises because they are *overgeneralized* or just plain wrong. The presumption that jocks prefer sports-related courses to economics contains a kernel of truth, but is overblown. Individuals within the stereotyped group vary more than expected (Brodt & Ross, 1998).

Prejudice is a negative attitude; discrimination is negative behaviour. Thus, discrimination is the behavioural component of outgroup bias. Discriminatory behaviour often has its source in prejudicial attitudes (Dovidio et al., 1996; Wagner et al., 2008). However, attitudes and behaviour are often loosely linked, partly because our behaviour reflects more than our inner convictions. Prejudiced attitudes need not breed hostile acts, nor does all oppression spring from prejudice.

Connection:

> We discussed the link between attitude and behaviour in Module 8.

Racism and sexism are institutional practices that discriminate, even when there is no prejudicial intent. If word-of-mouth hiring practices in an all-male organization have the effect of excluding potential female employees, the practice could be called sexist—even if an employer intended no discrimination.

LO 2

HOW PERVASIVE IS PREJUDICE?

Is prejudice inevitable? Let's look at the most heavily studied examples—racial and gender prejudice.

Racial and Ethnic Attitudes

In the context of the world, every race is a minority. Non-Hispanic Whites, for example, are but one-fifth of the world's people and will be but one-eighth within another half century. Thanks to mobility and migration during the past two centuries, the world's races now intermingle in relations that are sometimes hostile, sometimes amiable. This trend is very strong in Canada as evidenced by the 2011 census, which reports that almost 21 percent of Canadians are foreign born, and visible minorities now make up over 19 percent of the Canadian population, accounting for over 6 million individuals. For more than 20 percent of the population, neither English nor French is their first language. When people living in Canada are asked to self-identify their ethnic identity on the census, it becomes clear we are a diverse group. As shown in Figure 15-1, after we remove the 5.6 million people who simply identify themselves as "Canadian," a very multicultural population remains (although the two single largest groups are English and French). Furthermore, when surveys of Canadians are conducted, multiculturalism is one of the core values that we identify for our society. Indeed, to support this multicultural ideal, Parliament passed the Multiculturalism Policy in 1971 (the formal Act was passed in 1987). The stated purpose of the policy was to encourage people from all cultural backgrounds in Canada to share their unique cultural heritage with all members of Canadian society. The main aim was to promote tolerance and understanding among all cultural groups in Canada.

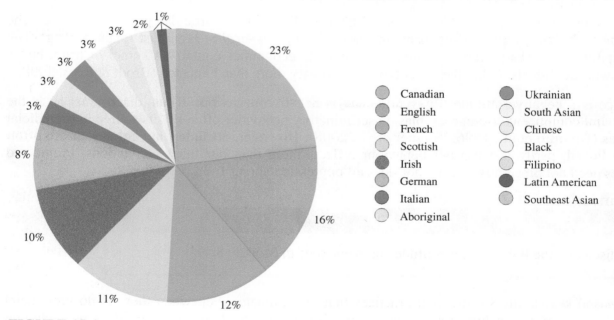

FIGURE 15-1

Self-Identified Ethnic Origin. 32 852 320 total respondents providing 48 149 805 total responses (some people gave multiple responses; and 6 264 800 self-identified as "Visible Minority").

Source: Data from 2011 Census, courtesy of Statistics Canada.

To a molecular biologist, skin colour is a pretty trivial human characteristic, one controlled by a minuscule genetic difference between races. Moreover, nature doesn't cluster races in neatly defined categories. It is we, not nature, who label Tiger Woods "African American" (his ancestry is 25 percent African) or "Asian American" (he is also 25 percent Thai and 25 percent Chinese)—or even as Native as Native American or Dutch (he is one-eighth each).

Historically, there has always been some level of conflict among ethnic groups in Canada. Since before Confederation, conflict between French and English Canadians has been a source of concern for the country. It is no secret that some French Canadians (especially in Quebec) have had concerns about their treatment at the hands of an Anglophone-dominated Canada. Indeed, two close separation votes in Quebec (the second of which Steven voted in and spent many hours watching the results of) have highlighted many of these issues. As an early attempt to deal with these issues, in the 1960s Prime Minister Lester Pearson made Canada an officially bilingual nation, and thus began a tradition of recognizing cultural uniqueness that has continued in the support and development of multiculturalism in Canada. In 2006 Parliament unanimously passed a declaration that Quebec is a "Nation within Canada," in an attempt to recognize Quebec's unique heritage.

Remarkably, especially since people tend to present themselves in the most positive manner possible in surveys, a substantial percentage of Canadians rate themselves as being racist to some degree (CBC, 2007). Forty-seven percent of Canadians rated themselves as at least somewhat racist, with Muslims being the most common target of racism. Interestingly, Québécois rated themselves as most racist, with 59 percent indicating some racist attitudes. Does this mean that Québécois really are the most racist, or does it mean they answered most honestly?

Despite these survey findings, multiculturalism has been highlighted as a distinctive element of Canadian society, making us distinct from other countries. More than 50 percent of Canadians are proud of Canada's multicultural identity, and almost 80 percent see a moderate to strong benefit from immigration in terms of benefits to cultural, cognitive, and intellectual resources (Parkin & Mendelsohn, 2003). Our major cities (particularly Toronto, Montreal, and Vancouver) have large and diverse multicultural communities that are encouraged to retain their ethnic identities. Indeed, in a PEW global attitudes survey (PEW, 2007), Canada ranked second among Western countries in terms of opposition to the restriction of immigration (Sweden was the most opposed to further restrictions). Sixty-two percent of Canadians are in favour of increasing immigration.

This stands in interesting contrast to the U.S. policy on the integration of immigrants and minorities: the United States has a specific policy of assimilation. When you move to the United States you become part of the "great melting pot," and it is assumed you will assimilate into the existing culture and society. In Canada, immigrants are expected to become Canadian but also to maintain and share their unique cultural heritage with the rest of the country. However, attempting to maintain multiple identities during this process of *acculturation* (i.e., when a person from one culture tries to re-establish his or her life in a new culture) can lead to personal conflict (see Berry, 1997). Sir Wilfrid Laurier, a French Canadian and our seventh prime minister, expressed this well when he said of his experience while trying to deal with issues surrounding full independence from Great Britain: "I am branded in Quebec as a traitor to the French, and in Ontario as a traitor to the English. In Quebec I am branded as a Jingo, in Ontario as a Separatist . . . I am neither. I am Canadian" (as quoted in Bliss, 2004, p. 46).

To a great extent, the multiculturalism policy seems to have been successful. John Berry and Rudolf Kalin, while they were at Queen's University, conducted an analysis of a national survey of attitudes toward different ethnic groups in Canada (Berry & Kalin, 1995). People's overall comfort levels with ethnic-group members were very positive, yet ethnic Canadians (people born and raised in Canada, regardless of ethnic origin) were rated more positively than immigrant Canadians. Douglas Palmer (1996), a social psychologist who works for Citizenship and Immigration Canada, found that Canadians, particularly younger Canadians, were often opposed to immigration. Interestingly, he found that prejudice was not a good predictor of attitudes toward immigration. He found that people's expectations about how immigration is related to increases in crime and how immigrants affect their employment opportunities were a better predictor of people's attitudes toward immigration than their level of prejudice. Similarly, in the United States, concerns about immigrants taking jobs are greatest among those with the lowest incomes (AP/Ipsos, 2006; PEW, 2006).

In a survey of students at 390 U.S. colleges and universities, 53 percent of African-American students felt excluded from social activities (Hurtado et al., 1994). (Such feelings were also reported by 24 percent of Asian Americans, 16 percent of Mexican Americans, and 6 percent of European Americans). Such majority–minority relationships transcend race. On NBA basketball teams, minority players (in this case, Whites) feel similarly detached from their group's socializing (Schoenfeld, 1995).

This phenomenon of *greatest prejudice in the most intimate social realms* seems universal. In India, people who accept the caste system will typically allow someone from a lower caste into their homes but would not consider marrying such a person (Sharma, 1981). In a national survey of Americans, 75 percent said they would "shop at a store owned by a homosexual," but only 39 percent would "see a homosexual doctor" (Henry, 1994). Similarly, although there is still overt prejudice and violence, attitudes toward minorities in general have changed. For example, while there were over 7000 reported hate crimes in the United States in 2004 (FBI, 2005), over 90 percent of Americans said they would vote for a Black presidential candidate in 2003 versus just over 50 percent in 1958 (Gallup, 2004). Yet race is still an issue. Substantial coverage of the 2008 presidential election focused on Barack Obama's racial background and Hillary Clinton's gender.

Dr. Victoria Esses, a professor at the University of Western Ontario, has been at the forefront of research on stereotyping and prejudice for a number of years. Her most recent work has focused on perceptions of immigrants. Even though Canadians report that multiculturalism is an important value, immigrants perceived themselves as not always being welcome in Canada. Dr. Esses found that immigrants often felt that their skills were being undervalued in the Canadian job market. Economists and sociologists call this skill discounting. Although the Canadian immigration program allots more "points" to a potential immigrant based on education level and work experience (more points means a greater likelihood of being allowed to immigrate to Canada), immigrants find that once they have arrived in Canada they often cannot obtain jobs in their field.

Connection:

We will discuss some of the reasons for prejudice in Module 16.

Along with a colleague in organizational behaviour, Joerg Dietz, Dr. Esses decided to use attitudes toward immigrants as a predictor of people's attitudes toward job applicants. Dr. Esses experimentally manipulated the country of origin (Canada, the United Kingdom, or India) of a potential job applicant but held education and ethnic background constant. In the study (see Esses et al., 2012), they manipulated the résumé of a potential job applicant. All résumés were for an applicant with the name "Anita Singh," who was described as speaking French, English, and Hindi.

Interestingly, if the applicant was described as being from Canada or the United Kingdom, participants' attitudes toward immigrants (positive or negative) had no impact on their ratings of the applicant's fit to the position or fit to the organization (two key evaluations made of any job applicant). However, if the applicant was described as being from India, attitudes were a significant predictor of evaluations—the more negative people's attitudes toward immigrants, the less the applicant was seen to "fit" the job and the organization. This suggested to Dr. Esses and her colleagues that people may feel more comfortable exhibiting prejudicial behaviours when they feel they can "get away" with it by appealing to the uncertainty of credentials obtained in India.

Subtle Forms of Prejudice

In 2005, an Ipsos-Reid poll reported that one in six Canadian adults (approximately 5 million people) felt they had been the victim of racism. Another national poll indicated that more than half of Canadians were aware of someone who had been discriminated against. In other words, although blatant and overt racism and discrimination may be on the decline, at minimum, perceived discrimination is still an issue (see Dion, 2002).

Thus, if prejudice and discrimination are less obvious, how are they manifested in society? As blatant prejudice subsides, automatic emotional reactions linger. Research indicates that conscious prejudice can affect our instant reactions (Macrae & Bodenhausen, 2000). But Patricia Devine and her colleagues (1989, 2000) report that those low and high in prejudice sometimes have similar automatic reactions. They differ because low-prejudice people consciously try to suppress prejudicial thoughts and feelings. It's like breaking a bad habit, says Devine. Try as we might to suppress unwanted thoughts—thoughts about food, thoughts about romance with a friend's partner, judgmental thoughts about another group—they sometimes refuse to go away (Macrae et al., 1994; Wegner & Erber, 1992). The result for all of us: unwanted (dissonant) thoughts and feelings often persist.

Dissimilarity breeds dislike: Like ethnic minorities elsewhere, Muslims living in Canada have encountered hostility. Here, Muslim women protest against the proposed Quebec Values Charter, which would have banned the wearing of religious symbols and clothing in public institutions.

All of this illustrates again the distinction between explicit (conscious) and implicit (automatic) attitudes toward the same target. Thus, we may retain from childhood a habitual, automatic fear or dislike of people for whom we now express respect and appreciation. Although explicit attitudes may change dramatically with education, Kerry Kawakami at York University reports that implicit attitudes may linger, changing only as we form new habits through practice (Kawakami et al., 2000).

A raft of experiments (e.g., Fazio et al., 1995; Greenwald et al., 2000; Nosek et al., 2005; Olson & Fazio, 2004; Jones & Fazio, 2010) have confirmed the phenomenon of automatic stereotyping and prejudice. These studies briefly flash words or faces that "prime" (automatically activate) stereotypes of some racial, gender, or age group. Without their awareness, the subjects' activated stereotypes may then bias their behaviour. Having been primed with images associated with Black people, for example, they may then react with more hostility to an experimenter's annoying request. In clever experiments by Anthony Greenwald and his colleagues (2000), nine out of ten White people took longer to identify pleasant words (such as *peace* and *paradise*) as "good" when associated with Black rather than White faces. The subjects, mind you, typically expressed little or no prejudice—only an unconscious, unintended response. Moreover, Hugenberg and Bodenhausen (2003) have demonstrated that the more strongly people exhibit such implicit prejudice, the readier they are to perceive anger in Black faces.

In separate experiments, Joshua Correll and his colleagues (2002, 2006), and Anthony Greenwald and his colleagues (2003) invited people to press buttons quickly to "shoot" or "not shoot" men who suddenly appeared on-screen holding either a gun or a harmless object such as a flashlight or bottle. The participants (both Blacks and Whites, in one of the studies) more often mistakenly shot targets who were Black. In a related series of studies, Keith Payne (2001) and Charles Judd and colleagues (2004) found that when primed with a Black rather than a White face, people think guns: they more quickly recognize a gun and they more often mistake tools, such as a wrench, for a gun. These studies help explain why Amadou Diallo (a Black immigrant in New York City) was shot 41 times by police officers for removing his wallet from his back pocket (Gladwell, 2005); or how Michael Brown, an unarmed black teenager in Ferguson, Missouri, was shot six times by a white police officer, reportedly while standing with his hands above his head (CBC, 2014).

Automatic prejudice: When Joshua Correll and his colleagues invited people to react quickly to people holding either a gun or a harmless object, race influenced perceptions and reactions.

Activity: Face-ism

Do the media portray men and women differently? Dane Archer at the University of California, Santa Cruz, thinks so. Archer and his colleagues (1983) showed that in the media, across 12 nations, photos of men emphasize their faces, whereas those of women emphasize their bodies. An examination of artwork over six centuries confirmed the pervasiveness of this difference in the portrayal of men and women.

You can attempt to replicate these findings by examining current issues of your favourite magazines. Do you find the same thing? Perhaps media portrayals have changed in the last three decades.

This possible bias may seem like a somewhat innocuous thing, but what impact might this be having on how we perceive men and women in our society?

Archer and his colleagues explored this in a final study, where they experimentally manipulated the degree of facial prominence in photographs. They found that the same person is perceived more favourably when the face is prominent than when it is not. Archer and his colleagues suggest that face-ism may perpetuate stereotyped conceptions of what's important about men and women.

It also appears that different brain regions are involved in automatic as well as consciously controlled stereotyping (Correll et al., 2006; Cunningham et al., 2004; Eberhardt, 2005). Pictures of outgroups that provoke the most disgust (such as drug addicts and the homeless) elicit more amygdala than frontal cortex activity (Harris & Fiske, 2006). This suggests that automatic prejudices involve primitive regions of the brain associated with fear, such as the amygdala, whereas controlled processing is more closely associated with the frontal cortex, which enables conscious thinking.

Sexuality and Prejudice

There is also widespread prejudice against homosexuals. In the most recent statistics available, it appears crimes against homosexuals may be on the rise. In 2010, Statistics Canada reported that in 2008 twice as many hate crimes were reported against homosexuals as in the previous year. Interestingly, these crimes may be more violent as well. Compared to race-based hate crimes reported, three-quarters of crimes against homosexuals (versus 38 percent) involved violence; 85 percent of the victims were men. It is likely that this increase is due in part to programs encouraging gay, lesbian, bisexual, and transgendered (LGBT) individuals to report these crimes, but estimates still suggest that up to 75 percent of hate crimes against these groups go unreported.

Connection:

We initially discussed sexuality identity and discrimination in Module 3.

Homophobia is also prevalent in schools, says a report by Catherine Taylor at the University of Winnipeg, Tracey Peter at the University of Manitoba, and Egale Canada, a group that does research and education on LGBT issues in Canada (Taylor & Peter, 2011). The report describes a three-year study on more than 3600 Canadian teens. According to the report, homophobic comments are common, and sometimes are directed at teens by teachers. Interestingly, this appears to be more of a problem for girls and young women than for boys and young men. One in ten straight teens has been on the receiving end of homophobic insults. Approximately 60 percent of straight teens find the comments directed at LGBT teens to be problematic.

Prejudicial attitudes toward gay men reflect the ideas studied by Melanie Morrison and Todd Morrison (at the University of Saskatchewan)—homonegativity and homopositivity (e.g., Jewell & Morrison, 2010; Morrison & Morrison, 2011; Morrison, Morrison & Franklin, 2009). These researchers have developed the Modern Homonegativity Scale to assess attitudes toward gays and lesbians. The idea here is that modern homonegativity is a more subtle form of prejudice; although overt prejudice against gays and lesbians is less acceptable, people may view these groups as making "unnecessary or illegitimate demands" because discrimination is no longer a real issue—gays and lesbians have received enough attention and special favours from the establishment and the media. Scores on the modern homonegativity scale predict discriminatory behaviour; for example, people who endorse modern homonegativity are less likely to vote for a gay mayoral candidate.

Gender Stereotypes and Prejudice

How pervasive is prejudice against women? Gender-role norms are people's ideas about how women and men *ought* to behave. Here we consider gender *stereotypes*—people's beliefs about how women and men *do* behave. Norms are *pre*scriptive, stereotypes are *de*scriptive.

Connection:

Remember that we discussed gender role norms in Module 3.

From research on stereotypes, two conclusions are indisputable: Strong gender stereotypes exist, and, as often happens, members of the stereotyped group accept the stereotypes. Men and women agree that you *can* judge the book by its sexual cover. In one survey, Mary Jackman and Mary Senter

(1981) found that gender stereotypes were much stronger than racial stereotypes. For example, only 22 percent of men thought the two genders were equally "emotional." Of the remaining 78 percent, those who believed females were more emotional outnumbered those who thought males were by 15 to 1. And what did the women believe? To within one percentage point, their responses were identical.

Connection:

In Module 14 we discussed the percentage of women in leadership positions in business and politics.

Applying Social Psychology: Modern Racism

Survey research shows a dramatic decline in prejudice against minorities over the last few decades. Nevertheless, indirect methods for assessing people's attitudes and behaviour reveal disguised racial bias. Racism may be subtler and more hypocritical than the blatant prejudice of 50 years ago. A survey by Patterson and Kim (1991) documented the phenomenon of greatest prejudice in the most intimate social realms, as described earlier in this module. So ask yourself the following:

- Could you fall in love with someone from a different ethnic group?
- How do you think your friends and parents would react if you married this person?
- You learn after an accident that you have received a blood transfusion from a gay person. Would that bother you?
- Does it make you uneasy to see a same-sex couple walking hand-in-hand?

McConahay (1981) argued that the following four beliefs underlie modern racism:

1. Minorities now have the freedom to compete in the marketplace and enjoy those things they can afford. Discrimination is really a thing of the past.

2. Minorities push too hard, too fast, and into places where they are really not wanted.

3. Both the demands and tactics that minorities use are unfair.

4. Our social institutions are giving minorities more attention and status than they deserve.

Do you agree with these statements? Would it apply equally to questions of gender or sexual orientation? McConahay noted that people who accept these ideas do not see themselves as prejudiced. In fact, they agree that racism is bad. Nonetheless, suggested McConahay, modern racism continues to generate negative racial affect, influences how people interpret new information, and perhaps most important, how people interact with minorities on a daily basis.

Research reveals that behaviours associated with leadership are perceived less favourably when enacted by a woman (Eagly & Karau, 2000). Assertiveness can seem less becoming in a woman than in a man (making it harder for women to become and succeed as leaders). Furthermore, women politicians who are seen as "power-seeking" (such as Hillary Clinton in the 2008 U.S. federal election) are perceived more negatively, and receive fewer votes. Men, however, are not seen more negatively if they are perceived as power-seeking (Okimoto & Brescoll, 2010).

Remember that stereotypes are generalizations about a group of people and may be true, false, or overgeneralized from a kernel of truth. (They may also be self-fulfilling.) In previous modules, we noted that the average man and woman do differ somewhat in social connectedness, empathy, social power, and aggressiveness. Do we then conclude that gender stereotypes are accurate? Often they are, observed Janet Swim (1994). She found that students' stereotypes of men's and women's restlessness, non-verbal sensitivity, aggressiveness, and so forth were reasonable approximations of actual gender differences. Moreover, such stereotypes have persisted across time and culture. Averaging data from 27 countries, John Williams and his colleagues (1999, 2000) found that people everywhere perceive women as more agreeable, and men as more outgoing. The persistence and omnipresence of gender stereotypes leads some evolutionary psychologists to believe they reflect innate, stable reality (Lueptow et al., 1995).

But individuals' accuracy varies widely, and stereotypes are sometimes misapplied (Hall & Carter, 1999). Moreover, gender stereotypes sometimes exaggerate small differences, as Carol Lynn Martin (1987) concluded after surveying visitors to the University of British Columbia. She asked them to check which of several traits described them and to estimate what percentage of North American males and females had each trait. Males were indeed slightly more likely than females to describe themselves as assertive and dominant and were slightly less likely to describe themselves as tender and compassionate. But stereotypes of these differences were exaggerated: The people perceived North American males as almost twice as likely as females to be assertive and dominant and roughly half as likely to be tender and compassionate. By leading to exaggerated perceptions that become self-fulfilling prophecies, small differences may grow.

Traditional gender stereotyping assumes that a father leaves a mother at home to perform child care while he goes to work (left) rather than other way around (right).

Alice Eagly and her associates (1991) and Geoffrey Haddock and Mark Zanna (1994) also report that people don't respond to women with gut-level, negative emotions as they do to certain other groups. Most people like women more than men. They perceive women as more understanding, kind, and helpful. Thus, a *favourable* stereotype, which Eagly (1994) dubs the *women-are-wonderful effect,* results in a favourable attitude.

Critical THINKING

So, given what you now know, what would it take to reduce gender discrimination? It is clear this is still occurring. Has it gotten better? Or is it just more subtle. Janet Swim and her colleagues (1995, 1997) have found a subtle ("modern") sexism that parallels subtle ("modern") racism. Have you ever experienced this in your life?

Sexism is not dead. We can also detect bias in behaviour. For example, members of a research team led by Ian Ayres (1991) visited 90 Chicago-area car dealers, using a uniform strategy to negotiate the lowest price on a new car that cost the dealer about $11 000. White males were given a final price that averaged $11 362; White females were given an average price of $11 504; Black males were given an average price of $11 783; and Black females were given an average price of $12 237.

Most women know that gender bias exists. They believe that sex discrimination affects most working women, as shown by the lower salaries for women and especially for jobs, such as child care, that are filled mostly by women. Garbage haulers (mostly men) make more than preschool teachers (mostly women). Consistent with research on prejudice, however, Faye Crosby and her colleagues (1989) have repeatedly found that most women deny feeling personally discriminated against (much like many minority group members). Discrimination, they believe, is something *other* women face. Their employers are not villainous. They are doing better than the average woman. Hearing no complaints, managers—even in discriminatory organizations—can persuade themselves that justice prevails.

Yet, around the world, people tend to prefer having baby boys. In the United States in 1941, 38 percent percent of expectant parents said they would prefer a boy if they could only have one child; 24 percent preferred a girl; and 23 percent said they didn't care. In 2003, the answers were virtually unchanged, with 38 percent still preferring a boy (Lyons, 2003; Simmons, 2000). With the widespread use of of ultrasound to determine the sex of a fetus and the growing availability of abortion, these preferences these preferences are affecting the number of boys and girls. Reports of the 2010 China census revealed 114 newborn boys for every 100 girls (CIA, 2010). In India the number is 112 newborn boys for every 100 girls.

CONCLUSIONS

Overt prejudice is far less common today than it was four decades ago. Nevertheless, techniques that are sensitive to subtle prejudice still detect widespread bias. And in parts of the world, gender and ethnic prejudice is, literally, deadly. We therefore need to look carefully and closely at the problem of prejudice and its causes. If we ignore the problem, we risk letting it get worse.

SUMMARY OF KEY POINTS

LO1. Define prejudice.

- Prejudice can be defined as a negative attitude toward a particular group. Prejudice is typically considered the affective or emotional component of outgroup bias.
- Stereotypes, the cognitive component, are beliefs about these groups that are typically overgeneralized, inaccurate, and resistant to new information.
- Discrimination is unjustifiable negative behaviour toward an outgroup.

LO2. Understand how pervasive prejudice is.

- Racial and ethnic attitudes are pervasive. Not all of these result in prejudice, but some do.
- Prejudice can be subtle, and can be directed at ethnic, social, or cultural groups, as well as resulting from sexuality and gender.

KEY TERMS

Discrimination   Unjustifiable negative behaviour toward a group or its members. Discrimination is the behavioural component of outgroup bias.

Prejudice   A negative attitude toward a group. Prejudice is typically considered the affective component of outgroup bias.

Racism   (1) An individual's prejudicial attitudes and discriminatory behaviour toward people of a given race, or (2) institutional practices (even if not motivated by prejudice) that subordinate people of a given race.

Sexism   (1) An individual's prejudicial attitudes and discriminatory behaviour toward people of a given gender, or (2) institutional practices (even if not motivated by prejudice) that subordinate people of a given gender.

Stereotypes   Beliefs about the personal attributes of a group of people. Stereotypes are sometimes overgeneralized, inaccurate, and resistant to new information. Stereotypes are the cognitive component of outgroup bias.

Causes of Stereotypes, Prejudice, and Discrimination

LEARNING OBJECTIVES After studying Module 16, you will be able to

LO **1** Explain the social sources of prejudice

LO **2** Understand how frustration can lead to aggression

LO **3** Understand the role of personality in prejudice

LO **4** Understand the cognitive sources of prejudice

Imagine you are driving your car (a new Lexus hybrid, perhaps?) through downtown Regina. It is late at night, the streets are empty, and you are slowly making your way home. Suddenly, looking in your rear-view mirror, you notice you are being followed by a police cruiser. How likely is it that you are going to be pulled over? Ten percent? Twenty percent? Fifty percent? Think about it, and come up with a number.

Interestingly, your response probably depends on your ethnic background. If you are Caucasian, you probably rated the likelihood lower than if you were non-Caucasian. Minorities expect to be the subject of discrimination. People perceive that the police engage in *racial profiling*—stopping people based on ethnic background rather than probable cause. Some Black Canadians have labelled this practice as being pulled over for a "DWB"—"Driving While Black." Although Canadian police and border officials steadfastly deny that they profile based on race, researchers at McMaster and the University of Toronto argue that they do, although they are able to rationalize what they do as "part of the job" rather than discrimination or prejudice (see Pratt & Thompson, 2008; Satzewich & Shaffir, 2009).

Is there any truth to these perceptions? Data released from the Kingston, Ontario, police found that Black motorists were 3.7 times more likely than Whites to be stopped, and Aboriginals were 1.4 times more likely than Whites to be stopped (CBC, 2005). Both the Toronto and Halifax police, as well as border security agents, have come under fire for perceived racial profiling. This is not limited to Canada. Similar statistics are reported in the United States, the United Kingdom, and other countries. Racial profiling also seems to be a concern for people of Arabic descent at airports worldwide, as a consequence of terrorist attacks.

Critical THINKING

In a well-publicized 2003 ruling, the Nova Scotia Human Rights Commission found that heavyweight boxer Kirk Johnson was discriminated against by the Halifax Regional Police when he was pulled over and had his car impounded. Johnson received an apology and $10 000, and the police had to revise their sensitivity-training practices. However, some people argue that this practice is not discrimination, insisting that certain groups are more likely to commit crimes and, therefore, increased attention is appropriate. Is there any validity to this argument?

Prejudice springs from several sources because it serves several functions. Prejudice may express our sense of who we are and gain us social acceptance. It may defend our sense of self against anxiety that arises from insecurity or inner conflict. And it may promote our self-interest by supporting what brings us pleasure and opposing what doesn't. Consider first how prejudice can function to defend self-esteem and social position.

LO 1

SOCIAL SOURCES OF PREJUDICE

Unequal Status

A principle to remember: *Unequal status breeds prejudice.* Masters view slaves as lazy, irresponsible, lacking ambition—as having just those traits that justify the slavery. Historians debate the forces that create unequal status. But once these inequalities exist, prejudice helps justify the economic and social superiority of those who have wealth and power. Stereotypes rationalize unequal status (Yzerbyt et al., 1997).

Connection:

We discussed attitudes toward Aboriginal peoples in Module 15.

Aboriginal peoples are often negatively stereotyped in Canada (Werhun & Penner, 2010). Much of that comes from perceptions of their lower social status (e.g., being poor or alcoholic; see Bell, Esses & Maio, 1996). When people think of Aboriginals, they typically conjure images of remote communities struggling with alcohol and substance abuse issues.

Gender stereotypes also help rationalize gender roles. After studying these stereotypes worldwide, John Williams and Deborah Best (1990a) noted that if women provide most of the care to young children, it is reassuring to think women are naturally nurturing. If males run the businesses, hunt, and fight wars, it is comforting to suppose that men are aggressive, independent, and adventurous. In experiments, people perceive members of unknown groups as having traits that suit their roles (Hoffman & Hurst, 1990).

But these gender attitudes can often be ambivalent, report Peter Glick and Susan Fiske (1996, 2001). In their surveys of 15 000 people in 19 nations, these researchers found that people often display a mix of this *benevolent* sexism (e.g., women are more nurturing; women are more moral), with more *hostile* sexism (e.g., women keep men on a short leash). Interestingly, the status of the women in question can also play a role. Theresa Veschio and her colleagues (2005) found that powerful men who stereotype their female subordinates give them plenty of praise, but few resources, thus undermining their performance. This distinction between benevolent and hostile sexism also extends to other prejudices as well. We tend to see "other" group members as either competent or likable, but not both. In the United States, Asians, Jews, Germans, non-traditional women, assertive African Americans, and gay men tend to be respected but not as well liked (Fiske et al., 1999), whereas subordinate African Americans and Hispanics, traditional women, effeminate gay men, and people with disabilities tend to be seen as less competent but likable.

Discrimination's Impact: The Self-Fulfilling Prophecy

Attitudes may coincide with the social hierarchy not only as a rationalization for it but also because discrimination affects its victims.

In *The Nature of Prejudice*, Allport (1958) catalogued 15 possible effects of victimization. Allport believed these reactions were reducible to two basic types—those that involve blaming oneself (withdrawal, self-hate, aggression against one's own group) and those that involve blaming external causes (fighting back, suspiciousness, increased group pride). If the net results are negative—say, higher rates of crime—people who discriminate can use them to justify their discrimination that helps maintain them.

Nevertheless, social beliefs *can* be self-confirming, as demonstrated in a clever pair of experiments by Word, Zanna, and Cooper (1974). In the first experiment, Princeton University White men interviewed White and Black research assistants posing as job applicants. When the applicant was Black, the interviewers sat farther away, ended the interview 25 percent sooner, and made 50 percent more speech errors than when the applicant was White. Imagine being interviewed by someone who sat at a distance, stammered, and ended the interview rather quickly. Would it affect your performance or your feelings about the interviewer?

To find out, the researchers conducted a second experiment in which trained interviewers treated students in the same manner that the interviewers in the first experiment had treated either the White or Black applicants. When videotapes of the interviews were later rated, those who were treated like the Blacks in the first experiment seemed more nervous and less effective. Moreover, the interviewees could themselves sense a difference; those treated like the Blacks judged their interviewers to be less adequate and less friendly. The experimenters concluded part of "the problem" of Black performance resides . . . within the interaction setting itself." As with other self-fulfilling prophecies, prejudice affects its targets (Swim & Stangor, 1998). One vehicle for its doing so is "stereotype threat."

Stereotype Threat

Placed in a situation in which others expect you to perform poorly, your anxiety may cause you to confirm the belief. Claude Steele and his colleagues call this phenomenon stereotype threat—a self-confirming apprehension that one will be evaluated based on a negative stereotype.

In several experiments, Steven Spencer, Claude Steele, and Diane Quinn (1999) gave a very difficult math test to men and women students who had similar math backgrounds. When told that there were *no* gender differences on the test and no evaluation of any group stereotype, the women's performance consistently equalled the men. Told that there *was* a gender difference, the women dramatically confirmed the stereotype (see Figure 16-1). Frustrated by the extremely difficult test questions, they apparently felt added apprehension, which undermined their performances. Recent work (e.g., Cook, Arrow & Malle, 2011) has shown that feeling stereotyped can also lead to feelings of being powerless, which leads to feeling inhibited.

Stereotype threat researchers have found that threat can motivate people to stereotype others as well. For example, Lisa Sinclair at the University of Winnipeg and Ziva Kunda at the University of Waterloo found that when our self-worth is threatened, we may devalue the source of that threat. For example, they found that people rated women as less competent than men when they had recently been negatively evaluated by a woman (see Sinclair & Kunda, 2000). These people activated and used a gender stereotype to protect their self-concept. However, people who were positively evaluated did not exhibit that stereotype. Interestingly, Sinclair and Kunda (1999) have also demonstrated that we can actively inhibit our stereotypes (if, for example, we receive praise from a group we hold a negative stereotype toward). Thus, the use and activation of stereotypes can depend on how the situation motivates our behaviour.

Might racial stereotypes be self-fulfilling? Steele and Joshua Aronson (1995) confirmed that they are when Whites and Blacks take difficult verbal abilities tests. Blacks underperformed Whites only when taking the tests under conditions high in stereotype threat. Jeff Stone and his colleagues (1999) report that stereotype threat affects athletic performance, too. Blacks did worse than usual when a golf task was framed as a test of "sports intelligence," and Whites did worse when it was a test of "natural athletic ability." "When people are reminded of a negative stereotype about themselves— 'White men can't jump' or 'Black men can't think'—it can adversely affect performance," Stone (2000) concluded.

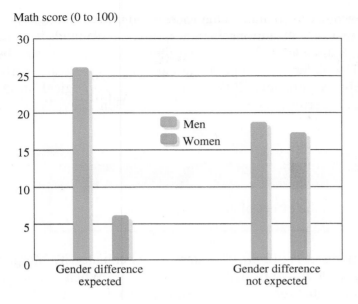

Math score (0 to 100)

FIGURE 16-1

Stereotype vulnerability and women's math performance. Steven Spencer, Claude Steele, and Diane Quinn (1999) gave equally capable men and women a difficult math test. When subjects were led to expect inferior performance by women, women fulfilled the stereotype by scoring lower.

If you tell students they are at risk of failure (as is often suggested by support programs), the stereotype may erode their performance, says Steele (1997), and cause them to "disidentify" with school and seek self-esteem elsewhere (see Figure 16-2). Moreover, students led to think they have benefited from gender- or race-based preferences in gaining admission to a post-secondary institution or an academic group tend to underperform compared to those who are led to feel competent (Brown et al., 2000). Better, therefore, to challenge students to believe in their potential, observes Steele.

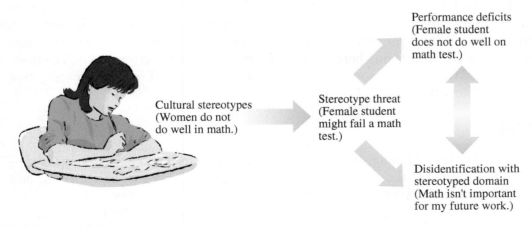

FIGURE 16-2

Stereotype threat. Threat from facing a negative stereotype can produce performance deficits and disidentification.

But how does stereotype threat undermine performance? One route is cognitive. Stereotype threat is distracting: the effort it takes to dismiss its allegations increases mental demands and decreases working memory (Croizet et al., 2004; Schmader & Johns, 2003; Steele et al., 2002). Another effect is motivational: worrying about mistakes under stereotype threat can impair a person's performance (Keller & Dauenheimer, 2003; Seibt & Forster, 2004), and the physiological arousal that accompanies stereotype threat can impair performance on difficult tests (Ben-Zeev, Fein & Inzlicht, 2005; O'Brien & Crandall, 2003).

Connection:

Recall from Module 12 that we discussed the effect of arousal from others.

If stereotype threats can disrupt performance, could *positive* stereotypes enhance it? Margaret Shih, Todd Pittinsky, and Nalini Ambady (1999) confirmed this possibility. When Asian-American females were asked biographical questions that reminded them of their gender identity before taking a math test, their performance plunged (compared to that of a control group). When similarly reminded of their Asian identity, their performance rose. Negative stereotypes disrupt performance, and positive stereotypes, it seems, facilitate performance.

Does how we expect other people to view us affect how we view them? Of course, it does. If we think someone likes us, we will tend to like them. Dr. Jacquie Vorauer wondered if this also applied to how we view other groups in society. Do our expectations of how another ethnic group views us influence our perceptions of them as a group? To answer this question, Dr. Vorauer and her colleagues decided to investigate people's beliefs about how other people perceive us in intergroup situations, which are called meta-stereotypes (Vorauer et al., 1998). These researchers demonstrated that White Canadians collectively hold a negative meta-stereotype about Aboriginals. In a second paper, they demonstrated that Whites' concerns about being judged in light of stereotypes may often be unwarranted and that members of lower-status groups (e.g., Aboriginals) as well as higher-status groups (e.g., Whites) tend to take an outgroup member's behaviour personally, as reflecting an evaluation of themselves, during intergroup interaction (see Vorauer & Kumhyr, 2001). However, the implications seem clear. If Whites presume that outgroups are perceiving them negatively, this may result in Whites interpreting ambiguous behaviour from members of the outgroup as negative, which could result in negative feelings toward these groups, and could perpetuate negative stereotypes and beliefs in the long run.

SOCIAL IDENTITY

Humans are a group-bound species. Our ancestral history prepares us to feed and protect ourselves—to live—in groups. Humans cheer for their groups, kill for their groups, die for their groups. Not surprisingly, we also define ourselves by our groups, note Australian social psychologists John Turner (1987, 1991, 2004), Michael Hogg (2003, 2008), and their colleagues. Self-concept—our sense of who we are—contains not just a *personal identity* (our sense of our personal attributes and attitudes) but a complex social identity (Chen et al., 2006). What is your social identity?

Working with the late British social psychologist Henri Tajfel, Turner proposed *social identity theory*. Tajfel and Turner (1979) observed that:

- *We categorize*: We find it useful to put people, ourselves included, into categories. To label someone as a Hindu, a Scot, or a bus driver is a shorthand way of saying some other things about the person.

- *We identify*: We associate ourselves with certain groups (our ingroups), and gain self-esteem by doing so.

- *We compare*: We contrast our groups with other groups (outgroups), with a favourable bias toward our own group.

We evaluate ourselves partly by our group memberships. Having a sense of "we-ness" strengthens our self-concepts. It *feels* good. We seek not only *respect* for ourselves but also *pride* in our groups (Smith & Tyler, 1997). Moreover, seeing our groups as superior helps us feel even better. When people's personal and social identity becomes fused—when the boundary between the self and the group blurs—people become more willing to fight or die for their group (Swann et al., 2009).

Intergroup relations are an essential part of Canadian social and political life, so it is perhaps not surprising that intergroup relations have provided a distinctive research focus for Canadian social psychologists. Jim Cameron at Saint Mary's University discovered early on that social identity theory is a useful framework for understanding perennial Canadian issues, such as immigration and multiculturalism. He was especially intrigued by the fact that while researchers agreed that social identity reflects various contributions of social group membership to the self-concept, they didn't always agree on what exactly those contributions are. As a result, measures of social identification, which are crucial for testing the hypotheses of social identity theory and other theories of intergroup relations, were often based on imprecise definitions of the construct.

Dr. Cameron determined that they could capture the various meanings of social identification in a single, multidimensional measure (Cameron & Lalonde, 2001). The research suggested dimensions of social identity correspond to three types of questions: "How important is this group to who I am?" "How does being a member of this group make me feel?" and "Do I feel like I belong with other members of this group?" Dr. Cameron found that the three-factor model of social identity applied to other group memberships as well, including ethnicity, nationality, and university (Cameron, 2004; Harris, Cameron & Lang, 2010).

Connection:

We first discussed this measure of social identity in Module 3.

Ingroup Bias

The group definition of who you are—your ethnic background, religion, gender, academic major—implies a definition of who you are not. The circle that includes "us" (the ingroup) excludes "them" (the outgroup). Thus, the mere experience of being formed into groups may promote ingroup bias. Ask children, "Which are better, the children in your school or the children at [another school nearby]?" Virtually all will say their own school has the better children. For adults, too, the closer to home, the better things seem. Merely sharing a birthday with someone creates enough of a bond to evoke heightened cooperation in a laboratory experiment (Miller et al., 1998).

Ingroup bias is one more example of the human quest for a positive self-concept. We are so group conscious that, given any excuse to think of ourselves as a group, we will do so—and will then exhibit ingroup bias. In one study, Tajfel and Billig (1974) had British teenagers evaluate modern abstract paintings and then told them that they and some others had favoured the art of Paul Klee over that of Wassily Kandinsky. Finally, without ever meeting the other members of their "Klee" group, the teens divided some money among members of both groups.

In this and other experiments, defining groups even in this trivial way produced ingroup favouritism. David Wilder (1981) summarized the typical result: "When given the opportunity to divide 15 points [worth money], subjects generally award 9 or 10 points to their own group and 5 or 6 points to the other group." This bias occurs with both genders and with people of all ages and nationalities, though especially with people from individualist cultures (Gudykunst, 1989). People in communal cultures identify more with all their peers and so treat everyone more the same.

We also are more prone to ingroup bias when our group is small and lower in status relative to the outgroup (Ellemers et al., 1997; Mullen et al., 1992). To be a foreign student, to be gay or lesbian, or to be of a minority race or gender at social gatherings is to feel one's social identity more keenly and to react accordingly.

Critical THINKING

This sign for a Whites-only beach in South Africa in the 1980s during the Apartheid era is an example of the unequal status of Blacks in that country, a status that bred flagrant prejudice and racism. What forms does racism take in today's society? Have you experienced racism yourself? How about someone you know? Do you think that would have affected your answer to the question we asked you at the beginning of the module (about being profiled)?

Conformity

Once established, prejudice is maintained largely by inertia. If prejudice is socially accepted, many people will follow the path of least resistance and conform to the fashion. They will act not so much out of a need to hate as out of a need to be liked and accepted.

Thomas Pettigrew's (1958) studies of Whites in South Africa and the American south revealed that, during the 1950s, those who conformed most to other social norms were also most prejudiced; those who were less conforming mirrored less of the surrounding prejudice. Prejudice may not be a manifestation of "sick" personalities but simply of social norms.

Conformity also maintains gender prejudice. "If we have come to think that the nursery and the kitchen are the natural sphere of a woman," wrote George Bernard Shaw in an 1891 essay, "we have done so exactly as English children come to think that a cage is the natural sphere of a parrot—because they have never seen one anywhere else." Children who *have* seen women elsewhere—children of employed women—have less-stereotyped views of men and women (Hoffman, 1977). If you ever wonder about this yourself, picture the following: What is a "good" father? You probably think this is someone who works hard, plays with his kids, and goes to the occasional school meeting. But what makes a "good" mother? Probably a lot more dedication. Also, it is much easier to be considered a "bad" mother. One mistake and you may be tarnished for life. Fathers are given much more leeway.

LO 2

FRUSTRATION AND CONFLICT

Although prejudice is bred by social situations, emotional factors often add fuel to the fire: frustration can feed prejudice. Pain and frustration (the blocking of a goal) often evoke hostility. When the cause of our frustration is intimidating or unknown, we often redirect our hostility. This phenomenon of "displaced aggression" may have contributed to the lynchings of African Americans in the south after the American Civil War (Hepworth & West, 1988; Hovland & Sears, 1940). Following their defeat in World War I and their country's subsequent economic chaos, many Germans saw Jews as villains. Long before Hitler came to power, one German leader explained: "The Jew is just convenient. . . . If there were no Jews, the anti-Semites would have to invent them" (quoted by G.W. Allport, 1958, p. 325). In earlier centuries, people vented their fear and hostility on witches, whom they sometimes burned or drowned in public. Americans felt more anger and fear after the 9/11 attacks and expressed greater intolerance toward immigrants and people from the Middle East (Skitka et al., 2004). People who are in unhappy moods often think and act more negatively toward outgroups (Esses & Zanna, 1995; Forgas & Fiedler, 1996). Passions provoke prejudice.

One source of frustration is competition. When two groups compete for jobs, housing, or social prestige, one group's goal fulfillment can become the other group's frustration. Thus, the realistic group conflict theory suggests that prejudice arises when groups compete for scarce resources (Maddux et al., 2008; Riek et al., 2006; Sassenburg et al., 2007). In Western Europe, for example, some people agree that they have been worse off economically than members of their countries' minority groups (Pettigrew & Meertens, 1995; Pettitgrew et al., 2008). Consistent with this, in

Canada, opposition to immigration since 1975 has gone up and down with the unemployment rate (Palmer, 1996). When interests clash, prejudice—for some people—pays.

Connection:

Remember our discussion of skill discounting in Module 15.

Interestingly, Michael Wohl at Carleton University and his colleagues (e.g., Wohl, Branscombe, & Reysen, 2010) have found that existential threats cause groups to work to strengthen themselves. The researchers found that the extent to which French Canadians felt threatened by English Canada predicted their desire to do group-strengthening behaviours, such as marrying another French Canadian, sending their children to French schools, and supporting French-Canadian organizations. Similarly, when Jews were reminded of the Holocaust, they supported similar group-strengthening behaviours. Might these behaviours also lead to bias against outgroups?

LO 3

PERSONALITY DYNAMICS

Any two people with equal reason to feel frustrated or threatened will often not be equally prejudiced. This suggests that prejudice serves other functions besides advancing competitive self-interest.

Need for Status, Self-Regard, and Belonging

Status is relative: to perceive ourselves as having status, we need people below us. Thus, one psychological benefit of prejudice, or of any status system, is a feeling of superiority. Most of us can recall a time when we took secret satisfaction in another's failure—perhaps seeing a brother or sister punished or a classmate failing a test. In Europe and North America, prejudice is often greater among those low or slipping on the socioeconomic ladder and among those whose positive self-image is being threatened (Lemyre & Smith, 1985; Pettigrew, 1997; Thompson & Crocker, 1985).

But other factors associated with low status could also account for prejudice. Imagine yourself as one of the Arizona State University students who took part in an experiment by Robert Cialdini and Kenneth Richardson (1980). You are walking alone across campus. Someone approaches you and asks your help with a five-minute survey. You agree. After the researcher gives you a brief "creativity test," he deflates you with the news that "you have scored relatively low on the test." The researcher then completes the survey by asking you some evaluative questions about either your school or its traditional rival, the University of Arizona. Would your feelings of failure affect your ratings of either school? Compared with those in a control group whose self-esteem was not threatened, the students who experienced failure gave higher ratings to their own school and lower ratings to their rival. Apparently, asserting one's social identity by boasting about one's own group and denigrating outgroups can boost one's ego.

James Meindl and Melvin Lerner (1984) at the University of Waterloo found that a humiliating experience—accidentally knocking over a stack of someone's important materials—provoked English-speaking Canadian students to express increased hostility toward French-speaking Canadians. And Teresa Amabile and Ann Glazebrook (1982) found that Dartmouth College men who were made to feel insecure judged others' work more harshly.

In study after study, it's been shown that thinking about one's own mortality—by writing a short essay on dying and the emotions aroused by thinking about death—also provokes enough insecurity to intensify ingroup favouritism and outgroup prejudice (Greenberg et al., 1990, 1994; Harmon-Jones et al., 1996; Schimel et al., 1999; Solomon et al., 2000; Arndt & Vess, 2008). We might also recede into our own culture. Identifying with our culture gives us a stronger sense of "place" and makes us think about our values (see Kashima, 2010).

But there are risks as well. Ingroup identification plays a role in how deprived we feel. Researchers in California (Tropp & Wright, 1999) have found that people who identify more strongly with their ingroup feel that both they as individuals and the ingroup are more deprived (both for themselves and their group). This may result in more attempts to seek justice. These feelings can be particularly enhanced with increased contact with the "mainstream." In a study of Inuit in Nunivik conducted by a group of McGill University researchers (Poore et al., 2002), the researchers found that this group, as a whole, did not perceive their group to be particularly deprived, but perceptions of deprivation increased the more contact they had with mainstream Canadian culture.

Authoritarian Personality

The emotional needs that contribute to prejudice are said to predominate in the "authoritarian personality." In the 1940s, University of California Berkeley researchers—two of whom had fled Nazi Germany—set out on an urgent research mission to uncover the psychological roots of anti-Semitism that caused the slaughter of millions of Jews and turned many millions of Europeans into indifferent spectators. In studies of American adults, Theodor Adorno and his colleagues (1950) discovered that hostility toward Jews often co-existed with hostility toward other minorities. Prejudice appeared to be a way of thinking about those who are different, rather than simply an attitude toward one specific group. Moreover, these judgmental, ethnocentric people shared authoritarian tendencies.

Although the original work on authoritarianism was criticized, decades of research conducted by Bob Altemeyer at the University of Manitoba using the Right-Wing Authoritarianism scale has confirmed the basic elements of the authoritarian personality. According to Altemeyer, high authoritarianism is reflected by the co-occurrence of the following (Altemeyer, 1996, 2006):

1. *Authoritarian submission*—a submission to the legitimate authorities in a society.

2. *Authoritarian aggression*—a general level of aggressiveness that is directed at specific groups; importantly, this is directed at groups that the person believes those "legitimate authorities" see as appropriate to aggress against (e.g., non-conventional individuals; see Smith & Kalin, 2006).

3. *Conventionalism*—a high degree of adherence to the social conventions established by authorities.

According to Adorno, as children, authoritarian people often were harshly disciplined. This supposedly led them to repress their hostilities and impulses and to "project" them onto outgroups. The insecurity of authoritarian children seemed to predispose them toward an excessive concern with power and status and an inflexible right–wrong way of thinking that made ambiguity difficult to tolerate. Such people therefore tended to be submissive to those with power over them and aggressive or punitive toward those beneath them.

Activity: How authoritarian are you?

For each of the questions, indicate whether or not you agree.

1. Gays and lesbians are just as healthy and moral as anybody else.

2. Women should have to promise to obey their husbands when they get married.

3. There is no "one right way" to live life; everyone needs to find their own way.

4. Our country needs free thinkers who have the courage to defy traditional ways, even if this upsets many people.

5. The only way our country can get through the crisis ahead is to get back to our traditional values, put some tough leaders in power, and silence the troublemakers spreading bad ideas.

6. The "old-fashioned ways" and "old-fashioned values" still show the best way to live.

These items are from a recent version of the Right-Wing Authoritarianism scale (Altemeyer, 2006). If you agreed with items 1, 3, and 4, and disagreed with 2, 5, and 6, this suggests you are low in authoritarianism. However, if the opposite is true, you may have some authoritarian tendencies. So, how authoritarian are you really?

Authoritarian tendencies, sometimes reflected in ethnic tensions, surge during threatening times of economic recession and social upheaval (Doty et al., 1991; Sales, 1973). In Russia, individuals scoring high in authoritarianism have tended to support a return to communist ideology and to oppose democratic reform (McFarland et al., 1992, 1996). Moreover, contemporary studies of right-wing authoritarians by Bob Altemeyer (1988, 1992, 2004) confirm that there *are* individuals whose fears and hostilities surface as prejudice. Feelings of moral superiority may go hand in hand with brutality toward perceived inferiors.

Different forms of prejudice—toward Blacks, gays and lesbians, women, old people, fat people, AIDS victims, the homeless—*do* tend to co-exist in the same individuals (Bierly, 1985; Crandall, 1994; Peterson et al., 1993; Snyder & Ickes, 1985). As Altemeyer concludes, right-wing authoritarians tend to be "equal opportunity bigots." The same is true of those with a *social dominance orientation*—who view people in terms of hierarchies of merit or goodness. Further, in an analysis of 6600 Canadian students and their parents, Altemeyer (2004) found that people who are both high in authoritarianism and high in social dominance orientation are some of the most prejudiced individuals in society. Further, they tend to hold the economic and social power to influence public policy. By contrast, those with a more communal or universal orientation—who attend to people's similarities and presume "universal human rights" enjoyed by "all God's children"—are more welcoming of affirmative action and accepting of those who differ (Phillips & Ziller, 1997; Pratto et al., 1994, 2000; Sidanius et al., 1996; Whitley, 1999).

Applying Social Psychology

You just completed a few of the Right-Wing Authoritarian items. But what is the Right-Wing Authoritarian scale, and what does authoritarianism really have to do with prejudice? Christie (1991) suggested that the best short authoritarianism scale is Lane's (1955) four-item measure. So, considering your own personality, do you agree or disagree with each of the following items? How do you think your parents would answer?

1. What young people need most of all is strict discipline by their parents.

2. Most people who don't get ahead just don't have enough will power.

3. A few strong leaders could make this country better than all the laws and talk.

4. People sometimes say that an insult to your honour should not be forgotten.

In a 1952 version of this example, 76 percent agreed with the first statement, 64 percent agreed with the second statement, 51 percent agreed with the third statement, and 25 percent agreed with the fourth statement. These items are a decent assessment of the specific authoritarian tendencies cited in the text. How did you fare?

LO 4

COGNITIVE SOURCES OF PREJUDICE

Little attention was paid to the cognitive sources of prejudice before the 1990s, but a new look at prejudice has been fuelled by more than 2100 articles on stereotyping that were conducted during that decade. The basic point is this: stereotyped beliefs and prejudiced attitudes exist not only because of social conditioning and because they enable people to displace hostilities, but also as by-products of normal thinking processes. Many stereotypes spring less from malice of the heart than the machinery of the mind. Like perceptual illusions, which are by-products of our knack for interpreting the world, stereotypes can be by-products of how we simplify our complex worlds.

Categorization

One way we simplify our environment is to *categorize*—to organize the world by clustering objects into groups (Macrae & Bodenhausen, 2000). A biologist classifies plants and animals. A human classifies people. Having done so, we think about them more easily. If individuals in a group share some similarities—if most MENSA members are smart, most basketball players tall—knowing their group memberships can provide useful information with minimal effort (Macrae et al., 1994). Stereotypes sometimes offer "a beneficial ratio of information gained to effort expended" (Sherman et al., 1998). Customs inspectors and airplane anti-hijack personnel are therefore given "profiles" of suspicious individuals (Kraut & Poe, 1980). But as we learned earlier, this can lead to racial profiling based more on race than actual risk.

We find it especially easy and efficient to rely on stereotypes when we are

- pressed for time (Kaplan et al., 1993)
- preoccupied (Gilbert & Hixon, 1991)
- tired (Bodenhausen, 1990)
- emotionally aroused (Esses et al., 1993b; Stroessner & Mackie, 1993)
- too young to appreciate diversity (Biernat, 1991)

Ethnicity and gender are, in our current world, powerful ways of categorizing people. We label people of widely varying ancestry as simply "Black," "White," "Indian," or "Asian." When subjects view different people making statements, they often forget who said what, yet they remember the race of the person who made each statement (Hewstone et al., 1991; Stroessner et al., 1990; Taylor et al., 1978). By itself, such categorization is not prejudice, but it does provide a foundation for prejudice.

Perceived Similarities and Differences

Picture the following objects: apples, chairs, pencils. There is a strong tendency to see objects within a group as being more uniform than they really are. Were your apples all red? Your chairs all straight-backed? Your pencils all yellow? It's the same with people. Once we assign people to groups—athletes, drama majors, math professors—we are likely to exaggerate the similarities within the groups and the differences between them (S. E. Taylor, 1981; Wilder, 1978). Mere division into groups can create an outgroup homogeneity effect—a sense that *they* are "all alike" and different from "us" and "our" group (Ostrom & Sedikides, 1992). Because we generally like people we think are similar to us and dislike those we perceive as different, the natural result is ingroup bias (Byrne & Wong, 1962; Rokeach & Mezei, 1966; Stein et al., 1965).

When the group is our own, we are more likely to see diversity. For example, many non-Europeans see the Swiss as a fairly homogeneous people. But to the people of Switzerland, the Swiss are diverse, encompassing French-, German-, and Italian-speaking groups. Many Anglo-Americans lump "Latinos" together. Mexican Americans, Cuban Americans, and Puerto Ricans see important differences, especially between their own subgroup and the others (Huddy & Virtanen, 1995).

In general, the greater our familiarity with a social group, the more we see its diversity (Brown & Wootton-Millward, 1993; Linville et al., 1989). The less our familiarity, the more we stereotype.

Perhaps you have noticed: they—the members of any racial group other than your own—even *look* alike. Many of us can recall embarrassing ourselves by confusing two people of another racial group, prompting the person we've misnamed to say, "You think we all look alike." Experiments by John Brigham, June Chance, Alvin Goldstein, and Roy Malpass in the United States and by Hayden Ellis in Scotland reveal that people of other races do in fact *seem* to look more alike than do people of one's own race (Chance & Goldstein, 1981, 1996; Ellis, 1981; Meissner and Brigham, 2001). Blacks more easily recognize another Black person than they do a White person (Bothwell et al., 1989). Hispanics more readily recognize another Hispanic whom they saw a couple of hours earlier than they do a Caucasian (Platz & Hosch, 1988).

Connection:

We will discuss the issue of cross-race eyewitness identification in greater detail in Module 22.

It's true outside the laboratory as well, as Daniel Wright and his colleagues (2001) found after either a Black or a White researcher approached Black and White people in South African and English shopping malls. When later asked to identify the researcher from lineups, people better recognized those of their own race. It's not that we cannot perceive differences among faces of another race. Rather, when looking at a face from another racial group we often attend first to race ("that man is Black"), rather than to individual features. When viewing someone of our own race, we are less race-conscious and more attentive to individual details (Bernstein et al., 2007; Levin, 2000; Shriver et al., 2008; Smith & Stinson, 2008).

Distinctiveness and Attention

Distinctive people and vivid or extreme occurrences often capture attention and distort judgments. As with the outgroup homogeneity effect, this innocent-seeming phenomenon sometimes breeds stereotypes.

Have you ever found yourself in a situation where you were the only person present of your gender, race, or nationality? If so, your difference from the others probably made you more noticeable and the object of more attention. Being East Indian in an otherwise White group, a man in an otherwise female group, or a gay person in an otherwise straight group seems more prominent and influential and to have exaggerated good and bad qualities (e.g., Crocker & McGraw, 1984; S. E. Taylor et al., 1979). This occurs because when someone in a group is made salient (conspicuous), we tend to see that person as causing whatever happens (Taylor & Fiske, 1978).

Have you noticed that people also define you by your most distinctive traits and behaviours? Tell people about someone who is a skydiver and a tennis player, report Lori Nelson and Dale Miller (1997), and they will think of the person as a skydiver. People also take note of those who violate expectations (Bettencourt et al., 1997). Such perceived distinctiveness makes it easier for highly capable job applicants from low-status groups to get noticed, though they must also work harder to prove that their abilities are genuine (Biernat & Kobrynowicz, 1997).

Ellen Langer and Lois Imber (1980) cleverly demonstrated the attention paid distinctive people. They asked Harvard students to watch a video of a man reading. The students paid closer attention when they were led to think he was out of the ordinary—a cancer patient, a millionaire, or a homosexual. They detected characteristics that other viewers ignored, and their evaluation of him was more extreme.

Sometimes we perceive others as reacting to our distinctiveness when actually they aren't. At Dartmouth College, researchers Robert Kleck and Angelo Strenta (1980) discovered this when they led college women to feel disfigured. The women thought the purpose of the experiment was to assess how someone would react to a facial scar created with theatrical makeup; the scar was on the right cheek, running from the ear to the mouth. Actually, the purpose was to see how the women themselves, when made to feel deviant, would perceive others' behaviour toward them. After applying the makeup, the experimenter gave each subject a small hand mirror so she could see the authentic-looking scar. When she put the mirror down, he then applied some "moisturizer" to "keep the makeup from cracking." What the "moisturizer" really did was remove the scar.

The scene that followed was poignant. A young woman, feeling terribly self-conscious about her supposedly disfigured face, talked with another woman who sees no such disfigurement and knows nothing of what has gone on before. Compared to women who were led to believe their conversational partners merely thought they had an allergy, the "disfigured" women became acutely sensitive to how their partners were looking at them. They rated their partners as more tense, distant, and patronizing. In fact, observers who later analyzed videotapes of how the partners treated "disfigured" persons could find no such differences in treatment. Self-conscious about being different, the "disfigured" women misinterpreted mannerisms and comments they would otherwise not have noticed.

Our minds also use distinctive cases as a shortcut to judging groups. Are Blacks good athletes? "Well, there's Donovan Bailey and Jarome Iginla. Yeah, I'd say so." Note the thought processes at work here: given limited experience with a particular social group, we recall examples of it and generalize from those (Sherman, 1996). Moreover, encountering exemplars of negative stereotypes (say, a hostile Middle-Eastern person) can prime such stereotypes, leading people to minimize contact with the group (Henderson-King & Nisbett, 1996). Such generalizing from single cases can cause problems. Vivid instances, though more available in memory, are seldom representative of the larger group. Exceptional athletes, though distinctive and memorable, are not the best basis for judging the distribution of athletic talent among an entire group.

Those in a numerical minority, being more distinctive, also may be numerically overestimated by the majority. Consider a 1990 Gallup poll conducted in the United States. In the poll, American respondents estimated that the Black and Hispanic populations of the U.S. were 30 and 19 percent of the total population, respectively. Yet the actual numbers are significantly lower (see Figure 16-3). A 2002 Gallup poll found that the average person thought 21 percent of men are gay and 22 percent of women are lesbians. Yet actual numbers suggest that only 3 or 4 percent of men and 1 to 2 percent of women have a same-sex orientation (National Center for Health Statistics, 1991; Smith, 1998; Tarmann, 2002).

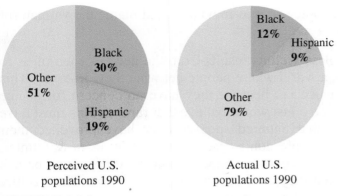

FIGURE 16-3

Overestimating minority populations.

Source: 1990 Gallup Poll (Gates, 1993).

Attribution: Is It a Just World?

In explaining others' actions, we frequently commit the fundamental attribution error. We attribute their behaviour so much to their inner dispositions that we discount important situational forces. The error occurs partly because our attention focuses on the people, not the situation. A person's race or sex is vivid and gets attention; the situational forces working upon that person are usually less visible. Until recently, the same was true of how we explained the perceived differences between women and men. Because gender-role constraints were hard to see, we attributed men's and women's behaviour solely to their innate dispositions. The more people assume that human traits are fixed dispositions, the stronger are their stereotypes (Levy et al., 1998, Williams & Eberhardt, 2008). In a series of experiments conducted at the Universities of Waterloo and Kentucky, Melvin Lerner and his colleagues (Lerner & Miller, 1978; Lerner, 1980) discovered that merely *observing* another innocent person being victimized is enough to make the victim seem less worthy. Juvenal, the Roman satirist, anticipated these results: "The Roman mob follows after Fortune . . . and hates those who have been condemned."

Numerous studies have confirmed this just-world phenomenon (Hafer & Begue, 2005). Imagine that you, along with some others, are participating in one of Lerner's studies—supposedly on the perception of emotional cues (Lerner & Simmons, 1966). One of the participants, a confederate, is selected by lottery to perform a memory task. This person receives painful shocks whenever she gives a wrong answer. You and the others note her emotional responses. After you see her receive these painful shocks, you are asked to evaluate her. How do you respond? With compassion? Apparently not. In these experiments, when the observers were unable to help the victim, they often rejected and devalued the victim. In other words, the victim "got what they deserved."

Linda Carli and her colleagues (1989, 1999) report that the just-world hypothesis colours our impressions of rape victims as well. Carli had people read detailed descriptions of interactions between a man and a woman. For example, a woman and her boss meet for dinner, go to his home, and each have a glass of wine. Some read a scenario that has a happy ending: "Then he led me to the couch. He held my hand and asked me to marry him." In hindsight, people find the ending unsurprising and admire the man's and woman's character traits. Others read the same scenario with a different ending: "But then he became very rough and pushed me onto the couch. He held me down on the couch and raped me." Given this ending, people see it as inevitable and blame the woman for behaviour that seems faultless in the first scenario.

Lerner (1980) noted that such disparaging of hapless victims results from the need of each of us to believe, "I am a just person living in a just world, a world where people get what they deserve." This suggests that people are indifferent to social injustice not because they have no concern for justice but because they see no injustice. Those who assume a just world believe that rape victims must have behaved seductively (Borgida & Brekke, 1985), that battered spouses must have provoked their beatings (Summers & Feldman, 1984), that poor people don't deserve better (Furnham & Gunter, 1984), and that sick people are responsible for their illnesses (Gruman & Sloan, 1983). Such beliefs enable successful people to reassure themselves that they, too, deserve what they have. The wealthy and healthy can see their own good fortune, and others' misfortune, as justly deserved. Linking good fortune with virtue and misfortune with moral failure enables the fortunate to feel pride and to avoid responsibility for the unfortunate.

But how can the just-world phenomenon influence our biases? When might we blame the victim? Domestic abuse and sexual abuse are a serious problem, particularly among youth. Up to one in five girls in high school are in abusive relationships. Sixty percent of sexual assault victims are under 18. These statistics are only estimates, as less than 20 percent of sexual assaults are reported to police. Why are these crimes so prevalent, and why do they largely go unreported? One reason that has been suggested is this belief in a just world—if these young women are victims, they must have done something to bring it on themselves.

Domestic abuse is also a difficult subject to address. About a year after being very publicly assaulted by her then-boyfriend Chris Brown, pop star Rihanna released a single with rap star Eminem entitled "Love the Way You Lie," which depicts a troubled and abusive relationship. The woman in the song proclaims "I like the way it hurts." Is this an ironic criticism of domestic abuse, or does it implicitly normalize abusive relationships? How the media depicts relationships is important to how we expect our relationships to work.

Connection:

We will discuss the role of media in relationships further in Module 21.

Self-Protection

A relatively new and fascinating approach to explain stereotyping comes for the work of Mark Schaller at the University of British Columbia, and his colleagues (e.g., Faulkner, Schaller, Park, & Duncan, 2004; Neuberg, Kenrick, & Schaller, 2011). They have demonstrated that people who are chronically worried about disease have more negative feelings about unfamiliar immigrant groups, and are more likely to associate these groups with "danger." In addition, experimental manipulations of fear of disease also results in less positive attitudes toward outgroups, and more endorsement of policies that would limit the immigration of unfamiliar foreign peoples.

Interestingly, these researchers also demonstrated that these negative attitudes exist toward the obese (Park, Schaller & Crandall, 2007) and older adults (Duncan & Schaller, 2009). Perhaps this social response is not surprising, in that self-protection is very important. Our immune system itself becomes more active when we simply *see* other people's disease symptoms (see Schaller et al., 2010). Perhaps the social response is a natural consequence of that activation.

CONCLUSIONS

Social psychologists have been more successful in explaining prejudice than in alleviating it. Because prejudice results from many interrelated factors, there is no simple remedy. Nevertheless, we can now anticipate techniques for reducing prejudice (discussed further in modules to come). If unequal status breeds prejudice, then we can seek to create cooperative, equal-status relationships. If prejudice often rationalizes discriminatory behaviour, then we can mandate non-discrimination. If outgroups seem more unlike one's own group than they really are, then we can make efforts to personalize their members. These are some of the antidotes for the poison of prejudice.

A number of these antidotes have been applied, and racial and gender prejudices have indeed diminished. It now remains to be seen whether, during this new century, progress will continue—or whether, as could easily happen in a time of increasing population and diminishing resources, antagonisms will again erupt into open hostility.

SUMMARY OF KEY POINTS

LO1. Explain the social sources of prejudice.

- Social sources of prejudice include unequal status between groups, self-fulfilling prophecies, and stereotype threat.
- Social identification leads to ingroup bias, which is perpetuated through conformity, and can reinforce prejudice beliefs.

LO2. Understand how frustration can lead to aggression.

- Realistic group conflict theory can explain why perceptions of scarcity can lead to disparaging of outgroups and subsequent prejudice.

LO3. Understand the role of personality in prejudice.

- The need for status, self-regard, and belonging can increase the development of prejudicial beliefs.
- People who are authoritarian tend to believe in the superiority of their own group over others.

LO4. Understand the cognitive sources of prejudice.

- Because we naturally categorize people into ingroups and outgroups, and because we perceive members of ingroups to be more dissimilar to each other, we tend to overgeneralize our beliefs about outgroup members.
- Negative attributions about others, self-protection, and a belief in a just world, can also lead us to be prejudiced against outgroups.

KEY TERMS

Authoritarianism   A personality style characterized by submission to legitimate authority, a general level of aggressiveness toward outgroups, and a high degree of adherence to social conventions.

Ethnocentrism   A belief in the superiority of one's own ethnic and cultural group, and a corresponding disdain for all other groups.

Ingroup   "Us"—a group of people who share a sense of belonging, a feeling of common identity.

Ingroup bias   The tendency to favour one's own group.

Just-world phenomenon   The tendency of people to believe the world is just and that people therefore get what they deserve and deserve what they get.

Outgroup   "Them"—a group that people perceive as distinctively different from or apart from their ingroup.

Outgroup homogeneity effect   Perception of outgroup members as more similar to one another than are ingroup members. Thus "they are alike; we are diverse."

Realistic group conflict theory   The theory that prejudice arises from competition among groups for scarce resources.

Social identity   The "we" aspect of our self-concept. The part of our answer to "Who am I?" that comes from our group.

Stereotype threat   A disruptive concern, when facing a negative stereotype, that one will be evaluated based on a negative stereotype. Unlike self-fulfilling prophecies that hammer one's reputation into one's self-concept, stereotype threat situations have immediate effects.

MODULE SEVENTEEN

Conflict and Dispute Resolution

LEARNING OBJECTIVES   After studying Module 17, you will be able to

LO **1**   Define social dilemmas

LO **2**   Understand the role of various factors in conflict

LO **3**   Understand how to promote dispute resolution

A Canadian soldier and a Mohawk warrior come face-to-face in a tense standoff at the Kanesatake Reserve in Oka, Quebec, in September 1990.

"We love peace, but there are people in the world who hate us for what we value. Therefore, we must defend ourselves against attack. We will do that by attacking and destroying the enemy before they destroy us." We hear arguments like this made about Iraq, Libya, Syria, Afghanistan, Darfur, and Kosovo. When Russia invaded Ukraine in 2014, they argued they were just protecting "Russians living in Ukraine." How we perceive others' violent intentions lead to our pre-emptive defensive actions. Not surprisingly, the countries we attack see us as the aggressors, which further escalates the behaviour of those we are in conflict with. This is a vicious cycle.

Critical THINKING

Before you begin this module, think back—can you think of a conflict you have been in recently? How did you respond? Did your actions escalate the tensions? Or did you act to reduce them? What factors played a role?

The elements of conflict (a perceived incompatibility of actions or goals—importantly, these perceptions may or may not be accurate) are similar at all levels—from civil wars, to national conflicts where ethnic or cultural groups compete for access to natural resources, to international conflicts, to corporations vying for market share, to executives fighting for jobs within a company, to people's troubled relationships with their spouses or partners. They all share a common underlying process. Let's consider these conflict elements.

LO 1

SOCIAL DILEMMAS

Several of the problems that most threaten our human future—nuclear arms, global warming, overpopulation, natural resource depletion—arise as various parties pursue their self-interests, ironically to their collective detriment. Often, choices that are individually rewarding become collectively punishing. We end up with a dilemma: How can we reconcile individual rights and well-being with communal well-being?

To isolate and illustrate this dilemma, social psychologists have used laboratory games that expose the heart of many actual social conflicts. By showing us how well-meaning people become trapped in mutually destructive behaviour, they illuminate some fascinating, yet troubling, paradoxes of human existence. "Social psychologists who study conflict are in much the same position as the astronomers," notes conflict researcher Morton Deutsch (1999). "We cannot conduct true experiments with large scale social events. But we can identify the conceptual similarities between the large scale and the small, as the astronomers have between the planets and Newton's apple." Consider two examples: the Prisoners' Dilemma and the Tragedy of the Commons.

The Prisoners' Dilemma

One dilemma derives from an anecdote concerning two suspects questioned separately by a Crown prosecutor (Rapoport, 1960). The suspects are both guilty; however, the Crown prosecutor only has enough evidence to convict them of a lesser offence. So the Crown prosecutor creates an incentive for each to confess privately: if one suspect confesses and the other doesn't, the Crown prosecutor will grant the confessor immunity (and will use the confession to convict the other of a maximum offence). If both confess, each will receive a moderate sentence. If neither confesses, each will receive a light sentence. The matrix of Figure 17-1 summarizes the choices.

To minimize their own sentences, many would confess, despite the fact that mutual confession elicits more severe sentences than mutual non-confession. In some 2000 studies (Dawes, 1991), university students have faced variations of the Prisoners' Dilemma with the outcomes being not prison terms but chips, money, or course points. How do you think you would do with the Prisoners' Dilemma? As the figure illustrates, on any given decision a person is better off defecting (because such behaviour exploits the other's cooperation or protects against the other's exploitation). However—and here's the rub—by not cooperating, both parties end up far worse off than if they had trusted each other and thus had gained a joint profit. This dilemma often traps each one in a maddening predicament in which both realize they *could* mutually profit but, unable to communicate and mistrusting one another, become "locked in" to not cooperating.

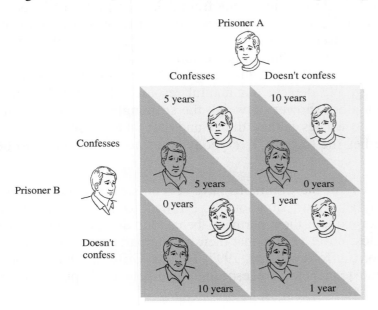

FIGURE 17-1

The Prisoners' Dilemma. In each box, the number above the diagonal is Prisoner A's outcome. Thus, if both prisoners confess, both get five years. If neither confesses, each gets a year. If one confesses, that prisoner is set free in exchange for evidence used to convict the other of a crime, bringing a ten-year sentence. If you were one of the prisoners, unable to communicate with your fellow prisoner, would you confess?

Punishing another's lack of cooperation may seem like a smart strategy, but research shows it leads to retaliation (Dreber et al., 2008). Punishers may feel they are being defensive, but recipients see it as aggressive and tend to escalate the aggression (Anderson et al., 2008). Furthermore, people tend to be paranoid in these types of situations and tend to pick competitive positions, rather than cooperative ones (Ellet et al., 2013). That said, if prisoners are given the opportunity to confirm the decision of the other, this dramatically increases cooperation (Attanasi et al., 2013).

The Tragedy of the Commons

Many social dilemmas involve more than two parties. Global warming stems from widespread deforestation and from the carbon dioxide emitted by the world's cars, oil furnaces, and coal-fired power plants. Each gas-guzzling car contributes infinitesimally to the problem, and the harm each does is diffused over many people. In an attempt to reduce worldwide greenhouse gas emissions, the United Nations sponsored the Kyoto Accord, which promised to significantly reduce greenhouse gas emissions by 2012 and was signed by more than 100 countries worldwide. Unfortunately, two of the world's worst contributors to greenhouse gas emissions, Canada and the United States, rejected the Accord as too difficult to achieve and have reported failing to reach the targets (CBC, 2013). After the 2010 Copenhagen conference, Canada and the United States were still resistant to change. To model such social predicaments, researchers have developed laboratory dilemmas that involve multiple people.

A metaphor for the insidious nature of social dilemmas is what ecologist Garrett Hardin (1968) called the "Tragedy of the Commons." He derived the name from the centrally located pasture area in old English towns, but the "commons" can be any shared and limited resource. If we use the resource in moderation, it may replenish itself as rapidly as it's harvested. Many real predicaments are analogous to a "commons." Environmental pollution is the sum of many minor pollutions, each of which benefits the individual polluters much more than they could benefit themselves (and the environment) if they stopped polluting. We deplete our natural resources because the immediate personal benefits of, say, taking a long, hot shower outweigh the seemingly inconsequential costs. Whalers knew others would exploit the whales if they didn't and that taking a few whales would hardly diminish the species. Therein lies the tragedy. Everybody's business (conservation) became nobody's business.

The Prisoners' Dilemma and the Tragedy of the Commons have several similar features. First, both tempt people to explain their own behaviour situationally ("I had to protect myself against exploitation by my opponent") and to explain their partners' behaviour dispositionally ("She was greedy," "He was untrustworthy"). Most never realize that their counterparts are viewing them with the same fundamental attribution error (Gifford & Hine, 1997; Hine & Gifford, 1996). People with self-inflating, self-focused, narcissistic tendencies are especially unlikely to display empathy for others' perspectives (Campbell et al., 2005).

Second, motives often change. At first, people are eager to make some easy money, then to minimize their losses, and finally to save face and avoid defeat (Brockner et al., 1982; Teger, 1980). We see this in international conflict as well. In both the Vietnam and Iraq wars, the initial logic behind the war was to protect democracy, freedom, and justice (and in the case of Iraq, find weapons of mass destruction). In both Vietnam and in Iraq there was an apparent shift, to avoid the shame of "losing" a war.

Third, most real-life conflicts, like the Prisoners' Dilemma and the Tragedy of the Commons, are non–zero-sum games. The two sides' profits and losses need not add up to zero. Both can win; both can lose. Each game pits the immediate interests of individuals against the well-being of the group. result. Each is a diabolical social trap that shows how, even when individuals behave "rationally," harm can No malicious person planned for the earth's atmosphere to be warmed by a blanket of carbon dioxide.

Resolving Social Dilemmas

In those situations that are indeed social traps, how can we induce people to cooperate for their mutual betterment? Research with laboratory dilemmas reveals several ways (Gifford & Hine, 1997).

If taxes were entirely voluntary, how many would pay their full share? Surely many would not, which is why modern societies do not depend on charity to pay for schools, parks, and social and military security. We also develop laws and regulations for our common good. An International Whaling Commission sets an agreed-upon "harvest" that enables whales to regenerate.

There is another way to resolve social dilemmas: make the group small (Kerr & Kaufman-Gilliland, 1997). In small groups, people feel more identified with a group's success. Anything that enhances group identity will also increase cooperation. Even just a few minutes of discussion, or just believing that one shares similarities with others in the group, can increase the "we feeling" and cooperation (Brewer, 1987; Orbell et al., 1988).

Connection:

Remember our discussion of group identity in Module 16.

To escape a social trap, people must communicate. Although group communication sometimes degenerates into threats and name calling (Deutsch & Krauss, 1960), more often communication enables groups to cooperate—much more (Bornstein et al., 1988, 1989). Discussing the dilemma forges a group identity, which enhances concern for the group's welfare. It devises group norms and consensus expectations and puts pressure on members to follow them. And especially when people are face-to-face, it enables them to commit themselves to cooperation (Bouas & Komorita, 1996; Drolet & Morris, 2000; Kerr & Kaufman-Gilliland, 1994; Kerr et al., 1997; Pruitt, 1998). Without communication, those who expect others not to cooperate will usually refuse to cooperate themselves (Messé & Sivacek, 1979; Pruitt & Kimmel, 1977).

Cooperation also rises when experimenters change the payoff matrix to make cooperation more rewarding and exploitation less rewarding (Komorita & Barth, 1985; Pruitt & Rubin, 1986). Changing payoffs also helps resolve actual dilemmas. In some cities, freeways clog and skies smog because people prefer the convenience of driving themselves directly to work. Each knows that one more car does not add noticeably to the congestion and pollution. To alter the personal cost–benefit calculations, many cities now give carpoolers incentives, such as designated freeway lanes or reduced tolls.

Chinese women wear masks on Tiananmen Square in thick haze in Beijing, China.

When cooperation obviously serves the public good, one can usefully appeal to the social-responsibility norm (Lynn & Oldenquist, 1986). When, for example, people believe public transportation can save time, they will be more likely to use it if they also believe it reduces pollution (Van Vugt et al., 1996). In the struggle for civil rights, many marchers willingly agreed, for the sake of the larger group, to suffer harassment, beatings, and jail. In wartime, people make great personal sacrifices for the good of their group. As Winston Churchill, prime minister of the U.K. during World War II, said of the Battle of Britain, the actions of the Royal Air Force pilots were genuinely altruistic: a great many people owed a great deal to those who flew into battle knowing there was a high probability—70 percent for those on a standard tour of duty—that they would not return (Levinson, 1950).

LO 2

FACTORS AFFECTING CONFLICT

Competition

Racial hostilities often arise when groups compete for jobs and other benefits. When interests clash, conflict erupts.

Connection:

Recall that we discussed attitudes toward Aboriginals, and the attitudes of Québécois in Modules 15 and 16.

As Canadians, we are collectively no strangers to these types of conflicts. There are perpetual negotiations that attempt to resolve centuries-old land claim issues between the federal government and numerous Aboriginal groups, with no resolution at hand. Some French Canadians in Quebec have perceived themselves to be so ill-treated that the Parti Québécois has held two referendums to decide whether Quebec should separate from the rest of Canada. Ultimately, the loss of the "Yes" side in the 1995 rally was blamed on ". . . money, and the ethnic vote" by Jacques Parizeau, then Quebec's premier and the leader of the Parti Québécois. (As an interesting side note, in 2013 Parizeau came out against the proposed Charter of Values as being too extreme such that it would drive minorities away from the separatists.)

But does competition by itself provoke hostile conflict? Real-life situations are so complex that it is hard to be sure. If competition is indeed responsible, then it should be possible to provoke in an experiment. We could randomly divide people into two groups, have the groups compete for a scarce resource, and note what happens. This is precisely what Muzafer Sherif (1966) and his colleagues did in a dramatic series of experiments with typical 11- and 12-year-old boys.

In one such study, he divided 22 unacquainted boys into two groups, took them to a Boy Scout camp in separate buses, and settled them in bunkhouses about a kilometre apart at Oklahoma's Robber's Cave State Park. For most of the first week, they were unaware of the other group's existence. By cooperating in various activities—preparing meals, camping out, fixing up a swimming hole, building a rope bridge—each group soon became close-knit. They gave themselves names: "Rattlers" and "Eagles."

In the days leading up to the 1995 sovereignty referendum in Quebec, federalists organized a unity rally in Montreal.

Jacques Parizeau, then premier of Quebec, blamed the loss on outsiders.

Group identity thus established, the stage was set for the conflict. Toward the end of the first week, the Rattlers "discovered the Eagles on 'our' baseball field." When the camp staff then proposed a tournament of competitive activities between the two groups (baseball games, tugs-of-war, cabin inspections, treasure hunts, and so forth), both groups responded enthusiastically. This was win–lose competition. The spoils (medals, knives) would all go to the tournament victor.

The result? The camp gradually degenerated into open warfare. It was like a scene from William Golding's novel *Lord of the Flies*, which depicts the social disintegration of boys marooned on an island. In Sherif's study, the conflict began with each side calling the other names during the competitive activities. Soon it escalated to dining hall "garbage wars," flag burnings, cabin ransackings, and even fistfights. Asked to describe the other group, the boys said "they" were "sneaky," "smart alecks," "stinkers," while referring to their own group as "brave," "tough," "friendly."

The win–lose competition had produced intense conflict, negative images of the outgroup, and strong ingroup cohesiveness and pride. However, we cannot forget the impact that the groups and social identity forces may have (e.g., Tajfel & Turner, 1979), which we discussed in the context of the previous two modules. Group polarization no doubt exacerbated the conflict. In experiments, groups behave more competitively than individuals in competition-fostering situations (see Wildschut et al., 2003). All this occurred without any cultural, physical, or economic differences between the two groups and with boys who were their communities' "cream of the crop." Sherif noted that, had we visited the camp at this point, we would have concluded these "were wicked, disturbed, and vicious bunches of youngsters" (1966, p. 85). When people see resources (such as jobs, money, or power) as zero-sum games, this can result in negative attitudes. Palmer (1996) and Vicki Esses and her colleagues (2005) have shown that people will develop negative attitudes toward immigrants if they are perceived to be competing for jobs and resources. Fortunately, Sherif not only made strangers into enemies; he then, as we will see, made the enemies into friends.

Connection:

Remember that we discussed the role of competition for resources in ethnic attitudes in Modules 15 and 16.

PERCEIVED INJUSTICE

"That's unfair!" "What a ripoff!" "We deserve better!" Such comments typify conflicts bred by perceived injustice. But what is justice? According to some social-psychological theorists, people perceive justice as equity—the distribution of rewards in proportion to individuals' contributions (Walster et al., 1978). If you and I have a relationship (employer–employee, teacher–student, husband–wife, colleague–colleague), it is equitable if

$$\frac{\text{My outcomes}}{\text{My inputs}} = \frac{\text{Your outcomes}}{\text{Your inputs}}$$

Connection:

Recall that we discussed the role of self-serving biases in perceptions of equity in relationships in Module 3. We will discuss it again in Module 20.

If you contribute more and benefit less than I do, you will feel exploited and irritated; I may feel exploitative and guilty. Chances are, though, that you, more than I, will be sensitive to the inequity (Greenberg, 1986; Messick & Sentis, 1979). Nonetheless, knowing that you are over-benefiting from a situation can trigger collective guilt. To restore a sense of justice, such guilt can provoke an apology and/or compensation (Mallet & Swim, 2003). Collective guilt may be part of the reason that in 2007 and 2008, Prime Minister Stephen Harper, on behalf of Canada, apologized to the Chinese community (for a head tax imposed in the early 1900s), to the East Indian community (for a 1914 incident where a boat full of East Indian refugees was turned away), and to the Aboriginal community (for abuse in residential schools; CBC, 2008).

But how do those who are exploited react? Elaine Hatfield, William Walster, and Ellen Berscheid (1978) detected three possibilities. They can accept and justify their inferior position ("We're poor; it's what we deserve, but we're happy"). They can demand compensation, perhaps by harassing, embarrassing, even cheating their exploiter. If all else fails, they may try to restore equity by retaliating.

Since 1970, professional opportunities for women have increased significantly. However, true equity has not been attained. The Canadian Department of Justice (2004) reports that women are consistently paid less than men (see Table 17-1). In 2014, the U.S. government reported that women earn approximately 80 percent of what men earn. But how are these inequities perceived? As long as women compared their opportunities and earnings with those of other women, they felt generally satisfied—as they still do with their disproportionate share of family labour (Jackson, 1989; Major, 1989, 1993). Research by Serge Desmarais and his colleagues at the University of Guelph has found that since women are now more likely to see themselves as men's equals, their sense of relative deprivation has grown (see Desmarais & Curtis, 2001). Although these data do not control for time in service, age, and other factors, the difference is real, and significant.

Connection:

Remember that we discussed relative deprivation in Module 14.

TABLE 17-1	Average Salaries of Women Working Full-Time as a Percentage of Average Salaries of Men
Banking	64.4%
Transportation	73.6%
Communications	86.9%
Other sectors	78.1%
All sectors	**77.6%**

Source: Adapted from Canadian Human Rights Commission, *2004 Employment Equity Annual Report.*

MISPERCEPTION

It is important to understand that conflict is a *perceived* incompatibility of actions or goals. Many conflicts contain only a small core of truly incompatible goals; the bigger problem is the misperceptions of the other's motives and goals. In earlier modules we considered the seeds of such misperception. The *self-serving bias* leads individuals and groups to accept credit for their good deeds and shuck responsibility for bad deeds, without according others the same benefit of the doubt. A tendency to *self-justify* further inclines people to deny the wrong of their evil acts that cannot be shucked off.

Thanks to the *fundamental attribution error*, each side sees the other's hostility as reflecting an evil disposition. One then filters the information and interprets it to fit one's *preconceptions*. Groups frequently *polarize* these self-serving, self-justifying, biasing tendencies. One symptom of groupthink is the tendency to perceive one's own group as moral and strong, and the opposition as evil and weak. Terrorist acts that are despicable brutality to most people are "holy war" to others. Indeed, the mere fact of being in a group triggers an ingroup bias. And negative stereotypes, once formed, are often resistant to contradictory evidence.

Connection:

Remember that we discussed the fundamental attribution error in Module 6.

So it should not surprise us, though it should sober us, to discover that people in conflict form distorted images of one another. Even the types of misperception are intriguingly predictable.

Mirror-Image Perceptions

To a striking degree, the misperceptions of those in conflict are mutual. People in conflict attribute similar virtues to themselves and vices to the other. Negative mirror-image perceptions have been an obstacle to peace in many places:

- Both sides of the Arab–Israeli conflict insisted that "we" are motivated by our need to protect our security and our territory, while "they" want to obliterate us and gobble up our land (Rouhana & Bar-Tal, 1998; Aslan, 2010). Both sides in this conflict believe that the land has been promised to them by God. This is obviously a difficult claim to verify and leaves the different sides firmly entrenched in their positions.

- As the United States and Iraq prepared for war, each repeatedly spoke of the other as "evil." To George W. Bush, Saddam Hussein was a "murderous tyrant" and "madman" who was threatening the civilized world with weapons of mass destruction. To Iraq's government, the Bush government was a "gang of evil" that lusted for Middle Eastern oil.

- One 2001 public opinion poll found 98 percent of Palestinians agreeing that the killing of 29 Palestinians by an assault-rifle-bearing Israeli at a mosque constituted terrorism, yet 82 percent disagreed that the killing of 21 Israeli youths by a Palestinian suicide bomber was terrorism (Kruglanski & Fishman, 2006).

Mirror-image perceptions have continued in the Arab–Israeli conflict despite many attempts to intervene.

Such conflicts, notes Philip Zimbardo (2004), engage "a two-category world—of good people, like US, and of bad people, like THEM." Opposing sides in a conflict tend to exaggerate their differences, note David Sherman, Leif Nelson, and Lee Ross (2003). However, people's actual views are not as extreme as their opponents believe (Chambers et al., 2006). Each side overestimates the extremity of the other's views, especially those of the group seeking change. And each presumes that "our" beliefs follow from the facts while "their" ideology dictates their interpretation of facts (Keltner & Robinson, 1996; Robinson et al., 1995). To resolve conflicts, it helps to understand the other's mind. But it isn't easy, notes Robert Wright (2003): "Putting yourself in the shoes of people who do things you find abhorrent may be the hardest moral exercise there is."

Yet, if misperceptions accompany conflict, they should appear and disappear as conflicts wax and wane. They do, with startling regularity. The same processes that create the enemy's image can reverse that image when the enemy becomes an ally. The Germans, who over the course of two World Wars were hated, then admired, and then again hated, were once again admired—apparently no longer plagued by what earlier was presumed to be cruelty in their national character. As long as Iraq was attacking Iran, even while using chemical weapons and massacring its own Kurds, many nations supported it: Our enemy's enemy is our friend. When Iraq ended its war with Iran and invaded oil-rich Kuwait in 1990, Iraq's behaviour suddenly became "barbaric."

LO 3

RESOLVING DISPUTES

We have seen how conflicts are ignited by social traps, competition, perceived injustices, and misperceptions. Although the picture is grim, it is not hopeless. Social psychologists have focused on four strategies for helping enemies become comrades. We can remember these as the Four Cs of peacemaking: contact, cooperation, communication, conciliation.

Contact

Might putting two conflicting individuals or groups into close contact enable them to know and like each other? We have seen why it might. We have seen that proximity—and the accompanying interaction, anticipation of interaction, and mere exposure—boosts liking. Until 1954, schools in the United States were segregated: Blacks and Whites went to separate schools. A 1954 Supreme Court decision (strongly influenced by the input of social scientists) desegregated the schools. Thus Blacks and Whites were forced to share space. Was this effective?

The overall evidence suggests that contact predicts tolerant attitudes. In a painstakingly complete analysis, Linda Tropp and Thomas Pettigrew (2004, 2005, 2006) assembled data from 515 studies of 250 513 people in 38 nations. In 94 percent of studies, *increased contact predicted decreased prejudice*. The correlation holds not only for interracial contacts, but also contacts with the elderly, psychiatric patients, homosexuals, and children with disabilities, notes Miles Hewstone (2003).

When Does Contact Improve Ethnic Attitudes?

There are clear issues associated with simple contact. Indeed, in a recent review of the impact of contact on racial attitudes, John Dixon, Kevin Durrheim, and Colin Tredoux (2005) have pointed out that contact is not always a good thing. The context in which contact occurs is very important.

Canada has had its share of racial and ethnic tensions both in the past and today. Although there was never an official segregation policy, many would argue that the federal government policy of relocating Aboriginals to reserves was a *de facto* segregation policy. Nonetheless, Canada has worked hard for many years to promote its multiculturalism policy. Yet ethnic groups often choose to segregate themselves. Most large cities have neighbourhoods that are dominated by specific ethnic groups—many new immigrants choose to move into areas where they are surrounded by people similar to themselves. In one study that tracked the attitudes of more than 1600 European students, over time, contact did serve to reduce prejudice, but prejudice also minimized contact (Binder et al., 2009).

Self-imposed segregation was evident in a South African desegregated beach, as Dixon and Durrheim (2003) discovered when they recorded the location of Black, White, and Indian beachgoers one midsummer afternoon (see Figure 17-2). Efforts to facilitate contact sometimes help, but sometimes fall flat. "We had one day when some of the Protestant schools came over," explained one Catholic youngster after a Northern Ireland school exchange (Cairns & Hewstone, 2002). "It was supposed to be like . . . mixing, but there was very little mixing. It wasn't because we didn't want to; it was just really awkward."

FIGURE 17-2

Desegregation needn't mean contact. After this Scottburgh, South Africa, beach became "open" and desegregated in the new South Africa, Blacks, Whites, and Indians tended to cluster with their own races.

Source: From Dixon & Durrheim, 2003.

Among North American students who studied in Germany or Britain, the more their contact with host country people, the more positive their attitudes (Stangor et al., 1996). In experiments, those who form friendships with outgroup members develop more positive attitudes toward the outgroup (Pettigrew & Tropp, 2000; Wright et al., 1997). It is not just knowledge of other people that matters, however—the emotional ties that form with intimate friendships serve to reduce anxiety (Hewstone, 2003; Pettigrew & Tropp, 2000, 2008). This drop in anxiety is physiological, and can be measured (Page-Gould et al, 2008).

Surveys of nearly 4000 Europeans reveal that friendship is a key to successful contact: if you have a minority-group friend, you become much more likely to express sympathy and support for the friend's group, and even somewhat more support for immigration by that group. It's true of Germans' attitudes toward Turks, French people's attitudes toward Asians and North Africans, Netherlanders' attitudes toward Surinamers and Turks, and Britishers' attitudes toward West Indians and Asians (Brown et al., 1999; Hamberger & Hewstone, 1997; Pettigrew, 1997). Likewise, anti-gay feeling is lower among people who know gays personally (e.g., Collier et al., 2012; Hodson et al., 2009). This may help explain the fact that as the trend has been for homosexuals to be more open, approval for same-sex marriage has increased as well—hitting a 53 percent approval rate in 2014 in the United States (*USA Today*, 2014). Additional studies of attitudes toward the elderly, the mentally ill, AIDS patients, and those with disabilities confirm that contact often predicts positive attitudes (Pettigrew, 1998).

The social psychologists who advocated contact never claimed that contact of *any* sort would improve attitudes. They expected poor results when contacts were competitive, unsupported by authorities, and unequal (Pettigrew, 1988; Stephan, 1987). For many years in South Africa under apartheid, Blacks and Whites had extensive contact—yet Whites invariably were in dominant positions and Blacks were in menial ones. Such unequal contacts breed attitudes that merely justify the continuation of inequality. So it's important that the contact be equal-status contact, like that between store clerks, soldiers, neighbours, prisoners, and summer campers.

Cooperation

Although equal-status contact can help, it is sometimes not enough. It didn't help when Muzafer Sherif stopped the Eagles versus Rattlers competition and brought the groups together for non-competitive activities, such as watching movies, shooting off fireworks, and eating. By this time, their hostility was so strong that mere contact only provided opportunities for taunts and attacks. When an Eagle was bumped by a Rattler, his fellow Eagles urged him to "brush off the dirt." Obviously, desegregating the two groups had hardly promoted their social integration.

Consider, too, the competitive situation in the typical classroom. Is the following scene familiar? Students compete for good grades, teacher approval, and various honours and privileges. The teacher asks a question. Several students' hands shoot up; other students sit, eyes downcast, trying to look invisible. When the teacher calls on one of the eager faces, the others hope for a wrong answer, giving them a chance to display their knowledge. The losers in this academic sport often resent the "nerds" or "geeks" who succeed. The situation abounds with both competition and painfully obvious status inequalities; we could hardly design it better to create divisions among the children (Aronson, 2000).

Does competitive contact divide and *cooperative* contact unite? Consider what happens to people who together face a common predicament.

Common External Threats

Have you ever been in a natural disaster that has shut down your town? When the ice storm of 1998 hit southern Ontario and Quebec, hundreds of thousands of people were left without power for days. A massive power failure struck Ontario and eight U.S. states in August 2003, leaving 50 million people without power. When Hurricane Juan hit Halifax in 2003, most of the city was without power for the better part of a week. What happened? News reports were filled with stories of people helping others in their communities—often, people they had never met. The Canadian Forces moved in, not to enforce law and order but to help remove downed trees and repair power poles. Such friendliness and camaraderie is common among people who have experienced a shared threat (see Lanzetta, 1955).

Hurricanes, like other natural disasters, can draw communities together or rip them apart.

Having a common enemy unified the groups of competing boys in Sherif's camping experiments— and in many subsequent experiments (Dion, 1979; Blake & Moulton, 1979). Membership in civic organizations "has historically grown rapidly during and immediately after major wars," reports Robert Putnam (2000, p. 267). Soldiers who face combat together often maintain lifelong ties with their comrades (Elder & Clipp, 1988). Times of interracial strife may therefore be times of heightened group pride. For Chinese university students in Toronto, facing discrimination heightens a sense of kinship with other Chinese (Pak et al., 1991). Just being reminded of an outgroup (say, a rival school) heightens people's responsiveness to their own group (Wilder & Shapiro, 1984). When keenly conscious of who "they" are, we also know who "we" are.

However, we cannot forget that external threats can cause real conflict as well. In the aftermath of Hurricane Katrina in New Orleans in 2005, looting, murders, and roving gangs of gun-toting vigilantes were a frequent sight on the evening news. Residents had little support, and real threats and conflicts were present. These issues, combined with the lack of law enforcement, caused the situation to rapidly descend into chaos.

Superordinate Goals

Closely related to the unifying power of an external threat is the unifying power of **superordinate goals**—goals that compel all in a group and require cooperative effort. To promote harmony among his warring campers, Sherif introduced such goals. He created a problem with the camp water supply, necessitating the cooperation of both groups to restore the water. Given an opportunity to rent a movie, one expensive enough to require the joint resources of both groups, they again cooperated. When a truck "broke down" on a camping trip, a staff member casually left the tug-of-war rope nearby, prompting one boy to suggest that they all pull the truck to get it started. When it started, a backslapping celebration ensued over their victorious "tug-of-war against the truck."

After working together to achieve such superordinate goals, the boys ate together and enjoyed themselves around a campfire. Friendships sprouted across group lines. Hostilities plummeted. On the last day, the boys decided to travel home together on one bus. During the trip they no longer sat in their original groups—instead, Eagles and Rattlers mixed together. With isolation and competition, Sherif made strangers into bitter enemies. With superordinate goals, he made enemies into friends.

Extending these findings, Samuel Gaertner, John Dovidio, and their collaborators (1993, 2000) report that working cooperatively has especially favourable effects under conditions that lead people to define a new, inclusive group that dissolves their former subgroups. Old feelings of bias against another group diminish when members of the two groups sit alternately around a table (rather than on opposite sides), give their new group a single name, and then work together under conditions that foster a good mood. "Us" and "them" become "we."

Cooperative Learning

Thus, there appear to be clear social benefits of successful, cooperative contacts between members of rival groups. So does this suggest a constructive alternative to traditional school desegregation practices? Several independent research teams have wondered whether, without compromising academic achievement, we could promote interracial friendships by replacing competitive learning situations with cooperative ones.

One research team, led by Elliot Aronson (1978, 2000, 2002; Aronson & Gonzalez, 1988), elicited group cooperation with a "jigsaw" technique. In experiments in Texas and California elementary schools, the researchers assigned children to racially and academically diverse six-member groups. The subject was then divided into six parts, with each student becoming the expert on his or her part. In a unit on Chile, one student might be the expert on Chile's history, another on its geography, another on its culture. First, the various "historians," "geographers," and so forth got together to master their material. Then they returned to the home groups to teach it to their classmates. Each group member held, so to speak, a piece of the jigsaw. The self-confident students therefore had to listen to and learn from the reticent students, who in turn soon realized they had something important to offer their peers.

There were other benefits as well. Cross-racial friendships began to blossom. The exam scores of minority students improved (perhaps because academic achievement is now peer-supported). After the experiments were over, many teachers continued using cooperative learning (D.W. Johnson et al., 1981; Slavin, 1990). So, cooperative, equal-status contacts exert a positive influence on boy campers, industrial executives, and schoolchildren. Does the principle extend to all levels of human relations? Other research suggests that it does (e.g., Brewer & Miller, 1988; Desforges et al., 1991, 1997; Deutsch, 1985, 1994). Thus, an important challenge facing our divided world is to identify and agree on our superordinate goals and to structure cooperative efforts to achieve them.

Communication

Conflicting parties have other ways to resolve their differences. When husband and wife, or labour and management, or nation X and nation Y disagree, they can **bargain** with one another directly. They can ask a third party to **mediate** by making suggestions and facilitating their negotiations. Or they can **arbitrate** by submitting their disagreement to someone who will study the issues and impose a settlement. In this section we will focus on the first two of these options.

Bargaining

Are you a good negotiator? If you want to buy or sell a new car, are you better off adopting a tough bargaining stance—opening with an extreme offer so that splitting the difference will yield a favourable result? Or are you better off beginning with a sincere "good-faith" offer?

Striking nurses protest outside the Halifax Infirmary in Halifax.

Experiments suggest no simple answer. On the one hand, those who demand more will often get more. Tough bargaining can lower the other party's expectations, making the other side willing to settle for less (Yukl, 1974). But toughness can sometimes backfire. Many a conflict is not over a pie of fixed size but over a pie that shrinks if the conflict continues. When a strike is prolonged, both labour and management lose. The National Hockey League, Major League Baseball, and most recently the National Football League learned this the hard way during labour disputes. In the 2004–2005 lockout, the NHL and the players lost hundreds of millions of dollars of income, as well as public support, when the season was cancelled. When a similar strike crippled baseball in 1994, it took almost ten years for the league to recover. Being tough can also diminish the chances of actually reaching an agreement. If the other party responds with an equally extreme stance, both may be locked into positions from which neither can back down without losing face.

Activity: **Being a good negotiator**

Do you want to be a good negotiator? We all do. Knowing some tricks of the trade could help you develop an advantage next time you find yourself in a negotiation position. Often, it is not as much about knowing what to do, but knowing what not to do. Max Bazerman (1986) described five common mistakes negotiators make and

(Continued)

suggested some strategies for avoiding them. Consider a typical negotiation you might get into: talking to a parent about borrowing a car, dividing chores with a roommate, discussing financial or child care arrangements with a spouse (or ex-spouse), coming to an agreement on a price for something with a salesperson.

1. *Expanding the fixed pie.* Too often, negotiators assume that only a fixed amount of profit or gain exists and that to win something, the other party must necessarily lose it. Sometimes this is true, but too often we assume it is without trying to think integratively. For example, purchasing goods is usually thought of in win–lose terms; however, another approach may be possible. A retailer may be willing to cut the price if payment is made in cash.

2. *Dehexing the winner's curse.* In some negotiations, we may find that the other party accepts our offer more quickly than we anticipated, and we wonder if we've been taken. A key factor in the winner's curse is that one side may have much better information than the other. To protect ourselves in negotiations of any sort, we may need to borrow expertise. For example, before buying a used car, you would be wise to get a mechanic's evaluation.

3. *De-escalating conflict.* Often, both sides in a conflict start with extreme demands, expecting to compromise somewhere in the middle; however, they get caught up in the conflict and take a hard line instead of a conciliatory or problem-solving approach. To prevent this kind of escalation, negotiators must constantly evaluate the benefits of continuing along the same course. Negotiators should also avoid pushing opponents into a corner, getting them angry, or making them feel as if they can't afford to give up the struggle.

4. *Undercutting overconfidence.* Bazerman noted that negotiators consistently expect the other side to concede more than objective analysis would suggest. Also, in final-offer arbitration, negotiators overestimate the likelihood that their final offer will be accepted. Negotiators should try to obtain objective assessments from outside experts to temper overestimation.

5. *Reframing negotiations.* There are important differences in how people respond to problems, depending on whether they are framed in terms of gains or losses. For example, given a choice between a small sure gain and a risky larger gain, most people take the sure thing; however, if the same situation is presented as a choice between a sure small loss and a possible larger loss, most will prefer to gamble. This framing effect suggests that if you are evaluating a settlement in terms of what might be lost, you should also consider what can be gained. It also suggests that a negotiator emphasize what the opposition has to gain from a risk-free settlement.

Now think back to the most recent negotiation you were involved in. Did you see these errors creep in? Now, consider the next negotiation you might be involved in. Can you think of ways to avoid those errors?

Conciliation

Mediation

A third-party mediator may offer suggestions that enable conflicting parties to make concessions and still save face (Pruitt, 1998). If your concession can be attributed to a mediator, who is gaining an equal concession from your antagonist, then neither of you will be viewed as caving in to the other's demands.

Mediators help resolve conflicts by facilitating constructive communication. Their first task is to help the parties rethink the conflict and gain information about others' interests (Thompson, 1998). Typically, people on both sides have a competitive win–lose orientation: they are successful if their opponent is unhappy with the result, and unsuccessful if their opponent is pleased (Thompson et al., 1995). The mediator aims to replace this win–lose orientation with a cooperative win–win orientation, by prodding both sides to set aside their conflicting demands and instead to think about each other's underlying needs, interests, and goals.

Communication often helps reduce self-fulfilling misperceptions. Perhaps you can recall when you have had an argument with a roommate or neighbour about how loud they play their TV or music. The outcome of such conflicts often depends on *how* people communicate their feelings to one another. Conflict researchers report that a key factor is *trust* (Ross & Ward, 1995). If you believe the other person is well-intentioned, you are then more likely to divulge your needs and concerns. Lacking such trust, you may fear that being open will give the other party information that might be used against you.

When the two parties mistrust each other and communicate unproductively, a third-party mediator—a marriage counsellor, a labour mediator, a diplomat—sometimes helps. Often the mediator is someone trusted by both sides. The mediator will therefore often structure the encounter to help each party understand and feel understood by the other. The mediator may ask the conflicting parties to restrict their arguments to statements of fact, including statements of how they feel and how they respond when the other acts in a given way: "I enjoy having music on. When you play it loud, I find it hard to concentrate. That makes me crabby." Also, the mediator may ask people to reverse roles and argue the other's position or to imagine and explain what the other person is experiencing. Experiments show that inducing empathy decreases stereotyping and increases cooperation (Batson & Moran, 1999; Galinsky & Moskowitz, 2000). Or the mediator may have them restate one another's positions before replying with their own: "My turning up the stereo bugs you."

In laboratory dilemma games, a successful strategy has proved to be simple "tit-for-tat," which begins with a cooperative opening play and thereafter matches the other party's last response (Axelrod & Dion, 1988; Komorita et al., 1992; Van Lange & Visser, 1999). Cooperate-unless-you've-just-been-exploited is another successful strategy that tries to foster cooperation and is forgiving, yet does not tolerate exploitation (Nowak & Sigmund, 1993). Repeated conciliatory acts *do* breed greater trust (although self-serving biases often make one's own acts seem more conciliatory and less hostile than those of the adversary). Maintaining an equality of power *does* protect against exploitation.

Conciliatory strategies have occasionally been tested outside the laboratory, with promising results. For example, in 1991, U.S. President George H. W. Bush ordered the elimination of all land-based U.S. tactical nuclear warheads and took strategic bombers off high alert, putting their bombs in storage. Although leaving intact his least vulnerable and most extensive nuclear arsenal—submarine-based missiles—he invited the U.S.S.R.'s Mikhail Gorbachev to reciprocate. Eight days later, Gorbachev did, taking his bombers off alert, storing their bombs, and announcing the removal of nuclear weapons from short-range rockets, ships, and submarines.

Applying Social Psychology

Now you have learned a bit more about negotiating, and the importance of cooperation and communication. But how would you negotiate if you were only interested in your own success. Machiavellians (named after Niccolo Machiavelli, a infamous Italian Renaissance political strategist) believe that people are only out for themselves, thus you can only gain by being exploitative and deceitful.

Christie (1991) developed the Machiavellian scale to measure the degree to which people believe others can be manipulated. Christie and his associates speculated that the perfect manipulator would use the following techniques:

- Be cool and detached with other people.
- Lack concern for conventional morality because rules often stand in the way of successful manipulation.
- Have low ideological commitment because means are more important than ends.
- Have no pathological disturbance or symptoms of neurosis or psychosis. A good manipulator must have an undistorted view of reality.

Research indicates that people scoring high in Machiavellianism ("high Machs") and low in Machiavellianism ("low Machs") behave differently when the situation (1) allows for improvisation (i.e., when there is ambiguity or a lack of structure), (2) involves face-to-face interaction, and (3) is emotionally arousing. Under these three conditions, high Machs are more successful than low Machs in achieving their ends.

The behavioural difference is probably caused by several factors. First, high Machs tend to concentrate on a task and their own private goal. Low Machs get carried away with interpersonal relationships that may have little to do with the task at hand. Second, high Machs resist social influence, whereas low Machs accept it. Finally, high Machs control the group, whereas low Machs accept the structure defined by others. So, are you Machiavellian? Yes or no? What will this say about your negotiation style?

Critical THINKING

Now that you have come to the end of this module, think back to what we asked at the beginning—what conflict have you been involved in recently? How would you respond differently now? How could your actions de-escalate the tensions? What factors or skills you have learned about could you use to resolve the situation?

CONCLUSIONS

Might conciliatory efforts also help reduce tension between individuals? There is every reason to expect so. When a relationship is strained and communication is non-existent, it sometimes takes only a conciliatory gesture—a soft answer, a warm smile, a gentle touch—for both parties to begin easing down the tension ladder, to a rung where contact, cooperation, and communication again become possible.

SUMMARY OF KEY POINTS

LO1. Define social dilemmas.

- Social dilemmas are when two groups or individuals have conflicting goals in a social situation.
- The Prisoners' Dilemma and the Tragedy of the Commons are two methods most commonly employed to explore conflict resolution.

LO2. Understand the role of various factors in conflict.

- Competition, perceived injustice, and misperceptions can all negatively influence the outcomes of social conflicts.

LO3. Understand how to promote dispute resolution.

- Contact, cooperation, communication, and conciliation are the fours Cs of conflict resolution.

KEY TERMS

Arbitration   Resolution of a conflict by a neutral third party who studies both sides and imposes a settlement.

Bargaining   Seeking an agreement through direct negotiation between parties to a conflict.

Conflict   A perceived incompatibility of actions or goals.

Equal-status contact   Contact made on an equal basis. Just as a relationship between people of unequal status breeds attitudes consistent with their relationship, so do relationships between those of equal status. Thus, to reduce prejudice, interracial contact should be between persons equal in status.

Mediation   An attempt by a neutral third party to resolve a conflict by facilitating communication and offering suggestions.

Mirror-image perceptions   Reciprocal views of one another often held by parties in conflict; for example, each may view itself as moral and peace-loving and the other as evil and aggressive.

Non–zero-sum games   Games in which outcomes need not sum to zero. With cooperation, both can win; with competition, both can lose. (Also called mixed-motive situations.)

Superordinate goals   Shared goals that necessitate cooperative effort; goals that override people's differences from one another.

Helping

Imagine yourself in the following situation: You are walking through town with a couple of your friends. You are having a good time, joking around and enjoying the weather. As you are crossing a bridge, you see a naked man (about your age) running toward you from the other side of the bridge. Cars slow down, people are staring, a few people are honking, but no one is stopping. Suddenly, the man jumps up onto the railing of the bridge, which has a 15-metre drop into running water. Would you say something to the man? Would you run up and try to stop him? Would you think it was all a joke? Would you encourage him to jump? In situations such as this, all sorts of things have happened. Sometimes people help; sometimes people do not. If you were in that situation, what would you do?

Or consider another situation: You are trolling through your favourite blogs over an early breakfast when you come across a thread entitled "This is it." Curious, you open up the thread see a picture and can read "Today at 11:30 GMT I will attack my school with arson and other forms of violence—

the bastards will pay!" You can see from the picture on the blog that the school is in a specific country, but you do not know which school. What do you do? Ignore it as ridiculous and meaningless threats? Or do you report it?

This was the dilemma faced by J.P. Neufeld in Montreal. What should he do? He could tell by the photo and a link on the blog that this person was in Norfolk, England. He decided to act—he Googled the Norfolk police department, found a number, and called. Feeling ridiculous, when the police department answered, he said, "Hi. I'm a guy from Canada . . . there is someone about to set fire to a school" (Fitterman & Bouquet, 2009, p. 63). Much to his surprise, they took his information and put detectives on the case. With the help of another tip, within the hour the Norfolk police arrested the young blogger outside of his school—he was carrying a flammable liquid, some matches, and a knife. The Internet is powerful—it can provide anonymity, but it can also empower people to act to help from the other side of the world.

What do people do when faced with emergencies? It all depends. Would you risk your life to save someone else? In November of 1998, passengers on a Toronto subway platform saw a man behaving oddly with two small children. At first many were not sure what was going on, but it became clear that he was trying to push one of the kids onto the subway track. The bystanders acted quickly, jumping on the man and restraining him until police arrived. Had they not intervened, at least one, if not both, of the children would have been killed by a speeding subway train.

In October of 2007, Robert Dziekanski, a Polish man coming to visit his mother, arrived in Vancouver. He did not speak any English. He spent almost ten hours in a holding area in the Vancouver airport. No one came to help him. After ten hours, agitated and tired, Dziekanski tried to leave. The RCMP was called. Within 45 seconds of their arrival, Dziekanski was shocked with a Taser. A short time later, he was dead. The police did not try to reason with him before he was shocked. Almost no one had tried to help him during the entire ordeal. Why not?

Zofia Cisowski, Robert Dziekanski's mother, grieves for her son, who died after being tasered by RCMP officers. Why did no one come to his aid before the final confrontation?

People can sometimes be incredibly generous. The 2004 South Asian tsunami that killed more than 225 000 people, the 2010 earthquake in Haiti killed hundreds of thousands, and Typhoon Haiyan, which devastated the Philippines in 2013, all resulted in help coming from all over the world. But sometimes people do not help those in need at all. What influences whether or not people help? Are you more likely to jump in a river to save a drowning stranger? Or are you more likely to give money to a good cause?

Critical THINKING

In this photo, we see people helping in the aftermath of Typhoon Haiyan in the Philippines. What are some of the factors that motivate people to act altruistically in times of crisis? Have you ever helped in such a crisis? What was it, and what did you do?

THE CASE THAT STARTED IT ALL

On March 13, 1964, bar manager Kitty Genovese was raped and murdered by a knife-wielding man as she returned to her Queens, New York, apartment house at 3:00 a.m. A newspaper report of the event two weeks later told a detailed and horrifying story of the event. According to the media report, her screams of terror and pleas for help aroused 38 eyewitnesses. Supposedly, many came to their windows and watched, while, for 35 minutes, she struggled to escape her attacker. But no one came to her aid. Not until her attacker departed did anyone so much as call the police. Soon after, she died. This story, widely reported in the media, and repeated often over the last five decades in every major social psychology textbook (see Manning, Levine & Collins, 2007), had a remarkable impact on the study of prosocial behaviour. In response to the uproar that followed the Genovese murder, Bibb Latané and John Darley (1968) embarked on a line of research that would change how we saw helping, and would help us understand why people choose to (or not to) help those in need.

Acts of comforting, caring, and helping abound: without asking anything in return, people offer directions, donate money, give blood, and volunteer time. Why, and when, will people perform altruistic acts? And what can be done to lessen indifference and increase altruism? Altruism is selfishness in reverse. An altruistic person is concerned and helpful even when no benefits are offered or expected in return.

Activity: **What is (and isn't) altruism?**

Indicate whether or not you think each of the items below is an example of helping behaviour.

Yes	Maybe	No		
_____	_____	_____	1.	Bob, a college student, spends three hours per week as a "Big Brother" to an eight-year-old boy.
_____	_____	_____	2.	Marie, a lawyer, stops to aid the victim of an automobile accident.
_____	_____	_____	3.	Bill notifies the bookstore manager when he sees a college student attempt to shoplift some notebook paper.
_____	_____	_____	4.	John, a firefighter, rescues an elderly woman from an apartment building fire.
_____	_____	_____	5.	Millie anonymously donates $500 to a local charity.
_____	_____	_____	6.	Sam attempts to save his three-year-old from drowning.
_____	_____	_____	7.	Sally buys a 50-50 ticket at a minor league hockey game.
_____	_____	_____	8.	Jim agrees to donate his organs for transplant after he dies.
_____	_____	_____	9.	Jill, a college student, gives a pint of blood.
_____	_____	_____	10.	Wanda, a police officer, arrests a bank robber who is fleeing the scene of the crime.
_____	_____	_____	11.	Believing that those who give will receive great blessings in return, Rick and Sophie contribute their family's monthly paycheque to their church fund drive.

Now that you have completed this activity, read the definition and explanation of altruism carefully. Go back and answer the questions again, but this time assessing whether or not these are true examples of altruism. Did your answers change? Why or why not?

LO 1

WHY DO PEOPLE HELP?

What motivates altruism? One idea, called social-exchange theory, is that we help after doing a cost–benefit analysis. As part of an exchange of benefits, helpers aim to maximize their rewards and minimize their costs. When donating blood, we weigh the costs (the inconvenience and discomfort) against the benefits (the social approval and noble feeling). If the anticipated rewards exceed the costs, we help.

You might object that social-exchange theory takes the selflessness out of altruism. It seems to imply that a helpful act is never genuinely altruistic; we merely call it "altruistic" when the rewards are inconspicuous. If we know people are tutoring only to alleviate guilt or gain social approval, we hardly credit them for a good deed. We laud people for their altruism only when we can't otherwise explain it.

From babyhood onward, however, people sometimes exhibit a natural empathy, by feeling distress when seeing others in distress and relief when their suffering ends. Loving parents (unlike child abusers and other perpetrators of cruelty) suffer when their children suffer and rejoice over their children's joys (Miller & Eisenberg, 1988). Although some helpful acts are indeed done to gain rewards or relieve guilt, experiments suggest that other helpful acts aim simply to increase another's welfare, producing satisfaction for oneself merely as a by-product (Batson, 1991).

Does being religious increase helping? Azim Shariff and Ara Norenzayan (2007) at the University of British Columbia asked people to share $10 with a stranger; they were allowed to keep as much or as little of the $10 as they wished. The researchers found that although self-reported religiosity (how religious people see themselves to be) did not predict how much people gave to anonymous strangers, those who unscrambled sentences containing words that would elicit the concept of God (e.g., spirit, divine, God, sacred, and prophet) were more generous. The authors hypothesized that part of this effect may be that people, reminded of "God," feel as though they are being "watched" and thus alter their behaviour accordingly.

Daniel Batson (2001; Batson & Powell, 2003) argues that our willingness to help is affected by both self-serving and altruistic motives. When we feel empathy we focus not so much on our own distress, but that of the sufferer (see Figure 18-1). This empathy comes naturally—even day-old infants cry more when they hear another infant cry (Hoffman, 1981). Most 18-month-olds, seeing an unfamiliar adult drop a marker or clothespin, will readily help the person if he or she is having trouble reaching it (Warnekan & Tomasello, 2006). Humans are not alone. Primates also exhibit empathy (deWaal, 2005). In a classic experiment, most rhesus monkeys refused to operate a device that gained them food if it caused another monkey to receive an electric shock (Masserman et al., 1964).

In order to separate egoistic distress reduction from empathy-based altruism (see Figure 18-1) Batson's research group conducted a number of studies. In one of these experiments, Batson (Batson et al., 1981) asked female university students to watch a young woman (a confederate) suffer while supposedly receiving electric shocks. Half the participants had been led to believe that the woman had similar values and interests as the participant. After the first round of shocks, the confederate told the experimenter and participant that a fall against an electric fence as a child had made her particularly sensitive to shock. The experimenter suggested that the participant take the woman's place. With their empathy aroused, nearly all agreed.

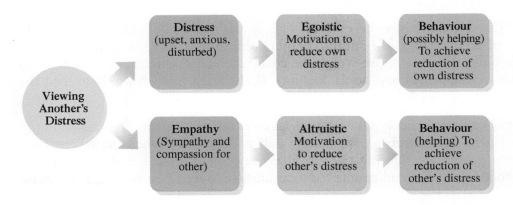

FIGURE 18-1

Egoistic and altruistic routes to helping. Viewing a person's distress can evoke a combination of inward-focused distress and/or outward-focused empathy. Researchers agree that distress triggers egoistic motives, but they debate whether empathy can trigger true altruistic motives, or if the role of motivation and emotion are at least equally important (see Carerra et al., 2013; Pavey et al., 2012).

Source: Adapted from Batson, Fultz, & Schoenrade, 1987.

But Mark Schaller and Robert Cialdini (1988) have doubted if this is true altruism. They argue that feeling empathy for someone's suffering makes one sad, and the motivation to reduce that sadness underlies helping. In one study (Schaller & Cialdini, 1988), these researchers told participants that their sadness could be relieved by listening to a comedy tape, instead of helping someone. In these conditions, people who did feel empathy were nonetheless not very helpful. Cialdini and his colleagues (Cialdini et al., 1991) argue that no helping experiment has ruled out all possible egoistic explanations for helping. But other studies suggest that genuine altruism does exist. With empathy aroused, people will help even when they believe no one will know about their helping (Fultz et al., 1986) and they will feel badly if their efforts to help are unsuccessful (Batson & Weeks, 1996). In the end, the evidence suggests that sometimes people do focus on others' welfare, not their own (Batson, 2001; Dovidio, 1991).

Social norms also motivate helping. They prescribe how we *ought* to behave. We learn the reciprocity norm, a version of the golden rule—we should do unto others as we would have them do unto us. In other words, if someone is nice to us, we should be nice to them. In the context of helping, this means that we should return help to those who have helped us. Thus, we expect that those who receive favours (gifts, invitations, help) should later return them. The reciprocity norm is qualified by our awareness that some people are incapable of reciprocal giving and receiving. Thus, we also feel a social-responsibility norm—that we should help those who really need it, without regard to future exchanges. When we pick up the dropped books for the person on crutches, we expect nothing in return.

But what happens when the potential costs of the situation conflict with these perceived norms? Sometimes the actual cost of a seemingly simple act (picking up a dropped object) is not what we expected. Sometimes we may be too embarrassed to help. In a clever study, Stuart McKelvie and James MacDonald (MacDonald & McKelvie, 1992) from Bishop's University explored helping in a real-world situation. In a shopping centre, they dropped either a mitten or a box of condoms in full view of people walking through the mall. The mitten was returned to the dropper 43 percent of the time, but the condoms were returned only 17 percent of the time. Thus, people avoided helping when the situation could cause embarrassment.

In addition, these suggested reasons for helping make biological sense. The empathy that parents feel for their children and other relatives promotes the survival of their shared genes. Likewise, say evolutionary psychologists, reciprocal altruism in small groups boosts everyone's survival.

Applying Social Psychology

How do we decide when to offer aid? Brickman and his colleagues (1982) argue that it depends on how we answer two questions: (1) Who is responsible for the problem? and (2) Who is responsible for the solution? The answers to these two questions form the basis for four models of helping:

1. In the *moral model*, actors are held responsible both for problems and solutions and are believed to need proper motivation. Historically, we have viewed criminality and addiction in this way: "You got yourself into this mess, now get yourself out." Helpers simply exhort people to assume responsibility for their problems and to work their own way out.

2. In the *compensatory model*, people are not seen as responsible for problems, but they are responsible for solutions. People need power, and the helper may provide resources or opportunities that the recipients deserve. Nonetheless, the responsibility for using this assistance rests with the recipient.

3. In the *medical model*, individuals are seen as neither responsible for the problem or for the solution. Helpers say, "You are ill, and I will try to make you better." This approach, of course, characterizes the health care system in all modern societies, and to some extent how addiction is more modernly viewed. Helping involves providing treatment and care.

4. In the *enlightenment model*, actors are seen as responsible for problems but as unable or unwilling to provide solutions. They are viewed as needing discipline. Helping means earning their trust and giving them guidance.

Think of how you have addressed the question of helping in your own past. Can you think of examples of using each model yourself?

Gender and Helping

Interestingly, gender has an impact both on who helps, and on who receives help. Alice Eagly and Maureen Crowley conducted a meta-analysis of the impact of gender on helping behaviour (1986). Across 172 studies, which looked at approximately 50 000 males and females, these researchers found that men were more likely to help in potentially dangerous situations where strangers need help (such as when someone has a flat tire or takes a fall in the subway). This may explain why 90 percent of Carnegie Medal winners, an award given for heroism in saving human life, have been men. Women are slightly more likely to help in safer situations, such as volunteering to help in an experiment or work with disabled children. Nonetheless, women are as or more likely than men to risk their lives, as Holocaust rescuers, or donating a kidney, or volunteering with the Peace Corps in the United States or with Doctors of the World (Becker & Eagly, 2004). Thus, clearly, this gender difference interacts with the particular situation.

Eagly and Crowley (1986) also found that women offered help equally to both men and women, whereas men offered more help when the people in need were women. For example, experiments in the 1970s found that women received more help for a disabled car than men (e.g., Penner et al., 1973). Eagly and Crowley argued that in most of these studies, the encounters were short-term encounters with strangers in need—the exact type of situation where men are expected to act in a "chivalrous" manner. But other factors may have played a role as well—men more frequently helped attractive than unattractive women (e.g., Mims et al., 1975). More recent studies have shown that women also seek more help (e.g., Addis & Mahalik, 2003). For example, women are twice as likely as men to seek medical and psychiatric help, and are more likely to accept help when it is offered (Nadler, 1991).

LO 2

WHEN DO PEOPLE HELP?

Social psychologists were curious and concerned about bystanders' lack of involvement during emergency events, so they undertook experiments to identify when people will help in an emergency. Then they broadened the question to ask: Who is likely to help in non-emergencies, such as by giving money, donating blood, or contributing time? Some people do little, perhaps giving money to a panhandler on the street or maybe dropping their change in the donation container in a coffee shop, but others do much more.

Craig Kielburger was born in 1982 in Thornhill, Ontario. Shocked by the reality of child labour in developing countries, at age 12 Kielburger founded "Free the Children" with a group of six other 12-year-old friends. Today, Free the Children is the world's largest network of children helping children through education and leadership development abroad and in North America. To date, his organization has built more than 650 schools around the world, which provide daily education for 55 000 children. It has touched more than 2.3 million people through its outreach and training programs in North America (Free the Children, 2014). In 2007, at the age of 24, Kielburger received the Order of Canada for his outstanding contributions to Canadian society.

Of course, Craig Kielburger may be an exception. He identified a problem when he was very young, and made it his life's mission to correct it. Although we can admire what he has done, researchers spend time focusing on the more day-to-day helpful acts. Thus, researchers have been very interested in discovering what encourages the average person to help others. In other words, what increases giving and helping? Among their answers is that helping often increases among people who are

- feeling guilty, thus providing a way to relieve the guilt or restore self-image
- in a good mood
- deeply religious (evidenced by higher rates of charitable giving and volunteerism)

Social psychologists also study the *circumstances* that enhance helpfulness. The odds of our helping someone increase in the following circumstances:

- We have just observed a helpful model.
- We are not hurried.
- The victim appears to need and deserve help.
- The victim is similar to ourselves.
- We are in a small town or rural area.
- There are few other bystanders.

LO 3

THE BYSTANDER EFFECT

Bystander passivity during emergencies has prompted social commentators to lament people's "alienation," "apathy," "indifference," and "unconscious sadistic impulses." By attributing the non-intervention to the bystanders' dispositions, we can reassure ourselves that, as caring people, we would have helped. But were the bystanders such inhuman characters?

Social psychologists Bibb Latané and John Darley (1970) were unconvinced. They staged ingenious emergencies and found that a single situational factor—the presence of other bystanders—greatly decreased intervention. By 1980, four dozen experiments had compared help given by bystanders who perceived themselves to be either alone or with others. In about 90 percent of these comparisons, involving nearly 6000 people, lone bystanders were more likely to help (Latané & Nida, 1981). In Internet communications, too, people are more likely to respond helpfully to a request (such as from someone seeking a link to the campus library) if they believe that they alone (and not several others) have received the request (Blair et al., 2005).

Sometimes the victim was actually less likely to get help when many people were around. When Latané, James Dabbs (1975), and 145 collaborators "accidentally" dropped coins or pencils during 1497 elevator rides, they were helped 40 percent of the time when one other person was on the elevator and less than 20 percent of the time when there were six passengers. Why? Latané and Darley surmised that as the number of bystanders increases, any given bystander is less likely to *notice* the incident, less likely to *interpret* the incident as a problem or emergency, and less likely to *assume responsibility* for taking action (see Figure 18-2).

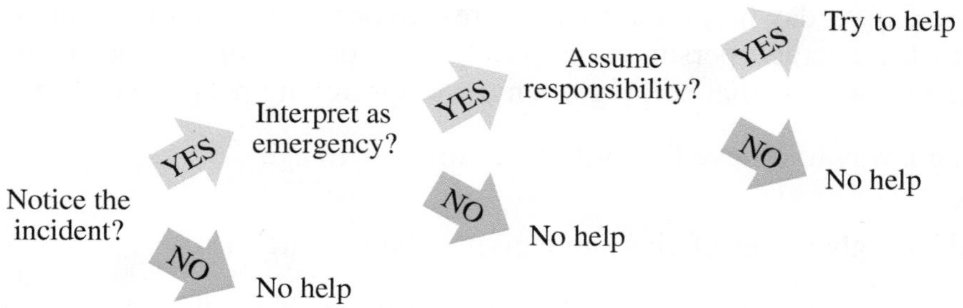

FIGURE 18-2

Latané and Darley's Decision Tree. Only one path up the tree leads to helping. At each fork of the path, the presence of other bystanders may divert a person down a branch toward not helping.

Source: Adapted from Darley & Latané, 1968

Noticing

In another study, Latané and Darley (1968) had Columbia University men fill out a questionnaire in a room, either by themselves or with two strangers. While they were working (and being observed through a one-way mirror), there was a staged emergency: smoke poured into the room through a wall vent. Solitary students, who often glanced idly about the room while working, noticed the smoke almost immediately—usually in less than five seconds. Those in groups kept their eyes on their work. It typically took them about 20 seconds to notice the smoke.

Interpreting

Remember the subway example we mentioned earlier? Imagine you were one of the bystanders on the Toronto subway platform that day. You are staring straight ahead, just like the other 200 waiting people, thinking about your day. You hear a child crying and an angry man yelling and struggling with his son. What would you do? No one else seems to be noticing or caring. Would you?

Once we notice an ambiguous event, we must interpret it. Put yourself in the room filling with smoke. Though worried, you don't want to embarrass yourself by getting flustered. You glance at the others. They look calm, indifferent. Assuming everything must be okay, you shrug it off and go back to work. Then one of the others notices the smoke and, noting your apparent unconcern, reacts similarly. This is yet another example of informational influence. Each person uses others' behaviour as clues to reality.

So it happened in Latané and Darley's experiment. When those working alone noticed the smoke, they usually hesitated a moment, then got up, walked over to the vent, felt, sniffed and waved at the smoke, hesitated again, and then went to report it. In dramatic contrast, those in groups of three did not move. Among the 24 men in eight groups, only one person reported the smoke within the first four minutes (see Figure 18-3). By the end of the six-minute experiment, the smoke was so thick it was obscuring the men's vision and they were rubbing their eyes and coughing. Still, in only three of the eight groups did even a single person leave to report the problem.

Proportion having reported smoke, percent

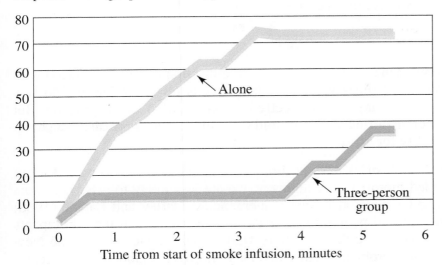

FIGURE 18-3

The Smoke-Filled-Room Experiment. Smoke pouring into the testing room was much more likely to be reported by individuals working alone than by three-person groups.

Source: Data from Latané & Darley, 1968.

Equally interesting, the group's passivity affected its members' interpretations. What caused the smoke? "A leak in the air conditioning." "Chemistry labs in the building." "Steam pipes." "Truth gas." Not one said, "Fire." The group members, by serving as non-responsive models, influenced each other's interpretation of the situation.

This experimental dilemma parallels dilemmas we all face. Are the shrieks outside merely playful antics or the desperate screams of someone being assaulted? Is the boys' scuffling a friendly tussle or a vicious fight? Is the person slumped in the doorway sleeping, high on drugs, or seriously ill—perhaps in a diabetic coma? That surely was the question confronting those who passed by Sidney Brookins (AP, 1993). Brookins, who had suffered a concussion when beaten, died after lying near the door to a Minneapolis apartment house for two days. A recent meta-analysis of bystander effect research has shown that the seemingly counterintuitive result that the bystander effect is reduced in dangerous situations. When the situation is obviously dangerous, people are more likely to provide help (Fischer et al., 2011). Why? Because a dangerous situation is easy to interpret. We know that a person needs help, so that overrides people's difficulty with interpreting the situation.

That may also have been the question for those who in 2003 watched Brandon Vedas overdose and die online. As his life ebbed, his audience, which was left to wonder whether he was putting on an act, failed to decipher available clues to his whereabouts and to contact police (Nichols, 2003). Amanda Todd, a 15-year-old from British Columbia, took her own life after being severely bullied online. Experts argued that passive bystanders were partly to blame (CBC, 2012). In Nova Scotia, this problem has been addressed head-on in the legal definition of bullying (which also applies to bullying online; CBC, 2013). Now, people who passively watch someone being bullied and do not act are also considered responsible and subject to sanctions.

Assuming Responsibility

Misinterpretation is not the only cause of the bystander effect—the inaction of strangers faced with ambiguous emergencies. What about those times when an emergency is obvious? Those who saw and heard Kitty Genovese's pleas for help may have correctly interpreted what was happening. But the lights and silhouetted figures in neighbouring windows told them that others were also watching. This may have diffused the responsibility for action.

Few of us have observed a murder. But all of us have at times been slower to react to a need when others were present. Passing a stranded motorist on a highway, we are less likely to offer help than on a country road. To explore bystander inaction in clear emergencies, Darley and Latané (1968) simulated the Genovese drama. They placed people in separate rooms from which the participants would hear a victim crying for help. To create this situation, Darley and Latané asked some New York University students to discuss their problems with university life over a laboratory intercom. The researchers told the students that to guarantee their anonymity, no one would be visible, nor would the experimenter eavesdrop. During the ensuing discussion, when the experimenter turned his microphone on, the participants heard one person lapse into an epileptic seizure. With increasing intensity and speech difficulty, he pleaded for someone to help.

Critical THINKING

Remember the "rape chant" incident discussed in Module 9: What struck many people was that there were about the same number of men and women singing the chant, and that it had apparently been going on for several years. Why would young women on university campuses, the most likely target of unwanted sexual advances, sing these chants? Were they suffering from the bystander effect? What could have encouraged them to speak out? Perhaps ironically, many of the student leaders who participated in the chant were subject to bullying themselves (CBC, 2013).

Connection:

We initially discussed the rape chant issue in Module 9.

Of those led to believe there were no other listeners, 85 percent left their room to seek help. Of those who believed four others also overheard the victim, only 31 percent went for help. Were those who didn't respond apathetic and indifferent? When the experimenter came in to end the experiment, she did not find this response. Most immediately expressed concern. Many had trembling hands and sweating palms. They believed an emergency had occurred but were undecided whether to act.

After the smoke-filled room and the seizure experiments, Latané and Darley asked the participants whether the presence of others had influenced them. We know the others had a dramatic effect. Yet the participants almost invariably denied the influence. They typically replied, "I was aware of the others, but I would have reacted just the same if they weren't there." This response reinforces a familiar point: *We often do not know why we do what we do*. That is why experiments are revealing. A survey of uninvolved bystanders following a real emergency would have left the bystander effect hidden.

These experiments raise again the issue of research ethics. Were the researchers in the seizure experiment ethical when they forced people to decide whether to abort the discussion to report the problem? Would you object to being in such a study? Note that it would have been impossible to get your "informed consent" without destroying the cover for the experiment.

Connection:

Remember our discussion of research ethics in Module 2—would it be an issue here?

In defence of the researchers, they were always careful to debrief the laboratory participants. After explaining the seizure experiment, probably the most stressful, the experimenter gave the participants a questionnaire. One hundred percent said the deception was justified and that they would be willing to take part in similar experiments in the future. None reported feeling angry at the experimenter. Other researchers confirm that the overwhelming majority of participants in such experiments say that their participation was both instructive and ethically justified (Schwartz & Gottlieb, 1981). In field experiments, an accomplice assisted the victim if no one else did, thus reassuring bystanders that the problem was being dealt with.

Remember that the social psychologist has a twofold ethical obligation: to protect the participants and to enhance human welfare by discovering influences upon human behaviour. Such discoveries can alert us to unwanted influences and show us how we might exert positive influences. The ethical principle seems to be: After protecting participants' welfare, social psychologists fulfill their responsibility to society by doing such research.

POSTSCRIPT: THE KITTY GENOVESE CASE REVISITED

As we mentioned at the beginning of the module, the rape and murder of Kitty Genovese was the catalyst for an entire line of research on helping. Because of this research, we now have a much better understanding of the factors that influence whether or not people will engage in prosocial behaviour, and when they will intervene in an emergency. We also now know the things we can do as the victims to encourage people to help us. Perhaps it is ironic then that the case that started it all turns out to have been misreported and misinterpreted from the time it happened (see Manning et al., 2007).

As it turns out, there were not 38 witnesses. There may have been as few as eight. Several witnesses saw a man and a woman talking on the street, some saw them on the ground, but only a couple seem to have seen the actual attack (i.e., there was some difficulty interpreting the events). After the initial attack on the street, Kitty Genovese cried out. One witness who saw the actual struggle yelled at the attacker (Winston Mosley) to leave (i.e., the person recognized the danger and intervened).

Mosley then ran away. Apparently, more than one person called the police immediately (i.e., identified the emergency situation and acted), but the police did not show up (apparently the attack occurred near a neighbourhood bar that was known for frequent fights and disturbances; this resulted in the police not recognizing the calls as an emergency). It was only after Kitty Genovese got up and stumbled away (perhaps sending a further message to the witnesses that the emergency had passed) and into her apartment building, that the attacker returned, raped her, and inflicted the wound that would ultimately kill her. In the entryway to her apartment building, she was no longer in sight of any of the witnesses, and her building neighbours were unlikely to have heard the struggle or her screams (i.e., no one could notice the crisis). Finally, the police did arrive at the scene, but Genovese was already mortally wounded. She died a short time later.

Thus, perhaps the iconic story of apathy in a big city, which led to more than 40 years of research on helping, was not as bleak a story as originally told. Indeed, some of the people who saw the problem and identified it as an emergency acted, just as we would predict based on the research literature.

WHAT TO DO WHEN YOU NEED HELP

If you are in an emergency situation, what should you do to increase the chances someone will help you? As highlighted earlier, the natural tendency of bystanders, especially when there are a lot of them, will be to ignore your emergency. They may not notice, they may interpret it incorrectly, they may not know how to help, or they may feel someone else has already helped. You, as the person in the middle of the situation, need to take action. Get the attention of a specific person. Point that person out and make eye contact. Make it clear, through your words, that you need help. This personal approach has been shown to be effective to get help in different situations: for blood donations (Foss, 1978), rides for hitchhikers (Snyder et al., 1974), and volunteers for AIDS workers (Omoto & Snyder, 2002). A personal approach reduces people's perceptions of anonymity and increases personal responsibility. Doing this, and identifying an individual, will reduce any ambiguity in the situation, and reduce any diffusion of responsibility.

CONCLUSIONS

We have heard of a number of cases where people ignored situations or even refused to help when people were in need. But could something as simple as a psychology class change people's behaviours in such situations? Recall the vignette at the beginning of the chapter of the man standing on the bridge railing. That very scenario unfolded in Ithaca, New York, in 1993. Pablo Salanova, Rob Lee, and Gretchen Goldfarb were walking through town when they saw a naked man leap onto the railing of a bridge. Initially they thought it was all a joke, but Gretchen, whose introductory psychology class had recently covered helping and prosocial behaviour, realized that it might be an emergency. At Gretchen's prompting, her two friends grabbed the man and kept him from jumping (likely to his death) from the bridge. Coincidentally, a similar thing has happened to one of this textbook's authors, David. A former student, now living in Washington, D.C., stopped by his office one day. The student mentioned that she had recently found herself as part of a stream of pedestrians striding past a man lying unconscious on the sidewalk. "It took my mind back to our social psych class and the accounts of why people fail to help in such situations. Then I thought, 'Well, if I just walk by, too, who's going to help him?'" So she made a call to an emergency help number and waited with the victim—and other bystanders who then joined her—until help arrived.

As you come to understand what influences people's responses, will your attitudes and your behaviour be the same? So, how will learning about social influences upon helping affect you? Will the knowledge you've gained affect your actions? We hope so.

SUMMARY OF KEY POINTS

LO1. Explain why people help.

- People help others when they feel empathy for them.
- At times, people are guided to help due to social-exchange principles—specifically, reciprocity, a social responsibility.

LO2. Explain when people help.

- People will help more when they are in a good mood, when they feel guilty (if helping will make them feel better), or if they are religious.
- Several contextual issues also increase helping.

LO3. Understand the bystander effect.

- The key to the effect occurring is tied to the observer noticing a person in need, interpreting the situation as requiring help, and assuming responsibility for providing help.

KEY TERMS

Altruism   A motive to increase another's welfare without conscious regard for one's self-interests.

Bystander effect   The finding that a person is less likely to provide help when there are other bystanders.

Empathy   The vicarious experience of another's feelings; putting oneself in another's shoes.

Reciprocity norm   An expectation that people will help, not hurt, those who have helped them.

Social-exchange theory   The theory that human interactions are transactions that aim to maximize one's rewards and minimize one's costs.

Social-responsibility norm   An expectation that people will help those dependent upon them.

MODULE NINETEEN

Interpersonal Attraction

How we meet and mate has been a major topic of social psychological research since the inception of the field. When does attraction happen and why? Is it different for men and women? Gay versus straight? What explains our attraction? Similarity? Differences? Genetic drivers hidden for eons in our DNA? A great deal of research has tried to address these issues.

What predisposes one person to like, or to love, another? So much has been written about liking and loving that almost every conceivable explanation—and its opposite—has already been proposed.

What factors nurture liking and loving? Does absence make the heart grow fonder? Or is someone who is out of sight also out of mind? Is it likes that attract? Or opposites?

Critical THINKING

Think back to your first romantic relationship. How did you meet him or her? What was it like? Was that person the only one you could think about? Did you agonize over what you would say when you saw him or her? Did you lose sleep? Now compare this to your relationship with your best friend. How did you meet him or her? How did you become friends? Is this someone who lived near you? Someone you met at school, at work, or in residence? Are they the same person?

Consider the simple but powerful *reward theory of attraction:* We like those whose behaviour is rewarding to us, and people we associate with rewarding events. Friends reward each other. Without keeping score, they do favours for one another. Likewise, we develop a liking for those whom we associate with pleasant happenings and surroundings. Thus, surmised researchers Elaine Hatfield and William Walster (1978), "If your relationship is to survive, it's important that you *both* continue to associate your relationship with good things."

Yet, as with most sweeping generalizations, the reward theory of attraction leaves many questions unanswered. What, precisely, *is* rewarding? Is it usually more rewarding to be with someone who differs from us or someone who is similar to us? To be lavishly flattered or constructively criticized? Do we have an innate need to belong?

LO 1

PROXIMITY

One of the most powerful predictors of whether any two people are friends is sheer proximity. Proximity can also breed hostility; most assaults and murders involve people living close together. But far more often, proximity kindles liking. Mitja Back and his colleagues (2008) confirmed this by randomly assigning students to seats in class and asking them to introduce themselves. One year later, these students reported being better friends with people who sat next to or near them than those who sat further away.

Though it may seem trivial to those pondering the mysterious origins of romantic love, sociologists have found that most people marry someone who lives in the same neighbourhood, or works at the same company or job, or sits in the same class (Bossard, 1932; Burr, 1973; Clarke, 1952; McPherson et al., 2001). In a Pew survey (2006), 38 percent of married people or those in long-term relationships met at work or school, and much of the rest met in their neighbourhood, church, gym, or while growing up. Look around. If you marry, it will likely be to someone who has lived or worked or studied within walking distance.

Interaction

Actually, it is not geographical distance that is critical but "functional distance"—how often people's paths cross. This was nicely illustrated in research by Leon Festinger and his colleagues (1952) in a study of married couples living in student apartments at the Massachusetts Institute of Technology. They found that people were most likely to be friends with next-door neighbours, and that people who lived in apartments in high-traffic areas were more likely to be listed by others as "friends."

Why does proximity breed liking? One factor is availability; obviously there are fewer opportunities to get to know someone who attends a different school or lives in another town. But there is more to it than that. Most people like their roommates, or those one door away, better than those two doors away. Those just a few doors away, or even a floor below, hardly live at an inconvenient distance. Moreover, those close by are potential enemies as well as friends. So why does proximity more often encourage affection than animosity?

Anticipation of Interaction

Already we have noted one answer: Proximity enables people to discover commonalities and exchange rewards. What is more, merely *anticipating* interaction boosts liking. John Darley and Ellen Berscheid (1967) discovered this when they gave University of Minnesota women ambiguous information about two other women, one of whom they expected to talk with intimately. Asked how much they liked each one, the women preferred the person they expected to meet. Expecting to date someone similarly boosts liking (Berscheid et al., 1976). Even voters on the losing side of an election will find their opinions of the winning candidate—whom they are now stuck with—rising (Gilbert et al., 1998).

The phenomenon is adaptive. Anticipatory liking—expecting that someone will be pleasant and compatible—increases the chance of forming a rewarding relationship (Klein & Kunda, 1992; Knight & Vallacher, 1981; Miller & Marks, 1982). It is good that we are biased to like those we often see. Our lives are filled with relationships with people whom we may not have chosen but with whom we need to have continuing interactions—roommates, siblings, grandparents, teachers, classmates, co-workers. Liking such people is surely conducive to better relationships with them, which in turn makes for happier, more productive living.

Mere Exposure

More than 200 experiments reveal that, contrary to the old proverb, familiarity does not breed contempt. Rather, it breeds fondness (Bornstein, 1989, 1999; Lee, 2001; Harmon-Jones & Allen, 2001). The mere exposure effect means that exposure to all sorts of novel stimuli—nonsense syllables, Chinese characters, musical selections, faces—boosts people's ratings of them. Do the supposed Turkish words *nansoma, saricik,* and *afworbu* mean something better or something worse than the words *iktitaf, biwojni,* and *kadirga*? University of Michigan students tested by Robert Zajonc (1968, 1970) preferred whichever of these words they had seen most frequently. The more times they had seen a meaningless word or a Chinese ideograph, the more likely they were to say it meant something good (see Figure 19-1). For example, what are your favourite letters of the alphabet? People of differing nationalities, languages, and ages prefer the letters appearing in their own names and those that frequently appear in their own languages (Hoorens et al., 1990; Kitayama & Karasawa, 1997; Nuttin, 1987). French students rate capital *W*, the least frequent letter in French, as their least favourite letter. Japanese students prefer not only letters from their names, but also numbers corresponding to their birthdates.

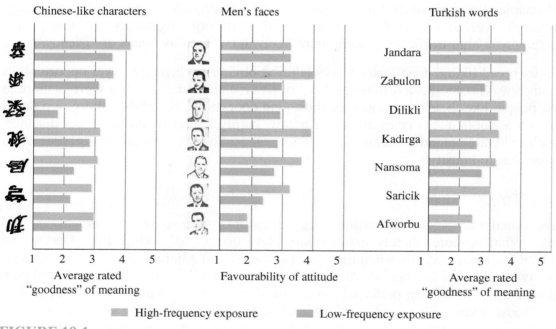

FIGURE 19-1

The Mere Exposure Effect. Students rated stimuli more positively after seeing them repeatedly.

Source: From Zajonc, 1968.

The mere exposure effect violates the common sense prediction that boredom *decreases* interest in repeatedly heard music or tasted foods (Kahneman & Snell, 1992). Unless the repetitions are incessant, liking usually increases. When completed in 1889, the Eiffel Tower in Paris was mocked as grotesque (Harrison, 1977). Today it is the beloved symbol of Paris. Such changes make one wonder about initial reactions to new things. Do visitors to the Louvre in Paris really adore the Mona Lisa, or are they simply delighted to find a familiar face? It might be both: To know her is to like her.

The mere exposure effect has "enormous adaptive significance," notes Zajonc (1998). It is a "hard-wired" phenomenon that predisposes our attractions and attachments. It helped our ancestors categorize things and people as either familiar and safe, or unfamiliar and possibly dangerous. Of course, the phenomenon's flip side is our wariness of the unfamiliar—which may explain the primitive, automatic dislike people often feel when confronting those who are different.

Connection:

Remember Module 16 and our fear of unfamiliar outgroups.

The mere exposure effect colours our evaluations of others: we like familiar people (Swap, 1977). We even like ourselves better when we are the way we're used to seeing ourselves. Theodore Mita, Marshall Dermer, and Jeffrey Knight (1977) photographed women and later showed each one her actual picture along with a mirror image of it. Asked which picture they liked better, most preferred the mirror image—the image they were used to seeing. (No wonder our photographs never look quite right.) When close friends of the subjects were shown the same two pictures, they preferred the true picture—the image *they* were used to seeing.

The mere exposure effect. If he is like most of us, Canadian Prime Minister Stephen Harper might prefer his familiar mirror-image (left), which he sees each morning while brushing his teeth, to his actual image (right).

Advertisers and politicians exploit this phenomenon. When people have no strong feelings about a product or a candidate, repetition alone can increase sales or votes (McCullough & Ostrom, 1974; Winter, 1973). If candidates are relatively unknown, those with the most media exposure usually win (Patterson, 1980; Schaffner et al., 1981). Political strategists who understand the mere exposure effect have replaced reasoned arguments with brief ads that hammer home a candidate's name and a sound-bite message.

LO 2

PHYSICAL ATTRACTIVENESS

What do (or did) you look for in a potential date? Sophisticated, intelligent people are unconcerned with such superficial qualities as good looks; they know "beauty is only skin deep" and "you can't judge a book by its cover." At least, they know that's how they *ought* to feel. As Cicero counselled,

"Resist appearance." Yet, there is now a file cabinet full of research studies showing that appearance *does* matter. The consistency and pervasiveness of this effect is disconcerting. Good looks are a great asset. Some say that the value of attractiveness rests in our genes.

Applying Social Psychology

The textbook uses reward theory as a simple principle for summarizing research on attraction. Newcomb (1961) came up with *balance theory*, another way to think about relationships. Balance theory, sometimes called the A-B-X model, proposes that there is a natural inclination for an actor (A) to organize thoughts about a person (B) and thoughts about another person, object, or issue (X) in a way that is harmonious or "balanced." Such relationships will prove more satisfying than those characterized by imbalance.

For example, if Adam likes Sarah and they both like rap music, a balanced state is said to exist in their relationship. Where Adam likes Sarah but they disagree about rap music, there is imbalance. Such a state is unpleasant, and Adam will be motivated to change Sarah's attitude toward rap music, his own attitude toward it, or his attitude toward Sarah. Thus attitude similarity will produce attraction.

Examples of *balanced* relationships are the following:

```
        1                 2                 3                 4
        A                 A                 A                 A
      +   +             +   -             -   +             -   -
    B   +   X         B   -   X         B   -   X         B   +   X
```

Examples of *imbalanced* relationships are the following:

```
      5                 6                 7                 8
      A                 A                 A                 A
    -   -             +   +             +   -             -   +
  B   -   X         B   -   X         B   +   X         B   +   X
```

One of the interesting tests of balance theory was provided by Aronson and Cope (1968). The title of their study was "My Enemy's Enemy Is My Friend" and was a specific test of Example 3 above. Participants, presumably participating in a study of creativity, wrote stories that the experimenter then evaluated negatively. The evaluation was delivered harshly to half the participants and kindly to the other half. A few seconds before completing his evaluation, the experimenter was called into the hallway by his supervisor and was given either lavish praise or a blistering condemnation for a report he had written. When later asked to do some work for the experimenter, participants were willing to work harder for the supervisor who treated the harsh experimenter harshly (my enemy's enemy is my friend) than for a supervisor who treated a harsh experimenter kindly (my enemy's friend is my enemy) or for a supervisor who treated a kind experimenter harshly (my friend's enemy is my enemy).

So what do you think? Can you think of some of your relationships that this theory would describe?

Understanding Gender and Mating Preferences

Noting the worldwide persistence of gender differences in aggressiveness, dominance, and sexuality, evolutionary psychologist Douglas Kenrick (1987) suggested, as have many others since, that "we cannot change the evolutionary history of our species, and some of the differences between us are undoubtedly a function of that history." Evolutionary psychology predicts no gender differences in all those domains in which the sexes faced similar adaptive challenges (Buss, 1995). But evolutionary psychology does predict gender differences in behaviours relevant to dating, mating, and reproduction.

Consider, for example, the male's greater sexual initiative. The average male produces many trillions of sperm in his lifetime, making sperm cheap compared to eggs. Moreover, while a female brings one fetus to term and then nurses it, a male can spread his genes by fertilizing many females. Thus, say evolutionary psychologists, females invest their reproductive opportunities carefully, by looking for signs of health and resources. Males compete with other males for chances to win the genetic lottery by sending their genes into the future. Women seek men who will be resourceful and monogamous caregivers, which has been referred to as the "dads versus cads" preference.

Moreover, evolutionary psychology suggests, physically dominant males gain more access to females, which over generations has enhanced male aggression and dominance. Whatever genetically influenced traits enabled Montezuma II to become an Aztec king were also perpetuated through offspring from some 4000 women (Wright, 1998). If our ancestral mothers benefited from being able to read their infants' and suitors' emotions, then natural selection may have similarly favoured emotion-detecting ability in females. Little of this process is conscious. No one stops to calculate, "How can I maximize the number of genes I leave to posterity?" Rather, say evolutionary psychologists, our natural yearnings are our genes' way of making more genes.

Evolutionary psychology also predicts that men will strive to offer what women will desire—external resources and physical protection. Male peacocks strut their feathers, and male humans their abs, Audis, and assets. "Male achievement is ultimately a courtship display," says Glenn Wilson (1994). Women (sometimes assisted by cosmetic surgery) strive to offer men the youthful, healthy appearance (connoting fertility) that men desire. Sure enough, note Buss (1994) and Alan Feingold (1992a), women's and men's mate preferences confirm these predictions. Consider this:

> Studies in 37 cultures, from Australia to Zambia, reveal that men everywhere feel attracted to women whose physical features, such as youthful faces and forms, suggest fertility. Women everywhere feel attracted to men whose wealth, power, and ambition promise resources for protecting and nurturing offspring. Men's greater interest in physical form also makes them the consumers of most of the world's visual pornography. But there are gender similarities, too: Whether residing on an Indonesian island or in urban San Paulo, both women and men desire kindness, love, and mutual attraction.

Reflecting on these findings, Buss (1999) reports feeling somewhat astonished "that men and women across the world differ in their mate preferences in precisely the ways predicted by the evolutionists. Just as our fears of snakes, heights, and spiders provide a window for viewing the survival hazards of our evolutionary ancestors, our mating desires provide a window for viewing the resources our ancestors needed for reproduction. We all carry with us today the desires of our successful forbearers."

Evolutionary psychologists argue that the features found attractive by both sexes are rooted in evolutionary processes. Thus evolutionary psychology is an approach to understanding people's behaviour. Fundamentally, both evolutionary psychologists and more theoretical-experimental psychologists want to understand the psychological mechanisms that allow people to deal with the things they encounter in their environment. The difference between evolutionary psychologists and others is that they use the theory of evolution as a basis for their research whereas other fields typically do not (see Crawford & Salmon, 2012, for a discussion).

Evolutionary psychology, as it has been allied to attraction, is not without its critiques (e.g., Barker, 2006; Gannon, 2002; Panksepp & Panksepp, 2000; Panksepp, 2006; Sternberg & Beall, 1991). For example, Hatfield and Rapson (1993) argue that the reason men prefer young attractive women has more to do with how they have been conditioned by the media than evolutionary processes. Rosenblatt (1974) has argued that women prefer men with money and power because traditionally, and across cultures, men have held those resources. Thus, the only way for women to gain access to them is to marry a man who has them. Consistent with Rosenblatt's argument, Gangestad (1993) (1993) has found that the more power women have in a particular culture, the more they value attractiveness in men. Further, evolutionary psychology does have some difficulty explaining homosexual relationships, and those among older couples, where reproduction is not a primary driver of decision-making.

In another interesting set of findings, Zebulon Silverthorne and Vern Quinsey (2000) at Queen's University have found that heterosexual and homosexual age preferences are remarkably consistent. Both gay and straight men preferred sexual partners younger than themselves, whereas this age difference was not as apparent for women (although lesbians preferred somewhat older partners).

Attractiveness and Dating

Like it or not, a young woman's physical attractiveness is a moderately good predictor of how frequently she dates. A young man's attractiveness is slightly less a predictor of how frequently he dates (Berscheid et al., 1971; Krebs & Adinolfi, 1975; Reis et al., 1980, 1982; Walster et al., 1966). Women more than men say they would prefer a mate who's homely and warm over one who is attractive and cold (Fletcher et al., 2004). Does this imply, as many have surmised, that women are better at following Cicero's advice? Or does it merely reflect the fact that men more often do the inviting? If women were to indicate their preferences among various men, would looks be as important to them as to men? Philosopher Bertrand Russell (1930, p. 139) thought not: "On the whole women tend to love men for their character while men tend to love women for their appearance."

In many experiments, men do put somewhat more value on opposite-sex physical attractiveness (Feingold, 1990, 1991; Sprecher et al., 1994). Perhaps sensing this, women worry more about their appearance and constituted nearly 90 percent of cosmetic surgery patients in the 1980s and 1990s (ASAPS, 2005; Crowley, 1996; Dion et al., 1990). But women, too, respond to a man's looks, and men appear to be noticing this. In 2012, the American Society of Plastic Surgeons reported that in that year 10 percent of all cosmetic surgeries were performed on men.

Relationship goals matter as well. Women who are looking for a short-term relationship do indeed prefer more masculine-looking and attractive men (e.g., Little et al., 2002; Li & Kenrick, 2006). For both sexes, preferences shift when considering longer-term relationships, with women preferring status over attractiveness (see Li et al., 2002). Lucia O'Sullivan and Sarah Vannier (2013) at the University of New Brunswick recently found that women find men who are "attached" as somewhat more attractive (but just as desirable) than those who are single; men find single women more desirable, but equally attractive as "attached" women.

Looks even influence voting, or so it seems from one study (Todorov et al., 2005). Princeton University students were shown photographs of candidates in almost 700 United States Senate and House of Representatives races. Based on looks alone, the students correctly identified the winners of 72 percent of the Senate races and 67 percent of the House races (both were significantly higher than chance). Interestingly, looks even influence medical judgments—more attractive patients were perceived as experiencing less pain than unattractive patients (e.g., Hadjistavropoulos et al., 1990).

To say that attractiveness is important, other things being equal, is not to say that physical appearance always outranks other qualities. Some people more than others judge people by their looks (Livingston, 2001). Moreover, attractiveness probably most affects first impressions. But first impressions are important—and are becoming more so as societies become increasingly mobile and urbanized and as contacts with people become more fleeting (Berscheid, 1981).

Interestingly, women who rate a man's face as attractive, masculine, or dominant tended to rate their bodies the same way—thus first impressions do play a role in later judgments (Fink, Taschner, Neave, Hugill & Dane, 2010). David Feinberg at McMaster University (Feinberg et al., 2008) found that for men, the same is true for voices and faces—attractive voices tend to be associated with attractive faces. Moreover, women who find masculine faces attractive also find masculine voices attractive.

Though interviewers may deny it, attractiveness matters in job interviews and compensation. Patricia Roszell and her colleagues (1990) looked at the attractiveness of a national sample of Canadians whom interviewers had rated on a 1 (homely) to 5 (strikingly attractive) scale. They found that for each additional scale unit of rated attractiveness, people earned, on average, an additional $1988 annually. Irene Hanson Frieze and her associates (1991) did the same analysis with 737 MBA graduates after rating them on a similar 1 to 5 scale using student yearbook photos. For each additional scale unit of rated attractiveness, men earned an added $2600 and women earned an added $2150.

The speed with which first impressions form, and their influence on thinking, helps explain why pretty prospers. Even a 0.013 second exposure—too brief to discern a face—is enough to enable people to guess a face's attractiveness (Olson & Marshuetz, 2005). Moreover, when categorizing subsequent words as either good or bad, an attractive face predisposes people to categorize good words faster.

Interestingly, what we know about a person can influence our perceptions of their attractiveness. Loriann Williams, Maryanne Fisher, and Anthony Cox at Saint Mary's University (2009) found that both men and women rated male and female photos as less attractive when the targets in the photos were said to have had more sexual experience and were looking for a short-term relationship. This effect was stronger for women than men.

The Matching Phenomenon

Not everyone can end up paired with someone stunningly attractive. So how do people pair off? Judging from research by Bernard Murstein (1986) and others, they pair off with people who are about as attractive as they are. Several studies have found a strong correspondence between the attractiveness of husbands and wives, of dating partners, and even of those within particular fraternities (Feingold, 1988; Montoya, 2008). People tend to select as friends and especially to marry those who are a "good match" not only to their level of intelligence but also to their level of attractiveness.

Experiments confirm this matching phenomenon. When choosing whom to approach, knowing the other is free to say yes or no, people usually approach someone whose attractiveness roughly matches their own (Berscheid et al., 1971; Huston, 1973; Stroebe et al., 1971). Good physical matches may also be conducive to good relationships, as Gregory White (1980) found that dating couples who were the most similar in physical attractiveness were the most likely, nine months later, to have fallen deeply in love. Interestingly, people who are narcissistic are more likely to believe that they are better looking than their partner, thus increasing dissatisfaction with their mate (Rohmann, et al., 2011).

Activity: **What do you look for in a relationship?**

What do you think is important in choosing a mate? Rate the following characteristics in terms of their importance to you in choosing a mate. Use the following scale:

3 = indispensable

2 = important but not indispensable

1 = desirable but not important

0 = irrelevant

_____   1. ambition and industriousness

_____   2. chastity (no previous experience in sexual intercourse)

_____   3. dependable character

_____   4. desire for home and children

_____   5. education and intelligence

_____   6. emotional stability and maturity

_____   7. favourable social status or rating

_____   8. good cook and housekeeper

_____   9. good financial prospect

_____ 10. good health

(Continued)

_____ 11. good looks

_____ 12. mutual attraction

_____ 13. pleasing disposition

_____ 14. refinement, neatness

_____ 15. similar education

_____ 16. similar religious background

_____ 17. similar political background

_____ 18. sociability

What factors do you identify as the most important? Has this been borne out in your relationships?

So who might we expect to be most closely matched for attractiveness—married couples or couples casually dating? White found, as have other researchers, that married couples are better matched. Perhaps this research prompts you to think of happy couples who are not equally attractive. In such cases, the less attractive person often has compensating qualities. Each partner brings assets to the social marketplace, and the value of the respective assets creates an equitable match. Personal ads exhibit this exchange of assets (Cicerello & Sheehan, 1995; Koestner & Wheeler, 1988; Rajecki et al., 1991). Men typically offer wealth or status and seek youth and attractiveness; women more often do the reverse: "Attractive, bright woman, 26, slender, seeks warm, professional male." Moreover, men who advertise their income and education, and women who advertise their youth and looks, receive more responses to their ads (Baize & Schroeder, 1995). The asset-matching process helps explain why beautiful young women often marry older men of higher social status (Elder, 1969).

Interestingly, homosexual men and women use personal ads in slightly different ways than heterosexuals (Gonzales & Meyers, 1993). Gay men are much more likely to refer to sexuality, and tend to want more short-term relationships than heterosexual men. Also, gay men emphasize physical characteristics most, whereas lesbians do it least. But heterosexual women mentioned attractiveness more than lesbians did. Thus, it is clear that homosexuals stress somewhat different characteristics when trying to find a mate. Heterosexuals were also more likely to mention financial security and sincerity.

Perhaps the discrepancy between what men and women want is no more evident than on the Internet. The online dating industry is big business, with estimated revenue of $500 million annually. But people lie online. Twenty-five percent of online daters (both men and women) admit to fabricating information to make themselves appear more attractive (CBC, 2004).

Connection:

We will discuss online relationships further in Module 20 and 21.

Levine (2000) argues that "virtual interactions" are unique in that people are much more anonymous online, people may perceive similar interests (because online, people may make claims that are difficult to confirm), and the regular cues to deception present in face-to-face interactions are absent. Yet meeting over the Internet first may well have benefits for people's relationships. McKenna and Bargh (2000) found that two people who initially met on the Internet actually liked each other more once they met in person than people who have had similar interactions face-to-face. Furthermore, the stigma associated with early online dating appears to be waning. Relationships developed through Facebook or other social networking sites are common and accepted.

Connection:

Remember our discussion of deindividuation in Module 12.

Perhaps part of the appeal is the extensive willingness to disclose personal information online (e.g., Nosko et al., 2007). This may make people better able to determine if the person they are in touch with might be a good match. However, there are risks to online social networks—in a 2010 study, the Truro, Nova Scotia, police trolled Facebook and pretended to be a teen new to the area. They sent "friend" requests to 296 teenagers. Only two refused to "friend" them. Thirty-five invited their new friend to their homes.

The Physical-Attractiveness Stereotype

Does the attractiveness effect spring entirely from sexual attractiveness? Clearly not, as Vicky Houston and Ray Bull (1994) discovered when they used a make-up artist to give an accomplice an apparently scarred, bruised, or birth-marked face. When riding on a Glasgow commuter rail line, people of *both* sexes avoided sitting next to the accomplice when she appeared facially disfigured. Moreover, much as adults are biased toward attractive adults, young children are biased toward attractive children (Dion, 1973; Dion & Berscheid, 1974; Langlois et al., 2000). To judge from how long they gaze at someone, even babies prefer attractive faces (Langlois et al., 1987).

Adults show a similar bias when judging children. Think of yourself as a playground supervisor having to discipline an unruly child. Might you, like the women studied by Karen Dion at the University of Toronto (1972), show less warmth and tact to an unattractive child? The sad truth is that most of us assume that homely children are less able and socially competent than their beautiful peers.

What is more, we assume that beautiful people possess certain desirable traits. Other things being equal, we guess beautiful people are happier, sexually warmer, and more outgoing, intelligent, and successful—though not more honest or concerned for others (Eagly et al., 1991; Feingold, 1992b; Jackson et al., 1995). In collectivist Korea, honesty and concern for others are highly valued and *are* traits people associate with attractiveness (Wheeler & Kim, 1997).

Added together, the findings define a physical-attractiveness stereotype: *What is beautiful is good.* Children learn the stereotype quite early. Snow White and Cinderella are beautiful—and kind. The witch and the stepsisters are ugly—and wicked. "If you want to be loved by somebody who isn't already in your family, it doesn't hurt to be beautiful," surmised one eight-year-old girl. Or as one kindergarten girl put it when asked what it means to be pretty, "It's like to be a princess. Everybody loves you" (Dion, 1979). If you think about popular children's movies, there are rarely unattractive heroes and the villains are almost always ugly (although the incredibly popular *Shrek* movies may provide an exception to this "rule").

Shrek and Fiona (above) are a rare exception to the "what is beautiful is good" phenomenon in films; Cinderella and Prince Charming (below) fit the typical mould.

If physical attractiveness is this important, then permanently changing people's attractiveness should change the way others react to them. But is it ethical to alter someone's looks? Such manipulations are performed millions of times a year by plastic surgeons and orthodontists. With nose and teeth straightened, hair replaced and dyed, face lifted, fat liposuctioned, and breasts enlarged, can a self-dissatisfied person now find happiness? It must have some effect. Approximately 200 000 Canadian women have had breast augmentation surgery. In 2012 in the United States, 12.6 million cosmetic procedures were conducted (ASAPS, 2013). In Beverly Hills, there are twice as many cosmetic surgeons as pediatricians (*People*, 2003).

Do beautiful people indeed have desirable traits? Or was Leo Tolstoy correct when he wrote that it's "a strange illusion . . . to suppose that beauty is goodness"? There is some truth to the stereotype. Attractive children and young adults are somewhat more relaxed, outgoing, and socially polished

(Feingold, 1992b; Langlois et al., 2000). Physically attractive individuals tend to be more popular, more outgoing, and more gender-typed (more traditionally masculine if male, more feminine if female; Langlois et al., 1996).

These small average differences between attractive and unattractive people probably result from self-fulfilling prophecies. Attractive people are valued and favoured, and so many develop more social self-confidence. By this analysis, what's crucial to your social skill is not how you look but how people treat you and how you feel about yourself—whether you accept yourself, like yourself, and feel comfortable with yourself.

Critical THINKING

Is what is beautiful good? Can you think of experiences in your life where this has been true? Incorrect? Do you know anyone that has used this to his or her advantage?

Despite all the advantages of being beautiful, attraction researchers Elaine Hatfield and Susan Sprecher (1986) report there is also an ugly truth about beauty. Exceptionally attractive people may suffer unwelcome sexual advances as well as resentment from those of their own gender. They may be unsure if others are responding to their performance or inner qualities, or just their looks, which in time will fade (Satterfield & Muehlenhard, 1997).

Who Is Attractive?

We have described attractiveness as if it were an objective quality like height, which some people have more of, some less. Strictly speaking, however, attractiveness is whatever the people of any given place and time find attractive. This, of course, varies. Culture influences the traits we find attractive, but do perceptions of beauty differ according to culture as well? Perhaps not as much as we might think. Karen Dion (2002) at the University of Toronto has found that although facial features may differ across cultures, what is considered attractive is surprisingly similar. For cultures with scarce resources and for poor or hungry people, plumpness seems attractive; for cultures and individuals with abundant resources, beauty more often equals slimness (Nelson & Morrison, 2005).

Despite such variations, there remains "strong agreement both within and across cultures about who is and who is not attractive," note Judith Langlois and her colleagues (2000). People's agreement about others' attractiveness is especially high when men rate women, and less so for men rating men (Marcus & Miller, 2003).

To be really attractive is, ironically, to be perfectly average (Rhodes, 2006). Research teams led by Langlois and Lorri Roggman (1990, 1994) at the University of Texas, and Anthony Little and David Perrett (2002) working with Ian Penton-Voak at the University of St. Andrews, have digitized multiple faces and averaged them using a computer. Inevitably, people find the composite faces more appealing than almost all the actual faces (see Figure 19-2). As this finding suggests, attractive faces are also perceived as more alike than unattractive faces (Potter et al., 2006). There are more ways to be homely than beautiful.

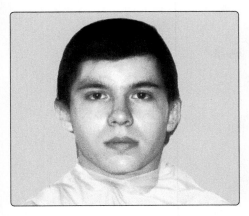 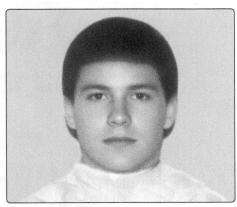

FIGURE 19-2

Is beauty merely in the eye of the beholder? Which of these faces is most attractive? People everywhere agree that the symmetrical face on the right (a composite of 32 male faces) is better looking, note Judith Langlois and her collaborators (1996). To evolutionary psychologists, such agreement suggests some universal standards of beauty rooted in our ancestral history.

Computer-averaged faces also tend to be perfectly symmetrical—another characteristic of strikingly attractive people (Gangestad & Thornhill, 1997; Mealey et al., 1999; Shackelford & Larsen, 1997). Research teams led by Gillian Rhodes (1999) and by Ian Penton-Voak (2001) have shown that if you could merge either half of your face with its mirror image—thus forming a perfectly symmetrical new face—you would boost your looks a tad. Averaging a number of such symmetrical faces produces an even better-looking face. So, in some respects, perfectly average is quite attractive. It's even true for dogs, birds, and wristwatches, report Halberstadt and Rhodes (2000). For example, what people perceive as your average dog they also rate as attractive.

The Contrast Effect

Although our mating psychology has biological wisdom, attraction is not all hardwired. What's attractive to you also depends on your comparison standards. Douglas Kenrick and Sara Gutierres (1980) had male confederates interrupt men in their residence rooms and explain, "We have a friend coming to town this week and we want to fix him up with a date, but we can't decide whether to fix him up with her or not, so we decided to conduct a survey. . . . Give us your vote on how attractive you think she is . . . on a scale of 1 to 7." The men were then shown a picture of an average young woman to rate. Those who had just been watching *Charlie's Angels* (the 1970s television show, not the later movies), rated her less attractive than those who hadn't.

*The original "Charlie's Angels."
Looking at beautiful people will
lower your perceptions of your
own partner.*

Laboratory experiments confirm this "contrast effect." To men who have recently been gazing at centrefolds, average women or even their own wives tend to seem less attractive (Kenrick et al., 1989). Viewing pornographic films similarly decreases satisfaction with one's own partner (Zillmann, 1989b). Being sexually aroused may *temporarily* make a person of the other sex seem more attractive to heterosexuals. But the lingering effect of exposure to perfect "10s," or of unrealistic sexual depictions, is to make one's own partner seem less appealing—more like a "6" than an "8."

It works the same way with our self-perceptions. After viewing a super-attractive person of the same sex, people feel *less* attractive than after viewing a homely person (Brown et al., 1992; Thornton & Maurice, 1997; Aubrey & Taylor, 2009; Trampe et al., 2007).

The Attractiveness of Those We Love

Let's conclude our discussion of attractiveness on an upbeat note. Not only do we perceive attractive people as likable, we also perceive likable people as attractive. Perhaps you can recall individuals who, as you grew to like them, became more attractive. Their physical imperfections were no longer so noticeable. Alan Gross and Christine Crofton (1977; see also Lewandowski et al., 2007) had students view someone's photograph after reading a favourable or unfavourable description of the person's personality. When portrayed as warm, helpful, and considerate, people *looked* more attractive. Discovering someone's similarities to us also makes the person seem more attractive (Beaman & Klentz, 1983; Klentz et al., 1987).

Moreover, love sees loveliness: the more in love a woman is with a man, the more physically attractive she finds him (Price et al., 1974). This is especially true if women have an attractive alternative to their partner available (Lydon et al., 2008)—the potential threat this poses to the relationship makes their partner seem more attractive—as though they were reassuring themselves they have made the right choice. And the more in love people are, the less attractive they find all others of the other sex (Johnson & Rusbult, 1989; Simpson et al., 1990).

LO 3

SIMILARITY VERSUS COMPLEMENTARITY

Do opposites attract? Many of you probably know a couple who are completely different yet completely in love. Yet sometimes the saying "birds of a feather flock together" is more apt—you can probably easily come up with examples of friends who seem almost identical to each other in terms of attitudes, personalities, and preferences. What do *you* find more important in a relationship—similarity or complementarity?

Do Birds of a Feather Flock Together?

Friends, engaged couples, and spouses are far more likely than randomly paired people to share common attitudes, beliefs, and values. Furthermore, the greater the similarity between husband and wife, the happier they are and the less likely they are to divorce (Byrne, 1971; Caspi & Herbener, 1990). Such correlational findings are intriguing. But cause and effect remain an enigma. Does similarity lead to liking? Or does liking lead to similarity?

Dr. Marian Morry at the University of Manitoba has been interested in determining if similarity leads to attraction or if the opposite is true—that attraction leads to perceptions of similarity. In one study (Morry, 2003), participants were asked to rate their own and their friends' locus of control and friendship satisfaction. As Dr. Morry expected, participants perceived their friends to be similar to themselves on locus of control and satisfaction, but these perceptions did not match the friends' self-ratings. Instead, participants' perceptions reflected a belief in their friends' similarity to themselves. In a later study (Morry, 2005), she manipulated participants' relationship satisfaction and found similar effects—more satisfied individuals rated their friends as more similar. This provides clear evidence that attraction can lead to perceptions of similarity.

The similarity–attraction effect has been tested in real-life situations by noting who comes to like whom. At the University of Michigan, Theodore Newcomb (1961) studied two groups of 17 unacquainted, male transfer students. After 13 weeks of boarding house life, those whose agreement was initially highest were most likely to have formed close friendships. One group of friends was composed of five liberal arts students, each a political liberal with strong intellectual interests. Another was made up of three conservative veterans who were all enrolled in the engineering college. The desire for similar mates outweighs the desire for beautiful mates (Buston & Emlen, 2003). Studies of newlyweds reveal that similar attitudes, traits, and values help bring couples together and predict their satisfaction (Gaunt, 2006; Gonzaga et al., 2007). Similarity breeds contentment—birds of a feather do flock together.

Do Opposites Attract?

Are we not also attracted to people who are in some ways *different* from ourselves, in ways that complement our own characteristics? Researchers have explored this question by comparing not only friends' and spouses' attitudes and beliefs but also their ages, religions, races, smoking behaviours, economic levels, educations, height, intelligence, and appearance. In all these ways and more, similarity still prevails (Buss, 1985; Kandel, 1978).

Are we not attracted to people whose needs and personalities complement our own? Would a sadist and a masochist find true love? Even the *Reader's Digest* has told us that "opposites attract . . . Socializers pair with loners, novelty-lovers with those who dislike change, free spenders with scrimpers, risk-takers with the very cautious" (Jacoby, 1986). Sociologist Robert Winch (1958) reasoned that the needs of someone who is outgoing and domineering would naturally complement those of someone who is shy and submissive. The logic seems compelling, and most of us can think of couples who view their differences as complementary. Some complementarity may evolve as a relationship progresses. Yet people seem slightly more prone to like and to marry those whose needs and personalities are *similar* (Botwin et al., 1997; Buss, 1984; Fishbein & Thelen, 1981a, 1981b; Nias, 1979). Perhaps we shall yet discover some ways (other than heterosexuality) in which differences commonly breed liking. Dominance/submissiveness may be one such way (Dryer & Horowitz, 1997). And we tend not to feel attracted to those who show our own worst traits (Schimel et al., 2000). But researcher David Buss (1985) doubts complementarity: "The tendency of opposites to marry, or mate . . . has never been reliably demonstrated, with the single exception of sex."

LO 4

LIKING THOSE WHO LIKE US

With hindsight, the reward theory explains our conclusions so far:

- *Proximity* is rewarding. It costs less time and effort to receive friendship's benefits with someone who lives or works close by.
- We like *attractive* people because we perceive that they offer other desirable traits and because we benefit by associating with them.
- If others have *similar* opinions, we feel rewarded because we presume that they like us in return. Moreover, those who share our views help validate them. We especially like people if we have successfully converted them to our way of thinking (Lombardo et al., 1972; Riordan, 1980; Sigall, 1970).

If we like those whose behaviour is rewarding, then we ought to adore those who like and admire us. Are the best friendships mutual admiration societies? Indeed, one person's liking for another does predict the other's liking in return (Kenny & Nasby, 1980). Liking is usually mutual.

But does one person liking another *cause* the other to return the appreciation? People's reports of how they fell in love suggest that it does (Aron et al., 1989). Discovering that an appealing someone really likes you seems to awaken romantic feelings (Berscheid & Walster, 1978). It is even better, as one speed-dating study found, if they like *you* more than any other (Eastwick et al., 2007). Interestingly, Berscheid and her colleagues (1969) found that students like a student who says eight positive things about them better than one who says seven positive things and one negative thing. We are sensitive to the slightest hint of criticism. Writer Larry L. King speaks for many in noting, "I have discovered over the years that good reviews strangely fail to make the author feel as good as bad reviews make him feel bad." (This is a sentiment your authors and your instructor can surely agree with!) Whether we are judging ourselves or others, negative information carries more weight because it grabs more attention (Yzerbyt & Leyens, 1991). People's votes are more influenced by their impressions of candidates' weaknesses than strengths (Klein, 1991), a phenomenon that has been used by those who design negative campaigns.

LO 5

OUR NEED TO BELONG

Aristotle called humans "the social animal"—we have an intense need to belong—to connect with others in enduring, close relationships. Social psychologists Roy Baumeister and Mark Leary (1995) illustrate the power of social attractions bred by our need to belong:

- For our ancestors, mutual attachments enabled group survival. When hunting game or erecting shelter, ten hands were better than two.
- For a woman and a man, the bonds of love can lead to children, whose survival chances are boosted by the nurturing of two bonded parents who support each other.
- For children and their caregivers, social attachments enhance survival. Inexplicably separated from each other, parent and toddler may both panic, until reunited in a tight embrace.
- Relationships consume much of a university student's life. How much of your waking time is spent talking with people? Researchers took samples from 10 000 recordings of 30-second periods of students' waking hours, using belt-worn recorders. The researchers found that these students were talking to someone 28 percent of the time (and that did not count listening time; Mehl & Pennebaker, 2003).
- Illustrating our need to stay connected, in 2013, Canadians sent 270 million text messages *per day*. Mobile data traffic is expected to increase up to nine times by 2018 (CTWA, 2014).
- For people everywhere, whatever their sexual orientation, actual and hoped-for close relationships preoccupy thinking and colour emotions. Finding a supportive soul mate in whom we can confide, we feel accepted and prized. Falling in love, we feel irrepressible joy. Longing for acceptance and love, we spend billions on cosmetics, clothes, and diets. Even seemingly dismissive people want to be accepted (Carvallo & Gabriel, 2006).
- Exiled, imprisoned, or in solitary confinement, people ache for their own people and places. Rejected, we are at risk for depression (Nolan et al., 2003). Time goes by more slowly and life seems less meaningful (Twenge et al., 2003).
- For the jilted, the widowed, and the visitor in a strange place, the loss of social bonds triggers pain, loneliness, or withdrawal. Reared under extreme neglect or in institutions without belonging to anybody, children become withdrawn, anxious creatures. Losing a soul-mate relationship, adults feel jealous, distraught, or bereaved, as well as more mindful of death and the fragility of life.
- Reminders of death in turn heighten our need to belong, to be with others, and hold close those we love (Mikulincer et al., 2003; Wisman & Koole, 2003). Facing the terror of 9/11, millions of North Americans called and connected with loved ones. Likewise, the shocking death of a classmate, co-worker, or family member brings people together, their differences no longer mattering.

We are, indeed, social animals. We need to belong. When we do belong—when we feel supported by close, intimate relationships—we tend to be healthier and happier.

Kipling Williams (2002) has explored what happens when our need to belong is thwarted by *ostracism* (acts of excluding or ignoring). Humans in all cultures, whether in schools, workplaces, prisons, or homes, use ostracism to regulate social behaviour. So what is it like to be shunned—to be avoided, met with averted eyes, or given the silent treatment? People (women especially) respond to ostracism with depressed mood, anxiety, hurt feelings, efforts to restore relationships, and eventual withdrawal. The silent treatment is "emotional abuse" and "a terrible, terrible weapon to use" say those who have experienced it from a family member or co-worker. In experiments, people who are left out of a simple game of ball tossing feel deflated and stressed.

Sometimes deflation turns nasty. In several studies, Jean Twenge and her colleagues (2001, 2002; Baumeister et al., 2002; Leary et al., 2006) gave some people an experience of being socially included. Others experienced exclusion: they were either told (based on a personality test) that they "were likely to end up alone later in life" or that others whom they'd met didn't want them in their group. People led to feel excluded became more likely to disparage or deliver a blast of noise to someone who had insulted them. If a small laboratory experience could produce such aggression, noted the researchers, one wonders what aggressive tendencies "might arise from a series of important rejections or chronic exclusion."

Williams and his colleagues (2000) were surprised to discover that even "cyberostracism" by faceless people whom one will never meet takes a toll. (Perhaps you have experienced this when feeling ignored in a chat room or when having your email messages go unanswered.) The researchers had 1486 participants from 62 countries play a Web-based game of throwing a flying disc with two others (actually computer-generated fellow players). Those ostracized by the other players experienced poorer moods and became more likely to conform to others' wrong judgments on a subsequent perceptual task. Williams and four of his colleagues (2000) even found ostracism stressful when each was ignored for an agreed-upon day by the unresponsive four others. Contrary to their expectations that this would be a laughter-filled role-playing game, the simulated ostracism disrupted work, interfered with pleasant social functioning, and "caused temporary concern, anxiety, paranoia, and general fragility of spirit." To thwart our deep need to belong is to unsettle our life.

CONCLUSIONS

So what does all of this tell us? There are many reasons why we become attracted to people. We can be complementary or we can be similar, or we can just be close by or around a lot. Either way, sometimes, being attracted to someone leads to a great friendship. But sometimes it leads to more, which is the topic of the next module.

SUMMARY OF KEY POINTS

LO1. Understand the role of proximity in attraction.

- We tend to be attracted to people and things we interact with, or expect to interact with.

LO2. Understand the role of physical characteristics in attractiveness.

- Physical attractiveness is important to both genders.
- Men find physical attractiveness most appealing, whereas women are more attracted to wealth, power, and ambition.
- People tend to date and mate with people of a similar level of attractiveness.
- People with "average" features are most attractive; we assume that attractive people are good people.

LO3. Understand the impact of similarity on attraction.

- We like those who are similar to us more than those who are less similar.

LO4. Understand the impact of liking on attraction.

- If someone likes us, we will tend to like them in return.

LO5. Understand the impact of our need to belong on attraction.

- We have a need to be liked by others.

KEY TERMS

Complementarity   The popularly supposed tendency, in a relationship between two people, for each to complete what is missing in the other.

Matching phenomenon   The tendency for men and women to choose as partners those who are a "good match" in attractiveness and other traits.

Mere exposure effect   The tendency for novel stimuli to be liked more or rated more positively after the rater has been repeatedly exposed to them.

Need to belong   A motivation to bond with others in relationships that provide ongoing, positive interactions.

Physical-attractiveness stereotype   The presumption that physically attractive people possess other socially desirable traits as well: What is beautiful is good.

Proximity   Geographical nearness. Functional distance powerfully predicts liking.

MODULE TWENTY

Romantic Relationships

LEARNING OBJECTIVES After studying Module 20, you will be able to

LO **1**   Describe the different kinds of love

LO **2**   Understand the steps to maintaining a close relationship

LO **3**   Understand why and how relationships end

The process of relationships leads us (and social psychologists) to many questions. What is this thing called love? Can passionate love endure? If not, what can replace it? Loving is more complex than liking, and thus more difficult to measure and more perplexing to study. People yearn for it, live for it, die for it. When asked what love means to them, people tend to list characteristics associated with both close friends and companions (e.g., warmth, intimacy, loyalty) and passionate relationships (e.g., euphoria, sexual attraction, obsessive thoughts). Which set of traits do you associate with love?

If North American romances flourished *randomly*, without regard to proximity and similarity, then most Sikhs would marry Christians, most minorities would marry Whites, and university graduates would marry high school dropouts. Typically, mixed marriages (e.g., by race, religion, education) are not the norm; similarity tends to dominate in these matters. Although same-race marriages are by far more common, recent Statistics Canada data suggests that the trend may be shifting. In the 2006 census, there were almost 300 000 mixed-race couples, a third more than in 2001 (Statistics Canada, 2010; CBC, 2008).

Critical THINKING

In the last module we asked you to think back to your first romantic relationship. Now we would like you to think about the first time you really fell in love. How did your passion for this person change as your relationship developed? Did it change as time wore on? Are you still together? Why or why not?

As we discussed in the previous module, first impressions are important, but long-term loving is not merely an intensification of initial liking. Social psychologists have therefore shifted their attention from the mild attraction experienced during first encounters to the study of enduring, close relationships.

LO 1

TYPES OF LOVE

Passionate Love

The first step in scientifically studying romantic love, as in studying any variable, is to decide how to define and measure it. Dr. Beverley Fehr at the University of Winnipeg wanted to know how individuals define and perceive love (Fehr, 1988). To test this, in one of her early studies she asked University of British Columbia students to list what they perceived to be characteristics of love. Students listed features such as warmth, intimacy, concern for the other person's well-being, loyalty, and caring—features we would expect to see in relationships with our best friends and companions. Students also listed characteristics we would see in passionate romantic relationships—obsessive thoughts, increased heart rate, euphoria, and sexual attraction. However, the "friendship" traits were consistently rated higher than the "love" traits by both men and women (see Fehr & Broughton, 2001).

Elizabeth Barrett Browning asked a similar question: "How do I love thee? Let me count the ways." Social scientists have counted various ways. Psychologist Robert Sternberg (1998) views love as a triangle, whose three sides (of varying lengths) are passion, intimacy, and commitment (see Figure 20-1). Drawing from ancient philosophy and literature, sociologist John Alan Lee (1988) and psychologists Clyde Hendrick and Susan Hendrick (1993) identify three primary love styles—*eros* (self-disclosing passion), *ludus* (uncommitted game-playing), and *storge* (friendship)—which, like the primary colours, combine to form secondary love styles. Some love styles, notably eros and storge, predict high relationship satisfaction; others, such as ludus, predict low satisfaction (Hendrick & Hendrick, 1997).

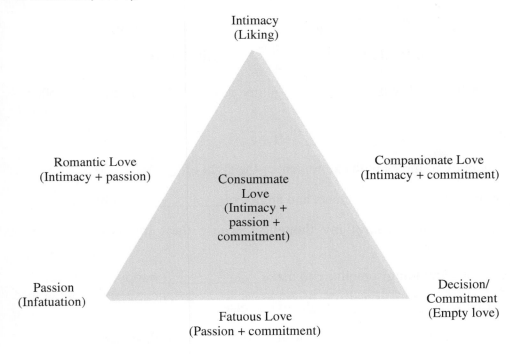

FIGURE 20-1

Robert Sternberg's (1988) conception of the kinds of loving as combinations of three basic components of love.

Some elements are common to all loving relationships, be they heterosexual, homosexual, or non-sexual friendships: mutual understanding, giving and receiving support, enjoying the loved one's company. Some elements are distinctive. If we experience passionate love, we express it physically, we expect the relationship to be exclusive, and we are intensely fascinated with our partner. You can see it in our eyes. Zick Rubin administered a love scale to hundreds of University of Michigan dating couples and timed eye-contact among "weak-love" and "strong-love" couples. His result will not surprise you: the strong-love couples gave themselves away by gazing into each other's eyes longer.

Passionate love is emotional, exciting, intense. Elaine Hatfield (1988) defined it as "a state of intense longing for union with another" (p. 193). If reciprocated, one feels fulfilled and joyous; if not, one feels empty or despairing. Like other forms of emotional excitement, passionate love involves a roller coaster of elation and gloom, tingling exhilaration and dejected misery. How passionately do you love? Go to the following activity to find out.

Activity Part I: How do you love?

Think of the person whom you love most passionately *right now*. If you are not in love right now, please think of the last person you loved passionately. If you have never been in love, think of the person whom you came closest to caring for in that way. Keep this person in mind as you complete this questionnaire. Try to tell us how you felt at the time when your feelings were the most intense. Use the following scale, placing a number in the blank to the left of each statement.

Do you want to know how passionate you are? Keep reading the module to find out.

1	2	3	4	5	6	7	8	9
Not at all true				**Moderately true**			**Definitely true**	

_____   1. Since I've been involved with _____, my emotions have been on a roller coaster.

_____   2. I would feel deep despair if _____ left me.

_____   3. Sometimes my body trembles with excitement at the sight of _____.

_____   4. I take delight in studying the movements and angles of _____'s body.

_____   5. Sometimes I feel I can't control my thoughts because they are obsessively on _____.

_____   6. I feel happy when I am doing something to make _____ happy.

_____   7. I would rather be with _____ than anyone else.

_____   8. I'd get jealous if I thought _____ were falling in love with someone else.

_____   9. No one else could love _____ like I do.

_____ 10. I yearn to know all about _____.

_____ 11. I want _____ —physically, emotionally, mentally.

_____ 12. I will love _____ forever.

_____ 13. I melt when looking deeply into _____'s eyes.

_____ 14. I have an endless appetite for affection from _____.

_____ 15. For me, _____ is the perfect romantic partner.

A Theory of Passionate Love

To explain passionate love, Hatfield notes that a given state of arousal can be steered into any of several emotions, depending on how we attribute the arousal. An emotion involves both body and mind—both the arousal and how we interpret and label the arousal. Imagine yourself with pounding heart and trembling hands: are you experiencing fear, anxiety, or joy? Physiologically, one emotion is quite similar to another. You may therefore experience the arousal as joy if you are in a euphoric situation, anger if your environment is hostile, and passionate love if the situation is romantic. In this view, passionate love is the psychological experience of being biologically aroused by someone we find attractive.

If, indeed, passion is a revved-up state that's labelled "love," then whatever revs one up should intensify feelings of love. In several experiments, college men aroused sexually by reading or viewing erotic materials had a heightened response to a woman (e.g., by scoring much higher on a love scale when describing their girlfriend; Carducci et al., 1978; Dermer & Pyszczynski, 1978; Stephan et al., 1971). The two-factor theory of emotion claims that emotional experience is a product of physiological arousal and how we cognitively label the arousal. Proponents of the two-factor theory of emotion, developed by Stanley Schachter and Jerome Singer (1962), argue that when the revved-up men responded to a woman, they easily misattributed some of their arousal to her.

According to this theory, being aroused by *any* source should intensify passionate feelings—providing the mind is free to attribute some of the arousal to a romantic stimulus. Donald Dutton and Arthur Aron (1974, 1989) invited University of British Columbia men to participate in a learning experiment. After meeting their attractive female partners, some were frightened with the news that they would be suffering some "quite painful" electric shocks. Before the experiment was to begin, the researcher gave a brief questionnaire "to get some information on your present feelings and reactions, since these often influence performance on the learning task." Asked how much they would like to date and kiss their female partners, the aroused (frightened) men expressed more intense attraction toward the women.

Connection:

We first discussed this study in Module 3.

Does this phenomenon occur outside the laboratory? Dutton and Aron (1974) had an attractive young woman approach individual young men as they crossed a narrow, wobbly, 137-metre-long suspension walkway hanging 70 metres above British Columbia's rocky Capilano River. The woman asked each man to help her fill out a class questionnaire. When he had finished, she scribbled her name and phone number and invited him to call if he wanted to hear more about the project. Most accepted the phone number, and half who did so called. By contrast, men approached by the woman on a low, solid bridge, and men approached on the high bridge by a *male* interviewer, rarely called. Once again, physical arousal accentuated romantic responses.

As you perhaps have noticed after scary movies, roller-coaster rides, and physical exercise, adrenaline makes the heart grow fonder. As this suggests, passionate love is a biological as well as a psychological phenomenon. Research shows (see Figure 20-2) that passionate love engages dopamine-rich brain areas associated with reward (Aron et al., 2005). The menstrual cycle also plays a role in brain activity. Women who are ovulating (versus other times of their cycle) show differing levels of brain activation, which encourages them to seek out different types of rewards.

The Capilano Bridge in Vancouver: Would crossing this bridge arouse you?

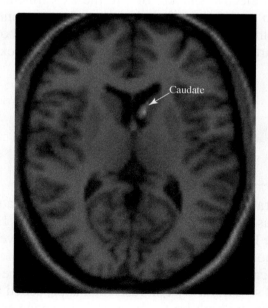

FIGURE 20-2

Love is in the brain. MRI scans from young adults intensely in love revealed that areas such as the caudate nucleus became more active when gazing at the loved one's photo, but not when looking at the photo of another acquaintance.

Source: From Aron et al., 2005.

Applying Social Psychology

So, do our relationships follow a predictable storyline? Robert Sternberg (2000), whose theory of love was recounted earlier, suggests a couple's rather foundational questions are entirely open. That is, "what makes a person the kind of lover they are?" and "what attracts them to other lovers?" Sternberg suggests the answers to these questions are found in people's "love stories." Sternberg suggests that people's stories can be categorized into a limited number of types (e.g., the business story—"I believe close relationships are like good partnerships," or the travel story—"I believe that beginning a relationship is like starting a new journey that promises to be both exciting and challenging"). Once we realize our own story, Sternberg suggests, we can begin to recognize elements of that story in the stories of potential mates. At the end of the article (which you can find online at *Psychology Today*), Sternberg asks the reader to choose between 12 different types of stories.

- Do you think a "story" can describe your relationship?
- Is his classification scheme too subjective to be called scientific?
- Can a theory of love be reduced to one storyline? Can Sternberg's?
- If we all have implicit theories of love, where do they come from?
- How well do the ideas expressed in this article fit with the theories mentioned in the text?

VARIATIONS IN LOVE

Time and Culture

It is always tempting to assume that most others share our feelings and ideas. People in Western cultures assume, for example, that love is a precondition for marriage. Within cultures, however, the very definition of marriage has been debated in recent years. In 2005, Canada became the fourth country in the world to formally recognize the right of homosexual couples to marry. Many homosexual couples have taken advantage of the opportunity: as of 2011, there were 21 015 same-sex couples legally married and living in Canada (nearly triple the number since 2006), along with over 43 560 common-law same-sex couples (Statistics Canada, 2012). It is likely that these figures underestimate the total number of same-sex marriages that have actually occurred in Canada to date. For example, in 2003 in British Columbia, which was one of the first provinces to legalize same-sex marriage, over half (55.9 percent) of same-sex marriages were between couples who lived outside Canada but came here to marry. Indeed, this has become a tourist trade. Rosie O'Donnell, who famously announced she was a lesbian shortly after her first talk show ended, holds annual "gay-friendly cruises." In July of 2005, the cruise docked in Halifax, and ten couples exchanged wedding vows (CTV, 2005). Toronto and other Canadian cities highlight their "gay-friendly" atmosphere to encourage tourism (e.g., Tourism Toronto, 2007).

People's ideas about love seem to be fairly consistent across cultures. Most cultures—89 percent in one analysis of 166 cultures—do have a concept of romantic love (love characterized in Sternberg's theory as having both passion and intimacy), as reflected in flirtation or couples running off together (Jankowiak & Fischer, 1992). But in some cultures, notably those practising arranged marriages, love tends to follow rather than precede marriage. Moreover, until recently, even in North America, marital choices, especially those by women, were strongly influenced by considerations of economic security, family background, and professional status.

Toronto Tourism promotes the gay-friendliness of Toronto.

Karen Dion and Kenneth Dion at the University of Toronto researched the role of culture on perceptions of love for a number of years (e.g., Dion & Dion, 1993; Dion, 2001). In one study (1993), they surveyed University of Toronto students who came from a wide range of cultures—Chinese, Vietnamese, English, Irish, Spanish, and German, among others. They found that people from Asian cultures were more likely to prefer a style of love that is more focused on a companionate, friendship-based romance that can be integrated into their existing family relationships. Thus, culture definitely influences people's preferences and expectations around love.

Gender and Sexuality

Do males and females differ in how they experience passionate love? Studies of men and women falling in and out of love reveal some surprises. Most people suppose that women fall in love more readily. However, it is actually *men* who tend to fall more readily in love (Dion & Dion, 1985; Peplau & Gordon, 1985). Men also seem to fall out of love more slowly and are less likely than women to break up a premarital romance. Women in love, however, are typically as emotionally involved as their partners, or more so. They are more likely to report feeling euphoric and are also somewhat more likely than men to focus on the intimacy of the friendship and on their concern for their partner. Men are more likely than women to think about the playful and physical aspects of the relationship (Hendrick & Hendrick, 1995). What women find appealing in men also varies according to their menstrual cycles (e.g., Dreher et al., 2007; Gangesta, Garver-Apgar, Simpson & Cousins, 2007; Salonia et al., 2005). Women who are ovulating prefer more masculine-looking men with deeper voices and men who act in a more creative and socially dominant manner.

There is a gender gap in sexual attitudes and assertiveness. First, the experience of intercourse can vary. Lily Tsui and Elena Nicoladis (2004) at the University of Alberta interviewed Canadian university students about their first intercourse experience. Although women typically rated the experience as more painful and less physically satisfying than men did, they did not differ in terms of how emotionally satisfying they found the experience. Although it is true that in their physiological and subjective responses to sexual stimuli, women and men are "more similar than different" (Griffitt, 1987), attitudes toward sex definitely differ. Yet 48 percent of men and 12 percent of women agreed in an Australian survey (Bailey et al., 2000) that "I can imagine myself being comfortable and enjoying 'casual' sex with different partners." Fifty-three percent of men, but only 30 percent of women agreed that "If two people really like each other, it's all right for them to have sex even if they've known each other for only a very short time" (Sax et al., 2002). In a survey of 3400 randomly selected 18- to 59-year-old Americans, half as many men (25 percent) as women (48 percent) cited affection for the partner as a reason for first intercourse. How often do they think about sex? "Every day" or "several times a day," said 19 percent of women and 54 percent of men (Laumann et al., 1994).

The gender difference in sexual attitudes carries over to behaviour. "With few exceptions anywhere in the world," report cross-cultural psychologist Marshall Segall and his colleagues (1990, p. 244), "males are more likely than females to initiate sexual activity." Moreover, among people of both sexual orientations, "men without women have sex more often, with more different partners, than women without men" (Baumeister, 1991, p. 151; Bailey et al., 1994). Compared to lesbians, gay men also report more interest in uncommitted sex, more responsiveness to visual stimuli, and more concern with partner attractiveness (Bailey et al., 1994). "It's not that gay men are oversexed," observes Steven Pinker (1997). "They are simply men whose male desires bounce off other male desires rather than off female desires."

Indeed, observe Roy Baumeister and Kathleen Vohs (2004; Baumeister et al., 2001), men not only fantasize more about sex, have more permissive attitudes, and seek more partners, they are also more quickly aroused, desire sex more often, masturbate more frequently, are less successful at celibacy, refuse sex less often, take more risks and expend more resources to gain sex, and prefer more sexual variety. One survey asked 16 288 people from 52 nations how many sexual partners they desired in the next month. Among those unattached, 29 percent of men and 6 percent of women wanted more than one partner (Schmitt, 2003). These results were nearly identical for both straight and gay people (29 percent of gay men and 6 percent of lesbians desired more than one partner). Interestingly, in population surveys of men and women in the United States, Canada, the United Kingdom, and France, there is substantial variability in terms of people's reported sexuality (i.e., homosexual versus heterosexual) and the content of their sexual fantasies (i.e., homosexual versus heterosexual content; e.g., Ellis, Robb & Burke, 2005; Sell, Wells & Wypij, 1995). These studies report that homosexual behaviour is perhaps rarer than expected (3 to 8 percent of men and 2 to 4 percent of women report being homosexual or having had homosexual experiences; Statistics Canada reported in 2009 that less than 2 percent of Canadians self-report as gay, lesbian, or bisexual), yet homosexual fantasies are more common (8 to 20 percent of men and 9 to 25 percent of women report such fantasies).

However, the sexual fantasies themselves also express gender differences (Ellis & Symons, 1990). In male-oriented erotica, sexual partners are unattached and lust-driven. In romance novels, whose primary market is women, a tender male is emotionally consumed by his devoted passion for the heroine. Social scientists aren't the only ones to have noticed. "Women can be fascinated by a four-hour movie with subtitles wherein the entire plot consists of a man and a woman yearning to have, but never actually having, a relationship," observes humorist Dave Barry (1995). "Men HATE that. Men can take maybe 45 seconds of yearning, and they want everybody to get naked. Followed by a car chase. A movie called 'Naked People in Car Chases' would do really well among men."

Comedian Jeff Foxworthy summed up the male psyche more succinctly—men "want a beer, and they want to see something naked."

Companionate Love

Although passionate love burns hot, it inevitably simmers down. After two years of marriage, spouses express affection about half as often as when they were newlyweds (Huston & Chorost, 1994). About four years after marriage, the divorce rate peaks in cultures worldwide and many gay and lesbian partnerships have likewise ended (Fisher, 1994). If a close relationship is to endure, it will settle to a steadier but still warm afterglow that Hatfield calls companionate love.

Elmer Lokkins, 84, and Gustavo Archilla, 88, who hid their sexual orientation for 58 years, were wed in Canada.

Unlike the wild emotions of passionate love, companionate love is lower key; it's a deep, affectionate attachment (Aron et al., 2005). The cooling of passionate love over time and the growing importance of other factors, such as shared values, can be seen in the feelings of those who enter arranged versus love-based marriages in India. Usha Gupta and Pushpa Singh (1982) asked 50 couples in Jaipur, India, to complete a love scale. They found that those who married for love reported diminishing feelings of love if they had been married more than five years. By contrast, those in arranged marriages reported *more* love if they were not newlyweds (see Figure 20-3).

The cooling of intense romantic love often triggers a period of disillusion, especially among those who regard such love as essential both for a marriage and for its continuation. Jeffry Simpson, Bruce Campbell, and Ellen Berscheid (1986) suspect "the sharp rise in the divorce rate in the past two decades is linked, at least in part, to the growing importance of intense positive emotional experiences (e.g., romantic love) in people's lives, experiences that may be particularly difficult to sustain over time." Compared to North Americans, Asians tend to focus less on personal feelings and more on the practical aspects of social attachments (Dion & Dion, 1988; Sprecher et al., 1994, 2002). Thus, they are less vulnerable to disillusionment. Asians are also less prone to the self-focused individualism that, in the long run, can undermine a relationship and lead to divorce (Dion & Dion, 1991, 1996; Triandis et al., 1988).

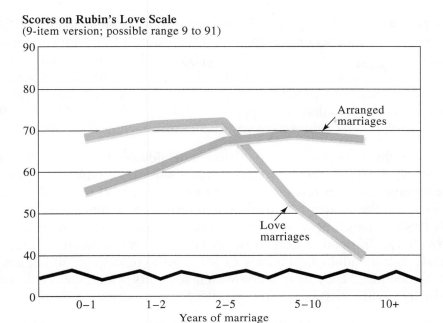

Scores on Rubin's Love Scale
(9-item version; possible range 9 to 91)

FIGURE 20-3

Romantic love between partners in arranged or love marriages in Jaipur, India.

Source: Data from Gupta & Singh, 1982.

The decline in intense mutual fascination may be natural and adaptive for species survival. The result of passionate love frequently is children, whose survival is aided by the parents' waning obsession with each other (Kenrick & Trost, 1987). Nevertheless, for those married more than 20 years, some of the lost romantic feeling is often renewed as the family nest empties and the parents are once again free to focus their attention on each other (Hatfield & Sprecher, 1986). "No man or woman really knows what love is until they have been married a quarter of a century," said Mark Twain. If the relationship has been intimate and mutually rewarding, companionate love rooted in a rich history of shared experiences deepens. But what is intimacy? And what is mutually rewarding?

LO 2

MAINTAINING CLOSE RELATIONSHIPS

What factors influence the ups and downs of our close relationships? Let's consider three: attachment style, equity, and intimacy (self-disclosure).

Attachment

Love is a biological imperative. There is strong evidence that oxytocin, a neural chemical released during stress, is an important moderator of anxiety and fear responses, and plays an important role in attachment (e.g., Kirsch et al., 2005). We are social creatures destined to bond with others. We are highly dependent on others as infants. This dependency strengthens our human bonds. Soon after birth we display various social responses—love, fear, anger. As babies, we prefer familiar faces and voices. By eight months, we crawl toward our parents and typically cry when they are separated from us. Once reunited, we cling to them again. All of this can be defined as our social attachments. They serve as powerful survival impulses. Researchers have compared the nature of attachment between various close relationships: friends, lovers, parents, and children (Davis, 1985; Sternberg & Grajek, 1984). Phillip Shaver and his colleagues (Shaver et al., 1988) noted that, like infants, lovers welcome physical affection, feel distress when separated, express intense affection when reunited, and take great pleasure in the significant other's attention and approval. Shaver and Cindy Hazan (1993, 1994), wondered if attachment style in infants would have any impact on attachment in adulthood.

About 70 percent of infants and adults exhibit secure attachment (Baldwin et al., 1996; Jones & Cunningham, 1996; Mickelson et al., 1997). Securely attached infants will play comfortably in novel environments (often called the strange situation task) when their mother is near. If the mother leaves they will become distressed, but when the mother returns they will resume play (after running to the parent for comfort first). This trusting attachment style, argue many researchers, forms a working model for relationships thorough the lifespan, where trust sustains the relationship in times of conflict (Miller & Rempel, 2004). Secure adults find it easy to get close to others and do not tend to get too dependent or fear being abandoned. They tend to enjoy their sexuality within the relationship, and their relationships tend to be long and satisfying (Feeney, 1996; Simpson et al., 1992).

Kim Bartholomew and Leonard Horowitz (1991) proposed an influential attachment model that categorizes styles according to their image of self (positive or negative) and of others (positive or negative). Secure people's positive image of self and others, and their strong sense of self lead them to believe others will accept and respond to their love. People with preoccupied attachment style (also called *anxious–ambivalent*) have positive expectations of others but a negative sense of their own worth. In strange situations, the anxious–ambivalent infant is more likely to cling to his or her mother. When she leaves, the infant may cry, but when she returns, the infant may be indifferent or even hostile to the mother. Anxious–ambivalent adults tend to be less trusting, more possessive, and jealous. They may break up with the same person several times. When dealing with conflicts, they can get emotional and angry (Cassidy, 2000; Simpson et al., 1996).

People with negative views of others exhibit either dismissive or fearful attachment styles. Both of these attachment styles are *avoidant*. Although avoidant infants become internally aroused, they show little outward distress when left alone, and little clinging when they are reunited with their parent. Adults with avoidant attachment styles tend to be less invested in relationships and more likely to leave them. They are also more likely to engage in "one-night stands" and be willing to have sex without love. Recent work (Del Guidice, 2011) has shown that, overall, men tend to be more avoidant, and women tend to be more anxious. Interestingly, although avoidance tends to increase over time (as we age), anxiety tends to decrease, peaking in young adulthood.

These attachment styles have been explored across at least 62 cultures (Schmitt et al., 2004). But where do they come from? Although some researchers have argued that attachment styles come from inherent temperament (Harris, 1998; Donnellan et al., 2005), other researchers (e.g., Hazan, 2004) have argued that attachment styles are the result of parental responsiveness. Sensitive, responsive mothers instill a sense of basic trust in their world's reliability, resulting in secure attachments in their infants (Ainsworth, 1979; Erikson, 1963). Youth who have experienced nurturing and involved parenting end up having warm and supportive relationships with their romantic partners (Conger et al., 2000; Poulsen et al., 2013). And this may continue across generations as well. One study (Besser & Priel, 2000) of 100 Israeli grandmother–daughter–granddaughter threesomes found intergenerational consistency of attachment styles. Early attachment styles do seem to lay a foundation for future relationships.

Equity

If both partners in a relationship pursue only their personal desires, it will die. Therefore, our society teaches us to exchange rewards by what Elaine Hatfield, William Walster, and Ellen Berscheid (1978) have called an equity principle of attraction: What you and your partner get out of a relationship should be proportional to what you each put into it. If two people receive equal outcomes, they should contribute equally; otherwise one or the other will feel it is unfair. If both feel their outcomes correspond to the assets and efforts each contribute, then both perceive equity.

Strangers and casual acquaintances maintain equity by exchanging benefits: You lend me your class notes; later, I'll lend you mine. I invite you to my party; you invite me to yours. Those in an enduring relationship, including roommates and those in love, do not feel bound to trade similar benefits (Berg, 1984). They feel freer to maintain equity by exchanging a variety of benefits ("When you drop by to lend me your notes, why don't you stay for dinner?") and eventually to stop keeping track of who owes whom.

Is it crass to suppose that friendship and love are rooted in an equitable exchange of rewards? Don't we sometimes give in response to a loved one's need, without expecting any sort of return? Indeed, those involved in an equitable, long-term relationship are unconcerned with short-term equity. Margaret Clark and Judson Mills (1979, 1993; Clark, 1984, 1986) argue that people even take pains to *avoid* calculating any exchange benefits. When we help a good friend, we do not want instant repayment. If someone has us over for dinner we wait before reciprocating, lest the person attribute the motive for our return invitation to be merely paying off a social debt. True friends tune in to one another's needs even when reciprocation is impossible (Clark et al., 1986, 1989). As people observe their partners sacrificing self-interest, their sense of trust grows (Wieselquist et al., 1999). One clue that an acquaintance is becoming a close friend is that the person shares when sharing is unexpected (Miller et al., 1989). Happily married people tend *not* to keep score of how much they are giving and getting (Buunk & Van Yperen, 1991).

We can also look at equity and exchange in love and relationships from a more evolutionary perspective. As Charles Crawford at Simon Fraser University and his colleague Catherine Salmon at the University of Redlands described in their recent work (Crawford & Salmon, 2012), in an ideal relationship, we might have *cooperative mating* where both individuals gain reproductively from the relationship. In *exploitive* mating, either the male or the female uses threats or coercion to gain a reproductive advantage. For men, a relevant example would be rape, whereas for women the reproductive advantage is more often seen through deception (e.g., having an affair with another fertile male). In the final category, called *detrimental mating,* both sides lose, such as in incestuous relationships. However, we would expect this category to be the most rare, as it is not likely to be selected evolutionarily.

Overall, equity in relationships is beneficial. Those in an equitable relationship are more content (Fletcher et al., 1987; Hatfield et al., 1985; Van Yperen & Buunk, 1990). Those who perceive their relationship as *in*equitable feel discomfort: The one who has the better deal may feel guilty and the one who senses a raw deal may feel strong irritation. (Given the self-serving bias—most husbands perceive themselves as contributing more housework than their wives credit them for—the person who is "over-benefited" is less sensitive to the inequity.)

Robert Schafer and Patricia Keith (1980) surveyed several hundred married couples of all ages, noting those who felt their marriages were somewhat unfair because one spouse contributed too little to the cooking, housekeeping, parenting, or providing. Inequity took its toll: those who perceived inequity also felt more distressed and depressed. During the child-rearing years, when wives often feel under-benefited and husbands feel over-benefited, marital satisfaction tends to dip. During the honeymoon and empty-nest stages, spouses are more likely to perceive equity and to feel satisfaction with their marriages (Feeney et al., 1994). When both partners freely give and receive, and make decisions together, the odds of sustained, satisfying love are good.

Do men and women differ in their memories of relationship events? Do our current relationship experiences shape our memories for past relationship events? Dr. Diane Holmberg and her colleagues wanted to know. In an early study (Holmberg & Ross, 1992), they found that women tended to have much more vivid memories of important events that couples share—a first date, a vacation, or a recent argument. Furthermore, women tended to assign more importance to the situations, and they reported reminiscing about the events more frequently than their male partners. They have further shown that women's memories about relationship events are not only more vivid, but also more complete, detailed, and accurate than men's (Holmberg et al., 2006).

Self-Disclosure

Deep, companionate relationships are intimate. They enable us to be known as we truly are and feel accepted. We discover this delicious experience in a good marriage or a close friendship—a relationship wherein trust displaces anxiety and we are therefore free to open ourselves without fear of losing the other's affection (Holmes & Rempel, 1989). Such relationships are characterized by what Sidney Jourard called self-disclosure (Derlega et al., 1993). As a relationship grows, self-disclosing partners reveal more and more of themselves to each other; their knowledge of each other penetrates to deeper and deeper levels until it reaches an appropriate depth. In relationships that flourish, these disclosures share successes and triumphs, and mutual delight over good things (Gable et al., 2006).

Experiments have probed both the *causes* and the *effects* of self-disclosure. When are people most willing to disclose intimate information concerning "what you like and don't like about yourself" or "what you're most ashamed and most proud of." And what effects do such revelations have upon those who reveal and receive them?

The most reliable finding is the disclosure reciprocity effect: Disclosure begets disclosure (Berg, 1987; Miller, 1990; Reis & Shaver, 1988). We reveal more to those who have been open with us. But intimacy is seldom instant. (If it is, the person may seem indiscreet and unstable.) Appropriate intimacy progresses like a dance: I reveal a little, you reveal a little—but not too much. You then reveal more, and I reciprocate.

Some people (most of them women) are especially skilled "openers"—they easily elicit intimate disclosures from others, even from those who normally don't reveal very much of themselves (Miller et al., 1983; Pegalis et al., 1994; Shaffer et al., 1996). Such people tend to be good listeners. During conversation they maintain attentive facial expressions and appear to be comfortably enjoying themselves (Purvis et al., 1984). They may also express interest by uttering supportive phrases while their conversational partner is speaking. They are what psychologist Carl Rogers (1980) called "growth-promoting" listeners—people who are *genuine* in revealing their own feelings, who are *accepting* of others' feelings, and who are *empathic*, sensitive, reflective listeners.

Intimate self-disclosure is one of companionate love's delights. Dating and married couples who most reveal themselves to one another express the most satisfaction with their relationship and are more likely to endure in it (Berg & McQuinn, 1986; Hendrick et al., 1988; Sprecher, 1987). Interestingly, disclosure can be in part predicted by attachment style. People with secure attachment styles disclose more to their intimate partners than to strangers, whereas this was not found for people with other attachment styles (Keelan, Dion & Dion, 1998). This may help explain why people with secure attachment styles may have higher-quality relationships.

Researchers have also found that women are often more willing to disclose their fears and weaknesses than men are (Cunningham, 1981). As Kate Millett (1975) put it, "Women express, men repress." Nevertheless, men today, particularly men with egalitarian gender-role attitudes, seem increasingly willing to reveal intimate feelings and to enjoy the satisfactions that accompany a relationship of mutual trust and self-disclosure. And that, say Arthur Aron and Elaine Aron (1994), is the essence of love—two selves connecting, disclosing, and identifying with one another; two selves, each retaining their individuality, yet sharing activities, delighting in similarities, and mutually supporting. The result for many romantic partners is "self–other integration": intertwined self-concepts (Slotter & Gardner, 2009).

Does the Internet Create Intimacy or Isolation?

As a reader of this textbook, you are almost surely one of the world's more than 2.4 billion Internet users (as of 2014; worldinternetstats.com). It took the telephone seven decades to go from 1 percent to 75 percent penetration of North American households. Internet access reached 75 percent penetration in a little more than seven years (Putnam, 2000). You—and over two billion others—enjoy email, blogs, browsing, and perhaps lurking as well on social-networking sites such as Tumblr, Instagram, Twitter, and Facebook.

So what do you think? Is computer-mediated communication within virtual communities a poor substitute for in-person relationships? Or is it a wonderful way to widen our social circles? Does the Internet do more to connect people with newfound soul mates or does it drain time from face-to-face relationships? Consider some of the statistics.

In 2013, 38 percent of single people used a dating site or mobile app (Pew, 2013). Even over 10 years ago, 7 million Canadians had visited dating sites, and over 1 million regularly used them (CBC, 2004). The online dating industry is big business, with estimated annual revenues of $500 million. Online dating is most popular with men and women ages 25–34.

Most Internet flirtations go nowhere. "Everyone I know who has tried online dating . . . agrees that we loathe spending (wasting?) hours gabbing to someone and then meeting him and realizing that he is a creep," observed one Toronto woman (Dicum, 2003). But friendships and romantic relationships that form on the Internet are more likely to last for at least two years (Bargh et al., 2002; McKenna & Bargh, 1998, 2000; McKenna et al., 2002). Robert Brym and Rhonda Lenton (2001) reported that of those who tried online dating, 60 percent had formed a long-term friendship, 63 percent had sex with at least one person they met online, 27 percent entered a long-term romantic relationship, and 3 percent eventually married that person.

Facebook pages, like this one from the CBC, have exploded in popularity in recent years.

Social relations involve networking, and the Internet is the ultimate network. It enables efficient networking with family, friends, and kindred spirits everywhere—including people we otherwise never could have found and befriended, be they fellow cancer patients, stamp collectors, or Harry Potter fans. There have been numerous cases where missing persons or emergency events have been highlighted and advertised on Twitter, Facebook, and similar sites.

Yet computer communication can be impoverished. For example, email lacks the nuances of eye-to-eye contact punctuated with non-verbal cues and physical touches. Except for simple emoticons—such as a :-) for a smile—electronic messages are devoid of gestures, facial expressions, and tones of voice. No wonder it's so easy to misread them. The absence of expressive e-motion makes for ambiguous emotion. For example, vocal nuances can signal whether a statement is serious, kidding, or sarcastic. Research by Justin Kruger and his colleagues (1999) shows that communicators often think their "just kidding" intent is equally clear, whether emailed or spoken, when it isn't. Thanks also to one's anonymity in virtual discussions, the occasional result is a hostile "flame war" or in the case of the workplace, sexual harassment or other lawsuits.

While Dr. Kimberly Matheson was an undergraduate and master's student at Carleton University (she is now a faculty member there), she began to program and work with computers in her research. Far from feeling anonymous and isolated, she found using computers—and communicating through them—to be entertaining and engaging. Matheson proposed that computer-mediated communications are very self-involving—even if you are isolated from other people, you are still (on one level at least) interacting with them. Matheson experimentally manipulated whether participants engaged in computer-mediated versus face-to-face interactions. Next, participants were assessed on both public and private self-consciousness (see Matheson & Zanna, 1988, 1990). Matheson found that in face-to-face communications, both private self-consciousness and public self-consciousness were high.

Conversely, computer-mediated communications reduced public self-consciousness (in other words, participants felt less inhibited), but private self-consciousness remained high (that is, deindividuation did not occur). Therefore, her research demonstrated that computer-mediated interactions are no more socially isolating than face-to-face communications. Both methods are self-involving. Matheson has suggested that inappropriate behaviour (such as sending flame emails) is much more likely to be the result of poor judgment rather than a deindividuation process.

Activity Part II: How passionate are you?

Passionate love is defined as a state of intense longing for union with another. Reciprocated love (union with the other) is associated with fulfillment and ecstasy, whereas unrequited love (separation) is associated with emptiness, anxiety, or despair. Passionate love is also a state of intense physiological arousal. How passionate are you?

What you completed in the first part of this activity was a shortened version of the Passionate Love Scale (PLS). The scale was designed to tap the cognitive, emotional, and behavioural components of passionate love (Hatfield & Sprecher, 1986). Add up your score. What components were you highest on? Lowest? Hatfield and Sprecher (1986) reported that PLS scores are significantly correlated with both Rubin's Love and Liking scales, satisfaction with the overall relationship, and satisfaction with the sexual aspect of the relationship. No overall gender differences were found in passionate love, although men do seem to love more passionately in the early stages of the relationship. For both genders, passionate love increases as the relationship goes from early states of dating to deeper levels of involvement, but then levels off. Does this reflect your score?

Cognitive components

1. Preoccupation with the partner (Item 5)

2. Idealization of the other or of the relationship (Items 7, 9)

3. Desire to know the other and be known (Item 10)

Emotional components

1. Attraction to other, especially sexual attraction

2. Negative feelings when things go awry (Items 1, 2, 8)

3. Longing for reciprocity (Item 14)

4. Desire for complete union (Items 11, 12)

5. Physiological arousal (Items 3, 13)

Behavioural components

1. Actions toward determining the other's feelings

2. Studying the other person (Item 4)

3. Service to the other (Item 6)

But the Internet, like television, diverts time from real relationships. Recent work has shown that time spent online can have a negative impact on your relationship. Everyone knows of stories where old flames have reunited on Facebook and rekindled their romance—often at the cost of their current relationship. An interesting study by Muise et al. (2009) at the University of Guelph found that the more time a person spent on Facebook, the more jealous they became in their own relationship. When Carnegie-Mellon University researchers followed 169 new Internet users for two years, they found increased loneliness and depression, and decreased social engagement (Kraut et al., 1998). A Stanford University survey found that 25 percent of more than 4000 adults surveyed reported that their time online had reduced time spent in person and on the phone with family and friends (Nie & Erbring, 2000). Nonetheless, most people don't perceive the Internet to be isolating. Another national survey found that "Internet users in general—and online women in particular—believe that their use of e-mail has strengthened their relationships and increased their contact with relatives and friends" (Pew, 2000). Internet use may displace in-person intimacy, but it also displaces television watching. And if one-click cyber-shopping is bad for your local bookstore, it frees time for relationships. Telecommuting does the same, enabling many people to work from home and to have more time for their families.

What's more, why say that computer-formed relationships are unreal? On the Internet your looks and location cease to matter. Your appearance, age, and race don't deter people from relating to you based on what's more genuinely important—your shared interests and values. In workplace and professional networks, computer-mediated discussions are less influenced by status and are therefore more candid and are equally participatory. Computer-mediated communication fosters more spontaneous self-disclosure than face-to-face conversation (Joinson, 2001). In addition, people who are shy are more likely to use social media like Facebook, as they can interact with people without the same level of risk (Orr et al., 2009; remember our discussion on deindividuation and anonymity). However, shy people had fewer Facebook friends than outgoing individuals.

Critical THINKING

Now that you know the statistics, what are your thoughts? Does the Internet promote intimacy? Do you have closer relationships now than you could have without Facebook, Twitter, Instagram, and all the other social media you use?

LO 3

ENDING RELATIONSHIPS

Often, love dies. What factors predict marital dissolution? How do couples typically detach or renew their relationships? In 1971, a man wrote a love poem to his bride, slipped it into a bottle, and dropped it into the Pacific Ocean between Seattle and Hawaii. A decade later, a jogger found it on a Guam beach:

> If, by the time this letter reaches you, I am old and gray, I know that our love will be as fresh as it is today.

It may take a week or it may take years for this note to find you . . . If this should never reach you, it will still be written in my heart that I will go to extreme means to prove my love for you. Your husband, Bob.

The woman to whom the love note was addressed was reached by phone. When the note was read to her she burst out laughing. And the more she heard, the harder she laughed. "We're divorced," she finally said, and slammed down the phone.

So it often goes. Comparing their unsatisfying relationship with the support and affection they imagine is available elsewhere, people are divorcing. Indeed, sometimes divorce seems inevitable. Headlines scream "Two-thirds of marriages end in divorce!" However, are these really accurate statements? It turns out that the statistics are a little more complicated. Using the most up-to-date numbers (from 2011), Statistics Canada reports that about 38 percent of all Canadian marriages will end in divorce. Although perceptions are that divorce rates are increasing, the divorce rate has been relatively steady for approximately 20 years. Common-law relationships are even more likely to end in separation. About half of the 2 million couples who separated between 2001 and 2006 had been in common-law relationships, even though common-law relationships represent only 17 percent of couples (Statistics Canada, 2011).

Who Divorces?

Divorce rates vary widely by country, ranging from 0.01 percent of the population in Bolivia, the Philippines, and Spain, to 4.7 percent annually in the world's most divorce-prone country, the United States. To predict a culture's divorce rates, it helps to know its values (Triandis, 1994). Individualistic cultures (where love is a feeling and people ask, "What does my heart say?") have more divorce than communal cultures (where love entails obligation and people ask, "What will other people say?"). Individualists marry "for as long as we both shall love," while collectivists more often marry for life. Individualists expect more passion and personal fulfillment in a marriage, which puts greater pressure on the relationship (Dion & Dion, 1993). "Keeping romance alive" was rated as important to a good marriage by 78 percent of American women surveyed and 29 percent of Japanese women (*American Enterprise*, 1992).

Interestingly, divorce in Canada depends on what province or territory you live in. Quebec had the highest divorce rate in Canada (in 2008) by far: 48 percent by year 30 of the marriage. Ontario, British Columbia, and the Yukon cluster together as the next group. Lower are the Maritime provinces (Nova Scotia, New Brunswick, and Prince Edward Island), the Prairies (Manitoba and Saskatchewan), and Nunavut and the Northwest Territories, which all have a similar rate of divorce. Finally, Newfoundland and Labrador wins as the province with the lowest divorce rate in Canada. Why do these differences exist? Could this be the result of cultural or religious differences among provinces? Or might it be due to the availability of alternatives? To date, no study seems to have addressed this issue.

Risk of divorce also depends on who marries whom (Fergusson et al., 1984; Myers, 2000; Tzeng, 1992). If these factors vary by province, this might explain some of the differences in divorce rates. People usually stay married if they

- married after age 20
- both grew up in stable, two-parent homes

- dated for a long while before marriage
- are well and similarly educated
- enjoy a stable income from a good job
- live in a small town or on a farm
- did not cohabit or become pregnant before marriage
- are religiously committed
- are of similar age, faith, and education

None of these predictors, by itself, is essential to a stable marriage. But if none of these things is true for someone, marital breakdown is an almost sure bet. If all are true, they are *very* likely to stay together until death. This list of predictors of marriage success is particularly relevant to one of your authors. While Steven was still a graduate student at Queen's University, Harry Reis, a renowned relationship researcher from the University of Rochester, visited the psychology department to give a guest lecture. During drinks afterward, Steven got to talking about his relationship with his then-fiancée, Isabel. Steven excitedly told Dr. Reis about his beautiful and charming fiancée, and at the end of the conversation Dr. Reis gave his prediction for their relationship. They differed in age, they had no stable income, they lived together before they were married, Isabel's parents were divorced, they were moving to a big city, and neither was religiously committed. Dr. Reis suggested that, according to the research, the relationship would not last. However, to date (15 years later) they are still happily married. Perhaps this illustrates the difficulty of predicting the outcome for an individual (or couple, in this case) from data based on a large group. Exceptions to the rule will always occur. Similarly, "anecdotal evidence" is not really evidence at all. We cannot use one example (or one couple) to prove (or disprove) the existence of a relationship between variables.

The Detachment Process

Severing bonds produces a predictable sequence of agitated preoccupation with the lost partner, followed by deep sadness, and eventually the beginnings of emotional detachment and a return to normal living (Hazan & Shaver, 1994).

Among dating couples, the closer and longer the relationship and the fewer the available alternatives, the more painful the break-up (Simpson, 1987). Surprisingly, Roy Baumeister and Sara Wotman (1992) report that, months or years later, people recall more pain over spurning someone's love than over having been spurned. Their distress arises from guilt over hurting someone, from upset over the heartbroken lover's persistence, or from uncertainty over how to respond. Among married couples, break-up has additional costs: shocked parents and friends, guilt over broken vows, and possibly restricted parental rights. Still, each year millions of couples are willing to pay such costs to extricate themselves from what they perceive as the greater costs of continuing a painful, unrewarding relationship. Such costs include, in one study of 328 married couples, a tenfold increase in depression symptoms when a marriage is marked by discord rather than satisfaction (O'Leary et al., 1994). When, however, a marriage is "very happy," life as a whole usually seems "very happy" (see Figure 20-4).

When relationships suffer, those without better alternatives or who feel invested in a relationship (through time, energy, mutual friends, possessions, and perhaps children) will seek alternatives to divorce. Caryl Rusbult and her colleagues (1986, 1987, 1998, 2004) have explored three other ways of coping with a failing relationship (see Table 20-1). Some people exhibit *loyalty*—by waiting for conditions to improve. The problems are too painful to speak of and the risks of separation are too great, so the loyal partner perseveres, hoping the good old days will return. Others (especially men) exhibit *neglect*; they ignore the partner and allow the relationship to deteriorate. When painful dissatisfactions are ignored, an insidious emotional uncoupling ensues as the partners talk less and begin redefining their lives without each other. Still others will *voice* their concerns and take active steps to improve the relationship by discussing problems, seeking advice, and attempting to change.

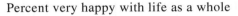

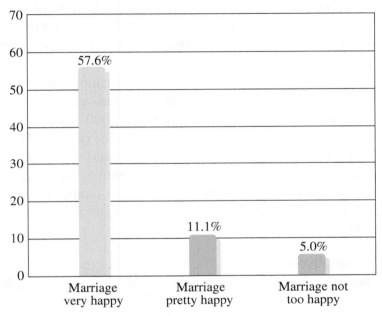

FIGURE 20-4

National Opinion Research Center Surveys of 23 076 married couples, 1972–2004.

TABLE 20-1	**Responses to Relationship Distress**	
	Passive	*Active*
Constructive	*Loyalty* Await improvement	*Voice* Seek to improve relationship
Destructive	*Neglect* Ignore the partner	*Exit* End the relationship

Source: Rusbult et al., 1986, 1987, 1998, 2001.

How does culture influence how we end relationships? Lisa Sinclair and Beverley Fehr at the University of Winnipeg asked that question. Recall that people from Western cultures tend to have independent self-construals—perceiving themselves to be independent and unique. People from Eastern cultures tend to have more interdependent self-construals—perceiving themselves more in terms of their relationships with others. With this different focus on relationships, should we expect a different preference for ending a relationship? These researchers (see Sinclair & Fehr, 2005) conducted two studies (one where self-construal was measured and one where it was manipulated). Across both studies, the researchers found that people with an independent self-construal tended toward the more active, constructive response of *voice*—expressing their dissatisfaction with the relationship in an attempt to improve it; whereas people with an interdependent self-construal tended to exhibit the more passive, constructive response of *loyalty*—optimistically waiting for conditions to improve.

Study after study—in fact, 115 studies of 45 000 couples—reveal that unhappy couples disagree, command, criticize, and put down. Happy couples more often agree, approve, assent, and laugh (Karney & Bradbury, 1995; Noller & Fitzpatrick, 1990). After observing 2000 couples, John Gottman (1994, 1998) noted that healthy marriages were not necessarily devoid of conflict. Rather, they were marked by an ability to reconcile differences and to overbalance criticism with affection. In successful marriages, positive interactions (smiling, touching, complimenting, laughing) outnumbered negative interactions (sarcasm, disapproval, insults) by at least a 5-to-1 ratio. Happy couples also tend to have positive illusions about their partners—finding them more attractive than they find themselves (Barleds & Dijkstra, 2009).

It's not distress and arguments that predict divorce, add Ted Huston and colleagues (2001) from their study on newlyweds through time, because most newlyweds experience conflict. Rather, it's coldness, disillusionment, and hopelessness that predict a dim marital future. This is especially so when inhibited men are coupled with critical women (Swann et al., 2003, 2006).

Successful couples have learned, sometimes aided by communication training, to restrain the cancerous putdowns and gut-level, fire-with-fire reactions, to fight fair (by stating feelings without insulting), and to depersonalize conflict with comments like "I know it's not your fault" (Markman et al., 1988; Notarius & Markman, 1993; Yovetich & Rusbult, 1994). Would unhappy relationships get better if the partners agreed to act more as happy couples do—by complaining and criticizing less? By affirming and agreeing more? By setting times aside to voice their concerns? By praying or playing together daily? As attitudes trail behaviours, do affections trail actions?

Joan Kellerman, James Lewis, and James Laird (1989) wondered. They knew that among couples passionately in love, eye gazing is typically prolonged and mutual (Rubin, 1973). Would intimate eye-gazing similarly stir feelings between those not in love? To find out, they asked unacquainted male–female pairs to gaze intently for two minutes either at one another's hands or in one another's eyes. When they separated, the eye gazers reported a tingle of attraction and affection toward each other. Simulating love had begun to stir it.

CONCLUSIONS

Researcher Robert Sternberg (1988) believes that by enacting and expressing love, the passion of initial romance can evolve into enduring love given the psychological ingredients of marital happiness—kindred minds, social and sexual intimacy, and equitable giving and receiving of emotional and material resources. It does, however, become possible to contest the French saying "Love makes the time pass and time makes love pass." But it takes effort to stem love's decay. It takes effort to carve out time each day to talk over the day's happenings. It takes effort to forgo nagging and bickering and instead to disclose and hear one another's hurts, concerns, and dreams. It takes effort to make a relationship into "a classless utopia of social equality" (Sarnoff & Sarnoff, 1989), in which both partners freely give and receive, share decision making, and enjoy life together.

SUMMARY OF KEY POINTS

LO1. Describe the different kinds of love.

- There are many types of love, which have been described by a number of theorists, including Sternberg's triangular theory of love.
- Love varies by time, culture, gender, and sexuality.

LO2. Understand the steps to maintaining a close relationship.

- Attachment theory has explored how people typically behave in romantic relationships.
- Equity and self-disclosure are important in maintaining strong relationships.

LO3. Understand why and how relationships end.

- Divorce is common, but the reasons relationships end are complex.
- Gender and culture influence how we end relationships, although they tend to follow a process dictated by constructive versus destructive, and active versus passive approaches.

KEY TERMS

Companionate love   The affection we feel for those with whom our lives are deeply intertwined.

Disclosure reciprocity   The tendency for one person's intimacy of self-disclosure to match that of a conversational partner.

Dismissive attachment   An avoidant relationship style marked by distrust of others.

Equity   A condition in which the outcomes people receive from a relationship are proportional to what they contribute to it. Note: Equitable outcomes need not always be equal outcomes.

Fearful attachment   An avoidant relationship style marked by fear of rejection.

Passionate love   A state of intense longing for union with another. Passionate lovers are absorbed in one another, feel ecstatic at attaining their partner's love, and are disconsolate on losing it.

Preoccupied attachment   Attachment marked by a sense of one's own unworthiness and anxiety, ambivalence, and possessiveness.

Secure attachment   Attachments rooted in trust and marked by intimacy.

Self-disclosure   Revealing intimate aspects of oneself to others.

Two-factor theory of emotion   Arousal label = emotion. (Emotional experience is a product of physiological arousal and how we cognitively label the arousal.)

PART FIVE: APPLYING SOCIAL PSYCHOLOGY

MODULE TWENTY-ONE

Media and Social Behaviour

LEARNING OBJECTIVES   After studying Module 21, you will be able to

LO 1   Understand the impact of pornography on perceptions and behaviour

LO 2   Understand the impact of television on perceptions and behaviour

LO 3   Understand the impact of video games on perceptions and behaviour

Have you ever seen something on TV or in a movie and wanted to try it out yourself? With the popularity of shows like *Glee*, glee clubs are becoming more common again (CNN, 2010). Teenagers have been hurt or killed trying out the stunts they saw on *Jackass* (MSNBC, 2007), which they film and post on YouTube. But how common is this type of copycat behaviour? Anyone who spends time with young children knows they will mimic the scenes they see on their favourite TV shows.

Clearly, the studios believe something is there as well, hence the frequently seen "Do not try this at home" disclaimers. These effects certainly seem to be causal—we watch the show, we engage in the act. But are they? What do you think? Can there be something else that explains this behaviour? If there is a relationship, what is the cause of it?

Connection:

Remember our discussion of correlation and causation in Module 2.

Critical THINKING

Does the media influence people's behaviour? Can watching violence on TV or playing violent video games affect how we behave in the real world? The answer depends on whom you ask. In 2006, Kimveer Gill shot 20 people, killing one, before turning the gun on himself at Dawson College in Montreal. Gill was a fan of the band Megadeath, and people quickly blamed the thrash-metal music for his behaviour. Gill was also a regular on VampireFreak.com, a gothic subculture website.

The prevailing view among people in the entertainment industry is that violent people are violent—what they watch is a symptom, not the cause of their behaviour. The media are simply giving us what we want. Guy Paquette at Université de Laval found that between 1993 and 2001, although there was significant pressure on broadcasters to reduce violence in their shows, the amount of violence depicted in the French- and English-language media consistently increased in Canada (Paquette, 2004). Despite this, Statistics Canada (2013) reports that the overall crime rate has dropped 22 percent since 1999. Violent crime rates are also down. In this module, we'll take a look at the social consequences of sexually explicit material, and the effects of modelling violence in movies, on television, and in video games.

LO 1

PORNOGRAPHY

What is **pornography**? It is often defined as any written or visual material that contains the description of or actual images of human sexual activity or sex organs, which is intended to stimulate erotic feelings, rather than focused on aesthetic or emotional reactions. Repeated exposure to fictional eroticism has several effects. It can decrease one's attraction to one's less exciting, real-life partner (Kenrick et al., 1989). It can also increase one's acceptance of extramarital sex and of women's sexual submission to men (Zillmann, 1989b). Music video images of macho men and sexually acquiescent women similarly colour viewers' perceptions of men and women (Hansen, 1989; Hansen & Hansen, 1988; St. Lawrence & Joyner, 1991). Increasingly, music videos show scantily clad young women being dominated by men. Indeed, the most popular video of 2013, Robin Thicke's "Blurred Lines," was steeped in controversy over the blatantly misogynistic content and lyrics.

Pornography has become big business. Every second, over $3000 is spent on pornography across the world. In Canada, over $1 billion is spent on pornography each year. In the United States, more money is spent on pornography than on professional football, baseball, and basketball combined— more than $13 billion per year. Worldwide, over $97 billion is spent on pornography in all its forms (e.g., video, Internet, novels, magazines, cable; Family Safe Media, 2011).

The Role of the Internet

The Internet is a huge money maker. And pornography is one of its biggest commodities. To date, there are more than 4.2 million pornography websites, representing more than 10 percent of all the websites on the Internet (and 4 percent of the 1 million most popular sites; National Research Council, 2002; Rich, 2001; Schlosser, 2003). Sixty million Americans visited porn sites in 2009— 70 percent of them kept it a secret (Family Safe Media, 2011). You can even get pornography downloaded to your cell phone for a fee from your service provider (CBC, 2007).

This high prevalence of Internet pornography is relevant, because we know that 98 percent of 16- to 24-year-old Canadians use the Internet. At least 85 percent of Grade 7 students surveyed in Montreal in 2006 were using the Internet for up to 10 hours per week (Barnett et al., 2008). Fifteen percent use the Internet more than 10 hours per week. Indeed, children typically get their first exposure to online pornography at age 11, and 90 percent of 8- to 16-year-olds have viewed online pornography (Greenfield, 2004). Canadians have ready access of high-speed Internet connections relative to other countries, and Canadians use the Internet about 43.5 hours per month, almost double the rate of the global average (23.1 hours per month; comScore, 2011). Thus, the potential for exposure is high.

Another risk for children and teens using the Internet is the potential for victimization by sex criminals. Child pornography is a $3 billion industry, with up to 20 000 new child-pornography images uploaded each week (Hughes, 2001; Sinclair & Sugar, 2005; enough.org, 2014). Child luring is also a big problem on the Internet. The Ontario Provincial Police have found that 25 percent of 13- and 14-year-olds who use Internet chat rooms are asked to meet a stranger face-to-face, and 15 percent of them do (OPP, 2007).

Connection:

Remember what the Truro Police Department did in 2010 (see Module 19).

People are willing to disclose personal information online. Child-luring online is common enough that sting operations have been featured on real-crime shows like *Cops*, and have even been developed into entire TV series, such as NBC's *To Catch a Predator*.

As we saw in the previous module, the Internet can be beneficial. Research has shown that much of the time young people, in particular, spend online is spent on social networking sites such as Twitter, Snapchat, Instagram, and Facebook. Teenagers spend on average five hours per day using their phones (CBC, 2014). Nineteen million Canadians log onto Facebook every month; 14 million do it every day (Canadian Press, 2013). People upload videos to Tumblr, Flickr, and YouTube and share them with the world. Ten-year-old Maria Aragon, of Winnipeg, became world-famous overnight after her version of Lady Gaga's "Born this Way" got the attention of the singer herself, and the video was posted on the Lady Gaga website. Ms. Aragon was invited to appear on the Ellen DeGeneres show, and ultimately sang with Lady Gaga herself in Toronto.

Connection:

Remember our discussion of online dating in Module 20.

Instant messaging has even developed its own language, punctuation, and abbreviations (see Provine et al., 2007).

There may also be a number of benefits for users of these social networking sites. For example, Nicole Ellison (Ellison et al., 2007) at Michigan State University found that people with low self-esteem and/or low life satisfaction might benefit most from using Facebook. Consistent with this, Paul Brunet and Louis Schmidt at McMaster University (2008) found that shyness predicted self-disclosures on the Internet only when people thought they were on a live webcam. When they did not, shyness did not predict self-disclosure. In other words, shy people were just as self-disclosing as outgoing people when they thought they were in a more anonymous situation.

Activity: **Text messaging abbreviations**

Below is a list of common text messaging abbreviations. Go through the list and see how many you can get.

?	2G2B4G	9	EZ	IMHO
182	411	AAAAA	F2F	LOL
20	4COL	AMAP	GTG	SYT

How did you do? Go to the end of the module to find out.

Source: From netlingo.com.

Interestingly (and as we might predict from previous modules), we are judged by the company we keep. The more attractive your "friends" are (i.e., the friends you have listed on your Facebook page), the more attractive you are assumed to be (Walther et al., 2008). In addition, Bernd Marcus at the University of Western Ontario (e.g., Marcus et al., 2006) found that people judge your personality from the content of your website. To some extent, this corresponds with your self-reported personality traits. In other words, your personality is likely to be reflected in your website. Thus, once again, we are what we present to the world.

Nonetheless, there have been significant concerns raised about how frequently children use the Internet. Ten hours per week for the average teenager is a lot of time, and much of this time may be unsupervised. Thus, a key recommendation by educators and law enforcement officers is not only to block problematic sites, but to keep the computer in a common room, so that use of the Internet can be monitored.

Distorted Perceptions of Sexual Reality

Social-psychological research on pornography has focused mostly on depictions of sexual violence. In a typical sexually violent episode, a man forces himself on a woman. At first she resists and tries to fight off her attacker. Gradually, she becomes sexually aroused, and her resistance melts. By the end she is in ecstasy, pleading for more. We have all viewed or read non-pornographic versions of this sequence: she resists, he persists. A dashing (or not) man grabs and forcibly kisses the protesting woman. Within moments, the arms that were pushing him away are clutching him tight, her resistance overwhelmed by her unleashed passion. This theme has been consistent for years through movies as diverse as *Gone With the Wind* and *Indiana Jones*, and through TV shows as diverse as *The Big Bang Theory* and *Downton Abbey*.

Social psychologists report that viewing such fictional scenes of a man overpowering and arousing a woman can (1) distort perceptions of how women actually respond to sexual coercion, and (2) increase men's aggression against women, at least in laboratory settings. Does viewing sexual violence and pornography reinforce the myth that some women would welcome sexual assault—that "no doesn't really mean no"? To find out, Neil Malamuth and James Check (1981) showed

University of Manitoba men either two non-sexual movies or two movies depicting a man sexually overpowering a woman. A week later, when surveyed by a different experimenter, those who saw the films with mild sexual violence were more accepting of violence against women.

Other studies confirm that exposure to pornography increases acceptance of rape myths (Oddone-Paolucci et al., 2000). William Fisher at the University of Western Ontario has pointed out that using pornography may be a sort of self-fulfilling prophecy for some individuals. People with antisocial personalities may seek out antisocial pornography, and as they become more exposed to these images, their views on what is appropriate sexual behaviour may become even more warped (Fisher & Barak, 2001).

Viewing slasher movies has much the same effect. Men shown films such as *The Texas Chainsaw Massacre* become desensitized to brutality and more likely to view rape victims unsympathetically (Linz et al., 1988). While spending three evenings watching sexually violent movies, male viewers in an experiment by Charles Mullin and Daniel Linz (1995) became progressively less bothered by the raping and slashing. Compared to others not exposed to the films, they also, three days later, expressed less sympathy for domestic violence victims and they rated the victims' injuries as less severe. In fact, said researchers Edward Donnerstein, Daniel Linz, and Steven Penrod (1987), what better way for an evil character to get people to react calmly to the torture and mutilation of women than to show a gradually escalating series of such films?

Viewing pornography can also affect our self-image. Research by Todd Morrison and Melanie Morrison at the University of Saskatchewan has shown that exposure to sexually explicit material is correlated with decreased genital self-esteem in men (i.e., people's own sense of "adequacy" in their genitals; Morrison et al., 2006) but is correlated overall positively with sexual self-esteem. In addition, increased exposure to sexually explicit material was related to decreased sexual anxiety (Morrison et al., 2004).

Aggression Against Women

Evidence also suggests that pornography may contribute to men's actual aggression toward women (Kingston et al., 2009). Correlational studies raise that possibility. John Court (1985) noted that across the world, as pornography became more widely available during the 1960s and 1970s, the rate of reported rapes sharply increased—except in countries and areas where pornography was controlled. (The examples that counter this trend, such as Japan, where violent pornography is available but the rape rate is low, remind us that other factors are also important.)

When interviewed, Canadian and American sexual offenders commonly admit pornography use. For example, William Marshall at Queen's University (1989) reported that Ontario rapists and child molesters used pornography much more than men who were not sexual offenders. A follow-up study with 341 child molesters confirmed this finding (Kingston et al., 2008). An FBI study also reports considerable exposure to pornography among serial killers, as does a report from the Los Angeles Police Department regarding most child sex abusers (Bennett, 1991; Ressler et al., 1988). And among university males, high pornography consumption has predicted sexual aggressiveness after controlling for other predictors of antisocial behaviour (Vega & Malamuth, 2007).

Although limited to the sorts of short-term behaviours that can be studied in the laboratory, controlled experiments reveal cause and effect. A consensus statement by 21 leading social scientists sums up the results: "Exposure to violent pornography increases punitive behaviour toward women" (Koop, 1987).

If the ethics of conducting such experiments trouble you, rest assured that these researchers appreciate the controversial and powerful experience they are giving participants. Only after giving their knowing consent do people participate. Moreover, after the experiment, researchers debunk any myths the films communicated. One hopes that such debriefing sufficiently offsets the vivid image of a supposedly euphoric rape victim. Judging from studies with University of Manitoba and Winnipeg students by James Check and Neil Malamuth (1984; Malamuth & Check, 1984), it does. Those who read erotic rape stories and were then fully debriefed became *less* accepting of the "women-enjoy-rape" myth than students who had not seen the film.

Connection:

Remember our discussion of research ethics from Module 2.

Justification for this experimentation is both scientific and humanitarian. Statistics Canada reports that one in four Canadian women will be sexually assaulted in their lifetime. Although rates of sexual assault have decreased in the last ten years, they are still high. Eighty-five percent of sexual assault victims are women and girls, and 60 percent of sexual offences reported to police involve people under 18 (Statistics Canada, 2009). In the United States, in surveys of 6200 college students nationwide and 2200 Ohio working women, Mary Koss and her colleagues (1985, 1988, 1990) found that 28 percent of the women reported an experience that met the legal definition of rape or attempted rape.

Surveys in other industrialized countries produce similar results. Three in four stranger rapes and nearly all acquaintance rapes went unreported to police. Careful surveys conducted by Statistics Canada estimate that upward of 90 percent of sexual assaults are never reported. Thus, the known rape rate *greatly* underestimates the actual rape rate. Moreover, many more women—half in one survey of college women (Sandberg et al., 1985)—report having suffered some form of sexual assault while on a date, and even more have experienced verbal sexual coercion or harassment (Craig, 1990; Pryor, 1987). Men who behave in sexually coercive, aggressive ways typically desire dominance, exhibit hostility toward women, and are sexually promiscuous (Anderson et al., 1997; Malamuth et al., 1995).

We must caution against oversimplifying the complex causes of rape—which is no more attributable to any one cause than is cancer. However, viewing violence, especially sexual violence, can have antisocial effects.

In the contest of individual versus collective rights, people in most Western nations typically side with individual rights. So, as an alternative to censorship, many psychologists favour "media awareness training." Recall that pornography researchers have successfully resensitized and educated participants to women's actual responses to sexual violence. Could educators similarly promote critical viewing skills? By sensitizing people to the view of women that predominates in pornography and to issues of sexual harassment and violence, it should be possible to counter the myth that women enjoy being coerced.

Is such a hope naive? As public consciousness changed, script writers, producers, and media executives decided that exploitative images of ethnic and sexual minorities were not good. Will we one day look back with embarrassment on the time when movies entertained people with scenes of exploitation, mutilation, and sexual coercion?

Picture this scene from one of Albert Bandura's experiments (Bandura et al., 1961). A Stanford nursery school child is put to work on an interesting art activity. An adult is in another part of the room, where there are Tinker Toys, a mallet, and a big, inflated "Bobo doll." After a minute of working with the Tinker Toys, the adult gets up and for almost 10 minutes attacks the inflated doll. She pounds it with the mallet, kicks it, and throws it, all the while yelling, "Sock him in the nose . . . Knock him down . . . Kick him."

Albert Bandura has conducted ground-breaking research on the role of social models on aggressive behaviour.

After observing this outburst, the child goes to a different room with many very attractive toys. But after two minutes the experimenter interrupts, saying these are her best toys and she must "save them for the other children." The frustrated child now goes into another room with various toys for aggressive and non-aggressive play, two of which are a Bobo doll and a mallet.

Seldom did children who were not exposed to the aggressive adult model display any aggressive play or talk. Although frustrated, they nevertheless played calmly. Those who had observed the aggressive adult were many times more likely to pick up the mallet and lash out at the doll. Watching the adult's aggressive behaviour lowered their inhibitions. Moreover, the children often reproduced the model's acts and said her words. Observing aggressive behaviour had both lowered their inhibitions and taught them ways to aggress. Thus, we learn through observing social models. If we watch aggression (and the model's aggression is rewarded), we will become more aggressive ourselves.

LO 2

TELEVISION

We have seen that watching an aggressive model can unleash children's aggressive urges and teach them new ways to aggress. Would watching aggressive models on television similarly affect children?

Consider these few facts about watching television. Today 99 percent of households have a TV set, more than have bathtubs or telephones. Two-thirds of homes have three or more TV sets, which helps explain why parents' reports of what their children watch correlate minimally with children's reports of what they watch (Donnerstein, 1998). With specialty channels and news networks spanning the globe, and *Modern Family, How I Met Your Mother,* and *CSI* (and its spin-offs) having billions of viewers in more than 152 countries, television is creating a global pop culture.

In the average home, the TV is on seven hours a day, with individual household members averaging four hours. The same study showing that Montreal teenagers spend 10 hours per day on the Internet, showed that 52 percent of boys and 39 percent of girls reported more than 23 hours per week of television watching (Barnett et al., 2008). However, among adults, women watch more than men, non-Whites more than Whites, preschoolers and retired people more than those in school or working, and the less educated more than the highly educated (Comstock & Scharrer, 1999).

During all those hours, what social behaviours are modelled? For a quarter century, George Gerbner and other TV watchers (1994) at the University of Pennsylvania sampled U.S. network prime-time and Saturday morning entertainment programs. From 1994 to 1997, bleary-eyed employees of the National Television Violence Study (1997) analyzed some 10 000 programs from the major networks and cable channels. Their findings? Six in ten programs contained violence ("physically compelling action that threatens to hurt or kill, or actual hurting or killing").

What does it add up to? By the end of elementary school, the average child views some 8000 TV murders and 100 000 other violent acts (Huston et al., 1992). One TV critic has estimated that if real people were murdered at the rate of TV characters, the population would be killed off in 50 days (Medved, 1995). So, does all this matter? Does prime-time crime stimulate the behaviour it depicts?

Television's Effects on Behaviour

Do viewers imitate violent models? Examples abound of people re-enacting television crimes. There are anecdotal reports that criminals are learning new tricks from shows such as *CSI* and *Law & Order*. Indeed, one RCMP officer told the story of how a criminal, in trying to avoid leaving footprints at a crime scene, covered his shoes in duct tape (Patry et al., 2006). Unfortunately for the criminal, he left the duct tape roll at the crime scene—covered in easy-to-read fingerprints.

Crime stories are not scientific evidence. Researchers therefore use correlational and experimental studies to examine the effects of viewing violence. One technique, commonly used with schoolchildren, asks whether their TV watching predicts their aggressiveness. To some extent it does. The more violent the content of the child's TV viewing, the more aggressive the child (Eron,

1987; Turner et al., 1986). The relationship is modest but consistently found in the United States, Europe, and Australia.

So can we conclude that a diet of violent TV fuels aggression? Perhaps you are already thinking that because this is a correlational study, the cause–effect relation could also work in the opposite direction. Maybe aggressive children prefer aggressive programs. Or maybe some underlying third factor, such as lower intelligence, predisposes some children both to prefer aggressive programs and to act aggressively.

Researchers have developed two ways to test these alternative explanations. They test the "hidden third factor" explanation by statistically pulling out the influence of some of these possible factors. For example, William Belson (1978; Muson, 1978) studied 1565 London boys. Compared to those who watched little violence, those who watched a great deal (especially realistic rather than cartoon violence) admitted to 50 percent more violent acts during the preceding six months (e.g., "I busted the telephone in a telephone box"). Belson also examined 22 likely third factors, such as family size. The heavy and light viewers still differed after equating them with respect to potential third factors. So Belson surmised that the heavy viewers were indeed more violent *because* of their TV exposure.

Similarly, Leonard Eron and Rowell Huesmann (1980, 1985) found that violence viewing among 875 eight-year-olds correlated with aggressiveness even after statistically pulling out several obvious, possible third factors. Moreover, when they restudied these individuals as 19-year-olds, they discovered that viewing violence at age eight modestly predicted aggressiveness at age 19, but that aggressiveness at age eight did *not* predict viewing violence at age 19. Aggression followed viewing, not the reverse. They confirmed these findings in follow-up studies of 758 Chicago-area and 220 Finnish youngsters (Huesmann et al., 1984). What is more, when Eron and Huesmann (1984) examined the later criminal conviction records of their initial sample of eight-year-olds, they found that, at age 30, those men who as children had watched a great deal of violent television were more likely to have been convicted of a serious crime (see Figure 21-1).

Huesmann and his colleagues (1984, 2003) confirmed these findings in follow-up studies of Chicago-area youngsters. Boys who as eight-year-olds had been in the top 20 percent of violence watchers were, 15 years later, twice as likely as others to acknowledge pushing, grabbing, or shoving their wives, and their violence-viewing female counterparts were twice as likely, as young women, to have thrown something at their husbands.

Adolescent viewing also clues us to future adult behaviours, as Jeffrey Johnson and his colleagues (2002) found when they followed more than 700 lives through time. Among 14-year-olds who watched less than an hour of TV daily, 6 percent were involved in aggressive acts (such as assault, robbery, or threats of injury) at ages 16 to 22, as were five times as many—29 percent—of those who had watched more than three hours a day.

Another fact to ponder: Where television goes, increased violence follows. Even murder rates increase when and where television comes. In Canada and the United States, the homicide rate doubled between 1957 and 1974 as violent television spread. In census regions where television came later, the homicide rate jumped later, too. In White South Africa, where television was not introduced until 1975, a similar near doubling of the homicide rate did not begin until after 1975 (Centerwall, 1989). And in a closely studied rural Canadian town where television came late, playground aggression doubled soon after (Williams, 1986).

Seriousness of Criminal Acts by Age 30

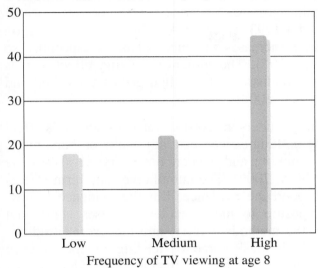

Frequency of TV viewing at age 8

FIGURE 21-1

Children's television viewing and later criminal activity. Violence viewing at age eight was a predictor of a serious criminal offence by age 30.

Source: Data from Eron & Huesmann, 1984.

Notice that these studies illustrate how researchers are now using correlational findings to *suggest* cause and effect. Yet, an infinite number of possible third factors could be creating a merely coincidental relation between viewing violence and aggression. Fortunately, however, the experimental method can control these extraneous factors. If we randomly assign some children to watch a violent film and others a non-violent film, any later aggression difference between the two groups will be due to the only factor that distinguishes them: what they watched.

TV Viewing Experiments

The trailblazing experiments by Albert Bandura and Richard Walters (1963) sometimes had young children view the adult pounding an inflated "Bobo" doll on film instead of observing it live—with much the same effect. Then Leonard Berkowitz and Russell Geen (1966) found that angry college students who viewed a violent film acted more aggressively than did similarly angered students who viewed non-aggressive films. These laboratory experiments, coupled with growing public concern, were sufficient to prompt the U.S. Surgeon General to commission 50 new research studies during the early 1970s. By and large, these studies confirmed that viewing violence amplifies aggression (Anderson & Bushman, 2002).

For example, research teams led by Ross Parke (1977) in the United States and Jacques Leyens (1975) in Belgium showed institutionalized American and Belgian delinquent boys a series of either aggressive or non-aggressive commercial films. Their consistent finding: "Exposure to movie violence . . . led to an increase in viewer aggression." Compared to the week preceding the film series, physical attacks increased sharply in cottages where boys were viewing violent films. Dolf Zillmann and James Weaver (1999) similarly exposed men and women, on four consecutive days, to violent or non-violent feature films. When participating in a different project on the fifth day, those exposed to the violent films were more hostile to the research assistant.

The aggression provoked in these experiments is not assault and battery; it's more on the scale of a shove in the lunch line, a cruel comment, a threatening gesture. Nevertheless, the convergence of evidence is striking. "The irrefutable conclusion," said a 1993 American Psychological Association youth violence commission, is "that viewing violence increases violence." This is especially so among people with aggressive tendencies (Bushman, 1995). The violence viewing effect also is strongest when an attractive person commits justified, realistic violence that goes unpunished and that shows no pain or harm (Donnerstein, 1998; Comstock, 2008).

All in all, conclude researchers Brad Bushman and Craig Anderson (2001), violence-viewing's effect on aggression surpasses the effect of passive smoking on lung cancer, calcium intake on bone mass, and homework on academic achievement. As with smoking and cancer, not everyone shows the effect—other factors matter as well (Ferguson & Kilburn, 2009). The cumulative long-term effects are what's worrisome, and corporate interests pooh-pooh the evidence. But the evidence is now "overwhelming," say Bushman and Anderson: "Exposure to media violence causes significant increases in aggression." The research base is large, the methods diverse, and the overall findings consistent, echoes a National Institute of Mental Health task force of leading media violence researchers (Anderson et al., 2003): "Our in-depth review . . . reveals unequivocal evidence that exposure to media violence can increase the likelihood of aggressive and violent behaviour in both immediate and long-term contexts."

Why Does TV Viewing Affect Behaviour?

The conclusion drawn by these researchers is *not* that television and pornography are primary causes of social violence. Rather, they say television is *a* cause. Even if it is just one ingredient in a complex recipe for violence, it is one that is potentially controllable (see Browne & Hamilton-Griachritsis, 2005). Given the convergence of correlational and experimental evidence, researchers have explored *why* viewing violence has this effect.

Consider three possibilities (Geen & Thomas, 1986). One is that it is not the violent content itself that causes social violence but the *arousal* it produces (Mueller et al., 1983; Zillmann, 1989a). As we noted earlier, arousal tends to spill over: one type of arousal energizes other behaviours.

Other research shows that viewing violence *disinhibits*. In Bandura's experiment, the adult's punching of the Bobo doll seemed to legitimate such outbursts and to lower the children's inhibitions. Viewing violence primes the viewer for aggressive behaviour by activating violence-related thoughts (Berkowitz, 1984; Bushman & Geen, 1990; Josephson, 1987). Listening to music with sexually violent lyrics seems to have a similar effect, predisposing younger males to accept the rape myth and to behave more aggressively (Barongan & Hall, 1995; Johnson et al., 1995; Pritchard, 1998).

Media portrayals also evoke *imitation*. The children in Bandura's experiments re-enacted the specific behaviours they had witnessed. The commercial television industry is hard-pressed to dispute that television leads viewers to imitate what they have seen: its advertisers model consumption.

Connection:

Remember our discussion of social learning from Module 14.

If the ways of relating and problem solving modelled on television do trigger imitation, especially among young viewers, then modelling **prosocial behaviour** should be socially beneficial. Happily, it is. Television's subtle influence can indeed teach children positive lessons in behaviour. Susan Hearold (1986) statistically combined 108 comparisons of prosocial programs with neutral programs or no program. She found that, on average, "if the viewer watched prosocial programs instead of neutral programs, he would [at least temporarily] be elevated from the 50th to the 74th percentile in prosocial behaviour—typically altruism."

In one such study, researchers Lynette Friedrich and Aletha Stein (1973; Stein & Friedrich, 1972) showed preschool children episodes of *Mister Rogers' Neighborhood* each day for four weeks as part of their nursery school program. During this viewing period, children from less-educated homes became more cooperative, helpful, and likely to state their feelings. In a follow-up study, kindergartners who viewed four *Mister Rogers* programs were able to state its prosocial content, both on a test and in puppet play (Friedrich & Stein, 1975; see also Coates et al., 1976).

Applying Social Psychology

The 1992 APA task force on television that provided guidelines for parents in helping them regulate their children's viewing habits seems as relevant now as ever (APA, 1992). They include the following:

- Maintain an activities time chart including TV viewing, playing with friends, and homework.
- Establish a weekly viewing limit. Assign points to specific programs and give a point total for the week. Less desirable programs may cost more to watch.
- Rule out TV at certain times (e.g., mealtimes or on school nights).
- Encourage the entire family to have a program choice before turning the TV on.
- Remember that you provide a model. If you watch lots of TV, chances are your child will, too.

In monitoring the violence children see, the report suggests that parents:

- Watch at least one episode of the programs their children watch to know its frequency and degree of violence.
- When viewing violence together, discuss why it occurs and how painful it is. Ask how conflict can be resolved without aggression.
- Explain how violence on programs is faked.
- Encourage children to watch programs with characters that cooperate and care for each other.

In your opinion, would these guidelines be easy to apply? Why or why not? Did your parents do this with you? Did it help? Would these rules apply equally to time spent online?

LO 3

VIDEO GAMES

Do video games influence behaviour? Illegal street racing has become a major problem in Canada. There have been a number of deadly crashes in recent years. For example, in February 2006 in Vancouver, three men in their 20s died when their BMW split in half after colliding with a metal light post during a street race. They had reached speeds of 160 km/h before the crash. The previous week, two 18-year-olds had raced down a Toronto street at 140 km/h—90 km/h over the posted limit. At the end of the race, a taxi driver was killed when one of the cars struck his cab as he tried to turn on to the street where the cars were racing. Police investigating the accident found a copy of the video game *Need for Speed* (which was made into a movie in 2014) in the backseat of one of the cars.

Street racing, frequently depicted in movies and video games, often leads to injuries and deaths in real life.

"The scientific debate over *whether* media violence has an effect is basically over," contend Douglas Gentile and Craig Anderson (2003). Researchers are now shifting their attention to video games, which have exploded in popularity and are also exploding with increasing brutality. Yet educational research shows that video games can also be excellent teaching tools. For example, Ian Spence and Jing Fung (2010) at the University of Toronto found that people who play action video games learn multiple object tracking and object rotation, and can apply these skills to other tasks. Video games have also been used to teach medical students how to do home visits (Duque et al., 2008).

The Games Kids Play

Since the first video game in 1972, we have moved from electronic Ping-Pong to splatter games (Anderson, 2004; Gentile & Anderson, 2003).

Today's mass murder simulators are not obscure games. *Grand Theft Auto* is well known as one of the most violent video games available. A player can kill pedestrians, carjack innocent bystanders, do drive-by shootings, pick up a prostitute, have sex in the car, kill the woman, and then get his money back (Gentile, 2004). *Grand Theft Auto V,* released in 2013, was the fastest-selling entertainment product of all time, selling over 34 million copies (Telegraph, 2013). In 2010, over 200 million games a year were being purchased, and the average 12- to 17-year-old is playing video games seven hours a week. And this may be an underestimate—Simon Tobin and Simon Grondin (2009) at Université de Laval found that kids playing video games tended to underestimate how long they had been playing. Furthermore, in one survey of Grade 4 students, 59 percent of girls and 73 percent of boys reported that their favourite games were violent ones (Anderson, 2003, 2004). Games rated "M" (mature) are supposedly intended for sale only to those 17 and older but often are marketed to those younger. The U.S. Federal Trade Commission found that in four out of five attempts, underage children could easily purchase them (Pereira, 2003).

Since its launch in 1997, the violent Grand Theft Auto *has become a bestseller.*

Effects of the Games Kids Play

Most smokers don't die of heart disease. Most abused children don't become abusive. And most people who spend hundreds of hours killing indiscriminately in video games live a gentle life. This enables video game defenders, like tobacco and TV interests, to say their products are harmless. "There is absolutely no evidence, none, that playing a violent game leads to aggressive behaviour," contended Doug Lowenstein (2000), president of the Interactive Digital Software Association. Gentile and Anderson (2003) nevertheless offer some reasons why violent game playing *might* have a more toxic effect than watching violent television. While game playing, players

- identify with, and play the role of, a violent character.
- actively rehearse violence, not just passively watch it.
- engage in the whole sequence of enacting violence—selecting victims, acquiring weapons and ammunition, stalking the victim, aiming the weapon, pulling the trigger.
- are engaged with continual violence and threats of attack.
- repeat violent behaviours over and over.
- are rewarded for effective aggression.

For such reasons, military organizations often prepare soldiers to fire in combat (which many in World War II reportedly were hesitant to do) by engaging them with attack simulation games.

But what does the available research actually find? Craig Anderson (2003, 2004; Anderson et al., 2004) offers statistical digests of three dozen available studies that reveal five consistent effects. Playing violent video games, more than playing non-violent games

- *increases arousal*—heart rate and blood pressure rise.

- *increases aggressive thinking*—for example, Brad Bushman and Anderson (2002) found that after playing games such as *Duke Nukem* and *Mortal Kombat*, university students became more likely to guess that a man whose car was just rear-ended would respond aggressively, by using abusive language, kicking out a window, or starting a fight; Anderson and his colleagues (2003) found that violent music lyrics also prime aggressive thinking, making students more likely to complete "h_t" as "hit" rather than "hat."

- *increases aggressive feelings*—frustration levels rise, as does expressed hostility; although these feelings can subside rapidly after stoppage of play (Bartlett et al., 2009), they can result in increased aggression up to 24 hours later (Englehart et al., 2011; Bushman & Gibson, 2012).

- *increases aggressive behaviours*—after violent game play, children and youth play more aggressively with their peers, get into more arguments with their teachers, and participate in more fights; the effect occurs inside and outside the laboratory, across self-reports, teacher reports, and parent reports (Hasan et al., 2013), and for reasons illustrated in Figure 21-2.

- *decreases prosocial behaviours*—after violent video game playing, people become slower to help a person whimpering in the hallway outside and slower to offer help to peers.

- *increases physical injury*—Craig Emes at McGill University (1997) reviewed the existing literature on the impact of video games on children and concluded that although video games can have a positive impact on children (similar to findings about prosocial TV), playing video games can have negative physical effects (e.g., causing seizures and tendonitis) and can lead to aggressive behaviour, particularly among younger children; Bartholow and his colleagues (2005) have found that, similar to TV viewing, exposure to video game violence *causes* increases in aggression.

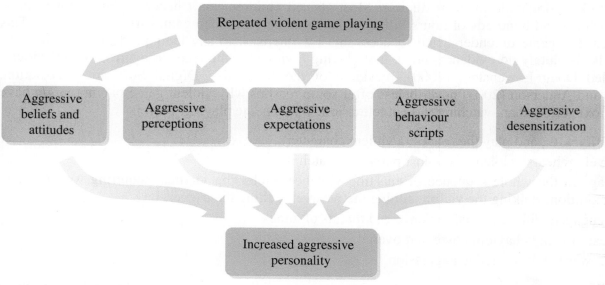

FIGURE 21-2

Violent video game influences on aggressive tendencies.

Source: Adapted from Craig A. Anderson and Brad J. Bushman, "Effects of violent video games on aggressive behavior, aggressive cognition, aggressive effect, psychological arousal and prosocial behavior: A meta-analytic review of the scientific literature," *Psychological Science, 12,* No. 5, pp. 353–359. Reprinted by permission of Blackwell Publishing.

Moreover, the more violent the games played, the bigger the effects. Video games *have* become more violent, which helps explain why newer studies find the biggest effects. Although much remains to be learned, these studies indicate that, contrary to the catharsis hypothesis, practising violence breeds rather than releases violence.

Critical THINKING

Now that you have read all of this information about the role of media in behaviour, what are your thoughts? Should we give up now and "shut down" the Internet? Or are there better ways to move forward. If you could, what would you recommend that parents do? Universities? High schools? What would do the most good?

Activity: **Answers**

Below are the answers for the items in the Activity box—if you have not completed the activity, please do so before checking the answers.

?	I have a question	**AMAP**	As many as possible, or as much as possible
182	I hate you	**EZ**	Easy
20	Location	**F2F**	Face-to-face
2G2B4G	Too good to be forgotten	**GTG**	Got to go
411	Information	**IMHO**	In my honest opinion
4COL	For crying out loud	**LOL**	Laughing out loud, or lots of love
9	Parent is watching	**SYT**	See you tomorrow
AAAAA	American Association Against Acronym Abuse		

So, how many did you get right? What do you think this says about you?

Source: netlingo.com.

CONCLUSIONS

When we think about the effect the media has on us and on society, we do have to remember some facts. Most people are not violent, and most people do watch television, play video games, and have been exposed to pornography. However, the more people watch or play, the more likely the negative behaviour will appear. As a concerned scientist, Anderson (2003, 2004; Anderson et al., 2008) therefore encourages parents to discover what their kids are ingesting and to ensure that their media diet, at least in their own home, is healthy. Parents may not be able to control what their child watches, plays, and eats in someone else's home, but they can oversee consumption in their own home and provide increased time for alternative activities. Networking with other parents can build a kid-friendly neighbourhood. And schools can help by providing media awareness education. Awareness helps.

SUMMARY OF KEY POINTS

LO1. Understand the impact of pornography on perceptions and behaviour.

- Repeated exposure to pornography can lead to distorted perceptions of sexuality and aggression against women.

LO2. Understand the impact of television on perceptions and behaviour.

- Many types of research have conclusively demonstrated that people learn through observing others behave—TV can make people more violent.
- Just as they can learn to be violent by watching others, they can learn prosocial behaviours as well.

LO3. Understand the impact of video games on perceptions and behaviour.

- Video games can have effects that are very similar to television—both prosocial and antisocial behaviour can be learned.

KEY TERMS

Pornography   Any written or visual material that contains the description of or actual images of human sexual activity or sex organs, which is intended to stimulate erotic feelings, rather than focused on aesthetic or emotional reactions.

Prosocial behaviour   Positive, constructive, helpful social behaviour; the opposite of antisocial behaviour.

MODULE TWENTY-TWO

Social Psychology and the Law

Tom Sophonow had been in Winnipeg at the time of a grisly murder. The murderer had entered a donut shop, locked the door, and proceeded to rob and murder the young woman working behind the counter. As he was leaving the crime scene, he ran into a man who was trying to enter the shop. He told the man the shop was closed. Nonetheless, the man soon discovered the dead teenager and ran outside to confront the murderer. The murderer threatened the witness with a knife and ran off. Later, the police interviewed Tom Sophonow and asked him if he would mind providing a photo to use in a lineup. Interestingly, the witness remembered that the man had worn a cowboy hat. Before police took a picture of Sophonow, they asked him to put on a cowboy hat.

Connection:

We discussed the Sophonow case in Module 1.

Critical THINKING

If you had been in Sophonow's situation, what would you have done? Would you have let the police take your photo? Would you have believed that you had nothing to worry about because you were innocent? Of course, you would. So did Sophonow. So do most innocent people (Kassin, 2005). But is this a mistake? Are you at more risk than you realize? Or was Sophonow a rare exception?

The police asked the witness from the coffee shop to try to identify the criminal from a photo lineup that included a picture of Sophonow in the cowboy hat. The witness was not able to do so. Nonetheless, police arrested Sophonow. After the witness saw Sophonow in custody and in handcuffs, he said he was "90 percent sure" Sophonow was the man he had seen leaving the crime scene. Sophonow was eventually convicted, based largely on the eyewitness testimony. Faced with a confident eyewitness, would you have convicted Sophonow?

Initially, you might think that there are not many areas where social psychology and the law intersect. The law is the law—black and white. However, in reality, moving through the legal system is a process of many interactions between many different groups of people, from how a victim experiences a crime, to how a lawyer, judge, or juror interprets the evidence (and the law), to how people, past experiences, and beliefs cloud the judgment of those people.

Connection:

In previous modules (e.g., Modules 3, 4, and 8), we have talked about making judgments and decisions.

In this module, we will explore how these factors influence judgments as they relate to the legal system. As we shall see, sometimes the mistakes we make and the things we bring with us into the crime or the courtroom can have devastating effects.

Tom Sophonow at a press conference in which police apologized for his wrongful conviction in the grisly murder of Barbara Stoppel in 1981.

Before you go on into the module, complete the following activity, which assesses your opinions about eyewitnesses.

Activity: **Attitudes toward eyewitnesses**

The following questions deal with your opinions of eyewitnesses in general. Please answer each question.

1	2	3	4	5
Strongly Disagree				**Strongly Agree**

1. Eyewitness testimony is an important part of most trials.	1 2 3 4 5
2. Eyewitnesses are reliable witnesses.	1 2 3 4 5
3. Eyewitness testimony provides crucial evidence in trials.	1 2 3 4 5
4. Eyewitnesses frequently misidentify innocent people just because they seem familiar.	1 2 3 4 5
5. Eyewitnesses generally give accurate testimony in trials.	1 2 3 4 5
6. The strongest evidence is provided by eyewitnesses.	1 2 3 4 5
7. Eyewitnesses can usually be believed.	1 2 3 4 5

(Continued)

8. Eyewitness testimony is more like fact than opinion.   **1   2   3   4   5**

9. Eyewitnesses generally do not give accurate descriptions.   **1   2   3   4   5**

This scale has been adapted from the work of Narby and Cutler (1994). Scoring is simple—items 4 and 9 are reverse scored, then responses are summed. The higher your score, the greater your belief in the importance and validity of eyewitnesses and eyewitness testimony. Why do you either believe or not believe in the usefulness and accuracy of eyewitness identifications?

Before you read the following section, make sure you have completed the activity.

As you read through this module, you have to understand that Tom Sophonow is far from alone. There are dozens of cases in Canada where innocent people have been charged and convicted of crimes. Here are just a few examples:

- John Labatt, the beer mogul, was kidnapped 10 minutes after leaving his cottage in Sarnia on his way to London, Ontario, on August 14, 1934. He was pulled over by three masked gunmen, blindfolded, and taken to a remote location, where he was held for three days while the kidnappers tried to get $150 000 in ransom from his brother. The kidnappers ultimately panicked and released Labatt unharmed. Why is this story here? Because Labatt identified David Meisner as one of his kidnappers. Meisner spent a year in prison before it became clear that he was the victim of mistaken identification. It was only after one of the kidnappers was killed and two others surrendered that Meisner was vindicated. He sued Labatt and settled out of court for $95 000.

- William Mullins-Johnson was convicted of killing (and possibly raping) his four-year-old niece. He spent 12 years in prison before it was found that the evidence he was convicted on, specifically the testimony of a pathologist who examined his niece's body, was likely incorrect. The pathologist has now been discredited, and hundreds of his cases are being re-examined. The pathologist, believing the people he was investigating were guilty, tended to find ambiguous evidence as indicative of guilt.

- In 1992, Robert Baltovich, a recent graduate of the University of Toronto, was convicted of killing his girlfriend, Elizabeth Bain, two years earlier. He was sentenced to life in prison. Although Bain had disappeared in 1990, no trace of her body was ever found. There was little forensic evidence in the case and Baltovich was ultimately convicted, in part, based on the "hypnotically enhanced memory" of a witness who testified against him. After winning a new trial in 2004, Baltovich was found not guilty in April of 2008, when the prosecution elected not to present any evidence at his retrial.

- In 1997, Simon Marshall, from Ste.-Foy, Quebec, was convicted of 15 counts of rape based on his confession. After being released in 2003, he was arrested again and charged with three more counts. Once again he confessed. DNA analysis showed he was in fact innocent. A further investigation showed he was also innocent of all of the previous crimes. Marshall, who is mentally handicapped, was ultimately awarded $2.3 million in compensation.

William Mullins-Johnson was convicted of killing his four-year-old niece. He was exonerated over a decade later.

Robert Baltovich was convicted of killing his girlfriend based on "hypnotically enhanced" evidence, even though there was no physical evidence corroborating the charges.

LO 1

THE FALLIBILITY OF EYEWITNESS TESTIMONY

These cases are just the tip of the iceberg of Canadian false-conviction cases. There is little evidence presented at trial that is more compelling than a confident eyewitness. Elizabeth Loftus, a pioneer in the eyewitness field (Loftus, 1974, 1979, 2013), conducted a study that shows the power of eyewitness testimony to influence trial outcomes. Students were presented with a hypothetical criminal case based on circumstantial evidence, or the same evidence and one eyewitness. When the case had only the circumstantial evidence, 18 percent of jurors voted for conviction. However, when there was a confident eyewitness, 72 percent voted for conviction. Interestingly, when the eyewitness was discredited (it turned out she was extremely nearsighted, with 20/400 vision), 68 percent of jurors still convicted. Thus, this is another good example of how our preconceptions can bias our thinking.

More recently, Dan Yarmey at the University of Guelph found that students' predictions about real-world eyewitness accuracy were no better than chance (Yarmey, 2004). Yet, if we believe an honest eyewitness is accurate (regardless of the reasons why he or she may not be accurate), then we increase the likelihood of making costly mistakes.

How Many Eyewitnesses Are Wrong?

There are hundreds of documented cases where honest eyewitness mistakes have led to false imprisonment. Can jurors tell when an eyewitness is mistaken? Gary Wells and Rod Lindsay (see Wells et al., 1979) conducted studies at the University of Alberta and found that both correct and incorrect eyewitnesses are believed about 80 percent of the time.

Although it is impossible to know how often eyewitnesses make mistakes, we know that mistakes get made. For example, of approximately 8000 sexual assault cases where DNA was tested by the U.S. Federal Bureau of Investigation, the suspect was exonerated about 25 percent of the time (Scheck et al., 2001). In most of those cases, eyewitness identification was the primary way in which suspects were identified. A group of lawyers out of a New York law school have developed what is called the Innocence Project. Students and professors investigate cases where DNA evidence is available but was not tested to determine if people who have been convicted of the crimes are actually innocent (testing of DNA was not common in all cases until 1993, when evidence rules changed). Of the (to date) 312 Innocence Project cases where people have been falsely imprisoned and subsequently exonerated, about 75 percent involved mistaken eyewitness identification (innocenceproject.org, 2014). Not surprisingly, improving the accuracy of eyewitness evidence has been a focus of social psychologists for many years.

Why are eyewitnesses so compelling? If an eyewitness has no reason to lie, and he or she claims to have seen someone commit a crime, juries will believe that person. This is particularly true when the witness is confident (Luus & Wells, 1994). Indeed, in the United States, the *Neil v. Biggers* criteria, used to assess eyewitness accuracy, specifically indicate that an eyewitness's confidence in his or her identification should be used to determine accuracy. However, the confidence–accuracy correlation (Sporer et al., 1995) is notoriously low, even at the best of times. Although the confidence–accuracy correlation varies wildly from study to study, it is typically around 0.30 (a relatively weak positive correlation). However, by the time a witness gets to trial, so many factors may have influenced their confidence that it is unlikely to predict accuracy at all (Wells & Bradfield, 1998; Wells et al., 2005).

Why Eyewitnesses Make Mistakes

Literally hundreds of studies have explored the accuracy of eyewitness identifications (see Wells, 1993; Wells et al., 2000, Loftus, 2013). These researchers have found that there are a number of different factors that can affect eyewitness accuracy. For example, children tend to do worse as eyewitnesses (e.g., Luus, Wells & Turtle, 1995), although not because their memory is poor, but because they are more likely to say "yes" when asked if a picture shown to them is the criminal. An important distinction that can be made among these factors is the difference between *system variables*—factors the legal system can control, and *estimator variables*—factors the legal system cannot control. With system variables, one can construct the situation so that errors may be avoided.

An example of an estimator variable is the race of the criminal relative to the witness (see Bothwell et al., 1989; Smith et al., 2001, 2004). Research has shown a consistent decrease in eyewitness accuracy if the witness and the suspect are of different races. Because this decrement is greater when the majority group member identifies a minority, relative to when a minority attempts to identify a majority group member, some researchers have suggested that familiarity with the other group may be the cause of the increased error (see Smith & Stinson, 2008, for a review). Essentially, researchers believe this is a perceptual deficit that is the result of the *outgroup homogeneity effect*.

Connection:

Remember we discussed the outgroup homogeneity effect in Module 16.

Other researchers have suggested that different racial groups focus on different facial features. However, a definitive cause has thus far eluded researchers (Ng & Lindsay, 1994; Smith et al., 2001, 2004). Importantly, there is little the legal system can do to alleviate this problem. Thus, many researchers have argued it may be best to focus on system variables as these are the factors that the legal system will be able to change. Two important elements that can be controlled by the legal system are how eyewitnesses are interviewed and how police lineups are constructed.

One example of a system variable is the impact of multiple witnesses. This is called the co-witness effect (see Luus & Wells, 1994; Goodwin et al., 2012). Elizabeth Brimacombe at the University of Victoria has been investigating the impact of multiple factors on eyewitness identification. Brimacombe found that co-witness information can have dramatic effects on witnesses. She found that witnesses who are told that another witness had identified the same suspect from a police lineup were significantly more confident than when no information was given about another witness. This is important because, although confidence can change, accuracy does not. A more confident witness at court is more convincing than one who is not, but will not necessarily be more accurate. How is this a system variable? Although we cannot control how many witnesses there will be to a crime, we can (to some extent) control the information we give to witnesses about what other witnesses have said or done.

Interviewing Eyewitnesses

Almost 2500 years ago, Plato argued that memory was a "wax tablet" upon which our everyday experiences left their impressions. An important consequence of this characterization, one that was accepted as truth for some time, is that once a memory is encoded it is set and unchangeable. Although a memory can be "forgotten" for some time, it could eventually be completely and accurately retrieved. The reality is much different. Memory is a constructive process. Memories change over time. They are influenced by our beliefs and expectations. You have probably all experienced this yourselves—think of the last time you and a friend got into an argument. Would you give different versions of the story? Probably—and you would both believe you were telling the complete and accurate truth.

Connection:

Recall that we discussed the confirmation bias in Module 7.

We ask questions in such a way that the answers we get will tend to confirm our expectations rather than disconfirm them—police do this as well. Not surprisingly, confirmation bias can have a significant effect on how we remember events. Elizabeth Loftus has demonstrated memory construction in a number of experiments. In one study (Loftus et al., 1978) she showed participants slides of a car accident. In one slide, a red Datsun is shown going through either a stop sign or a yield sign. Half of the participants were then asked if another car had passed the Datsun while it was at the stop sign. The other half of participants were asked the same question, but with "yield sign" substituted for "stop sign." Next, participants were presented with pictures from the slide show and asked to choose the picture they saw—either a picture with a stop sign or one with a yield sign. Participants who received the leading question were more likely to "remember" the incorrect information.

At times this can go so far that witnesses may develop completely false memories of events—these memories can be held with just as much confidence as true memories. The Martensville daycare case is an excellent example (*The Globe and Mail*, 2002). In 1991, the mother of one of the children being babysat by the Sterling family in the small Saskatchewan town found a suspicious rash on her child's bottom. She suspected her child had been abused and filed a complaint with Saskatchewan police, who began an investigation. Although there was no physical evidence of sexual abuse, the police eventually arrested nine people, including a police officer, and charged them with more than 40 crimes against a number of children.

John Yuille, an eyewitness researcher from the University of British Columbia, was an expert witness in the case and testified that the police interview tactics were flawed: there were leading and suggestive questions, children were cajoled into giving certain answers, and children were rewarded when they gave the "right answer." In the end, ten years later, all charges were dropped and the province was forced to pay compensation to those arrested.

Some therapists use "age-regression" (hypnotically putting people back in time to their infancy) to delve deeply into people's past to uncover long forgotten memories (usually of sexual abuse). However, Nicholas Spanos, at Carleton University, has shown that this can be a highly problematic procedure (Spanos et al., 1999). In one of his studies, 68 of 78 participants who were age-regressed eventually developed false memories from infancy (specifically of the day they were born). More than half of these participants reported strong beliefs that the memories were real and not just hypnotically induced fantasies. Spanos (1996) also points out that false memories can be very complex, as they are in some false memories of UFO abductions.

Because memories created during hypnotic procedures can create false memories that are indistinguishable from real memories (Spanos, 1996; Patry et al., 2009), researchers have sought to find ways to avoid the use of hypnosis, yet improve memory. Ron Fisher and his colleagues (e.g., Fisher et al., 1987) have designed the cognitive interview (CI) technique. In their initial research, Fisher and his colleagues found that after asking an open-ended question to a witness police often interrupted with closed-ended and often misleading questions (questions that could lead to misinformation and changes in memory). They designed the CI to improve how police interviewed witnesses. The CI is based on principles of cognitive psychology that have to do with cues that can help people to recall specific events. Thus, law enforcement officials are encouraged to establish rapport with the witnesses; encourage them to mentally "go back" to the event by having them visualize what they were thinking and feeling at the time of the event; encourage witnesses to give complete answers; ask only open-ended, non-leading questions (e.g., asking "What was the criminal wearing?" versus "Can you describe the guy in the black jacket?") and caution people against guessing about what they had witnessed.

Fisher and his colleagues trained numerous groups of detectives on the CI technique and found that it elicited 50 percent more information from witnesses without increasing the rate of incorrect information recalled (Fisher et al., 2002; Granhag et al., 2004). The effectiveness of the procedure has been demonstrated in numerous studies (e.g., Ginet et al., 2014; Dando et al., 2009). Fisher and Geiselman (2010) report that many police agencies in North America and Great Britain have adopted the CI and now include the interview technique in their standard training package.

Police Lineup Procedures

Every year in North America at least 75 000 people are identified from police lineups and subsequently prosecuted. The most common police lineups used are called simultaneous lineups—where photos are shown all at one time (see Figure 22-1). In Canada, the police use 12-person lineups, and they are almost always photo rather than live lineups. The vast majority of police lineups are simultaneous, but is this the best way for police to identify criminals? The simultaneous lineup has some problems (see Lindsay & Wells, 1985; Lindsay & Bellinger, 1999). You can

FIGURE 22-1

A police photo lineup.

conceive of a simultaneous lineup as much like a multiple-choice test—the right answer (that is, the suspect) is there, all you have to do is choose the right person. However, if an innocent suspect is chosen, this false identification can lead to an innocent person being imprisoned. Nonetheless, when presented with a lineup, witnesses often feel pressure to choose someone, and they will compare the photos and choose the one that looks most like what they remember. This is called a *relative judgment*, and it can lead to errors.

A better approach is to use sequential lineups—where photos are shown one at a time and witnesses have to make a yes or no decision before moving on. Gary Wells (at Iowa State University) and Rod Lindsay (at Queen's University; 1985) have shown that using a sequential lineup procedure can dramatically reduce error rates compared to other types of lineups (Carlson et al., 2008; Gronlund et al., 2009). These researchers have proposed that a sequential procedure forces people into *absolute judgment* strategies and reduces people's ability to compare among photos.

To further reduce errors during lineups, police should provide witnesses with unbiased instructions. Roy Malpass and Patricia Devine (1981) have demonstrated that biased lineup instructions (e.g., "The guy is in the lineup, all you have to do is pick him out") lead to more eyewitness errors (because people feel they have to choose someone) than unbiased instruction (e.g., "The criminal may or may not be present in the lineup"). Thus, whenever police present a witness with a lineup, the witness should be advised of the possibility that the criminal may not be there (current RCMP procedures already include such an instruction). Lineup types and instructions are both examples of system variables, whose use can be controlled by the legal system. Police should also avoid giving feedback to the eyewitness on whether or not they picked the suspect—once an eyewitness has received feedback, their confidence will change (e.g., Smith et al., 2004) and this makes it more difficult for observers (e.g., jurors or judges) to determine if they have made a correct decision (Smalarz & Wells, 2013).

Critical THINKING

You have now learned a lot about eyewitnesses and the errors they can make. Now, before you go on, go back and redo the activity on perceptions of eyewitnesses you did earlier in the module. Have your answers changed? Should they?

LO 2

THE PSYCHOLOGY OF POLICE INVESTIGATIONS

Lie Detection

Being able to tell if a witness is lying is a skill police would very much like to have. For a number of decades psychologists have been trying to identify ways to determine whether people are lying. However, research has typically shown that people rarely perform at better than chance levels at detecting deception (DePaulo et al., 1982; Memon & Gabbert, 2003), that people cannot effectively be trained to detect deception (Vrij, Edward, & Bull, 2001; Vrij et al., 2008), and that police, judges, psychiatrists, and other legal professionals perform no better than laypeople (Carlucci et al., 2012). Research conducted by Amy Leach at the University of Ontario Institute of Technology and her colleagues (Leach et al., 2008) has shown that even if people are able to detect deception in one context, they may not be able to in another. The cues to deception differ from situation to situation, but the research Leach and her colleagues have conducted suggests that people tend to rely on the same cues over and over. Also, Parliament and Yarmey (2002) have shown that when eyewitnesses were coached to lie about the identity of the criminal, they could do so consistently and convincingly.

Because of these failures, police often turn to mechanical means to determine if someone is deceiving them. The polygraph is by far the most commonly used and economical of these instruments. The polygraph does not measure lying per se, but is used to assess a number of physiological indices that are supposed to be a response to the anxiety and discomfort lying produces—including breathing rate, galvanic skin response (sweating), heart rate, and blood pressure. Police use the polygraph to verify witnesses' and suspects' versions of events. These are also used quite frequently in the assessment of potential police officers (to test for criminal and drug-related experiences). But how accurate is the polygraph? Although controversial, polygraph tests can accurately identify guilty suspects as guilty in as many as 85 percent of cases (Patrick & Iacono, 1991). However, the polygraph can misclassify innocent suspects as guilty in up to 25 percent of cases. Thus, the polygraph is not considered reliable enough to be admissible in Canadian courts (*R. v. Beland*, 1987).

Some researchers have argued that they may be able to detect deception far more accurately than the standard polygraph apparatus. A more recent development is a technique that measures *event-related brain potentials* (ERPs). When we encounter information that is infrequent or personally significant, there is activity in the cerebral cortex (that is, we show an ERP response). These electrical patterns in the brain can be measured by placing a series of electrodes on a person's scalp (see Allen et al., 1992; Rosenfeld et al., 1996). Presumably, when a guilty suspect is presented with information about the crime he or she will show an ERP response. However, an innocent person would not. In one study, Lawrence Farwell and his colleagues (e.g., Farwell & Donchin, 1991) were able to classify 18 of 20 of guilty suspects and 17 of 20 not-guilty suspects correctly. Rosenfeld and his colleagues have found overall correct classification rates of 92 percent for guilty participants and 87 percent for not-guilty suspects—seemingly an improvement over other methods. Some recent research (Lefebrve et al., 2007; Lefebrve et al., 2008) has shown that ERPs can be used to assess accuracy and deception in lineup identification as well. However, some caution must be maintained. Rosenfeld and his colleagues (Rosenfeld et al., 2004) have suggested that people who are knowledgeable about ERPs may be able to fake the tests. Thus, no method of detecting deception is infallible.

Confessions

We have already pointed out how mistaken eyewitness identifications are a major cause of false convictions and imprisonment. However, false confessions are another serious problem. Remember the case of Simon Marshall from earlier in the module? He is not alone, either. In the Innocence Project cases cited, approximately 25 percent have involved a false confession given by a suspect. It is important to point out that these were legally obtained confessions—they were not beaten out of the suspect. Most of you are probably thinking, "If you confess, you must be guilty—I would never confess to a crime I didn't commit!" When teaching, Steven regularly asks students in his classes to put up their hands if they think they would ever confess to a crime they did not commit. Only five or six out of a hundred will say they would. However, research by Saul Kassin (2005; Kassin et al., 2009) suggests that easily half of people could confess to crimes.

It is important to recognize the awesome power of the social situation when a suspect is being interrogated by police. During an interrogation police do everything they can (within the law) to extract a confession. Many people do not realize that the police are allowed to mislead people they are interviewing. Police can tell suspects that they have evidence (hair, fingerprints, DNA), say that there are witnesses to the crime, or tell suspects that they have failed a polygraph. As long as the police do not actually fabricate evidence, they are behaving within the law.

Police around the world are trained in the *Reid technique* (Inbau et al., 2001), an interview style designed to extract confessions from unwilling suspects. Saul Kassin and his colleagues (Kassin, 2005; Kassin & Gudjonsson, 2004) have found that this type of interrogation can put substantial social pressure on a suspect to confess. Police generally believe that suspects are guilty, and that if they deny their guilt then they are lying. Indeed, one experienced police detective was quoted as saying, "You can tell if a suspect is lying by whether he is moving his lips" (Leo, 1996). As mentioned earlier, police are no more skilled at detecting deception than the average person, but police are very confident in their judgments (Kassin, 2005). Finally, the Reid technique itself is specifically designed to overcome a suspect's assertions of innocence.

Applying Social Psychology

The Reid technique (Inbau et al., 2001) is specifically designed to get suspects to incriminate themselves through the application of three psychological processes: isolation of the witness from others, confrontation, and minimization. The Reid technique prescribes a nine-step process:

1. Confront the suspect with assertions of guilt: This includes thinking about and visualizing the crime, which can lead to confusion.

2. Develop "themes" that justify or excuse the crime: Minimization gives suspects a way out and functions as the equivalent of a promise of leniency.

3. Interrupt all efforts at denial.

4. Overcome the suspect's factual, moral, and emotional objections.

5. Ensure that the passive suspect does not withdraw.

6. Show sympathy and understanding; urge the suspect to cooperate.

7. Offer a face-saving alternative view of the alleged guilty act: "It was an accident, provoked, spontaneous," and so on.

8. Get the suspect to recount the details of the crime: vivid, detailed accounts can seem real after a while.

9. Convert statements into a full written confession.

The combination of seemingly overwhelming evidence with an aggressive and relentless interrogation technique results in a remarkable number of confessions (Kassin, 2005). Although this is an invaluable technique when the suspect is guilty, it is problematic if the suspect is innocent. This is particularly true because innocent people are also more likely than guilty suspects to waive their right to a lawyer (Kassin & Norwick, 2004), and innocent suspects tend to elicit aggressive interrogation styles because their protests of innocence cause police officers to become frustrated (Kassin et al., 2003). Youth, people under the influence of drugs or alcohol, and the developmentally disabled are particularly at risk of confessing falsely. Research suggests that video-taping interrogations (which is standard for most Canadian police agencies) may have a positive impact on this issue. Officers who know they are being video-taped while interrogating a suspect use fewer high-pressure tactics, and may be better at determining the honesty of those being interviewed (Kassin et al., 2013).

The Canadian system has a relatively unique approach called the "Mr. Big" technique (Smith, Stinson, & Patry, 2009, 2010). In this ploy, used primarily in high-profile cases (e.g., drug crimes, homicides) where a suspect has been identified but there is not enough evidence to make an arrest, police create an elaborate sting operation. The suspect (often out of work and ostracized by suspicious family members) is involved in a series of low-level crimes, as part of an organized crime group. Offered the opportunity to be "promoted," the suspect is brought to meet "Mr. Big," the boss of the organization. However, before the promotion (which often comes with lots of money and offers to make the police and any evidence "go away"), the suspect is told he or she must confess to the crime. Supposedly, this confession is needed so that the group "has something" on the suspect if he or she ever "turns" on the organization. Frequently, the person confesses, and this is used as evidence at trial. This tactic is very expensive (often costing over $300 000) and time consuming, but police argue it is effective 85 percent of the time.

Critical THINKING

Now that you have read about the Mr. Big strategy, ask yourself, "Is this a good strategy?" You can imagine the pressure to confess is enormous—money, friends, getting rid of evidence—and the cost seems low. The suspect has as much on the "crime gang" as they have on him or her. The pressure to confess is much higher than in a typical police interview, and we know many innocent suspects confess in those circumstances. Given these concerns, should the Mr. Big technique be legal in Canada? A recent Supreme Court case (*R. v. Hart,* 2014) has recognized there may be issues and has put some limitations on the admissibility of confessions obtained using the technique.

LO 3

THE PSYCHOLOGICAL INFLUENCES ON COURT JUDGMENTS

Defendant Characteristics

When juries are deciding the outcome of a criminal case, do factors such as attractiveness and similarity of the defendant to the jurors play a role? When Paul Bernardo was arrested for the grisly murders of two teenage girls, people were shocked. How could such a good-looking and charming man be accused of such heinous crimes? In the first O.J. Simpson case, a shocking number of jurors believed that O.J. could not have committed the murders he was charged with because he was an excellent football player (Wrightsman et al., 2001). Gillian Guess was a juror in the murder trial of Peter Gill. She openly flirted with the accused and ended up having an affair with him during the trial. She was ultimately convicted of obstruction of justice. Why do people react this way? Can this really have an effect in court?

Connection:

Remember that we discussed the "what is beautiful is good" hypothesis in Module 19.

Michael Efran at the University of Toronto wanted to test this hypothesis (1974). He gave students a description of a cheating case with the photo of the cheater attached. When the cheater was attractive, he was rated as less guilty and received a more lenient punishment. Other research has confirmed that attractiveness can influence trial outcomes, especially when the available evidence is ambiguous (Mazzela & Feingold, 1994). However, in Canada fewer than 20 percent of trials are held in front of a jury. Surely judges are not subject to these biases. To test this, Chris Downs and Phillip Lyons (1991) obtained attractiveness ratings of 1742 defendants in misdemeanour cases heard in front of 40 different judges. Regardless of the severity of the crime, judges gave more lenient bail amounts and fines to more attractive defendants (see Figure 22-2).

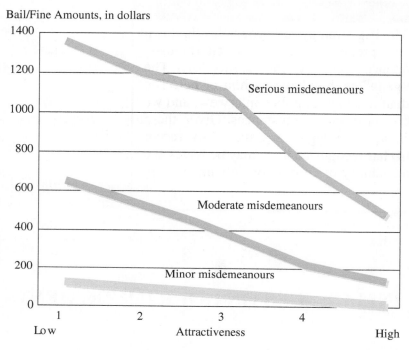

FIGURE 22-2

Attractiveness and legal judgments. Texas Gulf Coast judges set higher bails and fines for less attractive defendants.

Source: Data from Downs & Lyons, 1991.

Judge's Instructions

At the end of every jury trial, judges provide instructions to the jury in terms of the relevant aspects of the law, as well as what information they should consider in rendering their decision. However, we have all seen TV shows where one lawyer presents evidence he or she shouldn't have and opposing counsel shouts "I object!" The judge then quickly instructs the jury to "disregard that statement." Does this work? Evidence suggests the answer is no. For example, Stanley Sue and his colleagues (Sue et al., 1973) presented participants with a description of a crime and summaries of the defence and prosecution cases. Although the prosecution case was weak, in one condition of the study, participants heard a recording of an incriminating phone call made by the defendant. At the end of the trial, the judge instructed jurors that this evidence was inadmissible. Nonetheless, jurors in this condition were just as likely to convict as if no such instruction was given.

This has been supported by more recent work on information processing—people are not very good at correcting for the influence of potentially biasing information, and indeed their attempts to correct for the biasing information can actually lead to an increase in bias (Wegener et al., 2000). Perhaps famed defence attorney Jim Perruto summed it up best when he said that giving instructions to disregard evidence is like "putting a drop of ink into a jug of milk, shaking it, and then trying to take the ink back out again." Once the information is out there, the jury and the trial outcome have already been tainted.

A second element of the judge's instructions revolves around guidelines for the verdict. In a murder case, for example, a defendant can be found guilty of premeditated murder or manslaughter, acquitted, or found to have been defending himself or herself (that is, the murder was justified). Jurors must also understand statements such as "preponderance of evidence" and "beyond a reasonable doubt," which may have different meanings for legal professionals than for jurors (Kagehiro, 1990). Instructions can be quite complicated. Indeed, in order to avoid grounds for appeal, judges often read from legal texts that a typical juror will not necessarily understand. Even when they do this, the verdict can still be appealed—the decision in the first Robert William Pickton murder trial (the pig farmer who killed up to 49 women in and around Vancouver) was appealed because of arguments about the meaning of one of the judge's instructions.

Vicki Smith (1991) reports that, in the end, jurors might convict based on their own definitions of the crime rather than the instructions provided by the judge. To combat this problem, instructions to the jury should be written in clear, non-technical language (Halverson et al., 1997), and jurors should be allowed to take notes and review trial transcripts so they do not have to rely on their memories for details (Bourgeois et al., 1993).

LO 4

JURY DECISION MAKING

Jury Decision-Making Processes

Once a jury begins deliberating, how does it reach a verdict? Although it is legal in the United States, in Canada researchers are not allowed to question jurors about deliberations in specific cases. Jury decision-making research usually involves mock trials where every element of the deliberations can be observed. Typically, juries begin by having an initial vote. Although two-thirds of these juries will not agree on a verdict initially, eventually 95 percent will (Kalven & Zeisel, 1966). But how are these final verdicts achieved? Some intriguing work by James Davis, Norbert Kerr, and their colleagues (Davis et al., 1989; Kerr et al., 1976) tested a number of mathematical models to determine when juries would arrive at a verdict and when they would result in a hung jury. Although results varied depending specific circumstances, a "two-thirds rule" seemed to apply in most cases— if there was a two-thirds majority at the time of the initial vote, the final verdict was usually consistent with that initial vote. In addition, Kalven and Zeisel's work found that nine out of ten verdicts were consistent with the verdict of the majority in the initial vote.

A number of factors can affect the verdict, however. For example, when groups discuss an issue, individuals in the group can arrive at a more extreme position than they initially held—a process called *polarization* (e.g., Baron & Byrne, 1991). In the case of jury deliberations, this could mean a guilty verdict when some of the jurors initially might have been leaning toward acquittal. On the other hand, juries can sometimes show leniency biases (e.g., MacCoun & Kerr, 1988), whereby the jury may actually be more lenient once it has deliberated. As you might imagine, the outcomes of jury deliberations are not easy to predict.

Connection:

Remember our discussion of group polarization in Module 13.

Minority Influence

Many of you might remember the movie *12 Angry Men,* which tells the story of a man steadfastly arguing for the acquittal of the defendant (if you haven't seen it, you should—it's an excellent movie). In the film, a minority of one eventually convinces all 11 other members of the jury of the defendant's innocence. However, the work cited earlier suggests that such minorities rarely prevail. Nonetheless, minorities can be effective. As with any group, some individuals will contribute more than others. Research by Reid Hastie and his colleagues (1983) shows that if the minority is consistent, vocal, and persistent, then it will eventually prevail. This is also true in jury contexts. Indeed, many early group decision-making studies were conducted using juries as the group being examined.

Connection:

Remember we discussed the role of minority influence in Module 13.

CONCLUSIONS

The law and our legal system are constantly (if slowly) evolving. Thousands of people every year rely on our legal system to protect them as well as to punish people who violate the rights of others. However, social-psychological research tells us that we must remain vigilant about the impact of our very human biases and expectations on how people are treated within that system. Due process tells us that it is better for ten guilty people to go free than for one innocent person to be convicted. However, it should be clear from what we have presented in this module that there are many opportunities for innocent people to be falsely convicted. We must make sure that our legal system does its best to protect all those with whom it comes into contact. However, as John Turtle and his colleagues at Ryerson University have found, the legal system and the public can be resistant to the findings of research (e.g., Turtle & Want, 2008).

SUMMARY OF KEY POINTS

LO1. Understand the fallibility of eyewitness testimony.

- Eyewitnesses make mistakes.
- Mistakes can be caused by the context of the crime, or police procedures.
- Police procedures can also reduce errors.

LO2. Understand how psychology and police investigations intersect.

- Psychologists have long studied lie detection and have found that people cannot reliably determine if a person is lying.
- People sometimes confess to crimes they did not commit, and police interrogation tactics can increase or decrease that possibility.

LO3. Understand psychological influences on court judgments.

- Defendant characteristics and judges' instructions can influence trial outcomes.

LO4. Understand how psychology influences jury decision making.

- Group dynamics influence jury decisions making; vocal and consistent minorities can have a substantial influence on decisions.

KEY TERMS

Cognitive interview   An interview technique based in cognitive psychology, focusing on context reinstatement to enhance recall of events.

Confidence–accuracy correlation   The finding that the correlation between the confidence and accuracy of an eyewitness is weak to non-existent.

Sequential lineup   A lineup type where photos are presented individually.

Simultaneous lineup   A lineup type that presents photos together in one array.

Social Psychology and a Sustainable Future

LEARNING OBJECTIVES After studying Module 23, you will be able to

LO **1** Understand how to promote sustainability

LO **2** Understand materialism

LO **3** Understand the connection between economic growth and human morale

LO **4** Understand how we can move toward sustainability for ultimate survival

How much do you know about your impact on the environment? The media have been full of discussions about the validity of various claims. Read each question, and give your answer before you move on. You will know the answers to some questions, but probably not all of them.

- Is global warming real?
- If it is, would that be a bad thing?
- How do carbon emissions create a warmer planet?
- What effect will global warming have on Canada?
- Even if I want to change, how can I cut my greenhouse gas emissions?
- Would a hybrid vehicle be better than electric?
- Is ethanol a viable alternative fuel?
- What about wind power or solar power?

Critical THINKING

Think back to your childhood. To what extent has society's view of the world (and our impact on it) changed within your lifetime? What have you done (if anything) to be more environmentally friendly? Why is it that, despite the apparent threat to our climate and environment, many people are unwilling to change? Is it just economics (as many economic conservatives would have you think—going green will cost jobs) or is it something else?

From a broader perspective, environmental psychologists are interested in more than our impact on the world; they wonder how we perceive our impact and what creates changes in our perceptions and behaviour. They might ask the following question: What would a typical day be for you in your ideal world?

Perhaps the day starts with a nice hot shower, followed by a drive in the country in your Porsche convertible (or your SUV, or better yet a Porsche SUV). Would you spend the day surfing waves in California, or surfing the Internet in your Whistler home office before snowboarding down the hill in the afternoon? Many would be happy lounging in front of a 100-inch flat-panel HDTV watching movies on a surround-sound audio system. Life would be good. Indeed, compared to years past, life is good. Today, we enjoy luxuries unknown even to royalty in centuries past—hot showers, flush toilets, microwave ovens, jet travel, tablet computers with wireless Internet access, email, smartphones, and Post-it notes.

But there's a cost to this level of luxury. Perhaps no single individual has highlighted the problem of global warming more effectively than former U.S. vice president Al Gore, who won the 2007 Nobel Peace Prize (and an Academy Award) for his documentary *An Inconvenient Truth*. Although the movie generated significant controversy (some say he overstated certain claims), the film brought the

The Porsche Cayenne is some people's dream car, but it is not very fuel-efficient.

danger of global warming into sharp relief for many who had never thought much about it before. In 2014, the Intergovernmental Panel on Climate Change released a report warning of the dire consequences coming due to climate change: rising sea levels, extreme weather, economic hardships, reduced crop yields, and the forced migration of people from low-lying areas.

In 1950, Earth carried 2.5 billion people and 50 million cars. As of March 2014, it has more than 7.2 billion people and over 1 billion cars. The planet is on track to have over 9 billion people by 2050 (*National Geographic*, 2011). If world economic growth enabled all countries to match North Americans' present car ownership, the number of cars would multiply yet another 13 times (N. Myers, 2000). These cars, along with the burning of coal and oil to generate electricity and heat homes, produce greenhouse gases that contribute to global warming (Hileman, 1999).

The average world temperature has been above the global average (set from 134 years of measurement) for the last 37 years in row. The year 2010 was the hottest year ever, and 2013 tied as the fourth hottest ever. Greenland's ice sheets are melting at an accelerating rate, and ski resorts in St. Moritz (the site of two Winter Olympic Games) are going so far as to place reflective blankets on the icecaps to slow down their rate of melting (*National Geographic*, 2006; Jenkins, 2010). In Sochi, the site of the 2014 Winter Olympic Games, the air temperature was hotter than in 10 of the last 12 *summer* Olympics (CBC, 2014).

Equatorial insects and vegetation are migrating toward the poles. The Canadian Wildlife Service has found that the polar bear population around Hudson Bay is down 22 percent in the last 20 years—they are drowning due to long swims between ice floes (CBC, 2012). With the changing climate, extreme atmospheric events—including heat waves, droughts, and floods—are becoming more common. As precipitation falls more as rain and less as snow, the likely result will be more floods in rainy seasons and less melting snow and glaciers for rivers during dry seasons.

With world economic growth and population both destined to increase (even as birth rates fall), resource depletion and further global warming now seem inevitable. Indeed, in scientific gatherings sponsored by the United Nations, Britain's Royal Society, and the U.S. National Academy of Science, a consensus has emerged: Increasing population and increasing consumption have combined to overshoot Earth's carrying capacity (see Figure 23-1). Therefore, the need for more sustainable consumption has taken on "urgency and global significance" (Heap & Kent, 2000). In the summer of 2008, world gas prices hit record highs, with crude oil selling for over $140 per barrel and a litre of gas reaching $1.40. Although these prices subsequently dropped, in the winter of 2014, they reached those heights yet again.

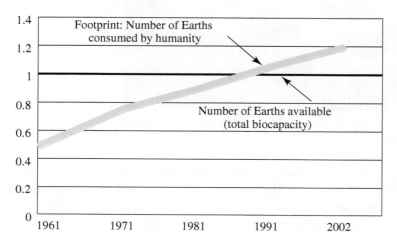

Total Ecological Footprint (number of Earths)

FIGURE 23-1

The ecological overshoot: The human demand for things such as timber, fish, and fuel is increasingly exceeding Earth's regenerative capacity.

Source: Data from footprintnetwork.org (2006).

Canadians do seem to care about environmental issues, rating the environment as the most important campaign issue in the 2004 federal election, and the second most important in the 2006 and 2008 federal elections. However, it took until the 2011 election for the Green Party's leader, Elizabeth May, to win the party's first seat in Parliament. Yet, winning a seat does not mean that the Green Party of Canada will be able to make environmental issues a priority in Parliament. Is it, as Gallup researcher Lydia Saad (2003) believes, because on a chilly winter day "global warming may sound, well, appealing"? Might people be more concerned about averting "global heating"? Language shapes thought.

Resource depletion will also affect the human future. Most of the world's original forest cover has been taken down, and what remains in the tropics is being cleared for agriculture, livestock grazing, logging, and settlements. With deforestation comes diminished absorption of greenhouse gases and sometimes flooding, soil erosion, changing rainfall and temperature, and the decimation of many animal species.

A growing population's appetite for fish, together with ecosystem destruction, has also led to decreasing annual catches in 11 of 15 major oceanic fishing areas and of 7 in 10 major fish species (Karavellas, 2000; McGinn, 1998). Due in part to overfishing, stocks of wild salmon, Atlantic cod, haddock, herring, and other species have suffered major depletion that has resulted in fishing bans off Canada's east coast (unfortunately, however, these bans do not apply to foreign ships in international waters).

LO 1

PROMOTING SUSTAINABILITY

So, what shall we do? Pursue self-interest to our collective detriment, as have so many participants in prisoners' dilemma games? ("Heck, on a global scale, my consumption is infinitesimal; it provides me pleasure at but a nominal cost to the world.") Those more optimistic about the future see two routes to sustainable lifestyles: (a) increasing technological efficiency and agricultural productivity, and (b) moderating consumption and decreasing population.

Connection:

Remember our discussion of the prisoner's dilemma in Module 17.

Increasing Efficiency and Productivity

One route to a sustainable future is through improving eco-technologies. In 2011, new refrigerators consume half the energy of those sold in the 1990s (Heap & Comim, 2005). Cars and cell phones are being made from recyclable materials. Already, we have replaced many incandescent bulbs with compact fluorescent bulbs, replaced printed and delivered letters and catalogues with email and ecommerce, and developed hybrid and electric cars. Indeed, it seems with today's high gas prices, hybrids and even electric cars are becoming the automotive status symbol rather than the sports car or SUV. Today's middle-aged adults drive cars that get twice the mileage and produce a twentieth the pollution of their first cars.

The Nissan Leaf is a 100 percent electric vehicle.

Activity: **How satisfied are you?**

Following are five statements that you may agree or disagree with. Using the 1–7 scale, indicate your agreement with each item by placing the appropriate number on the line preceding that item. Please be open and honest in your responses. However, before you respond, first estimate how much you make per year: $ _____.

1	2	3	4	5	6	7
Strongly Disagree	Disagree	Slightly Disagree	Neither Agree Nor Disagree	Slightly Agree	Agree	Strongly Agree

_____   In most ways, my life is close to my ideal.

_____   The conditions of my life are excellent.

_____   I am satisfied with my life.

_____   So far I have gotten the important things I want in life.

_____   If I could live my life over, I would change almost nothing.

The above is a brief, but well-researched "satisfaction with life" scale. To score the scale, simply sum the responses. How satisfied are you? The following markers may be helpful:

31–35	Extremely satisfied		15–19	Slightly dissatisfied
26–30	Satisfied		10–14	Dissatisfied
21–25	Slightly satisfied		5–9	Extremely dissatisfied
20	Neutral			

How do you score? What do you think this says about you? How do you think this affects your behaviour? Does being happy make you want less? Does being unhappy make you want more things? If you are satisfied, what is making you happy? If not, what would you need to be happier?

Plausible future technologies include diodes that emit light for 20 years without bulbs; ultrasound washing machines that consume no water, heat, or soap; reusable and compostable plastics; cars running on fuel cells that combine hydrogen and oxygen and produce water exhaust; extra-light materials stronger than steel; roofs and roads that double as solar energy collectors; and heated and cooled chairs that provide personal comfort control (N. Myers, 2000; Zhang et al., 2007).

Given the speed of innovation—who could have imagined today's world a century ago?—the future will surely bring solutions that we aren't yet imagining. Surely, say the optimists, the future will bring increased material well-being for more people requiring many fewer raw materials and much less polluting waste.

Reducing Consumption

The second route to a sustainable future is through reduced consumption. For example, although it accounts for only 5 percent of the world's population, the United States is responsible for 25 percent of consumption (USGS, 2006). Instead of more people consuming and polluting more, a stable population will need to consume and pollute less.

Due to family-planning efforts, the world's population growth rate has decelerated, especially in developed nations. Where food security has improved and women have become educated and empowered, birthrates have fallen. But even if birthrates everywhere instantly fell to replacement levels, the lingering momentum of population growth, fed by the bulge of younger humans, would continue for years to come.

Given that we have already overshot Earth's carrying capacity, individual consumption must also moderate. With our material appetites continually swelling—as people seek smaller and longer-playing MP3 players, are less tolerant of discomfort (e.g., with regard to cooling and heating), and want more (cheap) holiday travel—what can be done to moderate consumption?

One way is through public policies that harness the motivating power of incentives. As a general rule, what we tax we get less of, what we reward we get more of. If our highways are jammed and our air polluted, we can create fast lanes that reward carpooling and penalize driving solo. We can build bike lanes and subsidize mass transportation, thus encouraging alternatives to cars. We can shift taxes to gas, and reward recycling with a refundable deposit on soda cans and bottles. Gregg Easterbrook (2004) notes that if the United States had raised gas taxes by 50 cents 10 years ago, this would have resulted in smaller more fuel-efficient cars (as it has in Europe). Another strategy is to go the route the United Kingdom is taking, and installing "smart meters" that give immediate feedback on energy used and the associated cost (Rosenthal, 2008; Vollink & Meertens, 2010).

As the atmosphere warms, and oil and other resources become scarce, such a shift may be inevitable. Indeed, there are also some natural consumption controls. For example, with gas prices rising, sales of full-size SUVs (such as Ford Explorers) and trucks (such as GMC Sierras and Ford F-150s) fell over 35 percent in the first half of 2008 (CBC, 2008) and have stayed low since. Smaller SUVs are becoming more popular, however, especially as more hybrid models make it to showrooms.

Is there any hope that, before the crisis becomes acute, human priorities might shift from accumulating money to finding meaning, and from aggressive consumption to nurturing connections? Perhaps social psychology can help, by exposing our *materialism*, by informing people of the disconnect between *economic growth* and *human morale*, and by helping people understand *why materialism and money typically fail to satisfy*.

Applying Social Psychology

Who is happy? We study human happiness from different perspectives, ranging from the basic sciences up to integrative disciplines such as philosophy and religion. These various perspectives need not be conflicting. In fact, they can be complementary. What perspective is relevant depends on your primary interests.

For example, love can be described in multiple ways. A physiologist might portray love as a state of arousal. A psychologist might examine how the experience of love is influenced by such factors as belief similarity or physical attractiveness. A poet might extol the sublime experience that love can be. A theologian might describe love as the God-given goal of all human relationships. In short, successful explanations of human functioning at one level need not invalidate explanations at others.

So what does this tell us about happiness? Are you happy? What would make you happier? Would your answers have been different before you read this module?

LO 2

MATERIALISM

Does money buy happiness? No? Ah, but would a *little* more money make us a *little* happier? Many of us smirk and nod. There is, we believe, *some* connection between fiscal fitness and feeling fantastic. Indeed, the 2003 General Social Survey found that Canadians' happiness is to some extent related to their income; see Table 23-1 (Statistics Canada, 2004). But a careful look at the data shows that the vast majority of people rate themselves as "very" or "somewhat" happy, and the only meaningful shift in that percentage takes place at around $20 000 per year. After that, there is no real difference in happiness levels.

TABLE 23-1 Annual Income and Ratings of Happiness in Canada

Annual Income	Very or Somewhat Happy
<$20 000/year	89.5%
$20–40 000/year	94.8%
$40–60 000/year	96.4%
$60–80 000/year	97.6%
$80 000/year +	97.8%

Source: Adapted from Statistics Canada 2003 General Social Survey.

By 2005, three in four American students entering college—nearly double the 1970 proportion—considered it "very important" or "essential" that they become "very well-off financially" (see Figure 23-2). It's not just collegians. Money matters. "Whoever said money can't buy happiness isn't spending it right," proclaimed a Lexus ad.

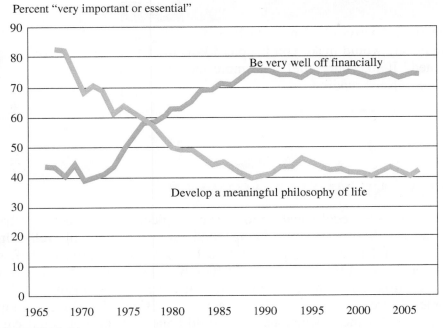

Percent "very important or essential"

FIGURE 23-2

Changing materialism, from annual surveys of more than 200 000 U.S. students entering college (total sample nearly 13 million students).

Source: Data from Dey, Astin, & Korn, 1991, and subsequent annual reports.

Jonathan Gardner and Andrew Oswald at the University of Warwick (2006) in the U.K. have found that Britons who win moderate lottery prizes ($2000–$240 000) were happier two years later. However, some research by Wendy Johnson and Robert Krueger (2006) at the University of Minnesota suggests that the money itself is not as important as people's perceptions of it. These researchers argue that the effect money has on happiness is accounted for by people's perceptions of their own wealth. In addition, winning money (or having more money) gives people a sense of control over their lives, which further increases happiness.

Ironically, however, those who most ardently seek money tend to live with lower well-being, a finding that "comes through very strongly in every culture I've looked at," reports research psychologist Richard Ryan (1999). Ryan's colleague, Tim Kasser (2000), concludes from their studies that people who instead seek "intimacy, personal growth, and contribution to the community" experience greater quality of life. People tend to value experiences with others over material possessions (Caprariello & Reis, 2013).

What's been the most satisfying event for you in the past month? When Ken Sheldon and his colleagues (2001) put such questions to university students, and also asked them to rate how much ten different needs were met by the satisfying event, the students were most likely to report that the event met their needs for self-esteem, relatedness to others, and autonomy. At the bottom of the list of satisfaction predictors were money and luxury.

Critical THINKING

So, have you done the scale in the activity? If not, do it now. Are you satisfied with life? What did you say would make you happier? Was money one of the things you mentioned? If so, your belief (that more money will make you happy) may not pan out. Keep reading.

LO 3

ECONOMIC GROWTH AND HUMAN MORALE

Materialism—lusting for more—exacts ecological and psychological costs. But perhaps unsustainable consumption is bad for the planet while being good for one's sense of well-being. Would people be happier if they could trade a simple lifestyle for one with a private chef, ski vacations, and travel on private jets? Would they be happier if they won the 6/49 lottery and could indulge in any luxury they chose? Roy Chua and Xi Zou (2009) at the Harvard Business School found that simply showing people pictures of luxury goods (such as watches and shoes) made people make more selfish choices, endorsing business decisions that would benefit them, but could cause harm to others. Luxury is a personal benefit, but can come at a collective cost.

We can observe the traffic between wealth and well-being by first asking if rich nations have more satisfied people. There is, indeed, some correlation between national wealth and well-being (indexed as self-reported happiness and life satisfaction). The Scandinavians have been mostly prosperous and satisfied; the Bulgarians are neither. But, similar to the Canadian data we discussed, early 1990s data revealed that once nations reached about $10 000 GNP per person, higher levels of national wealth were not predictive of increased well-being (see Figure 23-3; Inglehart, 2009).

Financial windfalls and increases in income temporarily boost happiness, and recessions create short-term psychological losses (Di Tella, MacCulloch & Oswald, 2001; Gardner & Oswald, 2006). But over time the emotions wane. Once comfortable, more and more money produces diminishing long-term returns. World values researcher Ronald Inglehart (1990, p. 242) therefore found the income-happiness correlation to be "surprisingly weak."

Next we can ask whether, over time, a culture's happiness rises with its affluence. Since 1960, we have seen the proportion of households with dishwashers rise from 7 to 50 percent, those with clothes dryers from 20 to 71 percent, and those with air conditioning from 15 to 73 percent. Ninety-nine percent of homes have at least one phone line. However, in 2004, 21 percent of Canadian homes had two phone lines, and an additional 28 percent had three phones or more. In 2014, 85 percent of Canadian households had Internet access. In 1987 there were 100 000 cell phones in use in Canada. Today, there are more than 26.5 million cell phones being used (by about 34.5 million Canadians; CWTA, 2014).

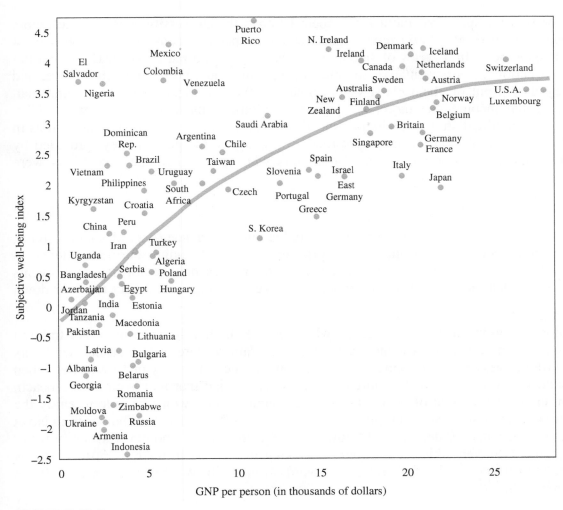

FIGURE 23-3

National Wealth and Well-Being, from 1995 World Bank data and the 2000 World Values Survey. Subjective well-being index combines happiness and life satisfaction (the average percentage of people rating themselves as (a) "very happy" or "happy" minus "unhappy," and (b) 7 or above on a 10-point scale minus percentage rating 4 or below).

Source: Reprinted by permission of Rafael M. Di Tella.

So, are the rich happier? Probably not. Economic growth has provided no boost to human morale.

Why Materialism and Money Fail to Satisfy

It is striking that economic growth in affluent countries has failed to satisfy. People who identify themselves with expensive possessions experience fewer positive moods, report Emily Solberg, Ed Diener, and Michael Robinson (2003). Such materialists tend to report a relatively large gap between what they want and what they have, and to enjoy fewer close, fulfilling relationships. The challenge for healthy nations, then, is to foster improving standards of living without encouraging a materialism and consumerism that displaces the deep need to belong. So, why have we not become happier?

One reason may be how we spend our money. Elizabeth Dunn at the University of British Columbia and her colleagues (Dunn et al., 2008) have argued that *how* people spent their money is most important to their happiness. In a series of studies published in the journal *Science*, Dunn and her colleagues asked a nationally representative sample of 632 Americans how happy they were, and how much money they spent on themselves versus others (gifts and donations). They found that, controlling for personal income, the more people spent on others, the happier they were. They replicated this in a longitudinal study on windfall spending (e.g., an unexpected bonus) as well as in an experimental study in a lab. Participants were randomly assigned to spend money (provided by the researchers) on themselves or on others. Participants who spent the money on others were significantly happier.

Our Human Capacity for Adaptation

The adaptation-level phenomenon is our tendency to judge our experience (e.g., of sounds, lights, or income) relative to a neutral level defined by our prior experience. We adjust our neutral levels—the points at which sounds seem neither loud nor soft, temperatures neither hot nor cold, events neither pleasant nor unpleasant—based on our experience. We then notice and react to up or down changes from these levels.

One of your authors experienced this phenomenon when he took his family on a trip to Australia in 2003. It was May, entering Australia's winter. Steven and his family were in Newcastle, two hours north of Sydney, where Steven was working with a colleague at the University of Newcastle. When the colleague asked where his wife and children were, Steven replied that they were at the beach. "It's too bad you came at this time of year," said his colleague. "They won't be able to enjoy the beach—the water is far too cold!" Steven replied, "But the water is 23 degrees!" (The ocean in Nova Scotia rarely gets warmer than 19 degrees.) "I know!" said the colleague (who never swam in water colder than 25 degrees). Steven's kids spent hours frolicking in the surf in their swimsuits, metres away from Australian surfers wearing full wetsuits to ward off the chill. What you are used to affects what you are happy with.

However, as our achievements rise above past levels we feel successful and satisfied. As our social prestige, income, or in-home technology surges, we feel pleasure. Before long, however, we adapt. What once felt good comes to register as neutral, and what formerly was neutral now feels like deprivation. As the good feelings wane, it takes a higher high to rejuice the joy.

So, could we ever create a social paradise? To be sure, adaptation to some events, such as the death of a spouse, may be incomplete, as the sense of loss lingers (Diener et al., 2006). But what if we work in a perfect world? Would that make us happy for the rest of our lives? Donald Campbell (1975) did not think so: If you woke up tomorrow to your utopia—perhaps a world with no bills, no ills, someone who loves you unreservedly—you would feel euphoric, for a time. Yet, before long, you would recalibrate your adaptation level and again sometimes feel gratified (when achievements surpass expectations), sometimes feel deprived (when they fall below), and sometimes feel neutral.

We also sometimes "miswant." When first-year university students predicted their satisfaction with various housing possibilities shortly before entering their school's housing lottery, they focused on physical features. "I'll be happiest in a beautiful and well-located residence," many students seemed to think. But they were wrong. When contacted a year later, it was the social features, such as a sense of community that predicted happiness, report Elizabeth Dunn and her colleagues (2003).

When focused on the short term and forgetting how quickly we adapt, we may think that the material features of our world predispose our happiness. Actually, report Leaf Van Boven and Thomas Gilovich (2003) from their surveys and experiments, positive *experiences* (often social experiences) leave us happier. The best things in life are not things.

Our Desire to Compare

Much of life revolves around social comparison. We are always comparing ourselves with others. As we learned when we discussed relative deprivation in earlier modules, this can have important impacts on our satisfaction. Our happiness is relative to our comparisons with others, especially with others within our own groups (Lyubomirsky, 2001; Zagefka & Brown, 2006). And whether we feel good or bad depends on who those others are. We are slow-witted or clumsy only when others are smart or agile. Let one baseball player sign a new contract for $15 million a year and his $8-million-per-year teammate may now feel less satisfied. "Our poverty became a reality. Not because of our having less, but by our neighbours having more," recalled Will Campbell in *Brother to a Dragonfly*.

Social comparisons help us understand the modest income–happiness correlation. Middle- and upper-income people in a given country, who can compare themselves with the relatively poor, tend to be slightly more satisfied with life than their less-fortunate compatriots. Nevertheless, once people reach a moderate income level, further increases do little to increase their happiness. Why? Because we tend to compare upward as we climb the ladder of success or income (Gruder, 1977; Suls & Tesch, 1978). Thus, "Napoleon envied Caesar, Caesar envied Alexander, and Alexander, I daresay, envied Hercules, who never existed. You cannot, therefore, get away from envy by means of success alone, for there will always be in history or legend some person even more successful than you are," noted Bertrand Russell (1930, pp. 68–69).

Rising income inequality, notes Michael Hagerty (2000), makes for more people markedly above us in our communities. And that helps explain why those living in communities with a large rich–poor gap tend to feel less satisfied. If you live in a 2000-square-foot house in a community filled with other 2000-square-foot houses, you likely are happier than if living in the same house amid 4000-square-foot homes. Television modelling of the lifestyles of the wealthy also serves to accentuate feelings of "relative deprivation" and desires for more (Schor, 1998).

The adaptation-level and social comparison phenomena give us pause. They imply that the quest for happiness through material achievement requires continually expanding affluence. But there's also good news: adaptation to simpler lives can also happen. If choice or necessity shrinks our consumption, we will initially feel pain, but it will pass. Indeed, thanks to our capacity to adapt and to adjust comparisons, the emotional impact of significant life events—losing a job, or even a disabling accident—dissipates sooner than most people suppose (Gilbert et al., 1998).

LO 4

TOWARD SUSTAINABILITY AND SURVIVAL

You will have noticed by now that many of our behaviours relating to the environment and sustainability have their roots in social psychological phenomena, and can be explained by social psychological theory (e.g., happiness, social comparison, relative deprivation, adaptation-level phenomena). Thus, social psychological principles can be used to understand the underlying cognitive and social processes related to our behaviours.

But how can social psychology have a positive influence when it comes to sustainability issues? How do we change current unsustainable attitudes and behaviours? We have already touched on this (e.g., increasing costs or taxes to change purchasing behaviour), but there are also more direct persuasion-based approaches that can be used. More intriguingly, how do we change people's perspectives about the environment and sustainability issues?

Changing People's Attitudes and Behaviour

Fundamentally, attitudes toward the environment, recycling, and sustainable behaviour are the same as any other attitude, and they can be changed using the same principles we have discussed previously.

Connection:

Remember that we have discussed persuasion principles in Modules 8 and 10.

Source characteristics (e.g., using experts like David Suzuki), message characteristics (making the message as clear as possible and the arguments as compelling as possible), and encouraging elaboration will result in attitude change. However, these are not the only routes.

In recent years, Robert Cialdini and his colleagues have conducted a number of studies trying to encourage people to engage in more environmentally friendly and sustainable behaviours (e.g., Bator & Cialdini, 2000; Goldstein et al., 2008) by focusing on the activation of social norms. We frequently look to others when making decisions about our behaviours. Descriptive norms describe what others in our social group are doing. For example, companies often try to sell a product by telling you it is the "best-selling product in its class." Injunctive norms tell you what you should do from a moral perspective (e.g., "don't be a litterbug" implies that littering is the "wrong" thing to do). Cialdini and his colleagues have argued that we rely on these social norms to make our decisions.

Connection:

Remember in Modules 8 and 18 that we discussed how we look to others when we make decisions about our behaviour.

If you have stayed in a hotel recently, you will certainly be aware of the signs you find in the bathroom and on the bed. These signs, designed to reduce the amount of laundry done by hotels (and consequently reduce water and electricity usage, and the release of soap into the environment), are now common in almost every hotel. The messages are clear—be ecologically friendly, reuse your towels and sheets. Cialdini, a frequent traveller, had seen these appeals in many hotels and convinced one hotel chain to test their effectiveness. The chain tested the hotel's standard message against descriptive and injunctive norms. They found that hotel guests who received the normative-based messages were 28 percent more likely to reuse their towels than people exposed to a standard message (Goldstein et al., 2008).

Interestingly, people may not be aware of how norms affect their behaviour. In a clever study of conservation behaviour in California, Cialdini and his colleagues (Goldstein et al., 2008) found that, although descriptive norms were the best predictors of people's environmental behaviours, people rated these as the least important element in their decisions. So, how do we use this to change behaviour? Rather than highlight the wasteful and unsustainable behaviours people are engaging in, focus on the positive things others are doing: "More people are buying smaller, fuel-efficient cars than ever!" will be a better argument than "Don't waste gas." Once enough people are engaging in pro-environmental and sustainable behaviours, we will reach what Malcolm Gladwell (2002) calls the "tipping point," where the social influence created by attention to and perceptions of people's behaviours will increasingly cause others to engage in the same behaviour. When the social trend moves to pro-environmental behaviours, more and more people will behave in pro-environmental ways. Changing perspectives on social norms are a large part of this process.

CONCLUSIONS

"If the world is to change for the better it must have a change in human consciousness," said Czech poet-president Vaclav Havel (1990).

Connection:

Remember our discussion of social dilemmas in Module 17.

Social psychology's contribution to a sustainable and survivable future will come partly through its consciousness-transforming insights into adaptation and comparison. Social psychology can also contribute through processes developed to solve social dilemmas. Legislating change, reducing competition, promoting cooperation, and communicating are all key factors that are necessary to resolve these issues.

One ingredient of well-being is the satisfaction of our deep need to belong. As social creatures, we are deeply motivated not only to eat, to procreate, and to achieve, but also to bond with important others. The 1998 General Social Survey (Statistics Canada, 1999) found that people who spent a lot of time by themselves were less likely to be happy. Positive traits—self-esteem, internal locus of control, optimism, extraversion—also mark happy times and lives (Myers, 2000b). Most of us are happier talking to friends than watching TV. Low-consumption recreations prove most satisfying. And that is indeed good news. The things that make for a genuinely good life—close, supportive relationships, a hope-filled faith community, positive traits, engaging activity—are enduringly sustainable.

SUMMARY OF KEY POINTS

LO1. Understand how to promote sustainability.

- Increasing efficiency and productivity while reducing consumption are key to promoting sustainability.

LO2. Understand materialism.

- Despite what people may believe, having more money (after a point) does not increase happiness.

LO3. Understand the connection between economic growth and human morale.

- People tend to adapt to the situation they are in, and tend to look to those who are better off as comparison points.

LO4. Understand how we can move toward sustainability for ultimate survival.

- Changing attitudes and behaviours is necessary, and the use of collective norms may be a valuable tool in persuasive appeals.

KEY TERMS

Adaptation-level phenomenon   The tendency to adapt to a given level of stimulation and thus to notice and react to changes from that level.

Descriptive norms   Norms that relate to the behaviours other people in your social group engage in.

Injunctive norms   Norms that relate to the behaviours you should engage in from a moral perspective.

MODULE TWENTY-FOUR

Social Psychology and Health

If you are a typical college or university student, there are times when you feel stressed. Indeed, the average post-secondary student in Canada has a higher overall stress level than the typical Canadian (Adlaf et al., 2001). But you are not alone! Stress (particularly work-related stress) is a pervasive element in our society. Perhaps it would not surprise you to learn that stress and health are related. Indeed, you may remember when feeling stressed out has left you feeling hopeless and even depressed. For some people, depression can be debilitating and may lead to medication and hospitalization. How do we deal with the stressors in our lives, and how can social psychology help us understand these processes?

Social psychology has begun to play an increasingly important role in the domain of personal health. To be fair, medical doctors have known for hundreds of years that the experiences of our everyday lives have an impact on our health. There are many areas where social psychology and health intersect. For example, industrial/organizational psychologists are interested in how the stressors we encounter in our everyday lives lead to stress and subsequent health outcomes.

Experiencing stress can lead to serious consequences, including negative health outcomes.

Clinical psychologists are interested in the causes and consequences of depression. Health professionals are interested in understanding how social-psychological principles can be applied to help us understand when we are ill, why the ill are sometimes stigmatized, and how to help people recover when illness strikes. Finally, persuasion researchers are interested in understanding how we can convince people to engage in healthier behaviours, like quitting smoking, getting regular breast screenings, or engaging in strenuous exercise.

In this module we will touch on all of these issues and delve into the field of health psychology, whose practitioners aim to incorporate the findings of psychological research to improve the lives and health of individuals. Although this chapter cannot cover all the many topics covered by health psychologists, we will address some topics that have received the most attention.

Critical THINKING

These labels have been developed by Health Canada to discourage smoking. Have they worked? Can social-psychological principles be used to change behaviour? How would you do it?

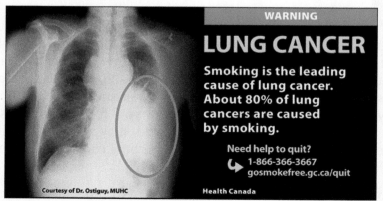

This is one of several warnings that can be found on Canadian cigarette packages.

LO 1

STRESS AND HEALTH

What is stress? Hans Selye (1976) at the Université de Montréal defined stress as the body's physiological response to events we perceive as threatening. Stressors are those factors that can potentially evoke a stress response in individuals. The key mediating factor (that is, the factor that determines whether a potential stressor causes stress) is one's ability to cope with the situation.

Individual Reactions to Stressors

Complete the scale in the activity that follows. The list is from Holmes and Rahe's (1967) Social Readjustment Rating Scale. Holmes and Rahe argue that the degree of stress we experience will depend on the extent to which we have to readjust our lives in response to external events. They assigned "life change units" to the events listed in the activity. The more change in your life the event causes, the more life change units you accumulate. Thus, the more areas of your life that are affected by the change, the more stressors (and subsequent stress) you will experience. Consistent with this reasoning, several studies (e.g., Seta et al., 1991; Tesser & Beach, 1998) have shown that higher scores on the Social Readjustment Rating Scale are related to increased rates of physical and mental illness. Other researchers (e.g., Morse et al., 1991) have shown that when people experience major change in their lives, their chance of dying increases. Thus the stress–illness relationship seems clear.

Activity: **Life stress**

Do you feel stressed? Thomas Holmes and Richard Rahe (1967) developed a checklist to assess how much stress a person is currently experiencing. Check the boxes that apply to you (things that have happened in the last year or so). When done, add up the values to get your score.

Life Events	Life Crisis Units	
Death of partner	100	❏
Martial separation	65	❏
Jail term	63	❏
Death of close family member	63	❏
Personal injury or illness	53	❏
Marriage	50	❏
Job loss	47	❏
Change in health of a family member	44	❏
Pregnancy	40	❏
Change in financial state	38	❏

(Continued)

Death of close friend	37	❏
Change in career	36	❏
Change in responsibilities at work	29	❏
Outstanding personal achievement	28	❏
Begin or end school	26	❏
Change in living conditions	25	❏
Trouble with boss	23	❏
Change in residence	20	❏
Change in sleeping habits	16	❏
Change in eating habits	15	❏
Vacation	13	❏
Important holidays alone	12	❏
Minor violations of the law	11	❏

So, are you stressed? Scores over 100 suggest you may be experiencing a somewhat elevated level of stress. But what impact does this have on your everyday life? Your health? Your relationships? Keep reading to find out. You will see that the stress you experience can have a potentially serious negative impact on your health (not to stress you out or anything . . .).

Importantly, you will notice from the examples provided in the scale that many of these events are happy ones. Getting a new job can be very exciting and rewarding, but it can mean a change in work schedule, a new home, and a complete disruption to your routine. Graduating from high school or university can also bring with it a number of stressors. Starting at a new school is equally disruptive (as many of you may be experiencing right now). However, we do adjust. Despite the fact that university students are more stressed than the general public, perceived stress reduces each year you spend at university (Adlaf et al., 2001).

Do stressful situations always lead to stress? As with many questions we have asked in this book, the answer is: it depends. How we deal with these stressors depends on a number of factors, both internal and external to ourselves. Essentially, our response will depend on how well we are able to cope with the situation.

Coping is an individual trait and how we deal with the stressors we are experience is called our coping style. As Lazarus (1966, 2000) has pointed out in his voluminous work on stress and reactions to stressful events, it is not just the stressor that matters; it is the reaction to that stressor. Two common coping styles are *problem-focused* coping, and *emotion-focused* coping. Problem-focused coping typically refers to situations where an individual identifies the problem and then works to overcome it. Emotion-focused coping refers to an approach where people try to make themselves "feel better" about the problem, either through social support or distraction.

Two people can experience the same event and have vastly different reactions. For example, you almost certainly have friends who react differently to midterm grades. You probably can think of one friend who would be happy with a "C" on the next social psychology midterm, and another who will only be happy with an "A." Imagine that the grades come back after the next midterm and both of your friends get a "B." The external stressor (a "B" in a midterm) is the same, yet the reactions of your two friends will differ. One will be ecstatically happy, the other will be distraught.

Now, let's consider the coping approach that the distraught friend might take. If she took a problem-focused approach, she might study more, work harder, or find other ways to improve her grades. However, in a more emotion-focused coping style, she might go out drinking with friends to forget her problems.

The context we are in can also play a role. Researchers in the United Kingdom (e.g., Haslam et al., 2009) report that people who have close ties to social groups, where those groups provide a sense of belonging or meaning, have more positive psychological outcomes, which can lead to better health outcomes. In addition, researchers at Sherbrooke University (Lefrançois et al., 2000; Couture et al., 2005) have demonstrated that social support cannot always be a buffer to stress experienced by the elderly (in this case, 81- to 86-year-olds). Negative social interactions and social isolation eliminate the buffering effect of social support.

Gender Differences in Coping

You may have heard of the fight-or-flight response before. Walter Cannon (1932) coined this expression to explain our response to a threat. We either attack (fight) or we run (flight). When we encounter a threat we get a sudden release of hormones that energize us (you will have experienced this if anyone has ever snuck up behind you to frighten you). Once energized, we have one of two alternatives—attack the threat or flee the situation. We respond to stressors in much the same way. People encountering a difficult work situation will release the same stress hormone as someone confronted with an angry and dangerous animal.

Shelley Taylor and her colleagues (2000) point out, however, that most of this research has been done on males, and typically the subjects have been male rats. Could human females respond differently than male rats? Taylor argues that they do. Specifically, she and her colleagues suggest that the fight-or-flight response pattern does not do a good job of explaining the behaviour of females, nor is it necessarily a good set of options for a gender that typically has all of the child-bearing and more of the child-rearing duties (this is true both in human and animal societies).

Taylor and her colleagues propose that females have developed a strategy to respond to stress by engaging in nurturing activities designed to be protective of themselves and their offspring, as well as developing social networks than can provide a protective barrier when the group is threatened. They labelled this the *tend-and-befriend* approach.

This effect may also have a biological basis. When women are under stress they are more likely to show increased oxytocin levels, a hormone that has calming properties and increases the likelihood of affiliation with others (e.g., see Taylor et al., 2000). Interestingly, in the context of romantic relationships, there is evidence that women are more likely than men to drink alcohol in response to relationship problems, perhaps reflecting a more emotion-focused coping style (Levitt & Cooper, 2010). However, it is worth noting that while the gender differences observed are significant, they are relatively small. In addition, the availability of social support is an important factor in stress management for both men and women.

When we encounter stressors, we naturally have a fight-or-flight response.

The Nature of the Stress–Illness Relationship

So far, all of the studies we have discussed concerning the stress–illness relationship are correlational in nature. For example, Stewart McCann at Cape Breton University (2001) looked at age of death across 23 samples of successful and powerful people across over a thousand years (over 1000 total people), His sample included prime ministers, presidents, Nobel Prize and Oscar winners, and many others. Overall, earlier peaks in career success led to shorter lives.

Could it be that it is not the stressors themselves that cause illness, but our reaction to them? Watson and Pennebaker (1989) have argued that personality traits are of vital importance in how we experience and deal with stressors. People who are more likely to experience negative moods also report more health problems. Could negative moods be the cause of illness, rather than the stressors themselves?

Our reaction to stressors can influence our susceptibility to illness.

In order to assess this, Cohen and colleagues (1991, 1993) devised a highly controlled study. They started by asking people to report information about their everyday life stressors and the major events that had occurred in their lives recently. They also assessed a variety of other factors that could lead to illness—age, gender, weight, and a variety of other factors. Next, the researchers exposed the participants to the common cold virus. On average, 20 to 60 percent of people exposed to the common cold virus become ill. Participants who had reported the least amount of negative stress were least likely to become ill (about 27 percent) whereas those who reported the highest stress were significantly more likely to become ill (50 percent). Consistent with this effect, John Cacioppo and his colleagues (e.g., Cacioppo et al., 1998) have shown that exposure to even minor stressors (such as solving math problems) can directly affect immune system function.

But this immune system response is not limited to contracting the common cold. When we experience negative events (and negative emotions), we respond by producing a stress hormone. This can then lead to all kinds of negative health outcomes (see Figure 24-1). For example, studies have shown that experiencing stress can lead to the development of plaque on the walls of the heart's arteries (e.g., see Smith & Ruiz 2002; Williams, 1993).

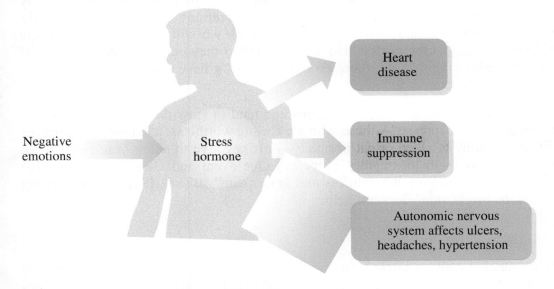

FIGURE 24-1

Stress-caused negative emotion may have various effects on health. This is especially true for depressed or anger-prone people.

In recent work, Jacob Vigil and his colleagues (Vigil et al., 2009; Vigil, Geary, Granger & Flinn, 2010) have found that following natural disasters (like Hurricane Katrina, which hit New Orleans in 2005) people, and particularly mothers, show lowered levels of salivary cortisol, and report higher rates of depressive symptoms, distress, and anxiety, as well as lower self-esteem.

Thus, it seems clear that the stressor–stress–illness relationship is causal, but affected by our interpretation of stressful events. For example, people who are anger-prone or highly competitive (i.e., "Type A" personalities) are most susceptible to this type of stress response (Smith & Ruiz, 2002; Williams, 1993).

LO 2

UNDERSTANDING DEPRESSION

The Public Health Agency of Canada (2002) reports that about 20 percent of Canadians will experience a mental illness in their lifetime. For half of those it will be a major depression. Women are almost twice as likely as men to be diagnosed with depression. In a very public series of events during the 2010–2011 academic year, six Queen's University students died, at least two by suicide. This resulted in a refocusing of mental health services at the university. According to a recent U.S. survey of university and college counselling services, the number of students requiring mental health support has been increasing (*Chronicle of Higher Education*, 2011).

Most of us have experienced mild depressions (also called dysphoria) in our lives. Maybe bad grades have got you down. Or you have broken up with your boyfriend or girlfriend. We brood about it and it makes us feel worse. You feel low, hopeless, worthless, unloved, unlovable. These feelings are normal, particularly after more serious events (such as the death of a partner, close friend, or family member). Fortunately, for most of us these are relatively transient feelings, and although we might feel bad for a time (and the loss may stay with us for some time), we will recover. But for some people, life's down times are not just temporary blue periods—rather they define a major depressive episode that can last for weeks. Interestingly, these do not necessarily have to be linked to any one negative life event.

People who feel depressed tend to think in negative terms and tend to view the world in a negative light. For those who are seriously depressed—those who are feeling worthless, lethargic, uninterested in friends and family, and unable to sleep or eat normally—this negative thinking is self-defeating. Their pessimistic outlook lends them to magnify every negative event and minimize the positive ones. As one woman put it, "the real me is worthless and inadequate" (Burns, 1980, p. 29). Telling these people to "look on the bright side" does not help.

Depressive Realism

Are depressed people unrealistically negative? To assess this, Lauren Alloy, Lyn Abramson, and their colleagues (Alloy & Abramson, 1979; Alloy et al., 2004) studied mildly depressed and non-depressed college students and asked them to judge whether or not their pressing of a button controlled a light. Interestingly, the mildly depressed students were more accurate in making estimates of their level of control. Non-depressive students exaggerated their level of control—they were more inaccurate. Alloy and Abramson dubbed this depressive realism. This "sadder-but-wiser" effect shows up in various self-judgments.

Shelley Taylor (1989) argues that people who are mildly depressed are more even-handed in their self-assessments. Remarkably, as Kate Harkness, Mark Sabbagh, and Jill Jacobson (2005) at Queen's University have found, the mildly depressed are even *more* attuned to others' feelings than non-depressed people. We tend to see ourselves in a positive light. The mildly depressed, on the other hand, see the wrinkles and pimples, as well as the rosy glow on their faces. Recently, researchers have found that overall, depressed people are more negative, and this can go beyond "realism" to a general negative perceptual bias (Carson et al., 2010).

Connection:

Remember our discussion of self-serving biases in Module 4.

Underlying the thinking of depressed people are their attributions of responsibility. If you fail an exam and blame yourself (something we have all done before), you may conclude that you are stupid, lazy, and just not cut out for higher education. Consequently, you might feel depressed. On the other hand, if you attribute the failure to something outside your control (such as an unfair exam, noisy roommates), then you will react with externally directed anger.

In over 100 studies involving 15 000 participants, depressed people have been more likely than non-depressed people to exhibit a negative **explanatory style** (Peterson & Steen, 2002; Sweeney et al., 1986). As you can see in Figure 24-2, this explanatory style attributed failure and setbacks to causes that are *stable* ("It's going to last forever"), *global* ("It's going to affect everything I do"), and *internal* (It's all my fault"). Abramson and her colleagues (1989) have found that the result of this pessimistic, over-generalized, and self-blaming thinking is a depressing sense of hopelessness.

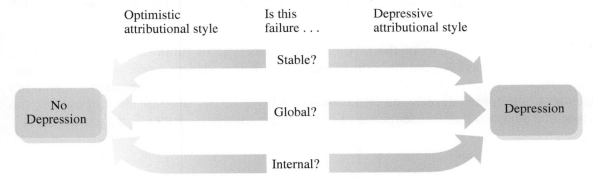

FIGURE 24-2

Depression is linked with a negative, pessimistic way of explaining and interpreting failures.

Is Negative Thinking the Root or Result of Depression?

Finding a relationship between negative thinking and depression raises an interesting question: Does depression cause negative thinking, or does negative thinking cause depression? This is a question that has been explored by a number of researchers over the years.

Connection:

Recall our discussion of mood and self-serving biases in Module 4.

Our moods can guide how we perceive our social worlds. When things are going well, we see only the positive in things. However, once our mood sours, our thoughts turn negative as well. A bad mood prods us to recall negative events (Bower, 1987; Johnson & Magaro, 1987). Our relationships seem to sour, our self-image tarnishes, and there seems little hope for the future (Brown & Taylor, 1986; Mayer & Salovey, 1987). As depression progresses, memories and expectations plummet; when depression lifts, thinking brightens (Barnett & Gotlib, 1988; Kuiper & Higgins, 1985). For example, currently depressed people are more likely than non-depressed people to recall their parents as being more rejecting and punitive, but formerly depressed people recall their parents no differently than those who are not depressed (Lewinsohn & Rosenbaum, 1987). Mood modifies memories.

A depressed mood also affects behaviour. The person who is depressed tends to be withdrawn, glum, and quick to complain. Strack and Coyne (1983) found that depressed people were realistic in thinking that others did not appreciate their behaviour; their pessimism and bad moods can thus trigger rejection from others (Carver et al., 1994). So, this evidence suggests that being depressed can cause certain cognitive and behavioural effects.

But does the opposite occur? Some level of depression after a negative event is natural. Divorce, losing a job, and other negative events can disrupt our sense of worth (e.g., Kendler et al., 1993). Nonetheless, the brooding that comes with depression can be adaptive. Sometimes the insights we gain at these times help us learn for the future. However, depression-prone people tend to respond to these situations with self-focused rumination and self-blame (e.g., Mor & Winquist, 2002; Pyszczynski et al., 1991).

So if we think back to the first part of the module—does this type of rumination explain people's response to even minor stress? As can be seen in Figure 24-3, this vicious circle is a real problem. Evidence suggests that when stress-induced rumination is filtered through a negative explanatory style, the frequent outcome is depression (Robinson & Alloy, 2003). Both inside and outside the laboratory, research suggests that this sequence of behaviour occurs (e.g., Sacks & Bugental, 1987).

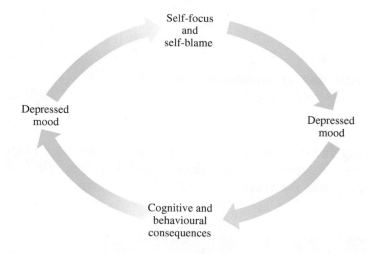

FIGURE 24-3

The vicious circle of depression.

People with a pessimistic explanatory style are more likely to become depressed when bad things happen. In one study, Robinson and Alloy (2003) followed university students for two and a half years. Of those with an optimistic explanatory style, only 1 percent had a first depressive episode, whereas 17 percent of those with pessimistic explanatory styles did. Moreover, patients who end therapy no longer feeling depressed yet retaining their pessimistic explanatory style are more likely to relapse (Seligman, 1992). Those with optimistic explanatory styles who do relapse are more likely to recover quickly (see Metalsky et al., 1993; Needles & Abramson, 1990).

This is also apparent in the transition from high school to university. Raymond Perry, Robert Stupinsky, and their colleagues (e.g., Perry et al., 2008; Stupinsky et al., 2007; Haynes et al., 2008) at the University of Manitoba studied attribution styles across five groups of first-year university students. They found that attribution style influenced both cognitive outcomes (e.g., expectations) and affective outcomes (e.g., shame, guilt), and ultimately the students' grades.

Martin Seligman (1998, 2002) believes that self-focus and self-blame help explain why depression levels are so high in the Western world today. In North America, young adults are three times more likely than their grandparents to have suffered depression. This is despite the fact that they experience a significantly greater standard of living (e.g., Swindle et al., 2000). Seligman argues that the growth of individualism has played a major part in the growth of hopelessness and self-blame when things do not go well. In non-Western cultures, where close-knit relationships and cooperation are the norm, major depression is less common and less tied to guilt and self-blame over perceived personal failures. In Japan, for example, depressed people are more likely to report feeling shame over the embarrassment they have brought on their families and co-workers. Thus, again, as we have seen with so many psychological effects, the results are not that simple.

So, clearly, having a pessimistic explanatory style may be problematic. If that is the case, how do we change someone's explanatory style? People who have optimistic explanatory styles attribute success to internal, stable, and global characteristics (e.g., "I did well on that exam because I am smart") and attribute failures to external, unstable, and specific causes (e.g., "I failed that exam because the professor made it too hard"; Buchanan & Seligman, 1995). Indeed, as we learned in Module 6, this type of optimistic view of ourselves may well be the norm.

Daniel Bailis and Judith Chipperfield at the University of Manitoba (e.g., Bailis, Segall & Chipperfield, 2010) have conducted extensive work on the role of the health locus of control and its impact on health outcomes. Self-efficacy is an important determinant of how hard people are willing to try at tasks, and how successful they are likely to be in their behaviours. These researchers have found that health locus of control changes over time—people become more external and less internal. Interestingly, however, the more autonomous people's health goals are (e.g., losing weight, staying fit, relieving stress) the less likely they were to come to believe that external factors controlled their health outcomes (see Haynes et al., 2009).

Connection:

Recall our discussion of self-efficacy from Module 5.

Eisner (1995) has suggested that being exposed to controllable events, and being successful at them, may lead to optimistic explanatory styles. From a health perspective, we know that people with high self-efficacy are more likely to stick to New Year's resolutions (Norcross et al., 2002), lose weight

(Annesi, 2007), practise safe sex (Abbey et al., 2006), and quit smoking (Baldwin et al., 2006). Thus, if you know someone who has a pessimistic explanatory style, putting them in situations where they can be successful is the best way to improve their perceptions of their own self-efficacy. If this occurs repeatedly, this will make people more willing to take on difficult tasks and make them more likely to succeed.

Applying Social Psychology

Depression is the leading psychological disorder on campuses. Roughly 25 percent of the student population suffers some symptoms at any given time. Suicides are 50 percent more frequent among university students than among non-students of the same age. Beck and Young (1978) suggest that university and college students may be especially prone to psychological problems because they simultaneously experience all the transitions that are major stresses in adulthood. Entering university, they lose family, friends, and familiar surroundings and are provided no ready-made substitutes. Furthermore, when in high school they were the able students. In university, they must compare their own abilities with equally able students.

Moreover, students' frequent misperceptions of these stresses may be as important a cause of depression as the stresses themselves. Although students do not hallucinate their problems of academic or social adjustment, they often inflate the importance of temporary setbacks and misjudge the severity of rejections. They may overestimate academic difficulties on the basis of one mediocre grade. They may grieve over their social isolation, even though they often have caring and supportive friends. Their pessimism and dissatisfaction may lead to clinical depression, which, in turn, interferes with actual performance. A vicious circle is created in which misperceptions of academic and social difficulties result in still poorer grades and greater social isolation. People also may misperceive illness as weakness and be less likely to seek help (Yap et al., 2011).

Thus, it is important to recognize the link between depression and suicide, and not treat it as though it is a "slump" people are going through. Depression has real and serious risks associated with it. If you are depressed, or someone you know is, do something about it. Seek help. University and college campuses have well-designed support mechanisms for students.

LO 3

NOTICING, TREATING, AND RECOVERING FROM ILLNESS

In the industrialized world, at least half of all deaths are linked with behaviour. Smoking cigarettes, drinking alcohol excessively, using drugs, and eating unhealthy foods are one set of problems. So are our reactions to stressors, lack of exercise, and not following medical advice. Both the interdisciplinary field of behavioural medicine and the psychological contributions to this field, health psychology, study how people respond to illness symptoms and how we understand illness.

Reacting to Symptoms

Here is a list of typical complaints: headache, nausea, stomach ache, mild rashes, diarrhea, constipation, sweating, loss of sleep, dizziness, joint stiffness. What do these symptoms mean? Are they meaningless? Does it mean you are about to die? It is hard to tell (Pennebaker, 1982). Have you ever experienced such symptoms and then tried to self-diagnose? Perhaps you went online to a medical website (such as WebMD) to get some outside help. Noticing and interpreting our body's signals is difficult.

For example, Baumann and Leventhal (1985) found that people judge their blood pressure based on how they feel, which typically has little relevance to actual blood pressure. Indeed, this is why high blood pressure is so problematic. Forty-three percent of Canadians who have high blood pressure do not know it (Heart & Stroke Foundation, 2011). There are typically no symptoms of high blood pressure until a significant amount of damage has been done to the body.

So how do we explain our symptoms, and how do we decide that we are ill? Is that a muscle spasm or is it a heart attack? It can be difficult to tell. Friedman and DiMatteo (1989) report that half of heart attack victims die without having sought medical attention. Once people notice their symptoms, they are more likely to seek treatment if they feel they have a physical versus a psychological cause (Bishop, 1987). Socio-economic status plays a role—wealthier people are more likely to seek help (Kaplan et al., 2013).

Gender plays a role as well. One study (Olfson & Pincus, 1994) found that women are more likely than men to seek professional advice on symptoms. This is interesting, considering that men are actually more likely to become ill (Statistics Canada, 2004). Why is there this gender difference? One suggestion is that women are less concerned about appearing "weak" by admitting to illness (Bishop, 1984). Others have suggested that women may just make more time to see a doctor (Marcus & Siegel, 1982).

The Stigma of Being Sick

People do not like to be sick. Being sick is not fun—you miss out on your work, school, family, or other activities. But for some people (and for some illnesses) there is another problem that must be dealt with. In our society, being sick can lead to stigmatization. You can lose your identity and be labelled as "a cancer survivor" or an "AIDS victim." Stigmas are very powerful. People define themselves by their salient characteristics. Someone who is ill can be defined by their illness. For most people, this is not pleasant.

Connection:

Remember our discussion of self-concept from Module 3.

People react negatively to illness and the ill. In a British study (Scambler, 1984), a group of 94 epileptics were interviewed about their reactions to their own diagnosis. The majority of these patients reacted with shock to the diagnosis itself, and became concerned that simply being labelled as "epileptic" would alter how others saw them. Someone with a mental illness may be labelled by the uninformed as "crazy" and this has numerous effects on how they are treated. In a classic study by Farina and Ring (1965), participants were led to believe their work partner was either a typical student or previously had a "nervous breakdown." Although performance on a subsequent task was unaffected by this disclosure, participants who believed their partner had suffered a nervous breakdown blamed their partner for errors, described them as less helpful, and indicated they would prefer to work alone in the future.

People with HIV/AIDS are frequently stigmatized (Triplet & Sugarman, 1987). When HIV/AIDS was first identified in the 1980s, people suffering from the disease were barred from schools, churches, and rental housing; were fired from jobs; and were generally treated poorly. Although knowledge of HIV/AIDS and how it is transmitted among the general public has increased (although is still not complete), HIV/AIDS patients are still seen as flawed, degenerate, or simply undesirable (Crawford, 1996).

Interestingly, people with HIV/AIDS are even more stigmatized than people with other illnesses. Why? Some reasons that have been suggested include that AIDS patients are seen as having caused their own illness (e.g., Herek & Glunt, 1988), that they have the potential to be contagious, or that the stigma is in part the result of homophobia (Triplet & Sugarman, 1987). But, as we have learned in previous modules, this may well be serving as a protective mechanism. If I can dislike and blame the victim for his or her illness, then I am at less risk. We dislike and disparage what we fear.

Recovering from Illness

What do you do when you get sick? Take a few days off, get some rest, and perhaps take some medication? If you are like most people, once you feel better, you get back to your daily routine. Normally, some rest may be "all that the doctor ordered." Sometimes however, more intervention is required. We mentioned earlier that high blood pressure is difficult for people to detect in themselves. High blood pressure (also known as hypertension) is actually fairly easy to treat. Changing diet, exercise, and the use of specific medications can safely reduce the danger posed by high blood pressure. Yet some studies (e.g., Leventhal & Hirschman, 1982) have found that up to 90 percent of people being treated for hypertension do not complete treatment. "I feel fine now, why do I need this anymore?"

Exercise programs and healthy diets are equally difficult to stick to. Can you think of a time when you promised yourself you would change your habits, yet one, two, or six months down the road found yourself back in the same old routine? You are not alone. Almost 90 percent of recovering alcoholics will relapse in their first four years of sobriety (National Institute on Alcohol Abuse and Alcoholism, 2008). But why does this happen? Over time, people commonly "slip" from their programs or goals. This type of deviation from a goal (be it losing weight, quitting drinking, or taking the entire dose of a prescribed antibiotic) is inevitable. Whether it means the end of the program or is simply a bump in the road depends on how people interpret the event.

Think back to our discussion of cognitive dissonance. People see the slip as inconsistent with their new self-image (e.g., a now ex-smoker having a cigarette) and must resolve this inconsistency (see Marlatt & Gordon, 1979). If the person sees the slip as a one-time event, he or she can stay on the path to recovery. However, if the person interprets it as an indication that he or she is really a smoker, that person will then start smoking again. Most people who successfully quit smoking have tried before and failed.

Connection:

Remember our discussion of cognitive dissonance in Module 8.

LO 4

HEALTH PROMOTION AND BEHAVIOUR CHANGE

As we mentioned earlier, it is clear that people's life choices have a significant impact on overall health and life expectancy. Health Canada, the Canadian Cancer Society, and a variety of other groups and agencies have been trying to convince Canadians to exercise, eat healthier, quit smoking, perform breast self-exams, engage in safer sex, and generally live healthier lives. For example, "Live Right Now" is a national initiative being sponsored by the CBC, the Heart and Stroke Foundation, the Canadian Diabetes Association, Participaction, and many other groups to help Canadians live well. It involves recipes, health information, a Facebook page, and a Twitter feed to try to reach Canadians of all ages. But before we can change people's behaviour to be healthier, we need to understand the process of change. Will the information on the "Live Right Now" website have the desired impact?

Models of Behaviour Change

Attitudes predict behaviour—sometimes. We discussed three approaches used by attitude researchers to deal with the argument that attitudes do not predict behaviour. One of those approaches was to develop models of the attitude-to-behaviour link. Our discussion focused on the theory of reasoned action (Fishbein & Ajzen, 2010), and the theory of planned behaviour (Ajzen, 1990; Ajzen & Albarracin, 2007; Ajzen & Fishbein, 2005), as these two models had received significant attention in the field. Perhaps not surprisingly, given their influence in the attitudes literature, health researchers have applied these models to a variety of health behaviours, such as cancer screening (Orbell et al., 2006), HIV prevention (Kalichman, 2007), exercise (Downs et al., 2006), and smoking prevention (Guo et al., 2007).

Connection:

Remember our discussion of the attitude–behaviour link in Module 8.

Another model of health behaviour that has received significant attention is the stages of change model (Prochaska et al., 1992). As can be seen in Figure 24-4, there are several separate (but overlapping) steps in the process to changing health behaviours. This model is very different from the theory of reasoned action and theory of planned behaviour because it does not deal with discrete behavioural episodes, but with a process of change. The major benefit of this type of approach is that it allows for interventions that target specific steps in the process, rather than one general behaviour such as "smoking" (Leamon, 2006; Lippke & Plotnikoff, 2006).

Stages of Change Model (Applied to quitting smoking)		
Stage	**Description**	**Example**
1. Precontemplation	Individuals in this stage are not yet ready to think about changing and may never even understand or be aware that they have a particular problem.	Someone who smokes does not accept that they are addicted, or that smoking may be harmful to them. "I only smoke socially." "I work out, so smoking isn't that bad for me."
2. Contemplation	Individuals at this stage have accepted that they have a problem, but they are not ready to make any specific changes.	A smoker at this stage recognizes that they have a problem and need to quit smoking, but are not yet sure if they want to. "I am sure I'll quit someday."
3. Preparation/ Determination	Individuals at this stage are preparing to take positive action.	A smoker at this stage will start to explore options about quitting. "Maybe I can cut down." "Would the nicotine patch work for me?"
4. Action/Willpower	At this stage individuals make a commitment to a behavioural change and enact a plan.	A smoker at this stage begins the quitting process and tries to maintain this over the short term. "I am quitting today."
5. Maintenance	Individuals at this stage (where opportunity for relapse is high) are successful in continuing their changed behaviour over time.	A smoker at this stage has refrained from smoking for a significant time (e.g., six months) and has developed coping strategies to deal with temptations to smoke. "I don't go to bars anymore."

FIGURE 24-4

Prochaska's stages of change model applied to smoking behaviour.

Source: Adapted from Prochaska et al., 1992; 1994.

In the *precontemplation* stage, people are not aware they have a problem. People who use drugs recreationally may be in this situation—they do not see their drug use as having any negative side effects or problems. Often, these people need some form of "consciousness raising" in order to highlight the problem of their behaviour. This often takes the form of a significant life event. Many women quit smoking when they become pregnant, or a drunk-driving charge may focus someone's thoughts about their drinking, or a bout of bronchitis might make a smoker think about quitting.

In the *contemplation* stage, people start to acknowledge that they have a behaviour that needs to be changed. However, even though the problem has been identified, they might not be willing to change. Someone who is overweight might say, "Sure, I'm fat, but I like being fat, and I love to eat."

A smoker might recognize that smoking is a problem, and be concerned about the amount of money spent on cigarettes, but not be willing to give them up yet.

In the *preparation/determination* stage, people are ready to take some positive action. They accept that they have a problem, they want to deal with it, and they try to come up with a strategy to solve the problem. For example, a drug user might start exploring rehab centres. An overweight person might start looking into gym memberships or Weight Watchers. Concrete plans for action are made: "I will quit on January 1st."

In the *action/willpower* stage, people take some action. They quit smoking, they stop taking drugs, they go to the gym, or they do whatever it is they have determined will help them stop their negative behaviour or engage in a positive one. Reinforcers are important at this stage to maintain success. Buying new clothes as the weight drops off, or a shopping spree with extra cigarette money are good ways of encouraging the positive health behaviours. Friends, family, and other members of a person's social network are an important source of support at this stage (Taylor, 2007). This may be why support groups have developed for many negative health behaviours (such as smoking, drug use, gambling) and why many people like to have a workout buddy. Having the support of others helps with changing the behaviour.

The *maintenance* stage is important. At this point, people's willpower has abated, but with a good plan they have figured out ways to avoid temptations. They may avoid old situations where the negative behaviour was common (e.g., casinos, bars, McDonald's), get all the junk food out of the house, and learn coping mechanisms when temptations do arise.

If they are lucky, people will achieve *transcendence* at this point, where they no longer have to fight to maintain their new lifestyle—it is simply a way of being. It is important to note that relapse is common (Prochaska & Norcross, 2007). However, as we mentioned earlier, how someone reacts to a relapse will be important. You have undoubtedly been in this situation before in your life. If you have a negative explanatory style, you might say, "I've failed. I'm a smoker—always have been, always will be. Why did I even try?" However, if you have a positive explanatory style, you might react by saying, "Well, I made a mistake. Nothing to lose my head over. I'll just make sure I don't get into that situation again. If I ever do end up in that situation, I will now have a plan to deal with it." Successful dieters, for example, are dieters who do not blame themselves when they have a relapse, but take the opportunity to learn from the experience (Phelan et al., 2003).

Although the stages of change model has been effectively applied to a number of health behaviours, including smoking (Shumann et al., 2006), exercise (Lippke & Plotnikoff, 2006), drug use (Walker et al., 2006) and others, it has not been without controversy (see Brug et al., 2004; Littrell & Girvin, 2002). Specifically, there is little evidence that the stages are mutually exclusive (e.g., you can imagine being in contemplation and preparation at the same time) nor are they necessarily sequential (e.g., one could jump directly from precontemplation to action). In addition, many of these stages really focus on attitudes, rather than the behaviours themselves. Thus, this model may be considered more as promoting readiness for change, rather than being a model of change, per se (West, 2005). Nonetheless, this model has been widely applied and has proved to be a very useful model for practitioners.

Approaches to Health Promotion

As we know, people engage in risky behaviour. Many Canadians smoke, there is a high level of binge drinking on Canadian university campuses (e.g., Weschler et al., 2002), 30 to 44 percent of young Canadians engage in risky sexual behaviour (Statistics Canada, 2005), and almost 60 percent of Canadians are considered overweight or obese (Statistics Canada, 2013).

The use of public service announcements by non-profit and governmental groups, with the aim of changing behaviour, is broadly referred to as health promotion, and this typically follows what is called a "social marketing" approach. Social marketing is different from what we would typically think of as marketing, as it is not trying to sell you a product, but is more focused on selling a way of life. Although social marketing can apply to a variety of domains (literacy, the environment, charity fundraising), here we will focus on how it is applied to health.

Despite the fact that people are exposed to social marketing messages on a regular basis, the messages are clearly not always effective. Some campaigns have worked. Seatbelt use is up; smoking is down. However, people still engage in many types of unhealthy behaviours. Perhaps it is not surprising, then, that persuasion researchers have spent considerable time and energy trying to understand how we can best alter people's behaviour to make them healthier.

FEAR-BASED PERSUASIVE APPEALS

One question that has been asked is whether or not frightening people will work to change their behaviour. In the 1970s and 1980s, one television advertisement showed a person being thrown from a vehicle in an accident because he did not have his seatbelt on. This likely motivated many people to put on their seatbelts.

Connection:

Recall our discussion of fear-based appeals in Module 10.

Critical THINKING

This type of fear-arousing advertising strategy has been used frequently, and MADD (Mothers Against Drunk Driving) and other anti–drunk driving groups have used similar fear-arousing advertisements to change people's driving habits. But will these advertisements work equally well? Another type of fear-based appeal was pictured earlier—anti-smoking ads. These warning labels, from Health Canada, use a fear-based appeal: If you smoke, you will die. Do these work? Under what circumstances?

Using a very similar fear-arousing campaign, Janis and Feshbach (1953) explored how fear influenced people's dental habits. They showed participants one of three appeals: an X-ray of a healthy mouth, a colour picture of a diseased mouth and gums, or a more "middle ground" appeal.

They found that high levels of fear arousal actually led to the least change, and the non–fear-arousing appeal was most effective. However, some later studies found the opposite, that as fear increased, change increased (e.g., Higbee, 1969; McGuire, 1969). Recently, a fear-based appeal that tried to warn Vancouver-area heroin users about the risks of overdosing on high-potency heroin actually increased users' desires for the drug (Kerr et al., 2013).

In reality, the relationship is a bit more complex (see Figure 24-5). As fear increases, change increases to a certain extent (we become aware of a problem and are motivated to change) but at some point, change decreases again (the appeals are so frightening that we may ignore them). Leventhal (1970) has argued that fear-based appeals must be accompanied by clear instructions on how to act effectively to deal with the problem or the message will be ignored or counterargued. Rogers (1975) has argued that people will react positively to the threat (i.e., a fear-based persuasive message) when each of these four factors are in place:

- The threat needs to be perceived as severe.
- People need to see themselves as vulnerable.
- The threat is accompanied by a specific recommended course of action.
- Taking that action will result in elimination of the threat (i.e., the action will be effective).

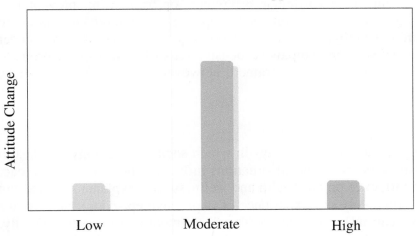

The Effect of Fear-Based Appeals

FIGURE 24-5

The impact of fear-based appeals.

Let's compare the two driving-related advertisements mentioned earlier. Would a seatbelt advertisement showing a person flying through a windshield work? Perhaps. It is fear-arousing, the threat is clearly severe, most people would see themselves as vulnerable, doing up your seatbelt is easy, and it will be effective in protecting you. But what about the drunk driving advertisement? A fear-based appeal may be less effective in this situation. People may feel they are less likely to be at risk ("I am fine after a few drinks"). In addition, not drinking and driving involves significantly more planning and thought than putting on a seatbelt. Thus, the effectiveness of a fear-based appeal on drunk driving may be limited.

MESSAGE FRAMING AND HEALTH PROMOTION

A somewhat different approach to designing health messages has focused on how to "frame" the message (i.e., message framing). If you consider the examples we used earlier, these have generally been *loss-framed*, meaning that they focus on what you can lose by not changing. Thus, a safer-sex ad showing a person who has contracted AIDS would be loss-framed. Alternatively, *gain-framed* messages focus on the benefits of engaging in that particular behaviour. For example, showing someone being active and healthy would show the benefits of quitting smoking or losing weight.

Is one of these approaches more effective? Again, it depends. If you want to focus on prevention (e.g., convincing women to perform breast self-examinations in order to detect cancer early, or convincing men to obtain digital rectal exams to assess prostate cancer risk), then a loss-framed appeal might be more effective (Rothman & Salovey, 1997; Salovey & Wegener, 2003). These messages bring a person's attention to the fact that they may have a problem, and that they have the means to assess and deal with the problem. For example, recent advertisements by the Canadian Cancer Society and the Canadian Breast Cancer Foundation have focused on the value of early detection, highlighting the high cure rates if cancers are caught early. Message framing appeals have also been used to encourage women to take more calcium (Gerend & Shepherd, 2013).

Alternatively, if the goal of the advertising campaign is to prevent the behaviour from ever beginning, a gain-framed appeal might be most effective. Gain-framed appeals focus on all of the benefits you will have from not engaging in a particular behaviour, or from using preventative methods to avoid illness. Thus, messages designed to convince people to use condoms or sunscreen should focus on the benefits of remaining healthy, rather than the consequences of contracting cancer or a sexually transmitted illness. Thus, persuasion campaigns focusing on social norms may prove to be a worthwhile direction to explore how messages are framed. However, no studies to date have explicitly tested this approach.

CONCLUSIONS

As we have seen in this module, there are a number of ways in which social psychology and health interact. How individuals approach stressors and stressful situations influences how our bodies react to these situations, which has a direct influence on our health and wellness. Our explanatory style can influence our level of self-worth and ultimately our experience of depressive episodes, and how we perceive the world and our symptoms can influence the course of treatment and recovery. Finally, social psychological principles can be brought to bear on how to change the less-than-healthy choices many of us are making on a day-to-day basis. How do you stay healthy? A positive attitude is always a good start!

SUMMARY OF KEY POINTS

LO1. Understand the link between stress and health.

- People have individual reactions to stress.
- There is some evidence that men and women can respond to stress differently.
- Increased stress can lead to increased illness.

LO2. Understand the causes and consequences of depression.

- A person's explanatory style can influence the sometimes-circular nature of depression.

LO3. Understand how we notice, treat, and recover from illness.

- Many people tend to dismiss symptoms and may even deny their illness, hampering the ability to get well.

LO4. Understand how to promote healthier behaviour.

- Different models of health behaviour change have been proposed.
- Using persuasion techniques can influence health attitudes and behaviour.

KEY TERMS

Behavioural medicine   An interdisciplinary field that integrates and applies behavioural and medical knowledge about health and disease.

Coping style   The manner in which individuals use available internal and external resources to effectively manage stressors.

Depressive realism   The tendency of mildly depressed people to make accurate rather than self-serving judgments, attributions, and predictions.

Explanatory style   One's habitual way of explaining life events. A negative, pessimistic, depressive explanatory style attributes failure to stable, global, and internal causes.

Fight-or-flight response   The term describing the response all mammals have to stress—either attacking the source of the stress (fight) or fleeing from the situation (flight).

Health psychology   The field of psychology dedicated to understanding and applying psychological principles to improve the health of individuals.

Message framing   Designing persuasive messages to either emphasize what may be lost or what may be gained.

Stress   The body's physiological response to events we perceive as threatening.

Stressors   Factors we encounter that can evoke a stress response.

Glossary

A

Actor–observer bias   When we are the actor, we tend to attribute behaviour to the environment, whereas when we observe others, we tend to underestimate the impact of the environment.

Adaptation-level phenomenon   The tendency to adapt to a given level of stimulation and thus to notice and react to changes from that level.

Aggression   Physical or verbal behaviour intended to hurt someone.

Altruism   A motive to increase another's welfare without conscious regard for one's self-interests.

Arbitration   Resolution of a conflict by a neutral third party who studies both sides and imposes a settlement.

Attitude   A general and enduring evaluation of some person, object, or issue along a continuum from positive to negative.

Attitude inoculation   Exposing people to weak attacks on their attitudes so that when stronger attacks come, they will have refutations available.

Attractiveness   Having qualities that appeal to an audience. An appealing communicator (often someone similar to the audience) is most persuasive on matters of subjective preference.

Attribution theory   The theory of how people explain others' behaviour—for example, by attributing it either to internal dispositions (enduring traits, motives, and attitudes) or to external situations.

Authoritarianism   A personality style characterized by submission to legitimate authority, a general level of aggressiveness toward outgroups, and a high degree of adherence to social conventions.

Availability heuristic   An efficient but fallible rule of thumb that judges the likelihood of things in terms of their availability in memory. If instances of something come readily to mind, we presume it is commonplace.

B

Bargaining   Seeking an agreement through direct negotiation between parties to a conflict.

Behavioural confirmation   A type of self-fulfilling prophecy whereby people's social expectations (based more on social beliefs than personal expectation) lead them to act in ways that cause others to confirm the expectations.

Behavioural medicine   An interdisciplinary field that integrates and applies behavioural and medical knowledge about health and disease.

Bystander effect   The finding that a person is less likely to provide help when there are other bystanders.

C

Catharsis   A belief, derived from instinct theories of aggression, that acting out violently will reduce the need or desire to be violent.

Central-route persuasion   Persuasion that occurs when interested people focus on the arguments and respond with favourable thoughts.

Certainty   Refers to the level of subjective confidence or validity a person attaches to his or her attitude.

Co-actors   Co-participants working individually on a non-competitive activity.

Cognitive dissonance theory   Cognitive dissonance is tension that arises when one is simultaneously aware of two inconsistent cognitions, as when we realize that we have, with little justification, acted contrary to our attitudes. Cognitive dissonance theory proposes that we act to reduce such tension, as when we adjust our attitudes to correspond with our actions.

Cognitive interview   An interview technique based in cognitive psychology, focusing on context reinstatement to enhance recall of events.

Collectivism   Giving priority to the goals of one's groups (often one's extended family or work group) and defining one's identity accordingly.

Companionate love   The affection we feel for those with whom our lives are deeply intertwined.

Complementarity   The popularly supposed tendency, in a relationship between two people, for each to complete what is missing in the other.

Confidence–accuracy correlation   The finding that the correlation between the confidence and accuracy of an eyewitness is weak to non-existent.

Confirmation bias   We are eager to verify our beliefs but less inclined to seek evidence that might disprove them.

Conflict   A perceived incompatibility of actions or goals.

Conformity   Changing one's perceptions, opinions, or behaviour in order to be more consistent with real or imagined group norms.

Coping style   The manner in which individuals use available internal and external resources to effectively manage stressors.

Correlational research   The study of the naturally occurring associations between two or more factors.

Correspondence bias   A tendency for people to view behaviour as coming from inner dispositions.

Credibility   Believability. A credible communicator is perceived as both expert and trustworthy.

Crowding   A subjective feeling that there is not enough space per person.

Cult   A group typically characterized by (1) distinctive rituals and beliefs related to its devotion to a god or a person, (2) isolation from the surrounding "evil" culture, and (3) a charismatic leader. (A sect, by contrast, is a spinoff from a major religion.)

Culture   The enduring behaviours, attitudes, and traditions shared by a large group of people and transmitted from one generation to the next.

D

Deindividuation   Loss of self-awareness and evaluation apprehension; occurs in group situations that foster responsiveness to group norms, good or bad.

Demand characteristics   Characteristics or cues in a study that suggest to participants what behaviour is expected.

Dependent variable   The variable being measured, so-called because it may depend on manipulations of the independent variable.

Depressive realism   The tendency of mildly depressed people to make accurate rather than self-serving judgments, attributions, and predictions.

Descriptive norms   Norms that relate to the behaviours other people in your social group engage in.

Disclosure reciprocity   The tendency for one person's intimacy of self-disclosure to match that of a conversational partner.

Discrimination   Unjustifiable negative behaviour toward a group or its members. Discrimination is the behavioural component of outgroup bias.

Dismissive attachment   An avoidant relationship style marked by distrust of others.

Displacement   The redirection of aggression to a target other than the source of the frustration. Generally, the new target is a safer or more socially acceptable target.

Dispositional attribution   Attributing behaviour to the person's disposition and traits.

Door-in-the-face technique   The tendency—based on the principle of reciprocity—for people who have first declined a large request to comply with a subsequent, smaller request.

E

Empathy   The vicarious experience of another's feelings; putting oneself in another's shoes.

Equal-status contact   Contact made on an equal basis. Just as a relationship between people of unequal status breeds attitudes consistent with their relationship, so do relationships between those of equal status. Thus, to reduce prejudice, interracial contact should be between persons equal in status.

Equity   A condition in which the outcomes people receive from a relationship are proportional to what they contribute to it. Note: Equitable outcomes need not always be equal outcomes.

Ethnocentrism   A belief in the superiority of one's own ethnic and cultural group, and a corresponding disdain for all other groups.

Evaluation apprehension   Concern for how others are evaluating us.

Experimental realism   The degree to which an experiment produces the real psychological experiences that it is intended to create.

Experimental research   Studies that seek clues to cause–effect relationships by manipulating one or more factors (independent variables) to determine their impact on other factors (dependent variables).

Explanatory style   One's habitual way of explaining life events. A negative, pessimistic, depressive explanatory style attributes failure to stable, global, and internal causes.

F

False consensus effect   The tendency to overestimate the commonality of one's opinions and one's undesirable or unsuccessful behaviours.

False uniqueness effect   The tendency to underestimate the commonality of one's abilities and one's desirable or successful behaviours.

Fearful attachment   An avoidant relationship style marked by fear of rejection.

Fight-or-flight response   The term describing the response all mammals have to stress—either attacking the source of the stress (fight) or fleeing from the situation (flight).

Foot-in-the-door phenomenon   The tendency for people who have first agreed to a small request to comply later with a larger request.

Free riders   People who benefit from the group but give little in return.

Frustration   The blocking of goal-directed behaviour.

Fundamental attribution error   The tendency for observers to underestimate situational influences and overestimate dispositional influences upon others' behaviour. This is also called the correspondence bias, because we so often see behaviour as corresponding to a disposition.

G

Gender   In psychology, the characteristics, whether biological or socially influenced, by which people define male and female.

Gender roles   Sets of behavioural expectations (norms) for males and females.

Group polarization   Group-produced enhancement of members' pre-existing tendencies; a strengthening of the members' average tendency, not a split within the group.

Groupthink   "The mode of thinking that persons engage in when concurrence-seeking becomes so dominant in a cohesive in-group that it tends to override realistic appraisal of alternative courses of action." Irving Janis (1971).

H

Health psychology   The field of psychology dedicated to understanding and applying psychological principles to improve the health of individuals.

Hindsight bias   The tendency to exaggerate, after learning an outcome, one's ability to have foreseen how something turned out. Also known as the I-knew-it-all-along phenomenon.

Hostile aggression   Aggression with the aim of injuring someone driven by anger.

Hypothesis   A testable proposition that describes a relationship that might exist between events.

I

Illusion of control   Perception of uncontrollable events as subject to one's control or as more controllable than they are.

Illusory correlation   Perception of a relationship where none exists, or perception of a stronger relationship than actually exists.

Independent variable   The experimental factor that a researcher manipulates.

Individualism   The concept of giving priority to one's own goals over group goals and defining one's identity in terms of personal attributes rather than group identifications.

Indoctrination   A process, used by a number of social groups, to teach members a partisan and uncritical acceptance of the group's perspective on issues.

Informational influence   When people change their opinions or actions because they believe that others have the information they need to make the right decisions.

Informed consent An ethical principle requiring that research participants be told enough to enable them to decide if they wish to participate.

Ingroup "Us"—a group of people who share a sense of belonging, a feeling of common identity.

Ingroup bias The tendency to favour one's own group.

Injunctive norms Norms that relate to the behaviours you should engage in from a moral perspective.

Instrumental aggression Aggression that provides a means to an end.

J

Just-world phenomenon The tendency of people to believe the world is just and that people therefore get what they deserve and deserve what they get.

L

Learned helplessness The hopelessness and resignation learned by humans or animals who perceive themselves as having no control over repeated bad events.

Locus of control The extent to which people perceive outcomes as internally controllable by their own efforts and actions, or as externally controlled by chance or outside forces.

Low-ball technique A tactic for getting people to agree to something. People who agree to an initial request will often still comply when the requester ups the ante. People who receive only the costly request are less likely to comply with it.

M

Matching phenomenon The tendency for men and women to choose as partners those who are a "good match" in attractiveness and other traits.

Mediation An attempt by a neutral third party to resolve a conflict by facilitating communication and offering suggestions.

Mere exposure effect The tendency for novel stimuli to be liked more or rated more positively after the rater has been repeatedly exposed to them.

Message framing Designing persuasive messages to either emphasize what may be lost or what may be gained.

Mirror-image perceptions Reciprocal views of one another often held by parties in conflict; for example, each may view itself as moral and peace-loving and the other as evil and aggressive.

Mundane realism The degree to which an experiment is superficially similar to everyday situations.

N

Need to belong A motivation to bond with others in relationships that provide ongoing, positive interactions.

Non–zero-sum games Games in which outcomes need not sum to zero. With cooperation, both can win; with competition, both can lose. (Also called mixed-motive situations.)

Normative influence When people change their opinions or actions because they want to fit in with the group (i.e., be normal).

O

Obedience Changes in behaviour elicited by the commands of an authority figure.

Observational research methods Research methods in which individuals are observed in natural settings, often without awareness, in order to provide the opportunity for objective analysis of behaviour.

Outgroup "Them"—a group that people perceive as distinctively different from or apart from their ingroup.

Outgroup homogeneity effect Perception of outgroup members as more similar to one another than are ingroup members. Thus "they are alike; we are diverse."

P

Peripheral-route persuasion Persuasion that occurs when people are influenced by incidental cues, such as a speaker's attractiveness.

Physical-attractiveness stereotype The presumption that physically attractive people possess other socially desirable traits as well: What is beautiful is good.

Pornography Any written or visual material that contains the description of or actual images of human sexual activity or sex organs, which is intended to stimulate erotic feelings, rather than focused on aesthetic or emotional reactions.

Prejudice A negative attitude toward a group. Prejudice is typically considered the affective component of outgroup bias.

Preoccupied attachment Attachment marked by a sense of one's own unworthiness and anxiety, ambivalence, and possessiveness.

Private self-awareness Being aware of our own internal states.

Prosocial behaviour Positive, constructive, helpful social behaviour; the opposite of antisocial behaviour.

Proximity Geographical nearness. Functional distance powerfully predicts liking.

Public self-awareness Being aware of how others are seeing us at a particular moment.

R

Racism (1) An individual's prejudicial attitudes and discriminatory behaviour toward people of a given race, or (2) institutional practices (even if not motivated by prejudice) that subordinate people of a given race.

Random assignment The process of assigning participants to the conditions of an experiment such that all persons have the same chance of being in a given condition. (Note the distinction between random assignment in experiments and random sampling in surveys. Random assignment helps us infer cause and effect. Random sampling helps us generalize to a population.)

Reactance A motive to protect or restore one's sense of freedom. Reactance arises when someone threatens our freedom of action.

Reactivity The degree to which a measure may itself influence the behaviour we are studying.

Realistic group conflict theory The theory that prejudice arises from competition among groups for scarce resources.

Reciprocity norm An expectation that people will help, not hurt, those who have helped them.

Regression toward the average The statistical tendency for extreme scores or extreme behaviour to return toward one's average.

Relative deprivation The perception that you are less well-off than others with whom you compare yourself.

Reliability The extent to which a measure yields the same result when used on more than one occasion to assess some relatively stable characteristic.

Representative samples Carefully selected samples used by survey researchers so that participant responses accurately reflect the responses of the population of interest.

Role A set of norms that define how people in a given social position ought to behave.

S

Secure attachment Attachments rooted in trust and marked by intimacy.

Selective attention The extent to which people's attitudes bias the attitude-relevant information they attend to, once exposed.

Selective exposure The extent to which people's attitudes bias the attitude-relevant information they expose themselves to.

Selective judgment The extent to which people's attitudes bias how they draw conclusions about the meaning or relevance of information.

Selective memory The extent to which people's attitudes bias recall and recognition of attitude-relevant information.

Selective perception The extent to which people's attitudes bias their encoding of information.

Self-concept A person's answers to the question, "Who am I?"

Self-disclosure Revealing intimate aspects of oneself to others.

Self-efficacy A sense that one is competent and effective.

Self-fulfilling prophecy The tendency for one's expectations to evoke behaviour in others that confirms the expectations.

Self-perception theory When unsure of our attitudes, we infer them—much as someone observing us would—by looking at our behaviour and the circumstances under which it occurs.

Self-presentation   Wanting to present a desired image both to an external audience (other people) and an internal audience (ourselves).

Self-reference effect   The tendency to process efficiently, and remember well, information related to oneself.

Self-schemas   Beliefs about self that organize and guide the processing of self-relevant information.

Self-serving bias   The tendency to perceive and present oneself favourably.

Sequential lineup   A lineup type where photos are presented individually.

Sexism   (1) An individual's prejudicial attitudes and discriminatory behaviour toward people of a given gender, or (2) institutional practices (even if not motivated by prejudice) that subordinate people of a given gender.

Simultaneous lineup   A lineup type that presents photos together in one array.

Situational attribution   Attributing behaviour to the environment.

Sleeper effect   A delay in the impact of a message; occurs when we remember the message but forget a reason for discounting it.

Social comparison   Evaluating one's opinions and abilities by comparing oneself to others.

Social facilitation   (1) Original meaning—the tendency of people to perform simple or well-learned tasks better when others are present. (2) Current meaning—the strengthening of dominant (prevalent or likely) responses in the presence of others.

Social identity   The "we" aspect of our self-concept. The part of our answer to "Who am I?" that comes from our group.

Social learning theory   The theory that we learn social behaviour by observing and imitating, and by being rewarded and punished.

Social loafing   The tendency for people to exert less effort when they pool their efforts toward a common goal than when they are individually accountable.

Social psychology   The scientific study of how people think about, influence, and relate to one another.

Social-exchange theory   The theory that human interactions are transactions that aim to maximize one's rewards and minimize one's costs.

Social-responsibility norm   An expectation that people will help those dependent upon them.

Stereotype threat   A disruptive concern, when facing a negative stereotype, that one will be evaluated based on a negative stereotype. Unlike self-fulfilling prophecies that hammer one's reputation into one's self-concept, stereotype threat situations have immediate effects.

Stereotypes   Beliefs about the personal attributes of a group of people. Stereotypes are sometimes overgeneralized, inaccurate, and resistant to new information. Stereotypes are the cognitive component of outgroup bias.

Stress   The body's physiological response to events we perceive as threatening.

Stressors   Factors we encounter that can evoke a stress response.

Subliminal messages   Messages presented in such a manner as to be below a person's threshold of conscious awareness.

Superordinate goal   A shared goal that necessitates cooperative effort; a goal that overrides people's differences from one another.

T

Theory   An integrated set of principles that explains and predicts observed events.

Two-factor theory of emotion   Arousal × label = emotion. (Emotional experience is a product of physiological arousal and how we cognitively label the arousal.)

V

Validity   The extent to which a measure assesses what it is intended to assess.

References

Abbey, A., Saenz, C., Buck, P. O., Parkhill, M. R., & Hayman, L. W., Jr., (2006). The effects of acute alcohol consumption, cognitive reserve, partner risk, and gender on sexual decision-making. *Journal of Studies on Alcohol, 67*(1), 113–121.

Abrams, D. (1991). AIDS: What young people believe and what they do. Paper presented at the British Association for the Advancement of Science conference.

Abrams, D., Wetherell, M., Cochrane, S., Hogg, M. A., & Turner, J. C. (1990). Knowing what to think by knowing who you are: Self-categorization and the nature of norm formation, conformity and group polarization. *British Journal of Social Psychology, 29,* 97–119.

Abramson, L. Y., Metalsky, G. I., & Alloy, L. B. (1989). Hopelessness depression: A theory-based subtype. *Psychological Review, 96,* 358–372.

Acitelli, L. K., & Antonucci, T. C. (1994). Gender differences in the link between marital support and satisfaction in older couples. *Journal of Personality and Social Psychology, 67,* 688–698.

Adair, J. G., Dushenko, T. W., & Lindsay, R. C. L. (1985). Ethical regulations and their impact on research practice. *American Psychologist, 40,* 59–72.

Adams, G., Garcia, D. M., Purdie-Vaughs, V., & Steele, C. M. (2006). The detrimental effects of a suggestion of sexism in an introduction situation. *Journal of Experimental Psychology, 42,* 602–615.

Addis, M. E., & Mahalik, J. R. (2003). Men, masculinity, and the contexts of help seeking. *American Psychologist, 58,* 5–14.

Adlaf, E. M., Gilksman, L., Demers, A., & Newton-Taylor, B. (2001). The prevalence of elevated psychological distress among Canadian undergraduates: Findings from the 1998 Canadian Campus Survey. *Journal of American College Health, 50*(2), 67–72.

Adler, R. P., Lesser, G. S., Meringoff, L. K., Robertson, T. S., & Ward, S. (1980). *The effects of television advertising on children.* Lexington, MA: Lexington Books.

Adorno, T., Frenkel-Brunswik, E., Levinson, D., & Sanford, R. N. (1950). *The authoritarian personality.* New York: Harper.

Aiello, J. R., Douthitt, E. Z. (2001). Social facilitation from Triplett to electronic performance monitoring. *Group Dynamics: Theory, Research, and Practice, 5,* 163–180.

Aiello, J. R., Thompson, D. E., & Brodzinsky, D. M. (1983). How funny is crowding anyway? Effects of room size, group size, and the introduction of humor. *Basic and Applied Social Psychology, 4,* 193–207.

Ainsworth, M. D. S. (1979). Infant-mother attachment. *American Psychologist, 34,* 932–937.

Ajzen, I. (1990). The theory of planned behavior. *Organizational Behavior and Human Decision Processes, 50,* 179–211.

Ajzen, I., & Albarracin, D. (2007). Predicting and changing behavior: A reasoned action approach. In I. Ajzen, D. Albarracin & R. Hornik (Eds.), *Prediction and change in health behavior* (pp. 1–18). Mahwah, NJ: Erlbaum.

Ajzen, I., & Fishbein, M. (2005). The influence of attitudes on behavior. In D. Albarracin, B. T. Johnson & M. P. Zanna (Eds.), *The handbook of attitudes.* (173–221). Mahwah, NJ: Erlbaum.

Alderson, K. G. (2003). The ecological model of gay male identity. *The Canadian Journal of Human Sexuality, 12*(2), 75–85.

Allee, W. C., & Masure, R. M. (1936). A comparison of maze behavior in paired and isolated shell-parakeets *(Melopsittacus undulatus Shaw)* in a two-alley problem box. *Journal of Comparative Psychology, 22,* 131–155.

Allen, J. J., Iacono, W. G., & Danielson, K. D. (1992). The identification of concealed memories using the event-related potential and implicit behavioral measures: A methodology for prediction in the face of individual differences. *Psychophysiology, 29*(5), 504–22.

Allison, S. T., Jordan, M. R., & Yeatts, C. E. (1992). A cluster-analytic approach toward identifying the structure and content of human decision making. *Human Relations, 45,* 49–72.

Allison, S. T., Messick, D. M., & Goethals, G. R. (1989). On being better but not smarter than others: The Muhammad Ali effect. *Social Cognition, 7,* 275–296.

Alloy, L. B., & Abramson, L. Y. (1979). Judgment of contingency in depressed and nondepressed students: Sadder but wiser? *Journal of Experimental Psychology: General, 108,* 441–485.

Alloy, L. B., Abramson, L. Y., Gibb, B. E., Crossfield, A. G., Pieracci, A. M., Spasojevic, J., & Steinberg, J. A. (2004). Developmental antecedents of cognitive vulnerability to depression: Review of findings from the cognitive vulnerability to depression project. *Journal of Cognitive Psychotherapy, 18,* 115–133.

Allport, F. H. (1920). The influence of the group upon association and thought. *Journal of Experimental Psychology, 3,* 159–182.

Allport, G. W. (1958). *The nature of prejudice* (abridged). Garden City, NY: Anchor Books.

Altemeyer, B. (1988). *Enemies of freedom: Understanding right-wing authoritarianism.* San Francisco, CA: Jossey-Bass.

Altemeyer, B. (1992). *Six studies of right-wing authoritarianism among American state legislators.* Unpublished manuscript, University of Manitoba.

Altemeyer, B. (1996). *The authoritarian specter.* Cambridge, MA: Harvard University Press.

Altemeyer, R. (2004). Highly dominating, highly authoritarian personalities. *Journal of Social Psychology, 144,* 421–447.

Altemeyer, R. (2006). *The authoritarians.* Robert Altemeyer: Winnipeg, MA. Retrieved from members.shaw.ca/jeanaltemeyer/drbob/TheAuthoritarians.pdf on April 20, 2008.

Altman, I. (1975). *The environment and social behavior: Privacy, personal space, territory, crowding.* The University of Michigan: Brooks/Cole Pub. Co.

Amabile, T. M., & Glazebrook, A. H. (1982). A negativity bias in interpersonal evaluation. *Journal of Experimental Social Psychology, 18,* 1–22.

American Enterprise. (1992, January/February). *Women, men, marriages & ministers,* p. 106.

American Psychological Association Task Force on Television and Society. (1992). *Report on televised violence.* Washington, DC: Author.

Anderson, C. A. (2003). Video games and aggressive behavior. In D. Ravitch and J. P. Viteritti (Eds.), *Kid stuff: Marketing sex and violence to America's children.* Baltimore: Johns Hopkins University Press.

Anderson, C. A. (2004). An update on the effects of violent video games. *Journal of Adolescence, 27,* 113–122.

Anderson, C. A., & Anderson, K. B. (1998). Temperature and aggression: Paradox, controversy, and a (fairly) clear picture. In R. G. Geen & E. Donnerstein (Eds.), *Human aggression: Theories, research, and implications for social policy.* San Diego, CA: Academic Press.

Anderson, C. A., Anderson, K. B., Dorr, N., DeNeve, K. M., & Flanagan, M. (2000). Temperature and aggression. In M. P. Zanna (Ed.), *Advances in experimental social psychology, Vol. 32,* (pp. 63–133). San Diego, CA: Academic Press.

Anderson, C. A., Benjamin, A. J., Jr., & Bartholow, B. D. (1998). Does the gun pull the trigger? Automatic priming effects of weapon pictures and weapon names. *Psychological Science, 9,* 308–314.

Anderson, C. A., & Bushman, B. J. (2001). Effects of violent video games on aggressive behavior, aggressive cognition, aggressive affect, physiological arousal, and prosocial behavior: A meta-analytic review of the scientific literature. *Psychological Science, 12,* 353–359.

Anderson, C. A., & Bushman, B. J. (2002). Media violence and the American public revisited. *American Psychologist, 57,* 448–450.

Anderson, C. A., Carnagey, N. L., & Eubanks, J. (2003). Exposure to violent media: The effects of songs with violent lyrics on aggressive thoughts and feelings. *Journal of Personality and Social Psychology, 84,* 960–971.

Anderson, C. A., Carnagey, N. L., Flanagan, M., Benjamin, A. J., Jr., Eubanks, J., & Valentine, J. C. (2004). Violent video games: Specific effects of violent content on aggressive thoughts and behavior. *Advances in Experimental Social Psychology, 36,* 199–249.

Anderson, C. A., Horowitz, L. M., & French, R. D. (1983). Attributional style of lonely and depressed people. *Journal of Personality and Social Psychology, 45,* 127–136.

Anderson, C. A., Lindsay, J. J., & Bushman, B. J. (1999). Research in the psychological laboratory: Truth or triviality? *Current Directions in Psychological Science, 8,* 3–9.

Anderson, K. B., Cooper, H., & Okamura, L. (1997). Individual differences and attitudes toward rape: A meta-analytic review. *Personality and Social Psychology Review, 23,* 295–315.

Anderson, S. L., Adams, G., & Plaut, V. C. (2008). He cultural grounding of personal relationship: The importance of attractiveness in everyday life. *Journal of Personality and Social Psychology, 95,* 352–368.

Annesi, J. J. (2007). Relations of changes in exercise self-efficacy, physical self-concept, and body satisfaction with weight changes in obese white and African-American women initiating a physical activity program. *Ethnicity and Disease, 17,* 19–22.

AP. (1993, June 10). Walking past a dying man. *New York Times* (via Associated Press), 485.

AP/Ipsos. (2006, May 4). Associated Press/Ipsos Poll data reported by personal correspondence with Michael Gross.

Archer, D., Iritani, B., Kines, D., & Barrios, M. (1983). Face-ism: Five studies of sex difference in facial prominence. *Journal of Personality and Social Psychology, 45,* 725–735.

Archer, J. (1991). The influence of testosterone on human aggression. *British Journal of Psychology, 82,* 1–28.

Archer, J. (2000). Sex differences in aggression between heterosexual partners: A meta-analytic review. *Psychological Bulletin, 126,* 651–680.

Arendt, H. (1963). *Eichmann in Jerusalem: A report on the banality of evil.* New York, NY: Viking Press.

Ariza, L. M. (2006). Virtual jihad. *Scientific American, 294*(1), 18–21.

Arkin, R. M., & Maruyama, G. M. (1979). Attribution, affect, and college exam performance. *Journal of Educational Psychology, 71,* 85–93.

Armor, D. A., & Taylor, S. E. (1996). Situated optimism: Specific outcome expectancies and self-regulation. In M. P. Zanna (Ed.), *Advances in experimental social psychology, Vol. 30.* San Diego, CA: Academic Press.

Arms, R. L., Russell, G. W., & Sandilands, M. L. (1979). Effects on the hostility of spectators of viewing aggressive sports. *Social Psychology Quarterly, 42,* 275–279.

Arndt, J., & Vess, M. (2008). Tales from existential oceans: Terror management theory and how the awareness of our mortality affects us all. *Social and Personality Psychology Compass, 2*(2), 909–928.

Aron, A., & Aron, E. N. (1994). Love. In A. L. Weber & J. H. Harvey (Eds.), *Perspective on close relationships.* Boston: Allyn & Bacon.

Aron, A., Dutton, D. G., Aron, E. N., & Iverson, A. (1989). Experiences of falling in love. *Journal of Social and Personal Relationships, 6,* 243–257.

Aron, A., Fisher, H., Mashek, D. J., Strong, G., Li, H., & Brown, L. L. (2005). Reward, motivation, and emotion system systems associated with early-stage intense romantic love. *Journal of Neurophysiology, 94,* 327, 337.

Aronson, E. (2000). *Nobody left to hate: Teaching compassion after Columbine.* New York, NY: Freeman/Worth.

Aronson, E. (2002). Building empathy, compassion, and achievement in the jigsaw classroom. In J. Aronson (Ed.), *Improving academic achievement: Impact of psychological factors on education.* San Diego, CA: Academic Press.

Aronson, E., Blaney, N., Stephan, C., Sikes, J., & Snapp, M. (1978). *The jigsaw classroom.* Beverly Hills, CA: Sage.

Aronson, E., Brewer, M., & Carlsmith, J. M. (1985). Experimentation in social psychology. In G. Lindzey & E. Aronson (Eds.), *Handbook of social psychology, Vol. 1.* Hillsdale, NJ: Erlbaum.

Aronson, E., & Cope, V. (1968). My enemy's enemy is my friend. *Journal of Personality and Social Psychology, 8,* 8–12.

Aronson, E., & Gonzalez, A. (1988). Desegregation, jigsaw, and the Mexican-American experience. In P. A. Katz & D. Taylor (Eds.), *Towards the elimination of racism: Profi les in controversy.* New York: Plenum.

ASAPS (2005). *Cosmetic surgery quick facts: 2004 ASAPS statistics.* The American Society for Aesthetic Plastic Surgery.

Ash, R. (1999). *The top 10 of everything 2000.* New York, NY: DK Publishing.

Asher, J. (1987, April). Born to be shy? *Psychology Today,* 56–64.

Aslan, R. (2010). *Beyond fundamentalism: Confronting religious extremism in the age of globalization.* New York, NY: Random House.

ATSB. (2005). Road deaths: Australia, 2004 statistical summary.

Attanasi, G., García-Gallego, A., & Montesano, A. (2013). An experiment on Prisoner's Dilemma with confirmed proposals. *Organizational Behavior and Human Decision Processes, 120*(2), 216–227.

Atwell, R. H. (1986, July 28). *Drugs on campus: A perspective.* Higher Education and National Affairs, 5.

Aubrey, J. S., & Taylor, L. D. (2009). The role of lad magazines in priming men's chronic and temporary appearance-related schemata: An investigation of longitudinal and experimental findings. *Human Communication Research, 35,* 28–58.

Axelrod, R., & Dion, D. (1988). The further evolution of cooperation. *Science, 242,* 1385–1390.

Ayres, I. (1991). Fair driving: Gender and race discrimination in retail car negotiations. *Harvard Law Review, 104,* 817–872.

Azrin, N. H. (1967, May). Pain and aggression. *Psychology Today,* 27–33.

BabyCentre. (2014). *Popular baby names in Canada.* Retrieved from http://www.babycenter.ca/popular-baby-names.

Baccus, J. R., Baldwin, M. W., & Packer, D. J. (2004). Implicit self-esteem through classical conditioning. *Psychological Science, 15,* 498–502.

Back, M. D., Schmukle, S. C., & Egloff, B. (2008). Becoming friends by chance. *Psychological Science, 19,* 439–440.

Bailey, J. M., Gaulin, S., Agyei, Y., & Gladue, B. A. (1994). Effects of gender and sexual orientation on evolutionary relevant aspects of human mating psychology. *Journal of Personality and Social Psychology, 66,* 1081–1093.

Bailey, J. M., Kirk, K. M., Zhu, G., Dunne, M. P., & Martin, N. G. (2000). Do individual differences in sociosexuality represent genetic or environmentally contingent strategies? Evidence from the Australian Twin Registry. *Journal of Personality and Social Psychology, 78,* 537–545.

Bailis, D., Feigenson, N. R., & Klein, M. P. (2006). *A cross-national comparison of perceived risks from terrorism and disease.* Unpublished manuscripts, University of Manitoba, Quinnipiac University, and University of Pittsburgh.

Bailis, D. S. (2001). Benefits of self-handicapping in sport: A field study of university athletes. *Canadian Journal of Behavioural Science, 33*(4), 213–223.

Bailis, D. S., Fleming, J., & Segall, A. (2005). Self-determination and functional persuasion to encourage physical activity. *Psychology & Health, 20*(6), 691–708.

Bailis, D. S., Segall, A., & Chipperfield, J. G. (2010). A longitudinal study of members of a health-promotion facility. *Journal of Health Psychology, 15*(3), 326–338.

Bailis, D. S., Segall, A., & Chipperfield, J. G. (2010). Age, relative autonomy and change in health locus of control beliefs: A longitudinal study of members of a health-promotion facility. *Journal of Health Psychology, 15*(3), 326–338.

Baize, H. R., Jr., & Schroeder, J. E. (1995). Personality and mate selection in personal ads: Evolutionary preferences in a public mate selection process. *Journal of Social Behavior and Personality, 10,* 517–536.

Baker, L. A., & Emery, R. E. (1993). When every relationship is above average: Perceptions and expectations of divorce at the time of marriage. *Law and Human Behavior, 17,* 439–450.

Baldwin, A. S., Rothman, A. J., Hertel, A. W., Linde, J. A., Jeffery, R. W., Finch, E. A., & Lando, H. A. (2006). Specifying the determinants of the initiation and maintenance of behavior change: An examination of self-efficacy, satisfaction and smoking cessation. *Health Psychology, 25,* 626–634.

Baldwin, M. W., Keelan, J. P. R., Fehr, B., Enns, V., & Koh-Rangarajoo, E. (1996). Social-cognitive conceptualization of attachment working models: Availability and accessibility effects. *Journal of Personality and Social Psychology, 71,* 94–109.

Bandura, A. (1979). The social learning perspective: Mechanisms of aggression. In H. Toch (Ed.), *Psychology of crime and criminal justice.* New York, NY: Holt, Rinehart & Winston.

Bandura, A. (1986). *Social foundations of thought and action: A social cognitive theory.* Englewood Cliffs, NJ: Prentice Hall.

Bandura, A. (1997). *Self-efficacy: The exercise of control.* New York, NY: Freeman.

Bandura, A., Pastorelli, C., Barbaranelli, C., & Caprara, G. V. (1999). Self-efficacy pathways to childhood depression. *Journal of Personality and Social Psychology, 76,* 258–269.

Bandura, A., Ross, D., & Ross, S. A. (1961). Transmission of aggression through imitation of aggressive models. *Journal of Abnormal and Social Psychology, 63,* 575–582.

Bandura, A., & Walters, R. H. (1959). *Adolescent aggression.* New York, NY: Ronald Press.

Bandura, A., & Walters, R. H. (1963). *Social learning and personality development.* New York, NY: Holt, Rinehart and Winston.

Barelds, D. P. H., & Dijkstra, P. (2009). Positive illusions about a partner's physical attractiveness and relationship quality. *Personal Relationships, 16*(2), 263–283.

Bargh, J. A., McKenna, K. Y. A., & Fitzsimons, G. M. (2002). Can you see the real me? Activation and expression of the "true self" on the Internet. *Journal of Social Issues, 58,* 33–48.

Barker, L. (2006). Teaching evolutionary psychology: An interview with David M. Buss. *The Teaching of Psychology, 33,* 69–76.

Barlett, C., Branch, O., Rodeheffer, C., & Harris, R. (2009). How long do the short-term violent video game effects last? *Aggressive Behavior, 35,* 225–236.

Barnett, P. A., & Gotlib, I. H. (1988). Psychosocial functioning and depression: Distinguishing among antecedents, concomitants, and consequences, *Psychological Bulletin, 104,* 97–126.

Barnett, T. A., O'Loughlin, J., Lambert, M., Gauvin, L., Kestens, Y., & Daniel, M. (2008). *Many teens spend 30 hours a week on 'screen time' during high school.* American Heart Association 48th Annual Conference.

Baron, R. A., & Bryne, D. (1991). *Social psychology: Understanding human interaction.* (6th ed.). Toronto: Allyn & Bacon.

Baron, R. M., Mandel, D. R., Adams, C. A., & Griffen, L. M. (1976). Effects of social density in university residential environments. *Journal of Personality and Social Psychology, 34,* 434–446.

Baron, R. S. (1986). Distraction-conflict theory: Progress and problems. In L. Berkowitz (Ed.), *Advances in experimental social psychology.* Orlando, FL: Academic Press.

Baron, R. S. (2000). Arousal, capacity, and intense indoctrination. *Personality and Social Psychology Review, 4,* 238–254.

Baron, R. S., David, J. P., Inman, M., & Brunsman, B. M. (1997). Why listeners hear less than they are told: Attentional load and the teller-listener extremity effect. *Journal of Personality and Social Psychology, 72,* 826–838.

Barongan, C., & Hall, G. C. N. (1995). The influence of misogynous rap music on sexual aggression against women. *Psychology of Women Quarterly, 19,* 195–207.

Barry, D. (1995, January). Bored stiff. *Funny Times, 5.*

Bartholomew, K., & Horowitz, L. M. (1991). Attachment styles among young adults: A test of a four-category model. *Journal of Personality and Social Psychology, 61*(2), 226–244.

Bartholow, B. C., & Heinz, A. (2006). Alcohol and aggression without consumption: Alcohol cues, aggressive thoughts, and hostile perception bias. *Psychological Science, 17,* 30–37.

Bartholow, B. C., Sestir, M. A., & Davis, E. B. (2005). Correlates and consequences of exposure to video game violence: Hostile personality, empathy, and aggressive behavior. *Personality and Social Psychology Bulletin, 31,* 1573–1586.

Bassili, J. N (1996). Inside the Political Mind. *PsycCRITIQUES, 41*(7), 699–701.

Bastian, B., & Haslam, N. (2006). Psychological essentialism and stereotype endorsement. *Journal of Experimental Social Psychology, 42,* 228–235.

Bator, R. J., & Cialdini, R. B. (2000). The application of persuasion theory to the development of effective proenvironmental public service announcements. *Journal of Social Issues, 56*(3), 527–541.

Batson, C. D. (2001). Addressing the altruism question experimentally. In S. G. Post, L. B. Underwood, J. P. Schloss, & W. B. Hurlbut (Eds.), *Altruism and altruistic love: Science, philosophy, and religion in dialogue* (pp. 89–105). New York, NY: Oxford University Press.

Batson, C. D. (2006). Not all self-interest after all: Economics of empathy-induced altruism. In D. De Cremer, M. Zeelenberg, & J. K. Maurnighan (Eds.), *Social psychology and economics* (pp. 281–299). Mahwah, NJ: Lawrence Publishers.

Batson, C., & Weeks, J. L. (1996). Mood effects of unsuccessful helping: Another test of the empathy-altruism hypothesis. *Personality and Social Psychology Bulletin, 22*(2), 148–157.

Batson, C. D. (1991). *The altruism question: Toward a social-psychological answer.* Hillsdale, NJ: Erlbaum.

Batson, C. D., Duncan, B. D., Ackerman, P., Buckley, T., & Birch, K. (1981). Is empathetic emotion a source of altruistic motivation? *Journal of Personality and Social Psychology, 40,* 290–302.

Batson, C. D., Fultz, J., & Schoenrade, P. A. (1987). Distress and empathy: Two qualitatively distinct vicarious emotions with different motivational consequences. *Journal of Personality, 55,* 19–40.

Batson, C. D., & Moran, T. (1999). Empathy-induced altruism in a prisoner's dilemma. *European Journal of Social Psychology, 29,* 909–924.

Batson, C. D., & Powell, A. A. (2003). Altruism and prosocial behavior. In T. Millon & M. J. Lerner (Eds.), *Handbook of psychology: Personality and social psychology, Vol. 5.* Hoboken, NJ: Wiley.

Baumann, L. J., & Leventhal, H. (1985). "I can tell when my blood pressure is up, can't I?" *Health Psychology, 4,* 203–218.

Baumeister, R. (1996). Should schools try to boost self-esteem? Beware the dark side. *American Educator, 20,* 14–19, 43.

Baumeister, R. F. (1991). *Meanings of life.* New York: Guilford.

Baumeister, R. F., Campbell, J. D., Krueger, J. I., & Vohs, K. D. (2003). Does high self-esteem cause better performance, interpersonal success, happiness, or healthier lifestyles? *Psychological Science in the Public Interest, 4*(1), 1–44.

Baumeister, R. F., Catanese, K. R., & Vohs, K. D. (2001). Is there a gender difference in strength of sex drive? Theoretical views, conceptual distinctions, and a review of relevant evidence. *Personality and Social Psychology Review, 5,* 242–273.

Baumeister, R. F., Catanese, K. R., & Wallace, H. M. (2002). Conquest by force: A narcissistic reactance theory of rape and sexual coercion. *Review of General Psychology, 6,* 92–135.

Baumeister, R. F., & Ilko, S. A. (1995). Shallow gratitude: Public and private acknowledgement of external help in accounts of success. *Basic and Applied Social Psychology, 16,* 191–209.

Baumeister, R. F., & Leary, M. R. (1995). The need to belong: Desire for interpersonal attachment as a fundamental human motivation. *Psychological Bulletin, 117,* 497–529.

Baumeister, R. F., Twenge, J. M., & Nuss, C. K. (2002). Effects of social exclusion on cognitive processes: Anticipated aloneness reduces intelligent thought. *Journal of Personality and Social Psychology, 83*(4), 817–827.

Baumeister, R. F., & Vohs, K. (2004). Sexual economics: Sex as female resource for social exchange in heterosexual interactions. *Personality and Social Psychology Bulletin, 8,* 339–363.

Baumeister, R. F., & Wotman, S. R. (1992). *Breaking hearts: The two sides of unrequited love.* New York: Guilford Press.

Baxter, T. L., & Goldberg, L. R. (1987). Perceived behavioral consistency underlying trait attributions to oneself and another: An extension of the actor-observer effect. *Personality and Social Psychology Bulletin, 13,* 437–447.

Bayer, E. (1929). Beitrage zur zeikomponenten theorie des hungers. *Zeitschrift fur Psychologie, 112,* 1–54.

Bazerman, M. H. (1986, June). Why negotiations go wrong. *Psychology Today,* 54–58.

BBC. (2008, November 21). Pirates "gained $150m this year" (news. bbc.co.uk).

Beaman, A. L., & Klentz, B. (1983). The supposed physical attractiveness bias against supporters of the women's movement: A meta-analysis. *Personality and Social Psychology Bulletin, 9,* 544–550.

Beaman, A. L., Klentz, B., Diener, E., & Svanum, S. (1979). Self-awareness and transgression in children: Two field studies. *Journal of Personality and Social Psychology, 37,* 1835–1846.

Beauvois, J. L., & Dubois, N. (1988). The norm of internality in the explanation of psychological events. *European Journal of Social Psychology, 18,* 299–316.

Beck, A. T., & Young, J. E. (1978, September). College blues. *Psychology Today,* pp. 80–92.

Becker, S. W., & Eagly, A. H. (2004). The heroism of women and men. *American Psychologist, 59*(3), 163–178.

Bell, D., Esses, V., & Maio, G. (1996). The utility of open-ended measures to assess intergroup ambivalence. *Canadian Journal of Behavioural Science/Revue canadienne des sciences du comportement, 28*(1), 12–18.

Bell, P. A. (1980). Effects of heat, noise, and provocation on retaliatory evaluative behavior. *Journal of Social Psychology, 110*, 97–100.

Belson, W. A. (1978). *Television violence and the adolescent boy.* Westmead, England: Saxon House, Teakfield Ltd.

Bem, D. J. (1972). Self-perception theory. In L. Berkowitz (Ed.), *Advances in experimental social psychology, Vol. 6.* New York: Academic Press.

Benjamin, L. T. Jr., & Simpson, J. A. (2009). The power of the situation: The impact of Milgram's obedience studies on personality and social psychology. *American Psychologist, 64*(1), 12–19.

Bennett, R. (1991, February). *Pornography and extrafamilial child sexual abuse: Examining the relationship.* Unpublished manuscript, Los Angeles Police Department Sexually Exploited Child Unit.

Ben-Zeev, T., Fein, S., & Inzlicht, M. (2005). Arousal and stereotype threat. *Journal of Experimental Social Psychology, 41*, 174–181.

Berg, J. H. (1984). Development of friendship between roommates. *Journal of Personality and Social Psychology, 46*, 346–356.

Berg, J. H. (1987). Responsiveness and self-disclosure. In V. J. Derlega & J. H. Berg (Eds.), *Self-disclosure: Theory, research, and therapy.* New York: Plenum.

Berg, J. H., & McQuinn, R. D. (1986). Attraction and exchange in continuing and noncontinuing dating relationships. *Journal of Personality and Social Psychology, 50*, 942–952.

Bergeron, S. M., & Senn, C. Y. (1998). Body image and sociocultural norms: A comparison of heterosexual and lesbian women. *Psychology of Women Quarterly, 22*, 385–401.

Berkowitz, L. (1968, September). Impulse, aggression and the gun. *Psychology Today*, 18–22.

Berkowitz, L. (1978). Whatever happened to the frustration-aggression hypothesis? *American Behavioral Scientists, 21*, 691–708.

Berkowitz, L. (1981, June). How guns control us. *Psychology Today*, 11–12.

Berkowitz, L. (1984). Some effects of thoughts on anti- and prosocial influences of media events: A cognitive-neoassociation analysis. *Psychological Bulletin, 95*, 410–427.

Berkowitz, L. (1989). Frustration-aggression hypothesis: Examination and reformulation. *Psychological Bulletin, 106*, 59–73.

Berkowitz, L. (1995). A career on aggression. In G. G. Brannigan & M. R. Merrens (Eds.), *The social psychologists: Research adventures.* New York: McGraw-Hill.

Berkowitz, L. (1998). Affective aggression: The role of stress, pain, and negative affect. In R. G. Geen & E. Donnerstein (Eds.), *Human aggression: Theories, research, and implications for social policy.* San Diego, CA: Academic Press.

Berkowitz, L., & Geen, R. G. (1966). Film violence and the cue properties of available targets. *Journal of Personality and Social Psychology, 3*, 525–530.

Bernstein, M. J., Young, S. G., Hugenberg, K. (2007). The cross-category effect. Mere social categorization is sufficient to elicit an own-group bias in face recognition. *Psychological Science, 18*, 706–712.

Berry J. W. (1997). Immigration, acculturation, and adaptation. *Applied Psychology, 46*, 5–34.

Berry, J. W., & Kalin, R. (1995). Multicultural and ethnic attitudes in Canada: An overview of the 1991 National Survey. *Canadian Journal of Behavioural Science/Revue canadienne des sciences du comportement, 27*(3), 301–320.

Berscheid, E. (1981). An overview of the psychological effects of physical attractiveness and some comments upon the psychological effects of knowledge of the effects of physical attractiveness. In W. Lucker, K. Ribbens, & J. A. McNamera (Eds.), *Logical aspects of facial form* (craniofacial growth series). Ann Arbor: University of Michigan Press.

Berscheid, E., Boye, D., & Walster (Hatfield), E. (1968). Retaliation as a means of restoring equity. *Journal of Personality and Social Psychology, 10*, 370–376.

Berscheid, E., Dion, K., Walster (Hatfield), E., & Walster, G. W. (1971). Physical attractiveness and dating choice: A test of the matching hypothesis. *Journal of Experimental Social Psychology, 7*, 173–189.

Berscheid, E., Graziano, W., Monson, T., & Dermer, M. (1976). Outcome dependency: Attention, attribution, and attraction. *Journal of Personality and Social Psychology, 34*, 978–989.

Berscheid, E., & Walster (Hatfield), E. (1978). *Interpersonal attraction.* Reading, MA: Addison-Wesley.

Berscheid, E., Walster, G. W., & Hatfield (Walster), E. (1969). *Effects of accuracy and positivity of evaluation on liking for the evaluator.* Unpublished manuscript. Summarized by E. Berscheid and E. Walster (Hatfield) (1978), Interpersonal attraction. Reading, MA: Addison-Wesley.

Besser, A., & Priel, B. (2005). The apple does not fall far from the tree: Attachment styles and personality vulnerabilities to depression in three generations of women. *Personality and Social Psychology Bulletin, 31*, 1052–1073.

Bettencourt, B. A., Dill, K. E., Greathouse, S. A., Charlton, K., & Mulholland, A. (1997). Evaluations of ingroup and outgroup members: The role of category-based expectancy violation. *Journal of Experimental Social Psychology, 33*, 244–275.

Bettencourt, B. A., & Miller, N. (1996). Gender differences in aggression as a function of provocation: A meta-analysis. *Psychological Bulletin, 119*, 422–447.

Bibby, R. (2004). *The Future Families Project: A survey of Canadian hopes and dreams.* The Vanier Institute of the Family: Ottawa.

Bierbrauer, G. (1979). Why did he do it? Attribution of obedience and the phenomenon of dispositional bias. *European Journal of Social Psychology 9*, 67–84.

Bierly, M. M. (1985). Prejudice toward contemporary outgroups as a generalized attitude. *Journal of Applied Social Psychology, 15*, 189–199.

Biernat, M. (1991). Gender stereotypes and the relationship between masculinity and femininity: A developmental analysis. *Journal of Personality and Social Psychology, 61*, 351–365.

Biernat, M., & Kobrynowicz, D. (1997). Gender- and race-based standards of competence: Lower minimum standards but higher ability standards for devalued groups. *Journal of Personality and Social Psychology, 72,* 544–557.

Binder, J., Zagefka, H., Brown, R., Funke, F., Kessler, T., Mummendey, A. . . . Leyens, J-P. (2009). Does contact reduce prejudice or does prejudice reduce contact? A longitudinal test of the contact hypothesis among majority and minority groups in three European countries. *Journal of Personality and Social Psychology, 96,* 843–856.

Bingenheimer, J. B., Brennan, R. T., & Earls, F. J. (2005). Firearm violence exposure and serious violent behavior. *Science, 308,* 1323–1326.

Bishop, B. (2004). The schism in U.S. politics begins at home: Growing gaps found from county to county in presidential race. *American Statesman,* November 22, 2004.

Bishop, G. D. (1984). Gender, role and illness behavior in a military population. *Health Psychology, 3,* 519–534.

Bishop, G. D. (1987). Lay conceptions of physical symptoms. *Journal of Applied Social Psychology, 17,* 127–146.

Björkqvist, K. (1994). Sex differences in physical, verbal, and indirect aggression: A review of recent research. *Sex Roles, 30,* 177–188.

Blair, C. A., Thompson, L. F., & Wuensch, K. L. (2005). Electronic helping behavior: The virtual presence of others makes a difference. *Basic and Applied Social Psychology, 27,* 171–178.

Blake, R. R., & Mouton, J. S. (1979). Intergroup problem solving in organizations: From theory to practice. In W. G. Austin & S. Worchel (Eds.), *The social psychology of intergroup relations.* Monterey, CA: Brooks/Cole.

Blass, T. (2004). *The man who shocked the world: The life and legacy of Stanley Milgram.* New York: Basic Books.

Blass, T. (2009). From New Haven to Santa Clara: A historical perspective on the Milgram obedience experiments. *American Psychologist, 64*(1), 37–45.

Bliss, M. (2004). *Right honorable men.* HarperCollins: Toronto.

Block, J., & Funder, D. C. (1986). Social roles and social perception: Individual differences in attribution and error. *Journal of Personality and Social Psychology, 51,* 1200–1207.

Bodenhausen, G. V. (1990). Stereotypes as judgmental heuristics: Evidence of circadian variations in discrimination. *Psychological Science, 1,* 319–322.

Bodenhausen, G. V. (1993). Emotions, arousal, and stereotypic judgments: A heuristic model of affect and stereotyping. In D. M. Mackie & D. L. Hamilton (Eds.), *Affect, cognition, and stereotyping: Interactive processes in group perception.* San Diego, CA: Academic Press.

Bohner, G., Bless, H., Schwartz, N., & Strack, F. (1988). What triggers causal attributions? The impact of valence and subjective probability. *European Journal of Social Psychology, 18,* 335–345.

Bolen, M. (2013, November). Canadian kids smoke most marijuana in Western World: UNICEF. *Hufflngton Post.* http://www. huffingtonpost.ca/2013/04/11/ canada-kids-marijuana-unicef_n_3062739.html.

Bonar, E. E., Rosenberg, H., Hoffmann, E., Kraus, S. W., Kryzak, E., Young, K. M. . . . Bannon, E. E. (2011). Measuring university students' self-efficacy to use drinking self-control strategies'. *Psychology of Addictive Behaviors, 25*(1), 155–161.

Bond, C. F., Jr., & Titus, L. J. (1983). Social facilitation: A meta-analysis of 241 studies. *Psychological Bulletin, 94,* 265–292.

Borgida, E., & Brekke, N. (1985). Psycholegal research on rape trials. In A. W. Burgess (Ed.), *Rape and sexual assault: A research handbook.* New York: Garland.

Borkenau, P., & Liebler, A. (1993). Convergence of stranger ratings of personality and intelligence with self-ratings, partner ratings, and measured intelligence. *Journal of Personality and Social Psychology, 65,* 546–553.

Bornstein, G., & Rapoport, A. (1988). Intergroup competition for the provision of step-level public goods: Effects of preplay communication. *European Journal of Social Psychology, 18,* 125–142.

Bornstein, G., Rapoport, A., Kerpel, L., & Katz, T. (1989). Within- and between-group communication in intergroup competition for public goods. *Journal of Experimental Social Psychology, 25,* 422–436.

Bornstein, R. E. (1999). Source amnesia, misattribution, and the power of unconscious perceptions and memories. *Psychoanalytic Psychology, 16,* 155–178.

Bornstein, R. F. (1989). Exposure and affect: Overview and meta-analysis of research, 1968–1987. *Psychological Bulletin, 106,* 265–289.

Bossard, J. H. S. (1932). Residential propinquity as a factor in marriage selection. *American Journal of Sociology, 38,* 219–224.

Bothwell, R. K., Brigham, J. C., & Malpass, R. S. (1989). Cross-racial identification. *Personality and Social Psychology Bulletin, 15,* 19–25.

Botvin, G. J., Schinke, S., & Orlandi, M. A. (1995). School-based health promotion: Substance abuse and sexual behavior. *Applied & Preventive Psychology, 4,* 167–184.

Botwin, M. D., Buss, D. M., & Shackelford, T. K. (1997). Personality and mate preferences: Five factors in mate selection and marital satisfaction. *Journal of Personality, 65,* 107–136.

Bouas, K. S., & Komorita, S. S. (1996). Group discussion and cooperation in social dilemmas. *Personality and Social Psychology Bulletin, 22,* 1144–1150.

Bourgeois, M. J., Horowitz, I. A., & Lee, L. F. (1993). Effects of technicality and access to trial transcripts on verdicts and information processing in a civil trial. *Personality and Social Psychology Bulletin, 19,* 219–226.

Bower, G. H. (1987). Commentary on mood and memory. *Behavioral Research and Therapy, 25,* 443–455.

Boyanowsky, E. (1999). Violence and aggression in the heat of passion and in cold blood: The Ecs-TC syndrome. *International Journal of Law & Psychiatry, 22,* 257–271.

Boyatzis, C. J., Matillo, G. M., & Nesbitt, K. M. (1995). Effects of the "Mighty Morphin Power Rangers" on children's aggression with peers. *Child Study Journal, 25,* 45–55.

Braverman, J. (2005). The effect of mood on detection of covariation. *Personality and Social Psychology Bulletin, 31,* 1487–1497.

Bray, S. R., Law, J., & Foyle, J. (2003). Team quality and game location effects in English professional soccer. *Journal of Sport Behavior, 26,* 319–334.

Brewer, M. B. (1987). Collective decisions. *Social Science, 72,* 140–143.

Brewer, M. B., & Miller, N. (1988). Contact and cooperation: When do they work? In P. A. Katz & D. Taylor (Eds.), *Towards the elimination of racism: Profiles in controversy.* New York: Plenum.

Brezina, T., & Topalli, V. (2012), Criminal self-efficacy exploring the correates and consequences of a "successful criminal" identity. *Criminal Justice and Behavior, 39*(8), 1042–1062.

Brickman, P., Rabinowitz, V. C., Coates, D., Cohn, E., & Kidder, L. (1982). Models of helping and coping. *American Psychologist, 37*, 364–384.

Broad, W. J., & Hulse, C. (2003, February 3). NASA dismissed advisers who warned about safety. *New York Times.* (http://www.nytimes.com).

Brockner, J., & Hulton, A. J. B. (1978). How to reverse the vicious cycle of low self-esteem: The importance of attentional focus. *Journal of Experimental Social Psychology, 14*, 564–578.

Brockner, J., Rubin, J. Z., Fine, J., Hamilton, T. P., Thomas, B., & Turetsky, B. (1982). Factors affecting entrapment in escalating conflicts: The importance of timing. *Journal of Research in Personality, 16*, 247–266.

Brodt, S. E., & Ross, L. D. (1998). The role of stereotyping in overconfident social prediction. *Social Cognition, 16*, 228–252.

Brooks, D. (2005, August 10). All cultures are not equal. *New York Times* (http://www.nytimes.com).

Brown, D. E. (1991). *Human universals.* New York: McGraw-Hill.

Brown, J. (2001). Anti-Arab passions sweep the U.S. *Salon.* Retrieved from http://www.salon.com/2001/09/13/backlash_2/.

Brown, J. D., Novick, N. J., Lord, K. A., & Richards, J. M. (1992). When Gulliver travels: Social context, psychological closeness, and self-appraisals. *Journal of Personality and Social Psychology, 62*, 717–727.

Brown, J. D., & Taylor, S. E. (1986). Affect and the processing of personal information: Evidence for mood-activated self-schemata. *Journal of Experimental Social Psychology, 22*, 436–452.

Brown, R., Maras, P., Masser, B., Vivian, J., & Hewstone, M. (2001). Life on the ocean wave: Testing some intergroup hypotheses in a naturalistic setting. *Group Processes and Intergroup Relations, 4*, 81–97.

Brown, R., Vivian, J., & Hewstone, M. (1999). Changing attitudes through intergroup contact: The effects of group membership salience. *European Journal of Social Psychology, 29*, 741–764.

Brown, R., & Wootton-Millward, L. (1993). Perceptions of group homogeneity during group formation and change. *Social Cognition, 11*, 126–149.

Brown, R., & Zagefka, H. (2006). Choice of comparisons in intergroup settings: The role of temporal information and comparison motives. *European Journal of Social Psychology, 36*(5), 649–671.

Brown, R. P., Charnsangavej, T., Keough, K. A., Newman, M. L., & Rentfrom, P. J. (2000). Putting the "affirm" into affirmative action: Preferential selection and academic performance. *Journal of Personality and Social Psychology, 79*, 736–747.

Browne, K. D., & Hamilton-Giachritsis, C. E. (2005). The influence of violent media on children and adolescents: A public health approach. *The Lancet, 365*, 702–710.

Browning, C. (1992). *Ordinary men: Reserve police battalion 101 and the final solution in Poland.* New York: Harper Collins.

Brug, J., Conner, M., Harre, N., Kremers, S., McKellar, S., & Whitelaw, S. (2004). The transtheoretical model and stages of change: A critique. Observations by five commentators on the paper by J. Adam and M. White, Why don't stage-based activity promotion interventions work? *Health Education Research, 20*, 244–258.

Brunet, P. M., & Schmidt, L. A. (2007). Is shyness context specific? Relation between shyness and online self-disclosure with and without a live webcam in young adults. *Journal of Research in Personality 41*, 938–945.

Brym, R. J., & Lenton, R. L. (2001). Love online: A report on digital dating in Canada. Retrieved from http://www.nelson.com/nelson/harcourt/sociology/newsociety3e/loveonline.pdf.

Buchanan, G. M. & Seligman, M. E. P. (1995). *Explanatory style.* Hillsdale, NJ: Erlbaum.

Buehler, R., & Griffin, D. (2003). Planning, personality, and prediction: The role of future focus in optimistic time predictions. *Organizational Behavior and Human Decision Processes, 92*, 80–90.

Buehler, R., Griffin, D., & Ross, M. (1994). Exploring the "planning fallacy": When people underestimate their task completion times. *Journal of Personality and Social Psychology, 67*, 366–381.

Buehler, R., Griffin, D., & Ross, M. (2002). Inside the planning fallacy: The causes and consequences of optimistic time predictions. In T. Gilovich, D. Griffin, & D. Kahneman (Eds.), *Heuristics and biases: The psychology of intuitive judgment* (pp. 87–88). Cambridge: Cambridge University Press.

Bui, N. H. (2012). False consensus in attitudes toward celebrities. *Psychology of Popular Media Culture, 1*(4), 236–243.

Burger, J. M. (1991). Changes in attributions over time: The ephemeral fundamental attribution error. *Social Cognition, 9*, 182–193.

Burger, J. M. (2009). Replicating Milgram: Would people still obey today? *American Psychologist, 64*, 1–11.

Burger, J. M., & Burns, L. (1988). The illusion of unique invulnerability and the use of effective contraception. *Personality and Social Psychology Bulletin, 14*, 264–270.

Burger, J. M., Soroka, S., Gonzago, K., Murphy, E., & Somervell, E. (2001). The effect of fleeting attraction on compliance to requests. *Personality and Social Psychology Bulletin, 27*, 1578–1586.

Burkholder, R. (2003, February 14). Unwilling coalition? Majorities in Britain, Canada oppose military action in Iraq. *Gallup Poll Tuesday Briefing* (http://www.gallup.com/poll).

Burn, S. M. (1992). Locus of control, attributions, and helplessness i n the homeless. *Journal of Applied Social Psychology, 22*, 1161–1174.

Burns, D. D. (1980). *Feeling good: The new mood therapy.* New York, NY: Signet.

Burnstein, E., & Kitayama, S. (1989). Persuasion in groups. In T. C. Brock & S. Shavitt (Eds.), *The psychology of persuasion.* San Francisco: Freeman.

Burnstein, E., & Vinokur, A. (1977). Persuasive argumentation and social comparison as determinants of attitude polarization. *Journal of Experimental Social Psychology, 13*, 315–332.

Burr, W. R. (1973). *Theory construction and the sociology of the family.* New York: Wiley.

Burson, K. A., Larrick, R. P., & Klayman, J. (2006). Skilled or unskilled, but still unaware of it: How perceptions of difficulty drive miscalibration in relative comparisons. *Journal of Personality and Social Psychology, 90,* 60–77.

Bushman, B. J. (1993). Human aggression while under the influence of alcohol and other drugs: An integrative research review. *Current Directions in Psychological Science, 2,* 148–152.

Bushman, B. J. (1995). Moderating role of trait aggressiveness in the effects of violent media on aggression. *Journal of Personality and Social Psychology, 69,* 950–960.

Bushman, B. J. (2002). Does venting anger feed or extinguish the flame? Catharsis, rumination, distraction, anger, and aggressive responding. *Personality and Social Psychology Bulletin, 28,* 724–731.

Bushman, B. J., & Anderson, C. A. (2001). Media violence and the American public: Scientific facts versus media misinformation. *American Psychologist, 56,* 477–489.

Bushman, B. J., & Anderson, C. A. (2002). Violent video games and hostile expectations: A test of the general aggression model. *Personality and Social Psychology Bulletin, 28,* 1679–1686.

Bushman, B. J., & Baumeister, R. (1998). Threatened egotism, narcissism, self-esteem, and direct and displaced aggression: Does self-love or self-hate lead to violence? *Journal of Personality and Social Psychology, 75,* 219–229.

Bushman, B. J., & Cooper, H. M. (1990). Effects of alcohol on human aggression: An integrative research review. *Psychological Bulletin, 107,* 341–354.

Bushman, B. J., & Geen, R. G. (1990). Role of cognitive-emotional mediators and individual differences in the effects of media violence on aggression. *Journal of Personality and Social Psychology, 58,* 156–163.

Bushman, B. J., & Gibson, B. (2011). Violent video games cause an increase in aggression long after the game has been turned off. *Social Psychological Personality Science, 2*(1), 29–32.

Buss, D. M. (1984). Toward a psychology of person-environment (PE) correlation: The role of spouse selection. *Journal of Personality and Social Psychology, 47,* 361–377.

Buss, D. M. (1985). Human mate selection. *American Scientist, 73,* 47–51.

Buss, D. M. (1994). *The evolution of desire: Strategies of human mating.* New York: Basic Books.

Buss, D. M. (1995). Psychological sex differences: Origins through sexual selection. *American Psychologist, 50,* 164–168.

Buss, D. M. (1999). Behind the scenes. In D. G. Myers, *Social psychology* (6th ed.). New York: McGraw-Hill.

Buston, P. M., & Emlen, S. T. (2003). Cognitive processes underlying human mate choice: The relationship between self-perception and mate preference in Western society. *Proceedings of the National Academy of Sciences, 100*(15), 8805–8810.

Butler, J. L., & Baumeister, R. F. (1998). The trouble with friendly faces: Skilled performance with a supportive audience. *Journal of Personality and Social Psychology, 75,* 1213–1230.

Buunk, B. P., & Van Yperen, N. W. (1991). Referential comparisons, relational comparisons, and exchange orientation: Their relation to marital satisfaction. *Personality and Social Psychology Bulletin, 17,* 709–717.

Byrne, D. (1971). *The attraction paradigm.* New York: Academic Press.

Byrne, D., & Wong, T. J. (1962). Racial prejudice, interpersonal attraction, and assumed dissimilarity of attitudes. *Journal of Abnormal and Social Psychology, 65,* 246–253.

Bytwerk, R. L. (1976). Julius Streicher and the impact of Der Stürmer. *Wiener Library Bulletin, 29,* 41–46.

Cacioppo, J. T., Berntson, G. G., Malarkey, W. B., Kiecolt-Glaser, J. K., Sheridan, J. F., Poehlmann, K. M., et al. (1998). Autonomic, neuroendocrine, and immune responses to psychological stress: The reactivity hypothesis. *Annals of the New York Academy of Sciences, 840,* 664–673.

Cacioppo, J. T., Petty, R. E., Feinstein, J. A., & Jarvis, W. B. G. (1996). Dispositional differences in cognitive motivation: The life and times of individuals varying in need for cognition. *Psychological Bulletin, 119,* 197–253.

Cairns, E., & Hewstone, M. (2002). The impact of peacemaking in Northern Ireland on intergroup behavior. In S. Gabi & B. Nevo (Eds.), *Peace education: The concept, principles, and practices around the world.* Mahwah, NJ: Erlbaum.

Calhoun, J. B. (1962, February). Population density and social pathology. *Scientific American,* 139–148.

Cameron, J. E. (2004). A three-factor model of social identity. *Self & Identity, 3,* 239–262.

Cameron, J. E., & Lalonde, R. N. (2001). Social identification and gender-related ideology in women and men. *British Journal of Social Psychology, 40,* 59–77.

Campbell, D. T. (1975). The conflict between social and biological evolution and the concept of original sin. *Zygon, 10,* 234–249.

Campbell, J. D., Fairly, P. J., & Fehr, B. (1986). Better than me or better than thee? Reactions to intrapersonal and interpersonal performance feedback. *Journal of Personality, 54*(3), 479–493.

Campbell, W. K., Bush, C. P., Brunell, A. B., & Shelton, J. (2005). Understanding the social costs of narcissism: The case of the tragedy of the commons. *Personality and Social Psychology Bulletin, 31*(10), 1358–1368.

Campbell, W. K., & Sedikides, C. (1999). Self-threat magnifies the self-serving bias: A meta-analytic integration. *Review of General Psychology, 3,* 23–43.

Canadian Centre on Substance Abuse. (1997). *Canadian profile: Alcohol, tobacco, and other drugs.* Ottawa: Canadian Centre on Substance Abuse.

Canadian Department of Justice. (2004). A statistical profile on vulnerable Canadians. Retrieved from http://www.justice.gc.ca/eng/rp-pr/jr/jr13/p6a.html#sec2.

Canadian Press. (2013). Facebook use in Canada: Over 19 million log on at least once a month. Retireived 09-14-2014.

Canadian Wireless Telecommunications Association (2014). Wireless phone subscribers in Canada 2012. Retrieved 2014-09-14.

Cannon, W. B. (1932). *The wisdom of the body.* New York: Norton.

Caprariello, P. A., & Reis, H. T. (2013). To do to have, or to share? Valuing experiences over material possessions depends on the involvement of others. *Journal of Personality and Social Psychology, 104*(2), 199–215.

Caputo, D., & Dunning, D. (2005). What you don't know: The role played by errors of omission in imperfect self-assessments. *Journal of Experimental Social Psychology, 41,* 488–505.

Carducci, B. J., Cosby, P. C., & Ward, D. D. (1978). Sexual arousal and interpersonal evaluations. *Journal of Experimental Social Psychology, 14,* 449–457.

Carli, L. L. (1999). Cognitive reconstruction, hindsight, and reactions to victims and perpetrators. *Personality and Social Psychology Bulletin, 25,* 966–979.

Carli, L. L., & Leonard, J. B. (1989). The effect of hindsight on victim derogation. *Journal of Social and Clinical Psychology, 8,* 331–343.

Carlson, C. A., Gronlund, S. D., & Clark, S. E. (2008). Lineup composition, suspect position, and the sequential lineup advantage. *Journal of Experimental Psychology: Applied, 14*(2), 118–128.

Carlson, M., Marcus-Newhall, A., & Miller, N. (1990). Effects of situational aggression cues: A quantitative review. *Journal of Personality and Social Psychology, 58,* 622–633.

Carlucci, M. E., Compo, N. S., & Zimmerman, L. (2013). Lie detection during high-stakes truths and lies. *Legal and Criminological Psychology, 18,* 314–323.

Carnahan, T., & McFarland, S. G. (2007). Revisiting the Stanford Prison Experiment: Could participant self-selection have led to the cruelty? *Personality and Social Psychology Bulletin, 33,* 603–614.

Carrera, P., Oceja, L., Caballero, A., Muñoz, D., López-Pérez, B., & Ambrona, T. (2013). I feel so sorry! Tapping the jont influence of empathy and personal distress on helping behavior. *Motivation and Emotion, 37*(2), 335–345.

Carson, R. C., Hollon, S. D., & Shelton, R. C. (2010). Depressive realism and clinical depression. *Behavior Research and Therapy, 48,* 257–266.

Carvallo, M., & Gabriel, S. (2006). No man is an island: The need to belong and dismissing avoidant attachment style. *Personality and Social Psychology Bulletin, 32*(5), 697–709.

Carver, C. S., Kus, L. A., & Scheier, M. F. (1994). Effect of good versus bad mood and optimistic versus pessimistic outlook on social acceptance versus rejection. *Journal of Social and Clinical Psychology, 13,* 138–151.

Caspi, A., & Herbener, E. S. (1990). Continuity and change: Assortative marriage and the consistency of personality in adulthood. *Journal of Personality and Social Psychology, 58,* 250–258.

Cassidy, J. (2000). The complexity of the caregiving system: A perspective from attachment theory. *Psychological Inquiry, 11*(2), 86–91.

Cassidy, W., Jackson, M., & Brown, K. N. (2009). Sticks and stones can break my bones, but how can pixels hurt me? Students' experiences with cyber-bullying. *School Psychology International, 30*(4), 383–402.

CBC. (1990). *Sikh Mounties allowed to wear turbans.* Retrieved from http://archives.cbc.ca/politics/rights_freedoms/clips/3302/.

CBC. (1996). *Chrétien extends a 'Shawinigan handshake.'* Retrieved from http://archives.cbc.ca/politics/federal_politics/clips/12796/.

CBC. (2003). Hurricane Juan on course for Nova Scotia. Retrieved from http://www.cbc.ca/canada/story/2003/09/27/hurricane_ns030927.html.

CBC. (2004). *Online dating facts and figures.* Retrieved from http://www.cbc.ca/marketplace/pre-2007/files/services/onlinedating/facts.html.

CBC. (2005). *Indepth: Forces of nature.* Retrieved from http://www.cbc.ca/news/background/forceofnature/.

CBC. (2005). *Police stop more Blacks, Ontario study finds.* Retrieved from http://www.cbc.ca/canada/story/2005/05/26/race050526.html.

CBC. (2005). *Understanding the violence.* Retrieved from http://www.cbc.ca/news/background/paris_riots/.

CBC. (2006). *The final showdown.* Retrieved from http://www.cbc.ca/sports/hockey/stanleycup2006/content/roundtable/05.html.

CBC. (2007). CBC Radio Podcasts. Downloaded from http://www.podcastdirectory.com/podcasts/33626.

CBC. (2007). *Hérouxville drops some rules from controversial code.* Retrieved from http://www.cbc.ca/news/canada/montreal/story/2007/02/13/qc-herouxville20070213.html.

CBC. (2007). *Kyoto protocol FAQs.* Retrieved from http://www.cbc.ca/news/background/kyoto/.

CBC. (2008). *Canada lowers 2008 GDP estimate.* Retrieved from http://www.cbc.ca/news/business/story/2008/01/24/bocreporthtml.

CBC. (2008). *Cyberbullying.* Retrieved from http://www.cbc.ca/news/background/bullying/cyber_bullying.html.

CBC. (2008). *Leaving reserve may be key to aboriginal success: Think-tank.* Retrieved from http://www.cbc.ca/news/canada/manitoba/story/2008/04/11/reserve-paper.html.

CBC. (2008). *The used-to-be Big 3.* Retrieved from http://www.cbc.ca/news/business/story/2009/02/17/f-bigthreeupdate.html.

CBC. (2010). *BP resumes "Top Kill" operation.* Retrieved from http://www.cbc.ca/news/world/story/2010/05/27/gulf-of-mexico-spill.html.

CBC. (2010). *Montreal mobs loot stores after Game 7 win.* Retrieved from http://www.cbc.ca/news/canada/montreal/story/2010/05/12/mtl-habs-fever-game-seven-penguins.html.

CBC. (2010). *Spanking linked to aggression in children.* Retrieved from http://www.cbc.ca/news/spanking-linked-to-aggression-in-children-1.874050.

CBC. (2011). *2010–2011 winter recap.* Retrieved from http://www.cbc.ca/nl/blogs/ryansnoddon/2011/04/20102011-winter-recap.html.

CBC. (2012). Hudson Bay polar bear numbers increase. CBC News online. Retrieved 09-14-2014.

CBC. (2013). *Bystanders key to tackling 'rape culture,' experts say: Saint Mary's University students attend conference after controversial frosh week chant.* Retrieved from http://www.cbc.ca/news/canada/nova-scotia/bystanders-key-to-tackling-rape-culture-experts-say-1.1855943.

CBC. (2013). *Pop drinking tied to aggression in 5-year-olds: Heavy consumption of soda linked to fights, destructive behavior.* Retrieved from http://www.cbc.ca/news/health/pop-drinking-tied-to-aggression-in-5-year-olds-1.1408511.

CBC. (2014). *Aboriginal women more likely to suffer violent death, RCMP says.* Retrieved from cbc.ca on Oct. 14, 2014.

CBC. (2014). *Countdown to Sochi 2014 Olympic Winter Games.* http://www.cbc.ca/live/countdown-to-the-winter-olympic-games.html.

CBS. (2009). Terrorists take recruitment effort online. Retrieved from http://www.cbsnews.com/stories/2007/03/02/60minutes/main2531546.shtml.

Centerwall, B. S. (1989). Exposure to television as a risk factor for violence. *American Journal of Epidemiology, 129,* 643–652.

Chaiken, S. (1979). Communicator physical attractiveness and persuasion. *Journal of Personality and Social Psychology, 37,* 1387–1397.

Chambers, J. R., Baron, R. S., & Inman, M. L. (2006). Misperceptions in intergroup conflict: Disagreeing about what we disagree about. *Psychological Science, 17,* 38–45.

Chan, A. C., & Au, T. K. (2011). Getting children to do more academic work: Foot-in-the-Door versus Door-in-the-Face. *Teaching and Teacher Education, 27*(6), 982–985.

Chance, J. E., & Goldstein, A. G. (1981). Depth of processing in response to own- and other-race faces. *Personality and Social Psychology Bulletin, 7,* 475–480.

Chance, J. E., & Goldstein, A. G. (1996). The other-race effect and eyewitness identification. In S. L. Sporer (Ed.), *Psychological issues in eyewitness identification* (pp. 153–176). Mahwah, NJ: Erlbaum.

Check, J., & Malamuth, N. (1984). Can there be positive effects of participation in pornography experiments? *Journal of Sex Research, 20,* 14–31.

Chen, B. & Marcus, J. (2012). Students' self-presentation on Facebook: An examination of personality and self-construal factors. *Computers in Human Behavior, 28*(6), 2091–2099.

Chen, H. C., Reardon, R., & Rea, C. (1992). Forewarning of content and involvement: Consequences for persuasion and resistance to persuasion. *Journal of Experimental Social Psychology, 28,* 523–541.

Chen, L. H., Baker, S. P., Braver, E. R., & Li, G. (2000). Carrying passengers as a risk factor for crashes fatal to 16- and 17-year-old drivers. *Journal of the American Medical Association, 283,* 1578–1582.

Chen, S., Boucher, H. C., & Tapais, M. P. (2006). The relational self revealed: Integrative conceptualization and implications for interpersonal life. *Psychological Bulletin, 132*(2), 151–179.

Chen, S. C. (1937). Social modification of the activity of ants in nest-building. *Physiological Zoology, 10,* 420–436.

Cheng, C., Cheung, S. F., Chio, J. H. M., &Chan, M. P. S. (2013). Cultural meaning of perceived control: A meta-analyis of locus of control and psychological symptoms across 18 cultural regions. *Psychological bulletin, 139*(1).

Chipperfield, J. G., Campbell, D. W., & Perry, R. P. (2004). Stability in perceived control: Implications for well-being among older individuals. *Journal of Aging and Health, 16,* 116–147.

Choi, I., & Choi, Y. (2002). Culture and self-concept flexibility. *Personality & Social Psychology Bulletin, 28,* 1508–1517.

Choi, I., Nisbett, R. E., & Norenzayan, A. (1999). Causal attribution across cultures: Variation and universality. *Psychological Bulletin, 125,* 47–63.

Christian, J. J., Flyger, V., & Davis, D. E. (1960). Factors in the mass mortality of a herd of sika deer, *Cervus nippon. Chesapeake Science, 1,* 79–95.

Christie, R. (1991). Authoritarianism and related constructs. In J. P. Robinson & P. R. Shaver (Eds.), *Measures of personality and social psychological attitudes* (pp. 501–571). San Diego, CA: Academic Press.

Chronicle Herald. (2013). *Bullying in N.S. includes bystanders.* Retrieved from http://thechronicleherald.ca/novascotia/669879-bullying-in-ns-includes-bystanders.

Chronicle of Higher Education (2011). *Almanac 2011: Student demographic.* Retrieved from http://chronicle.com/article/Almanac-2011-Students/128456/?m-nav.

Chua, R. Y. J., & Zou, X. (2009). *The devil wears Prada? Effects of exposure to luxury goods on cognition and decision making.* Harvard Business School Working Paper.

CIA. (2010). *The World Factbook.* Retrieved from http://www.cia.gov/library/publications/the-world-factbook/fields/2196.html.

Cialdini, R. (2006). *Influence: The psychology of persuasion.* New York, NY: HarperCollins.

Cialdini, R. B. (1988). *Influence: Science and practice.* Glenview, IL: Scott, Foresman/Little, Brown.

Cialdini, R. B. (1991). Altruism or egoism? That is (still) the question. *Psychological Inquiry, 2,* 124–126.

Cialdini, R. B., Cacioppo, J. T., Bassett, R., & Miller, J. A. (1978). Lowball procedure for producing compliance: Commitment then cost. *Journal of Personality and Social Psychology, 36,* 463–476.

Cialdini, R. B., Demaine, L. J., Barrett, D. W., Sagarin, B. J., & Rhoads, K. L. V. (2003). *The poison parasite defense: A strategy for sapping a stronger opponent's persuasive strength.* Unpublished manuscript, Arizona State University.

Cialdini, R. B., & Goldstein, N. J. (2004). Social influence: Compliance and conformity. *Annual Review of Psychology, 55,* 591–621.

Cialdini, R. B., & Richardson, K. D. (1980). Two indirect tactics of image management: Basking and blasting. *Journal of Personality and Social Psychology, 39,* 406–415.

Cialdini, R. B., Vincent, J. E., Lewis, S. K., Catalan, J., Wheeler, D. W., & Darby, B. L. (1975). Reciprocal concessions procedure for inducing compliance: The door-in-the-face technique. *Journal of Personality and Social Psychology, 31,* 206–215.

Cialdini, R. B., Wosinska, W., Dabul, A. J., Whetstone-Dion, R., & Heszen, I. (1998). When social role salience leads to social role rejection: Modest self-presentation among women and men in two cultures. *Personality and Social Psychology Bulletin, 24,* 473–481.

Cicerello, A., & Sheehan, E. P. (1995). Personal advertisements: A content analysis. *Journal of Social Behavior and Personality, 10,* 751–756.

Clancy, S. M., & Dollinger, S. J. (1993). Photographic depictions of the self: Gender and age differences in social connectedness. *Sex Roles, 29,* 477–495.

Clark, M. S. (1984). Record keeping in two types of relationships. *Journal of Personality and Social Psychology, 47,* 549–557.

Clark, M. S. (1986). Evidence for the effectiveness of manipulations of desire for communal versus exchange relationships. *Personality and Social Psychology Bulletin, 12,* 414–425.

Clark, M. S., & Bennett, M. E. (1992). Research on relationships: Implications for mental health. In D. Ruble & P. Costanzo (Eds.), *The social psychology of mental health.* New York: Guilford Press.

Clark, M. S., & Mills, J. (1979). Interpersonal attraction in exchange and communal relationships. *Journal of Personality and Social Psychology, 37,* 12–24.

Clark, M. S., & Mills, J. (1993). The difference between communal and exchange relationships: What it is and is not. *Personality and Social Psychology Bulletin, 19,* 684–691.

Clark, M. S., Mills, J. R., & Corcoran, D. M. (1989). Keeping track of needs and inputs of friends and strangers. *Personality and Social Psychology Bulletin, 15*(4), 533–542.

Clark, R. D., III, & Maass, A. (1990). The effects of majority size on minority influence. *European Journal of Social Psychology, 20,* 99–117.

Clark, R. D., III. (1995). A few parallels between group polarization and minority influence. In S. Moscovici, H. Mucchi-Faina, & A. Maass (Eds.), *Minority influence.* Chicago: Nelson-Hall.

Clarke, A. C. (1952). An examination of the operation of residual propinquity as a factor in mate selection. *American Sociological Review, 27,* 17–22.

CNN. (2001, September 17). *Hate crimes reports up in wake of terrorist attacks.* Retrieved from http://www.cnn.com/2001/US/09/16/gen.hate.crimes/.

CNN. (2010). *The "Glee" effect: Singing is cool again.* Retrieved from http://www.cnn.com/2010/LIVING/11/15/glee.effect.show.choir.comebackindex.html.

Coates, B., Pusser, H. E., & Goodman, I. (1976). The influence of "Sesame Street" and "Mister Rogers' Neighborhood" on children's social behavior in the preschool. *Child Development, 47,* 138–144.

Codol, J. P. (1976). On the so-called superior conformity of the self behavior: Twenty experimental investigations. *European Journal of Social Psychology, 5,* 457–501.

Cohen, J. (2006, March 8). *Poll: Americans skeptical of Islam and Arabs.* ABC News (http://www.abcnews.go.com).

Cohen, M., & Davis, N. (1981). *Medication errors: Causes and prevention.* Philadelphia: G. F. Stickley Co.

Cohen, S., Tyrrell, D. A. J., & Smith, A. P. (1991). Psychological stress in humans and susceptibility to the common cold. *New England Journal of Medicine, 325,* 606–612.

Cohen, S., Tyrrell, D. A. J., & Smith, A. P. (1993). Negative life events, perceived stress, negative affect, and susceptibility to the common cold. *Journal of Personality and Social Psychology, 64,* 131–140.

Collier, K. L., Bos, H. M. W., & Sandfort, T. G. M. (2012). Intergroup contact, attitudes towards homosexuality, and the role of acceptance of gender non-conformity in young adolescents. *Journal of Adolescence, 35*(4), 899–907.

Colvin, C. R., Block, J., & Funder, D. C. (1995). Overly-positive self evaluations and personality: Negative implications for mental health. *Journal of Personality and Social Psychology, 68,* 1152–1162.

ComScore. (2011). *The 2010 Canada digital year in review.* Retrieved from http://www.comscore.com/Press_Events/Presentations_Whitepapers/2011/2010_Canada_Digital_Year_in_Review.

Comstock, G. (2008). A sociological perspective on television violence and aggression. *American Behavioral Scientist, 51,* 1184–1211.

Comstock, G., & Scharrer, E. (1999). *Television: What's on, who's watching and what it means.* San Diego, CA: Academic Press.

Conger, R. D., Cui, M., Bryant, C. M., & Elder, G. H. (2000). Competence in early adult romantic relationships: A developmental perspective on family influences. *Journal of Personality and Social Psychology, 79,* 224–237.

Cook, J. E., Arrow, H., & Malle, B. F. (2011). The effect of feeling stereotyped on the social power and inhibition. *Personality and Social Psychology Bulletin. 37*(2), 165–180.

Cooper, D. P., Goldenberg, J. L., & Arndt, J. (in press). Examining the terror management health model: The interactive effect of conscious death thought and health-coping variables on decisions in potentially fatal health domains. *Personality and Social Psychology Bulletin.*

Cooper, H. (1983). Teacher expectation effects. In L. Bickman (Ed.), *Applied Social Psychology Annual, Vol. 4.* Beverly Hills, CA: Sage.

Correll, J., Park, B., Judd, C. M., & Wittenbrink, B. (2002). The police officer's dilemma: Using ethnicity to disambiguate potentially threatening individuals. *Journal of Personality and Social Psychology, 83,* 1314–1329.

Correll, J., Urland, G. R., & Ito, T. A. (2006). Event-related potentials and the decision to shoot: The role of threat perception and cognitive control. *Journal of Experimental Social Psychology, 42*(1), 120–128.

Cota, A. A., & Dion, K. L. (1986). Salience of gender and sex composition of ad hoc groups: An experimental test of distinctiveness theory. *Journal of Personality and Social Psychology, 50,* 770–776.

Cottrell, N. B., Wack, D. L., Sekerak, G. J., & Rittle, R. M. (1968). Social facilitation of dominant responses by the presence of an audience and the mere presence of others. *Journal of Personality and Social Psychology, 9,* 245–250.

Court, J. H. (1985). Sex and violence: A ripple effect. In N. M. Malamuth & E. Donnerstein (Eds.), *Pornography and sexual aggression.* New York: Academic Press.

Couture, M., Lariviere, N., & Lefrancois, R. (2005). Psychological distress in older adults with low functional independence: A multidimensional perspective. *Archives of Gerontology and Geriatrics, 41,* 101–111.

Craig, M. E. (1990). Coercive sexuality in dating relationships: A situational model. *Clinical Psychology Review, 10,* 395–423.

Craig, W. M., Vitaro, F., Gagnon, C., & Tremblay, R. E. (2002). The road to gang membership: Characteristics of male gang and nongang members from ages 10 to 14. *Social Development, 11*(1), 53–68.

Crandall, C. S. (1994). Prejudice against fat people: Ideology and self-interest. *Journal of Personality and Social Psychology, 66,* 882–894.

Crawford, A. M. (1996). Stigma associated with AIDS: A meta-analysis. *Journal of Applied Social Psychology, 26*(5), 398–416.

Crawford, C., & Salmon, C. (2012). Integrating social exchange and sexual selection theory in the study of mating interaction. In A. Goetz and T. Shakelford (Eds.), *Oxford Handbook of Sexual Conflict* (pp. 33–48). Oxford University Press.

Crocker, J. (1981). Judgment of covariation by social perceivers. *Psychological Bulletin, 90,* 272–292.

Crocker, J. (1994, October 14). *Who cares what they think? Reflected and deflected appraisal.* Presentation to the Society of Experimental Social Psychology meeting.

Crocker, J., & McGraw, K. M. (1984). What's good for the goose is not good for the gander: Solo status as an obstacle to occupational achievement for males and females. *American Behavioral Scientist, 27,* 357–370.

Crocker, J., & Park, L. E. (2004). The costly pursuit of self-esteem. *Psychological Bulletin, 130,* 392–414.

Croizet, J. C., Despres, G., Gauzins, M. E., Huguet, P., Leyens, J. P., & Meot, A. (2004). Stereotype threat undermines intellectual performance by triggering a disruptive mental load. *Personality and Social Psychology Bulletin, 30,* 721–731.

Crosby, F. J., Pufall, A., Snyder, R. C., O'Connell, M., & Whalen, P. (1989). The denial of personal disadvantage among you, me, and all the other ostriches. In M. Crawford & M. Gentry (Eds.), *Gender and thought.* New York, NY: Springer-Verlag.

Cross, S. E., Liao, M. H., & Josephs, R. (1992). *A cross-cultural test of the self-evaluation maintenance model.* Paper presented at the American Psychological Association convention.

Crowley, G. (1996, June 3). The biology of beauty. *Newsweek,* 61–69.

Crutchfield, R. S. (1955). Conformity and character. *American Psychologist, 1,* 191–198.

CTV. (2005). *Mistrial declared in Toronto murder trial.* Retrieved from http://www.cp24.com/servlet/an/local/CTVNews/20050216/johnathan_murder_050215?hubWinnipegHome.

CTV. (2005). *Rosie O'Donnell praises Canada, condemns Bush.* Retrieved from http://www.ctv.ca/CTVNews/2/20050712/rosie_halifax_050712/.

CTV. (2006). *Two gay RCMP officers plan to marry this summer.* Retrieved from http://www.ctv.ca/CTVNews/CTVNewsAt11/20060521/rcmp_marriage_060521/.

CTV. (2008). *Patrick, Jonathan Roy suspended over brawl.* Retrieved from http://toronto.ctv.ca/servlet/an/local/CTVNews/20080325/brawl_suspension_080325?hub=MontrealHome.

Cunningham, J. D. (1981). Self-disclosure intimacy: Sex, sex-of-target, cross-national, and generational differences. *Personality and Social Psychology Bulletin, 7,* 314–319.

Cunningham, W. A., Johnson, M. K., Raye, C. L., Gatenby, J. C., Gore, J. C., & Banaji, M. R. (2004). Separable neural components in the processing of black and white faces. *Psychological Science, 15*(12), 806–813.

Dabbs, J. M., Jr. (2000). *Heroes, rogues, and lovers: Testosterone and behavior.* New York: McGraw-Hill.

Dabbs, J. M., Jr., & Janis, I. L. (1965). Why does eating while reading facilitate opinion change? An experimental inquiry. *Journal of Experimental Social Psychology, 1,* 133–144.

Dabbs, J. M., Jr., & Morris, R. (1990). Testosterone, social class, and antisocial behavior in a sample of 4,462 men. *Psychological Science, 1,* 209–211.

Dabbs, J. M., Jr., Riad, J. K., & Chance, S. E. (2001). Testosterone and ruthless homicide. *Personality and Individual Differences, 31,* 599–603.

Dabbs, J. M., Jr., Strong, R., & Milun, R. (1997). Exploring the mind of testosterone: A beeper study. *Journal of Research in Personality, 31,* 577–588.

Dallaire, R. (2003). *Shake hands with the devil: The failure of humanity in Rwanda.* Toronto: Vintage Canada

Daly, M., & Wilson, M. (1996). Violence against stepchildren. *Current directions in Psychological Science, 5,* 77–81.

Daly, M., & Wilson, M. (1989). Killing the competition: Female/female and male/male homicide. *Human Nature, 1,* 81–107.

Dambrun, M. & Vatiné, E. (2010). Reopening the study of extreme social behaviors: Obedience to authority within an immersive video environment. *European Journal of Social Psychology, 40*(5), 760–773.

Dandeneau, S. D., & Baldwin, M. W. (2004). The inhibition of socially rejecting information among people with high versus low self-esteem: The role of attentional bias and the effects of bias reduction training. *Journal of Social and Clinical Psychology, 23,* 584–602.

Dando, C., Wilcock, R., & Milne, R. (2009). The cognitive interview: The efficacy of a modified mental reinstatement of context procedure for frontline police investigators, *Applied Cognitive Psychology, 23,* 138–147.

Darley, J. M., & Berscheid, E. (1967). Increased liking as a result of the anticipation of personal contact. *Human Relations, 20,* 29–40.

Darley, J. M., & Latané, B. (1968). Bystander intervention in emergencies: Diffusion of responsibility. *Journal of Personality and Social Psychology, 8,* 377–383.

Das, E. H. H. J., de Wit, J. B. F., & Stroebe, W. (2003). Fear appeals motivate acceptance of action recommendations: Evidence for a positive bias in the processing of persuasive messages. *Personality and Social Psychology Bulletin, 29,* 650–664.

Dashiell, J. F. (1930). An experimental analysis of some group effects. *Journal of Abnormal and Social Psychology, 25,* 190–199.

Davidson, R. J., Putnam, K. M., & Larson, C. L. (2000). Dysfunction in the neural circuitry of emotion regulation—A possible prelude to violence. *Science, 289,* 591–594.

Davis, B. M., & Gilbert, L. A. (1989). Effect of dispositional and situational influences on women's dominance expression in mixed-sex dyads. *Journal of Personality and Social Psychology, 57,* 294–300.

Davis, J. H., Kameda, T., Parks, C., Stasson, M., & Zimmerman, S. (1989). Some social mechanics of group decision making: The distribution of opinion, polling sequence, and implications from consensus. *Journal of Personality and Social Psychology, 57,* 1000–1012.

Davis, K. E. (1985, February). Near and dear: Friendship and love compared. *Psychology Today,* 22–30.

Davis, L., & Greenlees, C. (1992). *Social loafing revisited: Factors that mitigate—and reverse—performance loss.* Paper presented at the Southwestern Psychological Association convention.

Davis, M. H., & Stephan, W. G. (1980). Attributions for exam performance. *Journal of Applied Social Psychology, 10,* 235–248.

Dawes, M. E. (1998). Experimental evaluation of self-efficacy treatment on technical/scientific career outcomes. *Dissertation Abstracts International Section A: Humanities and Social Sciences, 59*(5-A), 1543.

Dawes, R. M. (1990). The potential nonfalsity of the false consensus effect. In R. M. Hogarth (Ed.), *Insights in decision making: A tribute to Hillel J. Einhorn.* Chicago: University of Chicago Press.

Dawes, R. M. (1991). Social dilemmas, economic self-interest, and evolutionary theory. In D. R. Brown & J. E. Keith Smith (Eds.), *Frontiers of mathematical psychology: Essays in honor of Clyde Coombs.* New York: Springer-Verlag.

Dawes, R. M. (1994). *House of cards: Psychology and psychotherapy built on myth.* New York: Free Press.

Dawson, N. V., Arkes, H. R., Siciliano, C., Blinkhorn, R., Lakshmanan, M., & Petrelli, M. (1988). Hindsight bias: An impediment to accurate probability estimation in clinicopathologic conferences. *Medical Decision Making, 8,* 259–264.

Deci, E. L., & Ryan, R. M. (1987). The support of autonomy and the control of behavior. *Journal of Personality and Social Psychology, 53,* 1024–1037.

De Hoog, N., Stroebe, W., & De Wit, J. B. F. (2007). The impact of vulnerability to and severity of a health risk on processing and acceptance of fear-arousing communications: A meta-analysis. *Review of General Psychology, 11,* 258–285.

Del Guidice, M. (2011). Sex differences in romantic attachment: A meta-analysis. *Personality and Social Psychology Bulletin. 37*(2), 193–214.

Demakis, G. J. (1997). Hindsight bias and the Simpson trial: Use in introductory psychology. *Teaching of Psychology, 24,* 190–191.

Dengerink, H. A., & Myers, J. D. (1977). Three effects of failure and depression on subsequent aggression. *Journal of Personality and Social Psychology, 35,* 88–96.

DePaulo, B. M., Charlton, K., Cooper, H., Lindsay, J. J., & Muhlenbruck, L. (1997). The accuracy-confidence correlation in the detection of deception. *Personality and Social Psychology Review, 1,* 346–357.

DePaulo, B. M., Lassiter, G. D., & Stone, J. I. (1982). Attentional determinants of success at detecting deception and truth. *Personality and Social Psychology Bulletin, 8,* 273–279.

Derlega, V., Metts, S., Petronio, S., & Margulis, S. T. (1993). *Self-disclosure.* Newbury Park, CA: Sage.

Dermer, M., & Pyszczynski, T. A. (1978). Effects of erotica upon men's loving and liking responses for women they love. *Journal of Personality and Social Psychology, 36,* 1302–1309.

Desforges, D. M., Lord, C. G., Pugh, M. A., Sia, T. L., Scarberry, N. C., & Ratcliff, C. D. (1997). Role of group representativeness in the generalization part of the contact hypothesis. *Basic and Applied Social Psychology, 19,* 183–204.

Desforges, D. M., Lord, C. G., Ramsey, S. L., Mason, J. A., Van Leeuwen, M. D., West, S. C., & Lepper, M. R. (1991). Effects of structured cooperative contact on changing negative attitudes toward stigmatized social groups. *Journal of Personality and Social Psychology, 60,* 531–544.

Desmarais, S., & Curtis, J. (2001). Gender and perceived income entitlement among full-time workers: Analyses for Canadian national samples, 1984 and 1994. *Basic and Applied Social Psychology, 23,* 157–168.

DeSteno, D. A., & Salovey, P. (1996). Jealousy and the characteristics of one's rival: A self-evaluation maintenance perspective. *Personality and Social Psychology Bulletin, 22,* 920–932.

Deutsch, M. (1985). *Distributive justice: A social psychological perspective.* New Haven, CT: Yale University Press.

Deutsch, M. (1994). Constructive conflict resolution: Principles, training, and research. *Journal of Social Issues, 50,* 13–32.

Deutsch, M. (1999). Behind the scenes. In D. G. Myers, *Social psychology* (6th ed.), (p. 519). New York, NY: McGraw-Hill.

Deutsch, M., & Krauss, R. M. (1960). The effect of threat upon interpersonal bargaining. *Journal of Abnormal and Social Psychology, 61,* 181–189.

Devine, P. G. (1989). Stereotypes and prejudice: Their automatic and controlled components. *Journal of Personality and Social Psychology, 56,* 5–18.

Devine, P. G., Plant, E. A., & Buswell, B. N. (2000). Breaking the prejudice habit: Progress and obstacles. In S. Oskamp (Ed.), *Reducing prejudice and discrimination.* Mahwah, NJ: Erlbaum.

Devos-Comby, L., & Salovey, P. (2002). Applying persuasion strategies to alter HIV-relevant thoughts and behavior. *Review of General Psychology, 6,* 287–304.

De Waal, F. B. M. (2005–2006, Fall-Winter). *The evolution of empathy: Greater good.* 6–9.

Dey, E. L., Astin, A. W., & Korn, W. S. (1991). *The American freshman: Twenty-five year trends.* Los Angeles: Higher Education Research Institute, UCLA.

DiBattista, D., & Sheppard, M. (1993). Primary school teachers' beliefs and advice to parents concerning sugar consumption and activity in children. *Psychological Reports, 72*(1), 47–55.

Dick, S. (2008). *Homophobic hate crime: The Gay British Crime Survey 2008.* Stonewall (http://www.stonewall.org.uk).

Dicum, J. (2003, November 11). Letter to the editor. *New York Times,* A20.

Diekmann, K. A., Samuels, S. M., Ross, L., & Bazerman, M. H. (1997). Self-interest and fairness in problems of resource allocation: Allocators versus recipients. *Journal of Personality and Social Psychology, 72*(5), 1061–1074.

Diener, E., & Crandall, R. (1979). An evaluation of the Jamaican anticrime program. *Journal of Applied Social Psychology, 9,* 135–146.

Diener, E., Lucas, R. E., & Scollon, C. N. (2006). Beyond the hedonic treadmill: Revising the adaption theory of well-being. *American Psychologist, 61*(4), 305–314.

Diener, E., & Wallbom, M. (1976). Effects of self-awareness on antinormative behavior. *Journal of Research in Personality, 10,* 107–111.

Dienstbier, R. A., Roesch, S. C., Mizumoto, A., Hemenover, S. H., Lott, R. C., & Carlo, G. (1998). Effects of weapons on guilt judgments and sentencing recommendations for criminals. *Basic and Applied Social Psychology, 20,* 93–102.

Dillard, A. J., Midboe, A. M., & Klein, W. M. P. (2009). The dark side of optimism: Unrealistic optimism about problem with alcohol predicts subsequent negative event experiences. *Personality and Social Personality Bulletin, 35*(11), 1540–1550.

Dindia, K., & Allen, M. (1992). Sex differences in self-disclosure: A meta-analysis. *Psychological Bulletin, 112,* 106–124.

Dion, K. (2002). Facial attractiveness: Evolutionary, cognitive, and social perspectives. In G. Rhodes & L. A. Zebrowitz (Eds.), *Advances in visual cognition* (pp. 239–259). Westport, CT: Ablex Publishing.

Dion, K. K. (1972). Physical attractiveness and evaluations of children's transgressions. *Journal of Personality and Social Psychology, 24,* 207–213.

Dion, K. K. (1973). Young children's stereotyping of facial attractiveness. *Developmental Psychology, 9,* 183–188.

Dion, K. K. (1979). Physical attractiveness and interpersonal attraction. In M. Cook & G. Wilson (Eds.), *Love and attraction.* New York: Pergamon Press.

Dion, K. K., & Berscheid, E. (1974). Physical attractiveness and peer perception among children. *Sociometry, 37,* 1–12.

Dion, K. K., & Dion, K. L. (1985). Personality, gender, and the phenomenology of romantic love. In P. R. Shaver (Ed.), *Review of personality and social psychology, Vol. 6.* Beverly Hills, CA: Sage.

Dion, K. K., & Dion, K. L. (1991). Psychological individualism and romantic love. *Journal of Social Behavior and Personality, 6,* 17–33.

Dion, K. K., & Dion, K. L. (1993). Individualistic and collectivistic perspectives on gender and the cultural context of love and intimacy. *Journal of Social Issues, 49,* 53–69.

Dion, K. K., & Dion, K. L. (1996). Cultural perspectives on romantic love. *Personal Relationships, 3,* 5–17.

Dion, K. L. (2001). Gender and relationships. In *Handbook of the psychology of women and gender* (pp. 256–274). New York, NY: Wiley.

Dion, K. L. (2002a). The social psychology of perceived prejudice and discrimination. *Canadian Psychology, 43,* 1–10.

Dion, K. L., & Dion, K. K. (1988). Romantic love: Individual and cultural perspectives. In R. J. Sternberg & M. L. Barnes (Eds.), *The psychology of love.* New Haven, CT: Yale University Press.

Dion, K. L., Dion, K. K., & Keelan, J. P. (1990). Appearance anxiety as a dimension of social-evaluative anxiety: Exploring the ugly duckling syndrome. *Contemporary Social Psychology, 14* (4), 220–224.

Dishion, T. J., McCord, J., & Poulin, F. (1999). When interventions harm: Peer groups and problem behavior. *American Psychologist, 54,* 755–764.

Di Tella, R. M., MacCulloch, R. J., & Oswald, A. J. (2001). Preferences over inflation and unemployment: Evidence from surveys of happiness. *American Economic Review 91,1,* 335–341.

Dixon, J., & Durrheim, K. (2003). Contact and the ecology of racial division: Some varieties of informal segregation. *British Journal of Social Psychology, 42,* 1–23.

Dixon, J., Durrheim, K., & Tredoux, C. (2005). Beyond the optimal contact strategy: A reality check for the contact hypothesis. *American Psychologist, 60,* 697–711.

Dollard, J., Doob, L., Miller, N., Mowrer, O. H., & Sears, R. R. (1939). *Frustration and aggression.* New Haven, CT: Yale University Press.

Dolnik, L., Case, T. I., & Williams, K. D. (2003). Stealing thunder as a courtroom tactic revisited: Processes and boundaries. *Law and Human Behavior, 27,* 265–285.

Donnellan, M. B., Larsen-Rife, D., & Conger, R. D. (2005). Personality, family history, and competence in early adult romantic relationships. *Journal of Personality and Social Psychology, 88,* 562–576.

Donnerstein, E. (1998). *Why do we have those new ratings on television?* Invited address to the National Institute on the Teaching of Psychology.

Donnerstein, E., Linz, D., & Penrod, S. (1987). *The question of pornography.* London: Free Press.

Doob, A. N., & Roberts, J. (1988). Public attitudes toward sentencing in Canada. In N. Walker & M. Hough (Eds.), *Sentencing and the public.* London: Gower.

Doty, R. M., Peterson, B. E., & Winter, D. G. (1991). Threat and authoritarianism in the United States, 1978–1987. *Journal of Personality and Social Psychology, 61,* 629–640.

Dovidio, J. F. (1991). The empathy-altruism hypothesis: Paradigm and promise. *Psychological Inquiry, 2,* 126–128.

Dovidio, J. R., Brigham, J. C., Johnson, B. T., & Gaertner, S. L. (1996). Stereotyping, prejudice, and discrimination: Another look. In N. Macrae, M. Hewstone, & C. Stangor (Eds.), *Stereotypes and stereotyping.* New York, NY: Guilford.

Downs, A. C., & Lyons, P. M. (1991). Natural observations of the links between attractiveness and initial legal judgments. *Personality and Social Psychology Bulletin, 17,* 541–547.

Downs, D. S., Graham, G. M., Yang, S., Bargainnier, S., & Vasil, J. (2006). Youth exercise intention and past exercise behavior: Examining the moderating influences of sex and meeting exercise recommendations. *Research Quarterly for Exercise and Sport, 77,* 91–99.

Dreber, A., Rand, D. G., Fudenberg, D., Nowak, M. A. (2008). Winners don't punish. *Nature, 452,* 348–351.

Dreher, J. C., Schmidt, P. J., Kohn, P., Furman, D., Rubinow, D., & Berman, K. F. (2007). Menstrual cycle phase modulates reward-related neural function in women. *Proceedings of the National Academy of Sciences, 104 (7),* 2465–2470.

Drolet, A. L., & Morris, M. W. (2000). Rapport in conflict resolution: Accounting for how face-to-face contact fosters mutual cooperation in mixed-motive conflicts. *Journal of Experimental Social Psychology, 36,* 26–50.

Dryer, D. C., & Horowitz, L. M. (1997). When do opposites attract? Interpersonal complementarity versus similarity. *Journal of Personality and Social Psychology, 72,* 592–603.

Duncan, L. A., & Schaller, M. (2009). Prejudicial attitudes toward older adults may be exaggerated when people feel vulnerable to infectious disease: Evidence and implications. *Analyses of Social Issues and Public Policy, 9,* 97–115.

Dunn, E. W., Aknin, L. B., & Norton, M. I. (2008). Spending money on others promotes happiness. *Science, 319*(5870), 1687–1688.

Dunn, E. W., Wilson, T. D., & Gilbert, D. T. (2003). Location, location, location: The misprediction of satisfaction in housing lotteries. *Personality and Social Psychology Bulletin, 29,* 1421–1432.

Dunning, D. (1995). Trait importance and modifiability as factors influencing self-assessment and self-enhancement motives. *Personality and Social Psychology Bulletin, 21,* 1297–1306.

Dunning, D. (2005). *Self-insight: Roadblocks and detours on the path to knowing thyself* (p. 87). London: Psychology Press.

Dunning, D., & Hayes, A. F. (1996). Evidence for egocentric comparison in social judgment. *Journal of Personality and Social Psychology, 71,* 213–229.

Dunning, D., Griffin, D. W., Milojkovic, J. D., & Ross, L. (1990). The overconfidence effect in social prediction. *Journal of Personality and Social Psychology, 58,* 568–581.

Dunning, D., Meyerowitz, J. A., & Holzberg, A. D. (1989). Ambiguity and self-evaluation. *Journal of Personality and Social Psychology, 57,* 1082–1090.

Dunning, D., Perie, M., & Story, A. L. (1991). Self-serving prototypes of social categories. *Journal of Personality and Social Psychology, 61,* 957–968.

Duque, G., Fung, S., Mallet, L., Posel, N., & Fleiszer, D. (2008). Learning while having fun: The use of video gaming to teach geriatric house calls to medical students. *Journal of the American Geriatrics Society, 56*(7), 1328–1332.

Dutton, D. G., & Aron, A. (1989). Romantic attraction and generalized liking for others who are sources of conflict-based arousal. *Canadian Journal of Behavioural Science, 21,* 246–257.

Dutton, D. G., & Aron, A. P. (1974). Some evidence for heightened sexual attraction under conditions of high anxiety. *Journal of Personality and Social Psychology, 30,* 510–517.

Eagly, A. H. (1987). *Sex differences in social behavior: A social-role interpretation.* Hillsdale, NJ: Erlbaum.

Eagly, A. H. (1994). *Are people prejudiced against women?* Donald Campbell Award invited address, American Psychological Association convention.

Eagly, A. H., Ashmore, R. D., Makhijani, M. G., & Longo, L. C. (1991). What is beautiful is good, but . . . : A meta-analytic review of research on the physical attractiveness stereotype. *Psychological Bulletin, 110,* 109–128.

Eagly, A. H., & Carli, L. L. (1981). Sex of researchers and sex-typed communications as determinants of sex differences in influenceability: A meta-analysis of social influence studies. *Psychological Bulletin, 90*(1), 1–20.

Eagly, A. H., & Chaiken, S. (1993). *The psychology of attitudes.* Fort Worth, TX: Harcourt Brace Jovanovich.

Eagly, A. H. & Crowley, M. (1986). Gender and helping behavior: A meta-analytic review of the social psychological literature. *Psychological Bulletin, 108,* 233–256.

Eagly, A. H., Diekman, A. B., Schneider, M., & Kulesa, P. (2003). Experimental tests of an attitudinal theory of the gender gap in voting. *Personality and Social Psychology Bulletin, 29,* 1245–1258.

Eagly, A. H., & Karau, S. J. (2000). *Few women at the top: Is prejudice a cause?* Unpublished manuscript, Northwestern University.

Eagly, A. H., Mladinic, A., & Otto, S. (1991). Are women evaluated more favorably than men? *Psychology of Women Quarterly, 15,* 203–216.

Eagly, A. H., & Wood, W. (1999). The origins of sex differences in human behavior: Evolved dispositions versus social roles. *American Psychologist, 54*(6), 408–423.

Easterbrook, G. (2004, May 25). The 50¢-a-gallon solution. *New York Times* (http://www.nytimes.com).

Eastwick, P. W., Finkel, E. J., Mochon, D., & Ariely, D. (2007). Selective versus unselective romantic desire. *Psychological Science, 18,* 317–319.

Eaton, A., Visser, P., Krosnick, J., & Anand, S. (2009). Social power and attitude strength over the life course. *Personality and Social Psychology Bulletin, 35*(12), 1646–1660.

Ebbesen, E. B., Duncan, B., & Konecni, V. J. (1975). Effects of content of verbal aggression on future verbal aggression: A field experiment. *Journal of Experimental Social Psychology, 11,* 192–204.

Eberhardt, J. L. (2005). Imaging race. *American Psychologist, 60,* 181–190.

Efran, M. G. (1974). The effect of physical appearance on the judgment of guilt, interpersonal attraction and severity of recommended punishment in a simulated jury task. *Journal of Research in Personality, 8,* 45–54.

Ehrlich, D., Guttman, I., Schönbach, P., & Mills, J. (1957). Postdecision exposure to relevant information. *The Journal of Abnormal and Social Psychology, 54*(1), 98–102.

Eiser, J. R., Sutton, S. R., & Wober, M. (1979). Smoking, seat-belts, and beliefs about health. *Addictive Behaviors, 4,* 331–338.

Eisner, J. E. (1995). The origins of explanatory style: Trust as a determinant of pessimism and optimism. In G. M. Buchanan & M. E. P. Seligman (Eds.), *Explanatory style* (pp. 49–55). Hillsdale, NJ: Erlbaum.

Elder, G. H., Jr. (1969). Appearance and education in marriage mobility. *American Sociological Review, 34,* 519–533.

Elder, G. H., Jr., & Clipp, E. C. (1988). Wartime losses and social bonding: Influences across 40 years in men's lives. *Psychiatry, 51,* 177–197.

Ellemers, N., Van Rijswijk, W., Roefs, M., & Simons, C. (1997). Bias in intergroup perceptions: Balancing group identity with social reality. *Personality and Social Psychology Bulletin, 23,* 186–198.

Ellet, L., Allen-Crooks, R., Stevens, A., Wildscut, T., & Chadwick, P. (2013). A paradigm for the study of paranoia in the general population: The Prisoner's Dilemma Game. *Cognition and Emotion, 27*(1), 53–62.

Ellickson, P. L., & Bell, R. M. (1990). Drug prevention in junior high: A multi-site longitudinal test. *Science, 247,* 1299–1305.

Ellis, B. J., & Symons, D. (1990). Sex difference in sexual fantasy: An evolutionary psychological approach. *Journal of Sex Research, 27,* 490–521.

Ellis, H. D. (1981). Theoretical aspects of face recognition. In G. H. Davies, H. D. Ellis, & J. Shepherd (Eds.), *Perceiving and remembering faces.* London: Academic Press.

Ellis, L., Robb, B., & Burke, D. (2005). Sexual orientation in the United States and Canada. *Archives of Sexual Behavior, 34,* 569–581.

Ellison, N. B., Steinfield, C., & Lampe, C. (2007). The benefits of Facebook "friends:" Social capital and college students' use of online social networking sites. *Journal of Computer-Mediated Communication, 12,* 1143–1168.

Emes, C. E. (1997). Is Mr. Pac Man eating our children? A review of the effect of video games on children. *Canadian Journal of Psychiatry, 42,* 404–414.

Engelhardt, C. R., Bartholow, B. D., Kerr, G. T., & Bushman, B. J. (2011). This is your brain on violent video games: Neual desensitization to violence predicts increased aggression following violent video game exposure. *Journal of Experimental Social Psychology, 47,* 1033–1036.

Engs, R., & Hanson, D. J. (1989). Reactance theory: A test with collegiate drinking. *Psychological Reports, 64,* 1083–1086.

Ennis, B. J., & Verrilli, D. B., Jr. (1989). Motion for leave to file brief of amicus curiae on behalf of Society for the Scientific Study of Religion, American Sociological Association, and others. U.S. Supreme Court Case No. 88–1600, Holy Spirit Association for the Unification of World Christianity, et al., v. David Molko and Tracy Leal. On petition for write of certiorari to the Supreme Court of California. Washington, DC: Jenner & Block.

Ennis, R., & Zanna, M. P. (1991). Hockey assault: Consitiutive versus normative violations. Paper presented at the Canadian Psychological Association convention.

Enough is Enough. (2014). Enough is Enough: Making the internet safer for children and families. Retrieved from http://enough.org/.

Environics. (2010). Environics Institute Newsletter. Why do we support gay rights? Because we know each other. http://www.environicsinstitute.org/news-events/news-events/why-do-we-support-gayrights-because-we-know-each-other.

Epley, N., & Huff, C. (1998). Suspicion, affective response, and educational benefit as a result of de ception in psychology research. *Personality and Social Psychology Bulletin, 24,* 759–768.

Epley, N., & Whitchurch, E. (2008). Mirror, mirror on the wall: Enhancement in self-recognition. *Personality and Social Psychology Bulletin, 34,* 1159–1170.

Epstein, J. A., & Botvin, G. L. (2008). Media refusal skills and drug skill refusal techniques: What is their relationship with alcohol use among inner-city adolescents? *Addictive Behavior, 33,* 528–537.

Erikson, E. H. (1963). *Childhood and society.* New York, NY: Norton.

Eron, L. D. (1987). The development of aggressive behavior from the perspective of a developing behaviorism. *American Psychologist, 42,* 425–442.

Eron, L. D., & Huesmann, L. R. (1980). Adolescent aggression and television. *Annals of the New York Academy of Sciences, 347,* 319–331.

Eron, L. D., & Huesmann, L. R. (1984). The control of aggressive behavior by changes in attitudes, values, and the conditions of learning. In R. J. Blanchard & C. Blanchard (Eds.), *Advances in the study of aggression, Vol. 1.* Orlando, FL: Academic Press.

Eron, L. D., & Huesmann, L. R. (1985). The role of television in the development of prosocial and antisocial behavior. In D. Olweus, M. Radke-Yarrow, & J. Block (Eds.), *Development of antisocial and prosocial behavior.* Orlando, FL: Academic Press.

Esser, J. K., & Lindoerfer, J. S. (1989). Groupthink and the space shuttle Challenger accident: Toward a quantitative case analysis. *Journal of Behavioral Decision Making, 2,* 167–177.

Esses, V. M., Brochu, P. M., & Dickson, K. R. (2012). Economic costs, economic benefits, and Atttudes toward immigrants and immigration, *Analyses of Social Issues and Public Policy, 12*(1), 133–137.

Esses, V. M., Dietz, J., & Bhardwaj, A. (2006). *The role of prejudice in the discounting of immigrant skills.* London: University of Western Ontario.

Esses, V. M., Haddock, G., & Zanna, M. P. (1993). The role of mood in the expression of intergroup stereotypes. In M. P. Zanna & J. M. Olson (Eds.), *The psychology of prejudice: The Ontario symposium, Vol. 7.* Hillsdale, NJ: Erlbaum.

Esses, V. M., Jackson, L. M., Dovidio, J. F. & Hodson, G. (2005). Instrumental relations among groups: Group competition, conflict and prejudice. In J. F. Dovidio, P. Glick & L. A. Rudman (Eds.), *On the nature of prejudice: Fifty years after Allport* (pp. 227–243). Maiden, MA: Blackport.

Esses, V. M., Wagner, U., Wolf, C., Preiser, M., & Wilbur, C. J. (2006). Perceptions of national identity and attitudes toward immigrants and immigration in Canada and Germany. *International Journal of Intercultural Relations, 30,* 653–669.

Esses, V. M., & Zanna, M. P. (1995). Mood and the expression of ethnic stereotypes. *Journal of Personality and Social Psychology, 69,* 1052–1068.

Evans, G. W. (1979). Behavioral and physiological consequences of crowding in humans. *Journal of Applied Social Psychology, 9,* 27–46.

Evelo, A. J., & Greene, E. (2013). Judgments about felony-murder in hindsight. *Applied Cognitive Psychology, 27*(3), 277–285.

Ezeonu, I. (2010). Gun violence in Toronto: Perspectives from the police. *The Howard Journal, 49*(2), 147–165.

Fabrigar, L. R., & Petty, R. E. (1999). The role of the affective and cognitive bases of attitudes in susceptibility to affectively and cognitively based persuasion. *Personality & Social Psychology Bulletin, 25,* 363–381.

Falk, C. F., Heine, S. J., Yuki, M., & Takemura, K. (2009). Why do Westerners self-enhance more than East Asians? *European Journal of Personality, 23*(3), 183–203.

Family Safe Media. (2011). Pornography statistics. Retrieved from http://www.familysafemedia.com/pornography_statistics.html

Farina, A., & Ring, K. (1965). The influence of per ceived mental illness on interpersonal relations. *Journal of Abnormal Psychology, 70,* 47–51.

Farrell, E. F. (2005, March 18). The battle for hearts and lungs. *Chronicle of Higher Education.*

Farwell, L., & Weiner, B. (2000). Bleeding hearts and the heartless: Popular perceptions of liberal and conservative ideologies. *Personality and Social Psychology Bulletin, 26,* 845–852.

Farwell, L. A., & Donchin, E. (1991). The truth will out: Interrogative polygraphy ("lie detection") with event-related brain potentials. *Psychophysiology, 28,* 531–547.

Faulkner, J., Schaller, M., Park, J. H., & Duncan, L. A. (2004). Evolved disease-avoidance mechanisms and contemporary xenophobic attitudes. *Group Processes and Intergroup Behavior, 7,* 333–335.

Faulkner, S. L., & Williams, K. D. (1996). *A study of social loafing in industry.* Paper presented to the Midwestern Psychological Association convention.

Fazio, R. H., (1995). Attitudes as object-evaluation associations: Determinants, consequences, and correlates of attitude accessibility. In R. E. Petty & J. A. Krosnick (Eds.) *Attitude strength: Antecedents and consequences,* 247–282.

Fazio, R. H., & Zanna, M. P. (1978). On the predictive validity of attitudes: The roles of direct experience and confidence. *Journal of Personality, 46*(2), 228–243.

FBI. (2005). Incidents, offences, victims and known offenders. Downloaded from http://www.fbi.gov/ucr/hc2007/table_01.htm

Feeney, J. A. (1996). Attachment, caregiving, and marital satisfaction. *Personal Relationships, 3,* 401–416.

Feeney, J., Peterson, C., & Noller, P. (1994). Equity and marital satisfaction over the family life cycle. *Personality Relationships, 1,* 83–99.

Fehr, B. (1988). Prototype analysis of the concepts of love and commitment. *Journal of Personality and Social Psychology, 55,* 557–579.

Fehr, B., & Broughton, R. (2001). Gender and personality differences in conceptions of love: An interpersonal theory analysis. *Personal Relationships, 8,* 115–136.

Fein, S., Hilton, J. L., & Miller, D. T. (1990). Suspicion of ulterior motivation and the correspondence bias. *Journal of Personality and Social Psychology, 58,* 753–764.

Fein, S., & Spencer, S. J. (1997). Prejudice as self-image maintenance: Affirming the self through derogating others. *Journal of Personality and Social Psychology, 73,* 31–44.

Feinberg, D. R., DeBruine, L. M., Jones, B. C., & Little, A. C. (2008). Correlated preferences for men's facial and vocal masculinity. *Evolution and Human Behavior 29,* 233–241.

Feinberg, J. M., & Aiello, J. R. (2006). Social facilitation: A test of competing theories. *Journal of Applied Social Psychology, 36,* 1–23.

Feingold, A. (1988). Matching for attractiveness in romantic partners and same-sex friends: A meta-analysis and theoretical critique. *Psychological Bulletin, 104,* 226–235.

Feingold, A. (1990). Gender differences in effects of physical attractiveness on romantic attraction: A comparison across five research paradigms. *Journal of Personality and Social Psychology, 59,* 981–993.

Feingold, A. (1991). Sex differences in the effects of similarity and physical attractiveness on opposite-sex attraction. *Basic and Applied Social Psychology, 12,* 357–367.

Feingold, A. (1992a). Gender differences in mate selection preferences: A test of the parental investment model. *Psychological Bulletin, 112,* 125–139.

Feingold, A. (1992b). Good-looking people are not what we think. *Psychology Bulletin, 111,* 304–341.

Felson, R. B. (1984). The effect of self-appraisals of ability on academic performance. *Journal of Personality and Social Psychology, 47,* 944–952.

Fenigstein, A. (1984). Self-consciousness and the overperception of self as a target. *Journal of Personality and Social Psychology, 47,* 860–870.

Ferguson, C. J., & Kilburn, J. (2009). The public health risks of media violence: A meta-analytic review. *Journal of pediatrics, 154*(5), 759–763.

Ferguson, M. J., & Hassin, R. R. (2007). On the automatic association between America and aggression for news watchers. *Personality and Social Psychology Bulletin, 11*(4), 1632–1647.

Fergusson, D. M., Horwood, L. J., & Shannon, F. T. (1984). A proportional hazards model of family breakdown. *Journal of Marriage and the Family, 46,* 539–549.

Feshbach, S. (1980). *Television advertising and children: Policy issues and alternatives.* Paper presented at the American Psychological Association convention.

Festinger, L. (1954). A theory of social comparison processes. *Human Relations, 7,* 117–140.

Festinger, L. (1957). *A theory of cognitive dissonance.* Stanford, CA: Stanford University Press.

Festinger, L., & Carlsmith, J. M. (1959). Cognitive consequences of forced compliance. *Journal of Abnormal & Social Psychology, 58,* 203–210.

Festinger, L., & Maccoby, N. (1964). On resistance to persuasive communications. *Journal of Abnormal and Social Psychology, 68,* 359–366.

Festinger, L., Pepitone, A., & Newcomb, T. (1952). Some consequences of deindividuation in a group. *Journal of Abnormal and Social Psychology, 47,* 382–389.

Fiedler, K., Semin, G. R., & Koppetsch, C. (1991). Language use and attributional biases in close personal relationships. *Personality and Social Psychology Bulletin, 17,* 147–155.

Fincham, F. D., & Jaspars, J. M. (1980). Attribution of responsibility: From man the scientist to man as lawyer. In L. Berkowitz (Ed.), *Advances in experimental social psychology, Vol. 13.* New York, NY: Academic Press.

Findley, M. J., & Cooper, H. M. (1983). Locus of control and academic achievement: A literature review. *Journal of Personality and Social Psychology, 44,* 419–427.

Fineberg, H. V. (1988). Education to prevent AIDS: Prospects and obstacles. *Science, 239,* 592–596.

Fink, B., Taschner, K., Neave, N., Hugill, N., & Dane, L. (2010). Male faces and bodies: Evidence of a condition-dependent ornament of quality. *Personality and Individual Differences, 49,* 436–440.

Finlay, W. M. L. (2005). Pathologizing dissent: Identity politics, Zionism and the 'self-hating Jew.' *British Journal of Social Psychology, 44,* 201–222.

Fischer, P., Krueger, J. I., Greitemeyer, T., Kastenmüller, A., Frey, D., Heene, M. . . . Kainbacher, M. (2011). The bystander-effect: A meta-analytic review on bystander intervention in dangerous and non-dangerous emergencies. *Psychological Bulletin, 137*(4), 517–537.

Fischer, R., & Chalmers, A. (2008). Is optimism universal? A meta-analytical investigation of optimism levels across 22 nations. *Personality and Individual Differences, 45,* 378–382.

Fischhoff, B. (1982). Debiasing. In D. Kahneman, P. Slovic, & A. Tversky (Eds.), *Judgment under uncertainty: Heuristics and biases* (p. 89). New York, NY: Cambridge University Press.

Fischhoff, B., & Bar-Hillel, M. (1984). Focusing techniques: A shortcut to improving probability judgments? *Organizational Behavior & Human Performance, 34,* 174–194.

Fishbein, D., & Thelen, M. H. (1981a). *Husband-wife similarity and marital satisfaction: A different approach.* Paper presented at the Midwestern Psychological Association convention.

Fishbein, D., & Thelen, M. H. (1981b). Psychological factors in mate selection and marital satisfaction: A review (Ms. 2374). *Catalog of Selected Documents in Psychology, 11,* 84.

Fishbein, M., & Ajzen, I. (1980). *Understanding attitudes and predicting social behavior.* Englewood Cliffs, NJ: Prentice-Hall.

Fishbein, M., & Ajzen, I. (2010). *Predicting and changing behavior: The reasoned action approach.* New York, NY: Psychology Press.

Fisher, H. (1994, April). The nature of romantic love. *Journal of NIH Research,* 59–64.

Fisher, R. P., & Geiselman, R. (2010). The cognitive interview method of conducting police interviews: Eliciting extensive information and promoting therapeutic jurisprudence. *International Journal of Law and Psychiatry, 33* (5–6), 321–328.

Fisher, R. P., Geiselman, R. E., Raymond, D. S., Jurkevich, L. M., & Warhaftig, M. L. (1987). Enhancing eyewitness memory: Refining the cognitive interview. *Journal of Police Science and Administration, 15,* 291–297.

Fisher, W. A., & Barak, A. (2001). Internet pornography: A social psychological perspective on Internet sexuality. *Journal of Sex Research, 38*(4), 312–323.

Fiske, S. T. (1999). Behind the scenes. In D. G. Myers, *Social Psychology* (6th ed.). New York, NY: McGraw-Hill.

Fiske, S. T. (2002, June). Envy, contempt, pity, and pride: Dangerous intergroup emotions on September 11th. Talk given at the APS symposium: Psychological science perspectives on September 11th.

Fiske, S. T., Harris, L. T., & Cuddy, A. J. C. (2004). Why ordinary people torture enemy prisoners. *Science, 306,* 1482–1483.

Fitterman, L. & Bouquet, T. (2009, September) Web of conscience. *Reader's Digest,* 60–64.

Fletcher, G. J. O., Fincham, F. D., Cramer, L., & Heron, N. (1987). The role of attributions in the development of dating relationships. *Journal of Personality and Social Psychology, 53,* 481–489.

Fletcher, G. J. O., Tither, J. M., O'Loughlin, C., Friesen, M., & Overall, N. (2004). Warm and homely or cold and beautiful? Sex differences in trading off traits in mate selection. *Personality and Social Psychology Bulletin, 30*(6), 659–672.

Ford, M. B., & Collins, N. L. (2010). Self-esteem moderates neuroendocrine and psychological responses to interpersonal rejection. *Journal of Personality and Social Psychology, 98,* 405–419.

Forgas, J. P. (2007). When sad is better than happy: Negative affect can improve the quality and effectiveness of persuasive messages and social influence strategies. *Journal of Experimental Social Psychology, 43,* 513–528.

Forgas, J. P., & Fiedler, K. (1996a). Mood effects on intergroup discrimination: The role of affect in reward allocation decisions. *Journal of Personality and Social Psychology, 70,* 28–40.

Forgas, J. P., & Fiedler, K. (1996b). Us and them: Mood effects on intergroup discrimination. *Journal of Personality and Social Psychology, 70,* 28–40.

Foss, R. D. (1978). *The role of social influence in blood donation.* Paper presented at the American Psychological Association convention.

Foster, E. M., & McCombs-Thornton, K. (2013). Child welfare and the challenge of causal inference. *Children and Youth Services Review, 35*(7), 1130–1142.

Fowler, S. P., Williams, K., Hunt, K. J., Hazuda, H. P., & Stern, M. P. (2005). Diet soft drink consumption is associated with increased incidence of overweight and obesity in the San Antonio Heart Study. San Antonio, TX: Annual Meeting of the American Diabetes Association.

Fowler, S. P., Williams, K., Resendez, R. G., Hunt, K. G., Hazuda, H. P., & Stern, M. P. (2008). Fueling the obesity epidemic? Artificially sweetened beverage use and long-term weight gain. *Obesity, 16*(8), 1894–1900.

Frank, M. G., & Gilovich, T. (1989). Effect of memory perspective on retrospective causal attributions. *Journal of Personality and Social Psychology, 57,* 399–403.

Frank, M. G., & Gilovich, T. (1988). The dark side of self and social perception: Black uniforms and aggression in professional sports. *Journal of Personality and Social Psychology, 54,* 74–85.

Freedman, J. L., & Fraser, S. C. (1966). Compliance without pressure: The foot-in-the-door technique. *Journal of Personality and Social Psychology, 4,* 195–202.

Freedman, J. L., & Perlick, D. (1979). Crowding, contagion, and laughter. *Journal of Experimental Social Psychology, 15,* 295–303.

Freedman, J. L., & Sears, D. O. (1965). Warning, distraction, and resistance to influence. *Journal of Personality and Social Psychology, 1,* 262–266.

Freedman, J. L., Birsky, J., & Cavoukian, A. (1980). Environmental determinants of behavioral contagion: Density and number. *Basic and Applied Social Psychology, 1*(2), 155–161.

FreeTheChildren.com. (2014). Downloaded from website Sept 4, 2014.

French, J. R. P. (1968). The conceptualization and the measurement of mental health in terms of self-identity theory. In S. B. Sells (Ed.), *The definition and measurement of mental health.* Washington, DC: Department of Health, Education, and Welfare. (Cited by M. Rosenberg, 1979, *Conceiving the self.* New York, NY: Basic Books.)

Friedman, H. S., & DiMatteo, M. R. (1989). *Health psychology.* Englewood Cliffs, NJ: Prentice-Hall.

Friedrich, L. K., & Stein, A. H. (1973). Aggressive and prosocial television programs and the natural behavior of preschool children. *Monographs of the Society of Research in Child Development, 38* (4, Serial No. 151).

Friedrich, L. K., & Stein, A. H. (1975). Prosocial television and young children: The effects of verbal labeling and role playing on learning and behavior. *Child Development, 46,* 27–38.

Frieze, I. H., Olson, J. E., & Russell, J. (1991). Attractiveness and income for men and women in management. *Journal of Applied Social Psychology, 21,* 1039–1057.

FTC. (2003, June 12). Federal Trade Commission cigarette report for 2001 (http://www.ftc.gov/opa/2003/06/2001cigrpt.htm).

Fultz, J., Batson, C., Fortenbach, V. A., McCarthy, P. M., & Varney, L. L. (1986). Social evaluation and the empathy-altruism hypothesis. *Journal of Personality and Social Psychology, 50*(4), 761–769.

Furnham, A. (1982). Explanations for unemployment in Britain. *European Journal of Social Psychology, 12,* 335–352.

Furnham, A., & Gunter, B. (1984). Just world beliefs and attitudes towards the poor. *British Journal of Social Psychology, 23,* 265–269.

Gable, S. L., Gonzaga, G. C., & Strachman, A. (2006). Will you be there for me when things go right? Supportive responses to positive event disclosures. *Journal of Personality and Social Psychology, 91,* 904–917.

Gabrenya, W. K., Jr., Wang, Y.-E., & Latane, B. (1985). Social loafing on an optimizing task: Cross-cultural differences among Chinese and Americans. *Journal of Cross-Cultural Psychology, 16,* 223–242.

Gabriel, S., & Gardner, W. L. (1999). Are there "his" and "hers" types of interdependence? The implications of gender differences in collective versus relational interdependence for affect, behavior, and cognition. *Journal of Personality and Social Psychology, 77,* 642–655.

Gaertner, L., Sedikides, C., & Graetz, K. (1999). In search of self-definition: Motivational primacy of the individual self, motivational primacy of the collective self, or contextual primacy? *Journal of Personality and Social Psychology, 76,* 5–18.

Gaertner, S. L., Dovidio, J. F., Anastasio, P. A., Bachman, B. A., & Rust, M. C. (1993). The common ingroup identity model: Recategorization and the reduction of intergroup bias. In W. Stroebe & M. Hewstone (Eds.), *European Review of Social Psychology, Vol. 4.* London: Wiley.

Gaertner, S. L., Dovidio, J. F., Nier, J. A., Banker, B. S., Ward, C. M., Houlette, M., & Loux, S. (2000). The common ingroup identity model for reducing intergroup bias: Progress and challenges. In D. Capozza & R. Brown (Eds.), *Social identity processes: Trends in theory and research.* London: Sage.

Galanter, M. (1989). *Cults: Faith, healing, and coercion.* New York, NY: Oxford University Press.

Galanter, M. (1990). Cults and zealous self-help movements: A psychiatric perspective. *American Journal of Psychiatry, 147,* 543–551.

Galinsky, A. D., & Moskowitz, G. B. (2000). Perspective-taking: Decreasing stereotype expression, stereotype accessibility, and in-group favoritism. *Journal of Personality and Social Psychology, 78,* 708–724.

Galizio, M., & Hendrick, C. (1972). Effect of musical accompaniment on attitude: The guitar as a prop for persuasion. *Journal of Applied Social Psychology, 2,* 350–359.

Gallup, G., Jr. (2004). *The Gallup Poll: Public Opinion 2003.* Lanham, MD: Rowman & Littlefield Publishers Inc.

Gangestad, S. W. (1993). Sexual selection and physical attractiveness: Implications for mating dynamics. *Human Nature, 4,* 205–235.

Gangestad, S. W., Garver-Apgar, C. E., Simpson, J. A., & Cousins, A. J. (2007). Changes in women's mate preferences across the ovulatory cycle. *Journal of Personality and Social Psychology, 92,* 151–163.

Gangestad, S. W., & Thornhill, R. (1997). Human sexual selection and developmental stability. In J. A. Simpson & D. T. Kenrick (Eds.), *Evolutionary social psychology.* Mahwah, NJ: Erlbaum.

Gannon, L. (2002). A critique of evolutionary psychology. *Psychology, Evolution and Gender, 4,* 173–218.

Gardner, J., & Oswald, A. (2006). *Does money buy happiness? A longitudinal study using data on windfalls.* Working paper, Department of Economics, Cambridge University.

Gastorf, J. W., Suls, J., & Sanders, G. S. (1980). Type A coronary-prone behavior pattern and social facilitation. *Journal of Personality and Social Psychology, 8,* 773–780.

Gates, D. (1993, March 29). White male paranoia. *Newsweek,* 48–53.

Gates, M. F., & Allee, W. C. (1933). Conditioned behavior of isolated and grouped cockroaches on a simple maze. *Journal of Comparative Psychology, 15,* 331–358.

Gaunt, R. (2006). Couple similarity and marital satisfaction: Are similar spouses happier? *Journal of Personality, 74,* 1401–1420.

Gecas, V. (1989). The social psychology of self-efficacy. *Annual Review of Sociology, 15,* 291–316.

Geen, R. G. (1998). Aggression and antisocial behavior. In D. Gilbert, S. Fiske, & G. Lindzey (Eds.), *Handbook of Social Psychology* (4th ed.). New York, NY: McGraw-Hill.

Geen, R. G., & Gange, J. J. (1983). Social facilitation: Drive theory and beyond. In H. H. Blumberg, A. P. Hare, V. Kent, & M. Davies (Eds.), *Small groups and social interaction, Vol. 1.* London: Wiley.

Geen, R. G., & Quanty, M. B. (1977). The catharsis of aggression: An evaluation of a hypothesis. In L. Berkowitz (Ed.), *Advances in experimental social psychology, Vol. 10.* New York, NY: Academic Press.

Geen, R. G., & Thomas, S. L. (1986). The immediate effects of media violence on behavior. *Journal of Social Issues, 42,* 7–28.

Geisler, G. W. W., & Leith, L. M. (1997). The effects of self-esteem, self-efficacy and audience presence on soccer penalty shot performance. *Journal of Sport Behaviour, 20*(3), 322–337.

Gelinas, C., Lussier, Y., & Sabourin, S. (1995). Marital adjustment: The role of attribution and psychological distress /Adaptation conjugale: le role des attributions et de la detresse psychologique. *Canadian Journal of Behavioral Science/Revue canadienne des sciences du comportement, 27*(1), 21–35.

Gentile, D. A. (2004, May 14). Quoted by K. Laurie in *Violent games* (ScienCentral.com).

Gentile, D. A., & Anderson, C. A. (2003). Violent video games: The newest media violence hazard. In D. A. Gentile (Ed.), *Media violence and children.* Westport, CT: Ablex.

Gerbner, G. (1994). The politics of media violence: Some reflections. In C. Hamelink & O. Linne (Eds.), *Mass communication research: On problems and policies.* Norwood, NJ: Ablex.

Gerend, M. A., & Shepherd, M. A. (2013). Message framing, it does a body good: Effects of message framing and motivational orientation on young women's calcium consumption. *Journal of Health Psychology, 18*(10), 1296–1306.

Gerstenfeld, P. B., Grant, D. R., & Chiang, C. P. (2003). Hate online: A content analysis of extremist Internet sites. *Analyses of Social Issues and Public Policy, 3,* 29–44.

Gibbons, F. X., Eggleston, T. J., & Benthin, A. C. (1997). Cognitive reactions to smoking relapse: The reciprocal relation between dissonance and self-esteem. *Journal of Personality and Social Psychology, 72,* 184–195.

Gibson, B., & Sanbonmatsu, D. M. (2004). Optimism, pessimism, and gambling: The downside of optimism. *Personality and Social Psychology Bulletin, 30*(2), 149–160.

Gifford, R., & Hine, D. W. (1997). Toward cooperation in commons dilemmas. *Canadian Journal of Behavioural Science, 29,* 167–179.

Gifford, R., & Peacock, J. (1979). Crowding: More fearsome than crime-provoking? Comparison of an Asian city and a North American city. *Psychologia, 22,* 79–83.

Gigerenzer, G. (2004). Dread risk, September 11, and fatal traffic accidents. *Psychological Science, 15,* 286–287.

Gigone, D., & Hastie, R. (1993). The common knowledge effect: Information sharing and group judgment. *Journal of Personality and Social Psychology, 65,* 959–974.

Gilbert, D. (2007). *Stumbling on happiness.* New York: Knopf.

Gilbert, D. T., & Ebert, J. E. J. (2002). Decisions and revisions: The affective forecasting of changeable outcomes. *Journal of Personality and Social Psychology, 82*(4), 503–514.

Gilbert, D. T., & Hixon, J. G. (1991). The trouble of thinking: Activation and application of stereotypic beliefs. *Journal of Personality and Social Psychology, 60,* 509–517.

Gilbert, D. T., McNulty, S. E., Giuliano, T. A., & Benson, J. E. (1992). Blurry words and fuzzy deeds: The attribution of obscure behavior. *Journal of Personality and Social Psychology, 62,* 18–25.

Gilbert, D. T., Pelham, B. W., & Krull, D. S. (1988). On cognitive busyness: When person perceivers meet persons perceived. *Journal of Personality and Social Psychology, 54,* 733–740.

Gilbert, D. T., Pinel, E. C., Wilson, T. D., Blumberg, S. J., & Wheatley, T. P. (1998). Immune neglect: A source of durability bias in affective forecasting. *Journal of Personality and Social Psychology, 75,* 617–638.

Gilmor, T. M., & Reid, D. W. (1979). Locus of control and causal attribution for positive and negative outcomes on university examinations. *Journal of Research in Personality, 13,* 154–160.

Gilovich, T. (1987). Secondhand information and social judgment. *Journal of Experimental Social Psychology, 23,* 59–74.

Gilovich, T., Kerr, M., & Medvec, V. H. (1993). Effect of temporal perspective on subjective confidence. *Journal of Personality and Social Psychology, 64,* 552–560.

Gilovich, T., Medvec, V. H., & Savitsky, K. (2000). The spotlight effect in social judgment: An egocentric bias in estimates of the salience of one's own actions and appearance. *Journal of Personality and Social Psychology, 78,* 211–222.

Ginet, M., Py, J., & Colomb, C. (2014). The differential effectiveness of the cognitive interview instructions for enhancing witnesses' memory of a familiar event. *Swiss Journal of Psychology, 73*(1), 25–34.

Gladwell, M. (2002). *Blink.* Lebanon, IN: Little, Brown.

Gladwell, M. (2005). *Blink.* New York, NY: Back Bay Books; Little, Brown.

Glenn, N. D. (1980). Aging and attitudinal stability. In O. G. Brim, Jr. & J. Kagan (Eds.), *Constancy and change in human development.* Cambridge, MA: Harvard University Press.

Glenn, N. D. (1981). *Personal communication.*

Glick, P., & Fiske, S. J. (1996). The ambivalent sexism inventory: Differentiating hostile and benevolent sexism. *Journal of Personality and Social Psychology, 70,* 491–512.

Glick, P., & Fiske, S. J. (2001). An ambivalent alliance: Hostile and ambivalent sexism as complementary justifications for gender inequality. *American Psychologist, 56,* 108–118.

Globe and Mail. (2002, June 19). Saskatchewan to pay officer $1.3 million to settle Martensville lawsuit.

Globe and Mail. (2010). Women in power: Best of the series. Retrieved from http://www.theglobeandmail.com/news/national/time-to-lead/women-in-power/.

Goethals, G. R., Messick, D. M., & Allison, S. T. (1991). The uniqueness bias: Studies of constructive social comparison. In J. Suls & T. A. Wills (Eds.), *Social comparison: Contemporary theory and research.* Hillsdale, NJ: Erlbaum.

Goldhagen, D. J. (1996). *Hitler's willing executioners.* New York, NY: Knopf.

Goldman, J. (1967). *A comparison of sensory modality preference of children and adults.* Dissertation: Thesis (Ph.D.). Ferkauf Graduate School of Humanities and Social Sciences, Yeshiva University.

Goldstein, A. P., & Glick, B. (1994). Aggression replacement training: Curriculum and evaluation. *Simulation and Gaming, 25,* 9–26.

Goldstein, J. H., & Arms, R. L. (1971). Effects of observing athletic contests on hostility. *Sociometry, 34,* 83–90.

Goldstein, N. J., Martin, S. J., & Cialdini, R. B. (2008). *Yes!: 50 Scientifically Proven Ways to Be Persuasive.* New York, NY: Free Press.

Gonzaga, G. C., Campos, B., & Bradbury, T. (2007). Similarity, convergence, and relationship satisfaction in dating and married couples. *Journal of Personality and Social Psychology, 93,* 34–48.

Gonzales, M. H., & Meyers, S. A. (1993). "Your mother would like me:" Self-Presentation in the personals ads of heterosexual and homosexual men and women. *Personality and Social Psychology Bulletin, 19,* 131–142.

Goodhart, D. E. (1986). The effects of positive and negative thinking on performance in an achievement situation. *Journal of Personality and Social Psychology, 51,* 117–124.

Goodwin, K. A., Kukucka, J. P., & Hawks, I. M. (2012). Co-witness confidence, conformity, and eyewitness memory: An examination of normative and informational social influences. *Applied Cognitive Psychology, 27,* 91–100.

Gortmaker, S. L., Must, A., Perrin, J. M., Sobol, A. M., & Dietz, W. H. (1993). Social and economic consequences of overweight in adolescence and young adulthood. *New England Journal of Medicine, 329,* 1008–1012.

Gottman, J. (with N. Silver). (1994). *Why marriages succeed or fail.* New York, NY: Simon & Schuster.

Gottman, J. M. (1998). Psychology and the study of marital processes. *Annual Review of Psychology, 49,* 169–197.

Graham, K., LaRocque, L., Yetman, R., Ross, T. J., & Guistra, E. (1980). Aggression and barroom environments. *Journal of Studies on Alcohol, 41,* 468–485.

Graham, K., Osgood, D. W., Wells, S., & Stockwell, T. (2005). To what extent is intoxication associated with aggression in bars? A multilevel analysis: Social factors and prevention interventions. Centre for Addiction and Mental Health.

Graham, K., Wells, S., Bernards, S., & Dennison, S. (2010). "Yes, I do but not with you": Qualitative analyses of sexual/romantic overture-related aggression in bars and clubs. *Contemporary Drug Problems: An Interdisciplinary Quarterly, 37*(2), 197–240.

Granhag, P. A., Andersson, L. O., Stromwall, L. A., & Hartwig, M. (2004). Imprisoned knowledge: Criminals' beliefs about deception. *Legal and Criminological Psychology, 9*(1), 103–119.

Grant, P. R. (2008). The protest intentions of skilled immigrants with credentialing problems: A test of a model integrating relative deprivation theory with social identity theory. *British Journal of Social Psychology, 47,* 687–705.

Gray, J. D., & Silver, R. C. (1990). Opposite sides of the same coin: Former spouses' divergent perspectives in coping with their divorce. *Journal of Personality and Social Psychology, 59,* 1180–1191.

Greeley, A. M., & Sheatsley, P. B. (1971). Attitudes toward racial integration. *Scientific American, 225*(6), 13–19.

Greenberg, J. (1986). Differential intolerance for inequity from organizational and individual agents. *Journal of Applied Social Psychology, 16,* 191–196.

Greenberg, J., Pyszczynski, T., Solomon, S., Rosenblatt, A., Veeder, M., Kirkland, S., & Lyon, D. (1990). Evidence for terror management theory: II. The effects of mortality salience on reactions to those who threaten or bolster the cultural worldview. *Journal of Personality and Social Psychology, 58,* 308–318.

Greenberg, J., Pyszczynski, T., Solomon, S., Simon, L., & Breus, M. (1994). Role of consciousness and accessibility of death-related thoughts in mortality salience effects. *Journal of Personality and Social Psychology, 67,* 627–637.

Greenberg, J., Solomon, S., & Pyszczynski, T. (1997). Terror management theory of self-esteem and cultural worldviews: Empirical assessments and conceptual refinements. *Advances in Experimental Social Psychology, 29,* 61–142.

Greenfield, P. M. (2004). Inadvertent exposure to pornography on the Internet: Implications of peer-to-peer file-sharing networks for child development and families. *Applied Developmental Psychology, 25,* 741–750.

Greenwald, A. G., Banaji, M. R., Rudman, L. A., Farnham, S. D., Nosek, B. A., & Rosier, M. (2000). Prologue to a unified theory of attitudes, stereotypes, and self-concept. In J. P. Forgas (Ed.), *Feeling and thinking: The role of affect in social cognition and behavior.* New York, NY: Cambridge University Press.

Greenwald, A. G., Nosek, B. A., & Banaji, M. R. (2003). Understanding and using the implicit association test: I. An improved scoring algorithm. *Journal of Personality and Social Psychology, 85,* 197–216.

Grekul, J., & LaBoucane-Benson, P. (2008). Aboriginal gangs and their (dis)placement: Contextualizing recruitment, membership, and status. *Canadian Journal of Criminology and Criminal Justice, 50*(1), 59–82.

Griffin, B. Q., Combs, A. L., Land, M. L., & Combs, N. N. (1983). Attribution of success and failure in college performance. *Journal of Psychology, 114,* 259–266.

Griffitt, W. (1970). Environmental effects on interpersonal affective behavior. Ambient effective temperature and attraction. *Journal of Personality and Social Psychology, 15,* 240–244.

Griffitt, W. (1987). Females, males, and sexual responses. In K. Kelley (Ed.), *Females, males, and sexuality: Theories and research.* Albany, NY: State University of New York Press.

Griffitt, W., & Veitch, R. (1971). Hot and crowded: Influences of population density and temperature on interpersonal affective behavior. *Journal of Personality and Social Psychology, 17,* 92–98.

Groenenboom, A., Wilke, H. A. M., & Wit, A. P. (2001). Will we be working together again? The impact of future interdependence on group members' task motivation. *European Journal of Social Psychology, 31,* 369–378.

Gronlund, S. D., Carlson, C. A., Dailey, S. B., & Goodsell, C. A. (2009). Robustness of the sequential lineup advantage. *Journal of Experimental Psychology: Applied, 15*(2), 140–152.

Gross, A. E., & Crofton, C. (1977). What is good is beautiful. *Sociometry, 40,* 85–90.

Grove, J. R., Hanrahan, S. J., & McInman, A. (1991). Success/failure bias in attributions across involvement categories in sport. *Personality and Social Psychology Bulletin, 17,* 93–97.

Gruder, C. L. (1977). Choice of comparison persons in evaluating oneself. In J. M. Suls & R. L. Miller (Eds.), *Social comparison processes.* Washington, D.C.: Hemisphere Publishing.

Gruman, J. C., & Sloan, R. P. (1983). Disease as justice: Perceptions of the victims of physical illness. *Basic and Applied Social Psychology, 4,* 39–46.

Gudykunst, W. B. (1989). Culture and intergroup processes. In M. H. Bond (Ed.), *The cross-cultural challenge to social psychology.* Newbury Park, CA: Sage.

Gueguen, N., & Jacob, C. (2001). Fundraising on the Web: The effect of an electronic foot-in-the-door on donation. *CyberPsychology and Behavior, 4,* 705–709.

Guerin, B. (1993). *Social facilitation.* Paris: Cambridge University Press.

Guerin, B. (1994). What do people think about the risks of driving? Implications for traffic safety interventions. *Journal of Applied Social Psychology, 24,* 994–1021.

Guerin, B. (1999). Social behaviors as determined by different arrangements of social consequences: Social loafing, social facilitation, deindividuation, and a modified social loafing. *The Psychological Record, 49,* 565–578.

Guerin, B., & Innes, J. M. (1982). Social facilitation and social monitoring: A new look at Zajonc's mere presence hypothesis. *British Journal of Social Psychology, 21,* 7–18.

Guo, Q., Johnson, C. A., Unger, J. B., Lee, L., Xie, B., Chou, C. P. Palmer, P. H. et al. (2007). Utility of theory of reasoned action and theory of planned behavior for predicting Chinese adolescent smoking. *Addictive Behaviors, 32,* 1066–1081.

Gupta, U., & Singh, P. (1982). Exploratory study of love and liking and type of marriages. *Indian Journal of Applied Psychology, 19,* 92–97.

Haddock, G., & Zanna, M. P. (1994). Preferring "housewives" to "feminists." *Psychology of Women Quarterly, 18,* 25–52.

Hadjistavropoulose, H.D., Ross, M.A., & VonBaeyer, C. L. (1990). Are physicians' ratings of pain affected by patients' physical attractiveness? *Social Science Medicine, 31*(1), 69–72.

Hafer, C. L., & Begue, L. (2005). Experimental research on just-world theory: Problems, developments, and future challenges. *Psychological Bulletin, 131,* 128–167.

Hafer, C. L., Reynolds, K. L., & Obertynski, M. A. (1996). Message comprehensibility and persuasion: Effects of complex language in counter-attitudinal appeals of laypeople. *Social Cognition, 14,* 317–337.

Haferkamp, N., Eimler, S. C., Papadakis, A., & Kruck, J. V. (2012). Men are from Mars, women are from Venus? Examining gender differences in self-presentation on social networking sites. *Cyberpsychology, Behavior, and Social Networking, 15*(2), 91–98.

Hagerty, M. R. (2000). Social comparisons of income in one's community: Evidence from national surveys of income and happiness. *Journal of Personality and Social Psychology, 78,* 764–771.

Halberstadt, J., & Rhodes, G. (2000). The attractiveness of nonface averages: Implications for an evolutionary explanation of the attractiveness of average faces. *Psychological Science, 11,* 285–289.

Hall, J. A., & Carter, J. D. (1999). Gender-stereotype accuracy as an individual difference. *Journal of Personality and Social Psychology, 77,* 350–359.

Halverson, A. M., Hallahan, M., Hart, A. J., & Rosenthal, R. (1997). Reducing the biasing effects of judges' non-verbal behavior with simplified jury instruction. *Journal of Applied Psychology, 82,* 590–598.

Hamberger, J., & Hewstone, M. (1997). Inter-ethnic contact as a predictor of blatant and subtle prejudice: Tests of a model in four West European nations. *British Journal of Social Psychology, 36,* 173–190.

Hamblin, R. L., Buckholdt, D., Bushell, D., Ellis, D., & Feritor, D. (1969, January). Changing the game from "get the teacher" to "learn." *Transaction,* 20–25, 28–31.

Haney, C., & Zimbardo, P. (1998). The past and future of U.S. prison policy: Twenty-five years after the Stanford Prison Experiment. *American Psychologist, 53,* 709–727.

Hansen, C. H. (1989). Priming sex-role stereotypic event schemas with rock music videos: Effects on impression favorability, trait inferences, and recall of a subsequent male/female interaction. *Basic and Applied Social Psychology, 10,* 371–391.

Hansen, C. H., & Hansen, R. D. (1988). Priming stereotypic appraisal of social interactions: How rock music videos can change what's seen when boy meets girl. *Sex Roles, 19,* 287–316.

Hardin, G. (1968). The tragedy of the commons. *Science, 162,* 1243–1248.

Hardy, C., & Latané, B. (1986). Social loafing on a cheering task. *Social Science, 71,* 165–172.

Harkins, S. G. (1981). Effects of task difficulty and task responsibility on social loafing. Presentation to the First International Conference on Social Processes in Small Groups.

Harkins, S. G., & Jackson, J. M. (1985). The role of evaluation in eliminating social loafing. *Personality and Social Psychology Bulletin, 11,* 457–465.

Harkins, S. G., Latané, B., & Williams, K. (1980), Social loafing: Allocating effort or taking it easy? *Journal of Experimental Social Psychology, 16,* 457–465.

Harkins, S. G., & Petty, R. E. (1981). Effects of source magnification of cognitive effort on attitudes: An information-processing view. *Journal of Personality and Social Psychology, 40,* 401–413.

Harkins, S. G., & Petty, R. E. (1982). Effects of task difficulty and task uniqueness on social loafing. *Journal of Personality and Social Psychology, 43,* 1214–1229.

Harkins, S. G., & Szymanski, K. (1989). Social loafing and group evaluation. *Journal of Personality and Social Psychology, 56,* 934–941.

Harkness, K. L., Sabbagh, M. A., Jacobson, J. A., Chowdrey, N. K., & Chen, T. (2005). Enhanced accuracy of mental state decoding in dysphoric college students. *Cognition and Emotion, 19,* 999–1025.

Harmon-Jones, E., & Allen, J. J. B. (2001). The role of affect in the mere exposure effect: evidence from psychophysiological and individual differences approaches, *Personality and Social Psychology Bulletin, 27*(7), 889–898.

Harmon-Jones, E., Brehm, J. W., Greenberg, J., Simon, L., & Nelson, D. E. (1996). Evidence that the production of aversive consequences is not necessary to create cognitive dissonance. *Journal of Personality and Social Psychology, 70,* 5–16.

Harris, G., Cameron, J. E., & Lang, J. (2010). Identification with community-based HIV agencies as a correlate of turnover intentions and general self-efficacy. *Journal of Community & Applied Social Psychology, 20,* 1–14.

Harris, J. R. (1998). *The nurture assumption.* New York, NY: Free Press.

Harris, L. T., & Fiske, S. T. (2006). Dehumanizing the lowest of the low: Neuro-imaging responses to extreme outgroups. *Psychological Science, 17*(10), 847–853.

Harris, M. (2012). Bullying victim Amanda Todd's death a consequence of 'passive bystandeers,' says experts. Retrieved from http://o.canada.com/news/national/amanda-todds-death-judged-a-consequence-of-passive-bystanders/.

Harris, M. J., & Rosenthal, R. (1985). Mediation of interpersonal expectancy effects: 31 meta-analyses. *Psychological Bulletin, 97,* 363–386.

Harris, M. J., & Rosenthal, R. (1986). Four factors in the mediation of teacher expectancy effects. In R. S. Feldman (Ed.), *The social psychology of education.* New York: Cambridge University Press.

Harrison, A. A. (1977). Mere exposure. In L. Berkowitz (Ed.), *Advances in experimental social psychology, Vol. 10,* New York, NY: Academic Press.

Hasan, Y., Bègue, L., Scharkow, M., & Bushman, B. J. (2013). The more you play, the more aggressive you become: A long-term experimental study of cumulative violent video game effects on hostile expectations and aggressive behavior. *Journal of Experimental Social Psychology, 49,* 224–227.

Haslam, S. A., & Reicher, S. (2007b). Beyond the banality of evil: Three dynamics of an interactionist social psychology of tyranny. *Personality and Social Psychology Bulletin, 33,* 615–622.

Haslam, S. A., & Reicher, S. D. (2007a). Identity entrepreneurship and the consequences of identity failure: The dynamics of leadership in the BBC prison study. *Social Psychology Quarterly, 70,* 125–147.

Haslam, S. A., Jetten, J., Postmes, T., & Haslam, C. (2009). Social identity, health and well-being: An emerging agenda for applied psychology. *Applied Psychology: An International Review, 58*(1), 1–23.

Hastie, R., Penrod, S. D., & Pennington, N. (1983). *Inside the jury.* Cambridge, MA: Harvard University Press.

Hatfield (Walster), E., Walster, G. W., & Berscheid, E. (1978). *Equity: Theory and research.* Boston, MA: Allyn & Bacon.

Hatfield, E. & Rapson, R. L. (1993). *Love, sex and intimacy: Their psychology, biology, and history.* New York: HarperCollins.

Hatfield, E. (1988). Passionate and compassionate love. In R. J. Sternberg & M. L. Barnes (Eds.), *The psychology of love.* New Haven, CT: Yale University Press.

Hatfield, E., & Sprecher, S. (1986). *Mirror, mirror: The importance of looks in everyday life.* Albany, NY: State University of New York Press.

Hatfield, E., Traupmann, J., Sprecher, S., Utne, M., & Hay, J. (1985). Equity and intimate relations: Recent research. In W. Ickes (Ed.), *Compatible and incompatible relationships.* New York, NY: Springer-Verlag.

Havel, V. (1990). *Disturbing the peace.* New York, NY: Knopf.

Haynes, T. L., Daniels, L. M., Stupnisky, R. H., Perry, R. P., & Hladkyj, S. (2008). The effect of attributional retraining on mastery and performance motivation among first-y ear college students. *Basic and Applied Social Psychology, 30,* 198–207.

Haynes, T. L., Heckhausen, J., Chipperfield, J. G., Perry, R. P., & Newall, N. E. (2009). Primary and secondary control strategies: Implications for health and well-being among older adults. *Journal of Social and Clinical Psychology, 28*(2), 165–197.

Hazan, C. (2004). Intimate attachment/capacity to love and be loved. In C. Peterson & M. E. P. Seligman (Eds.), *The values in action classification of strengths and virtues*. Washington, DC: American Psychological Association.

Hazan, C., & Shaver, P. R. (1994). Attachment as an organizational framework for research on close relationships. *Psychological Inquiry, 5*, 1–22.

Headey, B., & Wearing, A. (1987). The sense of relative superiority—central to well-being. *Social Indicators Research, 20*, 497–516.

Heap, B., & Comim, F. (2005). *Consumption and happiness: Christian values and an approach towards sustainability*. Capability and Sustainability Centre, St. Edmund's College, University of Cambridge. Address to Christians in Science annual meeting.

Heap, B., & Kent, J. (Eds.). (2000). *Towards sustainable consumption: A European perspective*. London: The Royal Society.

Hearold, S. (1986). A synthesis of 1043 effects of television on social behavior. In G. Comstock (Ed.), *Public communication and behavior, Vol. 1*. Orlando, FL: Academic Press.

Heart and Stroke Foundation. (2011). (http://www.heartandstroke.com).

Hebl, M. R., & Heatherton, T. F. (1998). The stigma of obesity in women: The difference is black and white. *Personality and Social Psychology Bulletin, 24*, 417–426.

Hedley, A. (1994). Review essay, identity: Sense of self & nation. *Canadian Review of Sociology and Anthropology, 31*, 200–214.

Heider, F. (1958). *The psychology of interpersonal relations*. New York, NY: Wiley.

Heine, S. J. (2003). Making sense of East Asian self-enhancement. *Journal of Cross-Cultural Psychology, 34*(5), 596–602.

Heine, S. J. (2010). Cultural psychology. In S. T. Fiske, D. T. Gilbert, & G. Lindzey (Eds.), *Handbook of social psychology, Vol. 2* (5th ed.) (pp. 1423–1464). Hoboken, NJ: Wiley.

Henderson-King, E. I., & Nisbett, R. E. (1996). Anti-black prejudice as a function of exposure to the negative behavior of a single black person. *Journal of Personality and Social Psychology, 71*, 654–664.

Hendrick, C., & Hendrick, S. (1993). *Romantic love*. Newbury Park, CA: Sage.

Hendrick, S. S., & Hendrick, C. (1995). Gender differences and similarities in sex and love. *Personal Relationships, 2*, 55–65.

Hendrick, S. S., & Hendrick, C. (1997). Love and satisfaction. In R. J. Sternberg & M. Hojjat (Eds.), *Satisfaction in close relationships*. New York, NY: Guilford Press.

Hendrick, S. S., Hendrick, C., & Adler, N. L. (1988). Romantic relationships: Love, satisfaction, and staying together. *Journal of Personality and Social Psychology, 54*, 980–988.

Henry, W. A., III. (1994, June 27). Pride and prejudice. *Time*, 54–59.

Hepworth, J. T., & West, S. G. (1988). Lynchings and the economy: A time-series reanalysis of Hovland and Sears (1940). *Journal of Personality and Social Psychology, 55*, 239–247.

Herek, G. M., Cogan, J. C., & Gillis, J. R. (2009). Internalized stigma among sexual minority adults: Insights from a social psychological perspective. *Journal of Counseling Psychology, 56*(1), 32–43.

Herek, G. M., & Glunt, E. K. (1988). An epidemic of stigma: Public reactions to AIDS. *American Psychologist, 43*, 886–891.

Hergovich, A., Schott, R., & Burger, C. (2010). Biased evaluation of abstracts depending on topic and conclusion: Further evidence of a confirmation bias within scientific psychology. *Current Psychology, 29*(3), 188–209.

Hertwig, R., & Ortmann, A. (2008). Deception in experiments: Revisiting the arguments in its defense. *Ethics & Behavior, 18*(1), 59–92.

Hewstone, M. (2003). Intergroup contact: Panacea for prejudice? *The Psychologist, 16*, 352–355.

Hewstone, M., & Fincham, F. (1996). Attribution theory and research: Basic issues and applications. In M. Hewstone, W. Strobe, & G. M. Stephenson (Eds.), *Introduction to social psychology: A European perspective*. Oxford, UK: Blackwell.

Hewstone, M., Hantzi, A., & Johnston, L. (1991). Social categorisation and person memory: The pervasiveness of race as an organizing principle. *European Journal of Social Psychology, 21*, 517–528.

Higbee, K. L. (1969). Fifteen years of fear arousal: Research on threat appeals: 1953–1968. *Psychological Bulletin, 72*, 426–444.

Higbee, K. L., Millard, R. J., & Folkman, J. R. (1982). Social psychology research during the 1970s: Predominance of experimentation and college students. *Personality and Social Psychology Bulletin, 8*, 180–183.

Higgins, E. T., & Bargh, J. A. (1987). Social cognition and social perception. *Annual Review of Psychology, 38*, 369–425.

Higgins, N. C., & Bhatt, G. (2001). Culture moderates the self-serving bias: Etic and emic features of causal attributes in India and in Canada. *Social Behavior and Personality, 29*, 49–61.

Hileman, B. (1999, August 9). Case grows for climate change. *Chemical and Engineering News*, 16–23.

Hine, D. W., & Gifford, R. (1996). Attributions about self and others in commons dilemmas. *European Journal of Social Psychology, 26*, 429–445.

Hinsz, V. B., Tindale, R. S., & Vollrath, D. A. (1997). The emerging conceptualization of groups as information processors. *Psychological Bulletin, 121*, 43–64.

Hirschman, R. S., & Leventhal, H. (1989). Preventing smoking behavior in school children: An initial test of a cognitive-development program. *Journal of Applied Social Psychology, 19*, 559–583.

Hoaken, P. N. S., & Pihl, R. O. (2000). The effects of alcohol intoxication on aggressive responses in men and women. *Alcohol and Alcoholism, 35*, 471–477.

Hodges, B. H., & Geyer, A. L. (2006). A nonconformist account of the Asch experiments: Values, pragmatics, and moral dilemmas. *Personality and Social Psychology Review*, 102–119.

Hodson, G., Harry, H., & Mitchell, A. (2009). Independent benefits of contact and friendship on attit udes towards homosexuals among authoritarians and highly identified heterosexuals. *European Journal of Social Psychology, 39*, 509–525.

Hoffman, C., & Hurst, N. (1990). Gender stereotypes: Perception or rationalization? *Journal of Personality and Social Psychology, 58*, 197–208.

Hoffman, L. W. (1977). Changes in family roles, socialization, and sex differences. *American Psychologist, 32,* 644–657.

Hoffman, M. L. (1981). Is altruism part of human nature? *Journal of Personality and Social Psychology, 40,* 121–137.

Hoffrage, U., Hertwig, R., & Gigerenzer, G. (2000, May). Hindsight bias: A by-product of knowledge updating? *Journal of Experimental Psychology: Learning, Memory, and Cognition, 26,* 566–581.

Hofling, C. K., Brotzman, E., Dairymple, S., Graves, N., & Pierce, C. M. (1966). An experimental study in nurse-physician relationships. *Journal of Nervous and Mental Disease, 143,* 171–180.

Hogg, M. A. (2003). Social identity. In M. R. Leary & J. P. Tangey (Eds.), *Handbook of self and identity.* New York, NY: Guilford Press.

Hogg, M. A. (2008). Social identify processes and the empowerment of followers. In R. E. Riggio, I. Chaleff, & J. Lipman-Blumen (Eds.), *The art of followships: How great followers create great leaders and organizations.* San Francisco: Jossey-Bass.

Hogg, M. A., Turner, J. C., & Davidson, B. (1990). Polarized norms and social frames of reference: A test of the self-categorization theory of group polarization. *Basic and Applied Social Psychology, 11,* 77–100.

Holmberg, D., & Ross, M. (1992). Are wives' memories for events more vivid than their husbands' memories? *Journal of Social and Personal Relationships, 9,* 585–604.

Holmberg, D., Pringle, J. D., Shea, S. L., & Dodge, D. (2006). *She remembers it well: Evidence for superior female relationship memory.* Unpublished manuscript. Wolfville: Acadia University.

Holmes, J. G., & Rahe, R. H. (1967). The social readjustment rating scale. *Journal of Psychosomatic Research, 11,* 213–218.

Holmes, J. G., & Rempel, J. K. (1989). Trust in close relationships. In C. Hendrick (Ed.), *Review of personality and social psychology, Vol. 10.* Newbury Park, CA: Sage.

Homel, J. B. (2013). Does bullying others at school lead to adult aggression? The roles of drinking and university participation during the transition to adulthood. *Austrialian Journal of Psychology, 65*(2), 98–106.

Honeyman, J. C., & Ogloff, J. (1996). Capital punishment: Arguments for life and death. *Canadian Journal of Behavioral Science, 28,* 27–35.

Hong, Y., Wyer, R., & Fong, C. (2008). Chinese working in groups: Effort dispensability versus normative influence. *Asian Journal of Social Psychology, 11*(3), 187–195.

Hoorens, V., Nuttin, J. M., Herman, I. E., & Pavakanun, U. (1990). Mastery pleasure versus mere ownership: A quasi-experimental cross-cultural and cross-alphabetical test of the name letter effect. *European Journal of Social Psychology, 20,* 181–205.

Horowitz, J. L., & Newcomb, M. D. (2002). A multidimensional approach to homosexual identity. *Journal of Homosexuality, 42,* 1–19.

Houston, D. A., & Fazio, R. H. (1989). Biased processing as a function of attitude accessibility: Making objective judgments subjectively. *Social Cognition, 7*(1), 51–66.

Houston, V., & Bull, R. (1994). Do people avoid sitting next to someone who is facially disfigured? *European Journal of Social Psychology, 24,* 279–284.

Hovland, C. I., & Sears, R. (1940). Minor studies of aggression: Correlation of lynchings with economic indices. *Journal of Psychology, 9,* 301–310.

Hsee, C. K., & Hastie, R. (2006). Decision and experience: Why don't we choose what makes us happy? *Trends in Cognitive Sciences, 10,* 31–37.

Huddy, L., & Virtanen, S. (1995). Subgroup differentiation and subgroup bias among Latinos as a function of familiarity and positive distinctiveness. *Journal of Personality and Social Psychology, 68,* 97–108.

Huesmann, L. R., Moise-Titus, J., Podolski, C. L., & Eron, L. D. (2003). Longitudinal relations between children's exposure to TV violence and their aggressive and violent behavior in young adulthood: 1977–1992. *Developmental Psychology, 39,* 201–222.

Hugenberg, K., & Bodenhausen, G. V. (2003). Facing prejudice: Implicit prejudice and the perception of facial threat. *Psychological Science, 14,* 640–643.

Hughes, D. R. (2001). The impact of the use of new communications and information technologies on trafficking in human beings for sexual exploitation. Retrieved from http://www.popcenter.org/problems/trafficked_women/PDFs/Hughes_2001.pdf.

Hull, J. G., Levenson, R. W., Young, R. D., & Sher, K. J. (1983). Self-awareness-reducing effects of alcohol consumption. *Journal of Personality and Social Psychology, 44,* 461–473.

Hullett, C. R. (2005). The impact of mood on persuasion: A meta-analysis. *Communication Research, 32*(4), 423–442.

Hunt, P. J., & Hillery, J. M. (1973). Social facilitation in a location setting: An examination of the effects over learning trials. *Journal of Experimental Social Psychology, 9,* 563–571.

Hunt, R., & Jensen, J. (2007). *The experiences of young gay people in Britian's schools.* Stonewall (http://www.stonewall.org.uk).

Hurtado, S., Dey, E. L., & Trevino, J. G. (1994). *Exclusion or self-segregation? Interaction across racial/ethnic groups on college campuses.* Paper presented at the American Educational Research Association annual meeting.

Huston, A. C., Donnerstein, E., Fairchild, H., Feshbach, N. D., Katz, P. A., & Murray, J. P. (1992). *Big world, small screen: The role of television in American society.* Lincoln, NE: University of Nebraska Press.

Huston, T. L. (1973). Ambiguity of acceptance, social desirability, and dating choice. *Journal of Experimental Social Psychology, 9,* 32–42.

Huston, T. L., & Chorost, A. F. (1994). Behavioral buffers on the effect of negativity on marital satisfaction: A longitudinal study. *Personal Relationships, 1,* 223–239.

Huston, T. L., Niehuis, S., & Smith, S. E. (2001). The early marital roots of conjugal distress and divorce. *Current Directions in Psychological Science, 10*(4), 116–119.

Ickes, W., Layden, M. A., & Barnes, R. D. (1978). Objective self-awareness and individuation: An empirical link. *Journal of Personality, 46,* 146–161.

ILO. (1997, December 11). Women's progress in workforce improving worldwide, but occupation segregation still rife. International Labor Organization press release. Retrieved from http://www.ilo.org/public/english/bureau/inf/pr/1997/35.htm

ILO. (2010). *Women in labour markets: Measuring progress and identifying challenges.* Geneva: International Labour Organization.

Imai, Y. (1994). Effects of influencing attempts on the perceptions of powerholders and the powerless. *Journal of Social Behavior and Personality, 9,* 455–468.

Inbau, F. E., Reid, J. E., Buckley, J. P., & Jayne, B. C. (2001). *Criminal interrogation and confessions* (4th ed.). Gaithersburg, MD: Aspen.

Ingham, A. G., Levinger, G., Graves, J., & Peckham, V. (1974). The Ringelmann effect: Studies of group size and group performance. *Journal of Experimental Social Psychology, 10,* 371–384.

Inglehart, R. (1990). *Culture shift in advanced industrial society.* Princeton, NJ: Princeton University Press.

Inglehart, R. (2006). Cultural change and democracy in Latin America. In F. Hagopian (Ed.), *Contemporary Catholicism, religious pluralism and democracy in Latin America.* South Bend, IN: Notre Dame University Press.

Inglehart, R. (2009). Cultural change and democracy in Latin America. In F. Hagopian (Ed.), *Religious pluralism, democracy, and the Catholic Church in Latin America.* South Bend: University of Notre Dame Press.

Inglehart, R., Foa, R., Peterson, C., & Welzel, C. (2008). Development, freedom, and rising happiness: A global perspective (1981–2007). *Perspectives on Psychological Science, 3,* 264–285.

Inglehart, R., & Welzel, C. (2005). *Modernization, cultural change, and democracy: The human development sequence* (pp. 58–59, 156, 180). New York, NY: Cambridge University Press.

International Civil Aviation Organization. (ICAO). (2005). Retrieved from http://www.icao.int/cgi/goto_m.pl?/icao/en/jr/jr.cfm.

IPU. (2005). *Women in politics 1945–2005.* Geneva: Inter-Parliamentary Union.

IPU. (2011). Women in national parliaments. Retrieved from http://www.ipu.org/wmn-e/world.htm.

Isozaki, M. (1984). The effect of discussion on polarization of judgments. *Japanese Psychological Research, 26,* 187–193.

ISR Newsletter. (1975). Institute for Social Research, University of Michigan, *3,* 4–7.

Ito, T. A., Miller, N., & Pollock, V. E. (1996). Alcohol and aggression: A meta-analysis on the moderating effects of inhibitory cues, triggering events, and self-focused attention. *Psychological Bulletin, 120,* 60–82.

Iyengar, S. S., & Lepper, M. R. (2000). When choice is demotivating: Can one desire too much of a good thing? *Journal of Personality and Social Psychology, 79,* 995–1006.

Iyengar, S. S., Wells, R. E., & Schwartz, B. (2006). Doing better but feeling worse: Looking for the best job undermines satisfaction. *Psychological Science, 17,* 143–150.

Jackman, M. R., & Senter, M. S. (1981). Beliefs about race, gender, and social class, different therefore unequal: Beliefs about trait differences between groups of unequal status. In D. J. Treiman & R. V. Robinson (Eds.), *Research in stratification and mobility, Vol. 2.* Greenwich, CT: JAI Press.

Jacks, J. Z., & Cameron, K. A. (2003). Strategies for resisting persuasion. *Basic and Applied Social Psychology, 25,* 145–161.

Jackson, J. M., & Latané, B. (1981). All alone in front of all those people: Stage fright as a function of number and type of co-performers and audience. *Journal of Personality and Social Psychology, 40,* 73–85.

Jackson, L. A. (1989). Relative deprivation and the gender wage gap. *Journal of Social Issues, 45,* 117–133.

Jackson, L. A., Hunter, J. E., & Hodge, C. N. (1995). Physical attractiveness and intellectual competence: A meta-analytic review. *Social Psychology Quarterly, 58,* 108–123.

Jacoby, S. (1986, December). When opposites attract. *Reader's Digest,* 95–98.

Jamieson, D. W., Lydon, J. E., Stewart, G., & Zanna, M. P. (1987). Pygmalion revisited: New evidence for student expectancy effects in the classroom. *Journal of Educational Psychology, 79,* 461–466.

Janis, I. L. (1971, November). Groupthink. *Psychology Today,* 43–46.

Janis, I. L. (1982). Counteracting the adverse effects of concurrence-seeking in policy-planning groups: Theory and research perspectives. In H. Brandstatter, J. H. Davis, & G. Stocker-Kreichgauer (Eds.), *Group decision making.* New York, NY: Academic Press.

Janis, I. L., & Feshbach, S. (1953). Effects of fear-arousing communications. *Journal of Abnormal and Social Psychology, 1,* 17–27.

Janis, I. L., Kaye, D., & Kirschner, P. (1965). Facilitating effects of eating while reading on responsiveness to persuasive communications. *Journal of Personality and Social Psychology, 1,* 181–186.

Janis, I. L., & Mann, L. (1977). *Decision-making: A psychological analysis of conflict, choice and commitment.* New York, NY: Free Press.

Jankowiak, W. R., & Fischer, E. F. (1992). A cross-cultural perspective on romantic love. *Ethnology, 31,* 149–155.

Jellison, J. M., & Green, J. (1981). A self-presentation approach to the fundamental attribution error: The norm of internality. *Journal of Personality and Social Psychology, 40,* 643–649.

Jenkins, M. (2010, June). True colors: The changing face of Greenland. *National Geographic,* 34–67.

Jennings, D. L., Amabile, T. M., & Ross, L. (1982). Informal covariation assessment: Data-based vs. theory-based judgments. In D. Kahneman, P. Slovic, & A. Tversky (Eds.), *Judgment under uncertainty: Heuristics and biases.* New York, NY: Cambridge University Press.

Jetten, J., Spears, R., & Postmes, T. (2004). Intergroup distinctiveness and differentiation: A meta-analytic integration. *Journal of Personality and Social Psychology, 86*(6), 862–879.

Jewell, L. M., & Morrison, M. A. (2010). "But there's a million jokes about everybody . . .": Prevalence of, and reasons for, directing negative behaviors toward gay men on a Canadian university campus. *Journal of Interpersonal Violence, 25*(11), 2094–2112.

Johnson, B. T., & Eagly, A. H. (1989). Effects of involvement on persuasion: A meta-analysis. *Psychological Bulletin, 106,* 290–314.

Johnson, B. T., & Eagly, A. H. (1990). Involvement and persuasion: Types, traditions, and the evidence. *Psychological Bulletin, 107,* 375–384.

Johnson, D. J., & Rusbult, C. E. (1989). Resisting temptation: Devaluation of alternative partners as a means of maintaining commitment in close relationships. *Journal of Personality and Social Psychology, 57,* 967–980.

Johnson, D. W., Maruyama, G., Johnson, R., Nelson, D., & Skon, L. (1981). Effects of cooperative, competitive, and individualistic goal structures on achievement: A meta-analysis. *Psychological Bulletin, 89,* 47–62.

Johnson, J. D., Jackson, L. A., & Gatto, L. (1995). Violent attitudes and deferred academic aspirations: Deleterious effects of exposure to rap music. *Basic and Applied Social Psychology, 16,* 27–41.

Johnson, J. G., Cohen, P., Smailes, E. M., Kasen, S., & Brook, J. S. (2002). Television viewing and aggressive behavior during adolescence and adulthood. *Science, 295,* 2468–2471.

Johnson, M. H. & Magaro, P. A. (1987). Effects of mood and severity on memory processes in depression and mania. *Psychological Bulletin, 101,* 28–40.

Johnson, W., & Kruger, R. F. (2006). How money buys happiness: Genetic and environmental processes linking finances and life satisfaction. *Journal of Personality and Social Psychology, 90*(4), 680–691.

Joinson, A. N. (2001). Self-disclosure in computer-mediated communication: The role of self-awareness and visual anonymity. *European Journal of Social Psychology, 31,* 177–192.

Jonas, E., Schulz-Hardt, S., & Frey, D. (2005). Giving advice or making decisions in someone else's place: The influence of impression, defense, and accuracy motivation on the search for new information. *Personality and Social Psychology Bulletin, 31,* 977–990.

Jones, C. R., & Fazio, R. H. (2010). Person categorization and automatic racial stereotyping effects on weapon identification. *Personality and Social Psychology Bulletin, 36*(8), 1073–1085.

Jones, E. E. (1976). How do people perceive the causes of behavior? *American Scientist, 64,* 300–305.

Jones, E. E. (1990). *Interpersonal perception.* New York: W.H. Freeman.

Jones, E. E., & Davis, K. E. (1965). From acts to dispositions: The attribution process in person perception. In L. Berkowitz (Ed.), *Advances in experimental social psychology, Vol. 2.* New York, NY: Academic Press.

Jones, E. E., & Nisbett, R. E. (1971). *The actor and the observer: Divergent perceptions of the cases of behavior.* Morristown, NJ: General Learning Press.

Jones, J. T., & Cunningham, J. D. (1996). Attachment styles and other predictors of relationship satisfaction in dating couples. *Personal Relationships, 3,* 387–399.

Jordan, C. H., Spencer, S. J., & Zanna, M. P. (2005). Types of high self-esteem and prejudice: How implicit self-esteem relates to ethnic discrimination among high explicit self-esteem individuals. *Personality and Social Psychology Bulletin, 31,* 693–702.

Jordan, C. H., Spencer, S. J., Zanna, M. P., Hoshino-Browne, E., & Correll, J. (2003). Secure and defensive high self-esteem. *Journal of Personality and Social Psychology, 85,* 969–978.

Josephson, W. L. (1987). Television violence and children's aggression: Testing the priming, social script, and disinhibition predictions. *Journal of Personality and Social Psychology, 53,* 882–890.

Joshi, M. S., & Carter, W. (2013). Unrealistic optimism: East and west? *Frontiers in Psychology, 4*(6), 1–15.

Jourden, F. J., & Heath, C. (1996). The evaluation gap in performance perceptions: Illusory perceptions of groups and individuals. *Journal of Applied Psychology, 81,* 369–379.

Judd, C. M., Blair, I. V., & Chapleau, K. M. (2004). Automatic stereotypes vs. automatic prejudice: Sorting out the possibilities in the Payne (2001) weapon paradigm. *Journal of Experimental Social Psychology, 40,* 75–81.

Jussim, L. (1986). Self-fulfilling prophecies: A theoretical and integrative review. *Psychological Review, 93,* 429–445.

Kagan, J. (1989). Temperamental contributions to social behavior. *American Psychologist, 44,* 668–674.

Kagehiro, D. K. (1990). Defining the standard of proof in jury instructions. *Psychological Science, 1,* 194–200.

Kahneman, D., & Snell, J. (1992). Predicting a changing taste: Do people know what they will like? *Journal of Behavioral Decision Making, 5,* 187–200.

Kahneman, D., & Tversky, A. (1979). Prospect theory: An analysis of decision under risk. *Econometrica, 47*(2), 263–291.

Kalichman, S. C. (2007). The theory of reasoned action and advances in HIV/AIDS prevention. In I. Ajzen, D., Albarracin, & R. Hornick (Eds.), *Prediction and change of health behavior.* Mahwah, NJ: Erlbuam.

Kalvern, H., & Zeisel, H. (1966). *The American jury.* Boston, MA: Little, Brown.

Kamalski, J., Lentz, L., Sanders, T., & Zwaan, R. (2008). The forewarning effect of coherence markers in persuasive discourse: Evidence from persuasion and processing. *Discourse Processes, 45*(6), 545–579.

Kameda, T., & Sugimori, S. (1993). Psychological entrapment in group decision making: An assigned decision rule and a groupthink phenomenon. *Journal of Personality and Social Psychology, 65,* 282–292.

Kammer, D. (1982). Differences in trait ascriptions to self and friend: Unconfounding intensity from variability. *Psychological Reports, 51,* 99–102.

Kandel, D. B. (1978). Similarity in real-life adolescent friendship pairs. *Journal of Personality and Social Psychology, 36,* 306–312.

Kaplan, M. F., Wanshula, L. T., & Zanna, M. P. (1993). Time pressure and information integration in social judgment: The effect of need for structure. In O. Svenson & J. Maule (Eds.), *Time pressure and stress in human judgment and decision making.* Cambridge: Cambridge University Press.

Kaplan, S. A., Madden, V. P., Mijanovich, T., & Purcaro, E. (2013). The perception of stress and its impact on health in poor communities. *Journal of Community Health, 38*(1), 142–149.

Karau, S. J., & Williams, K. D. (1993). Social loafing: A meta-analytic review and theoretical integration. *Journal of Personality and Social Psychology, 65,* 681–706.

Karau, S. J., & Williams, K. D. (1997). The effects of group cohesiveness on social loafing and compensation. *Group Dynamics: Theory, Research, and Practice, 1,* 156–168.

Karavellas, D. (2000). Sustainable consumption and fisheries. In B. Heap & J. Kent (Eds.), *Towards sustainable consumption: A European perspective.* London: The Royal Society.

Karney, B. R., & Bradbury, T. N. (1995). The longitudinal course of marital quality and stability: A review of theory, method, and research. *Psychological Bulletin, 118,* 3–34.

Kashima, E. S. (2010). Culture and terror management: What is "culture" in cultural psychology and terror management theory? *Social and Personality Psychology Compass, 4*(3), 164–173.

Kasser, T. (2000). Two versions of the American dream: Which goals and values make for a high quality of life? In E. Diener & D. Rahtz (Eds.), *Advances in quality of life: Theory and research.* Dordrecht: Kluwer.

Kassin, S. M., & Norwick, R. L. (2004). Why people waive their Miranda rights: The power of innocence. *Law and Human Behavior, 28,* 211–221.

Kassin, S. M. (2005). On the psychology of confessions: Does innocence put innocents at risk? *American Psychologist, 60,* 215–228.

Kassin, S. M., Drizin, S. A., Grisso, T., Gudjonsson, G. H., Leo, R. A., & Redlich, A. D. (2009). Police-induced confessions: Risk factors and recommendations. *Law and Human Behavior, 34*(1), 3–38.

Kassin, S. M., Dror, I. E., & Kukucka, J. (2013). The forensic confirmation bias: Problems, perspectives, and proposed solutions. *Journal of Applied Research in Memory and Cognition, 2*(1), 42–52.

Kassin, S. M., Goldstein, C. C., & Savitsky, K. (2003). Behavioral confirmation in the interrogation room: On the dangers of presuming guilt. *Law and Human Behavior, 27,* 187–203.

Kassin, S. M., & Gudjonsson, G. H. (2004). The psychology of confessions: A review of the literature and issues. *Psychological Science in the Public Interest, 5,* 33–67.

Kaufman, J., & Zigler, E. (1987). Do abused children become abusive parents? *American Journal of Orthopsychiatry, 57,* 186–192.

Kawakami, K., Dovidio, J. F., Moll, J., Hermsen, S., & Russin, A. (2000). Just say no (to stereotyping): Effects of training in the negation of stereotypic associations on stereotype activation. *Journal of Personality and Social Psychology, 78,* 871–888.

Kawakami, K., Dunn, E., Kiarmali, F., & Dovidio, J. F. (2009). Mispredicting affective and behavioral responses to racism. *Science, 323,* 276–278.

Keating, J. P., & Brock, T. C. (1974). Acceptance of persuasion and the inhibition of counterargumentation under various distraction tasks. *Journal of Experimental Social Psychology, 10,* 301–309.

Keelan, J. P., Dion, K. K., & Dion, K. L. (1998). Attachment style and relationship satisfaction: Test of self-disclosure explanation. *Canadian Journal of Behavioural Science, 30*(1), 24–35.

Keizer, B. (2001, November). The Netherlands' drug policy. *Paper presented at the hearing of the Special Committee on Illegal Drugs,* Ottawa, ON.

Keller, J., & Dauenheimer, D. (2003). Stereotype threat in the classroom: Dejection mediates the disrupting threat effect on women's math performance. *Personality and Social Psychology Bulletin, 29,* 371–381.

Kellerman, J., Lewis, J., & Laird, J. D. (1989). Looking and loving: The effects of mutual gaze on feelings of romantic love. *Journal of Research in Personality, 23,* 145–161.

Kelley, H. H. (1973). The process of causal attribution. *American Psychologist, 28,* 107–128.

Keltner, D., & Robinson, R. J. (1996). Extremism, power, and the imagined basis of social conflict. *Current Directions in Psychological Science, 5,* 101–105.

Kendler, K. S., Neale, M., Kessler, R., Heath, A. & Eaves, L. (1993). A twin study of recent life events and difficulties. *Archives of General Psychiatry, 50,* 789–796.

Kenny, D. A., & Nasby, W. (1980). Splitting the reciprocity correlation. *Journal of Personality and Social Psychology, 38,* 249–256.

Kenrick, D. T. (1987). Gender, genes, and the social environment: A biosocial interactionist perspective. In P. Shaver & C. Hendrick (Eds.), *Sex and gender: Review of personality and social psychology, Vol. 7.* Beverly Hills, CA: Sage.

Kenrick, D. T., & Gutierres, S. E. (1980). Contrast effects and judgments of physical attractiveness: When beauty becomes a social problem. *Journal of Personality and Social Psychology, 38,* 131–140.

Kenrick, D. T., Gutierres, S. E., & Goldberg, L. L. (1989). Influence of popular erotica on judgments of strangers and mates. *Journal of Experimental Social Psychology, 25,* 159–167.

Kenrick, D. T., & Trost, M. R. (1987). A biosocial theory of heterosexual relationships. In K. Kelly (Ed.), *Females, males, and sexuality.* Albany, NY: State University of New York Press.

Kernis, M. H. (2003). High self-esteem: A differentiated perspective. In E. C. Chang & L. J. Sanna (Eds.), *Virtue, vice, and personality: The complexity of behavior.* Washington, DC: APA Books.

Kerr, N. L. (1983). Motivation losses in small groups: A social dilemma analysis. *Journal of Personality and Social Psychology, 45,* 819–828.

Kerr, N. L., Atkin, R. S., Stasser, G., Meek, D., Holt, R. W., & Davis, J. H. (1976). Guilt beyond a reasonable doubt: Effects of concept definition and assigned decision rule on the judgments of mock jurors. *Journal of Personality and Social Psychology, 34,* 282–294.

Kerr, N. L., & Bruun, S. E. (1981). Ringelmann revisited: Alternative explanations for the social loafing effect. *Personality and Social Psychology Bulletin, 7,* 224–231.

Kerr, N. L., & Bruun, S. E. (1983). Dispensibility of member effort and group motivation losses: Free-rider effects. *Journal of Personality and Social Psychology, 44,* 78–94.

Kerr, N. L., Garst, J., Lewandowski, D. A., & Harris, S. E. (1997). That still, small voice: Commitment to cooperate as an internalized versus a social norm. *Personality and Social Psychology Bulletin, 23,* 1300–1311.

Kerr, N. L., Harmon, D. L., & Graves, J. K. (1982). Independence of multiple verdicts by jurors and juries. *Journal of Applied Social Psychology, 12,* 12–29.

Kerr, N. L., & Kaufman-Gilliland, C. M. (1994). Communication, commitment, and cooperation in social dilemmas. *Journal of Personality and Social Psychology, 66,* 513–529.

Kerr, N. L., & Kaufman-Gilliland, C. M. (1997). ". . . and besides, I probably couldn't have made a difference anyway": Justification of social dilemma defection via perceived self-inefficacy. *Journal of Experimental Social Psychology, 33,* 211–230.

Kerr, T., Small, W., Hyshka, E., Maher, L., & Shannon, K. (2013). It's more about the heroin': injection drug users' response to an overdose warning campaign in a Canadian setting. *Addiction, 108*(7), 1270–1276.

Kessler, S. J., & McKenna, W. (1978). *Gender: An ethnomethodological approach.* Chicago, IL: University of Chicago Press.

Kiesler, C. A. (1971). *The psychology of commitment: Experiments linking behavior to belief.* New York, NY: Academic Press.

Kihlstrom, J. F., & Cantor, N. (1984). Mental representations of the self. In L. Berkowitz (Ed.), *Advances in experimental social psychology, Vol. 17.* New York, NY: Academic Press.

Kim, H., & Markus, H. R. (1999). Deviance of uniqueness, harmony or conformity? A cultural analysis. *Journal of Personality and Social Psychology, 77,* 785–800.

Kim, H. S., & Sherman, D. K. (2007). "Express yourself": Culture and the effect of self-expression on choice. *Journal of Personality and Social Psychology, 92,* 1–11.

Kimmel, A. J. (1998). In defense of deception. *American Psychologist, 53,* 803–805.

Kingston, D. A., Fedoroff, P., Firestone, P., Curry, S., & Bradford, J. M. (2008). Pornography use and sexual aggression: The impact of frequency and type of pornography use on recidivism among sexual offenders. *Aggressive Behavior, 34,* 341–351.

Kingston, D. A., Malamuth, N. M., Fedoroff, P., & Marshall, W. L. (2009). The importance of individual differences in pornography use: Theoretical perspectives and implications for treating sexual offenders. *Journal of Sex Research, 46,* 216–232.

Kirmeyer, S. L. (1978). Urban density and pathology: A review of research. *Environment and Behavior, 10,* 257–269.

Kirsch, P., Esslinger, C., Chen, Q., Mier, D., Lis, S., Siddhanti, S., et al. (2005). Oxytocin modulates neural circuitry for social cognition and fear in humans. *The Journal of Neuroscience, 25*(49), 11489–11493.

Kitayama, S., & Karasawa, M. (1997). Implicit self-esteem in Japan: Name letters and birthday numbers. *Personality and Social Psychology Bulletin, 23,* 736–742.

Kitayama, S., & Markus, H. R. (1995). Culture and self: Implications for internationalizing psychology. In N. R. Goldberger & J. B. Veroff (Eds.), *The culture and psychology reader.* New York, NY: New York University Press.

Klassen, R. (2010). Confidence to manage learning: The self-efficacy for self-regulated learning of early adolescents with learning disabilities. *Learning Disabilities Quarterly, 33,* 19–30.

Kleck, R. E., & Strenta, A. (1980). Perceptions of the impact of negatively valued physical characteristics on social interaction. *Journal of Personality and Social Psychology, 39,* 861–873.

Klein, J. G. (1991). Negative effects in impression formation: A test in the political arena. *Personality and Social Psychology Bulletin, 17,* 412–418.

Klein, W. M., & Kunda, Z. (1992). Motivated person perception: Constructing justifications for desired beliefs. *Journal of Experimental Social Psychology, 28,* 145–168.

Kleinke, C. L. (1977). Compliance to requests made by gazing and touching experimenters in field settings. *Journal of Experimental Social Psychology, 13,* 218–223.

Klentz, B., Beaman, A. L., Mapelli, S. D., & Ullrich, J. R. (1987). Perceived physical attractiveness of supporters and nonsupporters of the women's movement: An attitude-similarity-mediated error (AS-ME). *Personality and Social Psychology Bulletin, 13,* 513–523.

Klinesmith, J., Kasser, T., & McAndrew, F. T. (2006). Guns, testosterone, and aggression. *Psychological Science, 17*(7), 568–571.

Klopfer, P. H. (1958). Influence of social interaction on learning rates in birds. *Science, 128,* 903.

Knight, G. P., Fabes, R. A., & Higgins, D. A. (1996). Concerns about drawing causal inferences from meta-analyses: An example in the study of gender differences in aggression. *Psychological Bulletin, 119,* 410–421.

Knight, J. A., & Vallacher, R. R. (1981). Interpersonal engagement in social perception: The consequences of getting into the action. *Journal of Personality and Social Psychology, 40,* 990–999.

Knowles, E. S. (1983). Social physics and the effects of others: Tests of the effects of audience size and distance on social judgment and behavior. *Journal of Personality and Social Psychology, 45,* 1263–1279.

Koehler, D. J. (1991). Explanation, imagination, and confidence in judgment. *Psychological Bulletin, 110,* 499–519.

Koestner, R., & Wheeler, L. (1988). Self-presentation in personal advertisements: The influence of implicit notions of attraction and role expectations. *Journal of Social and Personal Relationships, 5,* 149–160.

Komorita, S. S., & Barth, J. M. (1985). Components of reward in social dilemmas. *Journal of Personality and Social Psychology, 48,* 364–373.

Komorita, S. S., Parks, C. D., & Hulbert, L. G. (1992). Reciprocity and the introduction of cooperation in social dilemmas. *Journal of Personality and Social Psychology, 62,* 607–617.

Konrad, A. M., Ritchie, J. E., Jr., Lieb, P., & Corrigall, E. (2000). Sex differences and similarities in job attribute preferences: A meta-analysis. *Psychological Bulletin, 126,* 593–641.

Koop, C. E. (1987). Report of the surgeon general's workshop on pornography and public health. *American Psychologist, 42,* 944–945.

Koriat, A., Lichtenstein, S., & Fischhoff, B. (1980). Reasons for confidence. *Journal of Experimental Social Psychology: Human Learning and Memory, 6,* 107–118.

Koss, M. P. (1990, August 29). *Rape incidence: A review and assessment of the data.* Testimony on behalf of the American Psychological Association before the U.S. Senate Judiciary Committee.

Koss, M. P., Dinero, T. E., Seibel, C. A., & Cox, S. L. (1988). Stranger and acquaintance rape. *Psychology of Women, 12,* 1–24.

Koss, M. P., & Gidycz, C. A. (1985). Sexual experiences survey: Reliability and validity. *Journal of Consulting and Clinical Psychology, 53*(3), 422–423.

Krackow, A., & Blass, T. (1995). When nurses obey or defy inappropriate physician orders: Attributional differences. *Journal of Social Behavior and Personality, 10,* 585–594.

Kraut, R., Patterson, M., Lundmark, V., Kiesler, S., Mukopadhyay, T., & Scherlis, W. (1998). Internet paradox: A social technology that reduces social involvement and psychological well-being? *American Psychologist, 53,* 1017–1031.

Kraut, R. E., & Poe, D. B. (1980). Behavioral roots of person perception: The deception judgments of customs inspectors and laymen. *Journal of Personality and Social Psychology, 39*(5), 784–798.

Kravitz, D. A., & Martin, B. (1986). Ringelmann rediscovered: The original article. *Journal of Personality and Social Psychology, 50,* 936–941.

Krebs, D., & Adinolfi, A. A. (1975). Physical attractiveness, social relations, and personality style. *Journal of Personality and Social Psychology, 31,* 245–253.

Krizan, Z., & Suls, J. (2008). Losing sight of oneself in the above-average effect: When egocentrism, focalism, and group diffuseness collide. *Journal of Experimental Social Psychology, 44,* 929–942.

Krosnick, J. A., & Alwin, D. F. (1989). Aging and susceptibility to attitude change. *Journal of Personality and Social Psychology, 57,* 416–425.

Krosnick, J. A., & Petty, R. E. (1995). *Attitude strength: Antecedents and consequences.* Ohio State University Series on Attitudes and Persuasion, 4, 1–24.

Krueger, J. (1996). Personal beliefs and cultural stereotypes about racial characteristics. *Journal of Personality and Social Psychology, 71,* 536–548.

Krueger, J., & Clement, R. W. (1994). The truly false consensus effect: An ineradicable and egocentric bias in social perception. *Journal of Personality and Social Psychology, 67,* 596–610.

Kruger, J., & Dunning, D. (1999). Unskilled and unaware of it: How difficulties in recognizing one's own incompetence lead to inflated self-assessments. *Journal of Personality and Social Psychology, 77,* 1121–1134.

Kruger, J., & Evans, M. (2004). If you don't want to be late, enumerate: Unpacking reduces the planning fallacy. *Journal of Experimental Social Psychology, 40,* 586–598.

Kruger, J., & Gilovich, T. (1999). "I cynicism" in everyday theories of responsibility assessment: On biased assumptions of bias. *Journal of Personality and Social Psychology, 76,* 743–753.

Kruglanski, A. W., & Fishman, S. (2006). The psychology of terrorism: Syndrome versus tool perspective. *Journal of Terrorism and Political Violence, 18*(2), 193–215.

Kruglanski, A. W., & Webster, D. M. (1991). Group members' reactions to opinion deviates and conformists at varying degrees of proximity to decision deadline and of environmental noise. *Journal of Personality and Social Psychology, 61,* 212–225.

Krull, D. S., Loy, M. H. M., Lin, J., Wang, C. F., Chen, S., & Zhao, X. (1999). The fundamental attribution error: Correspondence bias in individualist and collectivist cultures. *Personality and Social Psychology Bulletin, 25,* 1208–1219.

Kubany, E. S., Bauer, G. B., Pangilinan, M. E., Muroka, M. Y., & Enriquez, V. G. (1995). Impact of labeled anger and blame in intimate relationships. *Journal of Cross-Cultural Psychology, 26,* 65–83.

Kugihara, N. (1999). Gender and social loafing in Japan. *Journal of Social Psychology, 139,* 516–526.

Kuiper, N. A., & Higgins, E. T. (1985). Social cognition and depression: A general integrative perspective. *Social Cognition, 3,* 1–15

Kuiper, N. A., & Rogers, T. B. (1979). Encoding of personal information: Self-other differences. *Journal of Personality and Social Psychology, 37,* 499–514.

Kumkale, G., & Albarracín, D. (2004). The sleeper effect in persuasion: A meta-analytic review. *Psychological Bulletin, 130*(1), 143–172.

Kwan, V. S. Y., Bond, M. H., & Singelis, T. M. (1997). *Journal of Personality and Social Psychology, 73,* 1038–1051.

Ladouceur, R., & Sevigny, S. (2005). Structural characteristics of video lotteries: Effects of a stopping device on illusion of control and gambling persistence. *Journal of Gambling Studies, 21,* 117–131.

Lagerspetz, K. (1979). Modification of aggressiveness in mice. In S. Feshbach & A. Fraczek (Eds.), *Aggression and behavior change.* New York, NY: Praeger.

Lalonde, R. N. (1992). The dynamics of group differentiation in the face of defeat. *Personality and Social Psychology Bulletin, 18,* 336–342.

Lalonde, R. N. (2002). Testing the social indentity-intergroup differentiation hypothesis: "We're not American eh!" *British Journal of Social Psychology, 41,* 611–631.

Landers, A. (1969, April 8). Syndicated newspaper column. Cited by L. Berkowitz in *The case for bottling up rage. Psychology Today,* September 1973, 24–31.

Lane, R. (1955). Political personality and electoral choice. *American Political Science Review, 49,* 173–190.

Langer, E. J., & Imber, L. (1980). The role of mindlessness in the perception of deviance. *Journal of Personality and Social Psychology, 39,* 360–367.

Langer, E. J., Janis, I. L., & Wofer, J. A. (1975). Reduction of psychological stress in surgical patients. *Journal of Experimental Social Psychology, 11,* 155–165.

Langlois, J. H., Kalakanis, L., Rubenstein, A. J., Larson, A., Hallam, M., & Smoot, M. (2000). Maxims or myths of beauty? A meta-analytic and theoretical review. *Psychological Bulletin, 126,* 390–423.

Langlois, J., Kalakanis, L., Rubenstein, A., Larson, A., Hallam, M., & Smoot, M. (1996). *Maxims and myths of beauty: A meta-analytic and theoretical review.* Paper presented to the American Psychological Society convention.

Langlois, J. H., Roggman, L. A., Casey, R. J., Ritter, J. M., Rieser-Danner, L. A., & Jenkins, V. Y. (1987). Infant preferences for attractive faces: Rudiments of a stereotype? *Developmental Psychology, 23,* 363–369.

Lanzetta, J. T. (1955). Group behavior under stress. *Human Relations, 8,* 29–53.

Larsen, R. J., & Diener, E. (1987). Affect intensity as an individual difference characteristic: A review. *Journal of Research in Personality, 21,* 1–39.

Larsson, K. (1956). *Conditioning and sexual behavior in the male albino rat.* Stockholm: Almqvist & Wiksell.

Lassiter, D. G. (2010). Videotaped interrogations and confessions: What's obvious in hindsight may not be in foresight. *Law and Human Behavior, 34*(1), 41–42.

Lassiter, G. D., & Dudley, K. A. (1991). The a priori value of basic research: The case of videotaped confessions. *Journal of Social Behavior and Personality, 6,* 7–16.

Lassiter, G. D., Munhall, P. J., Berger, I. P., Wieland, P. E., Handley, I. M., & Geers, A. I. (2005). Attributional complexity and the camera perspective bias in videotaped confessions. *Basic and Applied Social Psychology, 27*, 27–35.

Latane, B., & Dabbs, J. M., Jr. (1975). Sex, group size and helping in three cities. *Sociometry, 38*, 180–194.

Latane, B., & Darley, J. M. (1968). Group inhibition of bystander intervention in emergencies. *Journal of Personality and Social Psychology, 10*, 215–221.

Latane, B., & Darley, J. M. (1970). *The unresponsive bystander: Why doesn't he help?* New York, NY: Appleton-Century-Crofts.

Latane, B., & Nida, S. (1981). Ten years of research on group size and helping. *Psychological Bulletin, 89*, 308–324.

Latane, B., Williams, K., & Harkins. S. (1979). Many hands make light the work: The causes and consequences of social loafing. *Journal of Personality and Social Psychology, 37*, 822–832.

Laumann, E. O., Gagnon, J. H., Michael, R. T., & Michaels, S. (1994). *The social organization of sexuality: Sexual practices in the United States.* Chicago, IL: University of Chicago Press.

Lazarus, R. S. (1966). *Psychological stress and the coping process.* New York, NY: McGraw-Hill.

Lazarus, R. S. (2000). Toward better research on stress and coping. *American Psychologist, 55*, 665–673.

Leach, A. M., Lindsay, R. C. L., Koehler, R., Beaudry, J. L., Bala, N. C., Lee, K., & Talwar, V. (2008). The reliability of lie detection performance. *Law and Human Behavior.* Retrieved from http://www.springerlink.com/content/2215530x4063474l/fulltext.pdf.

Leamon, M. H. (2006). When to refer patients for substance abuse assessment and treatment. *Primary Psychiatry, 13*, 46–51.

Leaper, C., & Smith, T. E. (2004). A meta-analytic review of gender variations in children's language use. *Developmental Psychology, 40*, 993–1027.

Leary, M. R. (1998). The social and psychological importance of self-esteem. In R. M. Kowalski & M. R. Leary (Eds.), *The social psychology of emotional and behavioral problems.* Washington, DC: American Psychological Association.

Leary, M. R. (1999). Making sense of self-esteem. *Current Directions in Psychology, 8*, 32–35.

Leary, M. R., Nezlek, J. B., Downs, D. (1994). Self-presentation in everyday interactions: Effects of target familiarity and gender composition. *Journal of Personality and Social Psychology, 67*, 664–673.

Leary, M. R., Twenge, J. M., & Quinlivan, E. (2006). Interpersonal rejection as a determinant of anger and aggression. *Personality and Social Psychology Review, 10*, 111–132.

Lee, A. Y. (2001). The mere exposure effect: An uncertainty reduction explanation revisited. *Personality and Social Psychology Bulletin, 27*(10), 1255–1266.

Lee, B. K., & Chen, L. (2000). Cultural communication competence and psychological adjustment: A study of Chinese immigrant children's cross-cultural adaptation in Canada. *Communication Research, 27*(6), 764–792.

Lee, F., Hallahan, M., & Herzog, T. (1996). Explaining real-life events: How culture and domain shape attributions. *Personality and Social Psychology Bulletin, 22*, 732–741.

Lee, J. A. (1988). Love-styles. In R. J. Sternberg & M. L. Barnes (Eds.), *The psychology of love.* New Haven, CT: Yale University Press.

Lefcourt, H. M. (1982). *Locus of control: Current trends in theory and research.* Hillsdale, NJ: Erlbaum.

Lefebvre, C. D., Marchand, Y., Smith, S. M., & Connolly, J. F. (2007). Determining eyewitness identification accuracy using event-related brain potentials (ERPs). *Psychophysiology, 44*, 894–104.

Lefebvre, C. D., Marchand, Y., Smith, S. M., & Connolly, J. F. (2008). *Use of event-related brain potentials (ERPs) to assess eyewitness accuracy and deception.* Unpublished manuscript.

Lefrancois, R., Leclerc, G., Hamel, S., & Gaulin, P. (2000). Stressful life events and psychological distress of the very old: Does social support have a moderating effect? *Archives of Gerontology and Geriatrics, 31*, 243–255.

Lemyre, L., & Smith, P. M. (1985). Intergroup discrimination and self-esteem in the minimal group paradigm. *Journal of Personality and Social Psychology, 49*, 660–670.

Lench, H. C., Quas, J. A., & Edelstein, R. S. (2006). My child is better than average: The extension and restricton of unrealistic optimism. *Journal of Applied Social Psychology, 36*(12), 2963–2979.

Lennon, A., Watson, B., Arlidge, C., & Fraine, G. (2011). "You're a bad driver but I just made a mistake": Attribution differences between the "victims" amd "perpetrators" of scenario-based aggressive driving incidents. *Transportation Research Part F: Traffic Psychology and Behaviour, 14*(3), 209–221.

Leo, R. A. (1996). Inside the interrogation room. *The Journal of Criminal Law and Criminology, 86*, 266–303.

Leon, D. (1969). The Kibbutz: A new way of life. London: Pergamon Press. Cited by B. Latané, K. Williams, & S. Harkins (1979), in Many hands make light the work: The causes and consequences of social loafing. *Journal of Personality and Social Psychology, 37*, 822–832.

Lerner, M. J. (1980). *The belief in a just world: A fundamental delusion.* New York, NY: Plenum.

Lerner, M. J., & Miller, D. T. (1978). Just world research and the attribution process: Looking back and ahead. *Psychological Bulletin, 85*, 1030–1051.

Lerner, M. J., & Simmons, C. H. (1966). Observer's reaction to the "innocent victim": Compassion or rejection? *Journal of Personality and Social Psychology, 4*, 203–210.

Leventhal, H. (1970). *Findings and theory in the study of fear communications. Advances in experimental social psychology,* vol. 5, L. Berkowitz, ed., New York: Academic Press, 111–186.

Leventhal, H., & Hirschman, R. S. (1982). Social psychology and prevention. In G. S. Sanders, & J. Suls (Eds.), *Social psychology of health and illness* (pp. 387–401). Hillsdale, NJ: Erlbaum.

Lever, J. (1978). Sex differences in the complexity of children's play and games. *American Sociological Review, 43*, 471–483.

Levin, D. T. (2000). Race as a visual feature: Using visual search and perceptual discrimination tasks to understand face categories and the cross-race recognition deficit. *Journal of Experimental Psychology: General, 129*, 559–574.

Levine, D. (2000). Virtual attraction: What rocks your boat. *CyberPsychology & Behavior, 3*(4), 565–573.

Levine, J. M. (1989). Reaction to opinion deviance in small groups. In P. Paulus (Ed.), *Psychology of group influence: New perspectives.* Hillsdale, NJ: Erlbaum.

Levine, J. M., & Moreland, R. L. (1985). Innovation and socialization in small groups. In S. Moscovici, G. Mugny, & E. Van Avermaet (Eds.), *Perspectives on minority influence.* Cambridge: Cambridge University Press.

Levine, J. M., & Russo, E. M. (1987). Majority and minority influence. In C. Hendrick (Ed.) *Group processes: Review of personality and social psychology Vol. 8.* Newbury Park, CA: Sage.

Levine, R. (2003). *The power of persuasion: How we're bought and sold.* New York, NY: Wiley.

Levinson, H. (1950). *The science of chance: From probability to statistics.* New York, NY: Rinehart.

Levitan, L. C., & Visser, P. S. (2008). The impact of the social context on resistance to persuasion: Effortful versus effortless responses to counter-attitudinal information. *Journal of Experimental Social Psychology, 44,* 640–649.

Levitt, A., & Cooper, M. (2010). Daily alcohol use and romantic relationship functioning: Evidence of bidirectional, gender- and context-specific effects. *Personality and Social Psychology Bulletin, 36*(12), 1706–1722.

Levy, S. R., Stroessner, S. J., & Dweck, C. S. (1998). Stereotype formation and endorsement: The role of implicit theories. *Journal of Personality and Social Psychology, 74,* 1421–1436.

Levy-Leboyer, C. (1988). Success and failure in applying psychology. *American Psychologist, 43,* 779–785.

Lewandowski, G. W., Jr., Aron, A., & Gee, J. (2007). Personality goes along way: The malleability of opposite-sex physical attractiveness. *Personal Relationships, 14,* 571–585.

Lewinsohn, P. M. & Rosenbaum, M. (1987). Recall of parental behavior by acute depressives, remitted depressives, and nondepressives. *Journal of Personality and Social Psychology, 52,* 611–619.

Leyens, J. P., Camino, L., Parke, R. D., & Berkowitz, L. (1975). Effects of movie violence on aggression in a field setting as a function of group dominance and cohesion. *Journal of Personality and Social Psychology, 32,* 346–360.

Li, N. P., Bailey, J. M., Kenrick, D. T., & Linsenmeier, J. A. W. (2002). The necessities and luxuries of mate preferences: Testing the tradeoffs. *Journal of Personality and Social Psychology, 82,* 947–955.

Li, N. P., & Kenrick, D. T. (2006). Sex similarities and differences in preferences for short-term mates: What, whether, and why. *Journal of Personality and Social Psychology, 90*(3), 468–489.

Lichacz, F. M., & Partington, J. T. (1996). Collective efficacy and true group performance. *International Journal of Sport Psychology, 27,* 146.

Lichtblau, E. (2003, March 18). U.S. seeks $289 billion in cigarette makers' profits. *New York Times* (http://www.nytimes.com).

Lichtenstein, S., & Fischhoff, B. (1980). Training for calibration. *Organizational Behavior and Human Performance, 26,* 149–171.

Lindsay, R. C. L., & Wells, G. L. (1985). Improving eyewitness identification from lineups: Simultaneous versus sequential lineup presentations. *Journal of Applied Psychology, 70,* 556–564.

Lindsay, R. L., & Bellinger, K. (1999). Alternatives to the sequential lineup: The importance of controlling the pictures. *Journal of Applied Psychology, 84*(3), 315–321.

Linville, P. W., Gischer, W. G., & Salovey, P. (1989). Perceived distributions of the characteristics of in-group and out-group members: Empirical evidence and a computer simulation. *Journal of Personality and Social Psychology, 57,* 165–188.

Linz, D. G., Donnerstein, E., & Penrod, S. (1988). Effects of long term exposure to violent and sexually degrading depictions of women. *Journal of Personality and Social Psychology, 55,* 758–768.

Lippke, S., & Plotnikoff, R. C. (2006). Stages of change in physical exercise: A test of stage discrimination and nonlinearity. *American Journal of Health Behavior, 30*(3), 290–301.

Little, A., & Perrett, D. (2002). Putting beauty back in the eye of the beholder. *The Psychologist, 15,* 28–32.

Little, A. C., Jones, B. C., Penton-Voak, I. S., Burt D. M., & Perrett, D. I. (2002). Partnership status and the temporal context of relationships influence human female preferences for sexual dimorphism in male face shape. *Proceedings of the Royal Society. B, 269,* 1095–1100.

Littrell, J. H., & Girvin, H. (2002). Stages of change: A critique. *Behavior Modification, 26,* 223–273.

Livingston, R. W. (2001). What you see is what you get: Systematic variability in perceptual-based social judgment. *Personality and Social Psychology Bulletin, 27,* 1086–1096.

Locke, D. & Pennington, D. (1982). Reasons and other causes: Their role in attribution processes. *Journal of Personality and Social Psychology, 42,* 212–223.

Lockwood, P., & Kunda, Z. (2000). Outstanding role models: Do they inspire or demoralize us? *Psychological Perspectives on Self and Indentity, 69,* 147–171.

Lockwood, P., Marshall, T. C., & Sadler, P. (2005). Promoting success or preventing failure: Cultural differences in motivation by positive and negative role models. *Personality and Social Psychology Bulletin, 31*(3), 379–392.

Loewenstein, G., & Schkade, D. (1999). Wouldn't it be nice? Predicting future feelings. In D. Kahneman, E. Diener, & N. Schwarz (Eds.), *Understanding well-being: Scientific perspectives on enjoyment and suffering.* New York, NY: Russell Sage Foundation.

Lofland, J., & Stark, R. (1965). Becoming a worldsaver: A theory of conversion to a deviant perspective. *American Sociological Review, 30,* 862–864.

Loftin, C., McDowall, D., Wiersema, B., & Cottey, T. J. (1991). Effects of restrictive licensing of handguns on homicide and suicide in the District of Columbia. *New England Journal of Medicine, 325,* 1615–1620.

Loftus, E. F. (1974, December). Reconstructing memory: The incredible eyewitness. *Psychology Today,* 117–119.

Loftus, E. F. (1979). *Eyewitness testimony.* Cambridge, MA: Harvard University Press.

Loftus, E. F. (2013). 25 years of eyewitness science. . . . . . Finally pays off. *Perspectives on Psychological Science, 8*(5), 556–557.

Loftus, E. G., Miller, D. G., & Burns, H. J. (1978). Semantic integration of verbal information into a visual memory. *Journal of Experimental Psychology, Human Learning and Memory, 4,* 19–31.

Lombardo, J. P., Weiss, R. F., & Buchanan, W. (1972). Reinforcing and attracting functions of yielding. *Journal of Personality and Social Psychology, 21,* 359–368.

Lord, C. G., Ross, L., & Lepper, M. (1979). Biased assimilation and attitude polarization: The effects of prior theories on subsequently considered evidence. *Journal of Personality and Social Psychology, 37,* 2098–2109.

Lorenz, K. (1976). *On aggression.* New York, NY: Bantam Books.

Lowenstein, D. (2000, May 20). Interview. *The World* (http://www.cnn.com/TRANSCRIPTS/0005/20/stc.00.html).

Lueptow, L. B., Garovich, L., & Lueptow, M. B. (1995). The persistence of gender stereotypes in the face of changing sex roles: Evidence contrary to the sociocultural model. *Ethology and Sociobiology, 16,* 509–530.

Luus, C. A. E., Turtle, J. W., & Wells, G. L. (1995). Child eyewitnesses: Seeing is believing. *Journal of Applied Psychology, 80*(2), 317–326.

Luus, C. A. E., & Wells, G. L. (October, 1994). The malleability of eyewitness confidence: Co-witness and perseverance effects. *Journal of Applied Psychology, 79,* 714–723.

Lydon, J., & Dunkel-Schetter, C. (1994). Seeing is committing: A longitudinal study of bolstering commitment in amniocentesis patients. *Personality and Social Psychology Bulletin, 20,* 218–227.

Lydon, J. E., Menzies-Toman, D., Burton, K., & Bell, C. (2008). If-then contingencies and the differential effects of the availability of an attractive alternative on relationship maintenance for men and women. *Journal of Personality and Social Psychology, 95*(1), 50–65.

Lykken, D. T. (1997). The American crime factory. *Psychological Inquiry, 8,* 261–270.

Lynch, B. S., & Bonnie, R. J. (1994). Toward a youth-centered prevention policy. In B. S. Lynch & R. J. Bonnie (Eds.), *Growing up tobacco free: Preventing nicotine addiction in children and youths.* Washington, DC: National Academy Press.

Lynn, M., & Oldenquist, A. (1986). Egoistic and nonegoistic motives in social dilemmas. *American Psychologist, 41,* 529–534.

Lyons, L. (2003, September 23). *Oh, boy: Americans still prefer sons.* Gallup Poll Tuesday Briefing (http://www.gallup.com).

Lyttle, J. (2001). The effectiveness of humor in persuasion: The case of business ethics training. *Journal of General Psychology, 128,* 206–216.

Lyubomirsky, S. (2001). Why are some people happier than others? The role of cognitive and motivational processes in well-being. *American Psychologist, 56*(3), 239–249.

Maass, A., & Clark, R. D., III. (1984). Hidden impact of minorities: Fifteen years of minority influence research. *Psychological Bulletin, 95,* 428–450.

Maass, A., & Clark, R. D., III. (1986). Conversion theory and simultaneous majority/minority influence: Can reactance offer an alternative explanation? *European Journal of Social Psychology, 16,* 305–309.

Maass, A., Volparo, C., & MucchiFaina, A. (1996). Social influence and the verifiability of the issue under discussion: Attitudinal versus objective items. *British Journal of Social Psychology, 35,* 15–26.

Maccoby, E. E. (2002). Gender and group process: A developmental perspective. *Current Directions in Psychological Science, 11,* 54–58.

MacCoun, R. J., & Kerr, N. L. (1988). Asymmetric influence in mock deliberation: Jurors' bias for leniency. *Journal of Personality and Social Psychology, 54,* 21–33.

MacDonald, D. J., & Standing, L. G. (2002). Does self-serving bias cancel the Barnum effect in self-perception? *Social Behavior and Personality, 30,* 625–630.

MacDonald, G., Zanna, M. P., & Holmes, J. G. (2000). An experimental test of the role of alcohol in relationship conflict. *Journal of Experimental Social Psychology, 36,* 182–193.

MacDonald, J., & McKelvie, S. (1992). Playing safe: Helping rates for a dropped mitten and a box of condoms. *Psychological Reports, 71,* 113–114.

Macdonald, M., & Perrier, J. (2004). Gambling households in Canada. *Journal of Gambling Studies, 20,* 187–236.

MacDonald, T. K., & Ross, M. (1999). Assessing the accuracy of predictions about dating relationships: How and why do lovers' predictions differ from those made by observers? *Society for Personality and Social Psychology, 25,* 1417–1429.

MacGregor, R. M. (2003). I am Canadian: National identity in beer commercials. *The Journal of Popular Culture, 37*(2), 276–286.

Mackie, D. (1987). Systematic and nonsystematic processing of majority and minority persuasive communications. *Journal of Personality and Social Psychology, 53,* 41–52.

Maclean's. (2008, May 28). It comes down to these four. Retrieved from http://www.macleans.ca/article.jsp?content20080528_96688_96688.

Macrae, C. N., & Bodenhausen, G. V. (2000). Social cognition: Thinking categorically about others. *Annual Review of Psychology, 51,* 93–120.

Macrae, C. N., Bodenhausen, G. V., Milne, A. B., & Jetten, J. (1994). Out of mind but back in sight: Stereotypes on the rebound. *Journal of Personality and Social Psychology, 67,* 808–817.

Maddux, J. E. (1991). Personal efficacy. In V. Derlega, B. Winstead, & W. Jones (Eds.), *Personality: Contemporary theory and research* (2nd ed.). New York, NY: Nelson-Hall.

Maddux, J. E., & Gosselin, J. T. (2003). Self-efficacy. In M. R. Leary & J. P. Tangney (Eds.), *Handbook of self and identity* (pp. 218–238). New York, NY: Guilford Press.

Maddux, W. W., Mullen, E., & Galinsky, A. D. (2008). Chameleons bake bigger pies and take bigger pieces: Strategic behavioral mimicry facilities negotiation outcomes. *Journal of Experimental Psychology, 44,* 461–468.

Madon, S., Jussim, L., & Eccles, J. (1997). In search of the powerful self-fulfilling prophecy. *Journal of Personality and Social Psychology, 72,* 791–809.

Magnuson, E. (1986, March 10). "A serious deficiency": The Rogers Commission faults NASA's "flawed" decisionmaking process. *Time* [international ed.], 40–42.

Major, B. (1989). Gender differences in comparisons and entitlement: Implications for comparable worth. *Journal of Social Issues, 45,* 99–116.

Major, B. (1993). Gender, entitlement, and the distribution of family labor. *Journal of Social Issues, 49,* 141–159.

Major, B., Kaiser, C. R., & McCoy, S. K. (2003). It's not my fault: When and why attributions to prejudice protect self-esteem. *Personality and Social Psychology Bulletin, 29,* 772–781.

Malamuth, N. M., & Check, J. V. (1984). Debriefing effectiveness following exposure to pornographic rape depictions. *Journal of Sex Research, 20*(1), 1–13.

Malamuth, N. M., & Check, J. V. P. (1981). The effects of media exposure on acceptance of violence against women: A field experiment. *Journal of Research in Personality, 15,* 436–446.

Malamuth, N. M., Linz, D., Heavey, C. L., Barnes, G., & Acker, M. (1995). Using the confluence model of sexual aggression to predict men's conflict with women: A 10-year follow-up study. *Journal of Personality and Social Psychology, 69,* 353–369.

Malett, R. K. & Swim, J. K. (2003). Collective guilt in the United States: Predicting support for social policies that alleviate social injustice. In N. Branscombe & B. Doosje (Eds.), *Collective guilt: International perspectives* (pp. 56–74). New York, NY: Cambridge University Press.

Malkiel, B. (2004). *A random walk down Wall Street: Completely revised and updated 8th ed.* (p. 88). New York, NY: Norton.

Malle, B. F. (2006). The actor-observer asymmetry in attribution: A (surprising) meta-analysis. *Psychological Bulletin, 132,* 895–919.

Malle, B. F. (2007). Attributions as behaviour explanations: Toward a new theory. In D. Chadee & J. Hunter (Eds.), *Current themes and perspectives in social psychology* (pp. 3–26). St. Augustine, Trinidad: SOCS, The University of the West Indies.

Malpass, R. S., & Devine, P. G. (1981). Eyewitness identification: Lineup instructions and the absence of the offender. *Journal of Applied Psychology, 66*(4), 482–489.

Mann, L. (1981). The baiting crowd in episodes of threatened suicide. *Journal of Personality and Social Psychology, 41,* 703–709.

Manning, R., Levine, M., & Collins, A. (2007). The Kitty Genovese murder and the social psychology of helping: The parable of the 38 witnesses. *American Psychologist, 62,* 555–562.

Marcus, A. C., & Siegel, J. M. (1982). Sex differences in the use of physician services: A preliminary test of the fixed role hypothesis. *Journal of Health and Social Behavior, 23,* 186–197.

Marcus, B., Machilek, F., & Schutz, A. (2006). Personality in cyberspace: Personal Web sites as media for personality expressions and impressions. *Journal of Personality and Social Psychology, 90*(6), 1014–1031.

Marcus, D. K., & Miller, R. S. (2003). Sex differences in judgments of physical attractiveness: A social relations analysis. *Personality and Social Psychology Bulletin, 29,* 325–335.

Marcus, S. (1974, January 13). Review of *Obedience to Authority. New York Times Book Review,* 1–2.

Marcus-Newhall, A., Pedersen, W. C., Carlson, M., & Miller, N. (2000). Displaced aggression is alive and well: A meta-analytic review. *Journal of Personality and Social Psychology, 78,* 670–689.

Markey, P. M., Wells, S. M., & Markey, C. N. (2002). Social and personality psychology in the culture of cyberspace. In S. P. Shohov (Ed.), *Advances in psychology research, Vol. 9,* (pp. 94–113). Huntington, NY: Nova Science.

Markman, H. J., Floyd, F. J., Stanley, S. M., & Storaasli, R. D. (1988). Prevention of marital distress: A longitudinal investigation. *Journal of Consulting and Clinical Psychology, 56,* 210–217.

Marks, G., & Miller, N. (1985). The effect of certainty on consensus judgments. *Personality and Social Psychology Bulletin, 11*(2), 165–177.

Marks, G., & Miller, N. (1987). Ten years of research on the false-consensus effect: An empirical and theoretical review. *Psychological Bulletin, 102,* 72–90.

Markus, H. (2001, October 7). Culture and the good life. Adress to the Positive Psychology Summit conference, Washington, DC.

Markus, H., & Kitayama, S. (1991). Culture and the self: Implications for cognition, emotion, and motivation. *Psychological Review, 98,* 224–253.

Markus, H., & Wurf, E. (1987). The dynamic self-concept: A social psychological perspective. *Annual Review of Psychology, 38,* 299–337.

Marlatt, G. R., & Gordon, J. R. (1979). Determinants of relapse: Implications for the maintenance of behavior change. In P. Davidson (Ed.), *Behavioral medicines: Changing health lifestyles* (pp. 410–452). New York, NY: Brunner/Mazel.

Marsden, P., & Attia, S. (2005). A deadly contagion? *The Psychologist, 18*(3), 152–155.

Marsh, H. W., & Young, A. S. (1997). Causal effects of academic self-concept on academic achievement: Structural equation models of longitudinal data. *Journal of Educational Psychology, 89,* 41–54.

Marshall, W. L. (1989). Pornography and sex offenders. In D. Zillmann & J. Bryant (Eds.), *Pornography: Research advances and policy considerations.* Hillsdale, NJ: Erlbaum.

Martens, A., Kosloff, S., Greenberg, J., Landau, M. J., & Schmader, T. (2007). Killing begets killing: Evidence from a bug-killing paradigm that initial killing fuels subsequent killing. *Personality and Social Psychology Bulletin, 33*(9), 1251–1264.

Martin, C. L. (1987). A ratio measure of sex stereotyping. *Journal of Personality and Social Psychology, 52,* 489–499.

Masserman, J. H., Wechkin, S., & Terris, W. (1964). "Altruistic" behavior in rhesus monkeys. *The American Journal of Psychiatry, 121,* 584–585.

Mastronianni, G. R., & Reed, G. (2006). Apples, barrels, and Abu Ghraib. *Sociological Focus, 39,* 239–250.

Masuda, T., & Kitayama, S. (2004). Perceiver-induced constraint and attitude attribution in Japan and the U.S.: A case for culture-dependence of correspondence bias. *Journal of Experimental Social Psychology, 40,* 409–416.

Matheson, K., & Zanna, M. P. (1988). The impact of computer-mediated communication on self-awareness. *Computers in Human Behavior, 4,* 221–233.

Matheson, K., & Zanna, M. P. (1990). Computer-mediated communications: The focus is on me. *Social Science Computer Review, 8,* 1–12.

Mayer, J. D., & Salovey, P. (1987). Personality moderates the interaction of mood and cognition. In K. Fielder & J. Forgas (Eds.), *Affect, cognition, and social behavior.* Toronto: Hogrefe & Huber.

Mazzella, R., & Feingold, A. (1994). The effects of physical attractiveness, race, socioeconomic status, and gender of defendants and victims on judgments of mock jurors: A meta-analysis. *Journal of Applied Social Psychology, 24,* 1315–1344.

McAlister, A., Perry, C., Killen, J., Slinkard, L. A., & Maccoby, N. (1980). Pilot study of smoking, alcohol and drug abuse prevention. *American Journal of Public Health, 70,* 719–721.

McCann, C. D., & Hancock, R. D. (1983). Self-monitoring in communicative interactions: Social cognitive consequences of goal-directed message modification. *Journal of Experimental Social Psychology, 19,* 109–121.

McCann, S. J. H. (2001). The precocity-longevity hypothesis: Earlier peaks in career achievement predict shorter lives. *Personality and Social Psychology Bulletin, 27*(11), 1429–1439.

McCauley, C. (1989). The nature of social influence in groupthink: Compliance and internalization. *Journal of Personality and Social Psychology, 57,* 250–260.

McCauley, C. (2004). Psychological issues in understanding terrorism and the response to terrorism. In C. E. Stout (Ed.) *The psychology of terrorism: Coping with the continuing threat, condensed edition* (pp. 3–29). Westport, CT: Praeger Greenwood.

McCauley, C. R. (2002). Psychological issues in understanding terrorism and the response to terrorism. In C. E. Stout (Ed.), *The psychology of terrorism, Vol. 3.* Westport, CT: Praeger/ Greenwood.

McCauley, C. R., & Segal, M. E. (1987). Social psychology of terrorist groups. In C. Hendrick (Ed.), *Group processes and intergroup relations: Review of personality and social psychology, Vol. 9.* Newbury Park, CA: Sage.

McClure, J. (1998). Discounting causes of behavior: Are two reasons better than one? *Journal of Personality and Social Psychology, 74,* 7–20.

McConahay, J. B. (1981). Reducing racial prejudice in desegregated schools. In W. D. Hawley (Ed.), *Effective school desegregation.* Beverly Hills, CA: Sage.

McCullough, J. L., & Ostrom, T. M. (1974). Repetition of highly similar messages and attitude change. *Journal of Applied Psychology, 59,* 395–397.

McDermott, T. (2005). *Perfect soldiers: The hijackers: Who they were, why they did it* (p. 205). New York, NY: HarperCollins.

McFarland, C., & Miller, D. (1990). Judgments of self-other similarity: Just like other people, only more so. *Personality and Social Psychology Bulletin, 16,* 475–484.

McFarland, S., & Carnahan, T. (2009). A Situation's First Powers Are Attracting Volunteers and Selecting Participants: A Reply to Haney and Zimbardo, *Personality and Social Psychology Bulletin, 35,* 815–818.

McFarland, S. G., Ageyev, V. S., & Abalakina-Paap, M. A. (1992). Authoritarianism in the former Soviet Union. *Journal of Personality and Social Psychology, 63,* 1004–1010.

McFarland, S. G., Ageyev, V. S., & Djintcharadze, N. (1996). Russian authoritarianism two years after communism. *Personality and Social Psychology Bulletin, 22,* 210–217.

McGinn, A. P. (1998, June 20). *Hidden forces mask crisis in world fisheries.* Worldwatch Institute (http://www.worldwatch.org).

McGuire, A. (2002, August 19). Charity calls for debate on adverts aimed at children. *The Herald* (Scotland), 4.

McGuire, W. J. (1964). Inducing resistance to persuasion: Some contemporary approaches. In L. Berkowitz (Ed.), *Advances in experimental social psychology, Vol. 1.* New York, NY: Academic Press.

McGuire, W. J. (1969). The nature of attitudes and attitude change. In G. Lindzey, & E. Aronson (Eds.), *The handbook of social psychology* (2nd ed.), *Vol. 3* (pp. 136–314). New York, NY: Addison-Wesley.

McGuire, W. J., & McGuire, C. V. (1986). Differences in conceptualizing self versus conceptualizing other people as manifested in contrasting verb types used in natural speech. *Journal of Personality and Social Psychology, 51,* 1135–1143.

McGuire, W. J., & Padawer-Singer, A. (1978). Trait salience in the spontaneous self-concept. *Journal of Personality and Social Psychology, 33,* 743–754.

McGuire, W. J., McGuire, C. V., & Winton, W. (1979). Effects of household sex composition on the salience of one's gender in the spontaneous self-concept. *Journal of Experimental Social Psychology, 15,* 77–90.

McKelvie, S. J. (1995). Bias in the estimated frequency of names. *Perceptual and Motor Skills, 81,* 1331–1338.

McKelvie, S. J. (1997). The availability heuristic: Effects of fame and gender on the estimated frequency of male and female names. *Journal of Social Psychology, 137,* 63–78.

McKenna, F. P., & Myers, L. B. (1997). Illusory self-assessments— Can they be reduced? *British Journal of Psychology, 88,* 39–51.

McKenna, K. Y. A., & Bargh, J. A. (1998). Coming out in the age of the Internet: Identity demarginalization through virtual group participation. *Journal of Personality and Social Psychology, 75,* 681–694.

McKenna, K. Y. A., & Bargh, J. A. (2000). Plan 9 from cyberspace: The implications of the Internet for personality and social psychology. *Personality and Social Psychology Review, 4,* 57–75.

McKenna, K. Y. A., Green, A. S., & Gleason, M. E. J. (2002). What's the big attraction? Relationship formation on the Internet. *Journal of Social Issues, 58,* 9–31.

McNeel, S. P. (1980). *Tripling up: Perceptions and effects of dormitory crowding.* Paper presented at the American Psychological Association convention.

McPherson, M., Smith-Lovin, L., & Cook, J. M. (2001). Birds of a feature: Homophily in social networks. *Annual Review of Sociology, 27,* 415–444.

Mealey, L., Bridgstock, R., & Townsend, G. C. (1999). Symmetry and perceived facial attractiveness: A monozygotic co-twin comparison. *Journal of Personality and Social Psychology, 76,* 151–158.

Medvec, V., Madey, S. F., & Gilovich, T. (1995). When less is more: Counterfactual thinking and satisfaction among Olympic medalists. *Journal of Personality and Social Psychology, 69*(4), 603–610.

Medved, M. (1995). *Hollywood versus America.* New York, NY: HarperCollins.

Mehl, M. R., & Pennebaker, J. W. (2003). The sounds of social life: A psychometric analysis of students' daily social environments and natural conversations. *Journal of Personality and Social Psychology, 84,* 857–870.

Meindl, J. R., & Lerner, M. J. (1984). Exacerbation of extreme responses to an out-group. *Journal of Personality and Social Psychology, 47,* 71–84.

Meissner, C. A., & Brigham, J. C. (2001). Thirty years of investigating the own-race bias in memory for faces: A meta-analytic review. *Psychology, Public Policy, and Law, 7,* 3–35.

Memon, A., & Gabbert, G. (2003). Improving the identification accuracy of senior witnesses: Do prelineup questions and sequential testing help? *Journal of Applied Psychology, 88,* 341–347.

Mendel, R. R., Traut-Mattausch, E. E., Jonas, E. E., Leucht, S. S., Kane, J. M., Maino, K. K., & . . . Hamann, J. J. (2011). Confirmation bias: Why psychiatrists stick to wrong preliminary diagnoses. *Psychological Medicine, 41*(12), 2651–2659.

Merari, A. (2002). *Explaining suicidal terrorism: Theories versus empirical evidence.* Invited address to the American Psychological Association.

Messé, L. A., & Sivacek, J. M. (1979). Predictions of others' responses in a mixed-motive game: Self-justification or false consensus? *Journal of Personality and Social Psychology, 37,* 602–607.

Messick, D. M., & Sentis, K. P. (1979). Fairness and preference. *Journal of Experimental Social Psychology, 15,* 418–434.

Metalsky, G. I., Joiner, T. E., Jr., Hardin, T. S., & Abramson, L. Y. (1993). Depressive reactions to failure in a naturalistic setting: A test of the hopelessness and self-esteem theories of depression. *Journal of Abnormal Psychology, 102,* 101–109.

Metcalfe, C. (2010, July 8). Vampires reach cult religion status. *Penwirth Press.*

Mewhinney, D. M., Herald, E. S., & Maticka-Tyndale, E. (1995). Sexual scripts and risk-taking of Canadian university students on spring break in Daytona Beach, Florida. *Canadian Journal of Human Sexuality, 4,* 273–288.

Michaels, J. W., Blommel, J. M., Brocato, R. M., Linkous, R. A., & Rowe, J. S. (1982). Social facilitation and inhibition in a natural setting. *Replications in Social Psychology, 2,* 21–24.

Mickelson, K. D., Kessler, R. C., & Shaver, P. R. (1997). Adult attachment in a nationally representative sample. *Journal of Personality and Social Psychology, 73,* 1092–1106.

Mikulincer, M., Florian, V., & Hirschberger, G. (2003). The existential function of close relationships: Introducing death into the science of love. *Personality and Social Psychology Review, 7,* 20–40.

Milgram, A. (2000). My personal view of Stanley Milgram. In T. Blass (Ed.), *Obedience to authority: Current perspectives on the Milgram paradigm.* Mahwah, NJ: Erlbaum.

Milgram, S. (1965). Some conditions of obedience and disobedience to authority. *Human Relations, 18,* 57–76.

Milgram, S. (1974). *Obedience to authority.* New York, NY: Harper and Row.

Milgram, S., & Sabini, J. (1983). On maintaining social norms: A field experiment in the subway. In H. H. Blumberg, A. P. Hare, V. Kent, & M. Davies (Eds.), *Small groups and social interaction, Vol. 1.* London: Wiley.

Miller, A. G. (2004). What can the Milgram obedience experiments tell us about the Holocaust? Generalizing from the social psychological laboratory. In A. G. Miller (Ed.), *The social psychology of good and evil.* New York, NY: Guilford Press.

Miller, A. G., Gillen, G., Schenker, C., & Radlove, S. (1973). *Perception of obedience to authority.* Proceedings of the 81st Annual Convention of the American Psychological Association, *8,* 127–128.

Miller, D. T., Downs, J. S., & Prentice, D. A. (1998). Minimal conditions for the creation of a unit relationship: The social bond between birthdaymates. *European Journal of Social Psychology, 28,* 475.

Miller, J. G. (1984). Culture and the development of everyday social explanation. *Journal of Personality and Social Psychology, 46,* 961–978.

Miller, K. I., & Monge, P. R. (1986). Participation, satisfaction, and productivity: A meta-analytic review. *Academy of Management Journal, 29,* 727–753.

Miller, L. C. (1990). Intimacy and liking: Mutual influence and the role of unique relationships. *Journal of Personality and Social Psychology, 59,* 50–60.

Miller, L. C., Berg, J. H., & Archer, R. L. (1983). Openers: Individuals who elicit intimate self-disclosure. *Journal of Personality and Social Psychology, 44,* 1234–1244.

Miller, L. C., Berg, J. H., & Rugs, D. (1989). *Selectivity and sharing: Needs and norms in developing friendships.* Unpublished manuscript, Scripps College.

Miller, N., & Marks, G. (1982). Assumed similarity between self and other: Effect of expectation of future interaction with that other. *Social Psychology Quarterly, 45,* 100–105.

Miller, N., Pedersen, W. C., Earleywine, M., & Pollock, V. E. (2003). A theoretical model of triggered displaced aggression. *Personality and Social Psychology Review, 7,* 75–97.

Miller, N. E. (1941). The frustration-aggression hypothesis. *Psychological Review, 48,* 337–342.

Miller, P. A., & Eisenberg, N. (1988). The relation of empathy to aggressive and externalizing/antisocial behavior. *Psychological Bulletin, 103,* 324–344.

Miller, P. C., Lefcourt, H. M., Holmes, J. G., Ware, E. E., & Saley, W. E. (1986). Marital locus of control and marital problem solving. *Journal of Personality and Social Psychology, 51,* 161–169.

Miller, P. J. E., & Rempel, J. K. (2004). Trust and partner-enhancing attributions in close relationships. *Personality and Social Psychology Bulletin, 30,* 695–705.

Millett, K. (1975, January). The shame is over. *Ms.,* 26–29.

Mims, P. R., Hartnett, J. J., & Nay, W. R. (1975). Interpersonal attraction and help volunteering as a function of physical attractiveness. *Journal of Psychology, 89,* 125–131.

Mishna, F., Saini, M., & Solomon, S. (2009). Ongoing and online: Children and youth's perceptions of cyber bullying. *Children and Youth Services Review, 31,* 1222–1228.

Mita, T. H., Dermer, M., & Knight, J. (1977). Reversed facial images and the mere-exposure hypothesis. *Journal of Personality and Social Psychology, 35,* 597–601.

Moghaddam, F. M. (2005). The staircase to terrorism: A psychological exploration. *American Psychologist, 60,* 161–169.

Montoya, R. M. (2008). I'm hot, so I'd say you're not: The influence of objective physical attractiveness on mate selection. *Personality and Social Psychology Bulletin, 34,* 1315–1331.

Moons, W. G., & Mackie, D. M. (2007). Thinking straight while seeing red: The influence of anger on information processing. *Personality and Social Psychology Bulletin, 33,* 706–720.

Moore, D. L., & Baron, R. S. (1983). Social facilitation: A physiological analysis. In J. T. Cacioppo & R. Petty (Eds.), *Social psychophysiology.* New York, NY: Guilford Press.

Moore, D. W. (2003a, March 11). *Half of young people expect to strike it rich: But expectations fall rapidly with age.* Gallup News Service (http://www.gallup.com/poll/releases/pr030311.asp).

Moore, D. W. (2003b, March 18). *Public approves of Bush ultimatum by more than 2-to-1 margin.* Gallup News Service (http://www.gallup.com).

Moore, R. (2009). *Understanding Jonestown and Peoples Temple.* Westport, CT: Praeger/Greenwood.

Mor, N., & Winquist, J. (2002). Self-focused attention and negative affect: A meta-analysis. *Psychological Bulletin, 128,* 638–662.

Morling, B., & Lamoreaux, M. (2008). Measuring culture outside the head: A meta-analysis of individualism-collectivism in cultural products. *Personality and Social Personality Bulletin, 12,* 199–221.

Morrison, D. M. (1989). Predicting contraceptive efficacy: A discriminant analysis of three groups of adolescent women. *Journal of Applied Social Psychology, 19,* 1431–1452.

Morrison, M. A., & Morrison, T. G. (2011). Sexual orientation bias toward gay men and lesbian women: Modern homonegative attitudes and their associations with discriminatory behavioural intentions. *Journal of Applied Social Psychology, 41,* 2573–2599.

Morrison, M. A., Morrison, T. G., & Franklin, R. (2009). Modern and old-fashioned homonegativity among samples of Canadian and American university students. *Journal of Cross-Cultural Psychology, 40*(4), 523–542.

Morrison, T. G., Ellis, S. R., Morrison, M. A., Bearden, A., & Harriman, R. L. (2006). Exposure to sexually explicit material and variations in body esteem, genital attitudes, and sexual esteem among a sample of Canadian men. *The Journal of Men's Studies, 14*(2), 209–222.

Morrison, T. G., Harriman, R., Morrison, M. A., Bearden, A., & Ellis, S. R. (2004). Correlates of exposure to sexually explicit material among Canadian post-secondary students. *The Canadian Journal of Human Sexuality, 13*(3–4), 143–156.

Morry, M. M. (2003). Perceived locus of control and satisfaction in same-sex friendships. *Personal Relationships, 10,* 495–509.

Morry, M. M. (2005). *Relationship satisfaction as a predictor of perceived similarity among cross-sex friends: A test of the attraction-similarity model.* Manuscript under review.

Morse, D. R., Martin, J., & Moshonov, J. (1991). Psychosomatically induced death: Relative to stress hypnosis, mind control, and voodoo: Review and possible mechanisms. *Stress Medicine, 7*(4), 213–232.

Moscovici, S. (1985). Social influence and conformity. In G. Lindzey & E. Aronson (Eds.), *The handbook of social psychology,* (3rd ed.) Hillsdale, NJ: Erlbaum.

Moscovici, S., Lage, S., & Naffrechoux, M. (1969). Influence of a consistent minority on the responses of a majority in a color perception task. *Sociometry, 32,* 365–380.

Moscovici, S., & Zavalloni, M. (1969). The group as a polarizer of attitudes. *Journal of Personality and Social Psychology, 12,* 124–135.

Moskowitz, D. S., Suh, E. J., & Desaulniers, J. (1994). Situational influences on gender differences in agency and communion. *Journal of Personality and Social Psychology, 66,* 753–761.

Moyer, K. E. (1976). *The psychobiology of aggression.* New York, NY: Harper & Row.

Moyer, K. E. (1983). The physiology of motivation: Aggression as a model. In C. J. Scheier & A. M. Rogers (Eds.), *G. Stanley Hall Lecture Series, Vol. 3.* Washington, DC: American Psychological Association.

MSNBC. (2007). Jackass movie copycat lands in hospital. Retrieved from http://www.msnbc.msn.com/id/17515065/ns/us_news-weird_news/t/jackass-movie-copycat-lands-hospital/.

Mueller, C. W., Donnerstein, E., & Hallam, J. (1983). Violent films and prosocial behavior. *Personality and Social Psychology Bulletin, 9,* 83–89.

Muise, A., Christofides, E., & Desmarais, S. (2009). More information than you ever wanted: Does Facebook bring out the green-eyed monster of jealousy? *CyberPsychology & Behavior, 12*(4), 441–444.

Mullen, B. (1986a). Atrocity as a function of lynch mob composition: A self-attention perspective. *Personality and Social Psychology Bulletin, 12,* 187–197.

Mullen, B. (1986b). Stuttering, audience size, and the other-total ratio: A self-attention perspective. *Journal of Applied Social Psychology, 16,* 139–149.

Mullen, B., & Baumeister, R. F. (1987). Group effects on self-attention and performance: Social loafing, social facilitation, and social impairment. In C. Hendrick (Ed.), *Group processes and intergroup relations: Review of personality and social psychology, Vol. 9.* Newbury Park, CA: Sage.

Mullen, B., Brown, R., & Smith, C. (1992). Ingroup bias as a function of salience, relevance, and status: An integration. *European Journal of Social Psychology, 22,* 103–122.

Mullen, B., Bryant, B., & Driskell, J. E. (1997). Presence of others and arousal: An integration. *Group Dynamics: Theory, Research, and Practice, 1,* 52–64.

Mullen, B., & Copper, C. (1994). The relation between group cohesiveness and performance: An integration. *Psychological Bulletin, 115,* 210–227.

Mullen, B., & Goethals, G. R. (1990). Social projection, actual consensus and valence. *British Journal of Social Psychology, 29,* 279–282.

Mullen, B., & Riordan, C. A. (1988). Self-serving attributions for performance in naturalistic settings: A meta-analytic review. *Journal of Applied Social Psychology, 18,* 3–22.

Mullen, B., Salas, E., & Driskell, J. E. (1989). Salience, motivation, and artifact as contributions to the relation between participation rate and leadership. *Journal of Experimental Social Psychology, 25,* 545–559.

Muller, S., & Johnson, B. T. (1990). *Fear and persuasion: A linear relationship?* Paper presented to the Eastern Psychological Association convention.

Mullin, C. R., & Linz, D. (1995). Desensitization and resensitization to violence against women: Effects of exposure to sexually violent films on judgments of domestic violence victims. *Journal of Personality and Social Psychology, 69,* 449–459.

Murphy, C. (1990, June). New findings: Hold on to your hat. *The Atlantic,* 22–23.

Murray, S. L., Gellavia, G. M., Rose, P., & Griffin, D. W. (2003). Once hurt, twice hurtful: How perceived regard regulates daily marital interactions. *Journal of Personality and Social Psychology, 84,* 126–147.

Murray, S. L., Holmes, J. G., & Griffin, D. W. (1996). The self-fulfilling nature of positive illusions in romantic relationships: Love is not blind, but prescient. *Journal of Personality and Social Psychology, 71,* 1155–1180.

Murray, S. L., Holmes, J. G., & Griffin, D. W. (2000). Self-esteem and the quest for felt security: How perceived regard regulates attachment processes. *Journal of Personality and Social Psychology, 78,* 478–498.

Murray, S. L., Holmes, J. G., Gellavia, G., Griffin, D. W., & Dolderman, D. (2002). Kindred spirits? The benefits of egocentrism in close relationships. *Journal of Personality and Social Psychology, 82,* 563–581.

Murray, S. L., Holmes, J. G., MacDonald, G., & Ellsworth, P. C. (1998). Through the looking glass darkly? When self-doubts turn into relationship insecurities. *Journal of Personality and Social Psychology, 75,* 1459–1480.

Murstein, B. L. (1986). *Paths to marriage.* Newbury Park, CA: Sage.

Muson, G. (1978, March). Teenage violence and the telly. *Psychology Today,* 50–54.

Myers, D. G. (2000). *The American paradox: Spiritual hunger in an age of plenty.* New Haven, CT: Yale University Press.

Myers, D. G., & Bishop, G. D. (1970). Discussion effects on racial attitudes. *Science, 169,* 778–789.

Myers, N. (2000b). Sustainable consumption: The meta-problem. In B. Heap & J. Kent (Eds.), *Towards sustainable consumption: A European perspective* (pp. 576, 579). London: The Royal Society.

Myers, T., Allman, D., Calzavara, L., Maxwell, J., Remis, R., Swantee, C., & Travers, R. (2004). *Ontario men's survey final report.* Toronto: University of Toronto Press.

Nadler, A. (1991). Help-seeking behavior: Psychological costs and instrumental benefits. In M. S. Clark (Ed.), *Prosocial behavior* (pp. 290–311). Newbury Park, CA: Sage.

Nadler, A., Goldberg, M., & Jaffe, Y. (1982). Effect of self-differentiation and anonymity in group on deindividuation. *Journal of Personality and Social Psychology, 42,* 1127–1136.

Nagar, D., & Pandey, J. (1987). Affect and performance on cognitive task as a function of crowding and noise. *Journal of Applied Social Psychology, 17,* 147–157.

Nail, P. R., MacDonald, G., & Levy, D. A. (2000). Proposal of a four-dimensional model of social response. *Psychological Bulletin, 126,* 454–470.

Nakao, T., Tokunaga, S., Takamura, M., Nashiwa, H., Hayashi, S., & Miyatani, M. (2012). Altruistic people show no self-reference effect in memory. *Journal of General Psychology, 139*(1), 22–41.

Narby, D. J., & Cutler, B. L. (1994). Effectiveness of voir dire as a safeguard in eyewitness cases. Journal of Applied Psychology, 79, 724–729.

National Center for Health Statistics. (1991). *Family structure and children's health: United States, 1988, Vital and Health Statistics, Series 10, No. 178,* CHHS Publication No. PHS 91-1506 by Deborah A. Dawson.

National Geographic. (2006, February). *Meltdown: The Alps under pressure.*

National Geographic. (2011, January). *Population 7 billion: How your world will change.*

National Institute on Alcohol Abuse and Alcoholism. (2008). *Alcohol dependence, withdrawal and relapse.* Retrieved from http://pubs.niaaa.nih.gov/publications/arh314/348-361.htm.

National Research Council. (2002). *Youth, pornography, and the Internet.* Washington, DC: National Academy Press.

National Television Violence Study. (1997). Thousand Oaks, CA: Sage.

Needles, D. J., & Abramson, L. Y. (1990). Positive life events, attributional style, and hopefulness: Testing a model of recovery from depression. *Journal of Abnormal Psychology, 99,* 156–165.

Nelson, L. D., & Morrison, E. L. (2005). The symptoms of resource scarcity: Judgments of food and finances influence preferences for potential partners. *Psychological Science, 16,* 246.

Nelson, L. J., & Miller, D. T. (1997). The distinctiveness effect in social categorization: You are what makes you unusual. *Psychological Science, 6,* 246.

Nemeth, C. (1979). The role of an active minority in intergroup relations. In W. G. Austin & S. Worchel (Eds.), *The social psychology of intergroup relations.* Monterey, CA: Brooks/Cole.

Nemeth, C., & Wachtler, J. (1974). Creating the perceptions of consistency and confidence: A necessary condition for minority influence. *Sociometry, 37,* 529–540.

Neuberg, S. L., Kenrick, D. T., & Schaller, M. (2011). Human threat management systems: Self-protection and disease-avoidance. *Neuroscience & Biobehavioral Reviews, 35,* 1042–1051.

Newcomb, T. M. (1961). *The acquaintance process.* New York, NY: Holt, Rinehart and Winston.

Newell, B., & Lagnado, D. (2003). Think-tanks, or think tanks. *The Psychologist, 16,* 176.

Newman, A. (2001, February 4). Rotten teeth and dead babies. *New York Times Magazine* (http://www.nytimes.com).

Newman, H. M., & Langer, E. J. (1981). Post-divorce adaptation and the attribution of responsibility. *Sex Roles, 7,* 223–231.

Newman, L. S. (1993). How individualists interpret behavior: Idiocentrism and spontaneous trait inference. *Social Cognition, 11,* 243–269.

Newport, F., Moore, D. W., Jones, J. M., & Saad, L. (2003, March 21). *Special release: American opinion on the war.* Gallup Poll Tuesday Briefing (http://www.gallup.com/poll/tb/goverpubli/s0030325.asp), p. 202.

Ng, W., & Lindsay, R. C. L. (1994). Cross-race facial recognition: Failure of the contact hypothesis. *Journal of Cross-Cultural Psychology, 25,* 217–232.

Nias, D. K. B. (1979). Marital choice: Matching or complementation? In M. Cook & G. Wilson (Eds.), *Love and attraction.* Oxford: Pergamon.

Nicholls, D., & Viner, R. (2009). Childhood risk factors for lifetime anorexia nervosa by age 30 years in a national birth cohort. *Journal of the American Academy of Child and Adolescent Psychiatry, 48,* 791–799.

Nichols, J. (2003, February 9). Man overdoses online as chatters watch him die. *Grand Rapids Press,* p. A20.

Nie, N. H., & Erbring, L. (2000, February 17). *Internet and society: A preliminary report.* Stanford, CA: Stanford Institute for the Quantitative Study of Society.

NIH. (2010). *Depression high among youth victims of school cyber bullying, NIH researchers report.* Retrieved from http://www.nih.gov/news/health/sep2010/nichd-21.htm.

Nolan, S. A., Flynn, C. & Garber, J. (2003). Prospective relations between rejection and depression in young adolescents. *Journal of Personality and Social Psychology, 85,* 745–755.

Noller, P., & Fitzpatrick, M. A. (1990). Marital communication in the eighties. *Journal of Marriage and the Family, 52,* 832–843.

Norcross, J. C., Mrykalo, M. S., & Blagys, M. D. (2002). Auld lang syne: Success predictors, change processes, and self-reported outcomes of New Year's resolvers and nonresolvers. *Journal of Clinical Psychology, 58,* 397–405.

Norem, J. K. (2000). Defensive pessimism, optimism, and pessimism. In E. C. Chang (Ed.), *Optimism and pessimism.* Washington, DC: APA Books.

Norem, J. K., & Cantor, N. (1986). Defensive pessimism: Harnessing anxiety as motivation. *Journal of Personality and Social Psychology, 51,* 1208–1217.

Norris, M. (2007). *The impact of information processing goals and capacity restrictions on attitude-memory.* Unpublished Master's Thesis. Queen's University.

Norris, M. E., Smith, S. M., Fabrigar, L. R., & Wegener, D. T. (2014). Attitude-memory biases from auditory information: Exploring the moderating roles of information processing goals and capacity restrictions. Poster presented at the 15th annual meeting of the Society for Personality and Social Psychology, Austin, TX.

Nosek, B. A., Greenwald, A. G., & Banaji, M. R. (2005). Understanding and using the implicit association test II: Method variables and construct validity. *Personality and Social Psychology Bulletin, 31,* 166–180.

Nosko, A., Wood, E., & Desmarais, S. (2007). Unsolicited online sexual material: What affects our attitudes and likelihood to search for more? *Canadian Journal of Human Sexuality, 16*(1–2), 1–10.

Notarius, C., & Markman, H. J. (1993). *We can work it out.* New York, NY: Putnam.

Nowak, M., & Sigmund, K. (1993). A strategy of win-stay, lose-shift that outperforms tit-for-tat in the Prisoner's Dilemma game. *Nature, 364,* 56–58.

Nuttin, J. M., Jr. (1987). Affective consequences of mere ownership: The name letter effect in twelve European languages. *European Journal of Social Psychology, 17,* 318–402.

O'Brien, L. T., & Crandall, C. S. (2003). Stereotype threat and arousal: Effects on women's math performance. *Personality and Social Psychology Bulletin, 29,* 782–789.

Oddone-Paolucci, E., Genuis, M., & Violato, C. (2000). A meta-analysis of the published research on the effects of pornography. In C. Violata (Ed.), *The changing family and child development.* Aldershot: Ashgate Publishing.

O'Driscoll, P. (1997, December 9). In hot pursuit of road rage. *USA Today,* p. 3A.

Ohbuchi, K., & Kambara, T. (1985). Attacker's intent and awareness of outcome, impression management, and retaliation. *Journal of Experimental Social Psychology, 21,* 321–330.

O'Hegarty, M., Pederson, L. L., Yenokyan, G., Nelson, D., & Wortley, P. (2007). Young adults' perceptions of cigarette warning labels in the United States and Canada. *Preventing Chronic Disease: Public Health Research, Practice, and Policy, 30,* 467–473.

Ohlert, J., & Kleinert, J. (2013). Social loafing during preparation for performance situations: The preloafing effect. *Social Psychology, 44*(3), 231–237.

Okimoto, T. G., & Brescoll, V. L. (2010). The price of power: Power seeking and backlash against female politicians. *Personality and Social Psychology Bulletin, 36*(7), 923–936.

O'Leary, K. D., Christian, J. L., & Mendell, N. R. (1994). A closer look at the link between marital discord and depressive symptomatology. *Journal of Social and Clinical Psychology, 13,* 33–41.

Olfson, M., & Pincus, H. A. (1994). Outpatient therapy in the United States: II. Patterns of utilization. *American Journal of Psychiatry, 151,* 1289–1294.

Olson, I. R., & Marshuetz, C. (2005). Facial attractiveness is appraised in a glance. *Emotion, 5*(4), 498–502.

Olson, J. M., & Hafer, C. L. (1996). Affect, motivation, and cognition in relative deprivation research. In R. M. Sorrentino, & E. Higgins (Eds.), *Handbook of motivation and cognition, Vol. 3: The interpersonal context* (pp. 85–117). New York, NY: Guilford Press.

Olson, J. M., Roese, N. J., & Zanna, M. P. (1996). Expectancies. In E. T. Higgins & A. W. Kruglanski (Eds.), *Social psychology: Handbook of basic principles* (pp. 211–238). New York, NY: Guilford Press.

Olson, J. M., & Zanna, M. P. (1981, November). Promoting physical activity: A social psychological perspective. Report prepared for the Ministry of Culture and Recreation, Sports and Fitness Branch, 77 Bloor St. West, 8th Floor, Toronto, Ontario M7A 2R9.

Olson, M. A., & Fazio, R. H. (2004). Reducing the influence of extra-personal associations on the Implicit Association Test: Personalizing the IAT. *Journal of Personality and Social Psychology, 86,* 653–667.

Olweus, D. (1979). Stability of aggressive reaction patterns in males: A review. *Psychological Bulletin, 86,* 852–875.

Olweus, D., Mattsson, A., Schalling, D., & Low, H. (1988). Circulating testosterone levels and aggression in adolescent males: A causal analysis. *Psychosomatic Medicine, 50,* 261–272.

Omoto, A. M., & Snyder, M. (2002). Considerations of community: The context and process of volunteerism. *American Behavioral Scientist, 45,* 846–867.

O'Neill, B. (2012, August). Tattoos were once a sign of rebellion—now they are evidence of craen conformity to cultural norms. *The Telegraph,* Retrieved from http://blogs.telegraph.co.uk/news/brendanoneill2/100175760/tattoos-were-once-a-sign-of-rebellion-now-they-are-evidence-of-an-individuals-craven-conformity-to-cultural-norms/.

Ontario Provincial Police (2007). Retrieved from http://www.sudburycrimestoppers.com/Crime%20Files/ART%20ChildInternetLuring.aspx, 09-14-2014.

Orbell, J. M., van de Kragt, A. J. C., & Dawes, R. M. (1988). Explaining discussion-induced cooperation. *Journal of Personality and Social Psychology, 54,* 811–819.

Orbell, S., Hagger, M., Brown, V., & Tidy, J. (2006). Comparing two theories of health behavior: A prospective study of noncompletion of treatment following cervical cancer screening. *Health Psychology, 25,* 604–615.

O'Reilly, T., & Tennant, M. (2009). *The age of persuasion: How marketing ate our culture.* Toronto: Knopf Canada.

Orenstein, P. (2003, July 6). Where have all the Lisas gone? *New York Times* (http://www.nytimes.com).

Orgaz, C., Estévez, A., & Matute, H. (2013). Pathological gamblers are more vulnerable to the illusion of control in a standard associative learning task. *Frontiers in Psychology, 4,* 1–7.

Orive, R. (1984). Group similarity, public self-awareness, and opinion extremity: A social projection explanation of deindividuation effects. *Journal of Personality and Social Psychology, 47,* 727–737.

Orr, E. S., Sisic, M., Ross, C., Simmering, M. G., Arseneault, J. M., & Orr, R. R. (2009). The influence of shyness on the use of Facebook in an undergraduate sample. *CyberPsychology & Behavior, 12*(3), 337–340.

Osberg, T. M., & Shrauger, J. S. (1986). Self-prediction: Exploring the parameters of accuracy. *Journal of Personality and Social Psychology, 51,* 1044–1057.

Osberg, T. M., & Shrauger, J. S. (1990). The role of self-prediction in psychological assessment. In J. N. Butcher & C. D. Spielberger (Eds.), *Advances in personality assessment* (p. 46). Vol. 8. Hillsdale, N.J.: Erlbaum.

Osterhouse, R. A., & Brock, T. C. (1970). Distraction increases yielding to propaganda by inhibiting counterarguing. *Journal of Personality and Social Psychology, 15,* 344–358.

Ostrom, T. M., & Sedikides, C. (1992). Out-group homogeneity effects in natural and minimal groups. *Psychological Bulletin, 112,* 536–552.

O'Sullivan, L. F., & Vannier, S. A. (2013). Playing the field? Does actual or perceived relationship status of another influence ratings of physical attractiveness among young adults? *Canadian Journal of Behavioural Science, 45*(3), 210–219.

Ott-Holland, C. J., Huang, J. L., Ryan, A. M., Elizondo, F., & Wadlington, P. L. (2013). Culture and vocational interest: The moderating role of collectivism and gender egalitarianism. *Journal of Counseling Psychology, 60*(4), 569–581.

Ozer, E. M., & Bandura, A. (1990). Mechanisms governing empowerment effects: A self-efficacy analysis. *Journal of Personality and Social Psychology, 58,* 472–486.

Padgett, V. R. (1989). Predicting organizational violence: *An application of 11 powerful principles of obedience.* Paper presented at the American Psychological Association convention.

Page, R. (2003, September 22). Dying to kill us. *New York Times.*

Page, S. (1998). Accepting the gay person: Rental accommodation in the community. *Journal of Homosexuality, 36,* 31–40.

Page, S. (1999). Accommodating persons with AIDS: Acceptance and rejection in rental situation. *Journal of Applied Social Psychology, 29*(2), 260–262.

Page-Gould, E., Mendoza-Denton, R., & Tropp, L. R. (2008). With a little help from my cross-group friend: Reducing anxiety in intergroup contexts through cross-group friendship. *Journal of Personality and Social Psychology, 95,* 1080–1094.

Pak, A. W., Dion, K. L., & Dion, K. K. (1991). Social-psychological correlates of experienced discrimination: Test of the double jeopardy hypothesis. *International Journal of Intercultural Relations, 15,* 243–254.

Palmer, D. L. (1996). Determinants of Canadian attitudes toward immigration: More than just racism? *Canadian Journal of Behavioral Science, 28*(3), 180–192.

Palmer, E. L., & Dorr, A. (Eds.). (1980). *Children and the faces of television: Teaching, violence, selling.* New York, NY: Academic Press.

Pandey, J., Sinha, Y., Prakash, A., & Tripathi, R. C. (1982). Right-left political ideologies and attribution of the causes of poverty. *European Journal of Social Psychology, 12,* 327–331.

Panksepp, J. (2006). Emotional endophenotypes in evolutionary psychiatry. *Progress in Neuro-Psychopharmacology & Biological Psychiatry, 30,* 774–784.

Panksepp, J., & Panksepp, J. B. (2000). The seven sins of evolutionary psychology. *Evolution and Cognition, 6,* 108–131.

Papastamou, S., & Mugny, G. (1990). Synchronic consistency and psychologization in minority influence. *European Journal of Social Psychology, 20,* 85–98.

Paquette, G. (2004). Violence on Canadian television networks. *Canadian Child and Adolescent Psychiatry Review, 13,* 13–15.

Park, J. H., Schaller, M., & Crandall, C. S. (2007). Pathogen-avoidance mechanisms and the stigmatization of obese people. *Evolution and Human Behavior, 28,* 410–414

Parke, R. D., Berkowitz, L., Leyens, J. P., West, S. G., & Sebastian, J. (1977). Some effects of violent and nonviolent movies on the behavior of juvenile delinquents. In L. Berkowitz (Ed.), *Advances in experimental social psychology, Vol. 10.* New York, NY: Academic Press.

Parkin, A., & Mendelsohn, M. (2003). A new Canada: An identity shaped by diversity. *CRIC Papers, No. 11.* Retrieved from http://www.cric.ca.

Parks, J., Konopasky, R., Fleming, M. T., & Smith, S. M. (2005). *Giving 158 percent: How authors judge the amount and type of contribution to academic journal articles.* Poster presented at the 67th annual conference of the Canadian Psychology Association, Montreal.

Parliament, L., & Yarmey, A. D. (2002). Deception in eyewitness identification. *Criminal Justice and Behavior, 29*(6), 734–746.

Pascual-Leone, A., Singh, T., & Scoboria, A. (2010). Using deception ethically: Practical research guidelines for researchers and reviewers. *Canadian Psychology, 51,* 241–248.

Patrick, C. J., & Iacono, W. G. (1991). Validity of the control question polygraph test: The problem of sampling bias. *Journal of Applied Social Psychology, 76,* 229–238.

Patry, M. W., Stinson, V. & Smith, S. M. (2009). Supreme Court of Canada addresses admissibility of post-hypnosis witness evidence: R. *v.* Trochym (2007). *Canadian Psychology, 50,* 98–105.

Patry, M. W., Stinson, V., & Smith, S. M. (2006). CSI Effect: Is popular television transforming Canadian society? In J. Greenberg & C. Elliott (Eds.), *Communication in Question: Canadian Perspectives on Controversial Issues in Communication Studies,* 291–298. Scarborough: Thomson-Nelson.

Patterson, G. R., Chamberlain, P., & Reid, J. B. (1982). A comparative evaluation of parent training procedures. *Behavior Therapy, 13,* 638–650.

Patterson, G. R., Littman, R. A., & Bricker, W. (1967). Assertive behavior in children: A step toward a theory of aggression. *Monographs of the Society for Research in Child Development, 32,* (Serial No. 113), 5.

Patterson, J., & Kim, P. (1991). *The day America told the truth: What people really believe about everything that really matters.* Michigan, United States of America: Prentice Hall Press.

Patterson, T. E. (1980). *The role of the mass media in presidential campaigns: The lessons of the 1976 election. Items 1980, 34(2),* 25–30. New York, NY: Social Science Research Council.

Pavey, L., Greitemeyer, T., & Sparks, P. (2012). "I help because I want to, not because you tell me to": Empathy increases autonomously motivated helping. *Personality and Social Psychology Bulletin, 38*(5), 681–689.

Payne, B. K. (2001). Prejudice and perception: The role of automatic and controlled processes in misperceiving a weapon. *Journal of Personality and Social Psychology, 81,* 181–192.

Pearsall, M. J., Ellis, A. J., & Stein, J. H. (2009). Coping with challenge and hindrance stressors in teams: Behavioral, cognitive, and affective outcomes. *Organizational Behavior and Human Decision Processes, 109*(1), 18–28.

Pedersen, W. C., Gonzales, C., & Miller, N. (2000). The moderating effect of trivial triggering provocation on displaced aggression. *Journal of Personality and Social Psychology, 78,* 913–927.

Peetz, J., Wilson, A. E., & Strahan, E. J. (2009). So far away: The role of subjective temporal distance to future goals in motivation and behaviour. *Social Cognition, 27,* 475–495.

Pegalis, L. J., Shaffer, D. R., Bazzini, D. G., & Greenier, K. (1994). On the ability to elicit self-disclosure: Are there gender-based and contextual limitations on the opener effect? *Personality and Social Psychology Bulletin, 20,* 412–420.

Pelham, B. W., Koole, S. L., Hardin, C. D., Hetts, J. J., Seah, E., & DeHart, T. (2005). Gender moderates the relation between implicit and explicit self-esteem. *Journal of Experimental Social Psychology, 41,* 84–89.

Pennebaker, J. W. (1982). *The psychology of physical symptoms.* New York, NY: Springer-Verlag.

Penner, L. A., Dertke, M. C., & Achenbach, C. J. (1973). The "flash" system: A field study of altruism. *Journal of Applied Social Psychology, 3,* 362–370.

Penton-Voak, I. S., Jones, B. C., Little, A. C., Baker, S., Tiddeman, B., Burt, D. M., & Perrett, D. I. (2001). *Symmetry, sexual dimorphism in facial proportions and male facial attractiveness.* Proceedings of the Royal Society of London, 268, 1–7.

People. (2003, September 1). Nipped, tucked, talking, 102–111.

Peplau, L. A., & Gordon, S. L. (1985). Women and men in love: Gender differences in close heterosexual relationships. In V. E. O'Leary, R. K. Unger, & B. S. Wallston (Eds.), *Women, gender, and social psychology.* Hillsdale, NJ: Erlbaum.

Pereira, J. (2003, January 10). Just how far does First Amendment protection go? *Wall Street Journal,* Bl, B3.

Perkins, K. A., Parzynski, C., Mercincavage, M., Conklin, C. A., & Fonte, C. A. (2012). Is self-efficacy for smoking abstinence a cause of, or a reflection on, smoking behavior change? *Experimental and Clinical Psychopharmacology, 20*(1), 56–62.

Perloff, L. S. (1987). Social comparison and illusions of invulnerability. In C. R. Snyder & C. R. Ford (Eds.), *Coping with negative life events: Clinical and social psychological perspectives.* New York, NY: Plenum.

Perry, R. P., Stupnisky, R. H., Daniels, L. M., & Haynes, T. L. (2008). Attributional (explanatory) thinking about failure in new achievement settings. *European Journal of Psychology and Education, 23*(4), 459–475.

Pessin, J. (1933). The comparative effects of social and mechanical stimulation on memorizing. *American Journal of Psychology, 45,* 263–270.

Pessin, J., & Husband, R. W. (1933). Effects of social stimulation on human maze learning. *Journal of Abnormal and Social Psychology, 28,* 148–154.

Peters, E., Romer, D., Slovic, P., Jamieson, K. H., Whasfield, L., Mertz, C. K., & Carpenter, S. M. (2007). The impact and acceptability of Canadian-style cigarette warning labels among U.S. smokers and nonsmokers. *Nicotine and Tobacco Research, 9,* 473–481.

Peterson, B. E., Doty, R. M., & Winter, D. G. (1993). Authoritarianism and attitudes toward contemporary social issues. *Personality and Social Psychology Bulletin, 19,* 174–184.

Peterson, C., & Steen, T. A. (2002). Optimistic explanatory style. In C. R. Snyder & S. J. Lopez (Eds.), *Handbook of positive psychology* (pp. 244–256). London: Oxford University Press.

Peterson, C., Schwartz, S. M., & Seligman, M. E. P. (1981). Self-blame and depression symptoms. *Journal of Personality and Social Psychology, 41,* 253–259.

Petrocelli, J. V., Seta, C. E., & Seta, J. J. (2013). Dysfunctional counterfactual thinking: When simulating alternatives to reality impedes experiential learning. *Thinking & Reasoning, 19*(2), 205–230.

Petrocelli, J. V., Seta, C. E., Seta, J. J., Prince, L. B. (2012). "If only I could stop generating counterfactual thoughts": When counterfactual thinking interferes with academic performance. *Journal of Experimental Social Psychology, 48,* 1117–1123.

Petrocelli, J. V., Tormala, Z. L., & Rucker, D. D. (2007). Unpacking attitude certainty: Attitude clarity and attitude correctness. *Journal of Personality and Social Psychology, 92*(1), 30–41.

Pettigrew, T. F. (1958). Personality and socio-cultural factors in intergroup attitudes: A cross-national comparison. *Journal of Conflict Resolution, 2,* 29–42.

Pettigrew, T. F. (1988). *Advancing racial justice: Past lessons for future use.* Paper for the University of Alabama Conference: Opening Doors: An Appraisal of Race Relations in America.

Pettigrew, T. F. (1997). Generalized intergroup contact effects on prejudice. *Personality and Social Psychology Bulletin, 23,* 173–185.

Pettigrew, T. F. (1998). Intergroup contact theory. *Annual Review of Psychology, 49,* 65–85.

Pettigrew, T. F., & Meertens, R. W. (1995). Subtle and blatant prejudice in Western Europe. *European Journal of Social Psychology, 25,* 57–76.

Pettigrew, T. F., & Tropp, L. R. (2000). Does intergroup contact reduce prejudice: Recent meta-analytic findings. In S. Oskamp, (Ed.), *Reducing prejudice and discrimination.* Mahwah, NJ: Erlbaum, 93–114.

Pettigrew, T. F., & Tropp, L. R. (2006). A meta-analytic test of intergroup contact theory. *Journal of Personality and Social Psychology, 90*(5), 751–783.

Pettigrew, T. F., & Tropp, L. R. (2008). How does intergroup contact reduce prejudice? Meta-analytic tests of three mediators. *European Journal of Social Psychology, 38,* 922–934.

Pettigrew, T. F., Wagner, U., & Christ, O. (2008). Who opposes immigration? Comparing German with North American findings. *DuBois Review, 4,* 19–40.

Petty, R. E., & Cacioppo, J. T. (1986). *Communication and persuasion: Central and peripheral routes to attitude change.* New York, NY: Springer-Verlag.

Petty, R. E., & Krosnick, J. A. (Eds.). (1995). *Attitude strength: Antecedents and consequences.* Hillsdale, NJ: Erlbaum.

Petty, R. E., Schumann, D. W., Richman, S. A., & Strathman, A. J. (1993). Positive mood and persuasion: Different roles for affect under high and low elaboration conditions. *Journal of Personality and Social Psychology, 64,* 5–20.

Petty, R. E., & Wegener, D. T. (1999). The elaboration likelihood model: Current status and controversies. In S. Chaiken & Y. Trope (Eds.), *Dual-process theories in social psychology* (pp. 41–72). New York, NY: Guilford Press.

Petty, R. E., Wheeler, S. C., & Bizer, G. Y. (2000). Attitude functions and persuasion: An elaboration likelihood approach to matched versus mismatched messages. In G. R. Maio & J. M. Olson (Eds.), *Why we evaluate: Functions of attitudes* (pp. 133–162). Mahwah, NJ: Erlbaum.

Pew. (2000). *Tracking online life: How women use the Internet to cultivate relationships with family and friends.* Retrieved from http://www.pewinternet.org/Press-Releases/2000/Tracking-online-life-How-women-use-the-Internet-to-cultivate-relationships-with-family-and-friends.aspx.

Pew. (2003). *Views of a changing world 2003.* The Pew Global Attitudes Project. Washington, DC: Pew Research Center for the People and the Press (people-press.org/reports/pdf/185.pdf).

Pew. (2006). *America's immigration quandary.* Pew Research Center (http://www.people-press.org).

Pew. (2007). *World publics welcome global trade—but not immigration.* Pew Global Attitudes Survey. Retrieved from http://pewglobal.org/reports/pdf/258.pdf.

Pew. (2008). *Public attitudes toward the war in Iraq: 2003–2008.* Retrieved from http://pewresearch.org.

Pew. (2010). Gender equality universally embraced, but inequalities acknowledged. Washington, DC: Pew Research Center.

Pew. (2013). *5 facts about online dating.* Pew Research Center (http://www.people-press.org).

Phelan, S., Hill, J. O., Lang, W., Dibello, J. R., & Wing, R. R. (2003). Recovery from relapse among successful weight maintainers. *American Journal of Clinical Nutrition, 78,* 1079–1084.

Phillips, S. T., & Ziller, R. C. (1997). Toward a theory and measure of the nature of nonprejudice. *Journal of Personality and Social Psychology, 72,* 420–434.

Pilkington, N. W., & D'Augelli, A. R. (1995). Victimization of lesbian, gay, and bisexual youth in community settings. *Journal of Community Psychology, 23,* 34–56.

Pingitore, R., Dugoni, B. L., Tindale, R. S., & Spring, B. (1994). Bias against overweight job applicants in a simulated employment interview. *Journal of Applied Psychology, 79,* 909–917.

Pinker, S. (1997). *How the mind works.* New York, NY: Norton.

Plaks, J. E., & Higgins, E. T. (2000). Pragmatic use of stereotyping in teamwork: Social loafing and compensation as a function of inferred partner-situation fit. *Journal of Personality and Social Psychology, 79,* 962–974.

Platz, S. J., & Hosch, H. M. (1988). Cross-racial/ethnic eyewitnesses identification: A field study. *Journal of Applied Social Psychology, 18,* 972–984.

Pliner, P., Hart, H., Kohl, J., & Saari, D. (1974). Compliance without pressure: Some further data on the foot-in-the-door technique. *Journal of Experimental Social Psychology, 10,* 17–22.

Pomerleau, O. F., & Rodin, J. (1986). Behavioral medicine and health psychology. In S. L. Garfield & A. E. Bergin (Eds.), *Handbook of psychotherapy and behavior change* (3rd ed.). New York, NY: Wiley.

Poore, A. G., Gagne, F., Barlow, K. M., Lydon, J. E., Taylor, D. M., & Wright, S. C. (2002). Contact and the personal/group discrimination discrepancy in an Inuit community. *Journal of Psychology: Interdisciplinary and Applied, 136*(4), 371–382.

Post, J. M. (2005). The new face of terrorism: Socio-cultural foundations of contemporary terrorism. *Behavioral Sciences and the Law, 23,* 238–259.

Postmes, T., & Spears, R. (1998). Deindividuation and antinormative behavior: A meta-analysis. *Psychological Bulletin, 123,* 238–259.

Potter, T., Corneille, O., Ruys, K. I., & Rhodes, G. (2006). S/he's just another pretty face: A multidimensional scaling approach to face attractiveness and variability. *Psychonomic Bulletin & Review, 14,* 368–372.

Poulsen, F. O., Holman, T. B., Busby, D. M., & Carroll, J. S. (2013). Physical attraction, attachment styles, and dating development. *Journal of Social and Personal Relationships, 30*(3), 301–319.

Pratkanis, A. R., & Aronson, E. (1992). *Age of propaganda: Everyday use and abuse of persuasion.* New York: W. H. Freeman.

Pratkanis, A. R., Greenwald, A. G., Leippe, M. R., & Baumgardner, M. H. (1988). In search of reliable persuasion effects: III. The sleeper effect is dead. Long live the sleeper effect. *Journal of Personality and Social Psychology, 54,* 203–218.

Pratt, A., & Thompson, S. K. (2008). Chivalry, "race" and discretion at the Canadian border. *The British Journal of Criminology, 48*(5), 620–640.

Pratto, F. (1996). Sexual politics: The gender gap in the bedroom, the cupboard, and the cabinet. In D. M. Buss & N. M. Malamuth (Eds.), *Sex, power, conflict: Evolutionary and feminist perspectives.* New York, NY: Oxford University Press.

Pratto, F., Liu, J. H., Levin, S., Sidanius, J., Shih, M., Bachrach, H., & Hegarty, P. (2000). Social dominance orientation and the legitimization of inequality across cultures. *Journal of Cross-Cultural Psychology, 31,* 369–409.

Pratto, F., Sidanius, J., Stallworth, L. M., & Malle, B. F. (1994). Social dominance orientation: A personality variable predicting social and political attitudes. *Journal of Personality and Social Psychology, 67,* 741–763.

Prentice-Dunn, S., & Rogers, R. W. (1989). Deindividuation and the self-regulation of behavior. In P. B. Paulus (Ed.), *Psychology of group influence* (2nd ed.). Hillsdale, NJ: Erlbaum.

Price, G. H., Dabbs, J. M., Jr., Clower, B. J., & Resin, R. P. (1974). *At first glance—Or, is physical attractiveness more than skin deep?* Paper presented at the Eastern Psychological Association convention. Cited by K. L. Dion & K. K. Dion (1979). Personality and behavioral correlates of romantic love. In M. Cook & G. Wilson (Eds.), *Love and attraction.* Oxford: Pergamon.

Priester, J. R., & Petty, R. E. (1995). Source attributions and persuasion: Perceived honesty as a determinant of message scrutiny. *Personality and Social Psychology Bulletin, 21,* 637–654.

Pritchard, I. L. (1998). *The effects of rap music on aggressive attitudes toward women.* Master's thesis, Humboldt State University.

Prochaska, J. O., DiClemente, C. C., & Norcross, J. C. (1992). In search of how people change: Applications to addictive behaviors. *American Psychologist, 47,* 1102–1114.

Prochaska, J. O., & Norcross, J. C. (2007). *Systems of Psychotherapy* (6th ed.). Belmont, CA: Wadsworth.

Prochaska, J. O., Norcross, J. C., & DiClemente, C. C. (1994). *Changing for good: A revolutionary six-stage program for overcoming bad habits and moving your life positively forward.* New York, NY: Avon Books.

Prohaska, V. (1994). "I know I'll get an A": Confident overestimation of final course grades. *Teaching of Psychology, 21,* 141–143.

Pronin, E., & Ross, L. (2006). Temporal differences in trait self-ascription: When the self is seen as an other. *Attitudes and Social Cognition. 90*(2), 197–209.

Provine, R. R., Spencer, R. J., & Mandell, D. L. (2007). Emotional expression online emoticons punctuate website text messages. *Journal of Language and Social Psychology, 26*(3), 299–307.

Pruitt, D. G. (1998). Social conflict. In D. Gilbert, S. T. Fiske, & G. Lindzey (Eds.), *Handbook of social psychology,* (4th ed.). New York, NY: McGraw-Hill.

Pruitt, D. G., & Kimmel, M. J. (1977). Twenty years of experimental gaming: Critique, synthesis, and suggestions for the future. *Annual Review of Psychology, 28,* 363–392.

Pruitt, D. G., & Rubin, J. Z. (1986). *Social conflict.* San Francisco, CA: Random House.

Pryor, J. B. (1987). Sexual harassment proclivities in men. *Sex Roles, 17,* 269–290.

Pryor, J. B., & Reeder, G. D. (1993). *The social psychology of HIV infection.* Hillsdale, NJ: Erlbaum.

Pryor, J. H., Hurtado, S., Saenz, V. B., Lindholm, J. A., Korn, W. S., & Mahoney, K. M. (2005). *The American freshman: National norms for fall 2005.* Los Angeles: Higher Education Institute, UCLA.

Public Health Agency of Canada. (2002). (http://www.phac-aspc .gc.ca).

Public Health Agency of Canada. (2002). *A report on mental illness.* Retrieved from http://www.phac-aspc.gc.ca/publicat/miic-mmac/sum-eng.php.

Public Opinion. (1984, August/September). *Vanity Fair, 22.*

Puente, M., & Castaneda, C. J. (1997). Rage starting to rule the nation's roads. *USA Today.* Retrieved from http://www .dialog.carl.org:2030/sgibin/cw.htm.

Putnam, R. (2000). *Bowling alone.* New York: Simon & Schuster.

Pyszczynski, T., Hamilton, J. C., Greenberg, J. & Becker, S.E . (1991). Self-awareness and psychological dysfunction. In C. R. Snyder & D. O. Forsyth (Eds.), *Handbook of social and clinical psychology: The health perspective.* New York, NY: Pergamon.

Qirko, H. N. (2004). Fictive kin and suicide terrorism. *Science, 304,* 49–50.

R. v. Hart. (2014). SCC 52.

Raine, A. (2008). From genes to brain to antisocial behavior. *Current Directions in Psychological Science, 17,* 323–328.

Raine, A., Lencz, T., Bihrle, S., LaCasse, L., & Colletti, P. (2000). Reduced prefrontal gray matter volume and reduced autonomic activity in antisocial personality disorder. *Archives of General Psychiatry, 57,* 119–127.

Raine, A., Stoddard, J., Bihrle, S., & Buchsbaum, M. (1998). Prefrontal glucose deficits in murderers lacking psychosocial deprivation. *Neuropsychiatry, Neuropsychology, & Behavioral Neurology, 11,* 1–7.

Raine. A. (2005). The interaction of biological and social measure in the explanation of antisocial and violent behavior. In D. M. Stoff & E. J. Susman (Eds.), *Developmental psychobiology of aggression.* New York: Cambridge University Press.

Rajecki, D. W., Bledsoe, S. B., & Rasmussen, J. L. (1991). Successful personal ads: Gender differences and similarities in offers, stipulations, and outcomes. *Basic and Applied Social Psychology, 12,* 457–469.

Rank, S. G., & Jacobson, C. K. (1977). Hospital nurses' compliance with medication overdose orders: A failure to replicate. *Journal of Health and Social Behavior, 18,* 188–193.

Rapoport, A. (1960). *Fights, games, and debates.* Ann Arbor, MI: University of Michigan Press.

Rassin, E., Eerland, A., & Kuijpers, I. (2010). Let's find the evidence: An analogue study of confirmation bias in criminal investigations. *Journal of Investigative Psychology & Offender Profiling, 7*(3), 231–246.

Ratliff, E. (2011). Taming the wild. *National Geographic,* March 2011 issue.

Regan, D. T., & Cheng, J. B. (1973). Distraction and attitude change: A resolution. *Journal of Experimental Social Psychology, 9,* 138–147.

Reid, A. (2013). Half of Americans would allow same-sex marriages. Retrieved from http://www.angusreidglobal.com/polls/half-of-americans-would-allow-same-sex-marriage/.

Reifman, A. S., Larrick, R. P., & Fein, S. (1991). Temper and temperature on the diamond: The heat-aggression relationship in major league baseball. *Personality and Social Psychology Bulletin, 17,* 580–585.

Reis, H. T., Nezlek, J., & Wheeler, L. (1980). Physical attractiveness in social interaction. *Journal of Personality and Social Psychology, 38,* 604–617.

Reis, H. T., & Shaver, P. (1988). Intimacy as an interpersonal process. In S. Duck (Ed.), *Handbook of personal relationships: Theory, relationships and interventions.* Chichester, England: Wiley.

Reis, H. T., Wheeler, L., Spiegel, N., Kernis, M. H., Nezlek, J., & Perri, M. (1982). Physical attractiveness in social interaction: II. Why does appearance affect social experience? *Journal of Personality and Social Psychology, 43,* 979–996.

Ressler, R. K., Burgess, A. W., & Douglas, J. E. (1988). *Sexual homicide patterns.* Boston, MA: Lexington Books.

Rhodes, G. (2006). The evolutionary psychology of facial beauty. *Annual Review of Psychology, 57,* 199–226.

Rhodes, G., Sumich, A., & Byatt, G. (1999). Are average facial configurations attractive only because of their symmetry? *Psychological Science, 10,* 52–58.

Rholes, W. S., Newman, L. S., & Ruble, D. N. (1990). Understanding self and other: Developmental and motivational aspects of perceiving persons in terms of invariant dispositions. In E. T. Higgins & R. M. Sorrentino (Eds.), *Handbook of motivation and cognition: Foundations of social behavior, Vol. 2.* New York, NY: Guilford Press.

Rice, B. (1985, September). Performance review: The job nobody likes. *Psychology Today,* 30–36.

Rich, F. (2001, May 20). Naked capitalists: There's no business like porn business. *New York Times* (http://www.nytimes.com).

Riek, B. M., Mania, E. W., & Gaertner, S. L. (2006). Intergroup threat and outgroup attitudes: A meta-analytic review. *Personality and Social Psychology Review, 10,* 3336–353.

Riordan, C. A. (1980). *Effects of admission of influence on attributions and attraction.* Paper presented at the American Psychological Association convention.

Robins, R. W., Mendelsohn, G. A., Connell, J. B., & Kwan, V. S. Y. (2004). Do people agree about the causes of behavior? A social relations analysis of behavior ratings and causal attributions. *Journal of Personality and Social Psychology, 86,* 334–344.

Robins, R. W., Spranca, M. D., & Mendelsohn, G. A. (1996). The actor-observer effect revisited: Effects of individual differences and repeated social interactions on actor and observer attributions. *Journal of Personality and Social Psychology, 71,* 375–389.

Robinson, M. D., & Ryff, C. D. (1999). The role of self-deception in perceptions of past, present, and future happiness. *Personality and Social Psychology Bulletin, 25,* 595–606.

Robinson, M. S., & Alloy, L. B. (2003). Negative cognitive styles and stress-reactive rumination interact to predict depression: A prospective study. *Cognitive Therapy and Research, 27*(3), 275–292.

Robinson, R. J., Keltner, D., Ward, A., & Ross, L. (1995). Actual versus assumed differences in construal: "Naive realism" in intergroup perception and conflict. *Journal of Personality and Social Psychology, 68,* 404–417.

Robinson, T. N., Wilde, M. L., Navracruz, L. C., Haydel, F., & Varady, A. (2001). Effects of reducing children's television and video game use on aggressive behavior. *Archives of Pediatric and Adolescent Medicine, 155,* 17–23.

Roehling, M. V. (2000). Weight-based discrimination in employment: Psychological and legal aspects. *Personnel Psychology, 52,* 969–1016.

Roehling, M. V., Roehling, P. V., & Odland, I. M. (2008). Investigating the validity of stereotypes about overweight employees. *Group and Organization Management, 23,* 392–424.

Roehling, P. V., Roehling, M. V., Vandlen, J. D., Blazek, J., & Guy, W. C. (2009). Weight discrimination and the glass ceiling effect among top U.S. male and female CEOs. *Equal Opportunities International, 28,* 179–196.

Roese, N. J., & Olson, J. M. (1996). Counterfactuals, causal attributions, and the hindsight bias: A conceptual integration. *Journal of Experimental Social Psychology, 32,* 197–227.

Rogers, C. R. (1980). *A way of being.* Boston, MA: Houghton Mifflin.

Rogers, R. W. (1975). A protection motivation theory of fear appeals and attitude change. *The Journal of Psychology, 91,* 93–114.

Rohmann, E., Bierhoff, H. W., & Schmohr, M. (2011). Narcissism and perceived inequality in attractiveness in romantic relationships. *European Psychologist, 16*(4), 295–302.

Rokeach, M., & Mezei, L. (1966). Race and shared beliefs as factors in social choice. *Science, 151,* 167–172.

Rose, J. P., Endo, Y., Windschitl, P. D., & Suls, J. (2008). Cultural differences in unrealistic optimism and pessimism: The role of egocentrism and direct cersus indirect comparison measures. *Personality and Social Bulletin, 34*(9), 1236–1248.

Rosenblatt, P. C. (1974). Cross-cultural perspectives on attraction. In T. L. Huston (Ed.). *Foundations of interpersonal attraction* (pp. 79–99). New York, NY: Academic Press.

Rosenfeld, J. P., Soskins, M., Bosh, G., & Ryan, A. (2004). Simple, effective countermeasures to P300-based tests of detection of concealed information. *Psychophysiology, 41,* 205–219.

Rosenfeld, J. P., Sweet, J. L., Chuang, J., Ellwanger, J., & Song, L. (1996). Detection of simulated malingering using forced choice recognition enhanced with event related potential recording. *Neurophysiology, 120,* 163–179.

Rosenthal, R. (1985). From unconscious experimenter bias to teacher expectancy effects. In J. B. Dusek, V. C. Hall, & W. J. Meyer (Eds.), *Teacher expectancies.* Hillsdale, NJ: Erlbaum.

Rosenthal, R. (1991). Teacher expectancy effects: A brief update 25 years after the Pygmalion experiment. *Journal of Research in Education, 1,* 3–12.

Rosenthal, R. (2002). Covert communication in classrooms, clinics, courtrooms, and cubicles. *American Psychologist, 57,* 839–849.

Rosenthal, R. (2003). Covert communication in laboratories, classrooms, and the truly real world. *Current Directions in Psychological Science, 12,* 151–154.

Rosenthal, R. (2006). Applying psychological research on interpersonal expectations and covert communication in classrooms, clinics, corporations, and courtrooms. In S. I. Donaldson, D. E. Berger, & K. Pezdek (Eds.), *Applied psychology: New frontiers and rewarding careers.* Mahwah, NJ: Erlbaum.

Rosenthal, R. (2008). Introduction, methods, results, discussion: The story of a career. In R. Levin, A. Rodriques, & L. Zelezny (Eds.), *Journeys in social psychology: Looking back to inspire the future.* New York: Psychology Press.

Ross, L. (1977). The intuitive psychologist and his shortcomings: Distortions in the attribution process. In L. Berkowitz (Ed.), *Advances in experimental social psychology, Vol. 10.* New York, NY: Academic Press.

Ross, L. (1981). The "intuitive scientist" formulation and its developmental implications. In J. H. Havell & L. Ross (Eds.), *Social cognitive development: Frontiers and possible futures.* Cambridge: Cambridge University Press.

Ross, L. (1988). Situationist perspectives on the obedience experiments. *Contemporary Psychology, 33,* 101–104.

Ross, L., & Ward, A. (1995). Psychological barriers to dispute resolution. In M. P. Zanna (Ed.), *Advances in experimental social psychology, Vol. 27.* San Diego, CA: Academic Press.

Ross, L., Amabile, T. M., & Steinmetz, J. L. (1977). Social roles, social control, and biases in social-perception processes. *Journal of Personality and Social Psychology, 35,* 485–494.

Ross, M., & Newby-Clark, I. R. (1998). Construing the past and future. *Social Cognition, 16*(1), 133–150.

Ross, M., & Sicoly, F. (1979). Egocentric biases in availability and attribution. *Journal of Personality and Social Psychology, 37,* 322–336.

Ross, M., Hildy, S., Siddiqui, A., Ram, A., & Ward, L. (2004). Perspectives on self and other children's representations of sibling conflict. *International Journal of Behavioral Development, 128,* 37–47.

Roszell, P., Kennedy, D., & Grabb, E. (1990). Physical attractiveness and income attainment among Canadians. *Journal of Psychology, 123,* 547–559.

Rothman, A. J., & Salovey, P. (1997). Shaping perceptions to motivate healthy behavior: The role of message framing. *Psychological Bulletin, 121*(1), 3–19.

Rotton, J., & Frey, J. (1985). Air pollution, weather, and violent crimes: Concomitant time-series analysis of archival data. *Journal of Personality and Social Psychology, 49,* 1207–1220.

Rouhana, N. N., & Bar-Tal, D. (1998). Psychological dynamics of intractable ethnonational conflicts: The Israeli-Palestinian case. *American Psychologist, 53,* 761–770.

Rowe, D. C., Almeida, D. M., & Jacobson, K. C. (1999). School context and genetic influences on aggression in adolescence. *Psychological Science, 10,* 277–280.

Ruback, R. B., Carr, T. S., & Hoper, C. H. (1986). Perceived control in prison: Its relation to reported crowding, stress, and symptoms. *Journal of Applied Social Psychology, 16,* 375–386.

Rubin, J. Z. (1986). *Can we negotiate with terrorists?: Some answers from psychology.* Paper presented at the American Psychological Association convention.

Rubin, Z. (1973). *Liking and loving: An invitation to social psychology.* London: Holt, Rinehart & Winston.

Rui, J., & Stefanone, M. A. (2013). Strategic self-presentation online: A cross-cultural study. *Computers in Human Behavior, 29*(1), 110–118.

Ruiter, R. A. C., Kok, G., Verplanken, B., & Brug, J. (2001). Evoked fear and effects of appeals on attitudes to performing breast self-examination: An information-processing perspective. *Health Education Research, 16,* 307–319.

Rule, B. G., Taylor, B. R., & Dobbs, A. R. (1987). Priming effects of heat on aggressive thoughts. *Social Cognition, 5,* 131–143.

Rusbult, C. E., Johnson, D. J., & Morrow, G. D. (1986). Impact of couple patterns of problem solving on distress and nondistress in dating relationships. *Journal of Personality and Social Psychology, 50,* 744–753.

Rusbult, C. E., Martz, J. M., & Agnew, C. R. (1998). The investment model scale: Measuring commitment level, satisfaction level, quality of alternatives, and investment size. *Personal Relationships, 5,* 357–391.

Rusbult, C. E., Morrow, G. D., & Johnson, D. J. (1987). Self-esteem and problem-solving behaviour in close relationships. *British Journal of Social Psychology, 26,* 293–303.

Rusbult, C. E., Olsen, N., Davis, J. L., & Hannon, P. A. (2004). Commitment and Relationship Maintenance Mechanisms. In H. T. Reis, C. E. Rusbult, H. T. Reis, C. E. Rusbult (Eds.), *Close relationships: Key readings* (pp. 287–303). Philadelphia, PA: Taylor & Francis.

Rusbult, C. E., Verette, J., Whitney, G. A., Slovik, L. F., & Lipkus, I. (1991). Accommodation processes in close relationships: Theory and preliminary empirical evidence. *Journal of Personality and Social Psychology, 60,* 53–78.

Rushton, J. P., Fulker, D. W., Neale, M. C., Nias, D. K. B., & Eysenck, H. J. (1986). Altruism and aggression: The heritability of individual differences. *Journal of Personality and Social Psychology, 50,* 1192–1198.

Russell, B. (1930/1980). *The conquest of happiness.* London: Unwin Paperbacks.

Russell, G. W. (1983). Psychological issues in sports aggression. In J. H. Goldstein (Ed.), *Sports violence.* New York, NY: Springer-Verlag.

Russell, G. W. (1992). Response of the macho male to viewing a combatant sport. *Journal of Social Behavior and Personality, 7,* 631–638.

Russo, J. E., & Schoemaker, P. J. (1989). *Decision traps: The ten barriers to brilliant decision-making and how to overcome them.* New York, NY: Simon & Schuster

Ruthig, J. C., Chipperfield, J. G., Perry, R. P., N ewall, N. E., & Swift, A. (2007). Comparative risk and perceived control: Implications for psychological and physical well-being among older adults. *The Journal of Social Psychology, 147*(4), 345–369.

Ryan, R. (1999, February 2). Quoted by A. Kohn, In pursuit of affluence, at a high price. *New York Times* (via http://www.nytimes.com).

Saad, L. (2003, April 22). Giving global warming the cold shoulder. *The Gallup Organization* (http://www.gallup.com).

Sacks, C. H., & Bugental, D. P. (1987). Attributions as moderators of affective and behavioral responses to social failure. *Journal of Personality and Social Psychology, 53,* 939–947.

Saewyc, E. M., Skay, C. L., Pettingell, S. L., Reis, E. A., Bearinger, L., Resnick, M., et al. (2006). Hazards of stigma: The sexual and physical abuse of gay, lesbian, and bisexual adolescents in the United States and Canada. *Child Welfare, 85*(2), 195–213.

Sagarin, B. J., Rhoads, K. V. L., & Cialdini, R. B. (1998). Deceiver's distrust: Denigration as a consequence of undiscovered deception. *Personality and Social Psychology Bulletin, 24,* 1167–1176.

Sageman, M. (2004). *Understanding terror networks.* Philadelphia, PA: University of Pennsylvania Press.

Saks, M. J. (1992). Do we really know anything about the behavior of the tort litigation system—and why not? *University of Pennsylvania Law Review, 140*(4), 1147–1292.

Sales, S. M. (1973). Threat as a factor in authoritarianism: An analysis of archival data. *Journal of Personality and Social Psychology, 28,* 44–57.

Salganik, M. J., Dodds, P. S., & Watts, D. J. (2006). Experimental study of inequality and unpredictability in an artificial cultural market. *Science, 311,* 854–956.

Salonia, A., Nappi, R. E., Pontillo, M., Daverio, R., Smeraldi, A., Briganti, A., Fabbri, F., et al. (2005). Menstrual cycle-related changes in plasma oxytocin are relevant to normal sexual function in healthy women. *Hormones and Behavior, 47,* 164–169.

Salovey, P., & Wegener, D. T. (2003). Communicating about health: Message framing, persuasion and health behavior. In Suls, J., & Wallston, K. A. (Eds.), *Social psychological foundations of health and illness* (pp. 54–81). Maiden, MA: Blackwell Publishing.

Sandberg, G. G., Jackson, T. L., & Petretic-Jackson, P. (1985). *Sexual aggression and courtship violence in dating relationships.* Paper presented at the Midwestern Psychological Association convention.

Sande, G. N., Goethals, G. R., & Radloff, C. E. (1988). Perceiving one's own traits and others': The multifaceted self. *Journal of Personality and Social Psychology, 54,* 13–20.

Sanders, G. S. (1981a). Driven by distraction: An integrative review of social facilitation and theory and research. *Journal of Experimental Social Psychology, 17,* 227–251.

Sanders, G. S. (1981b). Toward a comprehensive account of social facilitation: Distraction/conflict does not mean theoretical conflict. *Journal of Experimental Social Psychology, 17,* 262–265.

Sanders, G. S., Baron, R. S., & Moore, D. L. (1978). Distraction and social comparison as mediators of social facilitation effects. *Journal of Experimental Social Psychology, 14,* 291–303.

Sanitioso, R., Kunda, Z., & Fong, G. T. (1990). Motivated recruitment of autobiographical memories. *Journal of Personality and Social Psychology, 59,* 229–241.

Sarnoff, I., & Sarnoff, S. (1989). *Love-centered marriage in a self-centered world.* New York, NY: Hemisphere.

Sartre, J. P. (1946/1948). *Anti-Semite and Jew.* New York, NY: Schocken Books.

Sassenburg, K., Moskowitz, G. B., Jacoby, J., & Hansen, N. (2007). The carry-over effect of competition: The impact of competition on prejudice towards uninvolved outgroups. *Journal of Experimental Social Psychology, 43,* 529–538.

Satterfield, A. T., & Muehlenhard, C. L. (1997). Shaken confidence: The effects of an authority figure's flirtatiousness on women's and men's self-rated creativity. *Psychology of Women Quarterly, 21,* 395–416.

Satzewich, V., & Shaffir, W. (2009). Racism versus professionalism: Claims and counter-claims about racial profiling. *Canadian Journal of Criminology and Criminal Justice, 51*(2), 199–226.

Savitsky, K., Epley, N., & Gilovich, T. (2001). Do others judge us as harshly as we think? Overestimating the impact of our failures, shortcomings, and mishaps. *Journal of Personality and Social Psychology, 81,* 44–56.

Sax, L. J., Astin, A. W., Korn, W. S., & Mahoney, K. M. (1999). *The American freshman: National norms for Fall, 1999.* Los Angeles, CA: Higher Education Research Institute, UCLA.

Sax, L. J., Lindholm, J. A., Astin, A. W., Korn, W. S., & Mahoney, K. M. (2002). *The American freshman: National norms for Fall, 2002.* Los Angeles: Cooperative Institutional Research Program, UCLA.

Scambler, G. (1984). Perceiving and coping with stigmatizing illness. In R. Fitzpatrick, J. Hinton, S. Newman, G. Scrambler, & J. Thompson (Eds.), *The experience of illness* (pp. 203–226). London: Tavistock Publications.

Schachter, S. (1951). Deviation, rejection and communication. *Journal of Abnormal and Social Psychology, 46,* 190–207.

Schachter, S., & Singer, J. E. (1962). Cognitive, social and physiological determinants of emotional state. *Psychological Review, 69,* 379–399.

Schafer, R. B., & Keith, P. M. (1980). Equity and depression among married couples. *Social Psychology Quarterly, 43,* 430–435.

Schaffner, P. E., Wandersman, A., & Stang, D. (1981). Candidate name exposure and voting: Two field studies. *Basic and Applied Social Psychology, 2,* 195–203.

Schaller, M., & Cialdini, R. B. (1988). The economics of empathetic helping: Support for a mood management motive. *Journal of Experimental Social Psychology, 24,* 163–181.

Schaller, M., Miller, G. E., Gervais, W. M., Yager, S., & Chem, E. (2010). Mere visual perception of other people's disease symptoms facilitates a more aggressive immune response. *Psychological Science, 21*(5), 649–652.

Scheck, B., Neufeld, P., & Dwyer, J. (2001). *Actual innocence.* Colchester: Signet Publishing.

Scheier, M. F., & Carver, C. S. (1992). Effects of optimism on psychological and physical well-being: Theoretical overview and empirical update. *Cognitive Therapy and Research, 16,* 201–228.

Schiffenbauer, A., & Schiavo, R. S. (1976). Physical distance and attraction: An intensification effect. *Journal of Experimental Social Psychology, 12,* 274–282.

Schimel, J., Arndt, J., Pyszczynski, T., & Greenberg, J. (2001). Being accepted for who we are: Evidence that social validation of the intrinsic self reduces general defensiveness. *Journal of Personality and Social Psychology, 80,* 35–52.

Schimel, J., Pyszczynski, T., Greenberg, J., O'Mahen, H., & Arndt, J. (2000). Running from the shadow: Psychological distancing from others to deny characteristics people fear in themselves. *Journal of Personality and Social Psychology, 78,* 446–462.

Schimel, J., Simon, L., Greenberg, J., Pyszczynski, T., Solomon, S., & Waxmonsky, J. (1999). Stereotypes and terror management: Evidence that mortality salience enhances stereotypic thinking and preferences. *Journal of Personality and Social Psychology, 77,* 905–926.

Schimmack, U., Oishi, S., & Diener, E. (2005). Individualism: A valid and important dimension of cultural differences between nations. *Personality and Social Psychology Review, 9,* 17–31.

Schkade, D., & Sunstein, C. (2003, June 11). Judging by where you sit. *New York Times* (http://www.nytimes.com).

Schlosser, E. (2003, March 10). Empire of the obscene. *New Yorker,* 61–71.

Schmader, T., & Johns, M. (2003). Converging evidence that stereotype threat reduces working memory capacity. *Journal of Personality and Social Psychology, 85,* 440–451.

Schmitt, D. P. (2003). Universal sex differences in the desire for sexual variety: Tests from 52 nations, 6 continents, and 13 islands. *Journal of Personality and Social Psychology, 85,* 85–104.

Schmitt, D. P., et al. (2004). Patterns and universals of adult romantic attachment across 62 cultural regions: Are models of self and of other pancultural constructs? *Journal of Cross-Cultural Psychology, 35,* 367–402.

Schoenfeld, B. (1995, May 14). The loneliness of being white. *New York Times Magazine,* 34–37.

Schor, J. B. (1998). *The overworked American.* New York, NY: Basic Books.

Schumann, A., John, U., Rumpf, H., Hapke, U., & Meyer, C. (2006). Changes in the "stages of change" as outcome measures of a smoking cessation intervention: A randomized control trial. *Preventive Medicine: An International Journal Devoted to Practice and Theory, 43*(2), 101–106.

Schwartz, B. (2004). *The tyranny of choice.* New York, NY: Ecco/HarperCollins.

Schwartz, S. H., & Gottlieb, A. (1981). Participants' post-experimental reactions and the ethics of bystander research. *Journal of Experimental Social Psychology, 17,* 396–407.

Schwarz, N., Bless, H., & Bonner, G. (1991). Mood and persuasion: Affective states influence the processing of persuasive communications. In M. Zanna (Ed.), *Advances in experimental social psychology, Vol. 24.* New York, NY: Academic Press.

Schweinle, W. E., William, I., & Bernstein, I. H. (2002). Empathic inaccuracy in husband to wife aggression: The overattribution bias. *Personal Relationships, 9,* 141–158.

Sears, D. O. (1979). *Life stage effects upon attitude change, especially among the elderly.* Manuscript prepared for Workshop on the Elderly of the Future, Committee on Aging, National Research Council, Annapolis, MD, May 3–5.

Sears, D. O. (1986). College sophomores in the laboratory: Influences of a narrow data base on social psychology's view of human nature. *Journal of Personality and Social Psychology, 51,* 515–530.

Sedikides, C. (1993). Assessment, enhancement, and verification determinants of the self-evaluation process. *Journal of Personality and Social Psychology, 65,* 317–338.

Segall, M. H., Dasen, P. R., Berry, J. W., & Poortinga, Y. H. (1990). Human behavior in global perspective: An introduction to cross-cultural psychology. New York, NY: Pergamon.

Seibt, B., & Forster, J. (2004). Stereotype threat and performance: How self-stereotypes influence pro cessing by inducing regulatory foci. *Journal of Personality and Social Psychology, 87,* 38–56.

Seligman, M. E. P. (1975). *Helplessness: On depression, development and death.* San Francisco, CA: W. H. Freeman.

Seligman, M. E. P. (1991). *Learned optimism.* New York, NY: Knopf.

Seligman, M. E. P. (1992). Power and powerlessness: Comments on "Cognates of personal control." *Applied and Preventative Psychology, 1,* 119–120.

Seligman, M. E. P. (1998). The prediction and prevention of depression. In D. K. Routh & R. J. DeRubeis (Eds.), *The science of clinical psychology: Accomplishments and future directions.* Washington, DC: American Psychological Association.

Seligman, M. E. P. (2002). *Authentic happiness: Using the new positive psychology to realize your potential for lasting fulfillment.* New York, NY: Free Press.

Sell, R. L., Wells, J. A., & Wypij, D. (1995). The prevalence of homosexual behavior and attraction in the United States, the United Kingdom and France: Results of national population-based samples. *Archives of Sexual Behavior, 24*(3), 235–248.

Selye, H. (1976). *Stress in health and disease.* Woburn, MA: Butterworth.

Sentyrz, S. M., & Bushman, B. J. (1998). Mirror, mirror, on the wall, who's the thinnest one of all? Effects of self-awareness on consumption of fatty, reduced-fat, and fat-free products. *Journal of Applied Psychology, 83,* 944–949.

Seta, J. J. (1982). The impact of comparison processes on coactors' task performance. *Journal of Personality and Social Psychology, 42,* 281–291.

Seta, J. J., Seta, C. E., & Wang, M. A. (1991). Feelings of negativity and stress: An averaging-summation analysis of impressions of negative life experiences. *Personality and Social Psychology Bulletin, 17*(4), 376–384.

Shackelford, T. K., & Larsen, R. J. (1997). Facial asymmetry as an indicator of psychological, emotional, and physiological distress. *Journal of Personality and Social Psychology, 72,* 456–466.

Shaffer, D. R., Pegalis, L. J., & Bazzini, D. G. (1996). When boy meets girls (revisited): Gender, gender-role orientation, and prospect of future interaction as determinants of self-disclosure among same- and opposite-sex acquaintances. *Personality and Social Psychology Bulletin, 22,* 495–506.

Shariff, A. F., & Norenzayan, A. (2007). God is watching you: Priming God concepts increases prosocial behavior in an anonymous economic game. *Psychological Science, 18,* 803–809.

Sharma, N. (1981). Some aspect of attitude and behaviour of mothers. *Indian Psychological Review, 20,* 35–42.

Shaver, P., Hazan, C., & Bradshaw, D. (1988). Love as attachment: The integration of three behavioral systems. In R. J. Sternberg & M. L. Barnes (Eds.), *The psychology of love.* New Haven, CT: Yale University Press.

Shaver, P. R. & Hazan, C. (1994). Attachment. In A. L. Weber & J. H. Harvey (Eds.), *Perspectives on close relationships.* Boston, MA: Allyn & Bacon.

Shaver, P. R., & Hazan, C. (1993). Adult romantic attachment: Theory and evidence. In D. Perlman & W. Jones (Eds.), *Advances in personal relationships, Vol. 4.* Greenwich, CT: JAI.

Shavitt, S. (1990). The role of attitude objects in attitude functions. *Journal of Experimental Social Psychology, 26,* 124–148.

Sheldon, K. M., Elliot, A. J., Youngmee, K., & Kasser, T. (2001). What is satisfying about satisfying events? Testing 10 candidate psychological needs. *Journal of Personality and Social Psychology, 80,* 325–339.

Shepperd, J. A. (2003). *Interpreting comparative risk judgments: Are people personally optimistic or interpersonally pessimistic?* Unpublished manuscript, University of Florida.

Shepperd, J. A., Grace, J., Cole, L. J., & Klein, C. (2005). Anxiety and outcome predictions. *Personality and Social Psychology Bulletin, 31,* 267–275.

Shepperd, J. A., & Wright, R. A. (1989). Individual contributions to a collective effort: An incentive analysis. *Personality and Social Psychology Bulletin, 15,* 141–149.

Sherif, M. (1966). *In common predicament: Social psychology of intergroup conflict and cooperation.* Boston, MA: Houghton Mifflin.

Sherman, D. K., Nelson, L. D., & Ross, L. D. (2003). Naive realism and affirmative action: Adversaries are more similar than they think. *Basic and Applied Social Psychology, 25,* 275–289.

Sherman, J. W. (1996). Development and mental representation of stereotypes. *Journal of Personality and Social Psychology, 70,* 1126–1141.

Sherman, J. W., Lee, A. Y., Bessenoff, G. R., & Frost, L. A. (1998). Stereotype efficiency reconsidered: Encoding flexibility under cognitive load. *Journal of Personality and Social Psychology, 75,* 589–606.

Shih, M., Pittinsky, T. L., & Ambady, N. (1999). Stereotype susceptibility: Identity salience and shifts in quantitative performance. *Psychological Science, 10,* 80–83.

Shiue, Y., Chiu, C., & Chang, C. (2010). Exploring and mitigating social loafing in online communities. *Computers in Human Behavior, 26*(4), 768–777.

Showers, C., & Ruben, C. (1987). *Distinguishing pessimism from depression: Negative expectations and positive coping mechanisms.* Paper presented at the American Psychological Association convention.

Shrauger, J. S., Ram, D., Greninger, S. A., & Mariano, E. (1996). Accuracy of self-predictions versus judgments by knowledgeable others. *Personality and Social Psychology Bulletin, 22,* 1229–1243.

Shriver, E. R., Young, S. G., Hugenberg, K., Bernstein, M. J., & Lanter, J. R. (2008, February). Class, race, and the face: Social context modulates the cross-race effect in face recognition. *Personality and Social Psychology Bulletin, 34,* 260–274.

Sidanius, J., & Pratto, F. (1999). *Social dominance: An intergroup theory of social hierarchy and oppression.* New York, NY: Cambridge University Press.

Sidanius, J., Pratto, F., & Bobo, L. (1996). Racism, conservatism, affirmative action, and intellectual sophistication: A matter of principled conservatism or group dominance? *Journal of Personality and Social Psychology, 70,* 476–490.

Sieff, E. M., Dawes, R. M., & Loewenstein, G. F. (1999). Anticipated versus actual responses to HIV test results. *American Journal of Psychology, 112,* 297–311.

Sigall, H. (1970). Effects of competence and consensual validation on a communicator's liking for the audience. *Journal of Personality and Social Psychology, 16,* 252–258.

Silke, A. (2003). Deindividuation, anonymity, and violence: Findings from Northern Ireland. *Journal of Social Psychology, 143,* 493–499.

Silverman, C. (2004, March/April). Canadian cults: Blind faith or new religion? *The New Canadian Magazine, 1–4.* Retrieved 2006, June 1, from http://ordinary.blogs.com/clips/Cults.pdf.

Silverstone, Z. A., & Quinsey, V. A. (2000). Sexual partner age preferences of homosexual and heterosexual men and women. *Archives of Sexual Behavior, 29,* 67–76.

Simmons, W. W. (2000, December). *When it comes to having children, Americans still prefer boys.* The Gallup Poll Monthly, 63–64.

Simpson, J. A. (1987). The dissolution of romantic relationships: Factors involved in relationship stability and emotional distress. *Journal of Personality and Social Psychology, 53,* 683–692.

Simpson, J. A., Campbell, B., & Berscheid, E. (1986). The association between romantic love and marriage: Kephart (1967) twice revisited. *Personality and Social Psychology Bulletin, 12,* 363–372.

Simpson, J. A., Gangestad, S. W., & Lerma, M. (1990). Perception of physical attractiveness: Mechanisms involved in the maintenance of romantic relationships. *Journal of Personality and Social Psychology, 59,* 1192–1201.

Simpson, J. A., Rholes, W. S., & Nelligan, J. S. (1992). Support seeking and support giving within couples in an anxiety-provoking situation: The role of attachment styles. *Journal of Personality and Social Psychology, 62,* 434–446.

Simpson, J. A., Rholes, W. S., & Phillips, D. (1996). Conflict in close relationships: An attachment perspective. *Journal of Personality and Social Psychology, 71,* 899–914.

Sinclair, L., & Fehr, B. (2005). Voice versus loyalty: Self-construal and responses to dissatisfaction in romantic relationships. *Journal of Experimental Psychology, 41,* 298–304.

Sinclair, L., & Kunda, Z. (1999). Reactions to a Black professional: Motivated inhibition and activation of conflicting stereotypes. *Journal of Personality and Social Psychology, 77,* 885–904.

Sinclair, L., & Kunda, Z. (2000). Motivated stereotyping of women: She's fine if she praised me but incompetent if she criticized me. *Personality and Social Psychology Bulletin, 26,* 1329–1342.

Sinclair, R. L., & Sugar, D. (2005). The national child exploitation coordination center (NCECC) strategic and operations support services. Retrieved January, 2005, from Internet Based Sexual Exploitation of Children and Youth Environment. http://www.rcmp-grc.gc.ca/ncecc-cncee/index-accueil-eng.htm

Singer, M. (1979). *Cults and cult members.* Address to the American Psychological Association convention.

Sistrunk, F., & McDavid, J. W. (1971). Sex variable in conforming behaviour. *Journal of Personality and Social Psychology, 17*(2), 200–207.

Skitka, L. J. (1999). Ideological and attributional boundaries on public compassion: Reactions to individuals and communities affected by a natural disaster. *Personality and Social Psychology Bulletin, 25,* 793–808.

Skitka, L. J., Bauman, C. W., & Mullen, E. (2004). Political tolerance and coming to psychological closure following the September 11, 2001, terrorist attacks: An integrative approach. *Personality and Social Psychology Bulletin, 30,* 743–756.

Slavin, R. E. (1990, December/January). Research on cooperative learning: Consensus and controversy. *Educational Leadership,* 52–54.

Sleek, S. (1996, January). Psychologists build a culture of peace. *APA Monitor,* p. 1–33.

Sloan, J. H., Kellerman, A. L., Reay, D. T., Ferris, J. A., Koepsell, T., Rivara, F. P., et al. (1988). Handgun regulations, crime, assaults, and homicide: A tale of two cities. *New England Journal of Medicine, 319,* 1256–1261.

Slotter, E. B., & Gardner, W. L. (2009). Where do you end and I begin? Evidence for anticipatory, motivated self-other integration between relationship partners. *Journal of Personality and Social Psychology, 96,* 1137–1151.

Slovic, P., & Fischhoff, B. (1977). On the psychology of experimental surprises. *Journal of Experimental Psychology: Human Perception and Performance, 3,* 455–551.

Smalarz, L., & Wells, G. L. (2013). Post-identification feedback to eyewitnesses impairs evaluators' abilities to discriminate between accurate and mistaken testimony. *Law and Human Behavior,* Online publication, doi:10.1037/lhb0000067.

Smelser, N. J., & Mitchell, F. (Eds.) (2002). *Terrorism: Perspectives from the behavioral and social sciences.* Washington, DC: National Research Council, National Academies Press.

Smith, D. E., Gier, J. A., & Willis, F. N. (1982). Interpersonal touch and compliance with a marketing request. *Basic and Applied Social Psychology, 3,* 35–38.

Smith, H. J., & Tyler, T. R. (1997). Choosing the right pond: The impact of group membership on self-esteem and group-oriented behavior. *Journal of Experimental Social Psychology, 33,* 146–170.

Smith, J. L., Berry, N. J., Whiteley, P. (1997). The effect of interviewer-guise upon gender self-report responses as a function of interviewee's self-monitoring position. *European Journal of Social Psychology, 27,* 237–243.

Smith, S. M., & Kalin, R. (2006). Right-wing authoritarianism as a moderator of the similarity-attraction effect. *Canadian Journal of Behavioural Science, 38,* 63–71.

Smith, S. M., & Stinson, V. (2008). Does race matter? Exploring research on the cross-race effect in eyewitness identification. In S. E. Jones, J. Cardi, & G. Parks (Eds.), *Critical race realism: Intersections of psychology, race and law* (pp.102–114). New York, NY: The New Press.

Smith, S. M., Fabrigar, L. R., MacDougall, B. L., & Wiesenthal, N. L. (2008). The role of amount, cognitive elaboration, and structural consistency of attitude-relevant knowledge in the formation of attitude certainty. *European Journal of Social Psychology, 38,* 280–295.

Smith, S. M., Fabrigar, L. R., Powell, D. M., & Estrada, M. (2007). The role of information-processing capacity and goals in attitude-congruent selective exposure effects. *Personality and Social Psychology Bulletin, 33*(7), 948–960.

Smith, S. M., Lindsay, R. C. L., & Pryke, S. & Dysart, J. (2001). Postdictors of eyewitness errors: Can false identifications be diagnosed in the cross-race situation? *Psychology, Public Policy, and Law, 5,* 153–169.

Smith, S. M., Stinson, V., & Patry, M. W. (2009). The Mr. Big technique: successful innovation or dangerous development in the Canadian legal system? *Psychology, Public Policy, and Law, 15,* 168–193.

Smith, S. M., Stinson, V., & Patry, M. W. (2010). High risk interrogation: Using the "Mr. Big" technique to elicit confessions. *Law and Human Behavior, 34,* 39–40.

Smith, S. M., Stinson, V., & Prosser, M. A. (2004). Do they all look alike? An exploration of decision making strategies in cross-race identifications. *Canadian Journal of Behavioral Science, 36,* 146–154.

Smith, T. W. (1998, December). *American sexual behavior: Trends, socio-demographic differences, and risk behavior.* National Opinion Research Center GSS Topical Report No. 25.

Smith, T. W., & Ruiz, J. M. (2002). Psychosocial influences on the development and course of coronary heart disease: Current status and implications for research and practice. *Journal of Consulting and Clinical Psychology, 70,* 548–568.

Smith, V. L. (1991). Impact of pretrial instruction on jurors' information processing and decision making. *Journal of Applied Psychology, 76,* 220–228.

Snyder, C. R. (1980, March). The uniqueness mystique. *Psychology Today,* 86–90.

Snyder, C. R., & Fromkin, H. L. (1977). Abnormality as a positive characteristic: The development and validation of a scale measuring need for uniqueness. *Journal of Abnormal Psychology, 15,* 518–527.

Snyder, C. R., & Fromkin, H. L. (1980). *Uniqueness: The human pursuit of difference.* New York, NY: Plenum.

Snyder, C. R., & Higgins, R. L. (1988). Excuses: Their effective role in the negotiation of reality. *Psychological Bulletin, 104,* 23–35.

Snyder, M. (1984). When belief creates reality. In L. Berkowitz (Ed.), *Advances in experimental social psychology, Vol. 18.* New York, NY: Academic Press.

Snyder, M., & DeBono, K. G. (Eds.). (1989). Understanding the functions of attitudes: Lessons from personality and social behavior. In A. R. Pratkanis, S. J. Breckler, & A. G. Greenwald (Eds.), *Attitude structure and function.* Hillsdale, NJ: Erlbaum.

Snyder, M., & Ickes, W. (1985). Personality and social behavior. In G. Lindzey & E. Aronson (Eds.), *Handbook of social psychology* (3rd ed.). New York, NY: Random House.

Snyder, M., Grether J., & Keller, K. (1974). Staring and compliance: A field experiment on hitch-hiking. *Journal of Applied Social Psychology, 4,* 165–170.

Snyder, M., Tanke, E. D., & Berscheid, E. (1977). Social perception and interpersonal behavior: On the self-fulfilling nature of social stereotypes. *Journal of Personality and Social Psychology, 35,* 656–666.

Sokoll, G. R., & Mynatt, C. R. (1984). *Arousal and free throw shooting.* Paper presented at the Midwestern Psychological Association convention, Chicago.

Solberg, E. C., Diener, E., & Robinson, M. D. (2003). Why are materialists less satisfied? In T. Kasser & A. D. Kanner (Eds.), *Psychology and consumer culture: The struggle for a good life in a materialistic world.* Washington, DC: APA Books.

Solomon, S., Greenberg, J., & Pyszczynski, T. (2000). Pride and prejudice: Fear of death and social behavior. *Current Directions in Psychological Science, 9,* 200–203.

Spanos, N. P. (1996). *Multiple identities & false memories: A sociocognitive perspective.* Washington, DC: American Psychological Association.

Spanos, N. P., Burgess, C. A., Burgess, M. F., Samuels, C. & Blois, W. O. (1999). Creating false memories of infancy with hypnotic and non-hypnotic procedures. *Applied Cognitive Psychology, 13,* 201–218.

Sparrell, J. A., & Shrauger, J. S. (1984). *Self-confidence and optimism in self-prediction.* Paper presented at the American Psychological Association convention.

Spence, I., & Feng, J. (2010). Video games and spatial cognition. *Review of General Psychology, 14*(2), 92–104.

Spencer, S. J., Steele, C. M., & Quinn, D. M. (1999). Stereotype threat and women's math performance. *Journal of Experimental Social Psychology, 3,* 4–28.

Spencer, S., Fein, S., Wolfe, C., Fong, C., & Dunn, M. A. (1998). Automatic activation of stereotypes: The role of self-image threat. *Personality and Social Psychology Bulletin, 24,* 1139–1152.

Spivey, C. B., & Prentice-Dunn, S. (1990). Assessing the directionality of deindividuated behavior: Effects of deindividuation, modeling, and private self-consciousness on aggressive and prosocial responses. *Basic and Applied Social Psychology, 11,* 387–403.

Sporer, S. L., Penrod, S., Read, D., & Cutler, B. (1995). Choosing confidence and accuracy: A meta-analysis of the confidence-accuracy relation in eyewitness identification studies. *Psychological Bulletin, 118,* 315–327.

Sprecher, S. (1987). The effects of self-disclosure given and received on affection for an intimate partner and stability of the relationship. *Journal of Personality and Social Psychology, 4,* 115–127.

Sprecher, S., Aron, A., Hatfield, E., Cortese, A., Potapova, E., & Levitskaya, A. (1994). Love: American style, Russian style, and Japanese style. *Personal Relationships, 1,* 349–369.

Sprecher, S., Sullivan, Q., & Hatfield, E. (1994). Mate selection preferences: Gender differences examined in a national sample. *Journal of Personality and Social Psychology, 66,* 1074–1080.

Sprecher, S., & Toro-Morn, M. (2002). A study of men and women from different sides of Earth to determine if men are from Mars and women are from Venus in their beliefs about love and romantic relationships. *Sex Roles, 46,* 131–147.

Sprung, J. M., & Jex, S. M. (2012). Work locus of control as a moderator of the relationship between work stressors and counterproductive work behavior. *International Journal os Stress Management, 19*(4), 272–291.

St. Lawrence, J. S., & Joyner, D. J. (1991). The effects of sexually violent rock music on males' acceptance of violence against women. *Psychology of Women Quarterly, 15*(1), 49–63.

Standing, L. G. (2002). Modeling effects in students drinking and smoking, revisited after 24 years. *Social Behavior and Personality, 30,* 435–442.

Stangor, C., Jonas, K., Stroebe, W., & Hewstone, M. (1996). Influence of student exchange on national stereotypes, attitudes and perceived group variability. *European Journal of Social Psychology, 26,* 663–675.

Stanovich, K. E., & West, R. F. (2008). On the relative independence of thinking biases and cognitive ability. *Journal of Personality and Social Psychology, 94,* 672–695.

Stark, E., Kim, A., Miller, C., & Borgida, E. (2008). Effects of including a graphic warning label in avertisements for reduced-exposure products: Implications for persuasion and policy. *Journal of Applied Social Psychology, 38,* 281–293.

Stark, R., & Bainbridge, W. S. (1980). Networks of faith: Interpersonal bonds and recruitment of cults and sects. *American Journal of Sociology, 85,* 1376–1395.

Stasser, G. (1991). Pooling of unshared information during group discussion. In S. Worchel, W. Wood, & J. Simpson (Eds.), *Group process and productivity.* Beverly Hills, CA: Sage.

Statistics Canada. (1999). *Time alone.* Retrieved from http://www.statcan.gc.ca/studies-etudes/11-008/feature-caracteristique/5018782-eng.pdf.

Statistics Canada. (2000). *Youths and adults charged in criminal incidents, criminal code and federal statutes, by sex* (http://www.statcan.ca/english/pgdb/state/justice/legal14.htm).

Statistics Canada. (2004). *Results of 2003 General Social Survey.*

Statistics Canada. (2005). Crime Statistics. Retrieved June 2006, from http://www.statcan.ca/Daily/English/050721/d050721a.htm.

Statistics Canada. (2007). *Firearms and violent crime.* Statistics Canada - Catalogue no. 85-002-XIE, Vol. 28, no. 2.

Statistics Canada. (2009). *Criminal victimization in Canada.* Retrieved from http://www.statcan.gc.ca/pub/85-002-x/2010002/article/11340-eng.htm?fpv=2693.

Statistics Canada. (2010). *A portrait of couples in mixed unions.* Retrieved from http://www.statcan.gc.ca/pub/11-008-x/2010001/article/11143-eng.htm.

Statistics Canada. (2010). *Police-reported crime statistics in Canada, 2009.* Retrieved from http://www.statcan.gc.ca/pub/85-002-x/2010002/article/11292-eng.htm.

Statistics Canada. (2011). *Police reported crime statistics in Canada, 2010.* Retrieved from http://www.statcan.gc.ca/pub/85-002-x/2011001/article/11523-eng.pdf.

Statistics Canada. (2011). *Valentine's day—by the numbers.* Retrieved from http://www42.statcan.gc.ca/smr08/2011/smr08_151_2011-eng.htm.

Statistics Canada. (2012). *Portrait of Families and Living Arrangements in Canada.* Retrieved from http://www12.statcan.ca/census-recensement/2011/as-sa/98-312-x/98-312-x2011001-eng.cfm.

Statistics Canada. (2012). *Smoking,* Retrieved from http://www.statcan.gc.ca/pub/82-625-x/2013001/article/11844-eng.htm.

Statistics Canada. (2013). *Health in Canada.* Retrieved from http://www.statcan.gc.ca/eng/health/index.

Statistics Canada. (2013). *Police-reported crime statistics.* Retrieved from http://www.statcan.gc.ca/daily-quotidien/140723/dq140723b-eng.htm.

Steele, C. M. (1997). A threat in the air: How stereotypes shape intellectual identity and performance. *American Psychologist, 52,* 613–629.

Steele, C. M., & Aronson, J. (1995). Stereotype threat and the intellectual test performance of African Americans. *Journal of Personality and Social Psychology, 69,* 797–811.

Steele, C. M., & Southwick, L. (1985). Alcohol and social behavior I: The psychology of drunken excess. *Journal of Personality and Social Psychology, 48,* 18–34.

Steele, C. M., Spencer, S. J., & Aronson, J. (2002). Contending with group image: The psychology of stereotype and social identity threat. In M. P. Zanna (Ed.), *Advances in experimental social psychology* (pp. 34, 379–440). San Diego, CA: Academic Press.

Stein, A. H., & Friedrich, L. K. (1972). Television content and young children's behavior. In J. P. Murray, E. A. Rubinstein, & G. A. Comstock (Eds.), *Television and social learning.* Washington, DC: Government Printing Office.

Stein, D. D., Hardyck, J. A., & Smith, M. B. (1965). Race and belief: An open and shut case. *Journal of Personality and Social Psychology, 1,* 281–289.

Stephan, W. G. (1987). The contact hypothesis in intergroup relations. In C. Hendrick (Ed.), *Group processes and intergroup relations*. Newbury Park, CA: Sage.

Stephan, W. G., Berscheid, E., & Walster, E. (1971). Sexual arousal and heterosexual perception. *Journal of Personality and Social Psychology, 20,* 93–101.

Sternberg, R. J. (1988). Triangulating love. In R. J. Sternberg & M. L. Barnes (Eds.), *The psychology of love*. New Haven, CT: Yale University Press.

Sternberg, R. J. (1998). *Cupid's arrow: The course of love through time* (p. 408). New York, NY: Cambridge University Press.

Sternberg, R. J. (2000, July). What's your love story? *Psychology Today*. Retrieved from http://www.psychologytoday.com/articles/200007/whats-your-love-story.

Sternberg, R. J. (2003). A duplex theory of hate and its development and its application to terrorism, massacres, and genocide. *Review of General Psychology, 7,* 299–328.

Sternberg, R. J., & Beall, A. E. (1991). How can we know what love is: An epistemological analysis. In G. J. O. Fletcher & F. D. Fincham (Eds.), *Cognition and close relationships* (pp. 257–278). Hillsdale, NJ: Erlbaum.

Sternberg, R. J., & Grajek, S. (1994). The nature of love. *Journal of Personality and Social Psychology, 47,* 312–329.

Stone, A. A., Hedges, S. M., Neale, J. M., & Satin, M. S. (1985). Prospective and cross-sectional mood reports offer no evidence of a "blue Monday" phenomenon. *Journal of Personality and Social Psychology, 49,* 129–134.

Stone, J. (2000, November 6). Quoted by Sharon Begley, The stereotype trap. *Newsweek*.

Stone, J., Lynch, C. I., Sjomeling, M., & Darley, J. M. (1999). Stereotype threat effects on Black and White athletic performance. *Journal of Personality and Social Psychology, 77,* 1213–1227.

Stoner, J. A. F. (1961). *A comparison of individual and group decisions involving risk*. Unpublished master's thesis, Massachusetts Institute of Technology, 1961. Cited by D. G. Marquis in Individual responsibility and group decisions involving risk. *Industrial Management Review, 3,* 8–23.

Storms, M. D. (1973). Videotape and the attribution process: Reversing actors' and observers' points of view. *Journal of Personality and Social Psychology, 27,* 165–175.

Storms, M. D., & Thomas, G. C. (1977). Reactions to physical closeness. *Journal of Personality and Social Psychology, 35,* 412–418.

Strack, S., & Coyne, J. C. (1983). Social confirmation of dysphoria: Shared and private reactions to depression. *Journal of Personality and Social Psychology, 44,* 798–806.

Strahan, E. J., Spencer, S. J., & Zanna, M. P. (2002). Subliminal priming and persuasion: Striking while the iron is hot. *Journal of Experimental Social Psychology, 38,* 556–568.

Strahan, E. J., Spencer, S. J., & Zanna, M. P. (2005). Subliminal priming and persuasion: How motivation affects the activation of goals and persuasiveness of messages. In F. R. Kardes, P. M. Herr, & J. Nantel (Eds.), *Applying social cognition to consumer-focused strategy*. Mahwah, NJ: Erlbaum.

Straus, M. A., & Gelles, R. J. (1980). *Behind closed doors: Violence in the American family*. New York, NY: Anchor/Doubleday.

Stroebe, W., Insko, C. A., Thompson, V. D., & Layton, B. D. (1971). Effects of physical attractiveness, attitude similarity, and sex on various aspects of interpersonal attraction. *Journal of Personality and Social Psychology, 18,* 79–91.

Stroessner, S. J., & Mackie, D. M. (1993). Affect and perceived group variability: Implications for stereotyping and prejudice. In D. M. Mackie & D. L. Hamilton (Eds.), *Affect, cognition, and stereotyping: Interactive processes in group perception*. San Diego, CA: Academic Press.

Stroessner, S. J., Hamilton, D. L., & Lepore, L. (1990). *Intergroup categorization and intragroup differentiation: Ingroup-outgroup differences*. Paper presented at the American Psychological Association convention.

Stupnisky, R. H., Renaud, R. D., Perry, R. P., Ruthig, J. C., Haynes, T. L., & Clifton, R. A. (2007). Comparing self-esteem and perceived control as predictors of first-year college students' academic achievement. *Social Psychology of Education, 10,* 303–330.

Sue, S., Smith, R. E., & Caldwell, C. (1973). Effects of inadmissible evidence on the decisions of simulated jurors: A moral dilemma. *Journal of Applied Social Psychology, 3,* 345–353.

Suglia, S. L., & Briggs, R. D. (2013, August). Kindergartners' soda intake linked to aggression in study. *HealthyDay Reporter,* Retrieved from http://consumer.healthday.com/mental-health-information-25/behavior-health-news-56/kindergartners-soda-intake-linked-to-aggression-study-says-679300.html.

Suh, E. J., Moskowitz, D. S., Fournier, M. A., & Zuroff, D. C. (2004). Gender and relationships: Influences on a genetic and communal behaviors. *Personal Relationships, 11,* 41–59.

Suls, J., & Tesch, F. (1978). Students' preferences for information about their test performance: A social comparison study. *Journal of Applied Social Psychology, 8,* 189–197.

Summers, G., & Feldman, N. S. (1984). Blaming the victim versus blaming the perpetrator: An attributional analysis of spouse abuse. *Journal of Social and Clinical Psychology, 2,* 339–347.

Sunstein, C. R. (2001). Republic.com. Princeton, NJ: Princeton University Press.

Svenson, O. (1981). Are we all less risky and more skillful than our fellow drivers? *Acta Psychologica, 47,* 143–148.

Swann, W. B., Jr. (1996). *Self-traps: The elusive quest for higher self-esteem*. New York, NY: Freeman.

Swann, W. B., Jr. (1997). The trouble with change: Self-verification and allegiance to the self. *Psychological Science, 8,* 177–180.

Swann, W. B., Jr., & Gill, M. J. (1997). Confidence and accuracy in person perception: Do we know what we think we know about our relationship partners? *Journal of Personality and Social Psychology, 73,* 747–757.

Swann, W. B., Jr., Gómez, À., Seyle, D. C., Morales, J. F., & Huici, C. (2009). Identity fusion: The interplay of personal and social identities in extreme group behavior. *Journal of Personality and Social Psychology, 96,* 995–1011.

Swann, W. B., Jr., Rentfrow, P. J., & Gosling, S. D. (2003). The precarious couple effect: Verbally inhibited men + critical, disinhibited women = bad chemistry. *Journal of Personality and Social Psychology, 85,* 1095–1106.

Swann, W. B., Jr., Sellers, J. G., & McClarty, K. L. (2006). Tempting today, troubling tomorrow: The roots of the precarious couple effect. *Personality and Social Psychology Bulletin, 32*(1), 93–103.

Swap, W. C. (1977). Interpersonal attraction and repeated exposure to rewarders and punishers. *Personality and Social Psychology Bulletin, 3,* 248–251.

Sweeney, J. (1973). An experimental investigation of the free rider problem. *Social Science Research, 2,* 277–292.

Sweeney, P. D., Anderson, K., & Bailey, S. (1986). Attributional style in depression: A meta-analytic review. *Journal of Personality and Social Psychology, 50,* 947–991.

Swim, J. K. (1994). Perceived versus meta-analytic effect sizes: An assessment of the accuracy of gender stereotypes. *Journal of Personality and Social Psychology, 66,* 21–36.

Swim, J. K., Aikin, K. J., Hall, W. S., & Hunter, B. A. (1995). Sexism and racism: Old-fashioned and modern prejudices. *Journal of Personality and Social Psychology, 68,* 199–214.

Swim, J. K., & Cohen, L. L. (1997). Overt, covert, and subtle sexism. *Psychology of Women Quarterly, 21,* 103–118.

Swim, J. K., & Hyers, L. L. (1999). Excuse me—What did you just say?!: Women's public and private reactions to sexist remarks. *Journal of Experimental Social Psychology, 35,* 68–88.

Swim, J. K., & Stangor, C. (Eds.). (1998). *Prejudice: The target's perspective.* San Diego, CA: Academic Press.

Swindle, R., Jr., Heller, K., Bescosolido, B., Kikuzawa, S. (2000). Responses to nervous breakdowns in America over a 40-year period: Mental health policy implications. *American Psychologist, 55,* 740–749.

Symons, C. S., & Johnson, B. T. (1997). The self-reference effect in memory: A meta-analysis. *Psychological Bulletin, 121,* 371–394.

Tafarodi, R. W., Kang, J., Milne, A. B. (2002). When different becomes similar: Compensatory conformity in bicultural visible minorities. *Personality and Social Psychology Bulletin, 28,* 1131–1142.

Tafarodi, R. W., Lo, C., Yamaguichi, S., Lee, W. W.-S., & Katsura, H. (2004). The inner self in three countries. *Journal of Cross-Cultural Psychology, 35,* 97–117.

Tajfel, H., & Billig, M. (1974). Familiarity and categorization in intergroup behavior. *Journal of Experimental Social Psychology, 10,* 159–170.

Tajfel, H., & Turner, J. C. (1979). An integrative theory of intergroup conflict. In S. Worchel & W. G. Austin (Eds.), *Psychology of intergroup relations.* Monterey, CA: Brooks-Cole.

Tamres, L. K., Janicki, D., & Helgeson, V. S. (2002). Sex differences in coping behavior: A meta-analytic review and an examination of relative coping. *Personality and Social Psychology Review, 6,* 2–30.

Tannen, D. (1990). *You just don't understand: Women and men in conversation.* New York, NY: William Morrow.

Tarmann, A. (2002, May/June). Out of the closet and onto the Census long form. *Population Today, 30,* 1, 6.

Taylor, C. & Peter, T., with McMinn, T. L., Schachter, K., Beldom, S., Ferry, A., Gross, Z., & Paquin, S. (2011). *Every class in every school: The first national climate survey on homophobia, biphobia, and transphobia in Canadian schools.* Final report. Toronto, Egale Canada Human Rights Trust.

Taylor, D. M., & Doria, J. R. (1981). Self-serving and group-serving bias in attribution. *Journal of Social Psychology, 113,* 201–211.

Taylor, S. A. (2007). The addition of anticipated regret to attitudinally based, goal-directed models of information search behaviours under conditions of uncertainty and risk. *British Journal of Social Psychology, 46*(4), 739–768.

Taylor, S. E. (1981). A categorization approach to stereotyping. In D. L. Hamilton (Ed.), *Cognitive processes in stereotyping and intergroup behavior.* Hillsdale, NJ: Erlbaum.

Taylor, S. E. (1989). *Positive illusions:* Creative self-deception and the healthy mind. New York, NY: Basic Books.

Taylor, S. E., Crocker, J., Fiske, S. T., Sprinzen, M., & Winkler, J. D. (1979). The generalizability of salience effects. *Journal of Personality and Social Psychology, 37,* 357–368.

Taylor, S. E., & Fiske, S. T. (1978). Salience, attention, and attribution: Top of the head phenomena. In L. Berkowitz (Ed.), *Advances in experimental social psychology, Vol. 11.* New York NY: Academic Press.

Taylor, S. E., Fiske, S. T., Etcoff, N. L., & Ruderman, A. J. (1978). Categorical and contextual bases of person memory and stereotyping. *Journal of Personality and Social Psychology, 36,* 778–793.

Taylor, S. E., Klein, L. C., Lewis, B. P., Gruenewald, T. L., Gurung, R. A. R., & Updegraff, J. A. (2000). Biobehavioral responses to stress in females: Tend-and-befriend, not fight-or-flight. *Psychological Review, 107,* 411–429.

Taylor, S. P., & Chermack, S. T. (1993). Alcohol, drugs and human physical aggression. *Journal of Studies on Alcohol, Supplement No. 11,* 78–88.

Taylor, S. P., & Pisano, R. (1971). Physical aggression as a function of frustration and physical attack. *Journal of Social Psychology, 84,* 261–267.

techvibes.com. (2014). Retrieved from http://www.techvibes.com/blog/canadians-spending-less-time-online.

Teger, A. I. (1980). *Too much invested to quit.* New York, NY: Pergamon Press.

Telch, M. J., Killen, J. D., McAlister, A. L., Perry, C. L., & Maccoby, N. (1981). *Long-term follow-up of a pilot project on smoking prevention with adolescents.* Paper presented at the American Psychological Association convention.

Telegraph Newspaper. (2013). GTA V fastest selling game of all time. Retrieved 09-14-2014.

Terry Fox Foundation. (2010). Terry Fox and the Terry Fox Foundation. Retrieved from http://www.terryfox.org/Foundation/index.html.

Tesser, A., & Beach, S. R. H. (1998). Life events, relationship quality, and depression: An investigation of judgement discontinuity in vivo. *Journal of Personality and Social Psychology, 74,* 36–52.

Testa, M. (2002). The impact of men's alcohol consumption on perpetration of sexual aggression. *Clinical Psychology Review, 22,* 1239–1263.

Tetlock, P. E. (1998). Close-call counterfactuals and belief-system defenses: I was not almost wrong but I was almost right. *Journal of Personality and Social Psychology, 75,* 639–652.

Tetlock, P. E. (1999). Theory-driven reasoning about plausible pasts and probable futures in world politics: Are we prisoners of our preconceptions? *American Journal of Political Science, 43,* 335–366.

Thompson, L. (1998). *The mind and heart of the negotiator.* Upper Saddle River, NJ: Prentice-Hall.

Thompson, L., Valley, K. L., & Kramer, R. M. (1995). The bittersweet feeling of success: An examination of social perception in negotiation. *Journal of Experimental Social Psychology, 31,* 467–492.

Thompson, L. L., & Crocker, J. (1985). *Prejudice following threat to the self-concept. Effects of performance expectations and attributions.* Unpublished manuscript, Northwestern University.

Thomson, D. (2001). *Arab Americans feel backlash.* Retrieved from http://abcnews.go.com/US/story?id=92461&page=1.

Thornton, B., & Maurice, J. (1997). Physique contrast effect: Adverse impact of idealized body images for women. *Sex Roles, 37,* 433–439.

Tice, D. M., Butler, J. L., Muraven, M. B. (1995). When modesty prevails: Deferential favorability of self-presentation to friends and strangers. *Journal of Personality and Social Psychology, 69,* 1120–1138.

Timko, C., & Moos, R. H. (1989). Choice, control, and adaptation among elderly residents of sheltered care settings. *Journal of Applied Social Psychology, 19,* 636–655.

Tobin, S., & Grondin, S. (2009). Video games and the perception of very long durations by adolescents. *Computers in Human Behavior, 25,* 554–559.

Todorov, A., Mandisodza, A. N., Goren, A., & Hall, C. C. (2005). Inferences of competence from faces predict election outcomes. *Science, 308,* 1623–1626.

Tormala, Z. L., & Petty, R. E. (2002). What doesn't kill me makes me stronger: The effects of resisting persuasion on attitude change. *Journal of Personality and Social Psychology, 83,* 1298–1313.

Tormala, Z. L., Brinol, P., & Petty, R. E. (2006). When credibility attacks: The reverse impact of source credibility on persuasion. *Journal of Experimental Social Psychology, 42,* 684–691.

Toronto News (1977, July 26). 61.

Toronto Star/EKOS. (2002 September 11). Thin hindsight: Recovery and resolve. Retrieved from http://www.ekos.com/admin/articles/9sept2002.pdf.

Tourism Toronto. (2007). *Tourism Toronto Annual Report.* Retrieved from http://www.seetorontonow.com/web.cms/pdf/AnnualReport2007.pdf.

Trampe, D., Stapel, D. A., & Siero, F. W. (2007). On models and vases: Body dissatisfaction and proneness to social comparison effects. *Journal of Personality and Social Psychology, 92,* 106–118.

Travis, L. E. (1925). The effect of a small audience upon eye-hand coordination. *Journal of Abnormal and Social Psychology, 20,* 142–146.

Triandis, H. C. (1994). *Culture and social behavior.* New York, NY: McGraw-Hill.

Triandis, H. C., Bontempo, R., Villareal, M. J., Asai, M., & Lucca, N. (1988). Individualism and collectivism: Cross-cultural perspectives on self-ingroup relationships. *Journal of Personality and Social Psychology, 54,* 323–338.

Triplet, R. G., & Sugarman, D. B. (1987). Reactions to AIDS victims: Ambiguity breeds contempt. *Personality and Social Psychology Bulletin, 13*(2), 265–274.

Triplett, N. (1898). The dynamogenic factors in pacemaking and competition. *American Journal of Psychology, 9,* 507–533.

Trolier, T. K., & Hamilton, D. L. (1986). Variables influencing judgments of correlational relations. *Journal of Personality and Social Psychology, 50,* 879–888.

Tropp, L. R., & Pettigrew, T. F. (2004). Intergroup contact and the central role of affect in intergroup prejudice. In C. W. Leach & L. Tiedens (Eds.), *The social life of emotion.* Cambridge: Cambridge University Press.

Tropp, L. R., & Pettigrew, T. F. (2005a). Differential relationships between intergroup contact and affective and cognitive dimensions of prejudice. *Personality and Social Psychology Bulletin, 31,* 1145–1158.

Tropp, L. R., & Pettigrew, T. F. (2005b). Relationships between intergroup contact and prejudice among minority and majority status groups. *Psychological Science, 16,* 951–957.

Tropp, L. R., & Wright, S. C. (1999). Ingroup identification and relative deprivation: An examination across multiple social comparisons. *European Journal of Social Psychology, 29*(5–6), 707–724.

Trost, M. R., Maass, A., & Kenrick, D. T. (1992). Minority influence: Personal relevance biases cognitive processes and reverses private acceptance. *Journal of Experimental Social Psychology, 28,* 234–254.

Trzesniewski, K. H., Donnellan, M. B., & Robins, R. W. (2008). Do today's young people really think they are so extraordinary? An examination of secular trends in narcissism and self-enhancement. *Psychological Science, 19*(2), 181–188.

Tsang, J. A. (2002). Moral rationalization and the integration of situational factors and psychological processes in immoral behavior. *Review of General Psychology, 6,* 25–50.

Tsui, L., & Nicoladis, E. (2004). Losing it: Similarities and differences in first intercourse experiences of men and women. *Canadian Journal of Human Sexuality, 13,* 95–106.

Turner, C. W., Hesse, B. W., & Peterson-Lewis, S. (1986). Naturalistic studies of the long-term effects of television violence. *Journal of Social Issues, 42*(3), 51–74.

Turner, J. C. (1987). *Rediscovering the social group: A self-categorization theory.* New York, NY: Basil Blackwell.

Turner, J. C. (1991). *Social influence.* Milton Keynes: Open University Press.

Turner, J. C., & Reynolds, K. J. (2004). The social identity perspective in intergroup relations: Theories, themes, and controversies. In M. B. Brewer & M. Hewstone (Eds.), *Self and social identity.* Maiden, MA: Blackwell.

Turner, M. E., & Pratkanis, A. R. (1994). Social identity maintenance prescriptions for preventing groupthink: Reducing identity protection and enhancing intellectual conflict. *International Journal of Conflict Management, 5,* 254–270.

Turner, M. E., Pratkanis, A. R., Probasco, P., & Leve, C. (1992). Threat cohesion, and group effectiveness: Testing a social identity maintenance perspective on groupthink. *Journal of Personality and Social Psychology, 63,* 781–796.

Turtle, J., & Want, S. C. (2008). Logic and research versus intuition and past practice as guides to gathering and evaluating eyewitness evidence. *Criminal Justice and Behavior, 35*(10), 1241–1256.

Tversky, A., & Kahneman, D. (1973). Availability: A heuristic for judging frequency and probability. *Cognitive Psychology, 5,* 207–302.

Tversky, A., & Kahneman, D. (1974). Judgment under uncertainty: Heuristics and biases. *Science, 185,* 1123–1131.

Twenge, J. M. (2006). *Generation Me: Why today's young Americans are more confident, assertive, entitled—and more miserable than ever before.* New York, NY: Free Press.

Twenge, J. M., & Campbell, W. K. (2009). *The narcissism epidemic: Living in the age of entitlement.* New York, NY: Free Press.

Twenge, J. M., Baumeister, R. F., Tice, D. M., & Stucke, T. S. (2001). If you can't join them, beat them: Effects of social exclusion on aggressive behavior. *Journal of Personality and Social Psychology, 81,* 1058–1069.

Twenge, J. M., Catanese, K. R., & Baumeister, R. F. (2002). Social exclusion causes self-defeating behavior. *Journal of Personality and Social Psychology, 83,* 606–615.

Twenge, J. M., Catanese, K. R., & Baumeister, R. F. (2003). Social exclusion and the deconstructed state: Time perception, meaninglessness, lethargy, lack of emotion and self-awareness. *Journal of Personality and Social Psychology, 85,* 409–423.

Twenge, J. M., Konrath, S., Foster, J. D., Campbell, W. K., & Bushman, B. J. (2006). Egos inflating over time: A cross-temporal meta-analysis of the Narcissistic Personality Inventory. *Journal of Personality, 76*(4), 875–902.

Tyler, T. R. (1990). *Why people obey the law: Procedural justice, legitimacy, and compliance.* New Haven, CT: Yale University Press.

Tzeng, M. (1992). The effects of socioeconomic heterogamy and changes on marital dissolution for first marriages. *Journal of Marriage and the Family, 54,* 609–619.

Uleman, J. S. (1989). A framework for thinking intentionally about unintended thoughts. In J. S. Uleman & J. A. Bargh (Eds.), *Unintended thought: The limits of awareness, intention, and control* (pp. 425–449). New York, NY: Guilford.

UNHCR. 2008. *Report on Sudan.* Downloaded from http://www.unhcr.org/southsudan.html.

USA Today (2014). Poll: Attitudes towards gays changing fast. Downloaded Sept. 2, 2014, from http://www.usatoday.com/story/news/politics/2012/12/05/poll-from-gay-marriage-to-adoption-attitudes-changing-fast/1748873/.

USGS. (2006). *United States energy and world energy production and consumption statistics.* U.S. Geographical Survey.

Vail, K., III, Rothchild, Z., Weise, D., Solomon, S., Pyszczynski, T., & Greenberg, J. (2010). A terror management analysis of the psychological functions of religion. *Personality and Social Psychology Review, 14,* 84–89.

Valcour, M. (2007). Work-based resources as moderators of the relationship between work hours and satisfaction with work-family balance. *Journal of Applied Psychology, 92,* 1409–1413.

Vallone, R. P., Griffin, D. W., Lin, S., & Ross, L. (1990). Overconfident prediction of future actions and outcomes by self and others. *Journal of Personality and Social Psychology, 58,* 582–592.

Vallone, R. P., Ross, L., & Lepper, M. R. (1985). The hostile media phenomenon: Biased perception and perceptions of media bias in coverage of the "Beirut Massacre." *Journal of Personality and Social Psychology, 49,* 577–585.

Van Boven, L., & Gilovich, T. (2003). To do or to have? That is the question. *Journal of Personality and Social Psychology, 85,* 1193–1202.

Van Dijk, W. W., Finkenauer, C. & Pollmann, M. (2008). The misprediction of emotions in track athletics: Is experience the teacher of all things? *Basic and Applied Social Psychology, 30,* 369–376.

Van Knippenberg, D., & Wilke, H. (1992). Prototypicality of arguments and conformity to ingroup norms. *European Journal of Social Psychology, 22,* 141–155.

Van Lange, P. A. M. (1991). Being better but not smarter than others: The Muhammad Ali effect at work in interpersonal situations. *Personality and Social Psychology Bulletin, 17,* 689–693.

Van Lange, P. A. M., Taris, T. W., & Vonk, R. (1997). Dilemmas of academic practice: Perceptions of superiority among social psychologists. *European Journal of Social Psychology, 27,* 675–685.

Van Lange, P. A. M., & Visser, K. (1999). Locomotion in social dilemmas: How people adapt to cooperative, tit-for-tat, and noncooperative partners. *Journal of Personality and Social Psychology, 77,* 762–773.

Van Vugt, M., Van Lange, P. A. M., & Meertens, R. M. (1996). Commuting by car or public transportation? A social dilemma analysis of travel mode judgements. *European Journal of Social Psychology, 26,* 373–395.

Van Yperen, N. W., & Buunk, B. P. (1990). A longitudinal study of equity and satisfaction in intimate relationships. *European Journal of Social Psychology, 20,* 287–309.

Van Zomeren, M., Postmes, T., & Spears, R. (2008). Toward an integrative social identity model of collective action: A quantitative research synthesis of three socio-psychological perspectives. *Psychological Bulletin, 134*(4), 504–535.

Vasquez, E. A., Denson, T. F., Pederson, W. C., Stenstrom, D. M., & Miller, N. (2005). The moderating effect of trigger intensity on triggered displaced aggression. *Journal of Experimental Social Psychology, 41,* 61–67.

Vazire, S., & Mehl, M. R. (2008). Knowing me, knowing you: The accuracy and unique predictive validity of self-ratings and other-ratings of daily behavior. *Journal of Personality and Social Psychology, 95,* 1202–1216.

Vega, V., & Malamuth, N. M. (2007). Predicting sexual aggression: The role of pornography in the context of general and specific risk factors. *Aggressive Behavior, 33,* 104–117.

Vescio, T. K., Gervais, S. J., Snyder, M., & Hoover, A. (2005). Power and the creation of patronizing environments: The stereotype-based behaviors of the powerful and their effects on female performance in masculine domains. *Journal of Personality and Social Psychology, 88,* 658–672.

Veysey, B. M., & Messner, S. F. (1999). Further testing of social disorganization theory: An elaboration of Sampson and Groves's "Community structure and crime." *Journal of Research in Crime and Delinquency, 36,* 156–174.

Vigil, J., Carle, A. C., Geary, D., Granger, D., Flinn, M. V., & Pendleton, P. (2009). Maternal correlates of children's stress functioning following a major natural disaster. *Journal of Child and Adolescent Trauma, 2*(4), 287–296.

Vigil, J., Geary, D., Granger, D., & Flinn, M. V. (2010). Sex differences in salivary Cortisol, alpha-amylase, and psychological functioning following Hurricane Katrina. *Child Development, 82*(2), 1228–1240.

Vignoles, V. L., Chryssochoou, X., & Breakwell, G. M. (2000). The distinctiveness principle: Identity, meaning, and the bounds of cultural relativity. *Personality and Social Psychology Review, 4*(4), 337–354.

Viken, R. J., Treat, T. A., Bloom, S. L., & McFall, R. M. (2005). Illusory correlation for body type and happiness: Covariation bias and its relationship to eating disorder symptoms. *International Journal of Eating Disorders, 38,* 65–72.

Visser, P. S., & Krosnick, J. A. (1998). Development of attitude strength over the life cycle: Surge and decline. *Journal of Personality and Social Psychology, 75,* 1389–1410.

Völlink, T., & Meertens, R. (2010). The effect of a prepayment meter on residential gas consumption. *Journal of Applied Social Psychology, 40*(10), 2556–2573.

Vorauer, J. D., & Ross, M. (1999). Self-awareness and feeling transparent: Failing to suppress one's self. *Journal of Experimental Social Psychology, 35,* 415–440.

Vorauer, J. D., Main, K. J., & O'Connell, G. B. (1998). How do individuals expect to be viewed by members of lower status groups? Content and implications of meta-stereotypes. *Journal of Personality and Social Psychology, 75,* 917–937.

Vorauer, J., & Kumhyr, S. M. (2001). Is this about you or me? Self-versus other-directed judgments and feelings in response to intergroup interaction. *Personality and Social Psychology Bulletin, 27,* 706–719.

Vrij, A., Edward, K., & Bull, R. (2001). Police officers' ability to detect deceit: The benefit of indirect deception detection measures. *Legal & Criminological Psychology, 6*(2), 185.

Vrij, A., Mann, S. A., Fisher, R. P., Leal, S., Milne, R., & Bull, R. (2008). Increasing cognitive load to facilitate lie detection: The benefit of recalling an event in reverse order. *Law and Human Behavior, 32,* 253–265.

Wagner, R. V. (2006). Terrorism: A peace psychological analysis. *Journal of Social Issues, 62,* 155–171.

Wagner, U., Christ, O., & Pettigrew, T. F. (2008). Prejudice and group-related behavior in Germany. *Journal of Social Issues, 64,* 403–416.

Wagstaff, G. F. (1983). Attitudes to poverty, the Protestant ethic, and political affiliation: A preliminary investigation. *Social Behavior and Personality, 11,* 45–47.

Walker, M. P., & Stickgold, R. (2006). Sleep, memory and plasticity. *Annual Review of Psychology, Vol. 57.* Palo Alto, CA: Annual Reviews.

Wallace, C. P. (2000, May 8). Germany's glass ceiling. *Time,* B8.

Waller, J. (2002). *Becoming evil: How ordinary people commit genocide and mass killing.* New York, NY: Oxford University Press.

Walster (Hatfield), E., Aronson, V., Abrahams, D., & Rottman, L. (1966). Importance of physical attractiveness in dating behavior. *Journal of Personality and Social Psychology, 4,* 508–516.

Walster (Hatfield), E., Walster, G. W., & Berscheid, E. (1978). *Equity: Theory and research.* Boston, MA: Allyn & Bacon.

Walther, J. B., Van Der Heide, B., Kim, S., Westerman, D., & Tong, S. (2008). The role of friends' appearance and behavior on evaluations of individuals on Facebook: Are we known by the company we keep? *Human Communication Research, 34*(1), 28–49.

Warnecke, R. B., Morera, O. F., Turner, L. R., & Mermelstein, R. (2001). Self-efficacy and smoking behavior: Changes in self-efficacy and readiness for smoking cessation. *Advances in Immunology.* New York, NY: Academic Press.

Warneken, F., & Tomasello, M. (2006). Altruistic helping in human infants and young chimpanzees. *Science, 311,* 1301–1303.

Wason, P. C. (1960). On the failure to eliminate hypotheses in a conceptual task. *Quarterly Journal of Experimental Psychology, 12,* 129–140.

Watkins, D., Akande, A., & Fleming, J. (1998). Cultural dimensions, gender, and the nature of self-concept: A fourteen-country study. *International Journal of Psychology, 33,* 17–31.

Watson, D., & Pennebaker, J. W. (1989). Health complaints, stress, and distress: Exploring the central role of negative affectivity. *Psychological Review, 96,* 234–254.

Watson, R. I., Jr. (1973). Investigation into deindividuation using a cross-cultural survey technique. *Journal of Personality and Social Psychology, 25,* 342–345.

Webster, D. (1993). Modified augmentation and reduction of the over-attributed bias. *Journal of Personality and Social Psychology, 65,* 261–271.

Wegener, D. T., Kerr, N., Fleming, M., & Petty, R. E. (2000). Flexible corrections of juror judgments: Implications for jury instructions. *Psychology, Public Policy, and Law, 6,* 629–654.

Wegener, D. T., & Petty, R. E. (1996). Effects of mood on persuasion processes: Enhancing, reducing, and biasing scrutiny of attitude-relevant information. In L. L. Martin & A. Tesser, (Eds.), *Striving and feeling: Interactions among goals, affect, and self-regulation* (pp. 329–362). Hillsdale, NJ: Erlbaum.

Wegener, D. T., Petty, R. E., & Smith, S. M. (1995). Positive mood can increase or decrease message scrutiny: The hedonic contingency view of mood and message processing. *Journal of Personality and Social Psychology, 69,* 5–15.

Wegner, D. M., & Erber, R. (1992). The hyperaccessibility of suppressed thoughts. *Journal of Personality and Social Psychology, 63,* 903–912.

Weigel, R. H., & Newman, L. S. (1976). Increasing attitude-behavior correspondence by broadening the scope of the behavioral measure. *Journal of Personality and Social Psychology, 33,* 793–802.

Weiner, B. (1985). "Spontaneous" causal thinking. *Psychological Bulletin, 97,* 74–84.

Werner, B. (1995). *Judgments of responsibility: A foundation for a theory of social conduct.* New York, NY: Guilford.

Weinstein, N. D. (1980). Unrealistic optimism about future life events. *Journal of Personality and Social Psychology, 39,* 806–820.

Weinstein, N. D. (1982). Unrealistic optimism about susceptibility to health problems. *Journal of Behavioral Medicine, 5,* 441–460.

Weiss, J., & Brown, P. (1976). *Self-insight error in the explanation of mood.* Unpublished manuscript, Harvard University.

Wells, G. L. (1993). What do we know about eyewitness identification? *American Psychologist, 48,* 553–571.

Wells, G. L., & Bradfield, A. L. (1998). "Good, you identified the suspect": Feedback to eyewitnesses distorts their reports of the witnessing experience. *Journal of Applied Psychology, 83,* 360–376.

Wells, G. L., Charman, S. D., & Olson, E. A. (2005). Building face composites can harm lineup identification performance. *Journal of Experimental Psychology: Applied, 11*(3), 147–156.

Wells, G. L., Lindsay, R. C. L., & Ferguson, T. (1979). Accuracy, confidence, and juror perceptions in eye-witness identification. *Journal of Applied Psychology, 64,* 440–448.

Wells, G. L., Lindsay, R. C. L., & Ferguson, T. J. (1979). Accuracy, confidence, and juror perceptions in eyewitness identification. *Journal of Applied Psychology, 64,* 440–448.

Wells, G. L., Malpass, R. S., Lindsay, R. C. L., Fisher, R. P., Turtle, J. W., & Fulero, S. M. (2000). From the lab to the police station: A successful application of eyewitness research. *American Psychologist, 55,* 581–598.

Wener, R., Frazier, W., & Farbstein, J. (1987, June). Building better jails. *Psychology Today,* 40–49.

Werhun, C. D., & Penner, A. J. (2010). The effects of stereotyping and implicit theory on benevolent prejudice toward aboriginal Canadians. *Journal of Applied Social Psychology, 40*(4), 899–916.

Weschler, H. et al. (2002). Trends in college binge drinking during a period of increased prevention efforts: Findings from Harvard School of Public Health, College Alcohol Study surveys: 1993–2001. *Journal of American College Health, 50,* 203–217.

West, R. (2005). Time for a change: Putting the transtheoretical (stages of change) model to rest. *Addiction, 100,* 1036–1039.

Wester, S. R., Christianson, H., Vogel, D. L., & Wei, M. (2007). Gender role conflict and psychological distress: The role of social support. *Psychology of Men & Masculinity, 8*(4), 215–224.

Wheeler, L., & Kim, Y. (1997). What is beautiful is culturally good: The physical attractiveness stereotype has different content in collectivistic cultures. *Personality and Social Psychology Bulletin, 23,* 795–800.

White, G. L. (1980). Physical attractiveness and courtship progress. *Journal of Personality and Social Psychology, 39,* 660–668.

White, H. R., Brick, J., & Hansell, S. (1993). A longitudinal investigation of alcohol use and aggression in adolescence. *Journal of Studies on Alcohol, Supplement No. 11,* 62–77.

White, J. A., & Plous, S. (1995). Self-enhancement and social responsibility: On caring more, but doing less, than others. *Journal of Applied Social Psychology, 25,* 1297–1318.

White, J. W., & Kowalski, R. M. (1994). Deconstructing the myth of the nonaggressive woman. *Psychology of Women Quarterly, 18,* 487–508.

White, M. (2011). *Deaths by mass unpleasantness.* Retrieved from http://users.erols.com/mwhite28/warstat8.htm.

White, P. A., & Younger, D. P. (1988). Differences in the ascription of transient internal states to self and other. *Journal of Experimental Social Psychology, 24,* 292–309.

Whitley, B. E., Jr. (1999). Right-wing authoritarianism, social dominance orientation, and prejudice. *Journal of Personality and Social Psychology, 77,* 126–134.

Whitman, D. (1996, December 16). I'm OK, you're not. *U.S. News and World Report,* 24.

Whyte, G. (1993). Escalating commitment in individual and group decision making: A prospect theory approach. *Organizational Behavior and Human Decision Processes, 54,* 430–455.

Wicker, A. W. (1971). An examination of the "other variables" explanation of attitude-behavior inconsistency. *Journal of Personality and Social Psychology, 19,* 18–30.

Widom, C. S. (1989). Does violence beget violence? A critical examination of the literature. *Psychological Bulletin, 106,* 3–28.

Wiegman, O. (1985). Two politicians in a realistic experiment: Attraction, discrepancy, intensity of delivery, and attitude change. *Journal of Applied Social Psychology, 15,* 673–686.

Wieselquist, J., Rusbult, C. E., Foster, C. A., & Agnew, C. R. (1999). Commitment, pro-relationship behavior, and trust in close relationships. *Journal of Personality and Social Psychology, 77,* 942–966.

Wilder, D. A. (1978). Perceiving persons as a group: Effect on attributions of causality and beliefs. *Social Psychology, 41,* 13–23.

Wilder, D. A. (1981). Perceiving persons as a group: Categorization and intergroup relations. In D. L. Hamilton (Ed.), *Cognitive processes in stereotyping and intergroup behavior.* Hillsdale, NJ: Erlbaum.

Wilder, D. A. (1990). Some determinants of the persuasive power of in-groups and out-groups: Organization of information and attribution of independence. *Journal of Personality and Social Psychology, 59,* 1202–1213.

Wilder, D. A., & Shapiro, P. N. (1984). Role of out-group cues in determining social identity. *Journal of Personality and Social Psychology, 47,* 342–348.

Wildschut, T., Pinter, B., Vevea, J., Insko, G., & Schopler, J. (2003). Beyond the group mind: A quantitative review of the interindividual-intergroup discontinuity effect. *Psychological Bulletin, 129,* 698–722.

Williams, E. F., & Gilovich, T. (2008). Do people really believe they are above average? *Journal of Experimental Social Psychology, 44,* 1121–1128.

Williams, J. E. (1993). Young adults' views of aging: A nineteen nation study. In M. I. Winkler (Ed.), *Documents: Conferencia del XXIV Congreso Interamericano de Psicologia* (pp. 101–123). Santiago, Chile: Sociedad Interamericana de Psicologia.

Williams, J. E., & Best, D. L. (1990a). *Measuring sex stereotypes: A multination study.* Newbury Park, CA: Sage.

Williams, J. E., Satterwhite, R. C., & Best, D. L. (1999). Pancultural gender stereotypes revisited: The five factor model. *Sex Roles, 40,* 513–525.

Williams, J. E., Satterwhite, R. C., & Best, D. L. (2000). *Five-factor gender stereotypes in 27 countries.* Paper presented at the XV Congress of the International Association for Cross-Cultural Psychology, Pultusk, Poland.

Williams, K. D. (2002). *Ostracism: The power of silence.* New York, NY: Guilford Press.

Williams, K. D., Harkins, S., & Latané, B. (1981). Identifiability as a deterrent to social loafing: Two cheering experiments. *Journal of Personality and Social Psychology, 40,* 303–311.

Williams, K. D., & Karau, S. J. (1991). Social loafing and social compensation: The effects of expectations of coworker performance. *Journal of Personality and Social Psychology, 61,* 570–581.

Williams, K. D., Nida, S. A., Baca, L. D., & Latané, B. (1989). Social loafing and swimming: Effects of identifiability on individual and relay performance of intercollegiate swimmers. *Basic and Applied Social Psychology, 10,* 73–81.

Williams, L., Fisher, M., & Cox, A. (2009). The impact of sexual history and desired relationship duration evaluations of attractiveness and recall. *Journal of Evolutionary Psychology, 6*(1), 1–23.

Williams, M. J., & Eberhardt, J. L. (2008). Biological conceptions of race and the motivation to cross racial boundaries. *Journal of Personality and Social Psychology, 94,* 1033–1047.

Williams, T. M. (Ed.). (1986). *The impact of television: A natural experiment in three communities.* Orlando, FL: Academic Press.

Willis, F. N., & Hamm, H. K. (1980). The use of interpersonal touch in securing compliance. *Journal of Nonverbal Behavior, 5,* 49–55.

Willoughby, T., Anderson, S. A., Wood, E., Mueller, J., & Ross, C. (2009). Fast searching for information on the Internet to use in a learning context: The impact of domain knowledge. *Computers & Education, 52,* 640–648.

Wilson, A. E., Gunn, G. R., & Ross, M. (2009). The role of subjective time in identity regulation. *Applied Cognitive Psychology, 23,* 1164–1178.

Wilson, A. E., & Ross, M. (2001). From chump to champ: People's appraisals of their earlier and present selves. *Journal of Personality and Social Psychology, 80,* 572–584.

Wilson, G. (1994, March 25). Equal, but different. The Times Higher Education Supplement, *Times of London.*

Wilson, R. S., & Matheny, A. P., Jr. (1986). Behavior-genetics research in infant temperament: The Louisville twin study. In R. Plomin & J. Dunn (Eds.), *The study of temperament: Changes, continuities, and challenges.* Hillsdale, NJ: Erlbaum.

Wilson, T. D., & Gilbert, D. T. (2005). Affective forecasting: Knowing what to want. *Current Directions in Psychological Science, 14,* 131–134.

Wilson, T. D., Laser, P. S., & Stone, J. I. (1982). Judging the predictors of one's mood: Accuracy and the use of shared theories. *Journal of Experimental Social Psychology, 18,* 537–556.

Winch, R. F. (1958). *Mate selection: A study of complementary needs.* New York, NY: Harper & Row.

Wines, M. (2005, September 23). Crime in South Africa grows more vicious. *New York Times* (http://www.nytimes.com).

Winter, F. W. (1973). A laboratory experiment of individual attitude response to advertising exposure. *Journal of Marketing Research, 10,* 130–140.

Wisman, A., & Koole, S. L. (2003). Hiding in the crowd: Can mortality salience promote affiliation with others who oppose one's worldviews? *Journal of Personality and Social Psychology, 84,* 511–526.

Wohl, M. J. A., & Enzle, M. (2009). Illusion of control by proxy: Placing one's fate in the hands of another. *British Journal of Social Psychology, 48*(1), 183–200.

Wohl, M. J. A., & Enzle, M. E. (2002). The deployment of personal luck: Illusory control in games of pure chance. *Personality and Social Psychology Bulletin, 28,* 1388–1397.

Wohl, M. J. A., & Enzle, M. E. (2003). The effects of near wins and losses on self-perceived personal luck and subsequent gambling behavior. *Journal of Experimental Social Psychology, 39,* 184–191.

Wohl, M. J. A., Branscombe, N. R., & Reysen, S. (2010). Perceiving your group's future to be in jeopardy: Extinction threat induces collective angst and the desire to strengthen the ingroup. *Personality and Social Psychology Bulletin, 36*(7), 898–910.

Wolf, S. (1987). Majority and minority influence: A social impact analysis. In M. P. Zanna, J. M. Olson, & C. P. Herman (Eds.), *Social influence: The Ontario symposium on personality and social psychology, Vol. 5.* Hillsdale, NJ: Erlbaum.

Wolf, S., & Latané, B. (1985). Conformity, innovation and the psycho-social law. In S. Moscovici, G. Mugny, & E. Van Avermaet (Eds.), *Perspectives on minority influence.* Cambridge: Cambridge University Press.

Wood, J. V. Perunovic, W. Q. E., & Lee, J. W. (2009). Positive self-statements: Power for some, peril for others, *Psychological Science, 20,* 860–866.

Wood, J. V., Heimpel, S. A., & Michela, J. L. (2003). Savoring versus dampening: Self-esteem differences in regulating positive affect. *Journal of Personality and Social Psychology, 85,* 566–580.

Wood, J. V., Michela, J. L., & Giordano, C. (2000). Downward comparison in everyday life reconciling self-enhancement models with mood-cognition priming model. *Journal of Personality and Social Psychology, 35,* 563–579.

Wood, J. V., Taylor, S. E., & Lichtman, R. R. (1985). Social comparison in adjustment to breast cancer. *Journal of Personality and Social Psychology, 79,* 1169–1183.

Wood, N. L., & Cowan, N. (1995). The cocktail party phenomenon revisited: Attention and memory in the classic selective listening procedure of Cherry (1953). *Journal of Experimental Psychology: General. 124*(3), 243–262.

Wood, W., & Eagly, A. H. (2010). Gender. In S. T. Fiske, D. T. Gilbert, & G. Lindzey, (Eds.), in *Handbook of social psychology, Vol. 1* (5th ed.) (pp. 629–667). Hoboken, NJ: Wiley.

Wood, W., Lundgren, S., Ouellete, J. A., Busceme, S., & Blackstone, T. (1994). Minority influence: A meta-analytic review of social influence processes. *Psychological Bulletin, 115,* 323–345.

Wood, W., Pool, G. J., Leck, K., & Purvis, D. (1996). Self-definition, defensive processing, and influence: The normative impact of majority and minority groups. *Journal of Personality and Social Psychology, 71,* 1181–1193.

Wood, W., & Quinn, J. M. (2003). Forewarned and forewarmed? Two meta-analytic syntheses of forewarnings of influence appeals. *Psychological Bulletin, 129,* 119–138.

Woodward. B. (2006). *State of denial: Bush at war, part III.* New York, NY: Simon & Schuster.

Worchel, S., & Brown, E. H. (1984). The role of plausibility in influencing environmental attributions. *Journal of Experimental Social Psychology, 20,* 86–96.

Worchel, S., Rothgerber, H., Day, E. A., Hart, D., & Butemeyer, J. (1998). Social identity and individual productivity within groups. *British Journal of Social Psychology, 37,* 389–413.

Word, C. O., Zanna, M. P., & Cooper, J. (1974). The nonverbal mediation of self-fulfilling prophecies in interracial interaction. *Journal of Experimental Social Psychology, 10,* 109–120.

Worringham, C. J., & Messick, D. M. (1983). Social facilitation of running: An unobtrusive study. *Journal of Social Psychology, 121,* 23–29.

Wright, D. B., Boyd, C. E., & Tredoux, C. G. (2001). A field study of own-race bias in South Africa and England. *Psychology, Public Policy, & Law, 7,* 119–133.

Wright, R. (1998, February 2). Politics made me do it. *Time,* 34.

Wright, R. (2003, June 29). Quoted by Thomas L. Friedman, "Is Google God?" *New York Times* (http://www.nytimes.com).

Wright, S. C., Aron, A., McLaughlin-Volpe, T., & Ropp, S. A. (1997). The extended contact effect: Knowledge of cross-group friendships and prejudice. *Journal of Personality and Social Psychology, 73,* 73–90.

Wrightsman, L. S. (2001). *Forensic psychology.* Belmont, CA: Wadsworth.

Wylie, R. C. (1979). *The self-concept theory and research on selected topics, Vol. 2.* Lincoln, NE: University of Nebraska Press.

Yap, M. B. H., Wright, A., & Jorm, A. F. (2011). The influence of stigma on young people's help-seeking intentions and beliefs about the helpfulness of various sources of help. *Social Psychiatry and Psychiatric Epidemiology, 46*(12), 1257–1265.

Yarmey, A. (2004). Eyewitness recall and photo identification: A field experiment. *Psychology, Crime & Law, 10*(1), 53–68.

Ybarra, O. (1999). Misanthropic person memory when the need to self-enhance is absent. *Personality and Social Psychology Bulletin, 25,* 261–269.

Yik, M. S., Bond, M. H., & Paulhus, D. L. (1998). Do Chinese self-enhance or self-efface? It's a matter of domain. *Personality and Social Psychology Bulletin, 24,* 399–406.

Yovetich, N. A., & Rusbult, C. E. (1994). Accommodative behavior in close relationships: Exploring transformation of motivation. *Journal of Experimental Social Psychology, 30,* 138–164.

Yuchtman (Yaar), E. (1976). Effects of social-psychological factors on subjective economic welfare. In B. Strumpel (Ed.), *Economic means for human needs.* Ann Arbor: Institute for Social Research, University of Michigan.

Yukl, G. (1974). Effects of the opponent's initial offer, concession magnitude, and concession frequency on bargaining behavior. *Journal of Personality and Social Psychology, 30,* 323–335.

Yzerbyt, V., Rocher, S., & Schadron, G. (1997). Stereotypes as explanations: A subjective essentialistic view of group perception. In R. Spears, P. J. Oakes, N. Ellemers, & S. A. Haslam (Eds.), *The social psychology of stereotyping and group life.* Oxford: Basil Blackwell.

Yzerbyt, V. Y., & Leyens, J. P. (1991). Requesting information to form an impression: The influence of valence and confirmatory status. *Journal of Experimental Social Psychology, 27,* 337–356.

Zajonc, R. B. (1965). Social facilitation. *Science, 149,* 269–274.

Zajonc, R. B. (1968). Attitudinal effects of mere exposure. *Journal of Personality and Social Psychology, 9,* Monograph Suppl. No. 2, part 2.

Zajonc, R. B. (1970, February). Brainwash: Familiarity breeds comfort. *Psychology Today,* 32–35, 60–62.

Zajonc, R. B. (1998). Emotions. In D. Gilbert, S. T. Fiske, & G. Lindzey (Eds.), *Handbook of social psychology,* (4th ed.). New York, NY: McGraw-Hill.

Zajonc, R. B. (2000). *Massacres: Mass murders in the name of moral imperatives.* Unpublished manuscript, Stanford University.

Zajonc, R. B., & Sales, S. M. (1966). Social facilitation of dominant and subordinate responses. *Journal of Experimental Social Psychology, 2,* 160–168.

Zakaria, F. (2008). We need a wartime president. *Newsweek* (http://www.newsweek.com).

Zauberman, G., & Lynch, Jr., J. G. (2005). Resource slack and propensity to discount delayed investments of time versus money. *Journal of Experimental Psychology: General, 134,* 23–37.

Zebrowitz, L. A., White, B., & Wieneke, K. (2008). Mere exposure and racial prejudice: Exposure to other-race faces increases liking for strangers of that race. *Social Cognition, 26,* 259–275.

Zebrowitz-McArthur, L. (1988). Person perception in cross-cultural perspective. In M. H. Bond (Ed.), *The cross-cultural challenge to social psychology.* Newbury Park, CA: Sage.

Zhang, Y. F., Wyon, D. P., Fang, L., & Melikov, A. K. (2007). The influence of heated or cooled seats on the acceptable ambient temperature range. *Ergonomics, 50*(4), 586–600.

Zillman, D., & Weaver, J. (1999). Effects of prolonged exposure to gratuitous media violence on provoked and unprovoked hostile behavior. *Journal of Applied Social Psychology, 29*(1), 145–165.

Zillmann, D. (1989). Aggression and sex: Independent and joint operations. In H. L. Wagner & A. S. R. Manstead (Eds.), *Handbook of psychophysiology: Emotion and social behavior* (pp. 229–259). Chichester: Wiley.

Zillmann, D. (1989a). Aggression and sex: Independent and joint operations. In H. L. Wagner & A. S. R. Manstead (Eds.), *Handbook of psychophysiology: Emotion and social behavior.* Chichester: Wiley.

Zillmann, D. (1989b). Effects of prolonged consumption of pornography. In D. Zillmann & J. Bryant (Eds.), *Pornography: Research advances and policy considerations.* Hillsdale, NJ: Erlbaum.

Zillmann, D., & Paulus, P. B. (1993). Spectators: Reactions to sports events and effects on athletic performance. In R. N. Singer, N. Murphey, & L. K. Tennant (Eds.), *Handbook of research on sport psychology.* New York, NY: Macmillan.

Zillmann, D., & Weaver, J. B., III. (1998). Effects of prolonged exposure to gratuitous media violence on provoked and unprovoked hostile behavior. *Journal of Applied Social Psychology, 29,* 145–165.

Zillmer, E. A., Harrower, M., Ritzler, B. A., & Archer, R. P. (1995). *The quest for the Nazi personality: A psychological investigation of Nazi war criminals.* Hillsdale, NJ: Erlbaum.

Zimbardo, P. G. (1970). The human choice: Individuation, reason, and order versus deindividuation, impulse, and chaos. In W. J. Arnold & D. Levine (Eds.), *Nebraska symposium on motivation, 1969.* Lincoln, NE: University of Nebraska Press.

Zimbardo, P. G. (1971). *The psychological power and pathology of imprisonment.* A statement prepared for the U.S. House of Representatives Committee on the Judiciary, Subcommittee No. 3: Hearings on Prison Reform, San Francisco, CA, October 25.

Zimbardo, P. G. (1972). The Stanfarod Prison experiment. A slide/tape presentation produced by Philip G. Zimbardo, Inc., P.O. Box 4395, Stanford, CA 94305.

Zimbardo, P. G. (2002, April). Nurturing psychological synergies. *APA Monitor, 5,* 38.

Zimbardo, P. G. (2004). A situationist perspective on the psychology of evil: Understanding how good people are transformed into perpetrators. In A. G. Miller (Ed.), *The social psychology of good and evil.* New York, NY: Guilford.

Zimbardo, P. G. (2007, September). Person x situation x system dynamics. *The Observer* (Association for Psychological Science), p. 43.

Zoghbi-Manrique-de-Lara, P. (2009). Inequity, conflict, and compliance dilemma as causes of cyberloafing. *International Journal of Conflict Management, 20*(2), 188–201.

Zucker, G. S., & Weiner, B. (1993). Conservatism and perceptions of poverty: An attributional analysis. *Journal of Applied Social Psychology, 23,* 925–943.

Figure and Table Credits

Module 2
Figure 2-1: Data from Fowler et al., 2005.

Activity box: Adapted from Fowler, 2005, personal communication.

Module 3
Poem: © Molson Coors Canada

Figure 3-1: From Markus & Kitayama, 1991.

Figure 3-3: Data from the 2010 Pew Global Attitudes Survey.

Figure 3-4: Adapted from A. H. Eagly & W. Wood, 1991, "Explaining Sex Differences in Social Behavior: A Meta-Analytic Perspective," *Personality and Social Psychology Bulletin, 17*, pp. 306–315. Copyright © 1991. Reprinted by permission of Sage Publications, Inc.

Module 6
Figure 6-2: Data from Ross, et al., 1977.

Module 7
Figure 7-1: Adapted from R.P. Vallone, L.D. Ross, & M.R. Lepper, "The Hostile Media Phenomenon: Biased perception and perceptions of media bias in coverage of the 'Beirut massacre,'" in *Journal of Personality and Social Psychology, 49*, 1985, pp. 577–585. © 1985. Used by permission of Prof. Lee D. Ross.

Module 8
Figure 8-3: Data from Festinger & Carlsmith, 1959.

Module 9
Figure 9-2: http://en.wikipedia.org/wiki/Milgram_experiment

Figure 9-3: Figure 13: "Learner demands to be shocked" (p. 91) from OBEDIENCE TO AUTHORITY: AN EXPERIMENTAL VIEW by STANLEY MILGRAM. Copyright © 1974 by Stanley Milgram. Reprinted by permission of HarperCollins Publishers and by Pinter & Martin, Ltd.

Module 11
Figure 11-1: Data from McAlister et al., 1980; Telch et al., 1981.

Module 12
Figure 12-2: Data from Zajonc & Sales, 1966.

Module 13
Figure 13-2: Data from Janis & Mann, 1977, p. 132.

Module 14
Figure 14-1: Source: Based on Dollard et al., 1939; and Miller, 1941.

Figure 14-2: Source: Based on Dollard et al., 1939; and Miller, 1941.

Module 15
Figure 15-1: Data from the 2006 Census, courtesy of Statistics Canada: 31,241,030 responses providing 42,162,620 responses (some people gave multiple responses; and 5,068,090 self-identified as "Visible Minority").

Module 16
Figure 16-3: 1990 Gallup Poll (Gates, 1993).

Module 17
Table 17-1: Adapted from Canadian Human Rights Commission, 2004 Employment Equity Annual Report.

Figure 17-2: From Dixon & Durrheim, 2003.

Module 18
Figure 18-1: Adapted from Batson, Fultz, & Schoenrade, 1987.

Figure 18-2: Adapted from Darley & Latané, 1968.

Figure 18-3: Data from Latané & Darley, 1968.

Module 19
Figure 19-1: From Zajonc, 1968.

Module 20
Figure 20-2: From Aron et al., 2005

Figure 20-3: Source: Data from Gupta and Singh, 1982.

Figure 20-4: Used by permission of the National Opinion Research Center

Table 20-1: Source: Rusbult et al., 1986, 1987, 1998, 2001.

Module 21

Activity box: From www.netlingo.com

Figure 21-1: Data from Eron & Huesmann, 1984.

Figure 21-2: Adapted from Craig A. Anderson and Brad J. Bushman, "Effects of violent video games on aggressive behavior, aggressive cognition, aggressive effect, psychological arousal and prosocial behavior: A meta-analytic review of the scientific literature," *Psychological Science,* 12, No. 5, pp. 353–359. Reprinted by permission of Blackwell Publishing.

Module 22

Figure 22-2: Data from Downs and Lyons, 1991.

Module 23

Figure 23-1: www.footprintnetwork.org 2006

Table 23-1: Adapted from Statistics Canada, 2003 General Social Survey.

Figure 23-2: Source: Data from Dey, Astin, & Korn, 1991, and subsequent annual reports.

Figure 23-3: Reprinted by permission of Rafael M. Di Tella.

Module 24

Figure 24-4: Adapted from Prochaska et al., 1992, 1994.

Photo Credits